D1548226

The Upper Canadian Anglican Tory Mind

– A Cultural Fragment –

Robert W. Passfield

For my father, the late Cyril John Passfield, who inculcated in his eldest son a belief that work is a virtue and the precept that one must continually strive 'to be the best of whatever you are';

For my mother, the late Gertrude Violet Passfield, a true Christian and Churchwoman, who strove to raise her three children in the Anglican faith;

and

For my former wife, Lois Elaine Passfield (now Mrs. Lois Stubbs), who typed the draft chapters of a projected Ph.D. dissertation without which the present work would be lost to posterity.

———————————

Published by

Rock's Mills Press

www.rocksmillspress.com

Copyright 2018, Robert W. Passfield.
All rights reserved. Published by arrangement with the author.

For information, including Library and Archives Canada Cataloguing in Publication data, please contact the publisher at customer.service@ rocksmillspress.com.

Cover Design: Craig Passfield

Author's website: www.passrob.com

ISBN -13:978-1-77244-137-6

Table of Contents

Illustrations

"Portrait of the Reverend John Strachan",
artist unknown, n.d. Trinity College, University of Toronto.

Preface

The main body of this book is a cultural fragment that dates from over forty years' ago, when the author -- a graduate student in the History Graduate School of McMaster University in Hamilton, Ontario -- undertook to write a Ph.D. dissertation on "The Upper Canadian Tory Mind". It was to be a study in political thought that would focus on the Tories of the Province of Upper Canada in British North America. He failed to complete it. The present publication comprises a copy-edited version of the chapters of the abandoned dissertation and its Introduction, to which have been added a Preface, Acknowledgements, and a conclusion. The broader study covers the historical period from the close of the War of 1812 to the demise of Upper Canada as a separate province in February 1841 with the proclamation of the Act of Union that united the provinces of Upper Canada (Ontario) and Lower Canada (Quebec) in the new United Province of Canada.

The concept of the dissertation was to work up the worldview and the constitutional, religious and educational values, beliefs and principles of the Tories of Upper Canada -- in the two decades following the War of 1812, when an Anglican Tory elite governed the province – with the aim of reconstructing the underlying political philosophy of the Upper Canadian Tories. The overriding aim was, through an analysis of the Tory political thought, to determine whether the Upper Canadian Tories were true philosophical Tories in the church-state tradition of the Anglican theologian, Richard Hooker (1554-1600), or 18th Century 'Old Whigs'. In keeping with an assumption that 'ideas influence actions', it was contended as well that a reconstruction of the political philosophy of the Upper Canadian Tories would provide a better understanding of the Tory stance on the public issues of their day.

For this book, the typescripts of the dissertation chapters were scanned – with an optical character recognition scanner – and copy-edited, and several of the overly-long original chapters have been subdivided into two shorter chapters to render them more tightly focused and succinct. At the same time, an introductory paragraph has been added to each chapter to position the chapter with respect to its relevance to the broader treatment of the ideas of the Upper Canadian Anglican Tories.

For the most part, the book comprises an almost verbatim reproduction of the text of the chapters of the unfinished dissertation as it existed in May 1974, when the author left the History Graduate School at McMaster University to take up a position as a public historian with the Parks Canada Program (now the Parks Canada Agency) of the Canadian Government in Ottawa. At that time, the manuscript lacked a conclusion, and needed to be heavily edited, restructured and repositioned for presentation as a Ph.D. dissertation.

Herein, the original structure and writing approach of the dissertation have been retained. Hence, the book is written as a descriptive narrative that focuses on the constitutional, religious, and educational thought of the Upper Canadian Tories and their worldview. The numerous quotations in the original dissertation text have been retained, which convey in a vivid fashion the profound depth of the religious beliefs of the Upper Canadian Tories and the vitality of their worldview. In several chapters, additional historical information has been inserted to link the Tory ideas more closely with contemporary political events. Where the new historical inserts are concerned, the references in the Notes have been enclosed in square brackets to indicate a later insertion.

The chapters are grouped into five Parts, and each chapter is thoroughly referenced with the Notes grouped at the end of each part of the book. Thus, each part of this study is complete within itself. The Notes to the smaller sections – the Introduction, the conclusions, and the appendices – have been inserted as endnotes.

The Introduction remains as originally written with but several deletions and changes in phrasing. It sets forth the purpose of the original study, its perceived relevance to Canadian history, and the historiographical context as it existed at the time that the dissertation was in preparation. The Preface and the Acknowledgements were prepared to place the 'cultural fragment' – the forty-years-old dissertation text -- within a meaningful context with respect to its provenance, purpose, and significance.

The Conclusion comprises an intellectual analysis of Upper Canadian Toryism within the context of the history of English political thought and political behavior to determine whether, or not, the Tories of Upper Canada were in fact true Tories. It concludes the original study.

This study of the Upper Canadian Anglican Tory Mind is based primarily on the extant published writings and private papers of four prominent Upper Canadian Anglican Tories: a Loyalist, Richard Cartwright Jr. (1759-1815) of Kingston, Upper Canada; the Rev. John Strachan (1778-1867) of the established Church of England in Upper Canada, and two of his former students: John Beverley Robinson (1791-1863) of York and John Macaulay (1792-1857) of Kingston, Upper Canada, who were second- generation Loyalists. All four of these men were prominent High-Church Anglicans, and members of the political, religious, and social elite of Upper Canada, who held influential positions in various areas of public life: in the provincial government, the established Church of England, and/or the judiciary. Each was directly involved in the major public issues of their day and played a significant role in the public discourse.

The Loyalists of the American Revolution are not the subject of this work; nonetheless, Loyalism has a significance presence. The Upper Canadian Anglican Tories identified with the Loyalist experience of the American Revolution, and it was the Anglican Tories who possessed a philosophical basis for rejecting the Lockean-liberal principles and beliefs of the American revolutionaries. Moreover, it was the Anglican Tories who consciously strove to establish, maintain and defend, the traditional social, religious and political order within the 'Loyalist Asylum' of Upper Canada.

It is the contention of this book that the Upper Canadian Anglican Tories were true philosophical conservatives, who evolved a unique variant of English Anglican Toryism. The political thought of the Tories of Upper Canada was an amalgam of a political philosophy that embodied a Christian worldview, a theory of the union of church and state, and a concept of natural law as forged by the Anglican divine, Richard Hooker at the time of the English Reformation; the Old Tory concept of the sovereignty of the Crown and 'the 'rights of Englishmen'; and the 18th Century English Tory concept of the balanced British Constitution that grew out of the Glorious Revolution of 1688 and was distinctly different from 18th Century Whig parliamentarianism.

It was a Tory political philosophy that in Upper Canada was leavened by a belief in a meritocracy in which public offices, the National Church, and the professions were to be filled with well-educated young 'gentlemen' of a strong Christian moral character, well versed in science and the useful arts. To that end, the Tories believed in a 'national system' of education that would be open to all ranks of society, that would be under the direction of the Established Church, and that would have government bursaries provided for 'the clever poor' who excelled in elementary school to enable them to proceed to the District Grammar School, and beyond to university (once a projected King's College university were established). The concept of a 'national system' of education was derived from Scotland where the Rev. John Strachan was raised and educated. Otherwise, the Tory education system was based on Christian values, and had a broad Grammar School curriculum that embraced classical studies, the 'useful arts' and religious knowledge, and drew on the teaching methodology advocated by John Locke.

Overall, this study comprises three interrelated elements: an intellectual history study of the cultural values and beliefs of the Upper Canadian Anglican Tories and their underlying political philosophy (the original dissertation); a political history content written from the viewpoint of the ruling class; and an autobiographical comment on the conception and evolution of the study (the Acknowledgements). Indirectly, this is a study of the mind of the Rev. John Strachan – the Anglican Rector of York (1812-1827), Archdeacon of York (1827-1839), and Bishop of Toronto (1839-1867) -- of the established Church of England in Upper Canada. Although acting on a provincial stage, Bishop Strachan ranks among the great Church-statesmen of history – the chief ministers of Church and State -- in the older European tradition of clerical statesmen who shaped the religious, political and social development of their nation.

Cultural Fragment

The subtitle of the book – "a cultural fragment" – describes both its content and its nature. First, in the sense that the book treats the historical phenomenon of the Anglican Tory cultural fragment in the political culture of the Province of Ontario (formerly the Province of Upper Canada); and secondly, in the sense that the main body of the book comprises a cultural artefact in itself – a forty-year-old dissertation text -- that records the worldview, principles, values and beliefs inherent in a long-lost political philosophy: Upper Canadian Anglican Toryism.

Terminology

In this book, the term 'tory' is used to refer to those who were opposed to American democratic republicanism and believed in loyalty to the King, the British constitution, the unity of the British Empire, and the union of church and state. Thus, the term 'tory' is used in a generic sense for conservatives who, based on their Christian religious beliefs, supported the preservation of the traditional political and social order. In Upper Canada, the term 'tory' comprehended a good many, but not all, Anglicans, Church of Scotland adherents, Wesleyan Methodists, Lutherans, and the Scottish and English Roman Catholics, who upheld the established political, religious and social order and the balanced constitution, and either accepted or tolerated the existing church-state alliance; although they differed over the exclusive prerogatives and endowments that the Church of England enjoyed. The appellation 'Tory' is used herein specifically as a descriptor for the High Church Anglican Tories and, more particularly, for the Rev. John Strachan and his former students of the Cornwall District Grammar School (1803-1811) who formed the core of the social and political elite of Upper Canada following the War of 1812, and who lived and acted in accordance with Anglican Tory beliefs, principles and values.

The 'High Church Tories' were staunch supporters of the union of church and state and committed defenders of the exclusive prerogatives and endowments of the established Church of England in Upper Canada. There were also Anglicans who were 'moderate Tories'. They shared with the High Church Tories a belief in government based on Christian principles, values and beliefs, and in the principle of an established church, but held -- for the sake of social harmony – that all Protestant religious denominations ought to share in the endowments which the Crown had bestowed on the Church of England for the support of "a Protestant Clergy". Both the 'High Church Tories' and the 'moderate Tories' were strong defenders of the balanced British Constitution, 'the rights of Englishmen', the limited constitutional monarchy, the rule of law, and the British Imperial connection, and were believers in a 'natural' hierarchical social order.

The term 'conservative' is used in a much more comprehensive manner to include all groups and individuals, regardless of their religious affiliation, who supported the retention of the monarchy, the balanced British

Constitution, and the unity of Empire, and were opposed to American democratic republicanism. In sum, the term 'conservative' embraces High Church Anglican Tories and moderate Anglican Tories, as well as generic tories of different religious persuasions, and 'situational conservatives'. The latter category – which utilizes a term introduced by a political scientist, Samuel P. Huntington -- comprises those who supported the established social and political order of Upper Canada simply out of a force of habit and custom, or out of economic self-interest, rather than from any deeper philosophical or religious conviction.

In Upper Canada, the Tory provincial government administration was opposed by liberal-whigs, who were Lockean-liberals in their political beliefs and principles but otherwise were social conservatives, and by democratic radicals who demanded democratic elective institutions to empower 'the people'. The Tory establishment was also under attack by evangelical Protestant sectarians who demanded a complete separation of church and state and, as of the early 1830s, by egalitarian democratic republicans who were admirers of the American Republic and Jacksonian democracy. All four outgroups were encompassed within a provincial Reform Party.

The various outgroups were united in their hostility to the Tory governing establishment, and in their support of the Reform Party in its demand for 'responsible government'. It was a proposed new principle of government which, as expounded by the Reformers, required that the Crown must appoint members of the Executive Council who could command the support of a majority of the elected representatives in the House of Assembly, and that the representative of the Crown – the Lieutenant Governor – must take the advice of his Executive Council on local provincial matters. On their part, the Tories feared that the principle of responsible government would result -- if implemented -- in the overthrow of the balanced British Constitution through placing the majority party of the House of Assembly in control of the provincial government ministry, the provincial Crown revenues, and the distribution of Crown patronage. For the Tories of Upper Canada, the principle of 'responsible government' was equated with party government, partisan politics, and democracy (popular sovereignty).

In this study, the adherents of the Methodist Episcopal Church are referred to as 'American Methodists' in keeping with the terminology used by the Upper Canadian Anglican Tories. It was a terminology which was based on a recognition that the religious principles of the Episcopal Methodists – 'voluntaryism', 'religious equality', and the 'separation of church and state' -- were derived from American evangelical Protestantism and were introduced into Upper Canada by American itinerant preachers and the American sectarians who settled in the Province during the two decades prior to the War of 1812. Contrary to the assertions of the evangelical religious sects -- and their leading polemicist, the Rev. Egerton Ryerson -- the Church of England was an established church in Upper Canada, and it has been so treated in this study.

Mankind

In the writings of the Anglican Tories, the terms 'man' and 'mankind' were intended to be inclusive of both men and women, which is not to deny that the Tories viewed society as a patriarchy and held a paternalistic view of the role of males in society, government, the Church, and the family.

Acknowledgements

For the author, the selection of a Ph.D. dissertation topic -- while in graduate school -- and his approach to the writing of a dissertation, were a product of the evolution of his historical interests and his view of history. From an early age, he read histories of the early explorers of Canada, and in high school his historical interest focused on the achievements of great men in politics, engineering, and the military. Subsequently, upon entering a university undergraduate Arts program, he wanted to study history and become a high school history teacher.

While in Honours History, at the University of Western Ontario (1964-1968), the author became interested in pursuing graduate studies with the aim of pursuing a career in university teaching which would enable him to write scholarly works in the field of history. To that end, he entered the History Graduate School at McMaster University, but during his MA year in 1968-1969 experienced an intellectual crisis which had a decisive effect on his development as an historian.

As an undergraduate in history, the author had envisaged history as a grand edifice in which each book was a 'brick' that would endure for all time, and that would ensure the historian of a lasting place in the pantheon of men of achievement. In effect, unbeknownst to himself, the author was an adherent of the old 19th Century 'scientific school' of history, as championed by the German historian, Leopold von Ranke (1798-1886). It was a 'school' in which research was focused on primary sources, the facts were regarded as 'speaking for themselves', and history was viewed as the recording of 'what actually happened'. The writing of history was conceived as being objective and independent of the personal views and values of the historian. As an undergraduate, the author was aware that there were different interpretations of historical events; however, he had assumed that new interpretations were the product of a later discovery of additional primary source materials that yielded a deeper understanding of an historical event, or were the product of historians having chosen to emphasis different aspects of an historical event or of an historical period of study.

When studying historiography -- while completing his MA degree at McMaster University -- the discovery of the existence of bias in the writing of history, and the realization that each generation of historians re-writes history in keeping with its present outlook and changing perspectives, was very unsettling. For the author, it led to much self-questioning. Why pursue a career in history, if whatever one writes will be superseded by newer interpretations, will be ephemeral, and will soon be forgotten with the passage of time?

It was at such a time of uncertainty, and unease, that the author was struck by the contrasting reception of two works by Niccolo Machiavelli. His *History of Florence* (1532) had been superseded by numerous histories of Florence and was largely unread and forgotten, but his earlier political treatise, *The Prince* (1513), was still being studied in universities, had become recognized as a classic, and was a work of great renown. Hence, it dawned on the author that it was the histories of ideas that were lasting. Human nature did not change over time, and the problems faced by societies in seeking to secure 'peace, order and good government', or to ensure 'life, liberty and happiness', were universal and were faced by every generation in turn. At that point, a determination was made to study intellectual history to facilitate the writing of scholarly works in the history of ideas that would have a lasting value.

Hence, upon entering upon the Ph.D. studies program at McMaster University, the author was determined to write 'a great work' in the history of ideas, and had in contemplation a dissertation on the political ideas of the Tories of British North America. In the Ph.D. program, he read in a major field, Canadian History (Pre- and Post-Confederation), and three minor fields: Political Philosophy; Diplomatic History; and Modern European History. Once the orals were passed in all four fields, research commenced on the working up of a dissertation proposal. In that pursuit, the author was strongly influenced by the political ideas of a Canadian philosopher, George Grant, in his book, *Lament for a Nation: The Defeat of Canadian Nationalism* (1965), as well as by the writings of a Canadian historian, S.F. Wise, on Canadian conservatism.

Initially, what the author had in mind was a dissertation on 'The Evolution of British North American Toryism, 1780-1850', which would focus on a selected group of prominent tories in the provinces of Upper Canada and Nova Scotia. The intention was to work up the political ideas and attitudes that were expressed in their writings, and to trace the extent to which 18th Century British toryism was transformed in being transmitted to British North America. It was expected that there would be some differences in attitudes and outlook owing to the different circumstances of the tories in North America.

The original concept was to focus the study on seven prominent tories -- four from Upper Canada, and three from Nova Scotia. The men under consideration fell into two distinct sub-groups: British immigrants; and Loyalists, inclusive of the sons of Loyalists. The potential study subjects included both Church of England and Church of Scotland adherents. In commencing the preliminary research, the author had no intention of focusing on Anglican Tories or on religion. At that time, he viewed 'conservative' and 'tory' as interchangeable designations for the same mind set. However, the initial dissertation concept changed dramatically when the author became familiar with the works of the American intellectual historian, and Professor of American Literature, Perry Miller (1905-1963), through the reading of two of his works: *The New England Mind: From Colony to Province* (1953); and *Errand into the Wilderness* (1964).

What attracted the interest of the author was the assertion by Perry Miller that the Puritans of New England had a coherent worldview, which was based on their theology and which governed and guided their actions; and that the history of the establishment and development of the Massachusetts Bay Colony was an effort to work out their religious ideals in action. The author was equally impressed with Perry Miller's exclamation concerning his view of history:

> I have difficulty imaging that anyone can be a historian without realizing that history itself is part of the life of the mind; hence, I have been compelled to insist that the mind of man is the basic factor in human history. (*Errand*, ix.)

At that point, the author was motivated to investigate the Anglican Tory mind to determine whether the Anglican Tories of British North America had a distinctive and coherent worldview that was based on their theology, and that governed and guided their political actions. However, in consultation with his dissertation advisor, it was decided that the study should focus solely on the Province of Upper Canada to render the research more manageable; and that the author should prepare a proposal for a study of "the political ideas and attitudes of the Upper Canadian Tories".

The research would focus on four prominent Upper Canadian Tories: the Rev. John Strachan and John Beverley Robinson of York (Toronto), and Richard Cartwright and John Macaulay of Kingston. All four were men who had played a prominent role in the public life of Upper Canada, and had left extensive collections of private and public papers in archival records. Moreover, for the author, it was critically important that all four of the men were prominent Anglican Tories.

The undertaking of a study of the political thought of the Upper Canadian Anglican Tories soon took on a broader significance for the author personally. He began to think about a comment that had been made, about a year earlier, by a British exchange student who was taking a Canadian history course in the MA program at McMaster University. At that time, the author had asked the exchange student: "What do you think of Canadian history"? He had replied: "It's hollow at the core. It's a history of political agitations and protest movements".

It was a startling statement, but upon reflection the author came to a similar conclusion. The history of Upper Canada, and of Canadian history more generally, was written from the viewpoint of political agitators and outgroups who were attacking the governing establishment, and who were espousing liberal values in the pursuit of their own partisan self-interests. In truth, as interpreted in the historical works of liberal-whig historians, Canadian history was 'hollow at the core', and the Canada that they portrayed – where English Canada was concerned – lacked a soul. There was no clearly defined national culture.

In the histories of Canada that were produced in the late 19th and early 20th centuries, liberal-whig historians had focused their attention, and approval, on political agitators -- democratic radicals, religious sectarians, Lockean-liberal reformers, and anti-Imperialists. Collectively, they were viewed as having contributed directly to the attainment of 'responsible government' in Canada and/or to the subsequent growth in self-government and independence from Britain which was viewed as the essence of Canadian history. It was an imported progressive view of history that interpreted Canadian history in terms of the growth of freedom, national independence, and the march of civilization, and implicitly denied that English Canada had a distinct political culture that was worth articulating and preserving. Indeed, progress was equated with the spread of the tenets of classical liberalism which defined the political culture of the United States of America.

What the liberal-whig Canadian historians failed to realize was that they were denying the very essence of English Canada. It was founded as a Loyalist asylum within the British Empire by the defenders of a traditional social and political order that pre-dated the Lockean-liberalism of the 18th Century Enlightenment, and it was the Tories of Upper Canada who were defending that traditional order. In sum, the author in his musing became convinced that the true founders of English Canada were the Tories who were striving to build a traditional conservative 'nation' in North America, and who had been disparaged, denounced, and denigrated by liberal-whig historians.

In criticizing the supposed 'colonial mentality' of the Tories, what liberal-whig historians overlooked was that the tories of all stripes were realists. They believed that the provinces of British North America would unite one day, and that, as the united provinces grew in population, wealth and power, they would eventually form an independent nation within the British Empire in sharing with the mother country – the United Kingdom -- a common allegiance and loyalty to the Crown. However, the Upper Canadian Tories were convinced -- and conservatives, more generally, would remain convinced long after the founding of the Dominion of Canada in 1867 – that if Canada were totally independent from Britain, the result would be its annexation or absorption by the United States of America.

Based on his preliminary research, the author became further convinced that the Province of Upper Canada -- during the decades of the 1820s and 1830s -- was a Christian polity with an Established Church, wherein British subjects enjoyed a balanced constitution, the rule of law under a limited constitutional monarchy, and the protection and sustenance of the Imperial government within the British Empire. Hence, the projected dissertation was envisaged as a work that would lay the groundwork for a Tory history of Canada, that would foster the writing of histories of Canada which would restore its soul, and that would bring recognition to the true founders and defenders of what became the Dominion of Canada: viz. the Tories of the British North American provinces. It was decidedly an ambitious undertaking, and perhaps somewhat naïve in the aspirations that it gave rise to, but inspiring nonetheless. The 'Great Work' beckoned!

Having finally worked his way -- through reading and research -- to what he considered to be a viable dissertation topic, the author prepared a proposal that set forth the subject of the planned dissertation, the approach to be taken to the research and writing of the work, and its projected contribution to Canadian historiography. As finally conceptualized, the dissertation was to be a study of the 'Upper Canadian Tory Mind' that would focus on the worldview and the constitutional, religious, and educational ideas of the leading Anglican Tories of Upper Canada. The argument to be resolved was whether the Upper Canadian Tories were true Tories in the tradition of the Anglican Divine, Richard Hooker (1554-1600) or Old Whig parliamentarians. In keeping with the premise that 'ideas influence actions', it was held that the dissertation would make a further contribution to Canadian historiography by showing that the stands taken by the Upper Canadian Tories on the public issues of their day were readily understandable in terms of their Tory beliefs, values and principles.

It was to be left to others to analyze the extent to which the political thought of the Upper Canadian Tories was transformed in being transferred from Britain, and to place Upper Canadian Toryism within the broader field of the history of political thought. The dissertation proposal was focused exclusively upon a study of the Tories of Upper Canada. Moreover, the subject of the study was deliberately stated to be 'The Upper Canadian Tory Mind'. The author did not want to have to justify the undertaking of a dissertation focused exclusively upon Anglican Tories; although that was his decided intention.

In deciding to focus the dissertation strictly on Anglican Tories, the author had no personal identification with the subject. He was raised an Anglican, but when at university was only nominally so. His self-identification, at that time, was as 'a Canadian, from small-town southern Ontario'. He was going to research a subject of interest, and was motivated by a strong desire to produce a lasting work in intellectual history. It was only while working up the ideas of the Upper Canadian Anglican Tories – their principles, values and beliefs – that he came to the realize the extent to which he had been inculcated with Anglican Tory beliefs and values in his youth through his family and his attendance at St. Hilda's Anglican Church in St. Thomas, Ontario.

The approach that was taken to the research and writing of the dissertation was heavily influenced by Barbara Tuchman (1912-1989). Upon reading her popular history, *The Guns of August* (1962), the author was impressed by her particular approach to the writing of history: viz. Tuchman's insistence that historical works ought to be based on primary source research; that the writing should take the form of an historical narrative; and that the focus should be 'in the moment' -- based on the protagonists' understanding of their situation, rather than having a meaning imposed on the narrative by an omniscient historian in drawing on information not known to the participants in the actual event.

Tuchman's view of the historians' craft had a strong influence on the research and writing of the dissertation in the heavy use of primary sources, the historical narrative form, and the lack of an authorial voice interpreting the meaning of Upper Canadian Anglican Toryism throughout the dissertation. As written, the main text of the dissertation consists of a reproduction of the worldview, principles, beliefs and values of the Upper Canadian Anglican Tories as enunciated by the Tories themselves. Only in the conclusion did the author intend to present an analysis and interpretation of the Upper Canadian Anglican Toryism to prove that they were true Tories – based on their beliefs, values and principles -- and not Old Whigs.

A critical problem became evident as the study neared its completion. It was inherent in the approach taken by the author to the writing of the

Ph.D. dissertation. He was focused on writing 'a great work' in Canadian intellectual history, knew what he wanted to do, and had proceeded to follow his own path in a solitary manner. He had little knowledge of the requisite nature, character and structure of a Ph.D. dissertation. Moreover, he had had only a few meetings with his dissertation advisor at which the author had described the on-going results of his research and handed in several draft chapters for perusal. As the work progressed, there was no discussion as to how the dissertation ought to be structured, nor was there any discussion pertaining to the intellectual and historiographical framework within which the School of Graduate Studies would want a Ph.D. dissertation on Upper Canadian Toryism to be placed.

As of May 1974 -- when departing from the History Graduate School to take up a position as a public historian with the Canadian government -- the author had completed a draft of all the dissertation chapters and the Introduction, and was roughing out his concept for a conclusion. However, it was a period of great personal distress and disappointment. Several months earlier, following the completion of the Introduction, he had been informed that an Advisory Committee would review the dissertation chapters completed to that date and the initial draft of the Introduction. Following that review, the author was advised:

1) that each chapter needed to be "complete in itself with an introduction and a conclusion", and that the Tory beliefs needed to be tied to political events to provide an historical context;

2) that the chapters generally were too lengthy and overly-detailed, and needed to be shortened and made much more succinct;

3) that the use of quotations in the text had to be greatly reduced, and the citing of multiple sources in each endnote greatly simplified;

4) that the Introduction had to be made more succinct and to the point, and had to make clear the chronology of the period under study and "the distinction between the traditional philosophy associated with Richard Hooker, and the liberalism of the Enlightenment which was founded upon the writings of John Locke"; and lastly,

5) that the Conclusion would need "to synthesize the principal lines of argument", and to assess the significance of Upper Canadian Toryism "within the broader perspective of toryism and the historical period".

In sum, what was required -- as the author interpreted the comments of the Advisory Committee -- was a re-structuring and severe editing of the initial draft of the dissertation chapters, and a repositioning and expansion of the work. The Advisory Committee was demanding that the tenets of the traditional Anglican Tory political philosophy of Richard Hooker and the Lockean-liberal political philosophy of John Locke be clearly set forth in the Introduction; that the Upper Canadian Tory ideas, beliefs and values be related more directly to the political issues of their day; and that the conclusion would need to place Upper Canadian Toryism within the broader field of contemporary early 19th Century British tory political thought and to expound on the historical significance of Upper Canadian Toryism.

In retrospect, it is evident that the author should have requested a meeting with the Advisory Committee to discuss their comments, and to explain and defend his approach to the writing of the dissertation and his planned conclusion. Instead he withdrew into his office to contemplate what to do. He did not agree with the Advisory Committee on the need to place Upper Canadian Toryism within the broader field of British tory political thought; and he had no idea – at the time -- as to how to express the historical significance of Upper Canadian Toryism beyond what he had set forth in his draft Introduction. On the other hand, he had already accepted the offer of a history position with the Canadian government, and no longer felt any compulsion to rapidly complete the dissertation. He needed time to think.

Although he had posited in his dissertation proposal that 'ideas influence actions', and argued that the reconstruction of the worldview and the constitutional, religious and educational ideas of the Upper Canadian Tories would yield a better understanding of their position on various political issues, there had been no intention on his part to consistently link the Tory political ideas with particular historical issues. The dissertation was intended – as envisaged by the author -- to comprise a reconstruction of the political philosophy of the Upper Canadian Tories, and was regarded as an intellectual study which would resolve the disagreement among historians as to whether the 'Upper Canadian Tories' were true Tories or Old Whigs.

It was the author's intention, in the Conclusion, to provide the intellectual analysis requisite to prove that the Upper Canadian Tories were true Tories within the traditional political philosophy of Richard Hooker, rather than Old Whig parliamentarians, or even Lockean-liberals with a 'tory touch'. The Conclusion was envisaged as consisting of a comparative analysis of the beliefs, values and principles of the Upper Canadian Anglican Tories with: the pristine political philosophy of Anglican Toryism, as set forth by the Anglican theologian, Richard Hooker; the beliefs, values and principles of the Old Whigs of the 18th Century; and the Lockean-liberal political philosophy, as set forth in the works of John Locke.

Within the draft chapters of the dissertation, there were numerous references to contemporary politics in the Province of Upper Canada, but admittedly no consistent linking of the Tory political ideas to the major political issues of their era. Moreover, the author had had no intention of assessing 'the significance of Upper Canadian Toryism', or of placing Upper Canadian Anglican Toryism within the broader field of the history of contemporary British Toryism. Admittedly he had discussed both approaches initially, with his dissertation advisor, when contemplating the British North American tories as a potential dissertation topic, but the actual dissertation proposal had focused strictly on reconstructing the ideas, and the underlying political philosophy, of the Upper Canadian Tories. He had regarded such a study as a significant contribution to the intellectual history of Upper Canada, and had seen no need to place his work within a broader historical and intellectual context.

It was a disheartening blow to realize that the Advisory Committee did not agree with his approach to the writing of the dissertation, or to its existing structure and limited focus. To keep busy, he focused on completing the writing of the dissertation chapters and pursuing research for the writing of the projected conclusion, prior to his scheduled departure from the History Graduate School of McMaster University at the end of May 1974. By that time, he was beginning to come to terms with the situation. He would make the structural revisions and editorial work that were called for, and would undertake the additional research required to place the study within a broader intellectual and historical context. It would be done through part-time work while pursuing his professional career as a public historian with the Historic Sites Directorate of the Canadian Government in Ottawa.

As of the summer of 1976 -- despite receiving several letters of encouragements from his dissertation advisor -- the author began to feel totally overwhelmed by the magnitude of the work underway. A strong work ethic was not enough. It had become quite evident that the completion of the dissertation, in keeping with the advice of the Advisory Committee, would demand a concentrated period of research, reading, and additional thought that he was not able to provide while working full-time as a public historian. At the same time, he found that he was enjoying his work as a public historian. The projected 'great work' on the Upper Canadian Tory Mind ended with a whimper. The draft text of the dissertation and research notes were reluctantly put away in storage boxes, and the author withdrew fully from the Ph.D. program at McMaster University.

Despite entreaties from family and colleagues over the succeeding years, the author refrained from undertaking any additional work on the dissertation. He remained single-minded in the pursuit of his career as a public historian in researching, recording, and evaluating the significance of historic engineering works for Parks Canada, and in preparing reports on the national historic significance of various persons, places and events in Canadian history for the Historic Sites and Monuments Board of Canada. In that regard, he worked within the specialized fields of industrial archaeology, the history of technology, public works history, and Canadian history more generally, as well as in the heritage conservation field for Parks Canada. Upon retirement from the Parks Canada Agency, in August 2004, some consideration was given to reviving the dissertation work, but the author had several manuscripts in hand on subjects related to his research and recording work at Parks Canada that he wished to edit and publish. The dissertation chapters remained stored in boxes in his basement.

It was only when working -- in retirement -- on another book project, *Military Paternalism, Labour, and the Rideau Canal Project* (2013), that the situation changed. In seeking to set forth the significant differences between Anglican Toryism and Lockean liberalism in an appendix to that work, the author drew heavily on the knowledge that he had gained through his earlier research on his projected dissertation. In doing so, that exercise awakened anew the author's earlier ambition to produce a lasting work in intellectual history focused on the political philosophy of the Upper Canadian Anglican Tories. Moreover, there was now the added drive of a feeling of a debt owed -- as an historian -- to the Anglican Tories of Upper Canada by way of doing them justice in setting forth their beliefs and achievements in a published work. The contents of the basement storage boxes were examined to determine whether all the typescripts of the draft chapters of the dissertation were extant, and to ascertain whether they might lend themselves to publication as a book.

The typescripts of the Introduction and dissertation chapters were found extant, as well as the research notes. Upon perusal in February 2014, it was decided that the abandoned dissertation might well be publishable as a book. A conclusion would be needed, and the chapters would have to be copy-edited. Initially, the intention was simply to copy-edit and publish the extant work as written -- an intellectual study of the political thought of the Upper Canadian Anglican Tories that set forth the Tory worldview and their values, beliefs and principles as they pertained to the constitution of Upper Canada, religion and education.

After a forty-year hiatus, the author had no interest in undertaking a complete recasting and rewriting of the manuscript to shape it as a Ph.D. dissertation, nor any interest in placing the study within the context of the latest secondary works pertaining to the history of Upper Canada. The draft dissertation chapters would simply be copy-edited, with the insertion of some additional historical material, and published as a four-decades-old cultural fragment: a long-neglected historical document that recorded the political philosophy of Anglican Toryism in the Province of Upper Canada. In deciding to do so, the author was acutely aware of his long-held belief in the dictum that 'ideas transcend time'. A conclusion would be prepared in keeping with his original intention in the writing of the dissertation.

To reduce the length of an overly long, and rather unwieldy Introduction, two sections -- which set forth the intellectual connection between the Loyalists and Anglican Toryism, and the views of George Grant on the fate of conservatism in the modern era – were removed and placed in appendices. The problem posed by the physical bulk of the multiple sources cited in the endnotes, has been partially addressed by grouping the notes at the end of each part of the study, rather than all together at the back of the book. Several overly long chapters were simply divided and reworked as two separate chapters.

In sum, this work has evolved in a rather unorthodox fashion, but has retained an inner logic and coherence in the reconstruction of the values, beliefs and principles of the Upper Canadian Anglican Tories, a mention of the ideological struggles in which they were engaged, and in the setting forth of the Tory response to the various public issues of their day. As such, it is a noteworthy study of the Upper Canadian Anglican Tory Mind.

On a professional level, the author is indebted to his former dissertation advisor, the late Dr. Goldwin French of the Department of History, McMaster University, for his willingness to accord -- to a graduate student -- a complete freedom to conceptualize and define the original study in following wherever the research led. The exercise of that freedom has resulted in a substantial work – this publication – which, it is hoped, will have a truly lasting value. The advice of the Advisory Committee, on how to shape the original draft of this study into a presentable Ph.D. dissertation, has been followed to a some extent in the preparation of this publication.

Nonetheless, the original Introduction and structure of the work have been retained, as well as the historical narrative -- 'in the moment' -- writing approach of the original dissertation chapters. As such, this work does not conform to a conventional Ph.D. dissertation. In the main, it consists of the reconstruction of the beliefs and values, and principles and ideas of the Anglican Tories of Upper Canada, and the political philosophy that underlay their political ideas and that gave a coherence and purpose to their political actions. In sum, this is a monograph in intellectual history. It is not a political treatise or a philosophical work; although it partakes, in part, of both types of studies.

On a more strictly personal level, I would like to thank my brother, John Passfield, for his encouragement and his comments on the text during the copy-editing phrase. His comments have contributed to an improvement in the clarity of the writing. I am indebted as well to my nephew, Craig Passfield, for the design and preparation of the book covers, and to a good friend, Ken Watson, for the preparation of the sketch map of the Districts of the Province of Upper Canada circa 1815.

Once again, a debt of gratitude is owed to Susan James for her understanding and support as my retirement years continue to be devoted to a demanding muse – Clio – in the research and writing of historical works. Any errors, omissions or misconceptions in the present work are solely the responsibility of the author.

Robert W. Passfield

Ottawa, Ontario
September 2017

Introduction

The Historiographical Context

'Ideas influence Actions'

The Tory World View

The National Policy

The Focus of the Dissertation

The Tory Governing Elite

The Scope and Significance of the Study

"What, after all, of Bishop Strachan and the young Tories he schooled, what else of Strachan the politician can one say than that it is the most difficult thing in the world to imagine there ever was such a man. Politically, he believed (as Walter Bagot said of Lord Eldon) in everything it is impossible to believe in."

William Kilbourn, a Liberal Historian, in his Introduction to
*The Firebrand, William Lyon Mackenzie and the
Rebellion in Upper Canada* (1956).

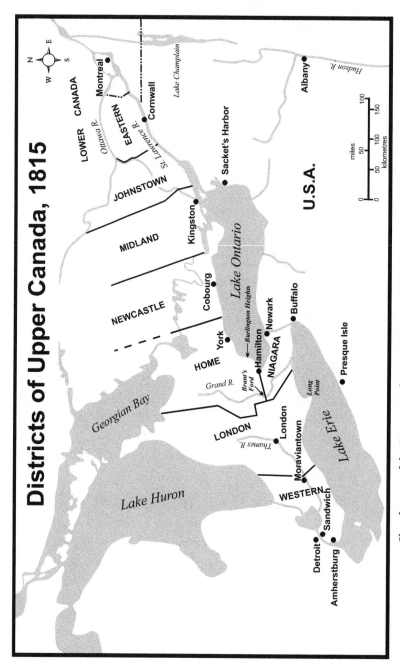

Districts of Upper Canada, 1815

Sketch map of the Districts of Upper Canada, 1815. By Ken W. Watson, 2018

Introduction

This Introduction to the projected Ph.D. dissertation was prepared during the winter of 1973-1974, while the author was striving to complete his study of the Upper Canadian Tory Mind. The Introduction incorporated the original dissertation proposal of October 1971, which had argued that an examination of the ideas, values, and beliefs of the Upper Canadian Tories with respect to the constitution, religion and education, would enable their underlying political thought -- their political philosophy – to be reconstructed. Such a study, it was maintained, would yield a better understanding of the positions that the Tories took on the public issues of their day, and would resolve an existing historiographical debate as to whether the Upper Canadian Tories were true Tories or Old Whigs.

The dissertation Introduction was produced at a time when the author felt on the defensive because several recently-published academic articles had argued that the Upper Canadian Tories were 'Old Whigs', rather than true Tories, and because of a growing concern that the concept of 'the Tory mind' might not be readily understood by Canadian historians. Hence, an effort was made in the Introduction to explain the approach taken to the writing of the dissertation, and to set forth the assumptions made by intellectual historians regarding the role of ideas in history, and the concept of 'the mind of an age' or the mind of a community. Above all, there was a concern to justify the significance of a study of the 'Upper Canadian Tory Mind' within the context of the then-prevailing liberal historiography in which the Tories were dismissed, disparaged, and denounced as reactionaries who had supposedly contributed little to the development of Canada.

The Dissertation Introduction

This study focuses on a select group of Upper Canadian Tories who played a leading role in formulating government policies and in guiding the development of the Province of Upper Canada in the two decades following the close of the War of 1812. It aims to arrive at a better understanding of the stances taken by the Upper Canadian Tories on the political issues of their era, and the rationale behind the 'national policy' that the Tories called for the provincial government to adopt. It will do so through a reconstruction of their worldview, and the ideas, values and beliefs that governed their response to the situation in which they found themselves in the Province of Upper Canada. In sum, this

3

study constitutes an effort to reconstruct the Upper Canadian Tory Mind as a body of political thought through an analysis of extant sermons, pamphlets, newspaper articles, and the private correspondence and the memoranda of four men who provided leadership to the Upper Canadian Tories of that era. Such a reconstruction has implications for achieving a better understanding of the conservative tradition in Canadian history, and for resolving an historiographical debate.

The Historiographical Context

The reconstruction of the ideas, beliefs and values of the Upper Canadian Tories as a unified body of political thought will permit a resolution of an historiographical debate as to whether the Upper Canadian Tories were genuine Tories who were defending a timeless traditional order, or Old Whig parliamentarians of the 18th Century who were defending a political and social order that pre-dated the American and French revolutions.

A Canadian philosopher, George Grant (*Lament for a Nation, The Defeat of Canadian Nationalism*, 1965), has asserted that the Canadian conservative tradition was "more than the covert liberalism" which passes for conservatism in the United States. It was derived from British Conservatism, which although "not philosophically explicit", nonetheless included a conception of the common good, of virtue, and of an eternal order; and it was these concepts which, among other characteristics, that distinguish a true conservative philosophy from Lockean-liberalism. In support of his assertion, Grant has noted that the Anglican Loyalists "appealed to the older political philosophy of Richard Hooker" to justify their rejection of the Lockean-liberalism of the American revolutionaries. (1)

In contrast, Terry Cook of Carleton University had argued ("John Beverely Robinson and the Conservative Blueprint for the Upper Canadian Community", *Ontario History*, 1972), that the Upper Canadian Tories were conservatives only in the context of their time. He maintained that the Old Whig values of the American colonial leaders were transformed during the American Revolution – under the influence of the writings of John Locke -- into liberal values that embraced "new and startling views of representation, consent, constitutions, and sovereignty"; and that

4

it was these novel political values and the "democratic excess" of the American and French revolutions which brought about a conservative reaction. For Cook the conservatives of Upper Canada were men who still clung to traditional values, but they were defenders of the "older whig notions" of order, authority, hierarchy, obedience and deference, "against the new heresies of democratic republicanism and popular sovereignty". According to Terry Cook, the so-called 'tories' of Upper Canada, were defending conservative values, but they were not "those of the pristine Toryism of Elizabeth and Hooker" which "did not survive the Glorious Revolution of 1688". (2)

In sum, Cook maintained that the Upper Canadian conservatives of the early nineteenth century – whom their contemporaries referred to as 'tories' -- were actually 18th Century whigs; whereas, to the contrary, George Grant has claimed that the Upper Canadian Tories were 'true Tories' -- defenders of a far older Tory system of beliefs and values as articulated in the works of the Anglican Divine, Richard Hooker (1554-1600) at the time of the English Reformation. It is a controversy that merits an examination and resolution.

A study of Toryism as a body of political thought will have value as well in contributing towards a better understanding of the current Canadian political culture because of the role which Toryism has played in its evolution. A Canadian political scientist, Gad Horowitz ("Conservatism, Liberalism and Socialism: An Interpretation", 1968) has argued that while English-Canadian and American societies are very similar in origin, nonetheless the political culture of Canada has important "un-American characteristics" which are "all related to the presence of toryism" in Canada. (3) In contrast, in the United States -- as pointed out by an American historian, William Nelson (*The American Tory*, 1961) -- Toryism did not reappear after the American Revolution. The United States, through its revolutionary experience, achieved "an alarming uniformity of outlook" -- a thoroughgoing Lockean-liberal political culture. (4)

From an historical viewpoint, a study of Upper Canadian Anglican Toryism has value because of the central role that the Tories played in the history of the Province of Upper Canada, and Canada more generally.

In several publications, Professor S.F. Wise of Carleton University has stressed that it was conservatives who, following the close of the War of 1812, provided "the leadership in economic and political nationalism" which was to sustain Canada throughout the better part of the nineteenth century. (5) It was the conservatives who were "acutely conscious of the military, economic and political menace of the United States", and who -- out of a concern for the survival of their distinct values -- formulated and pursued policies which transcended purely local interests to meet the dangers that were inherent in the peculiar position of Upper Canada. These 'national policies' were invested with "a special sense of mission" which the conservatives imparted to succeeding generations of Canadians during the developmental projects of the canal building era and, subsequently, during the railway construction era of the 1850s.

Ultimately, as argued by Professor Wise, "it was precisely this kind of developmental strategy, in the hands of a second generation of Upper Canadian conservatives, that was central to the scheme for the union of the British North American provinces in the 1860's and for the cementing of that union in the post-Confederation era." (6)

Moreover, the economic development policies of the Upper Canadian conservatives were directly related to the "total structure of conservative values" which, in turn, came to inform the tone, feeling, and character of Canadian politics as the reformers joined the tories in rejecting democratic radicalism. Professor Wise maintains that it was the fundamental attitudes and political values of the Upper Canadian tories, moderated somewhat over time, which by the 1850s permeated the bulk of the population of Upper Canada. (7) Furthermore, Professor Wise has argued that the conservative value system and outlook, and the 'nationalist assumptions' which it embodied, also provided the goals, as well as the means to carry forward Confederation and the nation-building efforts of Sir John A. Macdonald. (8)

Despite the important role which conservatism has played in the development of Canada and its political culture, no Canadian historian or political scientist has attempted to reconstruct in a comprehensive manner the political thought and outlook of the Anglican Tories of the Province of Upper Canada.

George Spragge, in his editor's introduction to *The John Strachan Letter Book: 1812-34* (1946), touched briefly upon the attitudes of a leading Upper Canadian Tory -- the Rev. John Strachan – towards education, religion, and government, and Strachan's views of the United States and Britain. However, the introductory remarks do not include any detail on the specific values that the Tories wished to conserve. (9) A study by H.G.J. Aitken (*The Welland Canal Company: A Study in Canadian Enterprise*, 1952) has commented upon the positive attitude of the Upper Canadian Tory 'oligarchy' towards business and economic development. (10) However, no one has reconstructed the broader political philosophy of the Anglican Tories of Upper Canada.

In several published articles, Professor Wise has sketched conservative arguments concerning "the vital social and political utility of religion", and some conservative social attitudes. He has discussed, as well, the wide ramifications of the tory conception of 'loyalty', and has explained how the providential outlook of the conservative Anglican and Presbyterian clergy governed their interpretation of the French Revolution and succeeding events. (11) Moreover, Terry Cook -- a graduate student of Professor Wise -- has commented briefly upon the economic attitudes, social outlook, and constitutional arguments of another leading 'conservative', John Beverley Robinson, in sketching Robinson's view of the ideal conservative community. (12)

In two additional articles in *Canada Views the United States* (1957), Professor Wise has delineated what he regarded as some of the negative aspects of Canadian toryism in the period 1812-1850, by showing what it was that Canadian conservatives were rejecting in the American experience as they saw it. However, Wise has readily admitted that his two articles omitted "the positive aspects" of Canadian beliefs, tory or otherwise, and did not give a coherence to the entire a body of conservative values. (13)

This latter is what has been lacking in the works published to date pertaining to Upper Canadian conservatism, and more particularly to Toryism in Upper Canada. Various Tory beliefs and values have been commented upon, or described, and their response to specific problems or events have been set forth, but no one has come to grips with the whole range of tory policies and the political philosophy that gave form and meaning to their principles and values. Nor has anyone traced the relationship between the ideas, hopes, and aspirations of the Upper Canadian Tories and their political actions.

Neither Upper Canadian Toryism, nor individual Tories, can be properly understood through studies which are confined to an articulation of the policies espoused by Upper Canadian Tories in isolation from their whole matrix of values. Such an understanding can come only from a reconstruction of the Tory worldview and the Tory political philosophy, which gave structure and meaning to their thoughts and, in large part, motivated and conditioned their political actions and reaction to events. Hence, a study of the study of the 'Upper Canadian Tory Mind' is requisite.

'Ideas Influence Actions'

This study rests upon an assumption, which has been made by intellectual historians, that the understanding of the history of a period, "its politics or public events", is dependent upon an awareness of "the climate of opinion" of the time: "the peculiar mixture of ideas and values that made up the mind of [the] age". It is a conviction that the actions of individuals and of peoples proceed in relation to a specific set of assumptions and ideas and take place within a particular conjunction of circumstances. Hence, it is from the manifold interaction of circumstances and ideas that the history of a period ought to be assessed and written. (14)

That is equally the case whether one is studying the history of an historical period or, on a more limited scale, the history of a community in any given historical period. The achievement of an historical understanding depends upon the recognition that:

> If ideas in politics more than elsewhere are the children of political needs, none-the-less, is it true, that the actual world is the result of men's thought. The existing arrangement of political forces is dependent at least as much upon ideas, as it is upon men's perception of their interests. (15)

Hence, ideas play a critical role in history, regardless of whether one fully accepts the assertion of the American intellectual historian, Perry Miller that "the mind of man is the basic factor in human history". (16)

The study of the mind of an age, or the mind of a group of particularly influential men, is a complex process. Such a study needs to embrace the conjunction of circumstances and ideas, as well as the legacy of traditional thought and the then-current ideas of the milieu within which the men acted. The ideas of individuals are not held in isolation, but rather are the expressions of a deeper coherent body of thought which provides a basic motivation for their actions. (17)

In sum, the actions of men are not merely an arbitrary response to various events or contingencies. Their response to events, and even their interpretation of the circumstances to which they respond, is determined by the intellectual framework of their mind: their worldview and their political philosophy, the latter of which embraces their basic principles, beliefs, and values which form their character and outlook. Hence, it is requisite that the body of thought that constitutes the mind of an age, or the mind of a specific historical community, be reconstructed and treated as a coherent whole. (18)

Within such a context, the intention of this study of The Upper Canadian Tory Mind is to facilitate the achievement of a better understanding of the conservatism tradition in present-day Ontario, through a reconstruction of the underlying body of thought which gave coherence to the political positions and actions of the Tory elite of the Province of Upper Canada in the two decades immediately following the War of 1812.

Within the political culture of Upper Canada, the Tory mind and the mind of Upper Canada were not one and the same. The Province never enjoyed a homogeneous political culture at any time of its existence. Indeed, if one accepts the Horowitz interpretation of the fragment theory of Louis Hartz – that the culture of English Canada differs from the Lockean-liberal political culture of the United States due to the presence of a Tory fragment within the Lockean-liberal Canadian culture – then Toryism deserves serious study for its cultural significance. Moreover, the Tories of Upper Canada, although a minority, were a very significant and powerful community who governed the Province for over two decades during a major period of development. (19)

On their part, the Tory elite of Upper Canada were aware that they were living in a revolutionary age wherein there were two different political systems in conflict – the traditional and the revolutionary – and that Upper Canada was not, and could not be, immune to the struggle.

They described their situation, as follows:

> Ever since the period when the French Revolution burst like a strange meteor upon the world, and startled nations, there has been no cessation of the conflict between anarchy and infidelity on the one hand, and subordination and true religion on the other. Wars have raged and ceased, but the din of battle has been succeeded by a conflict of opinion almost as desolating to the moral fabric of society, as the ravage of war to its political state. (20)

Thus, from the end of the War of 1812 until the political demise of the Province of Upper Canada in February 1841 – which is the period upon which the dissertation focuses -- Upper Canada was the scene of what the Tories regarded as a veritable 'battle of ideas'. And in such a situation, no equation can be made between the Tory mind and the mind of Upper Canada.

In seeking to reconstruct the mind of an identifiable community, the question arises as to whether the men themselves were conscious of possessing any guiding principles and values, or whether the historian, in reconstructing the body of their supposed thought, imputes a logic to their actions of which the actors themselves were unaware. Even if one accepts the premise that 'ideas influence actions', it does not imply that the actors were aware of any deeper coherent body of thought which underlay their ideas.

In defending a traditional order, the reactions of men may be based simply on commonly accepted ideas and beliefs or an emotional resistance to change that is unrelated to any conscious deeper thought. (21) Nonetheless, such an occurrence does not mean that the men who provided the leadership for their society or community were unaware of the deeper values being defended. In Upper Canada, the Tory political elite, enunciated their principles, values, and beliefs in defence of the traditional order, and expounded upon what they believed to be its deeper moral and religious essence and, in doing so, they revealed the philosophical content of their thought.

Given that the Tory elite of Upper Canada were conscious of the deeper meaning and significance of the principles, values, and beliefs which guided and provided a motivation for their public actions, there is a justification for seeking to reconstruct that body of thought. The objective is to gain a greater understanding of the deeper meaning and significance of the principles, values, and beliefs which were enunciated by the Tories of Upper Canada in response to the public issues of their day.

An example of this approach can be found in a treatment of Edmund Burke (1729-1797) -- the Old Whig parliamentarian and political pamphleteer -- by a Cambridge University historian, Charles Parkin (*The Moral Basis of Burke's Political Thought*, 1956). Parkin points out that studies which concentrate on the ideas of Edmund Burke simply in terms of their historical and immediate political context do not do justice to his thought and deprive his ideas of any meaningful content. In recognizing that ideas ought not to be divorced from the events and circumstances to which they were addressed, Parkin maintains that "while Burke's thought is by design a response to immediate contingencies, it is in no sense an uncontrolled or arbitrary response".

The ideas expressed by Edmund Burke in response to the political issues of his day were – in Parkin's words – "an expression of a coherent moral philosophy of man and community". Burke never set forth his governing beliefs in a formal treatise; yet Parkin has found it possible to reconstruct them as a single body of thought. (22) It is same situation with respect to the Tories of Upper Canada, and a similar treatment is requisite.

The Tory World View

When the provinces of Upper Canada and Lower Canada were united in the United Province of Canada in February 1841, it brought the political demise of Upper Canada and inaugurated what the Upper Canadian Tories regarded as "a strange new order of things" (23). In the depths of despondency, the leading Tories reaffirmed their conscientious adherence to "the principles of Church and State". They declared their determination to maintain their political beliefs "at every personal sacrifice" in knowing full well that a defence of such principles would bring down upon them the disfavour of the 'new men' of the government of the United Province of Canada, and of a large segment of the population. (24)

In defending the traditional order, both then and during the preceding two decades, the leading Tories used arguments that were leavened with references to such concepts as 'loyalty', 'subordination', 'deference', 'order', 'providence', 'true religion', 'church-state alliance', 'national church', and 'balanced constitution'. These concepts had a meaning for them which transcended their immediate historical context. In sum, they were – to paraphrase Parkin's comments on Burke's ideas – 'the expression of a coherent religious and moral philosophy of man and community'.

The Tory National Policy

In educating the sons of the social elite of Upper Canada -- at the District Grammar School in Cornwall, Upper Canada in the decade prior to the War of 1812 -- the Rev. John Strachan aspired to have his pupils achieve a future prominence in the public life and professions of the Province of Upper Canada. In the postwar decade, that aspiration was realized as the young Tory 'gentlemen' entered the professions and public life and, in comprising a well-educated elite in a pioneer society, they soon rose to positions of prominence in their respective fields. Once in positions of power and influence, the 'young Tories' – under the leadership of the Rev. John Strachan and his protégé, John Beverley Robinson – sought to implement a national policy program to guide the development of the young Province of Upper Canada, and to lay the foundations for a future nation within the British Empire.

Immediately following the close of the War of 1812, the leading Tories of Upper Canada began to call on the provincial government to implement the various aspect of their national policy, while trying to convince the British government to render its full support. The National Policy was intended to defend the existing order, to safeguard the well-being of the province, and to strengthen the "British national character" of the province. In presenting arguments in support of the proposed program, the Tories drew upon their fundamental principles and beliefs, and enunciated their basic values. In doing so, they provided a vehicle for comprehending the deeper body of thought of Anglican Toryism, which provided a unity and coherence to their political actions.

In presenting their arguments in favour of the implementation of their national policy in its various facets, the Anglican Tories made explicit what they regarded as the purpose of the various institutions of the state, and articulated the principles and values which they held ought to govern a well-ordered polity. They also revealed what they saw as threatening the existing institutions of the province and the social order, and their view of the purpose and efficacy of the institutions that they were defending. Thus, an understanding of the National Policy is central to any effort to understand the worldview, beliefs and values of the Upper Canadian Anglican Tories. It was formulated in response to the events of their time, and the circumstances in which the Tories found themselves, but drew on the deeper governing principles and values of the Tory mind. Hence, this study has a dual focus. It sets forth the Tory view of the events and circumstances which gave rise to the National Policy, and reconstructs the governing beliefs and values of the Anglican Tory mind as reflected in their arguments in support of their National Policy objectives. In setting forth the Tory beliefs and values, the study is sub-divided further in focusing on the Tory views of the constitution, the national church, and education, which were regarded as being "the three great pillars of the body politic". (25)

In one sense, the effort to separate out the several major elements of the Upper Canadian Anglican Tory Mind – the constitutional, the religious, and the educational -- is quite artificial. One of the primary characteristics of the Tory mind is its view of the body politic as being organic in nature. Tory political, religious, and educational ideas – as well as their social values -- were completely integrated, interdependent, and mutually sustaining; yet the various elements are differentiated in this study. That effort has resulted in some minor repetition in the various chapters, but an effort has been made to keep any repetition to an absolute minimum consistent with setting forth the essence of Tory political thought in the three critical areas.

The National Policy was born at a time when the Province of Upper Canada had narrowly escaped being overrun -- during the War of 1812 -- by a new revolutionary power, the United States of America. It was a republic that showed unmistakable signs of becoming even more powerful in the future, and that appeared to be committed to an extension of its democratic republicanism over the entire North American continent by force of arms. The future existence of the Province of Upper Canada appeared to be quite precarious. In facing such a threatening situation, several of the leading Tories of Upper Canada called upon the British Government to act, in conjunction with the Province government, to defend the existing institutions of state and the traditional order on which they depended, and to implement a unified plan of government action to develop the resources of the province and to maximize its strength and population.

To that end, the leading Tories had a very definite conception of what a 'national policy' should comprehend. In a succession of memoranda and lengthy letters -- which were submitted to the Colonial Office at intervals throughout the decade following the termination of the War of 1812, and at times of crisis thereafter -- the Tories elaborated on their ideas in detail. Over a period of two decades, they were to show a striking degree of consistency in the policies which they put forward as being necessary to the very survival of the province. The policies, which they advocated, constituted practical solutions to political problems that plagued the Province of Upper Canada.

The Tories argued that a concerted plan of action would be beneficial not only to the Province of Upper Canada, but also to the Mother Country upon whose unstinted aid and support the prescribed measures were dependent for their ultimate success. The Tories were convinced that the growing power of the United States, and its expansionist nature, made it impossible for the Province of Upper Canada to survive without a commitment from Great Britain to use its power in defence of the colony. However, the National Policy program was designed not only to prepare Upper Canada to resist foreign aggression in the form of American expansionism, but also to counteract an ideological threat: viz. the impact that the American democratic-republican ideas were having within the Province of Upper Canada.

One of the primary aims of the National Policy was to maintain, strengthen, and build a particular type of society in Upper Canada, and ultimately in British North America at large: viz. one having a "British national character". The experience of the war years, recent historical events, and the bias of the education which they had received, all combined to establish a fundamental dichotomy in the Upper Canadian

Tory mind. For the Anglican Tories, the aggressive and acquisitive American national character, and the democratic secular polity of the United States which they viewed as a 'mobocracy', represented all that they deplored in any people or in any society. In contrast, the British national character was viewed as the ideal for sustaining a polity based on 'peace, order and good government'. England was regarded as 'the good society' incarnate which Upper Canada should strive to emulate.

What the Anglican Tories sought to construct in Upper Canada was a society modeled on that of England. Upper Canada was to have a well-ordered polity, which would be peopled by subjects who possessed:

> the character of a perfect British citizen, who knows his rank, his place, his value, his duties, and his rights; and who will not step out of his own sphere unless he can do so in a constitutional manner -- one to whom *self-denial* is as dear a privilege as the protection of his person and property, because the detail of that virtue among his fellow citizens is his own security.

The Upper Canadian Tories were not unaware that England had shortcomings, but these were attributed to human frailties rather than to any imperfections in her institutions. From the vantage point of Upper Canada, it seemed that in England

> the comforts, the Knowledge and the virtues of social life have been carried to the highest perfection. The lofty sense of independence among her people, their truthful and vigorous morality, their sober and rational piety and the impartial decorous and laudable administration of their laws are all matters of joyful admiration.

The policies that the Tories wanted to see adopted as part of a national policy were aimed at establishing a foundation for the development of the Province in keeping with what they thought the Province of Upper Canada was, and ought to be. They believed that Upper Canada was founded as an asylum for the Loyalists of the American Revolution. It was an asylum where the Loyalists could continue to live as members of the British Empire, to be governed by British institutions, and to enjoy the unsurpassed benefits of British subjects and of British civilization within the British Empire.

For the Anglican Tories, the Province of Upper Canada was an integral part of 'the national family' of Great Britain and had as much of a claim to belong and to receive the benefits of her government as any county of England. Upper Canadians, as British subjects, were entitled to the same rights and security as British subjects in the United Kingdom. Thus, the Upper Canadian Tories did not hesitate to request the aid of Great Britain in support of their proposed national policy measures.

The National Policy program covered all areas of 'national life', including politics, religion, and education, as well as immigration, defence, and the economic development of the province. It involved the maintenance of the existing constitution -- the Constitutional Act of 1791 -- and the strengthening and extension of the Church of England which was held to be the established National Church of Upper Canada. A national system of education was to be established which would be open to all, but under the aegis of the provincial government and the direction of the Established Church. British emigration, particularly of men of means and good character, was to be encouraged to increase the population; whereas the influx of American settlers was to be curtailed until the national character was sufficiently formed to permit American immigrants to be safely absorbed.

Changes were to be made in the laws which governed the naturalization of foreigners to ensure that all public positions, including the positions governed by election as well as by appointment, would be kept in the hands of 'the loyal' for the immediate future. For the Tories, 'the loyal' were the *bona fide* Loyalist settlers, British immigrant settlers, and the men who had fought in the defence of Upper Canada during the recently concluded War of 1812, or had otherwise distinguished themselves in opposing the American invaders. Those who were to be excluded from public positions, were recent immigrants – primarily American settlers -- who had yet to become naturalized British subjects or had refused to take the Oath of Allegiance to the King. Many of the pre-war American settlers in Upper Canada had been disaffected during the War, and were viewed as being democratic republicans in their political beliefs. During the War, many of the pre-war American settlers had refused to fight in defence of the province against the American invading armies, some had joined the American invaders, and most had refused to support the war effort in defence of Upper Canada.

As part of the National Policy, the Tories advocated that the colonies of British North America be incorporated into a general political confederation under the Crown to foster the development of closer ties, both tangible and intangible, with the mother country. This development was envisaged as involving some form of imperial federation, which together with existing imperial trade preferences, would promote the development of a common national feeling. It was held that in time, the British connection of Upper Canada would be strengthened through the maintenance and sharing of a common character and outlook embodied in the British national character.

The French Canadians of the Province of Lower Canada were to be peaceably assimilated to the British national character in the proposed new general confederation of the British North American colonies. It was to be done by extending to French Canadians the benefits of a provincial education system – with bilingual teachers -- and by the opening of public offices to those who availed themselves of the opportunity to learn English. In the meantime, the representatives of the French Canadians in the elected House of Assembly of the proposed confederation government would be unable to block legislation aimed at promoting the economic development of the provinces or to oppose British emigration to the North American colonies. Where Upper Canada was concerned, various measures were proposed to foster the economic development of the province, and to establish essential war industries. The Tories also supported the plans prepared by the British military for strengthening the militia and the defences of Upper Canada. (26)

In the Tory mind, the various measures advocated in the National Policy program were interrelated and mutually sustaining. They could not be separated, one from another, without endangering the whole. Ultimately, the National Policy was a product of the Tory Mind: viz. of their worldview, their political philosophy, the circumstances in which they found themselves within the Province of Upper Canada, and their commitment to preserving the Loyalist asylum of Upper Canada and the traditional values on which it was founded.

The Focus of the Dissertation

The Upper Canadian Tories believed that the Christian religion was of the essence of Toryism, and of a true conservatism; and that both the public and private behavior of men ought to be governed by Christian principles. Hence, this dissertation examines the published writings of the Anglican Tories of Upper Canada for their religious, as well as their political and social content, in seeking to reconstruct the unifying body of political thought that underlay the principles, values and beliefs which the Tories espoused in defending the traditional order. More particularly, the sermons of a leading Anglican Tory, the Rev. John Strachan, have been consulted to determine the extent to which the preaching and teachings of the Church of England underlay the principles, values and beliefs of the Upper Canadian Tories, and provided a coherence and unity to their political thought.

One of the problems faced, in seeking to reconstruct the conservative mind in any given era, is that conservatives do not feel the need to articulate their most deeply-held beliefs. They "[assume] certain things to be immutably true and established", and take their legitimacy for granted. It is only when the traditional order is openly questioned, or its overthrow threatened, that the defenders of that order – the conservatives – see the need to articulate their basic principles and beliefs. They are enunciated only in response to a threatening challenge, and any study of conservatives must take that into account. (27)

In a time of crisis, whenever the traditional order may come under attack, the mind of the defenders of that order is revealed in two important ways: how the conservatives view their attackers, interpret their motives, and conceptualize the danger they pose; and secondly, how the conservatives propose to defend the existing order, and the principles that are cited to justify the actions which they propose to take. In such instances, conservative values, principles, and beliefs are set forth, but often they are not articulated within a coherent body of thought, or enunciated in sufficient detail to permit their reconstruction into a unified body of thought. However, that was not the case where the Upper Canadian Anglican Tories are concerned.

They lived in an age of revolutionary upheaval and social unrest wherein the traditional order was under siege. The spirit of anarchy and infidelity, which emanated from the French Revolution, and the democratic republican principles and expansionist policy of the new United States of America, were viewed as posing a constant threat to the political character of Upper Canada, as well as a threat – where the Americans were concerned -- to the very survival of Upper Canada as a province of the British Empire. It was a threatening situation which compelled the Tory elite to provide an articulate defence of the traditional order. In the frontier society of Upper Canada -- which was in a pioneer stage of development -- they had not only to defend the institutions which sustained the existing order, but had to act to establish, strengthen, and extend them, which involved an effort to explain and justify what they were striving to achieve to gain the support of the provincial and Imperial governments.

The Tory Governing Elite

Much of Tory politics in the post-war period was focused on the implementation of a national policy, which was formulated at the close of the War of 1812 to guide the development of the Province of Upper Canada. It was the Rev. John Strachan who, for the most part, was responsible for the formulation of the national policy. He was ably assisted by his former pupil and protégé, John Beverley Robinson, in working out the details of that policy, in securing provincial acts to further the national policy objectives, and in the seeking the aid of the British government in support of the various national policy initiatives. In many ways, the national policy consisted of a setting forth -- in a unified program -- of several initiatives that Richard Cartwright – an Anglican Loyalist, and close friend and associate of the Rev. John Strachan -- had urged on the provincial government in the years prior to the War of 1812 to protect the 'national interest' of the Province of Upper Canada. The Tory national policy was an embodiment of the governing principles of the Anglican Tory mind and, as such, the initiatives of the national policy program received a strong support from John Macaulay, a High Church Tory, the son of a Loyalist, and yet another former pupil of the Rev. John Strachan.

When the Rev. John Strachan entered public life following the War of 1812, it was to promote the interests of the Established Church of England and to defend the traditional social, religious, and political order. In that endeavour, he counted upon, and for the most part received, the support of the young men whom he had educated in his Cornwall District Grammar School (1803-1811) at Cornwall, Upper Canada. His former pupils were the sons of the leading Loyalists and prominent British immigrants whose families comprised the political, social, and economic elite of the province. Indeed, a significant number of his former pupils, who were among the most highly-educated young men in the province, were just entering the professions, the government, the Church, and public life in the immediate postwar period.

Within two years of the August 1818 arrival of a new governor in Upper Canada -- Lt. Governor, Major General Sir Peregrine Maitland – the members of a distinctive provincial Tory elite were becoming well established in the provincial government, in the judiciary at all levels, and in education. And they would remain in positions of power and influence until the demise of the Province of Upper Canada in 1841. The governing elite of the Province of Upper Canada comprised the Rev. John Strachan and his protégé John Beverley Robinson -- who provided the leadership in articulating a response to critical issues and challenges – and prominent young Tories who were educated by the Rev. John Strachan. They held public office together with men who shared their principles and values in being defenders of the traditional order.

For two decades, the provincial Anglican Tory elite struggled to carry forward a national policy program of provincial development, but were opposed by several opposition groups who were aligned in the House of Assembly under the umbrella of the Reform Party. Among the opposition groups were political radicals, liberal-whigs, evangelical sectarians and, as of the early 1830s, egalitarian democratic republicans. In seeking to implement a national policy program, the governing Tories were also plagued by the indifference, and often the outright opposition and/or the direct intervention in the politics of Upper Canada by the Colonial Office following the coming to power of the Whig Party reformers under Earl Grey in November 1830.

The Scope and Significance of this Study

Neither the national policy *per se*, nor the extent to which the Tories managed to implement their national policy program, are the subject of this study. The arguments, ideas, and principles that were expressed by the leading Tories -- in support of the various components of their national policy -- comprise simply the materials from which the political thought of the Upper Canadian Anglican Tories has been reconstructed, and an understanding gained of their worldview with respect to the circumstances in which they found themselves, and the nature of the forces which they perceived as threatening the overthrow the traditional order.

Because of the vast extent and quality of his writings, as well as the intellectual leadership that he provided for the Tory elite of Upper Canada, the bulk of this study rests firmly upon the thought of the Rev. John Strachan (later Bishop Strachan), and to a lesser extent upon the papers and writings of John Beverley Robinson and Richard Cartwright. Their writings have been supplemented by research in the published writings of John Macaulay. In several instances, the published writings of two other well-known Tories, the Rev. Alexander Neil Bethune and the Rev. Adam Hood Burwell were consulted to expand upon, corroborate, or fill gaps in the understanding of the political thought that gave a coherence and unity to the principles, values and beliefs which were enunciated by the leading Upper Canadian Tories. Both Bethune and Burwell were former pupils at the Cornwall District Grammar School, and were trained and ordained as Church of England clergy by the Rev. John Strachan. (28)

All the individuals on whom this study focuses were Anglicans, and many of the leading members of the Upper Canadian Tory elite were Anglicans. Whether, and to what extent, the worldview and political thought of the Anglican Tory elite was representative of the outlook and values of the broader body of conservatives in Upper Canada is not a concern of this study. During the postwar period, the Anglican Tories were in a minority in Upper Canada, but they were a very important, influential and powerful minority, whose most prominent members governed the Province of Upper Canada during the two post-War of 1812 decades upon which this study focuses.

It is not the purpose of this study to identify, in any broad sense, the Tory element in Upper Canada, the extent of its influence, or its relationship to other groups in that society. For example, not all Tory residents of Upper Canada were Loyalists, and not all Loyalists were Tories; yet the Upper Canadian Anglican Tory elite closely identified themselves with the Loyalist heritage of the American Revolution. Nonetheless, it was an identification that conveys little, nor is it intended to, about any connection at a deeper philosophical level between the Upper Canadian Anglican Tories and the Loyalists of the American Revolution. There was an intellectual connection; yet the extent of that connection is beyond the scope of this study.

This study is intended to yield a better understanding of the nature of Upper Canadian Anglican Toryism, to reveal the rationale for the positions that were taken by the Anglican Tories on the public issues of their day, and to provide a deeper meaning and significance for the principles, values and beliefs which were expressed by the leading Anglican Tories of Upper Canada in their defence of the traditional order. Most importantly, this study reconstructs -- within a unified body of thought -- the principles, values and beliefs which characterized the Anglican Tory cultural fragment which was absorbed into, and played a very important role in the shaping of the conservative tradition in the Canadian political culture. In a broader sense, if, as intellectual historians maintain, the 'mind of an age' is a basic factor in understanding the history of a period, then this study of the Anglican Tory mind of Upper Canada -- a study of a very significant group in an age of ideological diversity -- should contribute toward the writing of a more comprehensive history of Upper Canada than has been produced to date.

Finally, the insights and beliefs of the Anglican Tories in what constitutes the foundation of a stable political order might well give Canadians pause for reflection. The principles, values and beliefs of the Anglican Tories of Upper Canada provide an alternate view of the purpose of life, and of man's nature, to that of the man-centred Lockean liberalism which at present prevails in Canada. The Upper Canadian Anglican Tories judged men by their actions and sought always to act in keeping with what they regarded as an eternal moral order and eternal verities. The Christian principles and beliefs which governed their lives, and in which they felt compelled to instruct their fellow subjects in Upper Canada, embodied for them "the complete teaching for all men everywhere" independent of, and unaffected by, time or circumstance. (29)

Notes

The Dissertation Introduction

1. George Grant, *Lament for a Nation, The Defeat of Canadian Nationalism* (Toronto: McClelland & Stewart, 1965), 33, 63, 65, 69-70, 72-73, & 65, footnote #22. The reference to Richard Hooker is from page 64.

2. Terry Cook, "John Beverley Robinson and the Conservative Blueprint for the Upper Canadian Community", *Ontario History*, LXIV, June 1972, 72-94. The transformation of whiggism into liberalism during the American Revolution is admirably treated – as Cook points out – in Bernard Bailyn, *The Ideological Origins of the American Revolution* (Cambridge, Mass.: Harvard University Press, 1967).

3. Gad Horowitz, "Conservatism, Liberalism and Socialism: An Interpretation", *Canadian Journal of Economics and Political Science*, 32, 2, 1966, 143-171. Horowitz lists what he considered to be the un-American characteristics of English-Canadian society.

4 William Nelson, *The American Tory* (Boston: Beacon Press, 1961), 190.

5. S. F. Wise, "Conservatism and Political Development: The Canadian Case", *The South Atlantic Quarterly*, LXIX, 1970, 226-243; and S.F. Wise, "Upper Canada and the Conservative Tradition" in Edith Firth, ed., *Profiles of a Province, Studies in the History of Ontario* (Toronto: The Ontario Historical Society, 1967), 20-33.

Although Professor Wise makes several astute observations about the evolution and continued importance of conservatism in 19th Century Canada, his article on 'Conservatism and Political Development' is not concerned with conservatism *per se*. The article is an exercise in applying the techniques of political developmentalists to the British North American colonies of the early 19th Century. Wise points out the built-in bias in employing that economic theory, and its limitations.

6. Wise, 'Conservative Tradition', 30; and Wise, "Conservatism and Political Development', 241-242. The quotation is from page 242.

7. Wise, 'Conservative Tradition', 30-32. For a related commentary, see: S.F. Wise, "The Annexation Movement and Its Effect on Canadian Opinion, 1837-67", in S.F. Wise & R.C. Brown, *Canada Views the United States, Nineteenth-century Political Attitudes* (Toronto: Macmillan, 1967), 94 & 95 in which Wise points out that the democratic republicanism of men such as William Lyon Mackenzie and Louis-Joseph Papineau represented only a small minority of Canadians by mid-century. "However much the fortunes of nineteenth-century radicalism have attracted the interest and sympathy of later historians, the Canadian radical tradition is so episodic in character that it may scarcely be said to have existed". This statement is true of the short-lived democratic republicanism of Mackenzie and Papineau, but not of democratic radicalism *per se*.

8. Wise, "Conservatism and Political Development', 242. See also, Wise, 'Conservative Tradition', 31.

9. G.W. Spragge, ed., *The John Strachan Letter Book: 1812-1834* (Toronto: The Ontario Historical Society, 1946), i - xxviii. The interpretation that Spragge presents of the policies of the Rev. John Strachan is marred by two misconceptions: first, that Strachan's ultimate purpose was political – the maintenance and strengthening of the British connection – to which his education and religious plans were subservient (ix & xiv); and secondly, that the attitude of John Strachan toward government was that of a man who "to use modern jargon, ... believed in a totalitarian state" (xxv). Such was not the case on either point.

10. H.G.J. Aitken, "The Family Compact and the Welland Canal Company", *Canadian Journal of Economics and Political Science*, XVIII, 1952, 63-76.

11. S.F. Wise, "Sermon Literature and Canadian Intellectual History", *United Church of Canada Archives Bulletin*, XVII, 1965, 3-18; Wise, "Conservatism and Political Development', 232-234, and S.F. Wise, "God's Peculiar Peoples", in W. L. Morton, ed., *The Shield of Achilles, Aspects of Canada in the Victorian Age* (Toronto: McClelland & Steward, 1968), 38-61, and especially 45-49. In the article on Sermon literature, Professor Wise points out how valuable sermon literature is "as a medium for the expression of conservative ideas" (page 5), and comments as well upon the vital role which the sermons of the conservative clergy played in "the formation of a conservative political ideology" in Upper Canada" (pages 6 & 8).

12. Cook, 'Conservative Blueprint', 81-94.

13. The two articles by Professor Wise in *Canada Views the United States* (1967), are: "Colonial Attitudes from the Era of the War of 1812 to the Rebellions of 1837", 16-43; and "The Annexation Movement and Its Effect on Canadian

Opinion, 1837-67", 96 & 97. [For Professor Wise and his graduate students, the terms 'conservative' and 'tory' are treated as interchangeable when dealing with political alignments and political thought in the Province of Upper Canada. This study argues that there were different types of conservatives in Upper Canada, of which the High Church Anglican Tories were but one conservative element.]

14. R.N. Stromberg, *An Intellectual History of Modern Europe* (New York: Appleton-Century-Crofts, 1966), 1. [This historiographical analysis dates from 1974. More recently, Canadian historians have produced several studies on the political ideology of Upper Canada that comment on tory attitudes and beliefs. To date, none have treated Anglican Toryism as a unified body of thought, viz. as a political philosophy.]

15. J.N. Figgis, *Studies of Political Thought from Gerson to Grotius, 1414-1625* (Cambridge: Cambridge University Press, 1956 (First ed., 1907), as quoted by Stromberg, 1-2.

16. Perry Miller, *Errand into the Wilderness* (Cambridge, Mass.: Harvard University Press), 1956, ix.

17. Stromberg, *An Intellectual History*, 2.

18. Alan Heimert, *Religion and the American mind, From the Great Awakening to the Revolution* (Cambridge, Mass.: Harvard University Press, 1966), 21.

19. The Hartzian approach to the understanding of the political culture of new societies is to be found in Louis Hartz, *The Liberal Tradition in American, An Interpretation of American Political Thought Since the Revolution* (New York: Harcourt, Brace & world, 1955), and Louis Hartz, et al., *The Founding of New Societies, Studies in the History of the United States, Latin America, South Africa, Canada, and Australia* (New York: Harcourt, Brace & World, 1964). In the latter, its application to Canada is treated on pages 219-262. See also Gad Horowitz, *Canadian Labour in Politics* (Toronto: University of Toronto Press, 1968), 4-19, in which he discusses the Hartz cultural fragments theory as it applies to Canada.

20. Provincial Archives of Ontario (PAO), Strachan Sermons, Box C, Hebrews 12:11, "Chastening yieldeth Righteousness', 8-9, 16 March 1806; Strachan, *A Sermon Preached at York, Upper Canada, on the Third of June, Being the Day Appointed for a General Thanksgiving* (Montreal: William Gray, 1814), 25-29; *Kingston Chronicle* (John Macaulay editorial), 24 March 1820; and *The Church* (Rev. A.N. Bethune editorial), 3 November 1838. The quotation is from *The Church*, 3 November 1838. For a similar expression of the Tory view that they were living in a violent "age of revolutions" marked by "discontent & innovation", see: PAO, Strachan Sermons, Box C, St. Paul's Epistle to the Hebrews, 12:11, "Chastening yieldeth Righteousness", 8-9, 16 March 1806.

21. Karl Mannheim, *Essays on Sociology and Social Psychology* (New York: Oxford Press, 1953). In a chapter on "Conservative Thought", Mannheim contrasts 'traditionalism' and 'conservatism'. Traditionalism is defined as merely "a tendency to cling to vegetative patterns, to old ways of life", and "an instinctive fear of change, which is not related to any particular political thought". In contrast, conservatism is a "style of thought", "*an objective mental structure*". He defines 'modern conservatism' from a historicist approach, and insists that conservatism is "*not* objective in the sense of being eternally and universally valid". Rather it is objective in the sense that conservative action cannot be divorced from "*a concrete set of circumstances*", and therefore transcends "the subjectivity of the isolated individual" whose actions – either consciously or unconsciously – it guides. (Mannheim, 95-96, italics his.)

What the sociologist, Mannheim, defines as 'conservatism' is what political scientists categorize as 'situational conservatism'. However, neither the sociological nor political science definitions of 'conservatism' apply to Anglican Toryism' which embodies eternal certitudes that transcend time and circumstance. Similarly, the sociological definition of 'ideology' does not fully encompass Toryism as a political philosophy. For example, a sociologist, Joseph Roucek, maintains that the ideology or thought pattern of a social group is "always an expression of a specific social situation" in response to which the group "develops its own conceptual apparatus ... and a specific *style* of thinking adapted to its social position." (J.S. Roucek, "A History of the Concept of Ideology", *Journal of the History of Ideas*, V, 1944, 479-488, and especially 479-480.) Roucek cites the ideology of bourgeois liberalism as a case in point, but he does not address Toryism which, contrary to his argument, embodies timeless values. Nonetheless, one could argue that Anglican Toryism did express 'the specific social situation' of the Upper Canadian Tories, and did embody 'a specific style of thinking' that reflected their social aspirations, as well as their deeper religious beliefs. The specific social situation of the Tories in Upper Canada could be interpreted as accounting for why they continued to adhere strongly to a belief in the Christian value system when Lockean-liberal values were adopted by the intellectual elite in Europe and embraced by the new American republic.

22. Charles Parkin, *The Moral Basis of Burke's Political Thought* (New York: Russell & Russell, 1956), 1-3.

23. PAO, Macaulay Papers, reel 3, John Macaulay to Ann Macaulay, 24 December 1839.

24. *The Church* (Bethune editorial), 1 June 1839. For the Upper Canadian Anglican Tories, the political embodiment of Toryism was the unity of church and state. They proclaimed themselves to be 'Tories' based on their adherence to Christian moral values and their belief in an established church and a church-

state polity. Moreover, they continued to oppose secular liberalism long after the demise of Upper Canada. See PAO, Strachan Papers, reel 6, 61, John Macaulay to J.B. Robinson, 22 February 1850; PAO, Robinson Papers, Robinson Letterbook 1814-62, J.B. Robinson to Strachan, 8 April 1851; and PAO, Strachan Letterbook 1844-49, reel 12, Strachan to Robert Gillespie, 2 February 1848.

25. There are numerous references to the need for 'a national policy', and what such a policy should comprise, in the various letters and reports produced by Strachan and Robinson. On "the three great pillars of the body politic", see the *Kingston Chronicle*, 31 December 1831, "One of the People" [Rev. Adam Hood Burwell].

26. The economic development and defence policy components of the Tory national policy are not treated in this study. The quotations are from the *Kingston Chronicle*, [Rev. A.H. Burwell], "One of the People", 28 May 1831, and PAO, Strachan Sermons, Box E, Psalm 29:11, "Lord Will Give Strength", 4 November 1855, 4-5, respectively.

27. Wise, "Sermon Literature and Canadian Intellectual History", 15.

28. S.F. Wise ("God's Peculiar Peoples", 56), has noted that: "John Strachan, more than any other man, was responsible for the framing of Tory policy in church and state, and for the rationale by which it was defended". Elsewhere, Wise comments ("Sermon Literature", 14) with respect to the Rev. John Strachan: "His impact upon the Ontario community in its formative stage was very great ... and yet it cannot be said that his ideas have ever been adequately analyzed".

[There are now excellent online biographical sketches, with extensive bibliographies, for the leading Anglican Tories of this study in the *Dictionary of Canadian Biography*: viz. IX, G. M. Craig, "Strachan, John" & Robert E. Saunders, "Robinson, Sir John Beverley"; V, George Rawlyk and Janice Potter, "Cartwright, Richard"; and VIII, Robert Lochiel Fraser, "Macaulay (McAulay), John".]

29. The quoted phrase is from George Grant (*Lament for a Nation*, 95), and the point being made is dependent upon an understanding of Grant's discussion of the difference between ancient and modern philosophy. As Christians, the Anglican Tories did not forsake revealed religion or the traditional view of the Christian cosmos, and did not believe that human reason alone was the ultimate arbitrator of truth, virtue or goodness. In contrast, Lockean-liberalism is a man-centred, individualistic and rationalistic, modern political philosophy.

Part One

The Spectre of Revolution & Infidelity

"Never was the world agitated with so violent convulsions as at this moment. This indeed may be emphatically called the age of revolutions. ... the spirit of discontent & innovation has spread itself in every direction. For, if we cast our eyes over the map of the world, it will present a state of commotion never before known. ... For whosoever shall consider the changes that have happened since the colonial war [the American Revolution], must confess that the judgements of God are abroad upon the earth."

The Rev. John Strachan (1806)

Drawn by Major Bentai.

Published April 17th 1830 for J.W. LAIRD's Martial Achievements at Leadenhall St.

Prepared by T. Sutherlan

'Battle of Queenston Heights, 13 October 1812'. By Major James Dennis, engraved 1836. Toronto Reference Library.

Chapter One

The Age of Delusion

A key element, in seeking to understand the response of the Upper Canadian Anglican Tories to the political issues of their day, is the worldview of the Tories: viz. how they saw their situation in Upper Canada, their place in the wider world, and their interpretation of the major political events of their era. It was their worldview, which was derived from their deeper cultural values, that conditioned and guided their response to the forces which they perceived were threatening the existing political order and the very survival of the Province of Upper Canada. The Upper Canadian Tories were born into an age of political revolutions, and social unrest, wherein the very civilization which they knew, and valued, appeared to be threatened with a complete destruction. Political unrest and revolutionary upheaval was part of their heritage, even their family experience, and that heritage conditioned their very consciousness of what Upper Canada was intended to be, how it should be governed, and the critical importance of having a strong national church.

The Loyalist Province

For the Upper Canadian Tories, the Province of Upper Canada was pre-eminently a Loyalist asylum; a sanctuary which had been set aside by the Crown for the unfortunate Loyalists who had been reduced to poverty and driven into exile for their attachment to Britain during the American Revolution. In commenting upon the history of the early settlement of Upper Canada, the Tories were prone to stress that the province had been settled exclusively by men of tried and approved loyalty whom they divided into four general categories: first and foremost were the men of the Loyalist Provincial Corps who had fought for the Crown during the Revolutionary War and, secondly, the Loyalist families who had actively adhered to the Crown and quit the American colonies during the revolutionary struggle.

The third group comprised the known Loyalists who were forced to leave the newly-independent United States at the end of the war; and lastly the thousands of passive Loyalists – the so-called "Late Loyalists" -- who for a variety of reasons chose to leave the new American republic in the decade after the revolutionary war. It was believed that these four groups were comprised of men of firm loyalty and attachment to the

British Constitution and to the Unity of Empire. As a reward for their loyalty, the British government had welcomed them to settle on the waste lands of the Crown in British North America, and had created the Province of Upper Canada for them by the Constitutional Act of 1791, which divided the old Province of Quebec into the provinces of Upper and Lower Canada.

To the Tories, Upper Canada was intended to be a Loyalist haven wherein Loyalist principles would predominate as was attested to, as they believed, by several actions of the Crown. Among them were the bestowal, as a mark of honour and approbation, of the designation "United Empire Loyalist" upon those who had actively fought for the Crown and British sovereignty during the revolutionary war, the support provided to the Loyalists by the British government during their settling into the wilderness, and the pecuniary compensation paid the Loyalist for their losses incurred during the American Revolution. Moreover, the Loyalists were given free grants of Crown land, and their children were eligible for free land grants upon attaining their majority. For the men and officers of who had fought in the Provincial Corps the acreage of their grants depended on their rank. (1)

In responding to attacks from their detractors -- at a later date -- the Tories continued to maintain that the Loyalists had fought for the Crown and emigrated to Canada, not with an eye to receiving land, or benefiting from any potential commercial advantages, or from sordid mercenary motives, but rather out of pure patriotism and loyalty to the Crown and British Constitution. They were motivated by a sense of duty to support the established order, and ultimately by a desire to continue to live under English laws and the British government.

Far from being motivated by selfish interest, the men of the Loyalist Provincial Corps had responded with alacrity to fight for the Crown, and did so even in the absence of such traditional inducements as promises of land to be bestowed upon recruits at the termination of their enlistment. The Tories maintained that Loyalists had stood for, and many had fought for the constitutional rights of the Crown and the supremacy of Parliament which were regarded as coextensive with the British Dominions. They had sacrificed everything in seeking to defeat rebellion and maintain the unity of the Empire. For the Upper Canadian Tories, there was no doubt but that the Loyalists had acted from a spirit of loyalty in discharging their duty to God, to their Sovereign, and to their country in defending and/or standing up for what they believed to be right.

They were regarded as men who were scrupulous about forfeiting their allegiance and were opposed to a resort to arms to settle political disputes. They were men who had remained confident in the willingness of the Crown to redress all serious grievances, and who were bound to the Crown by a sense of duty, as well as feelings of affection and respect. Defeated in their efforts and sacrifices on behalf of the Empire, during the American Revolution, and faced with the hostility of the American rebels, they had emigrated to the wilds of the Province of Quebec from the American colonies. Through labouring in the wilderness, they had hoped to establish a society wherein their children could live as British subjects, in rending a dutiful obedience to their Sovereign, and enjoying all of the privileges and benefits of British laws and British institutions. (2)

From the beginning of settlement, even before the Province of Quebec was divided into Upper and Lower Canada in 1791, the leaders of the Loyalist settlements were deeply concerned to maintain both a British national character and British principles in their settlements. They were opposed to any promiscuous entry of settlers from the newly-established United States of America. Although anxious to build up the population of Upper Canada, and in favour of the government admitting settlers from the former American colonies, the Tories in their petitions to government were careful to insist that all such emigrants be required to furnish a proof of their loyalty before they were given a Crown land grant.

Many relatives of the Loyalists and other families -- passive Loyalists, who were not active in opposing the rebels during the Revolutionary War -- were allowed to settle in the western wilds of the Province of Quebec after the American Revolution. However, in 1789, in response to the petitions of the Loyalist communities, a Land Board was established in each of the four districts of the western part of province where the Loyalists were settled. The Land Boards were appointed to examine into the loyalty of prospective settlers from the United States, and to ascertain whether they were of good character, before issuing a certificate of location. Once accepted, a family was given a free grant of 200 acres of land. Loyalist entrepreneurs from the United States, who were prepared to establish a saw or grist mill and/or to found a new settlement by bringing in a party of settlers, were granted upwards of 1200 acres.

Initially, the Loyalists welcomed the accession of the 'Late Loyalists' to their population, but had soon experienced a considerable alarm. In 1794, during the administration of Lt. Governor John Graves Simcoe, the Land Boards were abolished. Under Lt. Governor Simcoe, the new provincial government of Upper Canada ceased to pay close attention to the character and past conduct of the American immigrants whom they allowed to obtain land grants in the province. Indeed, through what the Tory-Loyalists regarded as laxness on the part of the provincial government, a situation developed where "people were received promiscuously from the States without let or hindrance".

Many of the leaders of the Loyalist communities in Upper Canada forwarded memorials and petitions to successive Governors-in-Chief at Quebec in protest against the unrestricted influx of American settlers into the province. They expressed their astonishment and indignation that large sections of the province were being populated by Americans who had no claim whatsoever to being called Loyalists.

Not only was such a state of things a complete denial of the Loyalist belief that their lands had been bestowed upon them as a reward for their services and sacrifices on behalf of the Crown during the American Revolution, but it was a positive danger from a political point of view.

The concern of the Loyalist communities was expressed very forcibly by Richard Cartwright in a memorial to General Hunter in 1799, when the latter succeeded John Graves Simcoe in governing of Upper Canada.

> In all establishments of a political nature, it is of more consequence to lay a solid foundation than to give them a sudden and premature celebrity. In the founding of a colony, the character of the inhabitants seems to be much more material than their number; these, in the course of time, will

be sufficiently multiplied by natural causes, that, if originally
faulty, is not so easily changed. (3)

It was not denied that Americans were good settlers from a purely
agricultural standpoint. Indeed, it was admitted that they were the most
adept at meeting the demands of pioneer life; and that they were not
particularly hostile or treacherous in their attitude toward the government.
However, the political notions of the American settlers were considered to
be highly objectionable.

The influx of American settlers had evoked opposition from the Loyalists
– and the Anglican Tory Loyalists in particular -- because it was realized
that in coming to Upper Canada the American immigrants were not
motivated by any preference for, or attachment to, the civil and religious
institutions of the province. They had come into the province only to
better their circumstances by acquiring free land grants upon easy terms,
or to establish mills and other enterprises in keeping with their individual
'spirit of enterprise' or, in some cases, simply to escape prosecution for
crimes committed in the United States. In short, the Tory Loyalists held
that American settlers were entering the Province of Upper Canada for
every motive but loyalty.

More generally, the American settlers were regarded as having a tendency
towards insubordination, and were viewed as possessed of an affectation
for equality which boded ill for the development in Upper Canada of a
national character marked by a British tone and feelings, and a respect for
British institutions. Besides which, most of the settlers arriving from the
United States at the turn of the century were religious dissenters, rather
than adherents of the Anglican Church. Thus, in the minds of the Anglican
Tory Loyalists, the real danger in admitting American settlers to Upper
Canada was ideological.

The whole framework of American ideas and beliefs, and the attitudes
which they sustained, were regarded as a potential threat to the very being
of the Loyalist province. As expressed by Richard Cartwright, the Tory
Loyalists were acutely aware that:

> It is not to be expected that a man will change his political
> principles or prejudices by crossing a river, or that an oath of

allegiance is at once to check the bias of the mind, and prevent the predilection for those maxims and modes of estimating and conducting the concerns of the public to which he has been trained, from displaying itself, even without any sinister purpose, whenever an opportunity shall be presented.

The problem was inescapable, because such was the very nature of man. It was only natural that in the political sphere men would combine in support of the political principles and beliefs in which they had been raised. Hence, the presence in Upper Canada of American settlers in large numbers constituted 'a radical disease' that threatened to destroy the political health of the province. By the turn of 19th Century, the Tory Loyalists were convinced that the only effective remedy was to place an interdict on the grant of land to prospective American settlers "before their [numbers] become formidable and the evil incurable." However, that had not been done.

Later, during the War of 1812, the Upper Canadian Tories sought to address the threat posed to the British national character and security of Upper Canada by the large number of American settlers in the province. The Tories called for the British government to actively encourage discharged British army veterans to settle in Upper Canada as soon as the war was concluded. The British troops were regarded as men of a tried and true loyalty who were "bred up in habits of subordination", and who well suited to become orderly and well-affected settlers. If placed in the townships to the rear of the American settlements in large numbers, they would discountenance the affection for equality so discernible among the American settlers.

The foreboding of the Tories concerning the large numbers of American settlers in the province and the American affection for equality grew out of what they had observed in the American colonies. Great Britain had followed a free system of colonization in which religious dissenters from the national Church were permitted to emigrate to the colonies in contrast to the restrictive emigration policies of the other European colonial powers. However, rather than evoking gratitude and affection on the part of her colonial subjects, it had served to facilitate the fomenting of discontent and enmity towards the mother country and had culminated in a rebellion. (4)

The American Revolution (1765-1783)

What the Tories would continually seek to avoid in Upper Canada was the system of government and policies which in the American colonies had led to rebellion and a successful revolution. In that respect, they were heavily influenced by their interpretation of the origins and progress of the American Revolution which was derived from reading deeply in the contemporary histories of the Revolution, through hearsay from the Loyalists or, in the case of Richard Cartwright, from personal experience and observation. In contemplating the origins of the revolution, the Upper Canadian Tories were convinced that it was the product of the failings of British government policies in two general areas: the system of government established in the American colonies; and the lack of concern for the religious character of the colonies.

It was felt that, in the American colonies, Britain had allowed the colonists too much freedom and power in their local governments through laxness and neglect. In several instances, colonial governments were established that provided for the election of both houses of the legislature by the people and, given the widespread property ownership in the colonies, the colonial legislatures were thoroughly democratic. Such a form of government deprived the Crown of the protection and support of an appointed Upper House, and leaned too much towards popular government with the mother country having little control or influence at the local level.

But most importantly, it was the failure of the British government to provide support for the maintenance of an Anglican clergy in the colonies that was viewed as the basic fault of the British colonial policy. The Upper Canadian Tories believed that had the Anglican clergy been present in sufficient numbers in local parishes, they would have inculcated British principles and feeling among the colonial population, and thereby counteracted or precluded the development of any ardent desire to seek to separate, by force of arms, from the mother country.

The shortcomings in British government policy -- in the lack of support for the clergy of the National Church, in the lax governing of the colonies, and in the failure to establish a balanced constitution in all of the colonies -- were in time responsible for the development of a deplorable 'spirit of democracy and insubordination' that had fostered and reinforced a strong latent desire and longing for self-government and independence. It was that colonial frame of mind which the Tories saw, in retrospect, as the moving impulse behind American intransigence in their tax dispute with Great Britain. It was a desire for independence which, once awakened throughout the colonies, was such that nothing short of a complete despair of success could keep within bounds.

The conclusion drawn by the Upper Canadian Tories was that the American rebellion did not stem from the oppressive rule of Great Britain - which was non-existent - but rather that it was:

> the extreme mildness of the British government and the great liberty that was allowed [in the American colonies] that produced the revolution. (5)

When Britain had attempted to tax such highly-favoured colonies -- to help to alleviate the burden of the heavy national debt which she had assumed during the Seven Years' War (1756-1762) in defending the colonies against the France and its Indian allies -- the spirit of insubordination and latent desire for independence had broken forth in resistance. At that time, Britain paid the price for her lax administration, and for ignoring the religious character of the colonies. It was no accident that the resistance was led by the Massachusetts Bay Colony.

It was a colony that had been settled by men - Puritans - whose political and religious opinions were strongly tinged with the spirit of republicanism. Moreover, they had been allowed to conduct its government, from the time of the founding of the Massachusetts Bay Colony, "very much upon the plan of an independent Society". For years, the Province of Massachusetts had acted as if it were a sovereign independent state, engaging in free trade with the world in defiance of the Navigation Laws of the mother country. As a member of the New England League, Massachusetts had engaged in diplomatic negotiations with the French in 1643, and with the Dutch in 1650. Throughout the better part of the 18th Century, prior to the American Revolution, the Province of Massachusetts had continually acted as a sovereign power in seeking to deny the mother country any control over its affairs.

For the Upper Canadian Tories, it appeared indisputable that "the American rebellion grew out of the defection of the Puritans from the Church [of England]." From the commencement of their settlement in the New World, the Puritans had aimed continually at independence. They had submitted only with reluctance to the constitutional authority of the Crown. The republican disposition of the New England colonies was such that disaffection and discontent were rife. In such a situation, the outbreak of a rebellion in New England had been only a matter of time and circumstances. It was noted in retrospect that:

> the history of these colonies proves beyond dispute that they never were attached to the Parent State, never disposed to yield any obedience which they could avoid, and were only held in some sort of subjection by their own weakness and fear of the French.

The defeat of the French in 1763, which removed a hostile power from their very borders, and relieved the American colonies of their need for military and naval support from the mother country, provided the opportunity they were seeking. In judging that they had attained a sufficient strength to attempt to secure their independence, they did not hesitate to resist by force of arms all efforts on the part of the Imperial government to tax them. (7)

Although the Upper Canadian Tories maintained that the republican designs and desires of the Puritan settlers of New England were quite apparent from any reading of contemporary histories of the Puritan colonies, that factor was not considered as providing a complete explanation for the American Revolution. It did not account for why the other colonies, which were less deficient in their religious character, were moved to resort to rebellion to throw off the paternal rule of the mother country, particularly in the face of sustained efforts by the British government to conciliate the colonies. The Upper Canadian Tories gave this matter much serious study, and drew several conclusions of pertinence to the Province of Upper Canada in the early 19th Century.

Of itself, the British attempts to tax the colonies and the commercial restrictions of imposed by the Imperial government were not considered as capable of inducing a public discontent sufficient to incite a rebellion. The revolutionary fervent, which had gripped the colonies, was rather attributable to the manifold efforts of Massachusetts, regrettably all too successful, to induce a feeling of general indignation and to fan the flames of disaffection amongst the other colonies.

To serve their own selfish ends, and to attain the independence that they coveted, Massachusetts agitators had resorted to various artifices. Exaggerated accounts of fancied oppressions were circulated to the other colonies, as well as "false news" fabricated to win support for their struggle. The political agitators had not even shirked from engaging in criminal activities to promote their cause. However, in its effort to promote a rebellion, Massachusetts was aided immensely by the absence of any general government of the colonies, such as had been proposed by Governor Hutchinson of the Massachusetts colony in 1754.

Had such a government existed - or had the American colonies been given representation in the Imperial parliament - the Tories believed that not only would the other colonies have been kept informed of the machinations and ulterior motives of Massachusetts, but they would have dissociated themselves from them. Moreover, the British government would have enjoyed an opportunity of "learning the collective sense of the colonies" so that any real grievances could have been speedily redressed and the causes of dissention readily removed.

The conclusion drawn by the Upper Canadian Tories was that had the American colonies been united under a general government, and/or represented in the Imperial parliament at an early date, it would have precluded any discontent from escalating into a rebellion, and would have preserved the unity of Empire for generations to come. In the event, it was the system of government that inhibited the communication of the discontent of the colonists to parliament, and prevented the British government from providing effective leadership. In contrast, Massachusetts, ably assisted by various agitators and malcontents, was unhindered in her efforts to impart to the other colonies a spirit of rebellion which surfaced with the development of the taxation dispute.

In all colonies, discontented men and disappointed office seekers such as the Otis family connection, embezzlers, and ruined men such as Samuel Adams, joined together and formed factions to excite discontent and foment rebellion. Their aim was to attain positions of eminence under a new government which their misconduct had precluded them ever achieving under the existing system. These men in turn had been supported and countenanced by unscrupulous politicians and men of ambition, such as Dr. Franklin, John Hancock and John Adams, as well as by others who were motivated by various sordid interests such as a desire for plunder or to escape the debts which they owed to British merchants.

Aided by such men, Massachusetts had not only aimed at rebellion and independence from the very beginning of the taxation dispute, but her greatest fear throughout the developing crisis was that the Middle and Southern colonies would cease to maintain the spirit of opposition which had been so cleverly fostered. There was a fear that the other colonies would seek to become reconciled with the mother country.

Nonetheless, it was noted that such were the powers of faction to foment discontent when unopposed, and so compelling was such a bias of mind when once formed, that colonies with no real grievances had come to the support of Massachusetts. One of the best governed colonies, South Carolina, had no quarrel with its existing political constitution, and had no conflict of interest with the mother country, but was the first colony to act in support of Massachusetts by sending representatives to the Continental Congress. It provided a lesson that would not be forgotten by the Upper Canadian Tories when faced by the efforts of political agitators to foment discontent in Upper Canada. (8)

Amongst themselves, the Upper Canadian Tories differed as to whether Great Britain had a right to tax the colonies, given that the British government in 1778 had disclaimed any right to do so. In sum, there were Loyalists who agreed with the revolutionaries that the Imperial government had no right to tax the colonies. However, the Tories were united in believing that the attempt to tax the colonies was unwise, rather than motivated by any desire to oppress the colonies; and that, given the willingness of the British government to make concessions, there had been no justification for the rebellion of the American colonies.

During the early stages of the dispute, the sovereignty of parliament as the supreme governing and legislative power had not been questioned by the American colonists. Indeed, initially the unruly colonies had sought, with the encouragement of the parliamentary opposition in Britain, to establish a sham distinction between external taxes which they allowed were acceptable and internal taxation which was not. Yet when "a trifling tax on tea" was instituted on imports, that argument was hastily discarded. The colonies had turned to resistance under the leadership of Massachusetts, which wanted independence and nothing else.

To the Upper Canadian Tories, the British effort to tax the colonies was not an act of oppression, or an endeavour to lay the foundation for the exercise of arbitrary power. It was indicative only of a reasonable desire on the part of the Imperial government to raise revenues to reduce the large national debt that Great Britain had incurred during the fighting of two major wars in which the American colonies were defended against the French and their Indian allies: viz. The War of the Austrian Succession (1744-1748); and the Seven Years' War (1754-1763).

No matter how unwise the original decision to tax the American colonies might have been, once resistance flared up the British government had made a major mistake in continuing the attempt to conciliate the colonists. Given their aims, no concession short of an outright grant of independence would have satisfied them. Human nature was such that concessions made in the face of insurrection and defiance would merely increase the demands of the recipients and encourage further resistance.

Despite the British government making concessions "almost without limit", the colonists were not appeased. Once they had been seized by the spirit of disaffection, it would have been best to have simply left them to themselves. Yet, since such a course was politically inexpedient for the government of the day, the only recourse and proper policy was to rigorously enforce the law, and to leave concessions for a more settled time. (9)

The Upper Canadian Tories took issue with the statements in the American Declaration of Independence - a paper that they regarded as concocted to serve a party purpose - that the colonists had suffered a long train of abuses; and that Britain was seeking to impose an absolute tyranny over the American colonies. To the contrary, they held that an impartial examination of the different disputes between Britain and the American colonies, which ultimately culminated in rebellion, would show the colonies "in almost every case" were the aggressors. It was the colonists who were seeking to depart from the terms of their founding charters by acting and establishing laws inconsistent with the laws of the Imperial Parliament.

Economically, the American colonies had benefitted greatly from the Imperial connection. The colonies had been left to themselves to regulate all local commerce, and the overseas trade restrictions imposed by parliament were few. In return the colonists enjoyed access to the British home market and the markets of the other colonies of the British Empire, and benefitted from what amounted to a bounty on their exports through the higher duties placed on foreign products seeking entry into British markets. The Imperial trade regulation in force had been mutually beneficial for the Home country and the American colonies.

The Upper Canadian Tories were in sympathy with the American colonists who had objected to Britain putting restrictions upon colonial attempts to manufacture hats, paper and other products already manufactured in the mother country, and the imposition by Britain of trade regulations that were intended to confine colonial exports to the home market in Britain. However, the Tories held that the trade regulations had been imposed with the best of intentions. The science of political economy was not properly understood until David Hume wrote his essays, *Political Discourses* (1752), and Adam Smith published his book, *An Inquiry into the Nature and Causes of the Wealth of Nations* (1776). Thus, it was unfair to criticize Britain for imposing mercantilist restraints upon colonial trade when she did so from a general ignorance of the natural advantages that a free trade, unrestrained by government regulations, would yield. However, in defence of Great Britain, the Tories pointed out that the trade restrictions imposed on the American colonies by the Imperial Parliament were not nearly as illiberal as those enforced by the other colonial powers and were not oppressive.

Even if the new theories of political economy had been known, Great Britain could not have opened her ports to the trade of all nations while other markets continued to be protected by high duties and prohibitions. On balance, the Thirteen Colonies had received far more from the mother country than any benefits she received from them. It was pointed out that the colonies had been completely dependent upon British capital for their development; and that Britain, in defending the colonies and paying the interest on the national debt so contracted, had expended more than she gained in trade returns.

Nonetheless, such was the effect of "democratical jealousy" upon the American mind that once passions were aroused, reason was not heard. From 1765 onwards, even had Britain resisted a resort to coercive measures in response to colonial provocation, no reconciliation was possible. The prevalence of the 'spirit of democracy' had already rendered the American colonists incapable of even a moderate subordination. It was a spirit so strong that the colonies, having attained sufficient strength to rebel, did not hesitate to do so over a minor tax dispute.

For the Upper Canadian Tories, the American colonists were not resisting tyranny and oppression when they rebelled, but rather were acting according to the bias of their minds in response to imaginary grievances concocted by a particular province - Massachusetts - and various factions who had their own selfish interests to promote. Where the causes of the American Revolution were concerned, the Rev. John Strachan was moved to declare his belief that:

> future historians in relating this contest, will do justice to Great Britain, when the mania for undefined liberty and licentiousness shall have passed away. -- No longer biased by prejudice, the facts will not then bear the previous sentiments of those who relate them, and who will trace with coolness and precision the long train of miseries which have sprung from a rebellion nourished by faction and rendered successful through treachery. (10)

In sum, after studying the history of the American Revolution, the Rev. John Strachan and the young Tories whom he educated, were convinced that its origins were to be found in the restless 'democratic spirit' that had developed in all the colonies through the inadequacies of existing institutions, both political and religious. That inadequacy in turn had made it possible for a colony of republican sentiment - Massachusetts - to take advantage of a political dispute to foment discontent and a spirit of rebellion among all thirteen colonies. In assessing the reasons for the success of the rebellion, the Tories saw many of the same causes at work.

The continuation of the policy of concessions long after the outbreak of actual rebellion had merely increased the determination of the ill-disposed colonists to pursue their resistance, as did the foolish, half-hearted measures taken to crush the rebellion, and the encouragement given to the rebels by the opposition in the British Parliament. These factors were further compounded by a serious lack of judgment on the part of the British government which committed several major errors that had paved the way for a military defeat.

In the first place, the British government did not dispatch one-sixth of the number of troops required to maintain order, and protect the lives and property of the loyal population, while putting down the rebellion; and secondly, the British government ought to have foreseen the treacherous conduct of the two men appointed to command the King's forces. Both General William Howe and General John Burgoyne were political opponents of the Home government, and party men who had publicly stated that the war was unjust. They were not men who would prosecute a war to the utter defeat of their opponents, or who would welcome Loyalists to their standard.

Consequently, the Loyalists in the colonies had received neither protection, leadership, nor encouragement from the British Army to declare and fight for the Crown. To the contrary, on turning out to serve with the British army, they had been scorned for their loyalty, insulted and laughed at by its officers, with the result that thousands had returned home. Had the British army supported the Loyalists, and acted in concert with them, the rebellion would have been very soon put down. However, what was worse, in suffering rejection at the hands of the British Army, and receiving little protection from British troops, the loyal colonists were left with nowhere to turn.

The activities of the Revolutionary Committees were such that neutrality in the struggle was impossible. The loyal were faced with the prospect of declaring for the Crown and embracing personal ruin, or joining the rebels. The Tories believed that many were coerced into choosing the latter, and thereby augmented the forces of revolution and contributed to the ultimate success of the rebellion. (11)

In the absence of an effective government to maintain order, the colonists who did remain loyal to the Crown were left in a truly deplorable situation at the mercy of revolutionaries who conducted themselves in a shocking manner. The loyal subjects of the Crown were "hunted like wild beasts", stripped of their property, and "jailed or hanged without trial". In rejecting rebellion as a proper mode for settling grievances, the Loyalists had found themselves at the mercy of revolutionary mobs, and unprotected by any law. They were at the mercy of caprice and malice, where "discord reigned and all the miseries of Anarchy".

It was a cause of a great deal of vexation on the part of the Upper Canadian Tories that American and British historians in relating the history of the American Revolution ignored the persecution of the Loyalists - the former in consciously seeking to conceal their actions, and the latter out of ignorance. The Upper Canadian Tories were acutely aware of the magnitude of the suffering of the Loyalists. They pointed out that miseries inflicted on the Loyalists were comparable to what the French people had suffered during 'the Terror' of the French Revolution.

> The murders, imprisonments, and confiscations, perpetuated by the committee of Albany, equaled and far exceeded that of the committee of public safety in Paris, when the difference of population is taken into account.

Indeed, for Loyalists such as Richard Cartwright, and the Upper Canadian Tories who shared his views and sentiments, the American revolutionary struggle was not about liberty. True liberty was destroyed in the persecutions that the Loyalists suffered during the American Revolution. That experience had left the Loyalists of Upper Canada with a deep and abiding fear of disorder, and a strong concern for the maintenance of law and order and good government in any political society of which they formed a part. (12)

Of all the factors that the Tories cited to account for the American Revolution, and the suffering which the Loyalists had undergone, none was of any greater importance than the role which the dissenting ministers of religion and the evangelical sectarian preachers had played both in the origin and success of the revolution in Massachusetts and elsewhere. The experience of the revolution had left the leading Anglican Tories of Upper Canada with an acute consciousness of the danger which religious dissent and sectarianism posed to the political stability of a colony; and it generated a strong desire to strengthen the Established Church of England in the Province of Upper Canada.

In the American colonies, the British government had totally neglected to provide support for the clergymen of the Church of England, and in the absence of a regular clergy to furnish religious instruction, the people had come under the influence of dissenting ministers. During the rebellion, it was 'the dissenting ministers' - particularly in New England - who were among the most active and zealous proponents of the revolution. The Congregational ministers and the sectarian preachers had responded to appeals from the revolutionary Congress to preach the cause of revolution, "with the most hearty alacrity, inculcating sedition and treason fervently from their pulpits". In fact, not only had evangelical Calvinist preachers fomented discontent and rebellion; they had actively encouraged the fighting in that:

> the evangelical puritan ministers were plying the people with
> the Turkish doctrine, that whoever was killed by the King's
> troops in Battle was sure of going to heaven.

In stark contrast, the few clergymen of the Church of England who had made their way to America were imprisoned for their loyalty, and disparaged because they spoke of peace and abstained from politics in the pulpit. Yet, it was the members of the Anglican congregations who fought for the Crown throughout the rebellion.

The Tories were convinced that the dissenting ministers and evangelical sectarian preachers had contributed not a little to the opposition to the established colonial governments through their preaching and influence, and to the ultimate success of the revolution. For the leading Anglican Tories of Upper Canada, religious dissent and sectarianism was identified with the revolutionary upheaval of the American Revolution, and the Church of England with loyalty and the inculcation of British feelings and principles. In arguing for British government support for the training and establishment of Anglican priests in the parishes of Upper Canada, the Rev. John Strachan was moved to declare that had the British government properly supported a religious establishment in the American colonies, they would not have separated through a rebellion. (13)

Although the Upper Canadian Tories deplored the American Revolution, they did not believe that the American colonies were destined to remain a part of the British Empire forever had not the intrigues of faction incited a revolt. The resources of the American colonies, and their potential development, were so great that "the progress of natural causes must inevitably have led to their separation". Indeed, it was regarded as almost a maxim that colonies would, and should, join the nations of the world as equals whenever they attained the strength and capability to be self-sufficient in promoting the good of their people in an independent political union.

From the vantage point of the early decades of the 19th Century, the Upper Canadian Tories - unlike the Loyalists of an earlier generation - saw factors which they believed had made it inevitable that the American colonies would seek their independence sooner or later. Moreover, the Tories were aware that subsequently Britain had benefited ten times more from trading with an independent America than she had while bearing all the expense of governing and defending the Thirteen Colonies. Indeed, the Upper Canadian Tories came to argue, perhaps in seeking to make a virtue of necessity, that Great Britain was well rid of such insidious and ungrateful colonies which had yielded a dismal return to Britain for the millions of pounds spend in the quarrels of the colonists with the French and the Indians.

The Upper Canadian Tories came to regret the American Revolution not so much because it had fractured the unity of the Empire, but because of the way in which it had come about, the suffering that the revolution had inflicted upon the Loyalists, and its political repercussions. The American Revolution, by giving success to rebels, had been responsible for inflicting numerous miseries upon man. It had given birth to a veritable "age of delusion". Everywhere peoples were seen attempting to emulate the American experience in overthrowing their governments. And of all the revolutions, and attempted revolutions, none made a greater impression upon the Upper Canadian Tory mind than the French Revolution. (14)

The Age of Delusion

In the pre-War of 1812 period, the Upper Canadian Tories were well aware that they were living in a revolutionary age. In the American colonies the legitimate colonial governments had been overthrown during the American Revolution (1776-1783), and the traditional order and the rule of law was destroyed by the political leaders of the American Revolution who were advocating Lockean-liberal values: the pursuit of life, liberty and happiness, popular sovereignty, and the separation of church and state; whereas in France, the French Revolution (1789-1799) had witnessed the overthrow of the royal government, the installation of a democratic government, a Reign of Terror (1794) in which opponents of the new regime were executed by executive fiat and the Roman Catholic Church was persecuted by revolutionaries motivated by a rabid anti-clericalism. Moreover, in France a period of democratic anarchy had been succeeded by a ruthless military dictatorship, under Napoleon Bonaparte, that had plunged Europe into a series of revolutionary wars that were unprecedent in the loss of life and destruction of property. For the Tories, it was an 'Age of Delusion', for man to think that peace, order, and good government could be achieved by the rule of democrats and infidels who based their legitimacy on the support of the mob and their power to crush all opponents.

For the Upper Canadian Tories, who believed in a rational cosmic order, original sin, faith in Christ as the Redeemer, and God's moral law as revealed by reason and revelation, those who advocated that man could live a good life simply by 'following reason' (Locke), or his passions (Rousseau), or his 'emotions' (the evangelical sectarians), or majority opinion (the political democrats), or 'the general will' (Rousseau), were highly irrational men. For the Upper Canadian Tories, the so-called 'Age of Reason' of the 17th and 18th centuries was an irreligious and irrational age in which moral philosophy and political philosophy had degenerated from the philosophical works of the Ancients, and from the works of the medieval Scholastics -- such as Thomas Aquinas, who synthesized the philosophy of Artistotle on natural law and rational man with Christian theology -- and from the theology and political philosophy of Richard Hooker, the Anglican theologian. For the Tories, an age that believed in the pursuit of one's enlightened self-interest, individual happiness, and personal well-being as the proper goal of man, that viewed government as established only to protect life, liberty, and property without an overriding moral purpose and commitment to the promotion of the well-being of the people, that failed to acknowledge the concept of a 'common good', that rejected the Christian religion and Revelation, that embraced deism (infidelity) and ant-clericalism, and that regarded fallible human reason as the sole guide to virtue, the good, and morality, was truly an Age of Delusion. (15)

Chapter Two

The Onslaught of Revolution

The French Revolution made a deep impression upon the Upper Canadian Tory mind because it embodied political principles which were regarded as synonymous with chaos and disorder in any state: viz. the rejection of revealed religion and the natural hierarchical social order, the espousing of popular sovereignty, and the worship of human reason and the unbridled passions of man. The French Revolution had inspired religious dissenters, democrats, and infidels to attack the traditional social order and the established Christian churches of Europe. In the Tory view, the French Revolution – based on its revolutionary principles -- had followed a natural progression in descending into anarchy, and evolving into a military dictatorship. Once established, the military regime had threatened to overthrow the reigning dynasties of Europe and the international order.

In what was viewed as a critical struggle to preserve Christianity and true liberty, the Upper Canadian Tories saw Britain as standing alone -- in the period 1789-1815 -- in resisting domination by an anti-Christian revolutionary power and its successor a ruthless military dictator, while the established Church of England defended Christianity against the spread of democratic anarchy and infidelity. More immediately in Upper Canada, the Tories feared that the British national character of their Loyalist asylum was under threat, as well as the very survival of Upper Canada as a province of the British Empire. The nature of that threat – in both its ideological and military aspects – was evident in the Tory view of the revolutionary ideas being propagated abroad, recent events in Europe, and the growing influence and power of their immediate neighbour, the democratic republic of the United States of America.

The French Revolution (1789-1799)

From their vantage point in the early nineteenth century, the Upper Canadian Tories held that the French Revolution had proved itself to have been "the scourge of the world" from its commencement. It was interpreted as an abject example of the perils of bad government, and the dangers which any state faced in seeking to reform itself when its government lacked the will and the strength of character to resist demands for rash changes and hasty innovations in the face of a popular clamour.

The French Revolution was viewed as a product of shortcomings, both moral and religious, in the ruling class of France. It was the consequence of misgovernment and an unwillingness, or inability, of the Royal government to guide into legitimate channels a powerful desire for change which had been awakened among the French people. Once news of the American Revolution was introduced into such a situation, it had served as a catalyst that accelerated -- if it had not produced -- the revolution in France. (1)

In viewing the history of Europe prior to the French Revolution, the Rev. John Strachan was struck by the fact that, as of the mid-18th Century, western Europe appeared to be gripped by a spirit of improvement which permeated the people. Various reforms were made by several European governments in "actively promoting civilization". Laws were rendered less vindictive, and a greater concern was shown for the rights of the people. There was a greater religious toleration, and an increased attention paid to education and the spread of knowledge which held out the prospect of future improvements in the life of the people. However, despite some commendable efforts, the governments of Europe, particularly that of France, had failed to keep pace with the response of their subjects to the new spirit of improvement and desire for a better life. In France, a dangerous discrepancy had developed between a Royal government unwilling to grant substantial reforms and the rising expectations of the people.

Under King Louis XV (1710-1774), the stage had been set for the destruction of the French state when oppressive laws, and a rapacious and unjust royal government administration, were permitted to continue unreformed, while the King himself set a bad example for his subjects both in his personal conduct and that of his Court. The latter was marked by a general corruption of manners and "licentious morals", indicative of a complete lack of virtue. Such conduct among the Higher Orders, coupled with the various intrigues and selfish measures which they promoted, had undermined the State by weakening the authority of the Monarch and sowing discontent through all classes of society outside of the ruling circles.

Through misgovernment and a moral laxity, the King of France and his Court had produced a particularly dangerous situation at a time when a general increase in knowledge had produced a new consciousness amongst the people. It was a period of history when:

> the lower orders began to feel and appreciate their own importance; to be conscious of their right to greater freedom and happiness; and as these could not be immediately obtained, to nourish many pretensions, wishes, and desires, hostile to the established order of things. As their knowledge increased, their desires became the more vehement; and gave rise, at length, to a spirit of uneasiness, censoriousness, and disorder, which spread with astonishing rapidity. (2)

At that point, the American Revolution occurred and had such an impact on the people of France that it was -- so the Upper Canadian Tories believed -- "the chief cause of the French revolution". The role of the writings of Voltaire and the other philosophes in preparing the minds of the French for revolution was recognized, but it was pointed out that since most Frenchmen were illiterate, the influence of the philosophes was severely circumscribed. Their writings could have had little influence on the people at large compared to that of the American Revolution in bringing about the upheaval.

Thus, in accounting for the tremendous impact of the American Revolution upon France, two factors appeared pre-eminent to the Tories: the conduct of King Louis XVI (1774-1792) and his Court; and the return of the French soldiers from the fighting in America. In the first place, in giving military and political support to the American colonists -- subjects in arms against their lawful sovereign -- Louis XVI and his Court had done much to obliterate from the minds of Frenchmen their traditional "reverence and devotion for royalty".

The King of France and his Court, in defending the American rebellion and praising the declarations of the colonial revolutionaries, had caught the attention of the French people. Revolutionary ideas of liberty and democratic equality became popular within the nation, and a growing sympathy for American aims and ideals was inflamed by the French soldiers upon their return from the American colonies. The soldiers gave a revolutionary direction to the popular imagination by providing wondrous accounts of the rights and privileges, and happiness, which were supposedly enjoyed by the Americans, and in concocting fascinating descriptions of freedom and democracy. In doing so, they awakened "golden dreams of transatlantic felicity" in the French nation, with the result that:

the flame of blind enthusiasm was kindled in their breasts, and a desire for liberty excited which nothing could extinguish. (3)

Once a revolutionary situation developed among the French people, it was rendered even more acutely dangerous by the conduct of the soldiers. Having been exposed to the life, liberty and political equality of the American colonists, the soldiers had become turbulent, licentious, and insolent to their superiors, and furious for change. At that juncture, the monarchy and the ruling classes had received their chastisement, despite Louis XVI being a good king who – unlike his predecessor -- was motivated by an uncommon benevolence and love of his people.

The French State, which was plagued by financial difficulties and the opposition of the Parlement of Paris to the King, and was enfeebled by being deprived of its two strongest supports through the prevailing corruption of justice and religion, had tottered to destruction. It was unable to sustain itself when challenged by 'the new spirit' demanding change. The conduct of the Royal government in that time of crisis was a pregnant example of how not to deal with such a potentially revolutionary threat in that,

instead of meeting this spirit with a cautious firmness; conceding what appeared necessary; but opposing, with watchful energy, and circumspection improper innovations; the feeble administration of France, by changes too hasty, by unsteadiness of character; sometimes conceding too much, then violently retracting what had been given up, irritated the people, and produced such a fermentation, as ended in the destruction of the government, and the establishment of the most licentious anarchy. (4)

Two highly significant lessons were drawn from the events of the French Revolution. The most important lesson was that no government ought to deprive itself of the traditional supports of monarchy: viz. an established national religion; and the customary reverence for authority derived from good moral conduct and the exercise of a paternal rule on the part of those in authority. If a government did so, and sought to rule arbitrarily in denying God's moral law and the rights of the people, it would receive its chastisement at the hands of the people themselves. The second lesson was that "radical and organic changes, suddenly and rashly entered upon, must bring misery and ruin", as evidenced by the Reign of Terror in France (September 1793-July 1794).

The tragedy of the French Revolution underlined the fact that those possessed of the new vision of liberty, if unrestrained, would bring unparalleled wretchedness and desolation upon any state which experienced it. Thus, it was the task of government to maintain a spirit for change within proper bounds so that such a tragedy would not be repeated elsewhere. Such a task would be difficult for a government, but not impossible. The Tories believed that:

> Anarchy is the greatest of all evils, but anarchy is usually the climax of bad government. (5)

Thus, the real danger growing out of the French revolution, from the viewpoint of the Upper Canadian Tories, was to be found in the revolutionary spirit that it engendered, and the political principles which the revolutionaries embraced with all the zeal of converts. In France, the people had embraced anarchy in their pursuit of the form of American democracy and, in rejecting the Christian Church, had given birth to the "Beast of Infidelity". In doing so, the revolutionaries had united insubordination with infidelity, and had concocted a potent power which was hostile to every traditional government.

The madness of the French Revolution was such that the new revolutionary rulers of France had sought to follow Voltaire into infidelity. In doing so, they had presented the world with a spectacle altogether new: the efforts of a government to uproot Christianity, and substitute in its place the worship of 'the goddess of reason'. Indeed, the awful tragedy of the French revolution was to be found in its infidelity combined with its invocation to worship the passions. Under the influence of Voltaire and Jean-Jacques Rousseau, the French people had rejected God's revealed

Will as a standard of conduct for man and government, and turned to the mind of man. However, it was a mind which had been schooled by Rousseau "to deny the reality of truth and virtue, and to transfer the homage of [the heart] to the personifications of perverted human passions".

Rousseau had apotheosized the passions of man. Through the vicious and bewildering sentimentality of his writings, he had cleverly supplied the people of France with counterfeits of every truth as the guiding principle for all areas of life. Rousseau had taught them "to worship and serve their own disordered appetites – their inflamed and inflaming lusts". (6)

No country had proved to be immune to the moral plague of the age. Such was the rage for innovation that the French creed of revolution and atheism had secured many ardent adherents. Even England, with all the blessings that Englishmen possessed, had tottered on the verge of a precipice prior to the outbreak of the war with revolutionary France in 1793.

For the Upper Canadian Tories, it was truly astonishing that the revolutionary spirit had spread to England. They believed that the great liberty enjoyed by Englishmen under the British Constitution, and the general level of knowledge of the people, should have precluded revolutionary ideas having any appeal. It could only be accounted for by the very spirit of the age -- the "age of delusion" -- and the efforts of political agitators and polemicists who went to great lengths to blind the people to their true interests.

It was argued that paradoxically, it was the very well-being of England that had brought on such a crisis. The Tories believed that:

> Prosperity always tends to its own destruction, unless guarded with the greatest vigilance. Mankind are so apt to change their manners & disposition with the change of their affairs that to make a new man no more is needed than to make him prosperous.

England, in enjoying a free government and long years of prosperity, had grown careless in her ways, ungrateful, and indifferent to religion. She had abandoned the diligent industry and careful frugality which had produced her greatness. In wallowing in luxury, and giving themselves over to ostentatious extravagance, all classes have become less patriotic and more selfish. The ease and affluence of the nation, in the absence of the salutary influence of religion, had fostered a wayward disposition prone to find fault and to seek imaginary improvements. The public mind had become corrupted to the point where the people,

> continually aim at self-gratification, & when this is opposed, they breed the most rancorous discontent – They become the friends of change & innovation that amidst the disorders of society they may be satiated."

In that frame of mind, England had offered a fertile field for the revolutionary designs of such men as the renowned dissenting minister, Dr. Richard Price (1723-1791), and 'the prophet of vulgar infidelity', Thomas Paine (1732-1809).

The specific works, which the Tories regarded as being truly politically subversive, were an address, "Discourse on the Love of our Country", delivered by Dr. Price in November 1789, and a book by Tom Paine, *Rights of Man* (1791), in which Paine attacked the condemnatory view of the French Revolution as presented by the British Whig statesman, Edmund Burke, in his *Reflections on the Revolution in France* (1790). The Upper Canadian Tories denounced Paine for having imported the 'rights of man' principles of the French Revolution into Britain, where he had proceeded to advocate -- in their view -- "the general principle of revolutionizing everything". Dr. Price was denounced for his advocacy of religious dissent, popular sovereignty, and the right of the people to overturn the British constitution which was viewed as a veiled attempt to incite an uprising.

The Threat of religious dissent and revolutionary democracy: Dr. Price

In November 1789, Dr. Price presented a radical interpretation of the Glorious Revolution of 1688 at a gathering of dissenters in a London Meeting-House chapel. He argued that there were three basic principles that underlay the English Revolution. They were: the 'sacred right of liberty of conscience' possessed by the people, as individuals, to choose their own mode of religious worship and beliefs; the right of the people "to resist power when abused"; and the right,

"To choose our own governors;
To cashier them for misconduct; and
To frame a government for ourselves."

Price denounced the Anglican Tory doctrine of passive obedience, and argued that the Revolution of 1688 was incomplete. The Test Acts, which restricted Dissenters and Roman Catholics from public office needed to be repealed, and the franchise greatly extended. For Price, 'true liberty' required that the government be based on a universal male suffrage, and that all power be vested in the people's representatives in the House of Commons.

As a dissenting clergyman, Price shared with the Tories a belief in government based on moral principles and a belief that private and public virtue could not be separated in any man. They differed, however, in that the Tories were focused on the concept of a Christian nation which embraced a British national character, the balanced British Constitution, and the established National Church, and a Church-directed national education system. In contrast, the focus of Price was on the individual as a rational being with the right to choose his own mode of worship, to participate in government through his elected representatives, and to overthrow the government if it abused or denied the rights of the people. For Price, the 'true patriot' was 'a citizen of the world' who would respect the rights of the peoples of other nations.

For the Upper Canadian Tories, the insistence of Dr. Price that the people possessed a right to rebel, and the right to establish a constitution in keeping with their own wishes, constituted a serious revolutionary threat. It appeared to be aimed at inciting the English people to rebel in emulation of the French Revolution. Moreover, the Tories held a completely different view of the Glorious Revolution of 1688 than the interpretation espoused by Dr. Price. For the Tories, the Revolution of 1688 marked the culmination of a long struggle to establish the 'rights of Englishmen', and had produced the balanced British Constitution which was the guarantor of those rights within a limited constitutional monarchy. The argument that the English Revolution was incomplete, and that the constitution needed to be radically transformed by 'the people', was viewed by the

Upper Canadian Tories as being utterly subversive.

The Threat of democratic anarchy: Thomas Paine

In his refutation of Burke's conservative critique of the French Revolution, Thomas Paine drew on the principles of the "Déclaration des droits de l'homme et du Citoyen" of the National Constituent Assembly (August 1789) of revolutionary France. Paine argued that all men were created equal by God, and were possessed of irrevocable natural rights: liberty, property, security, and resistance to oppression. Furthermore, he maintained that the sole purpose of a national government was to preserve the natural rights of its citizens and, to that end, he supported the rule of law and equality before the law for all citizens.

Where Paine was truly revolutionary was in maintaining that the nation was 'the source of all sovereignty' (popular sovereignty), that the law was an 'expression of the will of the community' as expressed through their representatives, and that the purpose of the law was 'to prohibit only actions harmful to society'. There was no concept of the sovereignty of God, of the king being God's vicegerent, or of the Christian concept that the positive law ought to be based on God's moral law. For Paine, the law had no moral content or higher purpose. To the contrary, the law was only a vehicle to protect the natural rights of each citizen, and to prohibit what caused harm to others. Political liberty was defined as "the power of doing whatever does not injure another".

Paine rejected prescriptive rights and hereditary rights, and maintained that each generation had the right to act for itself to form its government in keeping with its current needs. He advocated the abolition of titles, the destruction of large estates through taxation and the repeal of the law of primogeniture, and the elimination of all social distinctions that were not based on a social utility. The aim was to achieve a society in which all men would be "of one degree" -- equal in their enjoyment of their natural rights. Religious differences were to be eliminated through the separation of church and state, the disallowance of tithes, and a complete toleration for all religious doctrines so long as their adherents did not disturb "the public order established by law".

Paine maintained that the only legitimate government was a government of and by the people: viz. a government composed of the representatives of the people, elected by means of a universal male suffrage, and seated in a unicameral legislature wherein the legislative body would direct the executive in the carrying out of its functions.

For the Upper Canadian Tories, the egalitarian social views of Thomas Paine were anathema. They were appalled by his call for the separation of church and state, for a government based on the principle of popular sovereignty, and for a secular government having no moral or religious purpose. His views were the direct antithesis of the beliefs of the Tories as to what the peace, order and well-being of a state required.

The Threat of Infidelity: Thomas Paine

Thomas Paine was held in further contempt by the Tories for another of his pamphlets, *The Age of Reason, Being an Investigation of True and Fabulous Theology* (1794), in which he attacked Christianity and the legitimacy of the Bible. The Christian churches, and religious creeds, were denounced by Paine for being simply a construct of man that had been established to terrify and control the people. Revolutionary France was praised for having abolished 'the national priesthood', along with religious observances and duties, and "compulsory articles of faith".

Paine denied that the Scriptures were the revealed Word of God. He argued that the Bible was compiled by writers who had not received a direct personal revelation from God, and that the passages were recorded second hand. The Bible contained sound moral concepts, but they were such as could have been produced by man without any 'supernatural intervention'. More particularly, Paine denied the divinity of Jesus Christ.

For Paine, Christ was a benevolent man, an outstanding moralist, and 'a revolutionist' who preached the equality of man. Rather than founding a system of religion, Christ had called on men to 'practice the moral virtues, and to believe in one God'. The 'story' of Christ being the son of God, Paine debunked. He claimed that it was a product of the tendency of 'ancient mythologists' to characterize men of extraordinary abilities and achievement as being the son of a god. As to the resurrection of

Christ, there was no compelling evidence for that claim. It was attested to by only a few followers of Christ, and lacked any public testimony.

While denying that the Bible was the revealed Word of God, Paine held that the true revelation of God was conveyed in His Works which were directly and universally available to all men to study, regardless of what language they might speak. Human reason alone was sufficient to read God's Creation, which was original and unchanging. For his part, man could understand all that he 'needed to know' of God's purpose in studying nature and "the principles of science in the structure of the universe". Hence, for Paine, true theology had to be founded on the study of nature – Natural Philosophy – rather than the Christian religion which, he maintained, obscured man's understanding of God.

Paine, a deist, declared that he believed in one God, in the equality of man in God's Creation, and in a religious duty to promote justice and mercy and the happiness of one's fellows, and that he hoped for an afterlife. He did not believe in anything more!

In the religious writings of Thomas Paine, the Tories faced a popular synthesis of the intellectual arguments against Christianity and the Bible which were developed by British deists in the early 18th Century, and which had reached their revolutionary potential in the infidelity and democratic anarchy of the French Revolution. From the Tory viewpoint, what Paine and the British deists lacked was faith in Christ as the savior of man, who died for man's sins, and a lack of understanding of the role of Christ's Church in the redemption of man from original sin into righteousness.

The Tories feared that Upper Canadians would be deluded into infidelity by the arguments presented by men such as Thomas Paine, if such writings were not counteracted. To that end, the Anglican clerics preached that the Bible was historical and allegorical and needed to be interpreted by a trained clergy, and that the New Testament gospels were written by men of a deep Christian faith who were possessed of, and inspired by, the spirit of the Holy Ghost. Paine had realized that there were mysteries beyond human understanding in nature, but he had failed to realize that there were also mysteries in the Christian religion that were beyond the fathoming of human reason. The mysteries of the

Christian religion could be known and understood only through faith in Christ and by studying the word of God as revealed in the Bible. Indeed, Anglicans -- and Protestants more generally -- believed in 'salvation through faith alone'.

The democratic radical threat

For the Upper Canadian Tories, Price and Paine personified the connection between religious dissent and democracy on the one hand, and democratic anarchy and infidelity on the other. The Tories were convinced that the democratic radicals had realized that Christianity, in the form of a national religious establishment, was the main obstacle to a successful revolution. Therefore, Dr. Price had sought to fragment the Church by advocating that every individual had 'a sacred right' to exercise his 'liberty of conscience' to set up a separate worship for himself independent of the National Church; while Paine, a deist, had tried to bring the Bible into contempt, and hence the Christian Church, by denying revealed religion and seeking to substitute in its place a natural religion based upon human reason and the study of nature. In denying all traditional authority in religion, the radical democrats maintained that 'truth' would emerge from the clash of the free opinions of rational men.

The Upper Canadian Tories were appalled by such doctrines which were believed to be subversive of traditional social values, political stability, morality, and the Christian religion, whether dispensed in England at the close of the 18th Century or in Upper Canada in the early decades of the 19th Century. (7) However, the ideological threat posed by the democratic radicals to the traditional order in Britain, and in its Dominions, was accompanied by an equally threatening military aspect as revealed by revolutionary France in the conduct of its international relations.

Total War & the 'New Man'

For the Upper Canadian Tories, the revolutionary government of France through placing a pre-eminent stress on ideology in their conduct toward other governments, had rejected the traditional limited aims of warfare between states, and the restraints commonly observed by the parties involved in a war. The French revolutionaries had inaugurated an age of 'total war'. Previously, European wars had been conducted between a limited number of belligerents over some object of contention, such as a colony, or they were fought to secure an indemnity for past wrongs. Conventional wars were often fought on the frontiers of a country or in the colonies, and the people of the several European nations involved in a war felt little or no interest in the struggle. For the most part, the belligerents did not attempt to interfere with the internal government or order of the enemy state, and the issues at stake in a war seldom threatened the existence of the belligerents as independent states. However, the French Revolution had brought about a revolutionary change.

In seeking to propagate their levelling principles, which were totally inconsistent with social order, the French revolutionaries had become "apostles of anarchy" who had not scrupled to hold out the promise of assistance to the disaffected of all nations to overthrow their legitimate governments. Great Britain, and the other countries of Europe, had been placed in a position where their governments were threatened with destruction in a struggle in which there was to be no neutrality. Countries had had either to fight for their independence, or submit to conquest. The revolutionary government of France had followed its ideological assault on the traditional order in France with a resort to military aggression and a declaration of war against all existing governments.

The wars which followed:

> were different from all others. The very foundations of Society were assaulted, existing Governments overthrown, the laws and policy of the conquered states disregarded, their independence swept away by annexing them to France, or making them tributary without regarding the feelings or wishes of the people. In this terrible context, everything dear to man was at stake, the whole of society was convulsed, and the meanest individual involved in calamity.

From the renewal of war in 1803, following the year-long Peace of Amiens, the armies of France under the direction of the new Emperor of France, Napoleon Bonaparte, had proceeded to conquer nation after nation in Europe. The nations, which did not readily succumb to his rule, were placed in a situation where they had to continually fight for their independence. (8)

The Upper Canadian Tories recognized that Britain was facing -- in Napoleon -- a new phenomenon altogether, rather than a traditional enemy. He was a man driven by a restless, illimitable ambition, who was bent on establishing a despotic universal dominion over mankind. It was evident that nothing would curb his aggressions, except his utter defeat and a complete loss of power.

The revolution in France, in destroying the old order and overthrowing the ruling classes, had witnessed the coming to power of the men of the revolution. They not only included regicides in their ranks, but were:

> for the most part illiterate upstarts of mean birth and of base manners inured to blood and delighting in carnage, men who regarded neither God or man.

The revolutionaries in France were viewed as being the 'new men' of a revolutionary age. They were men who were oblivious to all religious and moral restraints, who were driven solely by their own selfish interests in seeking personal fortune. They did not scruple to break every social tie, to massacre the king and nobility of France, and to trample on the Christian religion. They had shown themselves to be bereft of any ability except that of exciting tumult and encouraging rebellion against the established authorities. The exception was Napoleon Bonaparte, who united the 'satanic character' of the new man with extraordinary talents and superior powers. He had provided direction for the forces of revolution and through military aggression threatened Europe with a compete subjugation. In many ways, Napoleon, the Corsican usurper, was the epitome of the new man incarnate:

> Bonaparte is one of those bold, restless, enterprising spirits, who reckon every means lawful and good that appears necessary to promote the ends he has in view. He looks upon justice, probity, and sincerity, as empty names; and he has never had any scruples about employing lying, fraud, treachery, and perjury, to circumvent his neighbours. He thinks nothing of ruining nations for the purpose of extending his power; deems no sacrifice too precious to his ambitions; and acknowledges no rule for his actions; and no other God, but interest and fortune.

For the Upper Canadian Tories, Napoleon appeared to be the natural product of the progress of irreligion and the discarding of morality. He was viewed as lacking any magnanimity or virtue. A supposed favourite of the people, he was held to have resorted to innumerable crimes, murders and deceptions to advance himself, in being motivated by nothing more than insatiable ambition. Once in power, Napoleon had become a calculating and unrelenting tyrant, which was necessary to maintain his position. Lacking any moral virtue or legitimacy to retain the respect and support of his people, he was dependent upon a succession of victories in war and government by terror to maintain himself. Thus, Napoleonic France was a despotic military dictatorship in which liberty of opinion and free speech were proscribed.

The Tories did not deny that Napoleon had brought some benefits to France. However, they believed that whatever good he had accomplished was not attributable to paternalism on his part, but rather to a desire to promote his own selfish interests. Napoleon was recognized as a man of exceptional ability and talents, but they were talents continuously occupied in promoting evil. His actions were devoid of good intent, and were motivated by no higher purpose than his personal aggrandizement:

> Men were machines in his hands; he alone must project, command, reward and punish. From him everything must emanate; he must be the centre of all.

Under the iron rule of Napoleon, the French people had suffered for their revolutionary excesses, for the murder of King Louis XVI, and for their love of military glory. It was hoped that they, and others who observed their plight, would learn the lesson so written.

The intellectual climate of the times in conjunction with revolutionary upheavals had provided the opportunity for the exercise of such diabolical powers as were possessed by a Napoleon, and had in some measure determined the character of the man. In viewing the 'new men' whom the French Revolution had produced and brought to power, the Upper Canadian Tories were highly motivated to defend the traditional social order and system of government. (9)

A Struggle for Survival

In the great struggle being waged by Britain, and the other nations of Europe, to contain the unrelenting efforts of Napoleon to destroy them, Upper Canada had not been a passive spectator. At the time of the Napoleonic Wars, the Tories feared that if Great Britain were to be defeated by Napoleon, the fate of the Province of Upper Canada would be sealed as a British colony. Without the support of Great Britain, the Loyalist asylum would be unable to overcome the ideological danger posed by American democratic republicanism, or to defend itself against the military threat posed by the expansionist American republic.

The proximity of the United States facilitated the spread of American democratic republican ideals and levelling principles into Upper Canada and when coupled with the presence of a large numbers of American settlers in their midst, gave rise to fears for the survival of the British national character of the province. Moreover, there was a constant threat -- real or imagined -- of an American invasion leading to the conquest and annexation of Upper Canada to the United States. These potential dangers had caused the Upper Canadian Tories no end of anxiety throughout the whole period of the revolutionary wars in Europe. (10)

During the first decade of the 19th Century, the Upper Canadian Tories were thoroughly alarmed to observe that serious differences were developing between Great Britain and the United States over maritime rights and neutral rights. At issue were the Orders-in-Council of November 1807 by which the British government forbade its allies and neutrals from trading with Napoleonic France and its allies, and provided for its enforcement by a Royal Navy blockade of the seaports of Napoleonic Europe.

That alarm was heightened by the belligerent stance which was adopted by some segments of the American population, and their representatives in Congress. The Americans denounced the British trade embargo, and denied the right of the Royal Navy blockade ships to search ships on the high seas to recover Royal Navy sailors who had deserted to American commercial vessels. Moreover, the democratic republican government of the United States, under President Thomas Jefferson, was regarded as having virtually taken the side of Napoleon through the passage of an Embargo Act in December 1807. That Act forbade American ships to trade with Britain and France, but was regarded as aimed at weakening the power of Britain by stopping her lucrative wartime trade with the United States.

Under the administration of Jefferson's successor, President James Madison, Congress passed several warlike measures which were aimed -- so the Tories believed -- at facilitating the conquest of Upper Canada. Several leading members of Congress spoke openly of the ease with which Upper Canada could be invaded and conquered. Moreover, it was evident to the Tories that American 'War Hawks' in Congress were expecting the American settlers in Upper Canada - who comprised 3/5s of the population of the Province - to rally to the American cause, and did not expect any significant resistance from the remaining residents of the province. What caused the Upper Canadian Tories even more unease was their knowledge that the American assessment of the situation in Upper Canada was not all that questionable.

They noted that Upper Canadians, in the face of American threats, were succumbing to a general feeling of defeatism. Many Upper Canadians concluded that the American military strength was such that, in the event of a war, the province -- with its scattered settlements and slender population -- would be quickly overwhelmed; and that it would be worse than useless to offer any resistance.

Two of the leading Tories of Upper Canada, Richard Cartwright and the Rev. John Strachan, acted on their fears and were roused to give leadership, direction and encouragement to the loyal residents of Upper Canada, with the hope of preventing the Americans from achieving a conquest by default. Thus, while publicly attributing all utterances of defeatist views to cowardice or treachery, they set out consciously and deliberately to counteract the debilitating defeatism that had gripped the province. By means of letters placed in newspapers, speeches to the various militia units, sermons by the Rev. Strachan from the pulpit, and the publication of pamphlets, as well their personal influence on government, friends and associates, they sought to arouse a will to fight among Upper Canadians.

Their efforts were calculated to awaken Upper Canadians to their duty and obligations, to remind them of their Loyalist heritage and of the benefits which they derived from the British government. Cartwright and Strachan strove also to make Upper Canadians aware of the magnitude of the struggle against Napoleon in defending and preserving true liberty and Christianity, and the threat posed to Upper Canada by his North American ally, the United States of America. In the latter case, while warning of the imminent danger of an American attack on Upper Canada, the Tories sought to reassure Upper Canadians that their cause was not hopeless. They were assured by the Tories that in any war with the Americans, there was no doubt but that, ultimately, the United States would be defeated by British troops and the Royal Navy.

In addition to preparing the province psychologically for the possibility of a war with the United States, the stated rationale for such an effort was the belief that hesitation, timidity, and fear would merely encourage an attack by the United States. However, a united population, infused with patriotic zeal and ready to defend its life, property and independence, would have the contrary effect. As Richard Cartwright argued, it was a maxim of some validity that "the most effectual way to keep war at a distance is to be prepared to meet it".

To that end, with every means at their disposal, the Upper Canadian Tory leaders set out to influence public opinion, and to prepare the people of Upper Canada for the approaching war. It was an effort that emphasized the ideological and military threat which faced the province in its immediate environs, but also the significance of the struggle to the British Empire and western civilization. (11)

In their appeals to Upper Canadians, the Tories drew attention to the larger life and death struggle in which Great Britain was engaged in Europe. Upper Canadians were told that in coming forward to resist American aggression, they would be fighting not for themselves alone, but for the whole world. They would be contributing to the defeat of the most formidable conspiracy ever contrived against the civilization of man. It was a conspiracy that threatened a greater barbarism and misery than had followed the downfall of the Roman Empire.

Historical allusions aside, in the Tory worldview Britain was defending the civilized world in resisting in succession the threat of infidelity and democratic anarchy which was emanating from revolutionary France, and the efforts of Napoleon Bonaparte to impose his despotic military rule upon Europe. It was a battle that was still raging in Europe. For the Upper Canadian Tories, Great Britain represented the last bastion of civilization amidst the destruction of the nations of Europe, and the last sanctuary for true liberty. It was a Christian country that was standing alone against the onslaught of revolution and infidelity. The fruits of centuries of experience and development were threatened with destruction by men who were incapable of replacing it with anything other than either a "mob rule of the passions" or a military despotism.

It was argued that should Britain fall to Napoleon, the whole British polity of laws, religion, and civil institutions would be destroyed, and all love of liberty, of honour, and of virtue would be obliterated from the minds of man. The Tories admitted that Britain was not above reproach, but expressed their belief that:

> although Great Britain has many sins to deplore; yet, on a comparison with other nations, it will be found that she possesses more true liberty, more solid morality, and more true religion, than they.

The Anglican Tory clerics maintained that Britain was being chastised for its transgressions: a general decay of moral values, a growing indifference to religion, and the lack of thankfulness for the blessings that it had received. God had raised up an enemy to admonish the British people for the errors of their ways, and to convey to them the necessity of a moral regeneration. Such were the workings of Providence in the world; yet the situation was not hopeless. Britain was engaged in a good cause, and if she heeded the warning being delivered, it was believed that "the judgment which threatens us will be averted & made to promote our felicity".

Despite her failings, it was maintained that Britain remained superior to any other nation in the possession of a spirit of independence, intrepid virtue, and a rational piety, which was subsumed within the British national character. It was a character that was held to be marked by honesty, independence, and a disdain for meanness and fawning servility.

Such was the life and death struggle for civilization in which Upper Canadians were called upon to participate, to give their all, and to put "the general interests of humanity" before private advantage. They were exhorted to join in arms with their fellow British countrymen and to take the paths of virtue and glory. These exhortations were circulated in print at a time, just prior to the American declaration of war in June 1812, when the position of Britain appeared to be particularly desperate in Europe.

The effort of Napoleon to strangle British commerce through the imposition of a trade embargo – the Continental System -- was proving to be all but too effective in closing many British manufacturers and driving out specie, and the military situation was no better with both Austria and Prussia completely defeated, and Russia having been forced to sign an ignominious peace treaty.

In fine, Europe had virtually become the French Empire, and the whole force was directed against the British Isles. (12)

Despite a truly depressing state of affairs in Europe, the Upper Canadian Tories were convinced that the victories of the Royal Navy as sea, and the introduction of England's own version of the levée en masse, had rendered the country secure from invasion. Although the superiority of the French armies on land precluded an immediate successful issue of the war, Upper Canadians were assured that it was only a matter of time until the French Empire disintegrated.

In a pamphlet circulated within Upper Canada, *A Discourse on the Character of King George the Third*, (1810), the Rev. John Strachan argued that Napoleon through the vast extent of his conquests was overextending himself, and weakening the power of France by bringing more and more discontented subjects under his sway. It was not to be expected that France could hold the nations of Europe in subjection for long.

Strachan maintained that the unprecedented conquests by the French were the product of the political machinations of Napoleon, which were aided by the irresolute conduct of neighbouring states and the corruption and treachery of their ruling classes, rather than due to any supposed invincibility on the part of the French armies. Thus, Strachan declared his belief that:

> These things will change; repeated oppressions will rouse men of spirit and virtue to vindicate the cause of their country. How much these may effect appears from the example of the inhabitants of Spain. How insignificant the French would be, had the people a few men of conduct and abilities to direct their just indignation. -- Such men will appear; the present torpor that pervades the conquered nations will not always continue.

The Reverend Strachan maintained that good men would emerge in Europe to provide the leadership needed to restore the proper order of things. Although it was allowed that the talents of Napoleon were of such a magnitude that he might manage to hold the discordant parts together for some time, there was no doubt that even if he were successful in doing so, at his death the whole empire would disintegrate.

In contrast, the power of Great Britain was much more secure and permanent. The efforts of Napoleon to destroy British commerce through the imposition of his continental trade embargo (1806 and 1807) was proving to be far more costly to the French Empire and to the United States, which supported his efforts, than to Britain. The economy of Britain was based on both agriculture and commerce, and unlike Holland in modern times or Tyre in ancient times Britain could not be totally crippled by a trade blockage. Thus, the Rev. Strachan argued that despite all appearances to the contrary, Britain would emerge victorious from the struggle with her power intact. It was an argument calculated to give heart to the loyal population of Upper Canada, and to provide a rationale for caution and reflection on the part of any Upper Canadian settler who might be inclined to disaffection. (13)

With respect to the immediate threat of an American invasion, the Upper Canadian Tories were anxious in their public appeals to counteract the widespread belief that resistance was hopeless. To that end, they sought to disparage the American military forces, and draw attention to the internal political dissensions which they observed in the United States.

They argued that if Upper Canadians were united -- a rather significant qualification – the Province would be able to defeat any American invasion attempt. In the first place, the American regular army was not very numerous, their militia lacked proper officers and was exempted from service on foreign soil, and the Americans would have to garrison their own sea coast in any war because it was vulnerable to attack by the Royal Navy.

The logistics of supporting an army of regulars invading Upper Canada would tie up so many men that the Canadian provinces -- Upper and Lower Canada -- themselves would be able to provide, despite their paucity of population, at least a force equal in numbers to receive any American invasion force. Moreover, many experienced British army officers were settled in Upper Canada, and the militia could count on the support of British Army, the best disciplined troops in the world.

In any war with the United States, the Tories maintained that the Royal Navy would destroy American commerce and thereby deliver a telling blow to the very political stability and unity of the states of that union, as was shown by the repercussions of the less severe restrictions which the American national government had placed upon British trade in 1807. It was pointed out that the general government of the United States was feeble, and the different states had clashing interests. Moreover, their national politics was dominated by two warring parties – the Federalists and the Jeffersonian Democrats – which would threaten that country with disruption under the stresses of a war. Any British war against American commerce, and diversion of British trade away from America to other areas of the world, would greatly accelerate the decline of the United States of America.

Should the United States be so foolish as to declare war, the consequences for herself were such that:

> The country will be filled with discontent; discontent breeds faction; and the realm will dwindle into separate governments, which will be the more bitter enemies that they were once friends.

Whether the Upper Canadian Tories really believed in their hopeful assessment of what the United States would experience if it attacked

Upper Canada -- given that they were to experience an excruciating anxiety about the ultimate success of their cause throughout the War of 1812 -- is a moot point. However, whether based on false hopes, a calculated desire to give waverers and the disaffected cause for reflection, or a judicious appraisal of the situation, the Tory assessment proved remarkably prophetic in view of actual developments, both militarily and politically, in the United States during the War of 1812. Whatever the case, it was the Upper Canadian Tories who took the lead in the pre-war years in rousing a willingness among Upper Canadians to fight to preserve Upper Canada should the Americans launch an invasion attempt to conquer the Province.

Everything in which the Tories believed was at stake in the Loyalist asylum of Upper Canada. While fearing the outbreak of a war, the leading Upper Canadian Tories did everything possible to inculcate in Upper Canadians a confidence in ultimate victory, and a will to fight to achieve it, should a war be inflicted upon them by a democratic revolutionary power, the United States of America. (14)

Notes

Part One: The Spectre of Revolution

In documenting the dissertation text, the original practice was to cite most of the major sources in which a particular religious belief, principle, or argument was set forth to show that the Tory worldview, beliefs, values and principles were consistently held, and transcended time and circumstance.

During the copy-editing of the dissertation chapters, some additional historical information was inserted into the texts, as well as summaries of the beliefs of their radical and sectarian opponents of the Tories, to provide a more meaningful historical and ideological context, as well as to make clear the nature of the American threat to the survival of Upper Canada. Where additional historical information and the ideas of the ideological opponents of the Tories have been inserted into a dissertation chapter, the new sources are cited within square brackets in the Notes to differentiate them from the original dissertation references.

Part One: Divider

Quotation: Provincial Archives of Ontario, (PAO), Strachan Sermons, Box C, St. Paul's Epistle to the Hebrews, 12:11, "Chastening yieldeth Righteousness", 16 March 1806, 8-9.

Chapter One - The Age of Delusion

1. Queen's University, Douglas Library, Cartwright Letterbook, Vol. II, Richard Cartwright to Isaac Todd, 21 October 1792, and Richard Cartwright to His Excellency General Hunter, 23 August 1799; Public Archives of Canada (PAC), Anonymous [Richard Cartwright], *Letters from an American Loyalist in Upper Canada to His Friend in England on a pamphlet published by John Mills Jackson, Esquire: Entitled a View of the Province of Upper Canada* (1809), Letter Three; John Strachan, *A Letter to the Right Honourable Thomas Frankland Lewis, M.P.* (York: R. Stanton, 1830), 5-7; John Beverley Robinson, *Canada and the Canada Bill: Being an Examination of the Proposed Measure for the Future Government of Canada* (London: J. Hutchard & Son, 1840), 24; and *The Church*, 11 January 1840, "Speech of Attorney General Hagerman".

2. Cartwright Letterbook, Vol. II, Richard Cartwright to Isaac Todd, 21 October 1792; PAC (Public Archives of Canada), Anonymous [Richard Cartwright], *Letters from an American Loyalist*, Letter Three, 16-17; *Kingston Gazette*, Falkland [Richard Cartwright], 11 February 1812; Robinson, *Canada Bill*, 25-

26; *The Church*, 11 January 1840, Speech of Hagerman. The Tories pointed out that during the American Revolution, land had been promised to only one Loyalist regiment -- the 84th Regiment of Foot, a Scottish Highland Regiment -- as an inducement to enlist. The point being made was that the Loyalist regiments were motivated solely by loyalty to the Crown and the unity of the Empire in fighting against the American revolutionaries.

3. C.E. Cartwright, ed. *Life and Letters of the late Hon. Richard Cartwright* (Toronto: Belford Bros., 1876), 93-96, R. Cartwright to His Excellency General Hunter, 23 August 1799; Cartwright Letterbook, Vol. II, "Letter from the Magistrates to Sir John Johnson", 22 December 1787; G. W. Spragge, *The John Strachan Letter Book:1812- 1834*, (Toronto: The Ontario Historical Society, 1946), 165-166, Strachan to Colonel Harvey, 22 June 1818. The quotation is from Cartwright's letter to General Hunter, 23 August 1799, 95-96.

4. C.E. Cartwright, ed., *Life and Letters*, 74, Richard Cartwright to Messrs. Davison & Co., 4 November 1797, and 95-97, R. Cartwright to His Excellency General Hunter, 23 August 1799, as well as 85-89, Cartwright, " Representation respecting the State of landed Property in Upper Canada, Delivered to General Simcoe", July 1795; Strachan, *Letter to Thomas Frankland Lewis* , 8-9; E.A. Cruikshank, ed., *The Correspondence of Lieut. Governor John Graves Simcoe, , Vol. I, 1789-1793* (Toronto: Ontario Historical Society, 1923), 235, R. Cartwright to Lt. Governor Simcoe, 12 October 1793; and John Strachan, *A Discourse on the Character of King George the Third, Addressed to the Inhabitants of British America*, (Montreal: Nahum Mower, 1810), 38. The quotation is from Cartwright's letter to General Hunter, 23 August 1799, 96.

5. Strachan, *A Sermon on the Death of the Honourable Richard Cartwright, Preached at Kingston, 3 September 1815* (Montreal : W. Gray, 1816), 27; Strachan, *Discourse*, 54, 58 & 62; Robinson, *Canada Bill*, 2; Robinson, "A Letter to the Right Hon. Earl Bathurst, K.G., on the Policy of Uniting the British North-American Colonies", 26 December 1824, in *Four Pamphlets on Confederation and Union of the Canadas* (Toronto: Canadiana House, 1967), 34; and [Strachan], Document to the Colonial Office, 5 June 1824, reprinted in Spragge, *Strachan Letter Book*, xiv. The quotation is from Strachan, *Discourse*, 62.

6. *Kingston Chronicle*, 21 April 1820, [Strachan], Letter No. 10 to Robert Walsh Esq. quoting Marshall, *Life of Washington*, Vol. I, 101. The Upper Canadian Tory view of the origin of the American Revolution presented herein draws heavily upon the writings of the Rev. John Strachan. His views were formed through talks with Richard Cartwright, a Loyalist who had experienced the Revolution at first hand in the Colony of New York, as well as from a determined

effort by Strachan to familiarize himself with existing histories of the American Revolution in preparing to write a history of that event. The projected history of the American Revolution was never written; although Strachan passed on his interpretation and analysis of that event in his other writings, and in what he taught to his students.

Among the authors whom Strachan cited are: John Marshall, *The Life of Washington* (5 vols., 1804-1807); David Ramsay, *History of the American Revolution* (2 vols., 1789); Dr. William Robertson, *The History of America* (3 vols., 1777); and the Rev. William Gordon, *The History of the Rise, Progress, and Establishment, of the Independence of the United States of America* (1788).

7. Strachan, *Sermon on Death of Cartwright*, 1815, 27; *Kingston Chronicle*, 10 September 1831, "One of the People", [Rev. Adam Hood Burwell]; Strachan, *Discourse*, 1810, 31. The quote is from [Strachan], Letter no. 10 to Walsh, 21 April 1820. [During the American Revolution the Congregational Church was hesitant to support the revolutionaries, but did so based on Lockean-liberal political principles; whereas the evangelical Calvinist sectarians marshalled popular support for the revolution. For the political beliefs, rhetoric, and worldview of the evangelical Calvinist sectarians, and their ardent participation in the battles of the American Revolution (1776-1783), as well as their aggressive role in the persecution of the Loyalists in keeping with their religious belief in 'retributive justice', see, Alan Heimert, *Religion and the American Mind, From the Great Awakening to the Revolution* (Cambridge, Massachusetts: Harvard University Press, 1966), 454-509 & 510-524.]

8. Strachan, *Sermon on Death of Cartwright*, 1815, 27; *Kingston Chronicle*, 12 May 1820, [Strachan], Letter No. 11 to Robert Walsh; Robinson, "Letter to Earl Bathurst", 26 December 1824, 40-44; *Kingston Chronicle*, (Macaulay editorial), 11 June 1819. [On the democratic principles of the Puritans (Congregationalists), and their continual efforts to establish an independent government in the Massachusetts Bay Colony from its very founding with the granting of The Charter of 1629, see: Robert W. Passfield, *Phips' Amphibious Assault on Canada – 1690* (Amazon, 2011), Chapter Three, "Where Sovereignty Lay", 75-144.]

9, Strachan, *Discourse*, 1810, 31, 53-54 and 60; *Kingston Chronicle*, 21 April 1820 and 12 May 1820, [Strachan], Letter no. 10 & no. 11, to Robert Walsh; Strachan, *Sermon on Death of Cartwright*, 1815, 25-26; Robinson, "Letter to Earl Bathurst" 26 December 1821, 34; Robinson, *Canada Bill*, 1840, 24; *Kingston Chronicle*, (Macaulay editorial), 11 June 1819; PAO, Macaulay Papers, reel 1, John Bethune to John Macaulay, 21 December 1810 & 30 January 1811.

10. *Kingston Chronicle*, [Strachan], Letters to Robert Walsh: no. 5, 25 February 1820, no. 7, 17 March 1820, no. 9, 31 March 1820, & no. 10, 21 April 1820; and Strachan, *Discourse*, 57-61. The quotation is from Letter no. 10, 21 April 1820.

11. Public Archives of Ontario (PAO), Macaulay Papers, reel 1, John Bethune to John Macaulay, 30 January 1811; Strachan, *Discourse*, 1810, 62; *Kingston Chronicle*, 12 May 1820, [Strachan], Letter no.11 to Robert Walsh; Strachan, *Sermon on Death of Cartwright*, 1815, 27-28; and James [John] Strachan, *A Visit to the Province of Upper Canada in 1819*, (Aberdeen: D. Chalmers & Co.), 1820, 158.

12. Strachan, *A Visit to Upper Canada*, 1819, 157-158; Strachan, *Sermon on Death of Cartwright*, 1815, 27; and Cartwright Family Papers (private collection), Richard Cartwright, "A journey to Canada" (copy), [1777], 1 & 8. The quotation is from Strachan, *A Visit to Upper Canada*, 157-158.

13. PAO, Robinson Papers, 1823-37, Robinson, Memorandum to Wilmot Horton, 24 December 1828, 30-32; Strachan, *A Letter to the Rev. Thomas Chalmers D.D. Professor of Divinity at the University of Edinburgh, on the Life and Character of the Right Reverend Dr. Hobart, Bishop of New-York, North America* (New York: Swords, Stanford & Co., 1832), 4; Strachan, *Letter to Frankland Lewis*, 1830, 11-14; *Kingston Chronicle*, 8 October 1831, [Rev. Adam Hood Burwell] "One of the People"; Spragge, *Strachan Letter Book*, xiv, [Strachan], Document to the Colonial Office, 5 June1824.

In commenting upon the role of 'the dissenting ministers' in fomenting the American Revolution, the Upper Canadian Anglican Tories appear to have been referring to something which they regarded as common knowledge. Upon writing in 1828 to Robert Wilmot Horton (the former Under-Secretary of State for War and the Colonies), John Beverley Robinson prefaced his private remarks on that subject with a comment that: "It is perhaps 'illiberal' to remember these things -- or to call to mind ...." Such a comment indicates a general awareness of the facts related. In support of their comments on the role of 'the dissenting ministers' in fomenting the American Revolution, both Strachan and Robinson cited a book written by one of the dissenting ministers who actively supported the revolution: viz. the Rev. William Gordon (*History of the Rise, Progress and Establishment of the Independence of the United States of America, 1788*). Although Strachan constantly referred to 'the dissenting ministers' – primarily the ministers of the established Congregational churches of New England -- as being active supporters of the American rebellion, it was actually the preachers of the evangelical Calvinist separatist sects who were the most ardent supporters of the American revolutionaries. For an analysis of the intellectual process by which the evangelical sectarians conflated their religious principles with the political principles of the American Lockean-liberal revolutionaries, see Heimert, *Religion and the American Mind*, 294-519.

14. *Kingston Chronicle*, [Strachan], Letters to Walsh: no. 7, 17 March 1820 & no. 10, 21 April 1820; Strachan, *Discourse*, 1810, 31-32, and 7; Strachan, *Sermon on Death of Cartwright*, 1815, 28; Robinson, *Canada Bill*, 1840, 13-16; Robinson, "Letter to Earl Bathurst", *Four Pamphlets*, 26 December 1824, 45-47; and *Kingston Chronicle*, (Macaulay editorial), 11 June 1819.

15. The view of the Upper Canadian Tories that so-called 'Age of Reason' was really an 'Age of Delusion', is consistent with an argument made by an American political philosopher, Eric Voegelin (*The New Science of Politics* (Chicago: University of Chicago Press, 1952). Voegelin has argued that men who believed in a science of order -- "the classic and Christian science of man", wherein the given order of society and its representative institutions reflect a cosmic order that represents 'the truth' and that is inextricably bound up with the ultimate purpose of human existence -- must regard those who assail that order, and deny its validity, as being deluded.

Chapter Two – The Onslaught of Revolution

1. John Strachan, A *Discourse on the Character of King George the Third*, 1810, 32.

2. Strachan, *A Sermon Preached at York, Upper Canada on Third of June, Being the Day appointed for a General Thanksgiving* (Montreal: William Gray), 1814, 7-8; *Christian Recorder*, 1 June 1819, [Strachan], "Original Communication", 124; and Strachan, *Discourse*, 1810, 149-50. The quotation is from Strachan, *Discourse*, 8.

3. Strachan, *Sermon for General Thanksgiving*, 1814, 8; Strachan, *Discourse*, 1810, 32 and 64; and *The Church*, (Bethune editorial), 18 April 1840. The quotation is from Strachan, *Discourse*, 32.

4. Strachan, *Sermon for General Thanksgiving*, 1814; and Strachan, *Discourse*, 1810, 64. The quotation is from the sermon, 8.

5. *The Church*, (Bethune editorial) 29 May 1841; and *Kingston Chronicle* (editorial), 1 December 1820. The quotation is from the Kingston newspaper. The actual epigram quoted was not uttered with respect to the French Revolution; yet it is an apt statement of the Tory belief which applies directly to the conclusions which were drawn from that convulsion.

6. Strachan, *Sermon for General Thanksgiving*, 1814, 8; *The Church*, (Bethune editorial), 5 December 1840; Strachan, *Discourse*, 1810, 33; Strachan, "Memorial on King's College, autumn of 1843" in A.N. Bethune, *Memoir of the Right Reverend John Strachan, First Bishop of Toronto* (Toronto: Henry Rowsell), 1870, 238; and *Kingston Chronicle*, 14 January 1832, [Rev. Burwell], "One of the People".

7. Strachan, *Discourse*, 1810, 33; *The Church*, 11 November 1837, "Beilly Porteous, Bishop of London"; PAO, Strachan Sermons, Box C, St. Paul's Epistle to the Hebrews, 12:11, "Chastening yieldeth Righteousness", 16 March 1806, 7-8; Strachan, *Sermon for General Thanksgiving*, 1814, 9; *The Church*, (Bethune editorial), 5 December 1840; *Christian Recorder*, II, 290, October 1820, "Review of Harford's Life and Principles of Thomas Paine" (from *The Christian Observer*); and *Kingston Chronicle*, 14 January 1832, [Rev. Burwell], "One of the People", & 11 June 1819, (Macaulay editorial).

The first two quotes are from Strachan's *Sermon for General Thanksgiving*, 16 March 1806, 7; and the natural rights quote is from Dr. Price's "Discourse on the Love of our Country". It is quoted in Burke's *Reflections on the Revolution in France*, 27, and in Paine's, *The Rights of Man*, (New York: Doubleday & Co., 1961), 276, as well as paraphrased by "One of the people" [Rev. A. H. Burwell], 14 January 1832, and by John Macaulay in his editorial in the *Kingston Chronicle* of 11 June 1819. The Upper Canadian Tories believed that Dr. Richard Price and Thomas Paine were seeking to destroy Christianity through attacking the National Church so that they might promote a successful political revolution. However, Paine (*Age of Reason*) argued the reverse. He held that a change to a democratic government would bring about "a revolution in the system of religion".

[Brief references to the arguments of Price and Paine, in the original dissertation chapter, have been expanded for this publication with the insertion of summaries of their arguments drawn from the following primary sources: Richard Price, D.D., L.L.D., F.R.S., *A Discourse on the Love of Our Country, delivered on Nov. 4, 1789 at the Meeting House in the Old Jewry, to the Society for Commemorating the Revolution in Great Britain* (London: T. Cadell, 1790); Thomas Paine, *Rights of Man: Being an Answer to Mr. Burke's Attack on the French Revolution*, Sixth Edition (London: J.S. Jordan, 1791); and Thomas Paine, *The Age of Reason, Part the First, being An Investigation of True and Fabulous Theology* (London: Daniel Isaac Eaton, 1796).]

8. *Christian Recorder*, Vol. I, 124, June 1819, Strachan, "Original Communications"; Strachan, *Sermon for General Thanksgiving*, 1814, 9-12; *Kingston Gazette*, 11 February 1812, "Falkland" [Richard Cartwright]; and

Strachan, *Discourse*, 1810, 33-34. The quote is from the *Christian Recorder*, June 1819, vol. I, 124.

9. *Kingston Gazette*, 11 February 1812, "Falkland"; *Kingston Chronicle* (Macaulay editorial), 22 August 1821; Bethune, *Memoir*, Strachan, "Sermon to the Legislature", 2 August 1812, 4l; Strachan, *Sermon for General Thanksgiving*, 1814, 9-14; PAO, Strachan Sermons, Box B, Book of Scottish speeches 1795-1799, speech entitled "Whether a speedy peace or a continuance of the present war would be of more advantage to G. Britain", 114-115; Strachan, *Discourse*, 1810, 65-66 & 35; and *Kingston Chronicle* (Macaulay editorial), 22 August 1821. Both quotes are from Strachan, *Sermon for General Thanksgiving*, 1814, 12-13.

10. PAO, Cartwright Letterbook, 1793-1796, Richard Cartwright to Robert Hamilton, 9 May 1794; and C.E. Cartwright, ed., *Life and Letters*, 64-65, Richard Cartwright to Major Lothbridge, 10 October 1794.

11. Strachan, *Discourse*, 1810, 36-38, 73, 75-80, 84-85; *Kingston Gazette*, "Falkland", 4 February and 3 March 1812; *Kingston Gazette*, 12 May 1812, "John Bull Sen."; PAO, Robinson Papers, 1862-1905, John Beverley Robinson, "Address to the Militia of the Home District", n.d. [1813?]; Strachan, *Sermon on Death of Cartwright*, 3 September 1815, 35-36; Cartwright Family Papers, (Private Collection), Richard Cartwright to James Cartwright, 13 February 1808. The quote is from the "Falkland" letter of 3 March 1812.

The efforts of the Upper Canadian Tory elite, to raise and sustain the morale of Upper Canadians, continued throughout the war years. That effort, as well as the ideological implications of the struggle in which they were engaged, has been treated in R.A. Bowler, "Propaganda in Upper Canada, A Study of the Propaganda Directed at the People of Upper Canada during the War of 1812", (unpublished M.A. thesis, Queen's University, September 1964).

12. Donald C. MacDonald, "Honourable Richard Cartwright, 1759- 1815", Ontario Department of Public Records and Archives, *Three History Theses*, 1961, 69-170; "Address of the House of Assembly to the People of Upper Canada", reprinted in Bowler, "Propaganda in Upper Canada", Appendix II, 156-157; *Kingston Gazette*, "Falkand"; 11 February 1812; Kingston Gazette, [Strachan], "Address to the House of Assembly", 3 September 1811; Strachan, *Discourse*, 1810, 34-35; Bethune, *Memoir*, 41, extract from Strachan, "Sermon to the Legislature", 12 August 1812; and PAO, Strachan Sermons, Box C, 16 March 1806, St. Paul's Epistle to the Hebrews 12:11, "Chastening yieldeth righteousness" and PAO, Strachan Papers, Box B, Book of Scottish speeches, 1795-99, speech on "Peace or War", 116; and Strachan, *Sermon for General*

Thanksgiving, 1814, 6, 14 & 16. The quotations are from Richard Cartwright, "Address to the Militia", 15 December 1807; from the "Address of the House of Assembly to the People of Upper Canada", 5 Augusts 1812 as quoted by Bowler, 157; and Strachan, *Sermon for General Thanksgiving*, 6, respectively.

13. C. E. Cartwright, ed., *Life and Letters*, 64, R. Cartwright to Major Lothbridge, 10 October 1794; and Strachan, *Discourse*, 1810, 71-72. The quotation is from Strachan, *Discourse*, 71-72.

Strachan's comments were prescient. At that time, Stein and Hardenberg, and Scharnhorst and Gneisenau, were busy re-organizing and reforming Prussia and its army in preparation for a 'War of Liberation', which was launched against Napoleon in 1813 under their leadership.

14. *Kingston Gazette*, "Falkland" [Cartwright], 3 March 1812; *Kingston Gazette*, "John Bull Sen.", 12 May 1812; and Strachan, *Discourse*, 1810, 71-74 & 76. The quotation is from Strachan, *Discourse*, 74.

———————————

Part Two

Safeguarding Upper Canada

Chapter Three - The Postwar Outlook

Chapter Four - The American Threat

Chapter Five - A British National Character

———————————

"It should now be felt that we, in this generation, are laying the foundation of a social system, which is to extend its avails upon millions who will soon succeed. The responsibility upon us is great, & upon the measure in which we discharge our obligations, the very happiness of those who are to come afterwards may very well depend."

John Beverley Robinson
Chief Justice of Upper Canada

April 1834

'View of King Street East', York/Toronto, showing the District Court House, Jail and St. James' Anglican Church. By Thomas Young, 1834. Toronto Reference Library.

Chapter Three

The Post-war Outlook

In looking back over the reign of King George III (1760-1820) at the time of his death, the Upper Canadian Tories were very conscious of having escaped a great catastrophe which they believed had threatened the very existence of civilization. The period encompassing the American Revolution, the French Revolution, and the Napoleonic War years, was seen to have been a veritable age of revolutions that had been marked by a "spirit of discontent & innovation". A major concern of the Upper Canadian Tories was to examine the forces that had overwhelmed the nations of Europe and threatened the Loyalist asylum of Upper Canada, in seeking to understand how best to defend the established order.

In Upper Canada, the former pupils of the Rev. John Strachan of the Cornwall District Grammar School were just beginning to fulfill the hopes that he had long held out for them. The 'young Tories' were entering into the public life of the province and, in being among the best-educated individuals in the province and the sons of prominent families, they were securing government appointments and gaining election to the House of Assembly. Moreover, the Rev. Strachan had but recently been appointed to the Executive Council and to the Legislative Council of the province, and was well positioned to promote the public careers of his former pupils. They shared a common outlook on the threat posed to the traditional order by the democratic leveling principles and infidelity of the age of revolutions.

The revolutionary age had given birth to a social unrest and anarchy that had threatened the destruction of European civilization, and in North America, the Province of Upper Canada had narrowly escaped being conquered and annexed by a revolutionary power. In the postwar period, however, there were signs of improvement in the life of the common people and of a revitalization of the Christian religion that gave rise to hopes for a better future of peace and prosperity; although the Tories were determined to remain vigilant in defence of their principles and the institutions that sustained the traditional order.

A Promising Renewal

In reviewing the last forty years of the reign of George III, the Upper Canadian Tories were dumbfounded by the revolutionary outbursts that had threatened the ancient governments of Europe. Everywhere states and empires had appeared to be on the verge of chaos with their governments in danger of an imminent overthrow. China was wracked by internal upheavals, and the Turkish Empire appeared to be disintegrating from inertia. The world had presented a rather sorry spectacle wherein even Great Britain had had to fight for her very existence. It was a situation where:

> Kingdoms were convulsed, and thrones hurled from their foundations, while all around was darkness and dismay.

In that period of convulsion and disorder, Britain had been viewed as the only hope of stability and order amidst the destruction of nations which were overwhelmed by the eruptions of "the revolutionary volcano". In standing fast, Great Britain had made a major contribution to the salvation of Europe. In doing so, she had increased her stature immeasurably in the eyes of the young Tories of Upper Canada.

The revolutionary upheavals left a strong impression on the Upper Canadian Tory mind as expressed by John Macaulay.

> The mind is struck with the magnitude and character of the events to which it has given birth. The astonishing changes in the political world which marked this portion of History, stupendous as they were, scarcely require comment, as they must be engraven on the memory of all.

Years of war had visibly taken their toll in spreading misery and disorder among the nations, and in weakening their very moral fiber. War by its very nature was to be regretted because it changed the character of the people of every country through fostering a neglect of social duties and peaceful occupations. It appealed to the baser instincts in men and corrupted their moral habits. War also posed a threat to the state in that wars, when long continued, invariably led to a curtailing of civil liberties, and a concomitant increase in the military power over the civil authorities.

Great Britain, it was felt, had survived that danger with her constitution intact only because the she had had to resort to arming her citizens in defence of the country; and the citizen soldiers had "formed an equipoise to the regular army". Yet, despite the dangers which the years of war and revolution had posed to the very survival of civilization, there were other areas of life – the arts and the sciences -- that had witnessed great progress and discoveries that exceeded all former knowledge. The practical applications of the new knowledge had substantially increased the comforts of life.

The spread of knowledge, and an increasing contact between nations, ensured that all would benefit from new developments and improvements; yet that same ease of communication between nations had brought the age of total war. It had to be recognized that the development of better communications could be used for good or evil.

> Any great excitement that may be produced, is not therefore confined to one or two nations, which was the case some years ago, but circulate instantly through the civilized world. (1)

Religion and morality had suffered at the hands of "those malevolent spirits" who sought to undermine or displace Christianity, and thereby destroy all sense of moral obligation. Yet there was hope. Although the events of the past thirty years seemed to prove that there was a total want of religion among the leading nations of Europe and that man had a great capacity for wickedness, the true Christian could see a deeper meaning. As viewed by the Rev. John Strachan, the course of events revealed:

> that vast scheme for the salvation of mankind, which the whole providence of God is gradually promoting.

The philosophes had scoffed at religion, and there was a general apathy among all peoples towards religion in the pre-revolutionary period. However, in having witnessed the excesses of the French Revolution and the subsequent war years, governments were reacting by making unprecedented efforts to restore religion to its rightful place in society and the state. Moreover, the general increase in knowledge in all areas was supplying a new force to "the evidences of Christianity".

Spurred on by assaults on Christianity, and the ominous threat of infidelity, Christians had turned again to a study of the Bible to take stock of their beliefs. In doing so, men's understanding of Christianity had been expanded and deepened beyond what the reformers had attained during the Reformation of the 16th Century. Through new studies of the Bible, a purer religion had been recovered complete in its "native simplicity and beauty". Christians everywhere were now enabled to defend their faith through rational arguments.

Another encouraging sign was the fact that the attacks of infidels upon Christianity had brought together all denominations of Christians in various lands in support of Bible Societies. Prominent among them was the British and Foreign Bible Society, which was founded in Britain in 1804 for the distribution of Bibles and New Testaments. The enormous success of the Bible societies was made possible in turn by the better means of education which the lower classes were receiving, which fostered in turn a desire to read the Scriptures. Through the united efforts of the Christian churches, all peoples were provided with access to the Bible, and through missionary societies, were receiving religious instruction which was lacking earlier.

The union of Christian denominations was a potent force for good as was attested to by their united efforts – in Britain and within the British Empire -- in support of the successful struggle to abolish the slave trade. Such a development could not but be a harbinger of better things to come. (2)

Everywhere in Europe, among all ranks of society, convulsions in the moral and political world had turned the minds of men to religion, and greatly strengthened and increased the Christian spirit and principles among the nations. The age of revolutions had brought insecurity of life and property, and uncertainty which, ultimately, had moved men to look beyond themselves to religion where alone consolation was to be found. With the defeat of Napoleon, France -- the pivot of Europe -- was restored to her Ancient line of kings with a liberal constitution firmly established, which held out the promise that "the restless spirits of revolution" would be held in check.

King Louis XVIII had bound himself to rule in accordance with the Charter of 1814 at the head of a government which was animated by a

Christian spirit. He had abandoned the arbitrary measures of "Louis Le Grand" (Louis XIV) and his successors which had brought on the French Revolution. The restored monarchy recognized the rights of the French people. They were guaranteed liberty of the press, security of property and person, and religious toleration, under a government consciously dedicated to promoting their general welfare.

It was equally encouraging that the crown heads of Austria, Prussia and Russia – although of different religions – had professed their common Christian faith and had pledged, in joining the Holy Alliance of September 1815, to be guided by Christian principles and the truths of Christianity. In recognizing God's sovereignty over the Christian community, they had dedicated themselves to ruling their branch of that community in "a spirit of paternal tenderness" under God. Although not overly sanguine in expecting that princes would always live up to "such sublime principles", the Upper Canadian Tories, nonetheless, took heart in witnessing the public recognition that Christian principles were the foundation of the well-being of society.

Hope for the future prosperity and peace of Europe was raised by the fact that Great Britain, which had played the key role – with God's blessing -- in bringing about the restoration of a united Europe, now possessed the balance of power. Although able to maintain the balance, she was neither able nor willing to overthrow it. Her military power was not such as to constitute a danger to other states.

Britain had been chastised for her past sins, errors, and omissions through the suffering and dangers of the war years. It was to be hoped that Great Britain, which had been revitalized by the efforts of her various religious denominations in responding to the threat of infidelity and anarchy, would continue to exercise her power to "preserve the general tranquility and the liberty of all". That she would seek to extend the benefits of her trade "upon the most liberal principles" to all nations, and thereby secure a lasting security and peace for all nations. (3)

In regarding the European countries, which had experienced thirty or more years of war and revolutionary upheaval, the Upper Canadian Tories believed that the workings of God's judgment could be seen in the unfolding of events, and it provided a critical lesson for both rulers and subjects. Those in authority had been clearly admonished that their governments needed to be conducted on more liberal principles, and that they ought to be concerned with improving the prosperity and happiness of their people.

In sum, rulers had been taught that "the rights of the people" needed to be respected, and constitutions amended to guarantee them. That the harsh and savage penalties of the criminal law had to be made less severe, and fair and equitable taxation policies instituted. It was evident as well that the good of the people had to take precedence over the granting of special privileges for favoured individuals. If the existing governments were to survive, they must seek to promote the general good in destroying all monopolies and unmerited distinctions, in fostering the development of agriculture and industry, and in extending commerce. In sum, rulers should realize that "their true interest was comprised in the happiness of their people".

Subjects had been instructed as well, through bitter experience, to distrust the declamations of demagogues who declared themselves to be 'patriots' and who "busy themselves in exaggerating the faults of Rulers". Such men, it was now apparent to all, were merely seeking self-aggrandizement through degrading or destroying their superiors. And in the process, they had inflicted a great deal of misery upon mankind.

Subjects needed to realize that government, in being a work of man, could never be absolutely perfect in its structure, or faultless in its administration. Allowances had to be made for human failings. For it was evident that:

> Whatever may be the state of society in the several continental governments, it is not by sudden and violent alterations, such as the revolutionists contemplate, that the condition of the people is to be bettered. The awful example set by the French revolution is a sufficient warning against such changes.

To the contrary:

It is by peaceable and gradual steps, and not by revolutions, that the most solid improvements in the Science of government can be obtained. (4)

Only in tranquility could people be educated, laws reformed, and the public welfare promoted. Subjects must accept the fact that "labour is the lot of man"; and that there were limits to what governments could do, or be expected to do. No system of government could abolish the need for men to labour, or relieve mankind from all suffering. It had been shown that:

> No great and decided amelioration of the lower classes of society can be reasonably expected: much improved they certainly may be; but that foolish perfectibility with which they have been deluded, can never be realized. Events seem to confound the reasonings of all political reformers.

Both the American and the French experiments had totally failed in their attempt to constitute governments productive of virtue and happiness only. The revolution in France had produced horrific excesses, and had ended in a military despotism. The American Revolution had brought to power a democratic government which, in what was supposedly a free republic, had not scrupled to ally itself with a savage military despot. Such an alliance was an indication of the general decline that the United States was experiencing. Only the ultimate fate of the American republic remained to be resolved. From what they observed, the Upper Canadian Tories believed that the United States was:

> sinking fast into anarchy which will give rise either to a general despotism, or to a division.

A revolution would not change the realities of life, or achieve 'real liberty' for any nation. Only through the introduction of practical reforms in government approximating those of the British Constitution, and by means of serious efforts to educate the lower orders -- in a religiously-based education system -- could the condition of the people be improved in European Countries, or in any country for that matter.

Subjects could rest assured that governments had learned their lesson and, through various means, would "gradually introduce every amelioration compatible with social order". As for the Upper Canadian Tories, they could only indulge the hope that:

> the spirit of suspicious jealously which has so long separated the governed and governors, will now gradually subside; and the wish of both will be to promote the general good. (5)

Yet, all was not well in the worldview of the Upper Canadian Tories at the close of a generation of war. Although the efforts by revolutionary states to overturn all traditional governments -- by military aggression, --had been defeated, there remained still the task of combating 'the spirit of the age'. After the conclusion of the War of 1812, the Upper Canadian Tories were prepared to enter upon a struggle that they realized would be long and difficult, and which they viewed as a battle for civilization against the forces stemming from the French Revolution.

It was viewed as a "conflict between anarchy and infidelity on the one hand, and subordination and true religion on the other". In that struggle, military means were giving way to "a conflict of opinion almost as desolatory to the moral fabric of society, as the ravage of war to its political state". It was a struggle which offered no respite to those concerned to maintain the traditional order. The impact of the principles of the American and French revolutions had been such that wherever the Upper Canadian Tories paused to look -- to England, the United States, or in their own immediate surroundings in Upper Canada -- they were appalled by what they observed, and at the effect which the revolutionary credos were having upon the very constitution of society. (6)

One such phenomenon, which was prevalent in Upper Canada during the postwar decades, was a prevailing "rage for equality" which seemed to affect all areas of life, and occasioned a great deal of anxiety. It was observed that:

> the spirit of the present age is, generally speaking, too little inclined to those respectful usages which are necessary to the very being of society.

With respect to public life, not only were men of authority and eminence denied their customary respect and deference, but "republican ferocity" was such that their very character and abilities were traduced and ridiculed in attempts to destroy their dignity and bring all authority, whether civil or ecclesiastical, into contempt.

Democratic radicals, whom the Tories categorized as anarchists, were seen to be claiming for themselves "all sense, humanity, taste and genius", while persons of rank and dignity were depicted as men who were ignorant of the rights of humanity and possessed of a cruel and haughty demeanor, bereft of any sympathy for those less fortunate. Such an attitude, and the coarse invective which it gave rise to, was deeply deplored because, if left unchecked, it would destroy "all the outworks, and at length the very essence, of our civil and religious polity".

The danger was very real as no public office holders, including the judiciary, were exempt from attack and abuse at the hands of democrats and government detractors. The Tories were acutely conscious that:

> Names ... are, things; and it is very certain that the exterior forms of respect for any office have seldom been violated with impunity, without the office itself being soon exposed to contempt.

Open attacks upon public officials were never justified because office holders were unable to respond by entering into public debate to defend themselves against slander. If individual officers of the government, or members of the bench, deserved strong criticism or censure, there were legitimate channels of complaint and redress. Individual office holders were subject to removal, if found culpable. In view of their office, they should receive all "exterior marks of deference, and the ordinary language of respect" until such a time as any charges against them could be investigated, and individuals removed if found guilty of misconduct. Hurling insults and invective at those in authority, and openly speaking ill of them, would only make matters worse by destroying respect for the office itself. Moreover, it would discourage honourable men from seeking to serve the public.

A recourse to public denunciations of government officials by radicals was totally unjustifiable. Moreover, it was doubly deplorable in that for the most part such attacks were launched without proof or argument upon the merest suspicion, or were mere fabrications that were concocted 'by designing men' who were seeking to enhance their own reputation in the eyes of the unreflecting multitude.

If society were to function at all, it was essential that a civility and common courtesy be extended to one's fellows. In sum, decency, justice, Christian duty, and "the just balance of society", demanded that prescriptive usages of respect be maintained. To that end, it was regarded as essential that parents and teachers inculcate in children, through instruction in Christian precepts, a respect for their betters, not in a servile sense, but rather in the sense of rendering all men their due. Christian principles needed to be taught to counteract the designs of those who were seeking to instigate a political revolution, and to remind men of the necessity to 'fear God and honour the King'.

In retrospect, it was noted that politically, the new spirit had resulted in a general enfeeblement of authority. The Upper Canadian Tories were aware of the paradox that at a time when governments everywhere were becoming possessed of more and more power than ever before, their authority had become weaker. No longer did those in authority, in virtue of their office, receive on all sides a recognition of their legitimacy and right to rule. No longer did they elicit that former willing obedience which formed a necessary component of order in any society.

It was of the utmost importance that proper values be inculcated into the population of any state because once the legitimacy of authority was destroyed by revolution, the resultant anarchy could only be rectified, if then, by returning to the original state and polity. Otherwise, all that remained would be government by force and fear – an appalling prospect to the defenders of the traditional order of society, who believed in true liberty under the law. (7)

Long before the existing order in Upper Canada came under concentrated and persistent attack by democratic radicals and religious sectarians, the Upper Canadian Tories realized that in the province and elsewhere, an ideological struggle was being waged for "the mind of man"; and it was a struggle in which religion was of the essence. The spread of atheism and infidelity into Upper Canada in the immediate post-war years, and the growing magnitude of the threat in Britain, brought the Upper Canadian Tories face to face with that "frightful crisis". Initially, it spurred them to form a local chapter of the Society for Promoting Christian Knowledge to distribute Bibles, religious books and religious tracts throughout the province.

Such an effort -- which they instituted in 1819 -- was regarded as necessary by the Tories because of their awareness that infidels no longer confined their appeals exclusively to the middle class and/or to the aristocracy as the philosophes had done in the 18th Century. Infidels now sought to poison the mind of the masses. It was a situation where:

> the peculiar and more pressing danger of the moment arises from a diffusive circulation, amongst the lower classes, of short tracts, which, however otherwise to be despised, are but too well calculated, by bold fallacies and blasphemous assertions, to shake the faith of the ignorant and uninformed, and by an unceasing repetition of attacks in daily and weekly numbers finally to overthrow it. (8)

The Democratic Radical Threat

In seeking how best to defend the existing order of things, and to counteract the forces of revolution, both political and religious, the Tories were acutely conscious of the difficulties which they faced. That was particularly so with respect to the psychology which they observed at work in the potent appeal of all 'innovators' in Church and State. In facing the spectre of infidelity in 1819, and the onslaught of republican and ecclesiastical democracy over a decade later, the Tories were never far removed from a consciousness of the origins of the ideas which their opponents espoused. Hence, they turned to study the works of Jean-Jacques Rousseau and Thomas Paine to assess the reasons for the strong appeal and impact of their subversive ideas upon the popular mind.

Such men, it was noted, did not reason or argue but rather declaimed in employing "the language of irony, satire, and contempt" and "an insinuating eloquence" to rail against the traditional order. They consciously appealed to and played upon "the passions, the prejudices, and the very appetites and favourite indulgences" of those whom they addressed. In taking advantage of the "portion of credulity" which belonged to their age – with the pagan mythology of previous ages with its giants, magicians, fairies and heroes of romance having lost its impact --- the radicals sought to profit from man's propensity to respond to the marvelous and exciting. To do so, the radicals propounded new theories of politics, religion and morals, that were flattering to human pride and presumption.

The success of their efforts was understandable on several counts: first, their appeal was being directed to uninstructed minds; and, secondly, their efforts were directed to the passions rather than the understanding which gave them a greater impact because:

> it is far easier to feel strongly than to think correctly or argue rationally. The one requires neither truth nor reflection: the process of the others cannot be carried on without both.

Ultimately, as the Tories realized, it was the very bias of human nature and of the human mind with which they were contending. The writings of men such as Rousseau and Paine -- and their successors of the 19th Century who were attacking Christianity and the institutions which embodied its principles -- were effective in moving the popular mind because:

> It is so much easier to comprehend objections than solutions; so much more gratifying to human pride and the love of display, to attack what is revered and established, than to be contented with quietly defending it; so much more congenial to our fallen nature to wish to discard a system which enjoins humility, and watchfulness, and self-denial, than submissively to obey its dictates. (9)

Discontent and disquiet were also to be accounted for by the fact that innovation and change struck a responsive chord in the human mind which, because it partook in part of the divine nature, was marked by "a busy restless principle" ever seeking after perfection. For those who accepted Christianity, this principle was given a purposive direction and control in that both the object to be attained and the manner of pursuit were clearly set forth in the promise held out of a better life to come. However, the non-Christian was denied this unimpeachable guide to conduct and solace, with the result that:

> with the man of this world, the object is ideal-- the creature of his brain only; because not existing where alone he seeks for it -- in this world. Consequently, his search is the chase of a mere phantom, conjured up by a heated imagination, ever before his eyes, yet ever eluding his grasp. Ignorant that a perfect state is nowhere below the skies, he finds fault with what, in its very nature, cannot be otherwise than faulty. Discontented, because not godly, he spends his time in inquiring for, and planning some new thing; vainly hoping, like the seekers of old for the philosopher's stone, that every invention is to be the alchymy [sic]-- the secret power which by its touch, is to change the very nature of evil into good.

Such was the psychology which was held to be at work behind the appeal of all 'innovators' and men given to change, and what motivated their conduct. It was the same in every age, as human nature remained unchanged.

Motivated by pride, selfishness, envy, or discontent, men would always be found, and followers would not be lacking, who would object to whatever was -- though the product of the wisdom of centuries and based upon the revelation of God Himself -- and seek to overturn everything in the name of some fancied reform or improvement. The proof of this was apparent to the Upper Canadian Tories as they cast their eyes around them. In looking at Europe and Upper Canada during the third decade of the 19th Century and thereafter, they realized that they were living in a veritable age of innovation wherein "the great antiquity of any law, custom or institution is deemed by many, a sufficient reason for its abrogation".

The Tories in their writings pointed out the folly of such a bias of mind. Radicals, in frantically seeking perfection here on earth, were precluded from any enjoyment of what good the present condition of man was capable of yielding. Moreover, 'innovators' in seeking to destroy the existing order had nothing to put in its place. They were men who merely sought change to better themselves at the expense of the people who were left "without any reasonable expectation of obtaining a better order of things". Nonetheless, such was the madness of the people that there was "no creed so monstrous, which thousands, if unrestrained, will not espouse". (10)

Postwar Political Unrest in Europe and Britain

The credulity of the people was evidenced in the fact that although the American and French revolutions had proved to be miserable failures -- to the Tory mind at least -- the revolutionary spirit continued unabated among peoples everywhere. In England by 1820, the spirit of innovation and infidelity were seen to be sweeping through the manufacturing areas and making inroads into Scotland and Ireland; while on the Continent, political revolution again threatened the ancient monarchical governments. The revolution in Spain (January 1820) was seen to have had an "electric effect on the minds of neighbouring nations", and was quickly followed by revolutions in Portugal, Naples and Sardinia, by disturbances in Germany, revolutionary plots in France, and rebellions among the Spanish colonies of South America.

The uprisings were regarded as indicative of "a ferment in the public mind" which posed a continuing threat to the existence of all governments everywhere. The Upper Canadian Tories sympathized with the peoples who were demanding liberty, and who were suffering from oppression in the various states where discontent and rebellion were rampant. In regarding the liberal revolutions on the European continent in Spain, Portugal, Naples and Sardinia, the Tories were aware that each government that had been overthrown was "weak, corrupt, oppressive and full of abuses". However, the Tories firmly believed that revolution by force of arms would not bring about any amelioration of the condition of the oppressed peoples.

In sum, the Upper Canadian Tories were far from being blind supporters of established governments, regardless of their nature and conduct. To the contrary, they were ardent supporters of 'the rights of the people', and were ever anxious to see them properly secured, but the Tories believed that violent revolution was not a suitable means to achieve that end. As John Macaulay expressed it:

> The word liberty has a fascinating sound, and it truly is a glorious spectacle to witness a nation seeking for emancipation with firmness, moderation and constancy. But the means which were employed for the acquisition of freedom in the late revolutions cannot be commended.

The Tories also experienced a foreboding in the way in which the so-called 'liberal revolutions' were carried out. The attempts to establish liberal governments in the several European countries -- on the model of the abortive liberal Spanish Constitution of 1812 -- were not the result of the active exertion of the mind or the will of the people over time, or even at the time of the revolution. The revolutions were purely military undertakings which were effected through a "seduction of the soldiery". In each country, the people had remained as passive during their respective 'liberal revolutions' as they had under their former despotic governments – a fact which boded ill for their future liberty. (11)

In the view of the Tories, the situation in England was totally different. There, 'true liberty' had been long established, and the difficulties being experienced were basically economic in origin.

The cause was the heavy taxes levied to pay an immense national debt occasioned by years of war, and a postwar economic dislocation caused by the revival of European manufacturing and a reduced demand for British manufactures. These factors had combined to throw an already superabundant population into a state of distress, which fell particularly hard upon the lower classes.

In England, widespread unemployment and severe suffering had provided a fertile field for demagogues and 'designing individuals', such as the radicals William Cobbett and Henry Hunt, who worked their intrigues through "inflammatory speeches and resolutions exciting tumult and disorder". By their efforts, the poor were:

seduced into believing that a radical reform, or more properly speaking, a total subversion of the existing Constitution was required for the salvation of the country; and that the most violent measures should be adopted to this end.

One event made a singular impression on the Upper Canadian Tory mind. On 16 August 1819, over 60,000 people had gathered in St. Peter's Field in Manchester, England, to hear an address by Henry Hunt. They carried banners demanding political reforms: 'Annual Parliaments, Universal Suffrage, and Vote by ballot', as well as demands for a repeal the Corn Laws which, through restricting foreign wheat imports, were keeping bread prices artificially high.

An attempt by the military -- at the request of the local magistrates -- to arrest Hunt and the organizers of the gathering had resulted in a melee in which a cavalry regiment charged into the crowd and killed over a dozen people and wounded as many as 400 persons, men and women. Although newspapers and the British public almost universally condemned what became known derisively as the "Peterloo Massacre", the Tory government in London feared that England was on the verge of a rebellion. Cobbett and Hunt maintained that they sought only parliamentary reform, but the government feared that the large public meetings might ignite a popular insurrection or a revolution.

As viewed from afar, the Upper Canadian Tories were convinced that Cobbett and Hunt were men of a restless spirit who were seeking, under the pretense of reform, to plunge England into "all the horrors of a sanguinary revolution". They were aware, from English newspaper accounts, that thousands of men were secretly drilling and gathering at meetings in the manufacturing districts of England; that riots were occurring in some of the manufacturing centres; and that treasonable placards were being displayed everywhere.

Although concerned about the unrest in England, the Upper Canadian Tories remained convinced that there was no real danger of revolution in the Home country. The demands for radical reform were confined for the most part to the manufacturing classes. These were the people who were suffering the worst from the postwar economic malaise, but they formed only a small proportion of the English nation. Nonetheless, the Tories concluded that something had to be done to prevent riots and disorder.

What the Upper Canadian Tories favoured for England were 'judicious reforms' such as "a more liberal and equal representation in parliament, a more economical system of poor laws, and an amendment of some of the penal statutes" to render them less severe. However, the critical concern, and caution, was:

> how to attain these objects without opening a door to dangerous innovations which might ultimately subvert the venerable fabric of the British Constitution.

In the view of the Upper Canadian Tories, the overturning of the Constitution would not bring about any amelioration in economic conditions or the resultant social distress. On the contrary, a revolution would merely bring anarchy and bloodshed, and a further aggravation of suffering and misery.

It was evident to the Tories of Upper Canada that the ultimate solution to the political unrest in England was to secure new markets to foster the revival of British manufacturing. To that end, they expressed the hope that the contemporary revolutions in South America would result in the creation of several "free and enterprising States" which, despite their questionable origins, would hopefully escape falling into military dictatorships. The hope expressed was that the former Spanish colonies would provide an immense market for British manufactures, and relieve her trade from depression.

In the meantime, the Upper Canadian Tories approved the efforts of the British government to rigorously enforce the law. The arrest of the 'Jacobin' leaders was also welcome. It would prevent their organizing large public gatherings, and thereby preclude further violent encounters and loss of life on the scale of the Manchester tragedy, which the Upper Canadian Tories greatly deplored.

The Tories also supported, but not without some misgivings, the strong measures -- the Six Acts of November 1819 -- which parliament subsequently passed to maintain peace and order in the United Kingdom. The Acts placed restrictions on large public gatherings, forbade the training of civilians in military manoeuvres, empowered the magistrates to search for and confiscate weapons, speeded up the judicial process for prosecutions, placed a tax on political pamphlets and tracts, and strengthened the laws and penalties pertaining to authors who published "immoral and blasphemous writings".

Unusual circumstances required the exercise of extraordinary powers. When viewed from Upper Canada, it appeared to the Tories that the powers which had been granted to the British government by parliament, were no greater than what was needed "to crush the efforts of revolutionizing and deistical demagogues" and keep order in the state. Not all Upper Canadians were of the Tory view. There were liberal-whigs, political radicals and presumably moderate Tories, who shared the view of the British whigs that the Six Acts constituted a suppression of the rights and liberties of the people, and were an overreaction to a localized political unrest. (12)

Political Unrest in Upper Canada

During the early postwar years, the Upper Canadian Tories could not escape thinking about the problem of how to maintain peace and order in society. Everywhere they looked in the world, the revolutionary spirit appeared in evidence and Upper Canada itself was not immune to it. During the war, they had faced the problem of disaffection among the American settlers who preferred a democratic republican government and annexation to the United States to the existing monarchical form of government, and the American aliens who remained in the province continued to be regarded as a threat to the existing order. Moreover, Upper Canada had already experienced, and was experiencing, episodes of domestic political unrest.

In the pre-war period (1807-1810), discontent had been fomented by recent British immigrants, who comprised for the most part dissatisfied office seekers such as William Weekes, Joseph Willcocks, and Judge Robert Thorpe, and their associate John Mills Jackson. They were men who sought to assuage their disappointment at failing to attain the public positions which they coveted -- or in the case of Jackson, his failure to receive a major land grant -- by openly attacking members of the provincial government. Individual office holders were denounced at the bar of the House of Assembly in diatribes which were published in the local newspapers, and in addresses to juries by Judge Thorpe, and by denunciations which were uttered at public meetings. Various charges were hurled at the government administration which was accused of favouritism in land granting and the mismanagement of public monies.

To the Tories, the pre-War agitators were 'factious demagogues' who were bent on fomenting discontent among the settlers. Although the denunciations were embarrassing to the provincial government of the day, that earlier effort to discredit the leading members of the provincial government, had failed to engender any widespread public support. However, the fact that the pre-war leader of the opposition faction in the House of Assembly, Joseph Willcocks, and two of his prominent supporters in the Assembly, Benajah Mallory and Abraham Markle, had joined the American invasion forces during the War of 1812, left a vivid impression upon the Upper Canadian Tory mind.

In the immediate postwar period, Upper Canada experienced yet another disturbance of the peace of the province by an agitator who appeared bent on fostering discontent among the people. That effort was led by a newly-arrived British immigrant, Robert Gourlay who, in the view of the Tories, had attempted to put into practice the doctrines of the "Jacobinical School" of Richard Price, Thomas Paine, and Cobbett and Hunt. (13)

Within several months of his arrival in Upper Canada from Scotland -- to claim 866 acres of land which had been inherited by his wife -- Robert Gourlay published an address "To the Resident Land-owners of Upper Canada" (October 1817). His address called for responses from the residents of the districts of the province to a series of queries which he posed about the condition of the province, and how it might be improved.

Upon reading the proofs of the list of questions in the Address, the Rev. Strachan "saw through him at once", became alarmed at the "general tone and Spirit of the whole", and opposed its publication. Nonetheless, the Address was published in the government newspaper, the *Upper Canada Gazette*. In a Second Address of February 1818, Gourlay advocated the removal of restrictions on American immigration – an action which he maintained would double land values – and demanded that the Legislature undertake an enquiry into various charges which he hurled against the government over the administration of land granting system in the province. When his demands for a Legislative inquiry were not met, he published a Third Address of April 1818, in which he proposed that a provincial convention be organized to which delegates would carry petitions from township meetings to the ultimate end of petitioning the Prince Regent – the eldest son of King George III -- to institute reforms.

The escalating demands appeared to confirm the initial assessment of the Rev. Strachan as to the radical nature of the addresses published by Gourlay. The Tories witnessed what they regarded as attempts to stir up sedition through the fabrication of "down-right false assertions", inflammatory statements, and what the House of Assembly would later condemn as "scandalous, malicious and traitorous libel". Several public figures were publicly slandered by Gourlay, including the Rev. John Strachan. Nonetheless, in the absence of any law prohibiting district meetings, Gourlay proceeded to organize meetings in every district across the province. The only recourse for local magistrates was to launch a libel suit against him for his slanderous public abuse of members of the provincial government.

Something had to be done, for the leading Tories of the province believed:

> the safety and tranquillity [sic] of the Colony is at Stake. Indeed, no Govt. could stand were persons like Mr. Gourlay allowed to proceed without hinderance or opposition.

Finally, the provincial government responded to such concerns, and the Crown Officers were instructed to keep a watch on Robert Gourlay and his meetings. A surveillance of his activities was deemed to be necessary because the Third Address was regarded as almost a direct invitation for Upper Canadians to join the American Republic, or engage in some such radical political action. As John Macaulay observed:

> Are we not urged to affect a change (no matter what) in some way or other?

Gourlay had openly declared himself to be an admirer of Cobbett and Hunt; although, admittedly, he claimed to differ from them as to the means of effecting reform. Yet, Gourlay failed to make clear just what reforms he proposed to make, or by what means he would seek to institute his 'changes'. However, from his public declarations, it was quite evident that: "his object was *a radical change in the system*" of government. For the Tories, there was no other conclusion that could be drawn about an individual who took it upon himself to proselytize and excite discontent, and who:

> endeavors by various methods, to influence the public mind against the constituted authorities of the country and then projects the formation of a fourth power in the government, by which he might control or overset the other at his pleasure.

There was only one conclusion, which was quite apparent. Such methods were aimed at arousing the people to overturn the government of Upper Canada. (14)

Although the Tories regarded Gourlay as being "a bold and mischievous demagogue", they did not fear the man so much as experienced alarm at his method of pursuing reforms which was having an impact on the population of Upper Canada. As to Gourlay personally, his idiosyncrasies were such that he was compared to Cervantes' demented hero, Don Quixote. John Macaulay bestowed upon Gourlay the appellation "Knight of the Rueful Countenance", and observed:

> Our Political Quixote, like his famous prototype, was impatient to set out 'to redress grievances, to rectify wrongs, to reform abuses, and to remove doubts'. His followers, like Sancho Panza, were to be rewarded, not indeed with the Government of Islands and Kingdoms, but with the solid possession of countless acres. In his progress, he has converted poor innocent sheep into hostile armies, he has tilted at Benedictine friars, and had even sought to make the Laws themselves give way to his prowess. When he found difficulty in persuading his followers, that the bugbears of his diseased imagination were foes to his and their happiness, like the hero of La Mancha, he affirmed it with such vehemence that the simple folk at last believed him.

The latter was the real danger, and particularly so in a colony such as Upper Canada where large numbers of the residents were uneducated or semi-literate and, in the view of the Tories, possessed no spirit of inquiry, and were prone to believe whatever they heard or had read to them.

People would give credence to the falsehoods that were being preached in the absence of any denial or contrary argument and/or legal action against the instigator. It was feared that the provincial convention which Gourlay planned to hold, would agitate the colony by producing "uneasiness, irritations & exciting unreasonable hopes". Moreover, political unrest would discourage British emigrants -- who were needed to strengthen the province and promote its settlement and prosperity -- from coming to the colony. Thus, once sufficient evidence was attained by the government, the Attorney General, John Beverley Robinson, instituted a criminal libel charge against Robert Gourlay. He was arrested in June 1818, and released on bail to stand trial in August for the offense.

Although Gourlay was later acquitted at his trial by sympathetic jurors, the Tories were pleased to note that as of the summer of 1818 his efforts to stir up political unrest were failing. His provincial convention, which was held in York on 6 July 1818 under the close watch of the provincial government, had attracted only fourteen delegates and proved to be rather innocuous. Moreover, the new Lt. Governor, Major-General Sir Peregrine Maitland, immediately upon his arrival, publicly denounced the activities of Robert Gourlay and secured from the Legislature a law (October 1818) prohibiting the holding of political conventions.

The decisive actions of Lt. Governor Maitland succeeded in ending the public agitation. As of December 1818, the Rev. John Strachan noted that the province was in a peaceful state, which he attributed -- with some exaggeration -- to the fact that "as we have in truth no grievances the people are beginning to discover that it is so". Numerous loyalty addresses were received by the new Lt. Governor, which moved John Macaulay to observe that "the danger, if there ever existed any, was entirely blown over". The Gourlay agitation was regarded as finished, which it was, except for one unfortunate incident.

As the Tories interpreted it, Gourlay, in seeing his support fading away, resorted to "a stale trick", which was often used by radicals in England to draw attention to themselves when popular support for their cause was flagging. Thus, treasonable statements and malicious libels on the government were published anonymously in two articles in the *Niagara Spectator*. When the government moved to arrest the editor, Gourlay came forward and claimed authorship while -- as was the wont of radicals -- denouncing the government for attacking the liberty of the press. In that way, a potentially popular grievance was brought to the fore, and the instigator assured of being restored to prominence.

Much to the chagrin of Macaulay and Strachan, who felt that the best response at that stage was to simply ignore Gourlay -- who was no longer seen as a threat -- two members of the Legislative Council brought charges against him under the terms of the Sedition Act of 1804. Gourlay was subsequently arrested, found guilty before a magistrates' court, and sentenced to quit the province or be incarcerated under the terms of the Act. When Gourlay refused to leave the province, he was retained in custody from December 1818 to August 1819. When brought before the Chief Justice, and again ordered to leave the province, he did so.

The leading Tories did not question the legality of the action against Gourlay -- which was perfectly legal -- but rather the necessity of resorting to such an action, and the fact that it was impolitic. As John Macaulay noted:

> this persecution of Mr. Gourlay and his cause, has the most direct tendency further to inflame the mind of the people. We have had sufficient lessons to teach us moderation in such cases. Where had been Wilkes, but for the violence manifested against him by the Government -- and where had been Mr. Gourlay now, but for this new attack upon him? A little longer neglect [would have] consigned him to oblivion. (15)

Thus, Upper Canada itself was not immune to the political unrest of the postwar period, and the Gourlay episode reinforced the Tory concern about maintaining peace, order and social harmony in the province.

The start of the third decade of the 19th Century was for the Upper Canadian Tories a period of hope and planning for the future. It was a period of relief from the excruciating anxiety which had troubled their mind throughout the war years when the very survival of the Province of Upper Canada appeared to be in jeopardy.

With the fading of the Gourlay agitation, the Upper Canadian Tories were focused on furthering their plans for sustaining the existing traditional order and promoting the general good and wellbeing of the province. Under the direction of Lt. Governor Maitland, the Tories had a vigorous new administration in which the Rev. John Strachan and his protégé John Beverley Robinson were the most influential members of the provincial government.

At the commencement of the Maitland administration (August 1818 - November 1828), the Rev. John Strachan, held a seat in the Executive Council and in the Legislative Council, and his former pupils were entering public life. Among them, John Beverley Robinson, held the position of Attorney General of the province, and George Herkimer Markland was appointed to the Legislative Council. In the July 1820 provincial election, there were at least four of prominent former pupils of Strachan who entered the House of Assembly – Jonas Jones, Archibald McLean, Philip Vankoughnet, and John Beverley Robinson, who assumed the leadership of the conservative members who supported the provincial government. They were joined in government during the following decade by the appointment of additional 'young Tories' to the Executive Council and the Legislative Council, that enabled the Anglican Tories to dominate both bodies.

It was a Tory provincial government that -- from a policy perspective -- was devoted to strengthening the British national character of the province, to excluding prospective American settlers, to supporting and extending the ministrations of the established National Church, to promoting education, and to fostering the settlement and economic development of the province through British emigration and public works, while maintaining the British constitution of the province and the Imperial connection.

For the Tories, the future of the Province of Upper Canada looked promising as differences between the two houses of the Legislature were reconciled through eliminating a major public grievance involving the land granting system. In 1818, the system of giving large land grants to favoured individuals, in return for their promises to secure immigrants to settle the land, was ended and improvements were made as well in the efficiency of the administration of the land-granting system.

With the commencement of the decade of the 1820s, the House of Assembly appeared to have confidence in the management of public affairs by the government administration, and the members of the popular body were supportive the government policy of undertaking internal improvements. Differences still existed over questions of privilege in the House of Assembly, but disputes were becoming less frequent as the rules of parliamentary government were becoming better understood. The Tories were pleased to see that agriculture was beginning to prosper once again, and believed that commerce would soon revive. The colony was visibly increasing in wealth and was experiencing a general prosperity, which was aided by a rapidly growing number of British immigrants who were settling on the wastelands of the province.

Combating Discontent

Still the Gourlay episode had shown the obvious: that Upper Canada could be subject to the same political disorders as witnessed elsewhere. With respect to the pre-war political agitation, Richard Cartwright had observed "that there will be discontented People everywhere must be expected while human Nature remains as it is."

For the Tories, there was a constant need for a strong government to remain vigilant and ready to defend the existing order against political agitators, and they had no fear of empowering the provincial government to maintain public order. They were convinced that 'any democrat' would be pleased to realize how little influence the Lt. Governor could exert over an election, or over the conduct and opinions of the representatives of the people in the Assembly. It was evident that the rights of the people were secure from any possibility of oppression at the hands of the Lt. Governor but, on the other hand, political discontent could not be discounted where the people were concerned.

Despite enjoying a freedom from taxation and an absence of any real grievances, the Tories expected that self-proclaimed 'patriots' would always seek to do mischief and heap abuse upon those in authority. It was regarded as being inevitable that discontent would arise over "the Distribution of the Favours of the Crown" – government patronage -- as it was impossible to satisfy everyone. Those who were not gratified by a patronage appointment would seek to foster discontent. (16)

Hence, the Upper Canadian Tories were continually concerned about the problem of preserving order in a new colony. From the earliest years of settlement, they had taken actions which were calculated to strengthen the social order. One early effort, championed by Richard Cartwright, was the pre-war policy of installing half-pay officers of the British Army and Royal Navy in various public capacities at all levels of the civil administration: "Offices of Judges of the District Courts, Coriners [sic], Clerks of the Peace, Surrogates, Inspectors of Still & Tavern Licenses, Registers & Collectors". The object was to gain the influence that such men would have upon the tone and stability of society.

The Tories were always acutely aware that Upper Canada was a developing colony in a rather rude state of evolution, and therefore posed special problems where the maintenance of order was concerned. In the first place, the very population of the country was not homogeneous, but rather was composed of "peoples from different countries and of various classes". Hence, the province lacked the unity and cohesion of older established communities. In such circumstances, it was essential that the government should be brought near the people, to bring the influence and intelligence of the officers of government into play as a positive force in all spheres of public activity and development in the province.

With only the rudiments of a religiously-based education system, the National Church suffered from a dearth of clergymen, and the provincial government suffered through the lack of a peerage and landed gentry to take their part in government in the Legislative Council. In effect, the key influences on society in both a public and private capacity were weak or absent. In such circumstances, Upper Canada had much to fear from "the democratic leaven". Moreover, that was particularly so given the implications of the property franchise. In Upper Canada, almost every resident was an independent freeholder, and the property franchise amounted to a nearly universal manhood suffrage. Thus, Upper Canada was deficient in the means by which the existing order of things was sustained in Britain:

> with all the help of the vast patronage of Government... -- with all the influence of ancient and venerable institutions, and the traditionary [sic] respect for rank and family -- with all the substantial power of wealth, and the control of numerous landlords over a grateful tenantry.

Whether challenged in Upper Canada by demagogues such as Robert Gourlay, who espoused the doctrines of Thomas Paine, or by Cobbett and Hunt in Britain, who espoused a drastic program of parliamentary reform, for the Tories the problem always remained the same in its purely political aspect. It was the problem of balancing liberty and authority. Of protecting the 'true liberty' and 'the individual rights of the subject' safe from all "encroachments of power", while striving to "prevent that liberty from degenerating into licentiousness and anarchy".

The focus of the Tory effort to balance liberty and authority was the British Constitution, which was reproduced in the Constitutional Act of 1791 – the constitution of the Province of Upper Canada. Thus, the Upper Canadian Tories were determined to act:

> to preserve the nicely balanced powers of the Constitution, each within its proper sphere, by neither straining the prerogative of the Crown beyond its due limits, nor suffering the impetuosity of popular feeling to overstep the barriers fixed by law for the maintenance of order and the protection of society. (17)

The twin threats of infidelity and democratic anarchy had already made some inroads into a province where the supports for 'true religion' were woefully weak; and the battle for the mind of Upper Canada remained to be won to assure the province of a future enjoyment of peace, order and good government.

For the Upper Canadian Tories, the preservation of the traditional Christian order was essential because the progress of the French Revolution -- wherein infidel and levelling principles were inculcated in the minds of the young -- had proved that "no creature is so cruel as man, when freed from the restraints of religion". Once the public mind had been deprived of the salutary influence of Christianity that country had succumbed to a terrible anarchy. The pervasiveness of levelling principles in France had brought into power men who "regarded neither God or man", and who did not shirk from committing horrendous massacres and plunging the nations of Europe into war. The conclusion was inescapable that in any struggle to preserve the existing order of things, and the balance of the constitution, religion was of the essence.

Only Christian principles, when properly taught, could maintain tranquility and peace in any society. The Christian religion taught "patience, resignation and forbearance", a proper respect for those in authority, and commanded men to 'fear God and honour the king' and to *"meddle not with them that are given to change"*. Religion was the bulwark of the existing order which was itself an outgrowth of Christian principles, and a permanent bar to the levelling plans of those who were seeking to bring about a revolution in church and state. For the Tories, the church was the strongest support of the state. They were convinced that the infidels in attacking the church were seeking to destroy the hold which Christian principle had over the people, and were doing so as a conscious first step in towards the overthrow of the state itself.

Thus, the Rev. John Strachan could assert in 1819 that:

> the attention at present bestowed on the religious and moral
> instruction of youth, more effectually counteracts the schemes
> of infidelity, than millions of armed men. (18)

In combatting infidelity, and the dangers which it posed to political stability and true religion, a provincial system of moral and religious education was regarded as essential. So long as men were uninstructed in the truths of Christianity and ignorant of the Scriptures, they were open to corruption through the writings of infidels, such as Thomas Paine. Indeed, most men -- and not only the uneducated -- were incapable of distinguishing truth from falsehood where the truths of religion were concerned, because of the very nature of the subject.

Despite infidel appeals to the contrary, the common sense of man was insufficient to judge of such weighty matters. It was beyond the capacity of most men to "weigh arguments and sift objections", even if they were fairly and rationally presented. The most that one could expect from the common sense of humanity was that men would come to believe in Christianity because of its evident "adaptation to the wants and wishes of mankind", and, where disputes were raging, that men would judge of the character of the individuals who were involved, and defer to the learned in all questions demanding moral and theological knowledge.

Only "the intellectual mind" could comprehend the abundant evidences of Christianity by moral demonstration from the life of man. The bulk of mankind had no real choice but to accept such teachings on authority from men more competent to judge. In the nature of things, such was always the case in that:

> The argument of authority, in its various forms, is that which chiefly decides the opinions of the illiterate: the followers of Paine himself can, generally speaking, have no other argument for their 'no creed' than the assertions of their leader; for it surely will not be pretended that they are complete masters of his subject, and can judge how far his arguments rest on true propositions, and are cast in a truly logical mould. (19)

Where education was concerned -- specifically the inculcation of religious and moral values into the population through the instruction of youth -- the state could not bestow equal privileges upon atheists, or even tolerate the teaching of contrary values and principles among its subjects. Infidelity and democratic republican principles were, in all their attributes, antagonistic to those of 'true religion' and the monarchical form of government. If such discordant principles – infidelity and democratic republicanism – were permitted to take root in the province, with the state allowing its subjects to choose what was to be taught based on every "whim or inclination", it could only prove destructive of all harmony and peace in society.

To the contrary, the state must seek to promote the moral and intellectual improvement of youth through encouraging the teaching of traditional Christian values, and must stand fast against all innovators who demand radical change. The Rev. John Strachan summarized what he regarded as the proper attitude to take towards individuals who advocated a revolutionary change in church, state, or education:

> I am rather prejudiced in favor of antiquity, and shall without hesitation, premise it as a maxim from which it will never be found safe to depart: That practices and institutions of long standing should be carefully examined in all their bearings, before they are made to give way to speculative improvements which are not sanctioned by the test of experience. This rule does not prevent useful changes, it only insures caution in their introduction -- it does not prohibit necessary improvements, but it wishes them to be gradual. Its rigid application might not indeed please hasty innovators, because it would prove the propriety and wisdom of many ancient practices which they have denounced. (20)

Chapter Four

The American Threat

In seeking to defend the traditional political, social and religious order of the Loyalist asylum of Upper Canada against agitators and innovators, the Upper Canadian Tories were plagued by the presence of the archetype of the new revolutionary state -- the democratic republic of the United States of America -- on their very border. Immediately following the War of 1812, the Tories were acutely aware of their critical situation where the survival of Upper Canada was concerned. They faced an ideological threat, which was conveyed in the influx of American publications and polemics into the province, and they continued to fear the military threat that an expansionist American democratic republic posed to Upper Canada. Above all, they were haunted by the fear that Great Britain might abandon the inland colony of Upper Canada as being too difficult and costly to defend against any future American invasion.

Hence, the Tories made every effort to combat the impact of American publications on the public mind of Upper Canada and sought to publicly unmask the true character of the American democratic republic for the benefit of Upper Canadians who were viewed as being vulnerable to the lure of democratic republican propaganda. At the same time, the Tories strove to convince Great Britain that her North American colonies were a valuable commercial asset of strategic importance to the British Empire and well worth defending.

The American Ideological Threat

For the Upper Canadian Tories, there was much to fear in the presence in the province of numerous "scurrilous papers" and "spurious histories" of the American Revolution that were emanating from the United States. All such publications were adjudged to be particularly dangerous as they invariably denigrated the British government and praised American democracy and the revolutionary experience. The influx of American publications had become a subject of serious concern just prior to the outbreak of the War of 1812. At the time, it was noted that American principles were "beginning rapidly to find their way into this country and to corrupt the Loyalty of some of the best of our Subjects". Moreover, that concern continued unabated after the war. The objectionable publications reflected the bias of the democratic faction in the United States and were characterized as diatribes against the British Constitution and calumnies on the character of King George III.

The chief difficulty, as viewed by the Tories, was that there was a lack of sufficient means to educate the population of the province in the virtues of the British Constitution, "which requires only to be known to be beloved". It was a lamentable situation where "thousands have never heard the name of our good king coupled with anything but tyranny and oppression", and there was no opportunity for Upper Canadians to acquire the information which was necessary to form a more correct view. In effect, the historical interpretation, which was put forward by American books in glorifying the American Revolution and the principles for which it stood, was a complete denial of the whole raison d'être of the Loyalist province of Upper Canada and the motives of its Loyalist founders.

The influence of American principles and interpretations of the American Revolution had to be counteracted. To that end, John Strachan was moved to publish a *Discourse on the Character of George III* (1810), and to enter upon the writing of a history of the American Revolution. Such publications were felt to be necessary to disabuse the people of Upper Canada of their mistaken notions, and to expose the many falsehoods which were being fostered by American authors. Yet so Americanized was Upper Canada in the immediate pre-war years, that Strachan felt the need to emphasize -- in the publication -- that his "harsh comments" on the American government were aimed principally at the dominant democratic faction in that country, and not at the American people. Nonetheless, Strachan was openly criticized for his supposedly anti-American comments by American residents of the province, such as Barnabas Bidwell in his pamphlet *Friend to Peace*. Yet, this was at a time when several of the leading members of the American Congress were openly calling for an invasion of Upper Canada to annex the province to the United States. (1)

Much to the chagrin of the Tories, even in the aftermath of the War of 1812 Upper Canada continued to be plagued by pre-war American immigrants, such as Barnabas Bidwell and his son Marshall Spring Bidwell, who constantly looked to American institutions as "the *ne plus ultra* of perfection", and who held up the American government as an object of envy. Moreover, in 1820 the Tories were deeply concerned to discover that an Upper Canadian newspaper had published several articles on the American Revolution which were marked by the same abuse of Great Britain as was found in American newspapers: viz.

> the same spirit of relentless malignity against Great Britain, the same diligence in mistaking and colouring fact, in mixing truth with falsehood, in sometimes omitting important circumstances, and at other times in amplifying them.

Such arguments demanded a refutation. The Tories sought to publish their views in letters to the editors, and in editorials in newspapers that supported the government. In doing so, they put forth what they regarded as being "statements of *facts – incontrovertible facts*" about the revolution and the American colonial experience, which were intended to counteract the 'boasting' of Americans and their deluded Upper Canadian sympathizers.

John Macaulay, the editor of the *Kingston Chronicle*, expressed the complaint that the political radicals in Upper Canada were continually proselytizing Upper Canadians in praising American institutions to which they attributed the superior prosperity of the United States, its freedom of the press, its energetic government, and even the eloquence of their Presidents. All of which, it appeared to the Tories were being constantly raised "to be cast in our teeth". (2)

In consciously acting to counteract the influence of American ideas and values upon the population of Upper Canada, the Tories were not merely rejecting a set of values which they believed to be incompatible with their own, they were rejecting the very values themselves. They shared a general revulsion at the type of society which the United States was evolving, and the American experiment served for them as a plain and potent example of the workings and failures of a popular government in a democratic republic.

The Politics and Character of America

Whether "in philosophically viewing the structure of their polity" or merely passing events, the Tories continually professed to see "nothing to envy in the United States". In seeking to preserve Upper Canada from the miseries of anarchy and revolutionary bloodshed, they subjected the United States to scrutiny throughout the whole period of their lives and were continually drawing lessons from a comparison of the British society and government with that of the United States to the detriment of the latter.

The recent history of the two nations, and their divergent conduct during the convulsions in Europe, was regarded as ample proof of the difference between the British national character and the national character of the Americans. While Britons had made great sacrifices and fought alone in defence of the civilized world for the security, independence, and peace of all nations, the Americans by their actions had proven themselves to be "traitors to the peace and happiness of the world" and "the betrayer of the liberty and independence of mankind". When Britain was in dire straits, seemingly in imminent danger of succumbing to the overwhelming power of Napoleon Bonaparte, the United States -- "lost to every feeling of honor and glory", "blinded with ambition", and "tempted by views of immediate aggrandizement" -- had not hesitated to ally herself with that tyrant in seeking to partake of the spoils of victory by attacking Canada.

The American invasion of Upper Canada and the several years of fighting and suffering which it inflicted upon the province, and American attempts "to poison [Upper Canadians] with their crude and debasing principles", had resulted in the Tories thoroughly detesting the United States. The plundering of Upper Canada by the American invaders reinforced the Tory admiration for the British polity and the British national character, which was strengthen further by the workings of the American political system as the Tories perceived it.

In commenting upon the American system of government, the Tories were always careful to draw a distinction between American theories and professions and the political and social reality which they witnessed. The Rev. John Strachan for one, at a very early date, professed to one of his Scottish academic confrères:

> that the praises bestowed upon the United States ... are very much misplaced. A few months' residence in America would greatly chastise a man's political notions. I have profited by

my neighbourhood to Democracy. In point of real happiness, the British are far superior to the inhabitants of this celebrated republic.

The Upper Canadian Tories were quick to point out that several of the leading British radicals who had visited America– including William Cobbett -- for all their praise of America and the American system of government, had returned to Britain thoroughly disappointed and chastened after having viewed the actual workings of the American government and the American national character.

Everywhere the Upper Canadian Tories looked as of the early 1820s, they saw what they regarded as proof of the degeneracy of the United States. They were appalled by the American government excusing the unprovoked invasion and occupation of Spanish Florida by General Andrew Jackson, by the aggressiveness of the American Government in expropriating Spanish territory, and by the acquiescence of the American people in the Missouri Compromise of 1820 which failed to outlaw slavery in the new states being admitted into the American Union.

In March 1818, General Andrew Jackson -- at the head of a 4,000-man U.S. army (including militia and Indian allies) – had invaded Spanish Florida to put an end to Seminole Indian raids against settlers in Georgia. General Jackson destroyed Indian villages and several settlements of runaway slaves, seized the Spanish forts at St. Marks and Pensacola, and occupied Spanish Florida. Two British subjects, who were engaged in trade with the Indians – Robert Ambrister and Alexander Arbuthnot – were seized and executed on orders from General Jackson. Although Jackson was publicly denounced by several leading members of Congress for his unauthorized attack on Spanish Florida and the execution of the two British subjects, a motion of censure failed to pass the House of Representatives. The American government took no action against the popular military officer, General Jackson.

With Spain distracted by unrest and uprisings in New Spain (Mexico) and its South American colonies, and too weak to resist the American forces, a Transcontinental Treaty (February 1819) was signed between the United States and Spain. All Spanish lands east of the Mississippi

River – inclusive of Florida -- were ceded to the United States, and the southern boundary of the American Louisiana Purchase of 1803 was delineated from the Gulf of Mexico northwestward to the continental divide. West of the Rockies, Spain ceded its claim to the Oregon Country to the United States and agreed to recognize the 42 parallel of latitude as the southern boundary of the Oregon Country with New Spain from the Rockies to the Pacific Ocean.

In return, Spain received nothing. However, the delineation of the border between American lands and New Spain from the Mississippi River to the Pacific Ocean did imply that the United States recognized – or so it seemed -- the sovereignty of Spain over the Texas Territory and the territories of the South-West. The United States also agreed to pay U.S. citizens who were settled in Florida – primarily in West Florida (the Florida Panhandle) -- a sum of $5,000,000 to settle liability claims against Spain for damages supposedly suffered by the American settlers under Spanish rule before the American invasion.

As of 1819, the United States -- following the expansion of the American settlement frontier into the Ohio and Mississippi valleys -- had a balance of eleven slave-holding and eleven free states. A political crisis erupted when Missouri sought to enter the Union as a slave state. If admitted to the Union, Missouri would shift the balance of power in Congress in favour of the Southern slave states. The Missouri Compromise of 1820 avoided that situation. It enabled Missouri to enter the Union as a slave state, and the new state of Maine to enter as a free state, after the separation of the Maine territory from Massachusetts. The Compromise also prohibited slavery north of the 36 degrees/thirty minutes, parallel of latitude in the Louisiana Purchase territory west of the Mississippi River. However, there was an exception. Slavery was to be allowed within the borders of the projected state of Missouri, which was just north of that latitude. In sum, under the Missouri Compromise the balance between slave states and free states was maintained in the American Union, but an additional slave state was admitted to the American Union. However, there was a further problem.

The proposed Missouri State constitution banned free blacks and mulattoes from entering Missouri, and prohibited the state legislature from freeing slaves without the consent of their owners. The American Congress baulked at admitting Missouri into the Union with such a constitution. A second compromise was worked out which bound the new state legislature – in a rather ambiguous fashion -- to recognize the rights of the citizens of other states who entered Missouri. Ultimately, Maine was accepted into the Union in March 1821 and Missouri in August 1821 upon Congress accepting the second compromise.

For the Upper Canadian Tories, the lack of any condemnation of General Jackson by the American government for his unprovoked invasion of Spanish Florida, and the failure of the United States to prevent the extension of slavery into new states joining the American Union, constituted a "melancholy instance of the triumph of sordid interest over just principle" and "a satire upon true liberty and equal rights". The invasion of Spanish Florida and the extension of slavery in the American Union were regarded as mark of eternal disgrace and black blots on the entire American Republic. The United States, when viewed from Canada, offered nothing that the Upper Canadian Tories preferred to their own polity, or to the British institutions and the British national character which sustained it. (3)

In the immediate postwar period, and thereafter, both observation and experience had convinced the Upper Canadian Tories that in all essential points of good government the United States was a complete failure. It was a land of 'disjointed democracy' where supreme power was in the hands of "the many-voiced and unmanageable multitude". The people were virtually sovereign, and the government was seemingly deprived even of the power of enforcing its own decrees.

Despite American boasts about enjoying freedom and liberty, the Tories observed that the United States was a country "subject to the slavery of *popular opinion*". It was a slavery that the Tories characterized – in engaging in hyperbole -- as "more intolerable than the chains of corporeal slavery" which that 'heartless republic' also tolerated within its polity. For the Tories, government by the "incontrollable will of the rabble" was the worst form of tyranny, as John Macaulay asserted:

> I look on the tyranny of one man ... to be an intolerable evil, and
> on the tyranny of a hundred men to be a hundred times worse.

Under such a system, the executive government of the United States was powerless to maintain its authority and preserve order in the body politic. In times of public ferment, the most horrible public outrages were committed in defiance of the law. It was a country where:

> summary justice is not unfrequently [sic] inflicted by a lawless mob on a person suspected of crime, even after he had been acquitted by a jury of his peers. (4)

In the United States, liberty had degenerated into license, and the whole of their society was characterized by a complete moral disorganization. In the American Republic, as in Israel of old in the absence of her king, "every man did that which was right in his own eyes". The American people in having rejected the authority of their legitimate monarch -- God's representative -- through violent revolution, were even refusing to publicly recognize the authority of Almighty God.

As viewed by the Tories, the United States existed in the worst of all possible situations:

> While we have there the anarchy of a pure democracy, we have no acknowledgment, in a national religion, of Him who ruleth in the kingdoms of men -- no admission, but too positive a rejection, of the principle, that the State should be built upon the foundation of the Gospel.

Not only was the United States suffering from an enfeebled government, but it was plagued by a large and restless population which was uncontrollable because of the lack of any grounding in high moral principles. Moreover, the proper order of society was completely inverted in a country:

> where ignorance and incapacity are invested with the functions of wisdom, and where, worse than all, the passion and depravity of the untutored and irresponsible million are bowed to by the enlightened and the virtuous.

It was a country where all distinctions of society had been leveled, with the result that there was no social subordination. The popular nature of American institutions, supported by their 'atheistic constitution', had produced a population which believed that all men were equal, with the result that those in authority failed to receive their due deference and respect. Children were seldom taught to have "that profound reverence for, and strict obedience to their parents", which not only sustained the family, but the whole social organism. In the absence of parental authority, discipline had broken down in all areas of life. Farmers could not control their labourers, and teachers were unable to command their pupils, in a situation where everyone did as he pleased.

Devoid of any higher standard of conduct than that of the will of the majority and holding learning in low esteem, the population of the United States was regarded as being totally "lost to right feeling and blind to all considerations of honour". The great prosperity of the war years, in acting upon such a population, had produced an ambitious and arrogant people. More than any other nation, the Americans were characterized by a rapacious materialistic outlook on life in that "they are hurried on to any action provided they gain money by it".

Moreover, the Americans were marked by a conspicuous national vanity that was unequalled anywhere else. It was reflected in their publications which overflowed with claims of their superiority "in virtue, wisdom, valour, liberty, government and every other excellence" to European nations and to their colonies which were regarded as peopled with "ignorant paupers and dastardly slaves". Despite the loud protestations of the Americans to the contrary, the Tories were convinced that "the Character of the Americans is generally speaking bad"; and it was a character that was reflected in the kind of government which prevailed in the United States. (5)

From what they observed, the Tories concluded that the American system of government was totally unprincipled and marred by much corruption not only in its administration, but also in its very laws and policy. In Britain, government was conducted by men of high principles and education, who were moved by feelings of honour and a concern to maintain their public reputation through the principled nature and propriety of their actions in responding to an educated public opinion. In contrast, in the United States, ignorance and incapacity held sway, and the people suffered under a government of uneducated and unprincipled men who were unrestrained by any such considerations because they lacked any sense of a public character.

This was not to say that America lacked men of respectability and moral worth, but they were not to be found at the head of government in that country. Even the highest offices, such as the Presidency and Vice-Presidency, were filled with men who were elected through the machinations of the dominant faction, and who were bound to serve the partisan interests of that faction.

American government left much to be desired. Congress was often the scene of shameless jobbing, and American administrations and public measures were too often marked by a meanness of spirit and/or by craft and duplicity. In the United States, the intrigues and interests of faction permeated all aspects of American public life, and even the judiciary was not sacrosanct where the clamour of office seekers for the spoils of electoral victory was concerned.

Although the Upper Canadian Tories readily admitted that in Britain offices were filled too much by favouritism, rather than by merit, and that less corruption was desirable, yet in any comparison of the British and American governments, the British system was held to be far superior. Under their new republican system of government, the Americans had declined a good deal from the colonial period in all the tests of good government. That decline had reached its nadir under the rule of the democratic faction where true liberty was not to be found. It was a situation where:

> the dominion of the party, which now regulates everything, renders all pretensions to liberty ridiculous. It is a faction that has always been turbulent, cruel, and vindictive, discovering oppressions where none existed, supporting insolence, and trampling upon virtue. (6)

As the decade of the 1820s unfolded, democratic anarchy was seen to be increasing its sway in the United States. And the elements of a sound Christianity, which had been conveyed to America within the 'scattered principles' of the various Protestant sects, were fast becoming lost in the absence of an established church. In the United States, innovators and 'seekers after change' were having their effect as the religious community of the nation was marked by a wild disorganization. In the battle to gain adherents to this or that sect, "religious fanaticism and religious knavery" were coming to the fore with the continual promotion of new religions amidst "the excitements of changing creeds and every varying forms and modes of faith". Not only was religion in the United States in a continual ferment, but the religious sects in their struggle for supremacy did not have any scruples about organizing themselves to gain political power and political influence for their own ends.

In viewing the United States, the Upper Canadian Tories never varied in their preference for the orderly and stable government of British institutions over the democratic republican principles and government of the United States. In the view of the Upper Canadian Tories, the United States was a politically and religiously distracted country – a country "born in bitterness and nurtured in convulsion" – wherein the people lived in a constant state of agitation and momentary excitement. The Americans were totally devoid of that love of order and stability which characterized the British people; whereas in Britain,

> authority, and those gradations of rank which are necessary to its stability, are steadily looked at, and are approved of as good and beneficial. [In contrast, in the United States] from the domestic circle outward to the political, natural sentiments of deference are faint, and authority means very little beyond the limits of actual force. (7)

The American experiment with the democratic form of government had proven a failure in providing good government. Unable to protect and promote virtue or to restrain vice, or to honour and maintain its engagements, the American system of government was thoroughly repudiated by the thinking and disinterested elements of its own population. More generally, the American system of government was repudiated by all men who were astute enough to perceive behind the facade of loud and frequent appeals to the declaration of 'the inalienable rights of man', its many corruptions, its toleration of slavery, and its efforts to exterminate the Indian nations with whom it came in contact.

In viewing the innovations which Americans had made in church and state, and their denial or destruction of the traditional supports of good government and social order, the Tories were thoroughly convinced that the American experiment could not last. To the Tory mind, the repercussions of popular sovereignty in both politics and religion, and the democratic anarchy that it spawned, were such that they believed the collapse of the United States to be imminent. From what the Tories observed of the development of American democracy, it had inverted the natural social hierarchy and invested the people with a dangerous unrestrained power over the whole of society.

From the assertion of Richard Cartwright in 1812 that the collision of factions would soon result in the subjugation of America to some ambitious leader, to the assertion of John Macaulay in 1819 -- upon taking account of General Jackson's military exploits in Spanish Florida -- that the American experiment would terminate in the despotism of a military ruler, to the prediction by the Rev. John Bethune – much later in 1838 -- that the American democracy was top heavy and would ultimately collapse of its own unwieldiness, the Tories consistently maintained that the American experiment with democracy would not end well.

In rebuttal of those Upper Canadians who professed to admire the United States, and the American system of government, the Tories countered:

> it only lives by the absence of powerful neighbours -- and because
> its vast territory gives ample room for rebellious spirits to scatter
> and do as they please without much regard to law or order.

Of the two models of governments at hand for their perusal, there was no doubt in the mind of the Tories as to which form of government was best suited for promoting the wellbeing of the Province of Upper Canada. Yet, paradoxically, it was the very presence of the United States on the border of Upper Canada which, while it exposed to view the workings of democracy and reinforced the Tory antipathy to democratic leveling and the separation of church and state, also gave sustenance and encouragement to the opponents of the Tories in Upper Canada who were bent on importing American political principles and ideals into the province and overturning the existing order.

For the Upper Canadian Tories, the United States posed an ideological threat to the Loyalist asylum of Upper Canada as well as a continuing military threat. It was the external relations of Upper Canada with Britain and the United States which would ultimately determine whether the Province would survive as a political entity independent of the United States in North America. In sum, the Tories were acutely aware that the maintenance of the unity of the British Empire and a continued strengthening of the British connection was critical to all their hopes and aspirations. (8)

The American Military Threat

Although the War of 1812 had ended with the defeat of American invasion attempts, it had not resolved the ultimate question of the fate of the Province of Upper Canada. Time had been gained which could be turned to good purpose, and more time was available as the province was no longer viewed as being in any immediate danger of another attack from the United States. Nonetheless, the spectre of a future attack by the Americans, at a time of their own choosing, troubled the Tory mind. The United States continued to pose a real military threat to the very survival of Upper Canada; and it was the fear of that perceived military threat which conditioned to a very great extent the Tory response to the American Republic.

On the one hand, the Tory elite were filled with a feeling of pride in their war service, of admiration for British principles and institutions, and of gratitude for the role which Britain had played in defending Upper Canada during the war. They detested the American democrats, and thoroughly rejected the American experience. On the other hand, the Tories were acutely conscious of their perilous situation in postwar Upper Canada, and of a critical need to maintain a peacefully co-existence with the American behemoth.

The Province of Upper Canada had a population of just under 100,000 at the close of the War of 1812, and the two Canadian provinces – Upper Canada and Lower Canada – had a combined population of 300,000 British subjects. In contrast, New York State alone had a rapidly growing population of almost 1,000,000, and the entire population of the United States, as of 1820, was slightly more than 9,500,000 of whom 1,500,000 were slaves.

Thus, in the immediate postwar period the leading Tories were anxious that the spirit of hostility, which existed between Britain and the United States, be dampened. They also admonished Upper Canadians, as good Christians, to respond to Americans "with kindness and hospitality" and to put aside "all turbulent and hostile passions". The survival of Upper Canada was at stake.

In viewing the desperate situation of Upper Canada, John Beverley Robinson conveyed to the Colonial Office a rather wistful wish that an alliance might be concluded between Britain and the United States. He maintained that an alliance -- based on friendship, common origins, a common language, and common interests between two enterprising nations -- would prevent the calamity of any future war between them, and would promote the security, peace and happiness of the world, as well as of Upper Canada in particular. He expressed the rather forlorn hope that:

> If, indeed, an alliance so natural could be firmly and lastingly cemented, it would be happy for the interests of mankind; --- it would create a power which, while it would be competent to repress the designs of destructive ambition, would itself threaten no ill to the repose or the freedom of the world; and which might secure a happy progress to the cause of civilization, science, and rational religion. (9)

Nevertheless, Robinson realized that there were many unresolved differences which would preclude such an alliance; and that they "must not turn a pleasing hope into a dangerous delusion". Even the existence of a mutually-beneficial commercial intercourse between the Britain and the United States could not be counted on to provide an interest sufficient to maintain a peaceful relationship between them. Trade could be equally a potential source of conflict, as Britain had experienced already during the Napoleonic Wars.

Differences and disputes would invariably occur between the two countries. Although Britain -- as the Tories interpreted her actions -- had laboured diligently to settle all outstanding disputes with the United States prior to the War of 1812, the intransigence and corruption of the character of the American government could not be overcome. It was evident that the Americans respected only superior force in the resolution of disputes and differences, and they could not be expected to change their ways. In dealing with the Americans, one had to keep in mind that:

> if they are conscious of their ability to remove any check they experience, there is not, either in their past history or in their general temper, any assurance that they will forbear the attempt. (10)

The American temper was marked by a "lust for war, and ambition for extended rule" which was evident both during the War of 1812 and in their conduct thereafter. In 1812, at a time when Britain had been sorely pressed and seemingly in danger of imminent defeat, the United States had disregarded the best interests of the civilized world, allied herself with a European despot, and attacked Canada in the hopes of conquering the Canadian provinces. However, the defeat, which the United States suffered in that endeavour, had not curbed the American appetite for conquest.

Far from being satisfied with lands more extensive than needed for its present population, the United States was clearly bent on extending its boundaries at the expense of its neighbours. The Indian lands to the West and the Northwest, and the Spanish territories to the South were continually being encroached upon by American settlers, and the Tories were convinced that the Americans were "looking wistfully towards Canada on the north".

Both Spain in Florida and the Indian nations of the South and the Northwest had suffered from an aggressive American expansionism. U.S. troops were seen to be establishing forts in Indian territory as a prelude to a calculated extermination of the Indian tribes and the annexation of their lands to the United States. While elsewhere, the incursion of American settlers and adventurers into the Texas territory of the newly-independent Republic of Mexico boded ill for its future. Everywhere, the Americans had shown a blatant disregard for the rights of other nations. It was noted that:

> These nations are not in the territories of the United States, but the Americans go to seek them, build houses, & clear lands

within their precincts & when such are destroyed, they raise a
noise & make it a cause of war.

It appeared that such actions were condoned, if not initiated, by the
American government. Even General Jackson's arbitrary invasion of
Spanish Florida in 1818 -- which the Tories regarded, along with his
execution of the Englishmen Arbuthnot and Ambrister, as "a gross
outrage on humanity, a daring violation of the law of nations" -- had
been excused by the American government. Indeed, the American
government had taken advantage of the weakness of Spain to coerce that
country into ceding Florida and other Spanish territories to the United
States.

Such conduct and actions on the part of the Americans provided little
assurance that they would respect the integrity of the Province of Upper
Canada. Moreover, there was much evidence to the contrary. In the
immediate postwar period, the Americans were busy in establishing and
garrisoning military posts along the shores of the Great Lakes and on
Lake Champlain, and in constructing military roads to their northern
frontier, as well as in constructing defensive works along the Atlantic
Coast which would counteract British sea power in any future war.

Faced by these military developments and the known character of the
United States – as the Tories interpreted it -- John Macaulay was moved
to express the forlorn hope that the future development of British-
American trade might serve to abate American aggressiveness:

> that in short these benefits, while they serve to dispel the charm
> and false glare of conquest, may induce the people of those
> States to sit down contented with the vast territory they already
> possess, and allow their neighbours to enjoy similar privileges.
> (11)

In witnessing the ongoing efforts of the United States to erect new
fortifications along the Canadian frontier, the Upper Canadian Tories
were deeply concerned about the danger of a future American invasion.
Not only was there nothing in the American character or experience to
indicate a peaceful intent on their part, but it appeared that the Americans
were "continually plotting, directly or indirectly, the expulsion of the

British from North America". It was believed that behind American boastings about their military prowess and potential greatness, was a basic feeling of insecurity and uneasiness over the influence that Britain possessed over their country, particularly over the western territories through her friendship with the Indians.

Unfortunately, the insecurity of the Americans had given rise to an opinion amongst them – which the Tories found quite painful to contemplate – that so long as Britain continued to possess territory in North America, the American Union would never be secure. What was equally worrisome for the Tories was that the interests of the various States and territories of the Union, except for the South, were such as would lead them to favour the annexation of Upper Canada to the United States.

The Western territories, it was believed, wished to expel Britain to increase their control over the Indians whom they were engaged in exterminating; New York, Pennsylvania and Vermont desired to gain control over the St. Lawrence River communication; and the New England States wanted to gain a preponderance in Congress over the political alignment of the Western and Southern States by adding Upper Canada to the Union. Moreover, the conquest and annexation of the Canadian provinces – Upper Canada and Lower Canada -- would facilitate the effort to the United States to achieve its ultimate aim: the driving of Great Britain completely from the North American Continent. American hopes, fears, and interests all seemed to combine to one end: the fostering of a desire to conquer Upper Canada, as a prelude to expelling Great Britain from North America. (12)

The Crucial British Connection

In their concern for the survival of Upper Canada, the Tories were well aware that the province had almost succumbed to the American invasion of the summer of 1812 before British troops could be brought into the field, and that it was the British troops to whom they owed their preservation. Moreover, the war-like actions of the United States against Spanish Florida and the Indian nations showed clearly what Upper Canada could expect should she ever be deprived of the protection which was being furnished by Great Britain. It was only the knowledge of the cost and sacrifices which a war with England would bring that induced the Americans to introduce a little moderation into their relations with Upper Canada, and to refrain from launching yet another war of conquest. The only way that Upper Canada could find peace and security -- in the face of the threat of American expansionism – was for Great Britain to undertake to fortify the province, and to make it clear to the Americans that she intended to use all her power to defend the borders and the commerce of the province.

The Tories realized that the construction of a proper defensive system for Upper Canada would entail a great expense; and, as early as 1820, they were fully conscious of the fact that "unfortunately Great Britain has too many embarrassments to attend to this matter as amply as our perfect security would seem to require". However, they continued to call for Britain to fortify and garrison the province because of their conviction that sooner or later, whenever British forces were preoccupied elsewhere in the world, the Americans would launch an attack upon Upper Canada.

Regardless of whether the American government coveted Upper Canada or not, there was a real danger that if the province were too weak to defend itself, it would encourage some American adventurer to plan another Texas expedition. The American people were subject to ungovernable impulses. They were fierce and warlike when Britain was entangled in a multiplicity of foreign conflicts; yet moderate when British naval and military forces were uncommitted elsewhere. There was also a danger that "the temporary ascendancy of a particular party" over the government of the United States, might result in the United States starting a war that would be fatal to the continued existence of Upper Canada.

In sum, the Tory mind was besieged with fear and anxiety concerning the survival of the Loyalist asylum of Upper Canada. In assessing their plight, John Beverley Robinson was moved to voice the lament that Upper Canada:

> has unhappily for itself & its few inhabitants, to look forward to a constant struggle for independence agt [sic] a powerful & unprincipled neighbour who will obviously seize upon the moment when G. Britain is most embarrassed & most occupied

in other quarters, no matter in how good or glorious a cause she may be engaged, to attempt to rob her of her colonies. (13)

In viewing the United States, the Tories readily perceived its developing power and opulence. They were convinced that it was only a matter of time -- given the phenomenally rapid growth of the American population and its seemingly unlimited resources -- until the United States would be more powerful than any single state in Europe. That awesome potential power boded ill for the future security of Upper Canada.

For the immediate future, the danger was that "the Americans were always at home and ready to attack"; whereas Upper Canada was militarily weak, and its primary defender was 3,000 miles away. Thus, an absolute security was unattainable anywhere in the province, and there was no prospect of any immediate improvement in the military situation. The Tories realized that:

> it must continue to be so until years of rapidly increasing prosperity may give to Canada a population whose united efforts can suffice to withstand the first shock of invasion & maintain the contest till assistance can come.

The Province of Upper Canada could never hope to match American military resources, but with British support the Upper Canadian Tories were prepared to dedicate themselves to the struggle for the preservation of their Loyalist asylum. Nonetheless, they remained acutely conscious that:

> the unfortunate Inhabitants of Canada ... are doomed to a constant anxious speculation about the probable loss or preservation of everything they possess, of their very country. (14)

The anxiety felt by the Tories over the probability of a future American attack and their uneasiness over the relative weakness of Upper Canada, was in turn further aggravated by a parallel fear that Britain might abandon the province altogether.

Not only were the Whigs in Britain -- in following the lead of the *Edinburgh Review* -- showing a decided aversion to the maintenance of colonies, but several of the leading members of the Whig Party in parliament were openly advocating that Canada be *"given up"* to the Americans. Moreover, British public opinion was clearly opposed to spending monies for the benefit of the colonies; and that public attitude could not but have an influence on the British Parliament, even on a Tory government committed to the defence of the British Empire.

For the Upper Canadian Tories, it was readily understandable that the British public was opposed to heavy expenditures in the colonies. In the previous century, except for the French Revolutionary Wars, it was colonial disputes that had led to wars and the imposition of heavy tax levies on the people of Britain. Moreover, the Tories realized that the defence of Canada, given its inland location, proximity to the United States, and its exposed borders, would demand an expenditure of treasure and blood on a scale comparable to what had been expended by Britain in times past in defending its interests in wars upon the European continent.

In being aware of the heavy cost of defending Canada, the Tories were at great pains to convince successive British governments that the fate of Upper Canada was not a matter which should be decided purely upon pecuniary considerations. In their estimate, Britain was bound by national honour, and her past pledges of protection, to come to the defence of the province. The people of Upper Canada were British subjects, and were part of the national family as much as residents of the British Isles. Hence, the Canadian provinces were entitled to the same protection as British subjects at Home, regardless of any additional cost involved.

If she were to continue to receive the respect of other nations, Britain must defend her possessions against aggression, "just as an individual protects his property, even at the peril of his life". Moreover, Upper Canada was considered to have a binding claim upon British support in that a goodly portion of the population of the province consisted of Loyalists. Britain had encouraged the Loyalists to settle in Canada, and had granted them lands in recognition of their loyalty and the numerous sacrifices which they had made on her behalf at the time of the American rebellion.

To the Tories, there was no question, but that Great Britain was committed by honour and duty to the defence of the Loyalist Asylum of Upper Canada, and by a debt of gratitude to the Loyalists.

In declaring for the unity of the Empire, they hazarded their lives & lost their property. They are therefore connected with England by the nearest dearest ties, & it is not easy to name any sum of money when their claims for protection are considered that can justify their desertion by Great Britain. Indeed, she is pledged to protect the Inhabitants of Upper Canada in their lives & properties & in all the rights & privileges of Englishmen.

The Loyalists and their descendants had given proof of their continued loyalty and devotion during the War of 1812, and the postwar growth in population through an extensive British emigration was strengthening the province and its attachment to Britain. However, should the mother country choose to ignore the suffering and sacrifices of Loyalists and abandon them, it would be to her own great disgrace and would leave Upper Canadians feeling "exceedingly bitter". (15)

In maintaining that Britain had irrevocably committed herself to the preservation of Upper Canada, and ought to continue to live up to that commitment, the Tories did not see themselves as indulging in any special pleading. They sincerely believed that colonies were a definite asset to the Empire. Moreover, they thought that the North American colonies were destined to play an important role in the future prosperity of the Empire. Admittedly, that value was prospective rather than actual but, to the Tories, it was real nonetheless. In British North America, Upper Canada alone was envisaged as being capable of eventually supporting a population of seven or eight million people, who would eventually contribute appreciably to the strength of the British Empire.

Despite the financial burden which the retention of Canada imposed on Britain, that country was judged -- as early as 1822 -- to be well compensated for its financial outlays. The Canadian provinces were providing employment for British shipping, a market for British manufactures, and a home for Britain's surplus population. Moreover, greater benefits would accrue to Britain over time through the growth of population and the economic development of Canada.

Indeed, a decade later, John Beverley Robinson was to have the satisfaction of quoting statistics from the Board of Trade returns for 1836 which vindicated the Tory contention that the true national interest of Great Britain lay in the development of her colonial trade and the preservation of her colonies. The Board of Trade returns indicated that although the British government had sought -- as a deliberate matter of policy since 1823 -- to increase the market for British manufactures in Europe, the value of the trade with the British North American colonies was far greater. The North American colonial trade in the export of British manufactured goods was nearly £500,000 sterling greater than the total value of the exports to France, Spain, Prussia, Sweden and Denmark taken altogether, and was almost double Britain's exports to Russia.

A similar situation existed with respect to British shipping. The trade of Britain with her colonies had more than doubled over the previous twenty-five years. The tonnage of British shipping which was engaged in the Canadian trade alone exceeded that of the British trade with six foreign nations: France, Prussia, Sweden, Denmark, Norway and the United States of America.

For the Tories, the trade figures proved conclusively their long-held contention that the colonial trade was essential to the commercial wealth and national greatness of Great Britain. As for Upper Canadians, the Tories maintained that only the blind could fail to recognize the critical value of the British tie and not see:

> our true national interests, and the quarter from which we must look for our wealth, our security and independence in future times.

The Strategic Value of Colonies

What perplexed and dismayed the Upper Canadian Tories, as expressed by the Rev. John Strachan, was:

> that British Statesmen of all parties are totally unaware, I might say altogether ignorant, of the vast importance of our North American Provinces to the future strength and grandeur of the British Empire.

Britain should realize that she needed her colonies as much as they needed her. The naval supremacy of Great Britain, the very basis of her power and security, depended on the retention of her colonies. It was obvious that "without colonies, Great Britain would not command the seas. Her greatness & her colonies will go together."

Whether Britain was aware of it or not, the Upper Canadian Tories were convinced that the North American colonies were vital to her future security vis-à-vis the United States. It was a rising power, which, in the Tory view, was hostile to all the best interests of Great Britain. The United States was "a jealous and ambitious rival" of a formidable strength, which "must in time become *the most formidable* of all her opponents". (16)

The retention of the British North American colonies was essential to the security of Great Britain for several reasons. Strategically, the very position of the North American colonies, when combined with British control of the West Indies, gave Britain a complete command of the Atlantic Ocean, which would enable the Royal Navy to control the American seacoast in any future war.

Britain could only be threatened by a naval power, and the United States, despite its potential military power, was lacking in a solid basis for the development of a large navy. Unlike the British North American colonies on the Atlantic seaboard, with their commodious harbours, and their large fisheries which served as a very important nursery of seamen, the United States was lacking in such a potential accession to their naval strength. Only the coastal region from New York to Maine produced seamen in any numbers, and the length of the American coast was not half as extensive as that of the British North American colonies.

As viewed by the Tories, the mere retention of the North American colonies by Britain was of a great strategic value. It served to limit the potential growth of American naval power by denying them access to a large body of trained seamen who were capable of manning warships. Moreover, it was equally critical that the British North American colonies not be added to that "already overgrown confederation of republics" because the loss of the British North American colonies would certainly be followed by the loss of the colonies in the British West Indies. In turn, the loss of the British West Indies together with the loss of the British North American colonies, would greatly detract from the military capabilities of Great Britain in any future war with the United States, and would seriously erode the supremacy of the Royal Navy on the Atlantic seaboard of North America. (17)

The strategic value of the British North American colonies was also increasing in importance with their economic development. With their growing export trade, the North American colonies were becoming capable of supplying the needs of the West Indies and other parts of the British Empire, which would render them independent of the trade of the United States and the countries of northern Europe. The British North American colonies – and the Province of Upper Canada, in particular -- were fast approaching the time when their exports to the West Indies would be sufficient to free the British islands from their dependence upon the United States for lumber, fish and flour. Such a development would render the British West Indies independent of any American power to coerce them should that country, as a matter of policy, decide to withhold supplies to force them "to solicit the protection of the United States".

The late war had shown how vulnerable Britain was to a trade embargo. When the Baltic countries denied Britain access to their naval stores and lumber during the war, she had turned to her British North America colonies for her critical supplies. Yet had the British North American colonies become part of the United States, and were the United States allied with the Northern Powers, Britain would have found it difficult, if not impossible, to secure the supplies required for the Royal Navy on which her independence depended.

On all counts, it was obvious to the Tories that Britain ought to preserve and strengthen her North American colonies. Their abandonment would not only constitute a betrayal of the Loyalists, but was extremely short-sighted in that such an action:

> though of apparently small moment, strikes at the root of all our Colonial Policy & blasts forever that union of interests & independence of the whole Empire within itself, which the true Statesman desires to establish. (18)

Leaving aside all sentiment and obligation, for strategic reasons if nothing else, it was essential that Britain take advantage of the buttress which a protecting Providence – "the Almighty hand [which] rules the destinies of nations" – had provided to protect the British monarchy against future shocks.

Although the colonies of British North America were incapable of standing on their own against the power of the United States, it was evident that given the fertility of the soil, their rapidly growing population, and their increasing wealth and expanding trade, the North American colonies were advancing in all that constituted power. The ultimate question to be resolved, and the one which the Tories continually posed to the Colonial Office, was: would Britain sustain the colonies as a home for Englishmen, Irishmen and Scotchmen on a continent that might someday control the fate of nations, or would the colonies be abandoned to provide an even further accretion of strength to the American Union?

The Tories never sought to deny that that the fate of Upper Canada was in British hands. It was for Britain to decide whether the Province of Upper Canada was worth the expense which its defence would entail, and to weigh whether the advantages of its retention were exceeded by its liabilities. The Upper Canadian Tories called upon Britain to decide once and for all, and to let her intentions be known. No other course was consistent with honour and good faith. In short:

> If it be said however & truly said that Great Britain laments, but has not the power of defending Upper Canada, that the expence [sic] of giving us effectual assistance is too much for her finances, & that imperious necessity & not inclination decrees our abandonment, we bow in silence. We wish not to remain a burden, but let all this be fairly & candidly stated that we may provide as well as we can for our future security.

Despite such proud utterances, the Upper Canadian Tories were acutely aware that their security, and very survival, depended upon British military aid in time of war, and equally important on the maintaining of a conviction in the minds of both the American alien settlers and disaffected Upper Canadians that British support would invariably be forthcoming should the province be attacked.

The Tories were convinced that the Americans would not hesitate to attack Upper Canada, if it were left defenceless through Britain being unable or unwilling to come to its aid. In such a situation, it was evident that if the people of Upper Canada were not confident of receiving the support of Great Britain in any future war with the United States, they would succumb to discouragement and a want of confidence in their ability to preserve their country.

Hence, where the defence of the province was concerned, it was very important that the people receive an assurance from the British Government that Upper Canada would not be abandoned in wartime, or left open to invasion through a temporary strategic retreat of the British forces to Quebec. Otherwise, such fears would prove destructive of their affection and allegiance to the government. It was axiomatic that: "Protection and obedience are reciprocal".

For the Tories, it was imperative that Britain take every step possible to strengthen the defences of Upper Canada in keeping with some "deliberately settled plan" to provide evidence that Upper Canada would be defended in any future war. Hence, they called upon the British government to erect permanent defences in Upper Canada that would "speak plainly that they mean to keep the Country". The aim was not only to discourage an American attack, but to "quiet restless spirits, to animate the loyal and contented, and to restore the confidence of the province", which was periodically torn by doubts as to whether Upper Canada would, or could, survive as a province of the British Empire in the face of an aggressive American expansionism. (19)

The postwar Tory fears concerning the difficult of defending Upper Canada, and their doubts about the willingness of the British government to undertake the heavy cost of defending the province, were soon relieved to some extent by the Duke of Wellington, the Master General of the Board of Ordnance (1819-1827). In drawing on earlier reports on the state of the defences of Canada by the Duke of Richmond (Governor-in-Chief of British North America, 1818-1819) and Lt. Col. John Harvey (Aide-de-Camp to Richmond), Wellington developed a strategic plan for engineering a system of defence for Upper Canada.

The Wellington defence plan covered both Canadian provinces. It called for the erection of permanent fortification on the frontiers of

Upper and Lower Canada and the construction of an interior network of waterways and canals to interconnect with the defensive works and to link the frontier forts with the ocean port of Montreal. The forts were to be able to withstand a siege by American troops until the garrison troops and militia could be relieved by British troop reinforcement proceeding inland on the interior water communications network. The construction of the interior water communication was intended to enable British troops, munitions, and supplies to continue to be forwarded into the interior in wartime in the event of an American invasion force succeeding in cutting the upper St. Lawrence River communication and/ or the Americans succeeding in gaining a naval supremacy on the lower Great Lakes. (20)

Earlier, in November 1818, the Duke of Richmond, when faced with the seemingly overwhelmingly difficult task of defending Upper Canada, had recommended that the province be abandoned on the outbreak of war; and that British troops should be withdrawn to Kingston. It was his intention that the Province of Upper Canada would be recovered during the eventual peace negotiations in exchange for whatever gains the British forces might make elsewhere. (21) However, for the Upper Canadian Tories such a plan portended the destruction of the British national character of Upper Canada and the loyalty of the province, and would entail the dispossession and expulsion of the old Loyalists and the leading young Tories during any prolonged American occupation.

It was Lt. Col. Harvey, an English Anglican Tory -- and close friend and correspondent of the Rev. John Strachan -- who maintained that Upper Canada had to be defended in any future war with the United States, and who, in the immediate postwar period, prepared a plan of defence for doing so. (22). Subsequently, the Duke of Wellington, in working out his strategic plan for the defence of the Canadian provinces, took account of the arguments articulated by Lt. Col. Harvey against abandoning Upper Canada in wartime to be overrun by American invasion forces. (23) Thereafter, it was the Upper Canadian Tories who were the strongest supporters of the efforts of the Board of Ordnance in London to construct the fortifications and interior canals that were required to implement Wellington's grand defence strategy.

For the Tories, the implementation of the defence strategy of the Duke of Wellington was an integral component of their broader national policy by which they sought to strengthen and preserve the Province of Upper Canada against the threat posed by the democratic republicanism and expansionism of the new American Republic. It was a struggle for survival that had not only military implications, but political, religious and social ramifications.

Chapter Five

A British National Character

At the close of the War of 1812, the young native-born Tories of Upper Canada were very conscious of the need to strengthen the British national character of the Province. They were born into a period of revolutionary unrest and upheaval, and they had fought a defensive war against a revolutionary power – the United States – that was bent upon conquering Upper Canada. Hence, the Tories called upon the provincial government to implement a "National Policy", in conjunction with Great Britain, to safeguard and ensure the survival of the Loyalist province of Upper Canada. Only through a unified plan of government action could Upper Canada maximize its strength, and promote its own preservation, in the face of the rapidly growing power and influence of the neighboring American Republic.

On a deeper level, the national policy was intended to protect and strengthen the British national character of Upper Canada.

The Tory National Policy

The leading Upper Canadian Tories had a very definite conception of what a National Policy ought to include. In a succession of memoranda and lengthy letters to the Colonial Office -- submitted at intervals throughout the decade following the termination of the war in 1815 and at times of crisis long thereafter -- they produced detailed drafts of the policies which they wished to see implemented. Over a period of two decades, the Tories were to show a striking degree of consistency in the policies which they advocated as being necessary to the very survival of the Loyalist province, and as practical solutions to the political difficulties which continued to plague Upper Canada.

The Tories maintained that not only was a concerted plan of action necessary for the well-being of Upper Canada, but it would prove beneficial to the mother country as well, given its changing power relationship with the United States. They argued that the adoption of a national policy was essential to the maintenance of the supremacy of Great Britain upon whose unstinted aid all the prescribed measures were dependent for their ultimate success. The proposed National Policy ranged over all areas of the national life of Upper Canada: a proposed new political organization and institutional framework, religion, education, economic development, and defence in seeking to better ensure the security and survival of the Province of Upper Canada. One key element was the maintenance and strengthening of the British national character of the province which embodied the vital element of the national policy and the raison d'être for the existence of the Loyalist asylum of Upper Canada.

In addressing themselves to the Colonial Office, the Tories were anxious to convince British statesmen of the danger which the United States posed not only to the survival of Upper Canada, but to the future security and integrity of the Empire itself. They expressed their belief that, although American claims to power and greatness on behalf of their own nation had "deservedly attracted ridicule", nevertheless American resources were such that "in the natural progress of events" the new world would supersede the old world in "security, glory, and science". Such a transfer of power appeared to be inevitable, though the era might well be quite distant.

It was incumbent upon British statesmen to adopt a "great system of policy" to meet that future development. Not only did the best interests of Great Britain demand such a course of action, but it was argued that:

> If the seat of empire is to be transferred to the fertile regions of the west, it would seem a glorious purpose to provide for the continuance in the new world of those unequalled institutions which now command the admiration of the old, and to secure a scene in which the British character may maintain its existence, and manifest its excellence to the latest posterity. (1)

View of England & English Society

The desire to preserve Upper Canada, which was expressed in their call for the implementation of a national policy, was not merely a desire to maintain the political status quo. Its aim was to maintain, strengthen, and build a society of a particular type in Upper Canada: one having a "British national character". What they desired for Upper Canada was the establishment of an English society, which they viewed as a well-ordered polity, peopled by subjects who were possessed of:

the character of a perfect British citizen, who knows his rank, his place, his value, his duties, and his rights; and who will not step out of his own sphere unless he can do so in a constitutional manner --- one to whom self-denial is as dear a privilege as the protection of his person and property; because the detail of that virtue among his fellow citizens is his own security.

The experience of the war years, recent historical events and the bias of their education, all combined to establish a fundamental dichotomy in the Upper Canadian Tory mind. For the Tories, the American national character and polity represented all that they regarded as among the least admirable of any people of a civilized society; while Britain was viewed as the ideal, the 'good society' incarnate, which Upper Canada should seek to emulate. In rejecting the American experience, they were quite definite as to the shortcomings of the people and government of that society, and had a clear perception of the type of society which they wished to build in Upper Canada. However, that idealized society was not an exact replica of England, any more than their concept of a 'British national character' reflected the reality of the public character of Britain.

The Tory attitude toward England at the time of their propounding of the National Policy was rather complex, as can be seen best in the responses which England evoked in two young Tories, John Beverley Robinson and William Macaulay who, immediately following the war, migrated to that country to pursue higher education in their chosen professional fields of law and the Church, respectively.

Upon first arriving in England and having scarcely ventured beyond London itself, Robinson was filled with admiration for the country and 'enraptured' by the sight of its historic buildings and institutions of popular lore.

> The venerable monuments of antiquity, Westminster Abbey, the Hall itself & everything connected with it, the Tower, the ancient Statues & inscriptions, all these excite a delicious feeling one hour of which is worth a whole age of bare existence.

Such a pilgrimage, as indeed it proved to be, was a "grand and captivating" experience for young Robinson as he proceeded to draw upon the imaginings of his youth, and to "compare [his] ideas with the realities" that he saw before him. That "association of ideas" proved to be a "delightful task" as he viewed Oxford, "that great seat of learning" which for centuries had produced the most distinguished men in all areas of life, and for a time had been "the residence of our kings" and even of parliamentary deliberations. Similarly, he was enthralled in London by the Tower, which was built by "an absolute, arbitrary tyrant" – William the Conqueror -- and was associated with the countless men who had suffered in barbarous times to secure to their grateful posterity the blessings of "the present age of liberty & security".

Even the people of England evoked a similar response. Whether it was in meeting a group of disabled war veterans who had sacrificed much "in Some of those brilliant actions which have raised England to her glory & preserved her security", or in attending the Court at Westminster where he saw and heard -- as Robinson wrote to one of his former school mates -- "those very men whose names are so well known to us, & whose books even we have studied from".

First impressions had a marvelous affect upon a young Tory from Upper Canada as in every way England seemed to be "a perfect paradise". The estates of the nobles, and the state of the country in general, contrasted greatly with what Robinson had known:

> What a change from America. In manner, in splendor, in neatness, & in comfort. Everything is managed with such regularity, so much system in every branch of business -- travelling conducted in so superior a style that really all appears new to me.

It was a country that was possessed of numerous charitable institutions which served to provide "from the cradle to the Grave" for the needs of those who were afflicted with physical or mental disorders; all of which bespoke a religious population in keeping with such commendable efforts as the abolition of the slave trade, and the continuing concern to spread Christianity through missionary activity worldwide. In contemplating all that he viewed, Robinson was moved to exclaim:

> Could it be possible for any man even a mean, cunning, democrat --- a Yankee, to survey this ... & not admire & bless the nation that maintains it.

For the young Tories, England was their spiritual home, the cradle of their civilization, which they knew and valued. Their education and experiences during the war years had endowed them with a great historical consciousness and nurtured in them a strong attachment to England. However, what they admired, identified with, and desired to maintain contact with, was the England of history. It was the traditional English institutions, and the English heritage and culture embodying the "wisdom and experience" of their ancestors, which they regarded as being as much their heritage as it was that of an Englishman. (The Tories were avid readers of British history. John Macaulay lauded the efforts of the House of Commons in 1822 to print, at public expense, the "Ancient Histories of Great Britain".)

Nonetheless, the young Upper Canadian Tories were not blind to shortcomings in the England of their day, despite their having a deep-seated and profound admiration for the mother country. They believed that England had been saved only through God's "blessings & Providential interpositions" from succumbing to the infidelity and anarchy from which France – having sunk to the depths – was trying to extricate herself. Robinson, for one, was not carried away to the extent of believing that England, more than any other country, was above reproach. He realized that the superiority of England over all other nations needed to be viewed in relative not absolute terms; yet even that realization did not prepare Robinson for all that he witnessed in England. (2)

Any illusions he might have developed about the superior virtues of England were checked by:

> those vices which are too observable in this nation, & upon that
> lukewarmness in religion which characterizes the present age.

Robinson was shocked by some of the things which he observed during his sojourn in England and, most surprisingly, by the lack of a proper decorum in the English courts. In particular, "the gross prevarication" evident on the part of witnesses, and the "browbeating, cajoling, and insulting behavior" to which they were subjected by lawyers during cross-examination. The English court proceeding that he witnessed, filled him with disgust. Such a scene was thoroughly disagreeable, and destructive of all honourable feeling in witnesses. They could not but respond to the "cunning, insolence, buffoonery & threatening demeanor" of the lawyers with hostile and evasive replies. It was enough to "perplex an honest man". Why an English judge would tolerate such an abuse of the judicial system was beyond comprehension. As Robinson noted, "it certainly would not pass in Upper Canada".

Moreover, it was not only the conduct of the lawyers, but the attitude of the people towards the court that left much to be desired. In one court, Robinson witnessed the appalling conduct of a man who completely disrupted proceedings by his ranting and who, when ordered to leave, had the effrontery to forcibly resist all efforts to remove him. Yet, when finally put out of doors, the man had not even been arrested.

Such misconduct in a court of law was, to Robinson, "a shocking specimen of imbecility", which moved him to comment:

> Had I seen this in a ... Court in the States, I would with perhaps a little prejudice have talked about the blessed effects of their liberty and equality [and] said ... how soon that fellow would be taught better behaviour in England. Indeed. I scarcely could believe I was in an English Court of Justice.

Clearly, the public character and standards of conduct which the Upper Canadian Tories were bent upon inculcating in the population of Upper Canada, was what they had come to associate in their mind with English society in contrast to what they observed in the United States. Just as obviously, their mental image and understanding of the British national character was an ideal which did not necessarily reflect English realities. Distance it seems lent a lustre to the English name. (3)

Even with the passage of the years, and the numerous disappointments they were to experience in looking to Britain for support, the Upper Canadian Tories were to maintain their idealized concept of English society as their guide. As late as 1855, the Rev. John Strachan waxed enthusiastic about "the great number of God's people" in the mother country, which assured to England the continued receipt of His protection, guidance and beneficence. It was the standard -- in its idealized form -- against which Upper Canadians were expected, and encouraged, to measure themselves.

England exhibits such a beautiful and perfect model of public
& private prosperity as does not exist and never before existed
in the World .... It is so magnificent and at the same time so
durable a fabric of social happiness and national grandeur.

It was admitted that England had its obvious shortcomings, but they
were few and attributable to human frailties and the unavoidable
imperfections of human institutions. From the vantage point of Upper
Canada, it seemed that in England:

the comforts the Knowledge and the virtues of social life
have been carried to the highest perfection. The lofty sense of
independence among her people, their truthful and vigorous
morality, their sober and rational piety and the impartial
decorous and laudable administration of their laws are all
matters of joyful admiration.

The English were regarded as being a truly religious people, and their
national character – what was categorized as 'the British national
character' -- was what the Tories admired and wished to strengthen
and maintain in Upper Canada. Prior to the War of 1812, Anglican
Tory Loyalists, such as Richard Cartwright, had sought to preserve and
strengthen the British national character of the Loyalist province with
but little success, until the experience of the war years gave the young
Tories a new cause for hope. (4)

As British subjects, who were living in a province that was part of
the British Empire and who owed allegiance to the Crown, the Tories
regarded themselves as being true 'Britons". Upper Canada was for
them a part of "the national family" of Great Britain, with as much
claim to belong and receive the benefits of its government as any British
subject resident in the United Kingdom. Upper Canadians were advised
that they:

ought to give thanks to God that we are a portion of a nation
so estimable and renowned & from which we derive the more
prominent merits of our own characters --- the best of our
Institutions and the sources of our highest enjoyments.

A national or provincial character

Since the Upper Canadian Tories regarded themselves as "Britons", it was only natural that they should regard Britain as the very centre and source of all which they had come to value; yet they were not merely transplanted Englishmen, Scotchmen or Irishmen yearning for home. The war had given birth to what they referred to as "a national character and feeling" -- amongst the young Tories at least -- which they identified as being British, but it was one firmly rooted in Upper Canada.

The two young Tories, John Beverley Robinson and William Macaulay, mixed well with the best of English society, and were not the least out of place. Robinson was told on several occasions that he spoke "rather better English than [was] common here". However, they were always conscious of the fact that they were not Englishmen. Although both young men considered the prospect of pursuing their careers in England, neither could accept the prospect of abandoning Upper Canada for good. William Macaulay wrote to his brother John:

> With all my admiration for England somehow or other I have never felt a wish to pass my life here tho' I am constantly asked if such are not my plans.

The prospect of remaining in England for an extended period was welcome, particularly, if by doing so they could do something for Canada by way of promoting "the Interests of the province", but "not *forever.*" Upper Canada was their home, and both men chose to return there.

The emotional attachment of the young Tories to Upper Canada was evident again, at a later date in 1823, when the Colonial Office offered the Attorney General of Upper Canada, John Beverley Robinson, an appointment as Chief Justice of Mauritius. That offer was declined by Robinson on the grounds that:

> Attachments of a public & private nature lead me to prefer my present situation in Canada to one more lucrative in another Colony, in which I would probably take less interest & might therefore be less useful.

Not all Upper Canadian Tories felt that way, but it appears to have been a characteristic of the native-born in contrast to the British-born. The Rev. John Strachan, who was born and raised in Scotland, took a different view upon being informed of the important high-level connections which John Beverley Robinson was developing while in England. Strachan was at great pains to convince young Robinson to pursue his legal career there. Indeed, Strachan had declared his willingness to join Robinson in England, "if an adequate Provision" could be secured for himself in the Church of England.

Strachan urged Robinson to take the obvious opportunity that he enjoyed "of acting in more brilliant field", both in his legal career and public life. In Upper Canada, his efforts would not be appreciated. As Attorney General, he would bear the whole weight of public business; yet, he would be harassed constantly by a colonial assembly owing to the shortcomings to which such assemblies were prone. And all the while, he would experience "the mortification of beholding the Province getting more American and less attached to the Parent State".

In contrast, in England he might, once "in power, do infinite good to the British Empire", and be better positioned to promote "the general good". These were strong arguments which were calculated to appeal to the mind of a young Tory, but were not sufficient to convince Robinson. The young Tories were very conscious that they possessed what they described as a "national, or as it may perhaps be more properly termed, a Provincial character" which set them apart; and they were dedicated to making something of their native province.

The belief that they possessed a 'national or provincial character' was reflected over the years in various ways. It was evident in 1833 when Robert Stanton, a former pupil of the Rev. John Strachan, established a Canadian magazine to promote 'native talent' in the literary field, and in the recurrent Tory objection to public offices being filled by appointments from Britain. The latter objection was, of course, in the Tories' own self-interest, but it was motivated as well by a consciousness of a distinct difference between themselves and British-born appointees, and a belief on the part of the Tories in the future of their province. As early as 1823,

Robinson expressed his belief that "one day or other, we shall be a great people. That's certain. My boys may live to see it". (5)

The distinctive national or provincial character which the Upper Canadian Tories felt that they possessed was in no way incompatible with a British national character or the British connection. The 'national character' of Upper Canada was characterized by an allegiance to the British Crown through the Imperial relationship, a strong attachment to British institutions, inclusive of the national Church of England, and an admiration for English social and cultural values. However, ultimately the Upper Canadian Tories were attached to their province by feelings of 'patriotism', which they described as:

> a real love of our Country, an earnest desire for its moral and religious advancement and temporal prosperity hallowed by extending the affections and the pure and tender associations of the domestic circle.

Upper Canada and the British Empire

Within the Imperial relationship, there were certain political realities which had to be recognized. Indeed, the Tories freely admitted that if the interests of the Empire and those of Upper Canada ever came into conflict, the colony should yield:

> But this acquiescence has its limits & no sacrifice should be required that renders the Colony useless or its inhabitants miserable.

However, there was a common good to be realized, and the Imperial authorities should recognize that it was in their own interests to promote the welfare and happiness of the colony. Moreover, it was maintained that purely local concerns should be left exclusively in the hands of the local administration; and that the Imperial government should not act on any matter affecting the colony without first seeking its advice.

For the Tories, there were limits to the commitment of Upper Canada to the British Empire. It was a belief that was evident in the Tory argument that Upper Canada "ought not ... to be charged" with the cost of the War of 1812 because "the causes were national questions" affecting the interests of the Empire, and not just Upper Canada. Thus, although their view of England was somewhat idealized, the Upper Canadian Tories had a very definite concept of their 'national character' as Upper Canadians, of their commitment to the Province of Upper Canada, of what type of society they wished to build in Upper Canada, and its proper relationship to the Imperial power. Their proposed National Policy, in all its ramifications, was to be the means of realizing their own Upper Canadian objectives. (6)

The aim of the National Policy was not only to strengthen and preserve the British national character of a province within the Empire, but also to construct a viable political entity in North America with a strength and importance sufficient to permit Upper Canadians to play a significant role in the Empire which controlled their destiny. Upper Canada could not afford to risk going its own way. Moreover, all the best interests of the province, and the aspirations of the Tories, necessitated closer ties with the mother country and the other British North American colonies.

Union of the Canadas versus a BNA General Legislative Union

In 1822, a Union bill was introduced into the Imperial parliament to unite Upper and Lower Canada in a legislative union. The bill was introduced at the behest of the British Party of Lower Canada -- a 'party' led by the merchants of Lower Canada – to overcome a political deadlock in that assembly between the English-speaking representatives and a 'French party' led by Louis-Joseph Papineau. The union of the two provinces was envisaged as a means of overcoming the opposition of the French to the commercial development and improvement of the St. Lawrence River navigation, and to British immigrants being settled in the Eastern Townships. Moreover, the ultimate objective of the 'British Party' promoters of the union of the two Canadian provinces was to facilitate the assimilation of the French-Canadians within a larger British province.

For the Upper Canadian supporters of the proposed union of the Canadas, there were several benefits to be gained. It would facilitate the improvement of the St. Lawrence River navigation, and would serve to resolve an ongoing dispute over the division of the customs duties which were being collected by Lower Canada on imports proceeding inland to Upper Canada on the St. Lawrence River transport system. However, the two leading Tories of Upper Canada – the Rev. John Strachan and John Beverley Robinson -- were thoroughly alarmed by the prospect of political union of Upper and Lower Canada.

As it happened, when the Union Bill was introduced into Parliament, the Rev. John Strachan was in London to discuss a potential sale of some of the lands that the Crown had reserved in Upper Canada for the support of a Protestant Clergy -- the Clergy Reserves – and John Beverley Robinson was in London to secure the support of the British government for a resolution of the customs duties dispute between the two Canadian provinces. Both men immediately expressed their opposition to the proposed union of Upper and Lower Canada, in addresses to the Colonial Office.

On his part, Strachan was convinced that the establishment of a single united legislature would foster discontent and even rebellion. He feared that the anti-government minority in Upper Canada would join with the French-Canadian representatives of Lower Canada to form a solid bloc which would dominate a united assembly. As such, the proposed union would be contrary to British interests, and a real danger to the rights of Church of England. Subsequently, the Canada Bill of 1822 was withdrawn by the Colonial Office owing to the combined opposition of the leading Tories of Upper Canada and the French Canadians of Lower Canada who saw that it was aimed at assimilating them. The customs revenue dispute was settled by the Canada Trade Act (August 1822), which Robinson was instrumental in drafting for the Colonial Office.

In response to the Union bill, Robinson produced a pamphlet advocating a "General Legislative Union of the British Provinces of North America" (1824), which Strachan supported as a viable alternative to the union of Upper and Lower Canada. Over subsequent decades, the Upper Canadian Tories continued to call upon the British government to undertake -- as a matter of national policy – a general confederation of the British North American colonies on a plan set forth by Robinson and Strachan. The provinces to be encompassed in the proposed general legislative union were: Upper Canada; Lower Canada; New Brunswick; Nova Scotia; and Prince Edward Island; and perhaps Newfoundland.

The Tory argument, in favour of a general legislative union of all the British North American colonies, was expressed initially by Robinson. He maintained that circumstances necessitated the uniting of the various British North American colonies "into one territory or kingdom", and recommended that the united provinces be granted "a representation in the imperial parliament". Such an arrangement, in securing representation for the proposed 'kingdom' within parliament would make the united colonies an integral part of the British Empire on an equality with any of the united kingdoms of Great Britain. It would raise the British North American union to the rank of "a nation acting in unity and under the protection of the British Empire". It would secure each of the former separate colonies from internal upheaval, as well as from external aggression by discouraging encroachments by the American Republic.

With respect to the proposed general legislative union, it was suggested that if the united colonies were to remain a territory under the Crown, they might be called the "United Provinces of British North America". On the other hand, if the united provinces were exalted to the rank of a kingdom and governed by a viceroy -- which was what the Tories preferred – the new kingdom might be called the "Kingdom of British North America" or the "Kingdom of New Albion". It was proposed that under such a confederation or general union, the various colonies should retain their local legislatures for purely local concerns. The general legislature of the united provinces -- their parliament -- would legislate on matters of a general importance to all the colonies, and might be assembled annually or even triennially at Quebec.

As to the structure of the new general union government, it was proposed that it comprise, in addition to a Governor General or a Viceroy representing the sovereign, a Legislative Council to which the Governors of the respective provinces would each delegate three members from their local Legislative Councils, and an Assembly which would embody the elected representatives of the people. The general legislature would remain, however, subject to dissolution at the pleasure of the sovereign's representative.

It was suggested that the members of the Assembly of the general union parliament could be "chosen by the respective assemblies from their own body". On the other hand, if higher qualifications were demanded for members of the general assembly than those currently required for election to the local provincial assemblies, suitably qualified candidates could be elected directly by the people for a four-year term. Furthermore, it was proposed that the provinces might be represented in the general government House of Assembly on the ratio of: Lower Canada, twelve members; Upper Canada, ten members; Nova Scotia, ten members; New Brunswick, ten members; and Prince Edward Island, six members, with a further provision for Newfoundland to have six seats should she adhere to the confederacy.

In addition to setting forth a political framework for the proposed general legislative union of the British North American colonies, the Tory plan set forth a proposed division of powers between the different levels of government. It was maintained that the "general legislature or Parliament" should be given the power of making laws in certain designated areas, subject only to the restrictions which were placed on all colonial legislatures by the imperial parliament that any laws enacted not contradict the laws of the Imperial parliament. The legislative acts of the different provincial governments were to be confined to strictly local matters. All commercial regulations governing the trade of the colonies with one another, with the Empire and foreign nations, and all navigation laws, in the interest of uniformity, were to fall within the prerogative of the general union government and were not to conflict with the trade and navigation laws of Great Britain.

The general legislature would possess the right to "collect taxes, duties, imposts and excises" and would be responsible for the debts of the several provinces as well as for providing for their general peace and wellbeing. The local provincial governments would retain the right to levy assessments exclusively for local purposes such as a land tax or excise duties, but they should not be competent "to control or tax imports, or exports".

The general union government administration was to be supported by the establishment of a permanent civil list which would have the first call on the general revenues, after which the surplus revenue would be applied by the central government to cover other fields within its jurisdiction such as defence and the building of roads and canals to facilitate communications. Furthermore, the general government would be responsible for maintaining public order and curbing sedition. In addition, the general government ought to possess an exclusive right to enact laws pertaining to "Religion, or affecting any religious sect" subject to the restrictions of the Constitutional Act of 1791. In the Tory view, such an arrangement would preclude the Clergy Reserves of Upper Canada from being appropriated to any other use than the "maintenance and support of a protestant Clergy".

The proposed powers of the general union government were designed to address a number of the problems that had bedeviled the Tories in their governing of the Province of Upper Canada. In sum, it would facilitate the resolution of the customs revenue dispute with Lower Canada, and the dispute between the Assembly of Lower Canada and the Executive over the voting of the civil list. It raised the prospect of securing additional support in the general legislative union for the retention of the Clergy Reserves for the benefit of the Established Church of England in the Province of Upper Canada, as well as support for government efforts to construct arterial roads and canals to facilitate the economic development, and support for British immigration to promote the settlement of the provinces. Moreover, it was expected that a strong central government could deal effectively with disaffection, sedition, and treason in wartime, and would serve to lessen the impact of American settlers on the political system.

It was recognized that one difficulty in establishing a two-tier government in a general British North American union was the delineation of the jurisdictional boundaries between the general union legislature and the respective provincial legislatures so as to avoid areas of dispute. To that end, it was proposed that the Court of King's Bench be empowered to rule on any disputes that might arise over the new laws of the general union, and between individuals from the different provinces, and that a Court of Appeal ought to be established to rule on all appeals from the provincial courts.

It was also suggested that the Upper House of the general union government could serve as an intermediate court of appeal to the Judicial Committee of the Privy Council in England. The Upper House of the general government might also be given the power of impeachment over officers of the government and judiciary of the several provinces. Such a power in residing in the Upper House of the general government, would be once removed from the "influence of any prejudice or factious clamour", and would ensure that public servants received justice should any unwarranted charges be brought against them in the local provincial assemblies.

Benefits of a General Union of the Provinces

The Upper Canadian Tories were convinced that a general union of the British North American provinces – such as they recommended – would serve to resolve all the existing differences between Upper and Lower Canada, and would promote the general welfare of the individual provinces. And, most importantly, it would "increase their respectability". It was claimed that:

> the Colonies are at present so disjointed and have so little intercourse that they appear insignificant in every point of view, but, if united, they would assume in a short time a formidable attitude & would command the respect of our neighbours as well as of the Parent State.

The union of the British North American province would not entail the sacrifice of any "local advantage or convenience", but, on the contrary, would promote their security and foster the development of "a greater community of Interest and feeling among themselves". Moreover, the raising of the united colonies to the status of a kingdom could not but strengthen their attachment to the British Empire. It would bring them closer to a pure monarchical form of government, and consequently would deepen the distinctions which separated them from the republican institutions of the United States. Once formed, a western kingdom – "The Kingdom of New Albion" -- would strengthen and safeguard the colonies and ensure their continuance as part of the British Empire in remaining independent of the United States.

When united in one kingdom, the subjects of the new nation would be contented in:

possessing the same constitution and the same laws, and enjoying a community of rights and privileges, they would fully participate in all feelings, and all the glories of British subjects. (7)

A General Political Union and Imperial Federation

To the Tory mind, there was no doubt that if Britain would unite the provinces of British North America in a general legislative union enjoying the status of a kingdom under a Viceroy, and would grant the new kingdom a "direct representation in the imperial Parliament", it would immeasurably strengthen the British connection. What was proposed was that one or two representatives of the new confederation might be permitted to sit in the Imperial Parliament, and be empowered to propose and discuss measures of interest to the North American kingdom. The North American representative might be denied the right to vote in the Imperial Parliament, or could have a right to vote confined to colonial matters. In either case, the British Empire would be immeasurably strengthened, and the interest of the colonies better promoted and protected, through their becoming an actual part of the government of the United Kingdom.

In having their interests made known, through their own representatives in the Imperial Parliament, the colonies would cease to feel vague and unimportant. To the contrary, they would "feel that they were more truly British subjects" under a Parliament which, although distant, would be alive to their concerns. Such a political system would bring British North Americans closer to "the true nature and spirit of ... monarchical institutions", which – according to the Tories -- they already preferred over "the boasted republican institutions" of the Americans. Once united under the sovereign Crown in one general legislature, the colonists would become in time thoroughly attached "heart & soul" to the centre of the British Empire.

Through sharing in imperial councils, the former colonists would come to "cherish an intense affection ... for everything British", while identifying with the welfare and interests of the Empire and the various measures which might be required to sustain it. This was as it should be. The object of government measures should always be "to foster that national principle which ought to connect the people of the provinces with the parent state". It was after all only natural:

> that those who live at the extremities of an extensive empire or province, finding it necessary to keep up a connexion with those who live at the seat of government for protection, justice, or favour, and to request their assistance and support, should become attached to their benefactors; and where a regular intercourse of dependence is established, a union of measures, of views, and feelings must soon follow.

In time, as the provinces developed into mature societies, their "semblance of monarchy might be made more exact". Their patriotism and "reverence for monarchical government" might be strengthened by such means as the creation of an hereditary aristocracy as soon as the colonies could provide suitable materials for such distinctions to be properly bestowed.

Imperial federation, when combined with a general confederation of the North American colonies, would provide "a new field of laudable ambition" to which all young men of talent and ability could aspire. Better men – men of intelligence, ambition, and influence -- would be attracted to the government to serve for the good of their country. Seated in the House of Assembly or the Legislative Council of the general government of the provinces, such men could be counted upon to value the British connection. Their good sense, as well as their future hopes, would ensure that they would regard Britain rightly "as the palladium of their safety and civil rights".

Moreover, those who served in the Imperial Parliament as representatives of the united provinces of British North America would return to the general government with enlarged views and a better understanding of the problems of Empire. As a result, their influence would tend to promote "an identity of views and feelings" with the mother country, and infuse a British spirit into the united provinces.

Public order also would be strengthened as local discontents and the intrigues of faction would be isolated. And "malicious demagogues", though capable of misleading public opinion in one province and/

or gaining support in a local legislature, would be rendered incapable of blocking important public measures or of hurrying members into supporting illiberal or unconstitutional actions.

What is more, a general legislative union of the provinces had much to recommend it as:

> There [was] also every reasonable assurance that these members would be generally men of greater consideration for their property, intelligence, and standing in society, and would come to their duty with a more just sense of what the constitution demanded and be free from that jealous suspicion of the Government which prevails most with the least informed.

Men of such a calibre would understand the necessity of maintaining the balance of the constitution, as well as the British connection.

A general union of the provinces would tend also to promote the prosperity of the colonies. It would strengthen the ties of Empire by enabling them to participate more fully on an even larger scale in the Imperial trade system, and would foster the development of both internal and external transportation facilities to enable Upper Canada to benefit to an even greater extent from the Imperial market preferences.

And most importantly, a confederation of the provinces would increase the influence on the government of the Church of England – "the very heart of the constitution, the strongest bond of empire, and the pre-eminent support of social order". The Anglican Church was already established by provincial law in both Nova Scotia and New Brunswick; whereas, in Upper Canada, its establishment was under question by the political radicals and religious dissenters.

By means of a general political union of the British North American provinces, and representation in the Imperial Parliament, a perpetual union could be formed between Great Britain and her colonies, the people of whom were subjects of the same king. Their attachments and very interests, if a wise system of policy were to be followed, could be consolidated into one community. Once consciously united in spirit, feelings, and interest, such a union "would tend most materially to preserve the integrity of the Empire in all its parts".

Indeed, it was submitted that the union of British North American colonies could be regarded -- if one were to indulge in "attractive visions" -- as the forerunner of similar developments within the Empire as:

> perhaps it would not be found impracticable to group the colonial possessions of the empire into six or seven confederacies according to their situations, and to allow each of these confederacies a representative in Parliament. This actual consolidation of the British Empire would be at least a grand measure of national policy. (8)

Seeking British Government Support

The immediate post-war period was regarded as the most propitious time for laying the foundation for the proposed North American kingdom, which promised to be "a most valuable appendage to the British Empire".

The Upper Canadian Tories were convinced that circumstances were such that a proper policy needed only to be implemented to achieve desirable national ends. The Colonial Office was informed that the North American colonies had an industrious population, which was increasing substantially in numbers and wealth, and were possessed of a favourable climate and a fertile soil of a vast, though not unlimited extent. There was every reason to expect – if peace could be maintained -- that the united provinces would continue to grow in prosperity and strength under the protection of Great Britain which, following the defeat of Napoleonic France, was "first in glory, in wealth, in power, and in science, among the nations of the earth".

In the same vein, the Tories maintained that the loyalty of the colonies had been confirmed and strengthened during the War of 1812 through their adherence to the mother country, and the feelings engendered by the war were such as to prevent any leaning toward the United States. All the colonies, and Upper Canada in particular, were moved by a just pride in the contribution which they had made to the war effort, and were filled with a strong resentment against the Americans whose "unprovoked invasion" had occasioned the late bitter struggle.

For the Upper Canadian Tories, the time was fortuitous for a general union of the North American provinces, as the colonists were impregnated with "a proper spirit and feeling". And, if united in one nation under the Crown of Great Britain, they would soon "begin to pride themselves on the possession of a national character".

The Tories were convinced that the other colonies would regard such a scheme quite favourably, if it were presented to them. A general union of all the colonies in a system of imperial federation would flatter their self-esteem. It would enhance their respectability and "elevate them into an important and really integral part of the empire", and would not involve any "sacrifice of local advantage or convenience". Each colony would continue to govern its own internal economy, and continue to possess its legislative authority over local affairs.

All of the British North American colonies shared a common interest in preserving their independence from the common danger that was posed by the United States. Upper Canada was a Loyalist asylum, and Nova Scotia and New Brunswick were also "peopled chiefly by American loyalists" who were animated by a reverence for British institutions and the unity of Empire.

The French Canadians were expected to support a general union of the provinces as well. In addition to bearing "a determined hereditary dislike" for Americans, which was derived from the struggles waged in the days of New France, the French Canadians were of "tried fidelity". They had fought well against the Americans during the War of 1812. Moreover, the French Canadians were:

> fortified by prejudices in favor of civil and religious institutions which they must be convinced would not be so indulgently respected by any other government as that under which they have the happiness to live.

Robinson and Strachan believed that the French Canadians would support a general union of the provinces, which was not the case with respect to the proposed union of the two Canadian provinces. Indeed, one Upper Canadian Tory, John Macaulay, who favoured the proposed union of the Canadas in 1822 was chagrined to discover that French Canadians were opposed to a union with Upper Canada. He was taken aback to learn that French Canadians were convinced that: "The political and moral condition of the two Provinces differs ... essentially under every point of view". Not only were Upper Canadians English-speaking, rather than French-speaking, but the province was viewed by the French Canadians as being heavily populated with Americans who espoused republican principles, and with numerous American religious sects who were hostile to the Roman Catholic religion. For the French Canadians of the immediate postwar era, Upper Canada was viewed as having little in common with the monarchical and religious traditions of French Canada.

Macaulay hastened to express his dismay that the French should indiscriminately consider all Upper Canadians to be 'republicans'. His hope was that a direct union of the two provinces would promote harmony between French and English based upon their common principles and allegiance. In contrast to Strachan and Robinson, he did not foresee any future danger of an alliance of the French Canadians from Lower Canada with the anti-government reform faction of Upper Canada in a united Canadian legislature.

On the other hand, Strachan and Robinson, who were opposed to the lesser union of the two Canadian provinces, were convinced that similar principles, religious values, and a common fear of the United States, would bring the French Canadians to favour a general confederation of the British North American provinces. However, if the French failed to embrace a general union of the provinces, they could not justly complain if they were "placed on the same footing with their fellow subjects" of the several provinces in the proposed confederation. (9)

In seeking to secure the support of the British government for a general confederation of the British North American provinces, the Tories returned to their standard argument concerning the value of the colonies to Britain. Once again, they stressed that it was in her own best interest for Britain to strengthen the colonies and prevent her natural rival – the United States – from gaining additional power and resources.

They argued that, if once united with the support of Great Britain, there was no doubt that a kingdom so situated would, in time, form a most powerful check to the United States of America. Not only did the very strategic position of the proposed kingdom provide an effectual base for the Royal Navy to destroy American commerce in any future war, but the location of the provinces -- free from attack in the rear -- and their potential growth in population, rendered them capable of being defended, if united. The fisheries of the Atlantic colonies would furnish seamen and shipping to contribute to British strength; while, with an on-going British immigration, the inland colonies were developing a substantial population that would eventually yield a formidable military force. With the aid of British power and resources, the new confederation would be able to defend itself in any future war, and would be able to provide a powerful military presence in areas where the United States was inaccessible to attack by the warships of the Royal Navy.

In addition, the earlier argument was revived that the strengthening and retention of the colonies was in the best interests of Britain in a commercial sense. The resources of the colonies, such as timber, hemp, grain and the fisheries, provided a profitable field for the investment of British capital. Moreover, the colonies were a market for British manufactures which in turn created employment for British shipping, as well as a home within the Empire for the surplus population of the mother country.

With British aid, the extensive resources of British North America could be improved and developed, and the commerce of the Empire extended for the benefit of all. It was a common argument on the part of the Upper Canadian Tories, which was mustered in support of the benefits of a general union of the British North American colonies. The British government was advised that a union of the colonies "by consolidating the resources of the provinces and directing them with unity of design" would do much to inhibit American expansion northward. The colonies in being so united would "become more formidable in war", as well as more respectable in peace, and through being able to act in concert would discourage any encroachments by a foreign power. (10).

The Chimera of Independence

The Upper Canadian Tories went to great lengths to explain to the Colonial Office that a union of the British North American colonies would not serve simply to hasten the time of their departure from the Empire. Although the Tories were aware of the maxim that colonies should become nations in their own right "whenever they are so increased in numbers and strength as to be sufficient for all the good ends of a political union"; they believed that the circumstances of the North American colonies were such that independence was not a viable option. The circumstances of the provinces were such that even:

> Putting ... out of view all feelings of loyalty, and all obligation of duty, the event of Canada being a sovereign and independent power is surely not one which the world can ever be destined to see.

The geographical position of the colonies forbade them, even if united, from ever aspiring to possess a sufficient power and importance "to rationally hope to exist as an independent nation". They were situated next to a powerful neighbor who possessed boundless resources and a population which already numbered in the millions, as opposed to the several hundred thousand in the British colonies. Moreover, the British North American colonies were severely circumscribed by a limited amount of arable land, which rendered them incapable of supporting a population as large as the United States. In sum, with a limited population, the colonies would always be dependent upon British power to sustain them against a country which "must ever exceed them in power". Even the Canadian provinces, which would be able to eventually support a population sufficient to defend themselves with British aid, were in a weak position. They were confined to one outlet to the sea, which was frozen over for five months of each year, and were incapable of defending their own commerce against "even the weakest maritime nation of Europe".

Given the geographical position, and the limited population growth prospects of the British North American colonies in comparison with the United States, it was unrealistic to argue, as some British Whigs were doing, that England would only be hurrying on the day of independence. Moreover, that was equally the case with respect to the argument that the fostering of the economic development of the North American colonies, and their uniting in a single confederation, would only better enable them to revolt at some future date. To the contrary, the Tories argued that:

> The people of all these colonies know full well that, if their independence were granted to them, they could not maintain it, and that the only alternatives are their belonging to Britain or belonging to her greatest commercial rival.

Rather than strengthening the ability of the colonies to co-ordinate efforts to throw off the rule of the mother country in some future dispute, a general confederation would aid in preventing that very thing. The Tories argued that had the American colonies been so united, the members of the general government in coming from all the colonies "would have presented a more accurate account of the public mind", which would have permitted any misunderstanding in any one province to be rectified. Legitimate grievances could have been brought forward by the general government, and in coming from such a respectable body would have received the prompt attention of the British government. In the British American colonies, a general government of the colonies could have played a mediating role, and prevented discontent from developing to the point of an armed revolt.

Nevertheless, where the British North American colonies were concerned any declaration of independence from Great Britain was as "physically impossible, as it [was] morally ... improbable". The colonies had no reason to complain. Great Britain defended both their commerce and their territorial integrity at no expense to themselves, as well as provided their exports with preferences in the home market and other British colonial markets. The restrictions of Empire were not such as could be complained of when the very development of the colonies was dependent on British capital and British trade preferences. When all factors were taken into account, the British connection was in the best interests of the colonies. It provided them with "security and advantages unattainable under any other circumstances". (11)

In developing and improving her North American colonies, Britain did not have to fear that she was merely doing so for the ultimate benefit of the United States, whom they would join at some future date. The colonists were "most decidedly adverse to the American republic" and were animated by a firm loyalty and attachment to the mother country. Moreover, their patriotism, their best interests, and even their vanity would ensure their loyalty if the provinces were united in a larger confederation.

Once united into a kingdom and made an integral part of the United Kingdom, the British North American provinces would possess "all the substantial privileges of independent states". Invariably the new confederation government would "look to its own interest and to the continuance of its own Power", and these would be best promoted in maintaining the British Imperial connection. The government of the new kingdom would have much to lose in rejecting the benefits of empire, and nothing to gain in joining the United States. In becoming states of such an extensive country, they would be rendered comparatively insignificant in possessing little weight in its councils, and perhaps would find their own interests sacrificed to those of other parts of the United States.

Far from promoting the dismemberment of the Empire, whatever aid Great Britain could render to strengthen and improve its North American provinces would deepen their attachment to the mother country. Moreover, Britain could do no less because:

> it [was] an ungenerous and impracticable policy which would seek to hold countries in subjection by repressing their energies and retarding their improvement. (12)

Notes

Part Two: Safeguarding Upper Canada

Part Two Divider: The quotation is from PAO, Robinson Papers, Charges to the Grand Juries, 1829-1841, John Beverley Robinson, "Charge to the Grand Jury", Toronto, 1 April 1834, 9.

Chapter Three - The Postwar Outlook

1. *Kingston Chronicle* (Macaulay editorial), 24 March 1820; PAO, Strachan Sermons, Box C, St. Paul's Epistle to the Hebrews, 12:11, "Chastening yieldeth Righteousness", 16 March 1806, 8-9; Strachan, *Sermon Preached at York, Upper Canada on Third of June, Being the Day Appointed for a General Thanksgiving* (Montreal: William Gray, 1814), 31; and *Christian Recorder*, vol. I, 124, June 1819, Strachan, "Original Communications", 124. The first two quotations are from the Macaulay editorial of 24 March 1820, and the third quotation is from "Original Communications". Among the young Tories elected to the House of Assembly in the July 1820 provincial election were at least four former pupils of the Rev. John Strachan: John Beverley Robinson; Jonas Jones; Archibald McLean; and Philip Vankoughnet.

2. *Christian Recorder*, I, February 1820, "On the Increase of the Christian Spirit", 452-457, and II, March 1820, 61-62; *Kingston Chronicle*, (Macaulay editorial), 24 March 1820; *Christian Recorder*, II, December 1820, "Bible Society of Upper Canada", 359; and I, June 1819, [Strachan], "Universal Peace", 125. The quotations are from: "On the Increase of the Christian Spirit", 452.

3. *Christian Recorder*, II, March 1820, "On the Increase of the Christian Spirit", 59-60; Strachan, *Sermon for General Thanksgiving*, 3 June 1814, 22-27 and 32; *Kingston Chronicle*, (Macaulay editorial), 7 January 1820.

4. Strachan, *Sermon for General Thanksgiving*, 3 June 1814, 25-27 & 29; *Kingston Chronicle*, (Macaulay editorial), 6 December 1822. The quotations are from: Macaulay's editorial, and Strachan's Sermon, 29, respectively.

5. Strachan, *Sermon for General Thanksgiving*, 3 June 1814, 28-30; *Kingston Chronicle* (Macaulay editorial), 6 December 1822; Strachan, *Discourse*, 1810, 54-55. The quotations are from the *Sermon*, 29, the *Discourse*, 55, and the *Sermon*, 28, respectively.

6. *The Church*, (Rev. Alexander Neil Bethune editorial), 3 November 1838. Bethune was the son of a Loyalist minister of the Church of Scotland, and a former student at the Cornwall District Grammar School of John Strachan under whom Bethune subsequently studied divinity, and was ordained an Anglican priest in 1824. [See *DCB,* X, Arthur N. Thompson, "Bethune, Alexander Neil".]

7. *The Church*, (Bethune editorial), 3 November 1838; Strachan, *Discourse,* 1810, 47; *Christian Recorder*, vol II, 190-191, Strachan, "Respectful Demeanour towards constituted authorities, a Christian duty", July 1820; *The Church*, "Christian Loyalty", 22 December 1838; *The Church*, (Bethune editorial), 5 December 1840 & 29 May 1841. The quotations are from: the *Christian Recorder* article, 195 & 191, respectively.

8. *Christian Recorder*, II, March 1820, 78-80, "Society for Promoting Christian Knowledge", & October 1820, 296, "Harford's Life and Principles of Thomas Paine" (From the *Christian Observer*). The Quotations are from the SPCK article, 78.

9. *Kingston Chronicle*, vol. II, 14 January 1832, [Rev. Adam Hood Burwell], "One of the People"; *Christian Recorder*, vol. II, October 1820, "Harford's Life and Principles of Thomas Paine", 297-298 (From the *Christian Observer*). The quotations are from "One of the People", and the article on Thomas Paine, respectively. In analyzing the popular appeal of men such as Jean-Jacques Rousseau and Thomas Paine, the Tories of Upper Canada did not set forth a completely original interpretation of the phenomenon which they observed. The Rev. Burwell's analysis of Rousseau draws upon an analysis developed by Edmund Burke, which was derived in part from David Hume. The Tory analysis of the appeal of the writings of Thomas Paine comprised basically an excerpt -- that Strachan acknowledged that he extracted -- from an article in the *Christian Observer* in England which drew on a recently-published book: viz. John S. Harford, *Some Account of the Life, Death, and Principles of Thomas Paine, together with Remarks on his Writings, and on their intimate connection with the Avowed Objects of the Revolutionaries of 1798 and the Radicals of 1819* (Bristol: J.M. Gutch, 1819). Nevertheless, the point being made here is that the Upper Canadian Tories were seeking to understand the methods of such men as Rousseau and Paine, and the public appeal of their ideas, so that they could be more successfully combated in the future.

[The Rev. Adam Hood Burwell (1790-1849), was a former student of the Rev. John Strachan, who studied divinity under Strachan, was ordained an Anglican priest in 1827, and served in several parishes in Lower Canada. Between

March 1831 and February 1832, he published a series of article in the *Kingston Chronicle* as "One of the People". See *DCB*, VII, Michael Williams, "Burwell, Adam Hood".]

10. *The Church*, 22 December 1838, "Christian loyalty" & Editorial (Bethune), 18 July 1840; *Kingston Gazette*, [Strachan], Reckoner, No. 11, 12 March 1811; *Christian Recorder*, II, 299, October 1820, "Harford's Life and Principles of Thomas Paine", 299. The quotation is from "Christian loyalty", 22 December 1838.

11. *Kingston Chronicle* (Macaulay editorials), 19 November 1819, 7 January 1820, 28 April 1820, 13 October 1820 and 13 July 1821. The quotation is from the editorial of 13 July 1821.

12. *Kingston Chronicle* (Macaulay editorials) 10 September, 1 October and 19 November 1819, as well as 7 and 14 January, 18 February, 31 March, and 28 April 1820. The quotations are from the editorials of 1 October 1819 & 7 January 1820, respectively.

13. Spragge, ed., *Strachan Letter Book*,166, Strachan to Col. Harvey, 22 June 1818; Craig, *Upper Canada*, 9-63; PAQ, Cartwright Letterbook, IV, Cartwright to Lt. Governor Gore, 22 September 109, 327-328 & 2 October 1809, 329-330; and *Kingston Chronicle*, (Macaulay editorial),11 June 1819. [Robert Gourlay was a university-educated young Scot, who after participating in a statistical study of the condition of farm labourers in Britain, became an agrarian radical. In an earlier pamphlet, *A Specific plan for organizing the people, and for obtaining reform independent of parliament: Addressed by Robert Gourlay, Esq., to the people of Fife and of Great Britain* (London, 1809), Gourlay had set forth his visionary scheme. Parliament was viewed as controlled by a selfish governing class with the support of the Established Church clergy, but Gourlay had faith in 'the people'. He argued that if the poor were educated, it would facilitate the improvement of agriculture. He called for a national convention to bypass parliament and present a petition directly to the King to institute a land redistribution program. The land scheme developed by Gourlay and his proposal for a national convention to bypass parliament, were truly revolutionary. However, Gourlay believed that such a revolution could be carried out peacefully, and would inaugurate a new world order of virtue. See, *DCB*, IX, S.F. Wise, "Gourlay, Robert Fleming".]

14. *Kingston Chronicle*, (Macaulay editorials), 8 January and 11 June 1819; Craig, *Upper Canada*, 94- 96; Spragge, ed., *Strachan Letter Book*: 163-164 & 171, Strachan to Col. Harvey, 22 June 1818 & 27 July 1818 & 169, Strachan to the Administrator, 3 July 1818, & 185, Strachan to Dr. Brown, 1 December

1818. The first quotation is from Strachan to the Administrator, 3 July 1818, and the other two quotations are from the Macaulay editorial of 8 January 1819.

15. *Kingston Chronicle*, (Macaulay editorials), 8 January & 11 June 1819, and 27 December 1822; Craig, *Upper Canada*, 97-98; PAO, Macaulay Papers, reel 1, Strachan to John Macaulay, 30 January & 11 February 1819; Spragge, ed., *Strachan Letter Book*, 185, Strachan to Dr. Brown, 1 December 1818 & 171, Strachan to Col. Harvey, 27 July 1818 & 181-182, Strachan to the Hon. Francis Gore, 8 December 1818. The quotations are from the Macaulay editorials of 11 January 1819 and 8 January 1819, respectively.

[John Wilkes (1724-1797) was an English political radical, a member of parliament, and a libertine. He favored parliamentary reform -- equal representation of the people in parliament, elimination of the property franchise, and the disenfranchisement of rotten boroughs – and was a proponent of religious liberty, prisoners' rights, and freedom of the press. In his newspaper, *The North Briton*, he attacked the character of Lord Bute, the Prime Minister, and in one issue (No. 45) went so far as to libel King George III. Subsequently, he was accused of seditious libel and arrested on a general warrant. After a series of trials, the courts found general warrants to be illegal and freed Wilkes. In London, Wilkes became a cause célèbre among the political opposition who took up the cry "Wilkes and Liberty".

Once free, Wilkes published a salacious poem, which resulted in his being charged with obscene libel and blasphemy; and he fled to France. Four years later, in 1768, he returned to England and secured election to parliament where he claimed parliamentary immunity from prosecution for libel. Three times, Wilkes was expelled by parliament and each time the voters of Middlesex returned him in a bye-election, before the charges against him were finally expunged. In the American colonies, Wilkes came to be regarded as an icon of liberty for his political views, his tribulations at the hands of the British government, and his public support of the cause of the American rebels, who presumably knew nothing of his personal character. In Upper Canada, both John Macaulay and the Rev. John Strachan were quite aware that the earlier efforts of the British government to prosecute Wilkes had made him a popular hero and a political symbol for the opposition interests. Hence, they did not want to run the risk of arousing a popular support for Robert Gourlay by prosecuting him for libel.]

16. *Kingston Chronicle*, (Macaulay editorials), 30 July 1819, 7 January 1820, & 27 December 1822; Robinson, *Letter to Earl Bathurst*, 26 December 1824, 8; PAO, Cartwright Letterbook, IV, 327-328, Cartwright to Lt. Governor Gore, 22

September 1809 & 329-330, 2 October 1809. The quotation is from Cartwright to Gore, 22 September 1809, 327. [On the administration of Lt. Governor Maitland, see: DCB, VIII, Hartwell Bowsfield, "Maitland, Sir Peregrine".]

17. PAO, Cartwright Letterbook, IV, 335-336, Cartwright, "Representation respecting Half Pay Officers presented to Lt. Governor Gore, 24 February 1810; Robinson, "Future Government of Canada", *Canada Bill*, 12 & 135; *The Church*, (Bethune editorial), 29 February 1840; *Kingston Chronicle* (Macaulay editorials), 11 June & 19 November 1819, and 14 January 1820. The quotations are from: Robinson, "Future Government of Canada", 1840, 12, and the Macaulay editorial of 19 November 1819, respectively.

18. *Christian Recorder* (Strachan editorial), I, 266, September 1819; *The Church*, "Christian Loyalty", 22 December 1838; Strachan, *Discourse*, 1810, 33; PAO, Robinson Papers, John Beverley Robinson Diaries, 18 January, 1816, 149; PAO, Strachan Sermons, Book of Scottish speeches 1795-1799, speech entitled "Whether a speedy peace or a continuance of the present [French] war would be of more advantage to Great Britain", n.d., 114-115. The quotation is from the Strachan editorial, 266.

19. *Christian Recorder*, II, 297-300, "Harford's Life and Principles of Thomas Paine", October 1820. The quotation and the quoted phrases are taken from the published extracts in the *Christian Recorder*. Harford presents an excellent summary of the British Tory reasoning and attitude toward the teaching of religious and moral values which accords completely with the values and beliefs articulated by the Rev. John Strachan in his writings. Harford denounced the principles of Paine, as well as his low moral character. See John S. Harford, *Some Account of The Life, Death, and Principles of Thomas Paine, Together with Remarks on his Writings, and on their intimate connection with the avowed objects of the Revolutionists of 1793, and of the Radicals in 1819* (Bristol: J. M. Gutch, 1819). [For a recent study of Thomas Paine's works and the works of his contemporary critics, including Harford's book, see: Edward Larkin, *Thomas Paine and the Literature of Revolution* (N.Y.: Cambridge University Press, 2005).]

20. *The Church* (Bethune editorials), 18 July 1840 & 30 August 1844; and *Kingston Gazette*, [Strachan], "Reckoner No. 11", 12 March 1811. The quotation is from the Reckoner article, 12 March 1811. The Bethune editorials do not date from the immediate postwar period. However, they express attitudes which marked the Upper Canadian Tory mind at all periods, and which were quite in evidence in a myriad of ways in the immediate postwar period.

Chapter Four –The American Threat

1. Strachan, *Discourse*, 1810, iii-iv; and PAO, Macaulay Papers, reel 1, John Bethune to John Macaulay, 21 December 1810.

2. Strachan, *Sermon on the death of Cartwright*, 3 September 1815, 37; *Kingston Chronicle*, (Macaulay editorials), 14 and 11 June 1819; and *Kingston Chronicle*, [Strachan] "Letters to Robert Walsh Esq.", No. 8, 24 March and No. 10, 21 April 1820. The quotation is from Letter No. 8, 24 March 1820.

3. *The Church*, (Bethune editorial), 1 June 1839; Strachan, *Sermon on the death of Cartwright*, 3 September 1815, 38-39; Strachan, *Sermon for General Thanksgiving*, 3 June 1814, 33 & 37; PAO, Robinson Papers John Beverley Robinson Diaries, 1815-17, October 31, [1815], 62; *The Church*, (Bethune editorial), 17 November 1838; *Kingston Chronicle* (Macaulay editorials), 4 & 11 June 1819 and 31 March 1820; and Spragge, *Strachan Letter Book*, vii-viii, Strachan to Dr. Brown, 20 October 1807 and 21 October 1809. The Quotation is from Strachan to Brown, 21 October 1809, vii.

[On the American invasion of Spanish Florida, see Anderson, *The Dominion of War*, 237-238 & 240-246; and Internet: "Transcontinental Treaty" (Adams-Onis Treaty). Surprisingly, the Tories did not mention an earlier atrocity committed by Andrew Jackson in Spanish Florida during the War of 1812. In response to skirmishes between the 'Red Sticks' of the Creek nation and American settlers, Jackson led a militia force into West Florida that attacked and slaughtered the 'Red Sticks', and forced the Creeks, by the Treaty of Fort Jackson (9 August 1814), to cede over half of their territory – 23 million acres in present day Georgia and Alabama – to the United States. (Anderson, *The Dominion of War*, 231- 233. See also, A.J. Langguth, *Driven West, Andrew Jackson and the Trail of Tears to the Civil War* (New York: Simon & Schuster, 2010), 5-6, and Internet: "Missouri Compromise".]

4. Spragge, *Strachan Letter Book* ,viii, Strachan to Dr. Brown, 21 October 1809; Strachan, Sermon on the death of Cartwright, 3 September 1815, 28 & 38; *The Church*, (Bethune editorials), 31 March & 3 November 1838 and 13 February 1841; *The Church*, Speech by Christopher Hagerman, 21 November 1840; PAO, Macaulay Papers, reel 2, Reverend Robert D, Cartwright to John Macaulay, 4 July 1835; *Kingston Chronicle*, (Macaulay editorials), 4 & 11 June 1819; and PAC, Merritt Papers, vol. 13, John Beverley Robinson to W.H. Merritt, 27 December 1837. The quotations are from Macaulay's editorials of 14 & 11 June 1819, respectively.

[Christopher Hagerman (1792-1847) was a lawyer and second-generation Loyalist from Kingston. Although he was not a former pupil of John Strachan, he was a member of the provincial Tory elite, and an ardent supporter of the 'Established Church', the monarchy, and the British tie – a strong "Churchman and King's Man". He was an outspoken supporter of the government in the House of Assembly during the 1830s, and served as Solicitor General (1829-1837) and Attorney General (1837-1840). See Robert L. Fraser, "Hagerman, Christopher Alexander", *Dictionary of Canadian Biography*, VII.]

5. *The Church*, (Bethune editorials), 31 March & 17 November 1838, and 13 February 1841; *Kingston Chronicle*, [Strachan], Letter to Robert Walsh No. 13, 14 July 182O, Strachan, *Sermon for General Thanksgiving*, 3 June 1814, 33; and Spragge, *Strachan Letter Book*, viii, Strachan to Dr. Brown, 20 October 1807 and 9 October 1808. The quotations are from the Bethune editorials of 13 February 1841 and 31 March 1838, respectively.

[The Constitution of the United States of 1787 is a totally secular document that makes no mention of God in any capacity. The Preamble reads: "We, the people of the United States, in order to form a more perfect Union, establish justice, insure domestic tranquility, provide for the common defence, provide for the general welfare, and secure the blessings of liberty to ourselves and our posterity, do ordain and establish this Constitution for the United States of America."

Religion was mentioned only subsequently in the First Amendment of December 1791, which established the separation of Church and State and freedom of religion. It reads: "Congress shall make no law respecting an establishment of religion, or prohibiting the free exercise thereof, or abridging the freedom of speech, or of the press, or the right of the people peacefully to assembly, and to petition the government for a redress of grievances."]

6. Strachan, *Discourse*, 1810, iii-iv; Strachan, *Sermon on the death of Cartwright*, 3 September 1815, 27-28, 37-38 & 40; *Kingston Chronicle*, (Macaulay editorial), 11 June 1819; *The Church*, (Bethune editorial), 13 February 1841; Spragge, *Strachan Letter Book*, viii, Strachan to Dr. Brown, 9 October 1808 and 21 October 1809. The quotation is from the Strachan, *Sermon*, 3 September 1815.

7. *The Church*, (Bethune editorials) 31 March and 3 & 17 November 1838; and *The Church*, "England and America", 1 December 1838. The quotation is from the "England and America" article of 1 December 1838. The Tory view of the involvement of religious sects in American politics is in keeping with their earlier Tory view that the American evangelical sectarians in their belief in political activism and "ecclesiastical democracy" were a real threat to the traditional church-state monarchical polity of Upper Canada.. It was a view which the Tories held from a very early date and accounts for their striving to

combat the spread of American religious sects into Upper Canada.

8. *The Church*, (Bethune editorials), 3 and 17 November 1838; *The Church*, "Christian Loyalty", 22 December 1838; *York Gazette*, "Falkland" (Richard Cartwright), 26 February 1812; *Kingston Chronicle*, (Macaulay editorial), 11 June 1819; PAC, Merritt Papers, vol. 26, John Strachan to W.H. Merritt, 16 May 1856; and *The Church*, "England and America", 1 December 1838. The quotation is from Strachan to Merritt, 1 December 1838.

9. Robinson, *Canada Bill*, 1840, 15; Strachan, *Sermon for General Thanksgiving*, 3 June 1814, 34; *Kingston Chronicle*, (Macaulay editorial), 26 November 1819 and 8 December 1820; Strachan, *Sermon on the death of Cartwright*, 3 September 1815, 41; John Strachan and John Beverley Robinson, *Observations on the Policy of a General Union of all the British Provinces of North America* (London: W. Cloves, 1824), 5; John Beverly Robinson, *A Letter to the Right Hon. Earl Bathurst, K.G. on the Policy of Uniting the British North-American Colonies* (26 December 1824), 47- 49. The quotation is from Robinson pamphlet *Letter to Earl Bathurst*, 26 December 1824, 48.

[Census data has been inserted into the original dissertation text from Taylor, *The Civil War of 1812*, 140, and the Internet: U.S. Census Data for 1820.]

10. Spragge, Strachan Letter Book, 185, Strachan to Dr. Brown, 1 December 1818; *Kingston Chronicle*, (Macaulay editorial), 26 November 1819; Robinson, *Letter to Earl Bathurst*, 26 December 1824, 47- 49. The quotation is from Robinson, *Letter to Earl Bathurst*, 26 December 1824, 48.

11. *Kingston Chronicle*, (Macaulay editorials), 9 July, 26 November & 24 December 1819, and 8 December 1820, and 12 July & 30 August 1822, and 26 December 1824; Spragge, ed., *Strachan Letter Book*, 23, Strachan to Hon. Mr. Wilberforce, 1 November 1812. The quotations are from Strachan to Wilberforce, 1 November 1812, and *Kingston Chronicle*, 26 November 1819, respectively. As late as 29 March 1839, Robinson also expressed the hope that a growing intercourse between Britain and the United States would tend to restrain the Americans from a rupture with England; although earlier he had expressed a different opinion that trade relations would sooner or later provide some occasion for serious differences between the two powers because of the American temper. (PAO, Robinson Papers, 1839-1842, 19, Robinson to Marquess of Normanby, Secretary of State for War and the Colonies, on measures necessary for restoring security and confidence in Canada; and Robinson, *Letter to Earl Bathurst*, 26 December 1824, 48).

[On American expansionism, and its impact on Spanish Florida, the Indian tribes of the South and the North-West, and on Mexico, see Fred Anderson, *The Dominion of War, Empire and Liberty in North America, 1500-2000* (London: Penguin Books, 2005), 229-273. The Anderson study supports the far older Tory interpretation of American expansionism. See also Reginald C. Stuart, *United States Expansionism and British North America, 1775- 1871* (Chapel Hill, North Carolina: University of North Carolina Press, 1988). For Stuart, American expansionism, which grew out of the American Revolution, was a 'defensive expansionism' motivated primarily by a desire to attain security for the new Republic by removing Great Britain from North America by negotiation or by force.]

12. *Kingston Chronicle*, (Macaulay editorial), 26 November 1819 and 30 August 1822; Strachan and Robinson, *Observations on the Policy of a General Union*, 1824, 5; PAO, Robinson Papers 1813- 1817, 6-7, Strachan, "Reasons against removing the Seat of government of Upper Canada from York to Kingston", 1816; Spragge, *Strachan Letter Book*, 23, Strachan to Hon. Mr. Wilberforce, 1 November 1812, and 9, Strachan, "Remarks on the Subject of the removing the seat of Government to Kingston", October 1815.

[Immediately after the War of 1812, the British government proposed that the capital of the province be moved from York (Toronto) to Kingston, which was far more secure against attack in wartime. However, the Upper Canadian Tory elite in York opposed the move as they feared it would facilitate the abandonment of Upper Canada -- west of Kingston -- by the British Army in wartime. They also had vested interests in York. In opposing the British government proposal, the Tories elaborated on their view of the American military threat.]

13. *Kingston Chronicle*, (Macaulay editorials), 26 November & 24 December 1819, and 8 December 1820; Strachan and Robinson, *Observations on the Policy of a General Union*, 1824, 5; Robinson Paper, 18-19, Robinson to Marquess of Normanby on restoring security and confidence, 29 March 1839; PAO, Merritt Papers, vol. 13, J.B. Robinson to W.H. Merritt, 27 December 1837; *The Church*, (Bethune editorial), 13 February 1841; Robinson, *Canada Bill*, 1840, 49; and PAO, Robinson Papers, 1813-17, 14, John Beverley Robinson, "Draft argument against the Removal of the Seat of Government", 1816. The quote is from the Robinson, "Draft argument", 1816, 14.

14. Robinson, *Letter to Earl Bathurst*, 26 December 1824, 4 - 9; and Robinson, "Removal of the Seat of Government", 1816, 8-12. The quotations are from Robinson, "Removal", 1816, 8 & 10, respectively.

15. Robinson to Marquess Normanby, on restoring security and confidence, 29 March 1839, 20-24; PAO, Robinson Papers, J.B. Robinson Letterbook, 1814 - 1862, 11, Robinson to Strachan, 29 June 1822, and 241, Strachan to Robinson, 1 September 1822; PAO, Robinson Papers, 1813-17, 3 & 8, Strachan, " Reasons

against removing the seat of Government of Upper Canada from York to Kingston", 1816; and Robinson, *Letter to Earl Bathurst*, 26 December 1824, 6; and Spragge, *Strachan Letter Book*, 84, Strachan to Col. Harvey, February 1815. The quotation is from Strachan, "Reasons against removing the Seat of Government", 1816, 3.

16. Robinson, *Letter to Earl Bathurst*, 26 December,1824, 2 & 4; PAO, Strachan Papers, reel 3, Strachan to My Dear Sir, 18 January 1836; Robinson, "'Plan for General Legislative Union", 1822, 32; Strachan and Robinson, *Observations on the Policy of a General Union*, 1824, 5; PAO, Robinson Papers, J.B. Robinson Letterbook, 1814-1862, 241, Strachan to Robinson, 1 September 1822; and Robinson, *Canada Bill*, 1840, 75-79. The quotations are from Robinson, *Canada Bill*, 1840, 78, and the Strachan letters of 18 January 1836 and 1 September 1822, respectively.

17. Robinson, *Letter to Earl Bathurst*, 26 December 1824, 4; Strachan, *Remarks on Emigration from the United Kingdom, Addressed to Robert Wilmot Horton, Esq., m.p., Chairman of the Select Committee of Emigration in the last Parliament* (London: John Murray, 1827), 142; Strachan and Robinson, *Observations on the Policy of a General Union*, 1824, 5 & 7; and *Kingston Chronicle*, (Macaulay editorial), 30 August 1822.

18. Robinson Papers, 1813-1817, Strachan, "Reasons against removing the Seat of Government", 1816, 7 & 8; Spragge, *Strachan Letter Book*, 97, Strachan, "Remarks on the subject of removing the seat of Government to Kingston", October 1815; Robinson, "Plan for a General Legislative Union", 1822, 33; and Robinson, *Canada Bill*, 1840, 40- 41. The quotation is from Strachan, "Reasons against removing the Seat of Government", 1816, 7.

19. Robinson, *Canada Bill*, 1840, 40-41; Strachan, "Reasons against removing the Seat of Government", 1816, 2-3 & 8-9; Robinson, "Draft argument against the Removal of the seat of Government", 1816, 9-10; Charles R. Sanderson, ed., *The Arthur Papers*, vol. I, 417, J.B. Robinson to Lt. Governor Arthur, 5 December 1838; Spragge, *Strachan Letter Book*, 9, "Remarks on the subject of removing the seat of Government to Kingston", October 1815; *Kingston Chronicle*, (Macaulay editorial) 2 December 1819; Robinson, Plan for a General Legislative Union", 1822, 32; PAC, Merritt Papers, vol. 13, J.B. Robinson to William Merritt, 27 December 1837; and Robinson, "Letter to Marquess Normanby on restoring security and confidence", 29 March 1839, 20 & 29. The quotation is from Strachan, "Reasons against removing the Seat of Government", 1816, 3.

[The final section of this chapter has been added to the dissertation text, and is based on the references cited in the following endnotes.]

20. Wellington to My Dear Lord [Bathurst], "Memorandum on the Defence of Canada", London, 1 March 1819, in *Despatches, Correspondence, and Memoranda of Field Marshal Arthur, Duke of Wellington, K.G.*, vol. I (London: John Murray, 1867), 36-44.

21. Library and Archives Canada (LAC), MG11, CO42, vol. 179, reel B-141, 119-122, Duke of Richmond to Earl Bathurst, 10 November 1818.

22. LAC, MG11, CO42, vol. 358, reel B-297, 7-21, John Beverley Robinson to Lord Bathurst, 15 February 1816. The Tories concurred with Lt. Col Harvey who pointed out to the Colonial Office that a strategy of withdrawing British troops from Upper Canada upon the outbreak of war -- as advocated by the Duke of Richmond -- would do nothing to protect the persons and property of the loyal British subjects of Upper Canada. They would be left vulnerable to attack, harassment, and despoilment, at the hands of American marauders during any period of American occupation.

23. National Archives of Scotland, GD45/3/332, 1080- 1085, Lt. Col. Harvey, "Memorandum on the defence of the Canadas", 7 November 1818. The Library and Archives Canada has a microfilm copy of the Harvey Report (Dalhousie Muniments, MG24, A12, reel A533, Film 9, Section 3), but it is illegible in some parts. It was Lt. Col. Harvey who devised and led the surprise night attack by British troops -- at the Battle of Stoney Creek (6 June 1813) -- that stopped the American invasion army of Major-General Henry Dearborn in its advance against the Burlington Heights. See Phillip Buckner, "Harvey, Sir John", *Dictionary of Canadian Biography*, VIII.

Chapter Five – A British National Character

1. John Beverley Robinson, *Letter to the Rt. Hon. Earl Bathurst*, 26 December 1824, 149-150. The quotation is from the *Letter*, 149.

2. *Kingston Chronicle*, "One of the People", 28 May 1831; PAO, Robinson Papers, Private Letters of J.B. Robinson and Family Letter Book, J.B. Robinson to Thomas Ridout, 16 November 1815, 3, and J.B. Robinson to Rev. Strachan, 7 December 1815, 5; PAO, John Beverley Robinson Diaries, entries for November 10 & 29, and December 16 & 30, 1815, and January 18, 1816; *Kingston Chronicle*, (Macaulay editorial), 20 September 1822; and Strachan, *Sermon for General Thanksgiving*, 3 June 1814, 6. The first quotation is from

"One of the People", May 1831, 28, the second and third quotes from Robinson to Ridout, 16 November 1815, and the fourth quote from the Robinson diary entry of December 30, 1815, respectively.

3. PAO, J.B. Robinson Diaries, entries for 18 January 1816, 6 November 1815, and 5 December 1815. The quotations are from the diary entries of 18 January 1816, and 6 November 1815, respectively.

4. PAO, Strachan Sermons, Box E, Psalm 29:11, "Lord Will Give Strength", 4 November 1855, 4-5. The quotations are from the sermon, 4 and 4-5, respectively.

5. PAO, Strachan Sermons, Box E, Psalm 29:11, "Lord Will Give Strength", 4 November 1855, 4-5; PAO, Robinson Papers 1839- 1842, John Beverley Robinson to Marquess of Normanby, Secretary of State for the Colonies, on measures necessary for restoring the security and confidence of Canada, 29 March 1839, 22-23; *U.E. Loyalist*, (Robert Stanton editorial), 7 July 1827; PAO, J.B. Robinson Diaries, entry for 10 November 1815, 79; PAO, Macaulay Papers, reel 1, William Macaulay to John Macaulay, 2 February 1818; PAO, Robinson Papers, Letterbook, 15, J.B. Robinson, Copy of Note to Wilmot Horton, Under Secretary of State for the Colonies, 15 April 1823, and 12, Robinson to Strachan, 29 June 1822; PAO, Macaulay Papers, reel #2, Robert Stanton to John Macaulay, 16 January 1833; PAO, Strachan Papers, reel 3, Strachan, "Working of the Union", 6 March 1839, 7; and PAO, Macaulay Papers, reel 1, John Beverley Robinson to John Macaulay, 25 March 1823. The quotations are from the Strachan sermon of 4 November 1855, 5, from William Macaulay to John Macaulay, 2 February 1818, Robinson to Wilmot Horton, 15 April 1823, and Robinson to John Macaulay, 25 March 1823.

6. PAO, Strachan Sermons, Box D, John 4:16, "'Dwelleth in God", 20 January 1856, 19; Strachan, *A Letter to the Rev. Thomas Chalmers. D.D., Professor of Divinity at the University of Edinburgh, on the Life and Character of the Right-Reverend Dr. Hobart, Bishop of New-York, North America* (New York: Swords, Stanford & Co., 1832, 40-41; PAO, Robinson Papers, 1813-17, Strachan, "Reasons against removing the Seat of Government of Upper Canada from York to Kingston", 1816, 8; Spragge, ed., *Strachan Letter Book*, 84, Strachan to Col. Harvey, February 1815. The quotations are from the Strachan sermon of 20 January 1856, 19, and Strachan, "Reasons against removing the Seat of Government", 1816, 8, respectively.

7. J.B. Robinson, *A Letter to the Rt. Hon. Earl Bathurst*, 26 December 1824, 49-50, 56 & 59-62; Strachan and Robinson, *Observations on the Policy of a General Union of all the British province of North America* (London: W. Cloves, 1824), 16; J.B. Robinson, "Plan for a General Legislative Union of the British

Provinces in North America, Addressed to Lord Bathurst in 1822" in *Four Pamphlets on Confederation and Union of the Canadas* (Toronto: Canadiana House, 1967), 23-27 & 40; PAO, Strachan Papers, reel 2 (typescript), John Strachan to Robert Wilmot Horton, "Observations on the Policy of a General Union of all the British Provinces of North America", 25 May 1824, 1-2 & 6-8; PAO, Macaulay Papers, reel 1, Strachan to John Macaulay, 15 December 1824. The quotations are from Robinson, "Plan for a General Legislative Union", 1822, 40, Strachan to John Macaulay, 15 December 1824, and Robinson, *A Letter to the Rt. Hon. Earl Bathurst*, 26 December 1824, 6, respectively.

Strachan and Robinson consulted together in preparing their respective proposals for a union of the British North American provinces. Moreover, both men had read an earlier plan drafted by Chief Justice Sewell of Lower Canada for a union of the provinces of British North America. Strachan and Robinson were familiar also with the much earlier 'Plan of 1754' for a union of the American colonies, which was drafted by Governor Hutchinson of Massachusetts and modified by Benjamin Franklin. (See Robinson, *A Letter to the Rt. Hon. Earl Bathurst*, 140-141, and Strachan, "Observations on the Policy of a General Union", 2-3).

8. Robinson, "Plan for a General Legislative Union", 1822, 25, 31-32 & 39; Robinson, *A Letter to the Rt. Hon. Earl Bathurst*, 26 December 1824, 56-59; [Strachan], *Observations on a bill for Uniting the Legislative Councils and Assemblies of the Provinces of Lower Canada and Upper Canada in one Legislature* (London: W. Clowes, 1824), 1-2; PAO, Strachan Papers, reel 3, Strachan, "Working of the Union", 6 March 1839, 1 & 4-5; *Kingston Chronicle*, 10 September 1831, "One of the People", [Rev.A.H. Burwell]; and *Kingston Chronicle*, 3 September 1831, "Colonial representation in the Imperial Parliament", and 26 May 1832, editorial comments on David Chisholm, *Right of the British Colonies to representation in the Imperial Parliament* (Three Rivers: G. Stubbs, n.d.). The quotations are from [Strachan], *Observations on a bill for Uniting*, 1824, 2, Robinson, *Letter to Earl Bathurst*, 26 December 1824, 59, and Robinson, "Plan for a General Legislative Union", 1822, 39, respectively.

The Upper Canadian Tories were familiar with Adam Smith's book, *An Inquiry into the Nature and Causes of the Wealth of Nations* (1776), and were aware that Smith had written: "There is not the least probability that the British Constitution would be hurt by the union of Great Britain with her Colonies --- That Constitution, on the contrary, would be completed by it, and seems to be imperfect without it". Smith was quoted by the *Kingston Chronicle*, 3 September 1831, "Colonial Representation in the Imperial Parliament".

9. Robinson, *A Letter to the Rt. Hon. Earl Bathurst*, 26 December 1824, 7, 49-50 & 59; Spragge, ed., *Strachan Letter Book*, 84, Strachan to Col. Harvey, February 1815; Robinson, "Plan for a General Legislative Union" in *Four Pamphlets*, 28 &30-31; *Kingston Chronicle* (John Macaulay editorial), 23 June 1822. The quotations are from Robinson, "Plan for a General Legislative Union", 1822, 31.

In retrospect, George Grant in *Lament for a Nation, The Defeat of Canadian Nationalism* (Toronto: McClelland and Stewart, 1969, 69) has commented on the historic possibility in the 19th Century of a union of English Canadians and French Canadians on the basis of their common conservative principles and values: "Both the French and the British had limited common ground in their sense of social order -- belief that society required a high degree of law, and respect for a public conception of virtue. .... If their different conservatisms could have become a conscious bond, this nation might have preserved itself. An indigenous society might have continued to exist on the northern half of this continent."

In many ways, such a union would seem to have been perfectly natural, given the compatibility of the traditional religious and social values of the French Canadians and the Upper Canada Tories. Indeed, the Upper Canadian Tories admired the religiosity of the French Canadians and the work of the Roman Catholic parish priests. However, the opposition of 'the French party' leaders to commercial development and to British immigration, and their adopting of democratic republican political ideals (albeit to serve conservative ends) under the leadership of Louis-Joseph Papineau, acted against any possibility of a French Canadian-Tory alliance. Moreover, the Tory belief that the French Canadians, in their own best interests, should be assimilated, peacefully and gradually, but assimilated none-the-less to what the Tories regarded as a higher form of civilization, precluded such an alliance to attain conservative ends.

Following the rebellion of 1837, the gradual emergence during the 1840s of a new direction in French Canadian nationalism with its defence of the British connection and the monarchy, and the changed attitude of the French Canadian political leaders toward economic development, made possible a French-English conservative alliance, once English Canadian conservatives accepted 'the French fact'. The French *bleu*-English conservative alliance lasted from 1854 to the death of Sir John A. Macdonald in 1891. The Liberal-Conservative Party of Macdonald was a coalition formed of conservatives and moderate Reformers from Canada West (Upper Canada) – who rejected 'old fogey Toryism' -- with the French bloc from Canada East (Lower Canada). On the transformation of French Canadian nationalism after the rebellion of 1837-1838, see Jacques Monet, *The Last Cannon Shot: A study of French-Canadian*

Nationalism, 1837-1850 (Toronto: University of Toronto Press, 1969).

10. Strachan and Robinson, *Observations on the Policy of a Grand Union*, 1824, 16; Robinson, *Letter to the Rt. Hon. Earl Bathurst*, 26 December 1824,16; Strachan, *Sermon on the Death of Bishop Mountain*, 3 July 1825, 12; PAO, Strachan Papers, reel 3, "Working of the Union", 6 March 1839, 7; Robinson, *Canada Bill*, 1840, 18-19: PAO, Strachan Papers, reel 2, (typescript), Strachan to Robert Wilmot Horton, "Observations on the Policy of a General Union of all the British Provinces of North America", 25 May 1824, 1, 3-4 & 9-10.

11. Robinson, *Letter to the Rt. Hon. Earl Bathurst*, 26 December 1824, 143, 50-2; Robinson, "Plan for a General Legislative Union", 1822, 28 & 34-37; Robinson, *Canada Bill*, 1840, 17-19 & 22-23; Robinson to the Marquess of Normanby, "Measures necessary for restoring security and confidence to Canada", 29 March 1839, 18; PAO, Strachan Papers, reel 2 (typescript), Strachan, "Observations on the Policy of a General Union of all the British Provinces of North America", 25 May 1824, 11; and Strachan and Robinson, *Observations on the Policy of a General Union*, 1824, 13-14. The quotes are from: Robinson, *Canada Bill*, 1840, 18 & 19, respectively.

Throughout the first half of the 19th Century, the Tories held to their assessment that Canada, because of the real limits to her potential population growth, could never hope "to maintain itself as an independent nation upon the American continent". The only seeming exception was a comment by John Strachan in 1843 to the effect that it would be "a century ... before we are able to set up free & independent for ourselves". (PAO, Strachan Letter Book, 1839-43, reel 11, Strachan to Hon. Edward Ellice, [March 1843].

12. PAO, Strachan Papers, reel 2, (typescript), Strachan, "Observations on the Policy of a General Union", 25 May 1824, 11; Strachan and Robinson, *Observations on the Policy of a General Union*,1824,14; Robinson, *Letter to the Rt. Hon. Earl Bathurst*, 26 December 1824, 3; Robinson, "Plan for a General Legislative Union" in *Four Pamphlets*, 35-37 & 39; and Robinson, *Canada Bill*, 1840, 23. The quotations are from Robinson, "Plan for a General Legislative Union", 39.

Part Three

The Balanced Constitution

Chapter Six - The British Constitution

Chapter Seven - The Constitution of Upper Canada

".... according to the natural course of things, there will be found in every state, which has emerged from barbarism, three different orders of persons, each struggling for the supremacy, -- the King, anxious to establish the uncontrolled dominion of his own power, -- the Aristocracy, desirous of strengthening and extending the privileges of their order at the expense both of King and Commons, --and ... the People, struggling for additional liberty to themselves, and for the more effectual control of the other orders of the state with the implied, if not acknowledged, purpose of setting the government on a democratical basis. ... How are these evils to be prevented? ... Experience, ... has happily solved the problem [in the principles and workings of the balanced British Constitution.]"

Observations on the British Constitution
(Edinburgh & London, 1831).

"Chief Justice John Beverley Robinson". By George Theodore Berthon, 1846.
The Law Society of Upper Canada Art Collection

Chapter Six

The British Constitution

In seeking to foster a British national character in Upper Canada, the Upper Canadian Tories did not overlook the importance of the constitution of the province – the Constitutional Act of 1791 – which was based on the British Constitution. Indeed, in their minds the British national character of the province and the constitution were inseparable and interdependent. For the Tories, the constitution of a state -- and the institutions that supported it -- played a major role in shaping the national character of a people, in addition to maintaining the stability of the state and public order. What was more, the viability of the constitution was dependent in turn upon the character of the people.

The character of the people was not only shaped by the constitution of a state, but also was dependent on, and formed by, the matrix of religious, educational, and political institutions of a state, and the social habits and customs of the society, which needed to be maintained unimpaired for the benefit of succeeding generations. Since the constitution contributed to the formation of the national character, it was imperative as well that a proper knowledge of the principles and practical workings of the constitution be propagated amongst the people so that the government might continue to function properly for the benefit of the present and future generations.

In sum, one major components of the National Policy of the Upper Canadian Tories, was the need to protect and maintain the constitution of the Province of Upper Canada. In that effort, they strove to explain the origins, principles, and workings of its prototype – the British constitution – to the people of Upper Canada, within the context of God's scheme of things as they understood it.

The Sovereignty of God: Providence

For the government of man, as for life in general, the Tories believed that God had decreed certain immutable principles of justice and right which all nations were enjoined to follow. The Scriptures were not silent on a matter of such importance as the principles of government and politics. Far from being completely dominated by the will of man, government was subject to God's direction. The evolution of human government was not regarded as a process which was characterized by accident or contingency, or moulded by "man alone" acting solely in response to events. Government was neither the creature of man, nor purely the product of circumstances. Both government and human society were ordained and instituted by God "for His own purposes", and were under the control and direction of Providence. (1)

In a Christian community, living under God, there could be, and was, no other sovereign than the "Divine Saviour, Jesus Christ", the son of God, to whom all power belonged. God was the creator and the supreme sovereign and ruler of the universe, but He acted through his Son, who as the mediator between God and man, was "the Head and exemplar of all obedience". In God's scheme of things, religion could not be separated from public affairs because:

> God governs the world and rules over all things, human and divine.

God's moral law was everywhere supreme, and His moral governance was continually shaping the destinies of all peoples. The workings of providence were such that no nation could escape God's visitation and the certainty of retribution if a people refused to serve God. For nations and for men -- both as individuals and as citizens -- there was in all things a right and a wrong:

> it is not a matter of indifference which side a man takes, for all of us will be judged hereafter for the side we take.

Man would be punished for breaches of the moral law in all spheres of human activity -- and not just the religious -- either as a member of a nation which had aroused God's wrath, or as an individual. Whatever his situation, man was answerable to God for his actions. (2)

Only in subordination to God's Will -- as made known in the Bible -- could the blessings of Divine Providence be assured to any nation. Scriptures set forth all of man's duties and privileges in every walk of life, delineated his responsibilities, and provided rules to guide the conduct of both ruler and subjects. Neither the government of a Christian nation, nor the different social duties incumbent on man, could be separated from Christianity. The Christian religion supplied the only sure basis of happiness, morality, and freedom, because its precepts were those of justice, charity, and peace. Christian precepts were not intended to be confined solely to private life, they were such that:

they ought at the same time to direct the resolutions of princes, and to guide all their undertakings, as being the only means of giving stability to human institutions and remedying their imperfections.

It was not to be expected that rulers would always live up to the "sublime principles" of Christianity; but it was vastly important that they be made aware of the workings of Providence and the necessity of governing their conduct and actions by the principles which were essential to the wellbeing of society. (3)

The Origin of Society and Government

In the beginning, God created man -- both male and female -- in his own likeness, and "adopted their natural constitution" to suit the state of society for which He intended them. Through the holy estate of matrimony, and the authority which He gave to man over both his wife and children, the Creator founded "the fact of union in society". The head of the family was given authority over his wife and children:

to be ruled and governed and taught by him in subjection of their will to his, as he was bound to the will of God.

In acting for His own purposes, God thereby had constituted human society and placed human beings in the relations that He had ordained for them, so that they might fulfill the duties of this life, and partake of this life, according to His will.

In being born into a family, man was by his very nature a social being who was intended to live and act in society. To that end, God had further endowed man with the gift of language, the faculty of speech, and a basic reasoning capacity, which aided by the expansion of his intellectual capabilities over time, enabled him to "converse rationally" about his surroundings and his relationship to God, the Creator. Man was equipped by God to function as a member of society, and to tend to the needs and interests of society, with each individual acting "in his own sphere of duty", and responsible ultimately to God. (4)

In instituting human society, God had also instituted government through placing the woman and her children under the authority and governance of her husband. The family unit was in effect the very essence of society and government, for:

> Family stands in membership under *fatherhood*; to fatherhood government is committed. The family is the society: its government is parental. All these, by the act and order of God in the beginning, were set together and set up in one, and do, stand in the actual condition of *parentage* to all society and government for future times.

Human society and government were inseparable in their origin and being. Paternal authority and the domestic order, as ordained by God, were the very basis of civil government and the means by which all men were conditioned -- through being under direction and control from infancy -- to the subjection and subordination which government required. By its very nature, the family was "a miniature kingdom" both in the exercise of the authority of one over many, and the fostering of a disposition to govern and to be governed.

The conditioning which was received within the family was of the essence for the proper functioning of society, because human society could not continue without government. It was a fact that was attested to by the experience of even voluntary associations, which invariably found it necessary to adopt regulatory rules and to recognize a leader. The conclusion to be drawn from the Tory view of the origin of government was perfectly clear:

> namely that government under which society exists, is the ordinance and institution of God, and not of the people; that it was His outward personal act. (5)

Government was a gift from God to man to facilitate the carrying out of His purposes. Since it was God who created the world, he was consequently the proprietor, and all legitimate authority and power was derivative of His sovereignty. What could not be "traced up to Him" was unlawful and usurped. All power, regardless of rank, was granted from God for a His purposes.

In the first instance, through constituting the human family and establishing its order, God had installed Adam as the universal monarch of the human family, which for many generations remained but one family and one kingdom. God directly exercised his divine sovereignty in deputing a portion of his authority to man, and thereby entrusting to Adam the care of "all the interests of human society". Adam was acutely aware that in administering this "trust and charge", that he had received it from God; and that none of his children, who were placed in subordination to him, were free to reject his paternal authority without involving themselves in rebellion against God's sovereign power.

The source of all authority was found in the origin of society and government, and that authority had descended through "every marriage solemnized among men". It was embodied in the resultant family units that by a divine 'law of descent' bound father to son and son to father. Although marriage was a product of human society, it was nevertheless a divine institution and God played a real part in each union so consummated. Thus, the monarchical form of government was to be found in the earliest government, that of the family, from which all succeeding institutions of government were derived. (6)

The patriarchal rule of the father had sufficed for the purposes of government while the human race was comprised within one extended family, or one kingdom bound by familial affection. However, with an ever-increasing population, patriarchal rule became less and less effective in maintaining social cohesion and order. As society grew, a government making use of the coercive authority of magistrates and judges was required to make up the deficiency and keep society together:

> when that brotherly esteem which had induced [man] to regard
> the interest of each as the interest of the whole, had all but
> vanished....

As men came to be dispersed in distinct societies, each living under their own ruler, the lack of the ties of familial affection and the threat of violence, both external and internal, posed a danger to the peace, happiness and prosperity of the distinct societies and induced them to unite under a single monarch. In that way, at each stage of development, the monarchical form of government was applied in a different fashion to meet the evolving needs of human society. (7)

The historic evolution of power and authority was not a process in any way independent of God. It was indubitable that:

God is *a party* in everything that can possibly concern man, or
that man can possibly do either in detail or as bodies corporate.

Since all power was of God, it was by His "permissive providence, if not by command" that all governments arose. Such social and political relations as evolved were not purely the work of man, nor were they the "arbitrary appointments of God, having no relation or reference to what He is". Man was made in the image of God, and both the creation and the social constitution of man were of God, and a reflection of his being: "the *outactings of Himself in His creatures*". And the very constitution of human society was:

but the *out setting in external facts of that which was in God,
and with God, before the world began.*

In all aspects of life, in any state or nation, there were certain basic abstract truths which had to be recognized, and acted upon, for the continued welfare of society. With respect to government, they consisted of a recognition of its unity under God, and the resultant truths: that governments were in possession of rights bestowed from above by God, and not from below by the will of the people; that laws derived their substance and authority from their being embodiments of God's moral law, and not from any public vote; and that the form of government was sanctified by God, and not subject to the change at the whim of those "who fancy themselves displeased with it".

With respect to society, a basic truth was that society was naturally of a hierarchical order in the form of a pyramid – a very stable figure – comprising all ranks from the very lowest at its broad base to God's vicegerent, the monarch, at its apex. Such a social order was conducive, indeed necessary, to the proper functioning of society, and was not to be tampered with because:

while its constituent parts keep their respective places, a balance
of power and just rights are equally maintained in every part.

It was not for man to seek to overturn the social and political order and to make all authority responsible only to himself. Truth was unchangeable, and it was likewise the case in the relations between God and the human family. Indeed, it could not be otherwise:

> if God's work in setting up human society, under government,
> be the enunciation of eternal principles and relations, …. (8)

The evolution of government had been guided by God from the very beginning, as was witnessed by the Old Testament which declared Him to be:

> the sole and only Lawgiver of his people, their Sovereign King
> and Judge; [and] the Guide, Director, and Leader of all people
> in covenant with him, in all things that concern them.

The directions which God gave to man had taken many forms, among them written commandments, visions, messages through the prophets, and lastly Revelation. And the principles set forth -- justice, morality, and religion -- were such as could not be separated one from the other, or from the sacred eternal truth.

The principles of justice and of morality were derived not from man, but from the Christian religion and ultimately from God. Any system of jurisprudence -- if it were to be "just, and true to the wants of [man's] nature in a state of society" -- could not but embody the principles of the Christian religion:

> the ten commandments put into practice in keeping the public
> peace, and encouraging public virtue.

Neither the rulers who were set over man, nor the will of the fickle multitude, were to be looked to for guidance. They were incapable of sanctioning either a code of morality and justice or of providing the criteria of good government. The eternal principles of human society and government were "something too high for man" – either ruler or subject – to fully comprehend, and any human effort to begin anew was doomed to failure, if the established order were to be overthrown. (9)

Concept of Authority

All rulers derived their just authority from God, and were charged to act always in keeping with God's moral law. Rulers, as the servants of God, received:

> the Royal Power as God's Vicegerent upon earth and [were] His appointed instrument of blessedness to His people.

Hence, English kings were reminded in the Coronation address of the Archbishop of Canterbury that they were subject to Christ, and derived their power from God; and that the happiness and welfare of their subjects depended upon their seeking first, through Christ, the Kingdom of God from which all other blessings would flow.

In legitimate governments, the king had no will of his own to act independently in his executive capacity, but was subordinate to the Will of God and commanded to walk in His way. The words and actions of the king were "but a declaration of the public will, that is, public law whose principles are matter of revelation and divine bounty to man". The king was bound to govern in keeping with the true principles of justice, truth, morality and religion, rather than "the will of man". Having no independent will of their own, and being subject to human frailties -- besides being placed under greater temptations than most men – the king, if he were to carry out his duty successfully, required the gift of God's grace to give him the strength to do good.

For the Upper Canadian Tories, the human will alone was insufficient to bring and hold any man to the ways of God. If the royal power were to be properly exercised, it had to be by a Christian king, "a baptized man", conscious of his 'calling', and aware of his need of divine inspiration and the "spiritual gifts" which the Church -- in the Liturgy prayer for the king -- prayed God to bestow upon him. A good king needed to be in possession of an understanding heart, and hence capable of discerning between good and evil. Only a pious, God-fearing man could faithfully exercise the functions of kingship. (10)

Since all power was of God, rulers possessed an authority "neither of themselves nor for themselves". They were responsible for the exercise of their authority to a higher power. Scriptures taught that rulers were the ministers of God, appointed by God, and subordinate to God, in partaking of an authority that flowed naturally "down from above, and not upward from beneath". Rulers were commanded to fear God, and:

> to worship, and pray to God, and not worship nor pray to the people.

In the natural order of things, rulers were acting in trust in exercising a God-given power and authority, and were accountable to God for their conduct, and not to the people. They were counseled to be always conscious that they stood "in the person of God himself", and to be ever aware of their high and noble function and their final destination in this life. Rulers were charged to look beyond the "paltry self of the moment", and "the temporary and transient praise of the vulgar", and to seek a permanent fame and glory above the vicissitudes of the day. It was believed that:

> such sublime principles ought to be infused into persons of exalted stations; and religious establishments provided, that may continually revive and enforce them.

Although those placed in authority were responsible to God, and not the people, it did not mean that the relationship between ruler and subject was such that the obligations and duties were all one way. True, subjects were specifically commanded to fear their rulers, and "to pray for the Holy Ghost to bless all in authority". They were admonished that God had bestowed upon their governors "His sword of vengeance on the rebellious"; and that all who rebelled against a government ordained by God would receive damnation to themselves. However, rulers were also under constraints with respect to their subjects. The same duties which bound a king in subordination to God's will also obliged him to serve the best interests of his subjects. A king could not but be aware that;

> he is himself a subject, as well as his people, of a far higher tribunal than his own, and that all must follow the same road to virtue, to godliness, to immortality and glory.

The fact that king, and all those who were set in authority over men -- be they princes, magistrates or judges -- possessed more power than others, had consequences. It meant that they were under a much more severe obligation to accomplish greater good through always acting from generosity, wisdom, and impartiality.

To reign in peace and harmony, and secure a willing obedience from his subjects, a Christian prince had to be guided in his conduct by the principles of the Gospel. The proper relationship between ruler and subject was one of "rendering mutual services", tempered by a mutual affection and consciousness that all were members of a Christian nation under God. In sum, all government was parental. Kings occupied the position of the father of a family under a sacred obligation to govern their subjects "in the spirit of paternal tenderness", to protect them and seek always to promote their happiness and well- being. Subjects stood in the relation of children in that they were commanded by God "to honour and reverence and obey their fathers", who were the King and his ministers. (11)

Rejection of the compact theory of government

In believing that God's providence guided all facets of the life of man, and that society and government were coeval, and based upon the natural paternal family relationship which was ordained by God, the Upper Canadian Tories totally rejected the compact theory of the origin of government. They were motivated to do so by the realization that it was the compact theory on the origin of government that provided the rationale and justification for the belief in popular sovereignty by the democratic radicals: the belief that government was founded by the people; that it represented the people; and that all power was of the people.

The compact theory of John Locke (1632-1704) -- as the Tories understood it – posited that man had supposedly existed as an individual in a state of nature for some time prior to the formation of society and government. When man, as an individual, came to realize the value of cooperation in forwarding his personal interests, he came together with others to form "some original compact" of government. It was a compact between 'the people' and certain ones exalted thereby to rule over them. The compact, so formed, was considered to have involved each free individual:

mutually agreeing to surrender up each his natural liberty of doing as he pleased without restraint, and come under the control of a *public will*, submitting [to] a certain extent his own individual will to it, and consenting from it to receive law in all things touching reciprocal duties and relations.

Thus, according to the Lockean compact theory, both society and government originated in "a spontaneous act of the people" who agreed to put constraints upon their natural individual liberty in founding a government to better protect man's natural liberty and property.

For the Tories, the Lockean theory of the origin of society and government was "a pure deceit". Its basic premises were a fallacy, which entailed several inconsistencies in the theory. In the first place, it supposed that society and government were not coeval with the creation of man; that man had existed for some time in a solitary natural state where he was totally lacking in all social intercourse, marital relations, or parental government; and that human beings grew up as solitary individuals with individual rights and interests.

In the nature of things, such a situation was regarded as impossible by the Tories. Children could not be raised "to shift for themselves" outside of the structure of the family and paternal authority. In such a disassociated "ante- and anti-social state", man could not have come to any knowledge of the blessings of society; nor would he have developed his understanding and a common language. In a solitary state, man could not have acquired the knowledge and faculties which were required to establish a complex form of government and laws sufficient to attain the ends supposedly desired: the preservation of man's basic natural rights and property. A society and government could not be established in a moment of time simply by a general consent of individuals in a state of nature.

The problem of transition to society and government was complicated further – where the Lockean compact theory was concerned --when one considered the question of the nature of man. If a state of individual isolation was the natural state of man, as this theory held, then man could not have a natural tendency to rise beyond his primitive state. On the contrary, man would be "bound by the law of after his kind". In which case, it would have been:

as much his nature to continue in this condition as it is for a brute beast to continue in his [primitive natural] condition, and be incapable of himself to come out of it. Some animals were gregarious, and others were solitary, and they never become otherwise. They were so from the first.

The only possible explanation for the supposed transition from an original solitary individual state of nature to that of society and government – as espoused by Locke -- was that it might have occurred "by a simultaneous universal *miracle*": an act of God that had affected all men at the same time. However, this was a postulate that "the philosophical account" of the origin of society and government would not admit. (12)

Lockean political theory to the contrary, the Upper Canadian Tories believed that man was created as a social being by God and raised within a God-ordained family structure under the authority and governance of the father, from whence man derived his concepts and ideas concerning the value of society and government. As society and government evolved out of the family unit, higher forms of society and government were formed in response to changing circumstances and guided always by God the Father.

View of Human Nature

For the Tories, the balanced British constitution had evolved to meet the needs of human nature. As Christians, they believed in original sin: that the nature of man – from the Fall of Adam -- was morally and spiritually corrupted; and that man in his natural state was prone to evil. Man, of his own free will, was incapable of controlling his passions and persisting in the pursuit of 'the good' in keeping with God's revealed Will.

Moreover, as Anglicans, they believed that only through faith in Christ and baptism into the Christian Church – in entering into Christ, receiving God's saving grace, and being empowered by the Holy Spirit – could man be justified and enabled to live a life of good works, charity and self-restraint in obedience to the revealed Will of God. In sum, good works, charity and self-restraint, and the living of a moral, virtuous, and spiritual life, flowed of necessity from "a true and lively faith" in Christ and the attaining of justification and righteousness in the ways of God.

In Upper Canada, there were many non-believers and men who did not possess 'a true and lively faith'. Hence, the political concern for the Tories, given man's 'evil nature' in consequence of 'the Fall', was how to maintain the state of civilization -- which society had attained in Britain-- in the frontier settlements in the wilderness of Upper Canada. The problem was how to counteract the tendency of such men --- of which history provided ample evidence – to revert to a more savage state when left to themselves:

> for when left to their free choice, men in the mass always do
> that which tends to destroy one another and render society
> impossible.

In effect, the unredeemed man by his very nature was incapable of self-government, but rather required the continual exertion of a power distinct from and superior to himself to counteract his evil propensities and keep him in a state of society. Such a need was fully attested to by the obvious necessity of all human governments, throughout history, to employ physical force to maintain public order. (13)

To the Upper Canadian Tories, as of the 1830s, it appeared that the democratic radical proponents of the Lockean theory of the origin of society and government were motivated "by a hatred of Christianity". It was manifested in a concurrent desire to avoid all "acknowledgement of God and the Church" with respect to government, and everything which concerned man in the public sphere.

Once men were convinced that their society and government originated solely in "the will, wisdom, and work" of man, irrespective of God, it was but a small step to the conclusion that man did not require God's aid in human affairs at all. Through confining the act of Creation to a point in time, and viewing man as a creature "with certain blank capabilities" and a reasoning capacity sufficient to take care of all of his needs, God was removed from everyday life. According to the Lockean theory, man was able:

> to bring a living, self-sustaining order out of himself, the same
> as brute animals fulfill their destinies by the law of their several
> instincts.

For the Anglican Tories, such a belief was totally false and unscriptural. It was an outright denial of the need of God's active providence and for the necessity of conforming to God's moral law as laid down in the Bible. Whether it was called man's "natural liberty" or considered as an 'inner light' gift of God's grace, it was a fallacy to insist on acting:

> according to the rights and dictates of our own consciences over which there can be no outward law of control.

Such views of individual natural rights were a denial of God's dominion, and the teaching of His Church. The belief that man of his own volition and action created society and the state, could not but give rise to several corollaries: viz. that all political power resides in the people; and that:

> the people's will is the sole rule of law, and to them government should be responsible.

For the Tories, the political doctrines of the liberal-Whigs in England, which were based on the political thought and epistemology of John Locke, were clearly an outright denial of God's sovereignty. They were "atheistic" in the extreme (in the Scriptural sense of being 'without God', rather than a denial of God), and consequently were denounced and opposed by the Upper Canadian Tories. (14)

The Evolution of the British Constitution

The Tories believed that government was not the creation of man at a moment in time. It had evolved over time from the original parental government of the family which was ordained by God. Moreover, it had evolved "under the wise direction of God's overruling Providence" in response to the changing needs of man in each developing civilization. To this process, the British Constitution was no exception. It was, in its maturity, the product of "a thousand years" of effort and experience. (15)

The British Constitution was formed "by the exigencies of the times", but the underlying principles which guided its development were those of the Christian religion as the constitution grew to "consistency and perfection", in so far as anything of man could approach perfection. Given his corrupted nature, and his propensity to decline into savagery when left to his own devices, man could not of himself have evolved higher forms of government. To do so, he needed a uniform standard or sense to guide his effort, which the principles and values of the Christian religion provided.

In refining and improving deficient human laws, the builders of the British Constitution had had a revealed system of principles to draw upon through living in a Christian society, and in being imbued and inspired with the spirit of the Bible. Thus, the British Constitution "grew up in the light and liberty of the Gospel", and the principles of the constitution and the spirit of the laws were Christian principles. To the extent which the constitution and the laws approached perfection, they were based on the same principles of justice and morality as the Christian religion, and every legitimate system of jurisprudence was bound by those same realities. (16)

In England, it was through the means of the established National Church that the Christian principles and values, so essential to the evolution of the British Constitution, had been diffused throughout the population. And, over time, Christian principles had come to form the basis of the whole polity of the nation. As such, the established Church was inseparable from the state, and a part of its very essence, rather than a mere appendage. The connection between Church and state historically was such that the people of England considered the Established Church to be:

> the foundation of their whole constitution, with which, and
> with every part of which, it holds an indissoluble union.

The connection between the Church and State, as seen by the Tories in the evolution of the British Constitution, was a product of English history, as well as in keeping with God's scheme of things. On the one hand, the king and constitution were ordained by God -- the latter by His permissive providence, if not by His direct action -- to defend and guard His Church and people from all external danger and to ensure that all men were kept "within the reach of the Church and her ordinances". On the other hand, the Holy Catholic Apostolic Church – of which the Anglican Church was a member -- was commissioned by God to convey His Word and His Will to the king, office holders, and the people to instruct them:

in all things pertaining to human society and the true interests of mankind.

Otherwise, man was "left to his own ingenuity and industry" in all matters that were not directly concerned with the principles of truth, morality and justice. However, where truth, morality and justice were concerned, human reason was not sufficient for man's guidance. Given his corrupted reason and selfish passions, it was necessary that man be subject to the "authority of revelation". In effect, the British Constitution was the joint production of God and man, as was every production of human arts, because:

> man *creates* nothing, but he *builds* many things of materials made to his hand. Revealed principles are the abstract materials of truth, justice and morality, which he builds into the fabrick [sic] of human society. The proper adjustment of parts may be left to human judgment and experience. (17)

The whole of human life and government had to have reference to the eternal principles of truth, justice and morality, "and the facts founded on them". To "connect the human understanding and affections to the divine" was the role of the National Church, which from its founding in England expounded "a public standard of moral truth from which there was no appeal". The teachings of the National Church embodied the first principles of society and government.

Among the political principles which the National Church propagated, were: paternity in government; the need for subordination and obedience to God's ministers and His will; and the need of "a common centre for political and moral unity" for the nation, which was found in the King ruling in accordance with God's moral law. The Church taught that the government had a positive moral role to play in society, which involved "the recognition of human jurisprudence as the heaven-appointed guardian of the civil and moral interests" of mankind. Thus, government was to draw its vitality and moral values from the revealed truth, rather than deriving its sanction and principles from the people "whose conduct and whose interests it superintends". Such were the principles -- as taught by the National Church – upon which the British Constitution was founded and continued to receive its sustenance. (18)

Historically, the British Constitution -- in its evolution -- had witnessed many struggles in a successful effort to strike a proper balance through vindicating and defending "the natural rights of man" (in the sense of a right to paternal government based upon God's moral law and subordinate to God rather than to the earthly sovereign's arbitrary will), while acknowledging the "reasonable and high prerogative of supreme Executive power". It was continual struggle to achieve and maintain an equipoise to avoid succumbing to either the tyranny of the one or the tyranny of the many -- between royal absolutism and mob rule. Those who contended for "true and rational liberty" had been, and were continually, opposed by the proponents of either one or the other of the two extremes: despotism on the one hand; and anarchy and/or anarchism on the other.

The constitutional struggle, as viewed by the Tories, was marked by a series of attainments: the Magna Carta (1215), the right to petition the Crown (1406), the Petition of Right (1628), the Habeas Corpus Act (1679), the right of parliament to impeach the King's ministers for misconduct (1681), and finally -- following the Glorious Revolution of 1688 -- the Coronation Oath of 1689 and the Bill of Rights of 1689.

For the Upper Canadian Tories, the Magna Carta was the great guarantor of the 'ancient rights and liberties of Englishmen'. The great charter was drafted by Stephen Langton, the Archbishop of Canterbury, to resolve a conflict between King John III and his rebellious barons. It was sworn to by both parties in Runnymede meadow on June 15, 2015. The Charter guaranteed the rights and liberties of the English Church and its prerogatives, guaranteed the ancient liberties and free customs of the City of London and the boroughs, and granted merchants a right to a free travel and exercise of their commerce within and without of England, and established a right to trial by jury of one's peers according to the laws of England and the degree of the offense, as well as a right to justice without any undue delay. Moreover, the Charter forbade the confiscation of lands and properties, and the imposition of fines, contrary to the laws of the land, and concluded that:

> the men of our kingdom have and hold all the aforesaid liberties, rights and concessions, well and peacefully, freely

and quietly, fully and wholly, for themselves and their heirs ...
in all respects and all places forever.

Subsequently, the 'ancient rights and liberties of Englishmen' were incorporated into a series of parliamentary acts which were more specific in detail, although the Magna Carta maintained its lustre as the bedrock of 'the rights of Englishmen'. For the Tories of Upper Canada, the crowning achievement in the struggle to maintain the balance of the British constitution and 'the rights of Englishmen', were the acts of the constitutional settlement following the Glorious Revolution of 1688.

The revised Coronation Oath (1 Will. & Mary, c.6, 1688, enacted 1689) was administered to King William and Queen Mary upon their succeeding James II. It required the new joint monarchs, and their successors, to swear -- in keeping with "the Law and Ancient Usage of this Realme" -- to maintain the statute laws and customs of the kingdom, as well as the spiritual and civil rights and properties of all the people and inhabitants of the country; and to govern the people of "the Kingdome of England and the Dominions" in accordance with the statutes enacted by Parliament and the existing laws and customs.

Moreover, the monarchs swore to execute all laws and judgements with mercy; and to do the utmost in their power to "Maintaine the Laws of God, the true Profession of the Gospell and the Protestant Reformed Religion Established by Law", and the rights and privileges in law pertaining to the Established Church, its bishops and clergy, for the carrying out of the duties committed to their charge.

The Bill of Rights (1 Will. & Mary, c.2, 1688, enacted 1689), listed the charges against King James II who had 'abdicated' the throne, and the Bill re-iterated the "ancient rights and liberties" of Englishmen. It incorporated the rights and liberties of the earlier Petition of Right, while elaborating on the rights of Parliament and the limitations on the executive power of the king. The Bill of Rights declared that the king could not suspend or dispense with laws, or their execution, without the consent of Parliament; and reconfirmed that the imposition of taxes was illegal without the consent of Parliament.

Furthermore, the Bill of Rights reaffirmed the right of the subject to petition the King for redress; forbade the maintenance of a standing army in the Kingdom during peacetime without the consent of Parliament; permitted Protestant subjects to keep arms for their personal defence; required elections to be free of coercion by the government; and guaranteed freedom of speech, debate, and proceedings in Parliament.

The Bill of Rights Act also forbade the imposition of excessive bail or fines, and 'cruel or unusual punishments' by the king and the courts; required jurors to be properly impaneled and freeholders to serve on juries in high treason trials; ruled that all fines and forfeitures were illegal and void unless imposed by a due process of law; and demanded that Parliament be called at frequent intervals to redress grievances and to amend, strengthen, and preserve the laws.

Each of the historic constitutional enactments in turn, as cited by the Upper Canadian Tories, were regarded as having brought the British Constitution closer to its final perfection, which had been forged in the "Glorious Revolution of 1688", and its immediate aftermath. From that process, the British Constitution had emerged:

> as near the standard necessary for practical perfection, both
> moral and political, as wayward and imperfect man can arrive.

That perfection was found in the "limited constitutional monarchy" so established and the rule of law based on God's moral law. It was based upon a love of order, and embraced all the vital principles of society and government in a balanced form of government. The constitution of 1688-89 avoided the despotism of one man, as well as the tyranny of the populace which was considered by the Tories to be undeniably far worse. (19)

The constitution of 1688-89 corrected the abuses of the increasingly absolutist government of the Roman Catholic monarch, King James II, and denied that the king's free will alone was the source of all sovereignty. More specifically, it repudiated the old maxim of King James I – "*A Deo Rex, a rege lex*" – that royal power comes from God, while legal power comes from the King. To the contrary, the constitutional settlement of 1688-89 affirmed that there was:

> no *jure divino* right to legislate and rule by autocratical sway,
> -- by the whim or caprice of one individual.

The British Constitution -- as it had evolved as of 1688-89 -- supported a limited monarchy, which was confined by both public law – which was based on a God-given standard of morality and justice beyond human approach -- and "by the acknowledged right and influence of other parts of the body politic". (20)

The Balance of the Constitution

All government had to maintain a balance between liberty and authority. The very "infirmity of human nature" necessitated that power should always be limited. Both despotic government and the purely democratic were rejected by the Tories because they were based upon a common fallacy: the presumption that either an individual or mankind at large possessed the integrity of heart and sufficient "virtue, impartiality and soundness" to govern man without the necessity of extraneous checks or control. Prudence dictated that no human power should be left incontrollable, but rather should be restrained by a division of authority. It was preferable that human power be limited in a system of dynamic balance, such as that of the British constitution, wherein each authority could maintain itself and prevent either the monarch or the Commons attaining an unfettered ascendancy over the other.

With the balanced constitution, the people -- through their representatives -- had an essential role to play in controlling an authority which otherwise might become despotic. Yet, the people had no right to make all authority responsible to their own will. If the people usurped all governing power, they would work their own destruction as was clearly shown by the experience of the English republic under the Commonwealth (1649-1653), which had to rely upon the Army to maintain its control over the people.

It was requisite that some degree of power be exercised by the people in Parliament. However, all power could not be vested in the people, nor could they be excluded from a share of authority, because:

> they had their own place and value in the corporate body, which they did not incorporate and endue with life; though God in His providence had all along used them -- but under the Headship of the King, who is not *their* anointed --- and with

the co-working of other members which they did not originate or form, ….

In sum, the people were an essential component, in God's scheme of things, for the proper functioning of a perfect constitution of government, but were not the sovereign power. In its evolution under God, the British constitution had achieved:

> a happy equipoise of power – this balancing of prerogative and interests -- by which the wholesome control of the many is secured, while the exercise of any capricious executive authority is guarded against.

In its limited monarchy, the British Constitution had attained the aim of all constitutions in placing viable restraints upon undue influence though vesting power in places where it would be least liable to be able to attack "the vitals of the public community in its corporate state". Furthermore, through the representatives of the people and the corporate bodies of the realm being present in parliament, and the government being subject to a public moral law, the constitution embraced the principle of paternalism in ensuring that the wants of all classes of the people would receive attention as they arose.

For the Upper Canadian Tories, it was clearly the duty of the Christian subject, and true patriot, to maintain that equipoise of power by staunchly resisting any "encroachment upon the acknowledged rights of the people", on one hand, and any innovations tending to undermine the established prerogatives of the Crown, on the other hand. (21)

Under the British constitution, the supreme legislative authority was divided and balanced among the King, Lords and Commons with each branch of the Legislature to a large degree independent of the others, and capable of checking any encroachments one upon the other, while mutually uniting to foster the good of the whole nation. Such a balance was necessary in the legislature because of the recognition that "self goes a great way with most men". Although one branch of the legislature might be swayed to put forth measures solely in its own interest, the others could refuse their assent. Consequently, under a balanced constitution, one could be:

morally certain, that these three bodies will seldom concert in any measure that does not appear on the whole beneficial.

The Crown had its prerogatives; the House of Commons, which comprised the representatives of the people, had its privileges; and the House of Lords, which served as an intermediate control upon the Crown and the Commons, possessed its own peculiar rights as a separate estate of the realm. In possessing "a large and inalienable stake in the land", the nobility had a vital interest in government, as well as a hereditary claim to form a part of any government. The House of Lords not only weighed the measures of the Commons, but served to prevent a direct clash between prerogative and privilege. Moreover, through its Lords Spiritual, the House of Lords constituted "the connecting link between church and state" in conveying the Will of God to the King and all others in authority under him.

Although the functioning of the balanced constitution ensured, by a division of the legislative authority, that only measures which were beneficial to the whole nation would become law, the constitutional separation of powers did not impede the achievement of an effective government. Each branch had enough influence on the other to bring about, in the absence of any requirement in law, a "concurrence in opinion between the advisors of the Crown and the Representatives of the people in Parliament".

On the one hand, the King and the nobility possessed, and rightly so, a considerable influence over the House of Commons through various means -- among them the King's control of all appointments to office. On the other hand, the House of Commons, through its control over the voting of taxation and the civil list, had the very machinery of government at its mercy. The Tories observed that, practically speaking, the control of the Commons over the voting of taxes and the civil list, encouraged the King to choose ministers who were agreeable to the people's representatives in parliament. However, the King was under no obligation to appoint his ministers from among the leaders of a party that might attain a majority in the House of Commons.

Government was capable of functioning effectively while maintaining the balance of the constitution, but only so long as a Christian forbearance was exercised between the different branches of the government. It was recognized that in any direct clash between the royal prerogative and parliamentary privileges, the control of the House of Commons over the voting of supply was so great that the people -- through their elected members of parliament -- would inevitably prevail "whether the people be right or wrong". The representatives sent to parliament by the people, however, were expected to support measures for the improvement and common good of the nation as-a-whole; they were not considered to be representatives simply of their constituents.

For the Tories, the members of the House of Commons were not delegates to parliament who were bound to promote the peculiar interests of their riding, as determined by the local electorate. To the contrary, the members of parliament were regarded as being 'representatives of the people' who were elected to engage in rational debate in parliament to determine the measures that would promote the common good and well-being the nation, while making known the interests of their own riding in matters that would impinge directly on the welfare of their constituents. (22)

Unity of the State: Kingship

Every functional system, whether of government or otherwise, required a center or a head to give it unity and stability, and the British Constitution was no exception. In the constitution, the king occupied a position analogous to that of the sun in the solar system. The king was surrounded by bodies in a reciprocal relationship which was governed by the laws of the system, rather than the "caprice of one man". With respect to human society, the natural God-ordained social order was in the form of a pyramidal hierarchy, with the monarch at its crowning apex and the various ranks of society from the highest down to the lowest keeping their respective places below. In such a system, the king was the source of all honour, patronage and executive power, which he was obligated to bestow in a manner that would serve the general welfare – the common good -- and preserve the nation as one united family.

To that end, all executive power resided with the King. He possessed the right to appoint his own ministers, as well as enforce the law. Even the members of parliament, who were elected by the people, received their legislative character from him when sworn into office at the opening of parliament; and the calling and dissolution of parliament was a part of the king's prerogative. In effect, the king could call the legislature into being whenever he needed their advice and assistance or the voting of taxes.

Thus, the Crown was the very essence of unity in the state. The King was the head of the nation in law, and was "present everywhere in his Dominions". The king was a representative of the whole community in being above party spirit, and was supported from below by the loyalty of his subjects. In turn, he was bound to exercise his power and protection equitably for the benefits of his subjects in protecting their rights and maintaining the laws, liberty and property of all subjects. In addition, he was responsible for maintaining the prerogatives of the Crown unimpaired, within the framework of the balanced constitution which embodied a limited constitutional monarchy. (23)

Law and the Constitution

The British Constitution enshrined a government of law in two respects. In one aspect, it was composed of statutes which were fundamental inviolable laws. The statutes set out both the prerogatives of the Crown and the privileges of parliament, and the restrains on the various component powers of the government which were confined "each within its proper sphere". It was a relationship that was "fixed by law for the maintenance of order and the protection of society". While in another aspect, it was a constitution of free and equal laws which guaranteed and protected the life, property and rights of every individual within the state against either arbitrary acts of the sovereign or the "licentiousness of the people".

The King was the sovereign, and held the executive power, but he could not dispense with the Statute Law or the Common Law (case law or precedent developed by judicial decisions), as he was bound by the laws of the nation. As the supreme magistrate, the king's first care was to oversee the administration of the laws, which he did by delegating part of his prerogative to the judges of the realm. So far was the English monarch from seeking to augment its power, that George III, of his own volition, had made judges independent of the Crown by appointing them for life, rather than as previously, during the king's pleasure.

In England, the laws were paramount not only as enshrined in the constitution, but in the sense that all acts of government, as well as the constitutional principles themselves, were based not upon the will of man -- either that of the ruler or subject -- but upon the public law, which --in a legitimate government, such as the government of the United Kingdom -- was God's moral law, the principles of which were revealed in the Bible. (24)

For the Tories, neither the monarch nor the people had any right to violate such a constitution, or to dispense with any of its principles. It was inviolable on two grounds: that of prescriptive right; and that of its consistency with the Word of God and God's scheme of things. With respect to prescriptive rights, the Tories argued that the constitution was a product of centuries of experience and evolution in England; and it embraced "the collected wisdom of the ages". It was the product of a continuity which reached back beyond those who presently enjoyed its benefits. In effect, they were merely the "temporary possessors and life-renters of it". Consequently, they were bound to continue its blessings to their posterity in turn. They possessed no right, under the influence of the whim of the moment, to destroy the whole original fabric of their society. Secondly, and indeed inseparable from the former, was the belief that the British constitution in its maturity was as perfect as any human form of government could be. It was, so the Tories believed:

> a system of justice and truth, calculated to meet all the moral and civil necessities of the nation, and truly adapted in its theory to the moral and physical nature of man.

This was not to say that the Upper Canadian Tories were against any reform in the British government as they viewed it from afar. To the contrary, they recognized that there were defects, but these were the product of time and changing circumstances -- such as the existence of rotten boroughs and the lack of representation for some of the largest towns of England in parliament. It was held that these defects could be, and should be, rectified without infringing upon the integrity of the British Constitution.

In fact, one of the great benefits of the British Constitution was its inherent dynamism and flexibility, which allowed for and facilitated a continuing evolution of laws to meet new needs and circumstances as they emerged over time, without in any way infringing on its basic principles.

Despite all vicissitudes, there were certain basic principles which had to be adhered to, and maintained as inviolable. To the Tory mind:

> you can no more rule a nation by expediency than a private family. Either the constitution is something or nothing – if it be really a substance and not a shadow, it must have some pillars or landmarks – these ought to be preserved whatever new regulations may be introduced into the details."

In sum, the nation needed to maintain its constitutional bulwarks. (25)

The moral necessities and physical wants of man were such that he required a system of government which would place him "under the operation and discipline of moral truth and justice". Given his corrupted nature and his capacities for wrongdoing as a free intellectual agent, only the subordination of a people under a government based upon principles existing independently of and above man – God's moral law embodied in the constitution -- could keep him from disorder and anarchy. However, a balanced constitution was necessary to restrain the consequent tendency of all human governments to fluctuate between the extremes of dictatorship and oppression, on the one hand, and insubordination, resistance, and revolution, on the other hand.

It was requisite also that there be such a standard of morality and justice superior to all mere human authority, because if it were a product of human emanation then no one could claim any right to set standards and govern over other men. A situation would arise where one man's authority is as valid as any other's authority, and human pride being what it was, no authority would be found sufficient to demand and receive a submission that could not be questioned and set aside by aspiring men.

Such a high standard of morality and justice as was enshrined in the British Constitution, was particularly necessary in a revolutionary age -- such as the Upper Canadian Tories were living through -- wherein there were men who were bent on destroying every barrier of restraint, undermining all public authority, and trying to "obliterate every vestige of the principle of possession by prescriptive right". The British Constitution had proven its durability and efficacy over time, and would continue to meet the needs of the British nation in all circumstances, if kept intact and out of the hands of "visionary empiricks" [sic]. They would alter or destroy its basic principles, because "such men may destroy, but they can never build".

In their view of the British Constitution, the Upper Canadian Tories were at one with Edmund Burke. He was quoted to substantiate their view that the British Constitution and state were not based upon a mere partnership agreement or social contract formed at a point in time, but were part of "the great primoeval [sic] contract of eternal society" under God and subordinate to His will. The constitution was "a part of that moral and physical disposition of things" which man could not violate without bringing suffering and chaos upon himself. It was God's law -- embodied in the constitution and other institutions of the state -- which bound and held society together. And if man were going to live in society and approach the degree of perfection which his nature was capable of, he must act in subordination to God's Will. (26)

The Organic Constitution

The British Constitution could not be altered without destroying "the whole original fabric of ... society" – in a phrase borrowed from Edmund Burke -- because it was not just a mechanical contrivance to be altered at pleasure. It was by its very nature an organic constitution. It was an outgrowth of, and embodiment of, all the interests of British society, and was dependent for its continued vitality upon the maintenance of the social order that sustained it.

The maintenance of the balance of the constitution was dependent not only of the equipoise that it established in the legislature among the three branches of government, but also on the character of the people within the body politic of the nation. The constitution was dependent for its proper functioning, and continued maintenance, upon the values and attitudes inculcated into the people by various long-established "regulators of public opinion". Among the social supports of the constitution were a hereditary peerage, a country gentry, a Church-controlled education system, the influence of the commercial interests in favor of order in government, and lastly, and most preeminently, the established Church of England and the Monarchy. (27)

God had so ordered the world that no state could exist, or continue to prosper, without some form of religion. Moreover, it was undeniable that in England the very foundation of the constitution was the established Church of England; and it was that institution which continued to make an essential contribution to the support of the state and the conservation of its institutions.

To explain and illustrate the role of the church in the state, the Upper Canadian Tories adopted several analogies. Just as everything which was subject to motion required a regulator to govern and regulate its speed and the motion of its various parts, and just as a clock was kept in time by its weights and pendulum, so too the civil state needed a "moral regulator", namely religion, in the form of an established church. It was "the only fixed body in any country" capable of exercising a moral restraining influence on acts of government, while at the same time contributing to its stability and durability by inculcating, in the people, principles that were calculated to promote the public good.

A national religious establishment was of the essence in that the National Church taught "those principles only on which all Government ought to be conducted", and which were vital to the continued welfare and happiness of any state, as well as to the maintenance of its social order. (28)

Government could exist and continue to function effectively only if a mutual forbearance were practiced on the part of the sovereign, his subjects, and the various branches of government partaking of any share of authority. However, forbearance was of the very essence of Christianity. Christians were admonished by the Church to yield obedience to legitimately constituted authority. The moral weight and religious effect of the Church of England was such that by preaching mutual charity and brotherly love, and instructing the people in public virtue, the Christian religion provided an effective counterpoise to the rule of the human passions.

In its teachings, the Church placed restraints upon "the selfish mind and ambition of man". And in any state or society, such restraints were necessary because the human passions, if given free rein, would "weaken all the social affections and tend to dissolve the ties of civil obedience". If unrestrained by Christian teachings, human passions would give rise to an endless conflict which could not but reduce man to a "wild, lawless and brutal savage". On the other hand, religion served, through its influence upon the sovereign and society's natural rulers -- those of superior God-given talents – as a guide for their actions and a restraint upon all misconduct and misuse of authority.

In sum, the established Church of England was a requisite part of the constitution because:

> the great work of religion is to govern the passions and the will. It is from its very nature a restraint on all authority, unless purely and faithfully exercised, because it comes in the name of a divine Law. To subdue, mortify and direct human nature is its great object.

In its religious teachings, and in its very character, its prescribed rules for conducting the service, its fixed and systematic order of government and subordination within the Church hierarchy, and its general decorum, the Church of England was the mainstay of the British constitution and social order in the state. Through its influence and example, and its preaching and creeds, the Established Church made, and continued to make, a vital contribution to the formation of:

> the character of a perfect British citizen, who knows his rank, his place, his value, his duties, and his rights; and who will not step out of his own sphere unless he can do so in a constitutional manner -- one to whom *self denial* is as dear a privilege as the protection of his person and property; because the detail of that virtue among his fellow citizens is his own security. (29)

The very nature of man was such that religion and politics could not be separated. The maintenance of social order and the proper functioning and stability of government rested upon principles which were imbibed from the teachings of the National Church. It was evident that:

> those who reject religion and a salutary obedience to her commands, can never be good subjects, good citizens, nor good members of society.

From a strictly political perspective, there were three basic facts which – for the Upper Canadian Tories -- necessitated the union of Government, Religion, and Education (the latter controlled and directed by the Church) in a state. The basic facts were: that society and government were originally instituted by God for His own purposes; that society and government had evolved at the hands of man under the guidance of the "revealed principles" of truth, justice, and morality; and that government was charged with a responsibility for maintaining public morality. Hence, government, religion and education together formed "the three great pillars of the body politic".

In the abstract, every nation had to possess a recognized body of moral feeling if society were to maintain its cohesion, and in all nations, including those of Antiquity, a common religion had served the purpose of providing "a bond of Union among Citizens" and a means of fostering "a spirit of nationality". Among the Jews, religion was taught by a religious establishment which was duly provided for, and supported by, those in authority. The purpose was not purely to facilitate the carrying out of a religious function, but was:

> to form the citizen for his country by the influence of the religion of his country.

In that way, the national religion made a vital contribution to the development of the national character of a people, and ensured, as in the case of the Jews:

> that in all circumstances of religion and politics and national manners, every Israelite should be a *fac simile* of his countrymen.

Likewise, the established Church of England was an essential part of the British Constitution, and served the same end: the formation of "the national manners, and character, and heart, and soul" of all Britons, by means of the teaching of the Christian faith in church and school. (30)

In fostering patriotism and promoting a national spirit, the Established Church was not acting in opposition to the Christian message, or denying that benevolence and brotherhood should embrace all of mankind. On the contrary, the Church was recognizing the true nature of man and God's Will, as realized in man's moral and religious relations. In God's scheme of things, men were bound by ties of natural affection in the first place to their immediate family, then to relations, friends and acquaintances, and ultimately to the community of which they formed a part. Such an order of affection and interest in the family, the community, and the nation, was not un-Christian or unnatural, because:

> By instincts planted in our nature God has formed our hearts to enter readily into their interests and has thus first directed our benevolence to act within that sphere where its exertions can be most powerful and most useful.

Those who reserved their social affection for humanity at large -- to the extent of neglecting or denying the interests and welfare of their own family, community, and country -- would accomplish very little of value because their benevolence lacked any object of concentration. Indeed, such universal philanthropy was but a symptom of the absence of both affection for one's own people and a lack of religion. To the contrary, it was the charities of the domestic circle that were the source of all the virtues of life.

What was more natural than that these family virtues should carry over into the life of the nation and mould its character, and bind the nation together, through a common national spirit based upon a mutual affection and common interest and outlook.

Far from deprecating patriotism, the Scriptures sanctioned "friendship and the love of country". For what was one's country but a larger home, and the honour of one's parents and the extension of the social affections towards one's fellow citizens but "the first step towards considering all men our brethren". (31)

The Established Church -- both as a moral regulator and inculcator of a national spirit and character – and the King, the hereditary Aristocracy, and the Commons, each had a role to play in the proper functioning of the British Constitution. However, no government which lacked a unified executive power vested in a monarch could be assured of possessing real permanence and stability. Republics came and went, but monarchies endured. Monarchies were based upon the precepts of the Bible; whereas republics were based upon ephemeral theories which were derived from man's frail reason. Of all forms of government, monarchical government was the most proximate to the Godly.

The Character of a patriot King

Under all governments, social order was best maintained by the prevalence of public and private virtue among the populace. In turn, public virtue was inculcated into the people by the Church and the family through direct instruction, and by the actions and example set by those in authority, who consequently ought to be virtuous men.

For the Tories, the ideal monarch was a virtuous 'patriot king', such as – in their view -- King George the Third had proved to be. Their concept of kingship focused on the moral character of the monarch and nature of his exercise of the royal executive power. A true king would strive continually to earn the gratitude and affection of his subjects in attending constantly to the promotion of their welfare and happiness. He would seek, by his actions, to strengthen the natural loyalty, devotion, honest pride, and love which the people felt for a legitimate monarch. He would always be ready to accept the guidance of "the abilities and experience of his Parliament" in conducting a paternal administration, and ever mindful of extending his support and encouragement to agricultural improvement, the extension of commerce, and the advancement of the arts and sciences. A man of peace and moderation, he would uphold the constitution in church and state, would strictly maintain all existing rights, both civil and religious, and would actively encourage "the practice of true religion and virtue".

For the Tories, public virtue could not be separated from private virtue, and if the sovereign were to win the love and veneration of his subjects -- rather than ruling purely from fear -- he must first impress them with his integrity and piety in his capacity as a private gentleman. The king must set an example of virtuous conduct and "a pattern of the purest morals" and of personal piety, to inspire and reinforce such conduct among his subjects.

Virtuous conduct would secure to the king an attachment on the part of his subjects that would be based on affection, rather than merely an awe of power. In being a man of virtue and piety, and governing in accordance with God's moral law, the king would enjoy the affection and loyalty of the people to his person, which was the strongest support for the social order in a state. It was the personal attachment of the people to the king that gave monarchical government an element of stability and permanence which other forms of government, in wanting an executive vested in a hereditary monarch, could not provide. (32)

The mature British Constitution

In the view of the Upper Canadian Tories, the British constitution was the culmination of centuries of human effort, guided by Christian principles, in perfecting a constitution in keeping with the political and social needs of man, as well as his religious and moral being. The British constitution, as it had evolved, answered and fulfilled the needs and wants (deficiencies) of man as man, and guaranteed the proper functioning and good order of society and the stability of the state. In the proper functioning of the constitution, the character of the people was critically important, as were the institutions which formed that national character, and the social orders that sustained it and were represented in the workings of the constitution.

The dynamic balance of three branches of the Legislature not only prevented any one branch from overwhelming the others, but enabled them to work together to further the common good. However, the three branches of government – King, Lords, and Commons – were only a part of the constitution, which included a separate executive power in the person of the King, and the national Church and a Church-controlled education system which played a critical role in forming the national character and providing moral guidance. For the Upper Canadian Tories, all of the divers interests of a mature society were represented, and protected, in the workings of the British Constitution, and found their focus there.

In sum, the British constitution supported a limited monarchy under the rule of law, which was based on Christian principles of morality and virtue, and had evolved in keeping with God's scheme of things and the needs of human nature. In the Tory view, if Upper Canadians were to prosper and assure themselves of the enjoyment of peace, order and good government, they must strive to realize and conserve the benefits of the British Constitution, as it pertained to Upper Canada, and to maintain the integrity of the constitution unimpaired.

Chapter Seven

The Constitution of Upper Canada

To the Upper Canadian Tories, the ideal constitution for providing good government and responding to the needs of human nature was the British constitution, as it had evolved in England. At the close of the War of 1812, when the Tories articulated a series of policies – the National Policy -- to guide the development of the Province of Upper Canada, they did not elaborate on their view of the constitution of Upper Canada. Such a lacuna was readily understandable. Unlike their situation with respect to religion and education, where the implementation of the National Policy required a statement of their principles and beliefs, and positive action, what they regarded as a near-perfect constitution already existed: the Constitutional Act of 1791, which had founded the Province of Upper Canada.

Nevertheless, the Upper Canadian Tories were well informed of the workings of the balanced constitution of Upper Canada. Their view of the constitution and the function of its different supporting institutions was revealed in the arguments that they put forward during succeeding years when political radicals of the Reform Party sought to expand the powers of the House of Assembly at the expense of the executive power of the Crown. In defending the powers and prerogatives of the Crown against encroachments by the House of Assembly, the Tories also revealed their view of how the constitution reflected and reinforced the social structure, and how society needed to evolve to support the proper functioning of the constitution.

The Nature of the Constitution

The Upper Canadian Tories believed that the Constitutional Act of 1791 was "*the image and transcript of the British Constitution*"; and that it had bestowed upon Upper Canadians all the benefits and rights "of free born British subjects". The constitution of Upper Canada differed from the British constitution in some respects owing to the circumstances of the colony, and the fact that the Province of Upper Canada was not a sovereign and independent state.

The Tories felt a sense of gratitude and pride that the country – Great Britain -- to which they owed allegiance had bestowed upon an infant colony "such a liberal constitution". It embraced rights and privileges, and equitable laws, which were the culmination of centuries of struggle and experience in England. Having barely begun to emerge from a rude state of society, and lacking many of the essentials of civilization, Upper Canada at its very inception possessed a constitution second-to-none. Its residents enjoyed the right to elect their own members to the Assembly of the provincial parliament, lived under a government of laws of their own making, and their liberties – the 'rights of Englishmen' -- were protected by the "inestimable blessings" of the balanced British constitution.

Among 'the blessings' enjoyed by Upper Canadians were English civil and criminal law, and the statutes of the British parliament that included the Bill of Rights (1689) which guaranteed a freedom of elections, freedom of speech in parliament, and the right as British subjects to petition the King. Upper Canadians enjoyed the right to trial by jury, habeas corpus, freedom of the press, and the rule by law under a judicial system based on that of England. In the postwar period, the courts consisted of a superior court, at the provincial level, for trying civil and criminal cases – the Court of King's Bench -- which comprised the Chief Justice and initially two Puisné (Associate) Judges. In addition, in each of the eight districts of the province, there was a District Court and a Surrogate (Probate) Court.

At the local level, law enforcement was the responsibility of a Justice of the Peace, who was appointed by the Lt. Governor. The Justices of the Peace were assisted by an appointed constable – the sheriff of the district -- who was responsible for the collection of fines and payments due the court, the incarceration of convicted criminals and debtors, and the maintenance of the Goal (jail). More generally, the Justices of the Peace were the guardians of the peace and order of society, and the protectors of "the interests of the Crown". The more serious civil cases, and capital cases, were sent to the District Court – the Court of Quarter Sessions of the Peace—which was presided over by two or more Justices of the Peace. In each District, the Court met every three months and, initially, the cases were tried before a grand jury. When indictments were handed down to proceed to trial, the case was transferred to a superior court – the Court of Oyer and Terminer and General Goal Delivery.

When a major civil or criminal case was to be prosecuted, one of the judges of the Court of King's Bench was given a commission to try the case before a jury, in the spring or fall assize circuit, in the District concerned. There was no appeal from the Court of Oyer and Terminer and General Goal Delivery, but if the Chief Justice was not the presiding judge of the court, the execution of the court judgement was suspended temporarily pending receipt of the pleasure of the Lt. Governor for mercy or clemency. More generally, the verdict in all capital cases was reported to the Lt. Governor, who could exercise the Royal Prerogative of Clemency. In sum, Upper Canadians lived under the rule of law, with a judicial system based on the English court system. They benefitted as well from living under a limited constitutional monarchy that protected their rights and liberties – the 'ancient rights and liberties of Englishmen' -- from encroachment by either the monarch or the populace.

The Legislature of Upper Canada was modeled on that of Great Britain -- the balanced constitution of 'King, Lords and Commons' -- in that the legislative law-making process involved three branches of government: the Lt. Governor, who represented the King and possessed the right to assent to all acts before they became law, or to reserve them for the King's pleasure; the Legislative Council, which consisted of men appointed by the Crown from among "the principal inhabitants of the Province"; and the House of Assembly, which comprised members elected by the people. The provincial parliament, so constituted, enjoyed the right of voting money bills, which was the highest privilege that any parliament could have.

Thus, the Tories held that the constitution of Upper Canada was 'the image and transcript of the British Constitution', with perhaps the exception of the right of impeachment of ministers of the Crown for personal misconduct, by a joint action of the House of Assembly and the Legislative Council. The right of impeachment was not specifically granted in the constitution, but was not denied.

The Upper Canadian Tories were proud to be British subjects, and were strong supporters of the balanced constitution and His Majesty's

Provincial Government. They held that Upper Canadians were fortunate in having received -- through "the bounty of the mother country" -- free grants of Crown lands in a colony with a fertile soil, the facsimile of 'a perfect constitution', and numerous benefits to the extent that they "possessed more practical freedom, with fewer burthens, than any other people on the face of the globe". (1)

The Executive

Upper Canada was a province governed by law: the laws enacted by the provincial parliament and those of the British parliament. Normally, when a colony was founded by Englishmen, English law would be in force, but in a conquered colony -- such as Canada -- the established principle of law was such that the original laws remained in force until changed by the conqueror. In time, various acts of the British parliament – primarily the Quebec Act of 1774 –had superseded the old French system of law until the Constitutional Act of 1791 was enacted. It divided the old Province of Quebec by establishing Upper Canada and Lower Canada as separate provinces of the British Empire. Each province was headed by an appointed representative of the Crown, a Lt. Governor, under the overall command of a Governor-in-Chief, who was likewise appointed by the Crown.

Conquered territories were "a dominion of the King in right of his Crown and therefore [were] necessarily... subject to the Legislature of Great Britain". Upper Canada was no exception; and although its legislature was delegated the authority to make "laws for the Peace, welfare and good Government" of the province, it was a subordinate legislature, and its power of both making and repealing laws was specifically confined to internal laws and regulations. Upon the founding of Upper Canada, the laws of the old Province of Quebec remained in power except those expressly appealed by the Constitutional Act, or subsequently repealed or superseded by the laws enacted by the provincial parliament. Where the British Parliament was concerned, the general principle was that no local law in the colony could contradict or supersede an act of the British parliament; and that principle was enforced through the Crown's right of disallowance over colonial legislation. (2)

Once a Bill passed both houses of the Upper Canadian Legislature – the House of Assembly and the Legislative Council – the Lt. Governor had the authority, in the name of His Majesty, to either consent to the Bill, to withhold consent thereby rendering it null and void, or to reserve the Bill for the Signification of His Majesty's Pleasure. When a reserved Bill failed to receive the Royal assent within two years, it was null and void. On the other hand, when a Bill did receive the assent of the Lt. Governor, a copy was forwarded to the appropriate Secretary of State in London, with His Majesty reserving the right to disallow the Act within a two-year period and, if disallowed, the provincial government legislative enactment became null and void.

The Lt. Governor would present a government program to the Legislature in the Speech from the Throne at the opening of the provincial parliament, but it was the Attorney General who submitted government initiatives to the Legislature in requesting the passage of a bill with the requisite funding approval from the House of Assembly.

The sovereignty of the Crown was exercised by the Lt. Governor of Upper Canada, who as the King's representative formed a part of the Legislature, as well as possessed the sovereign executive power in the government. The Lt. Governor was solely responsible to the monarch for his political acts; although he was responsible under the law, as an individual, for any acts that violated the law or superseded his authority. That was clearly shown when a private individual, Charles Wyatt, secured a judgment at law in 1816 for £300 damages against Lt. Governor Gore personally for having dismissed him without sufficient cause from his post as Surveyor General of Upper Canada in 1807.

It was the Lt. Governor, in acting as the King's representative, who appointed the members of the Legislative Council, issued the writs of election for the House of Assembly, and appointed a Returning Officer for each district, county or town. And it was the Lt. Governor who summoned the provincial parliament and, at the opening of parliament presented a Speech from the Throne outlining government intentions and policies.

The executive consisted of the Lieutenant Governor, his appointed Crown Law Officers – the Attorney General and the Solicitor General -- and the appointed members of an Executive Council. In keeping with constitutional tradition, the Lt. Governor was expected to seek the advice of his Executive Council in governing the province, but there was no constitutional provision that he had to do so. However, the Upper Canadian Tories recognized that if any differences arose between the Lt. Governor and his advisors, he was bound:

> not to be guided by the advice of his Council, but by the Royal Instructions. This was a provision of the Constitution itself, ...

It was the Lt. Governor, acting on behalf of the King, who appointed the members of the Executive Council; and they served at the pleasure of His Majesty. Hence, the Executive Council was responsible solely to the King for their advice, rather than to the people. According to the Tory interpretation of its role, the Executive Council members were bound to be "guided by the King's Instructions", and were expected to provide advice to the Lt. Governor on how best to carry out the King's Instructions. For the Tories, it could not be otherwise because the King was the sovereign power and not the people. The Lt. Governor was the King's deputy in exercising a delegated authority. (3)

The role of the Executive Council in Upper Canada was based on tradition, rather than the Constitution. In the Constitutional Act, the Executive Council was mentioned several times, in separate clauses, in the content of the Lt. Governor being responsible for appointing the members, and acting "with the advice of his Executive Council". However, there was no stipulation provided in the Constitution as to the composition of the Executive Council, the number of members, or the limits and nature of the consultation process. It appears that it was expected to perform the role of a Cabinet in the British government system. On their part, the Upper Canadian Tories viewed its members as "the proper advisers" of the Lt. Governor on questions of policy and administration.

In Upper Canada, as of the mid-1820s, the Attorney General and the Solicitor General were not members of the Executive Council, and only one government office holder was traditionally a member, the Commissioner of Crown Lands. By tradition, when a Chief Justice was appointed, he became a member of the Executive Council to advise the

Lt. Governor on legal matters and the drafting of legislation. As of 1825, there were six members on the Executive Council. In addition, to the Chief Justice, the members were the Rev. John Strachan, and two of his former pupils, George Herkimer Markland and James Buchanan Macaulay, together with Peter Robinson, the elder brother of the Attorney General, John Beverley Robinson, and Samuel Smith, a former Administrator of the Province.

With the retirement in October 1825, of Samuel Smith, the Executive Council was reduced to five members in total: the Rev. John Strachan, and the two young Tories, together with Peter Robinson (who was subsequently appointed the Commissioner of Crown Lands), and the Chief Justice, William Campbell. Moreover, in April 1829, John Beverley Robinson joined the Executive Council upon his appointment as Chief Justice for the Province of Upper Canada to succeed Chief Justice Campbell, who had retired from the Bench and the Executive Council.

Where the government of the province was concerned, the Tories held the view that purely local measures "ought to be left to the Provincial Administration" to decide because they in no way threatened the interests of the mother country. Where the functioning of the provincial government executive was concerned, the Tories wanted the Colonial Office to introduce two changes. They wanted a directive instructing the Lt. Governor to consult his Executive Council "on all occasions", and wanted the individual members of the Executive Council to be "held responsible for their advice" to the Crown, as was the case with the King's ministers in Britain. Moreover, it was suggested that, upon the retirement of a Lt. Governor, the Executive Council be tasked with reporting to the Crown on his administration.

The Tories recognized that a situation might arise where measures to promote the general welfare of the Empire might clash with an immediate interest of Upper Canada in the broader areas of defence, the navigation laws, and Imperial trade, but it was recognized, and accepted for the sake of harmony and the unity of the Empire, that:

> the Colony ought certainly to yield. But this acquiescence has its limits & no sacrifice should be required that renders the Colony useless or its inhabitants miserable.

In the latter case, the leading Tories maintained that acquiescence would be contrary to the very purpose of government and society; and hence would be unacceptable.

The British government had no right to tax Upper Canadians. The Constitutional Act reaffirmed an earlier enactment of the British parliament at the time of the American Revolution – the Taxation of the Colonies Act (1778) -- whereby the King and Parliament renounced any right to impose taxes on his Majesty's colonies of North America. The sole exception was the imposing of customs duties, which were deemed necessary for the regulation of navigation and commerce within the Empire. Moreover, the net revenue collected from all such duties was to be used for the benefit of the two Canadian provinces, and applied to the purposes specified by His Majesty's provincial governments in acting with the advice of their respective executive councils and the consent of their respective legislatures. (4)

The Legislative Council

The Legislative Council members were appointed for life by the Sovereign – through his representative, the Lt. Governor -- from among inhabitants of the province who were distinguished for their abilities, independence, and integrity of character. The purpose of the Legislative Council was to serve as a moderating influence and as a balance between the Crown (represented by the Lt. Governor), and the House of Assembly. In enjoying an appointment for life, rather than at pleasure, and in being removable only upon conviction of high treason, the members of the Legislative Council were "independent alike of the crown and of the people". In the Tory view, they were the one body of the Legislature which, in its collective capacity, "could dare to do right, uninfluenced by the fear of offending any power or party". Thus, as a body they were entrusted with maintaining the balance of the constitution. The Legislative Council could resist arbitrary government acts by the Crown on the one hand, while serving as "a counterpoise to the rashness of the House of Assembly" on the other.

Appointment to the Legislative Council was held to be an honour, and a reward for "public spirit & exertions". There was no salary given to appointees. It was a form of public recognition and gratitude which the Tories held to be superior to "any sordid or pecuniary benefit". In appointing Upper Canadians of a high moral character and discernment to the Legislative Council, the intention was to attach a better type of man to government, and thereby establish "an influence different from that which is introduced by overgrown wealth". Such public recognition was intended to appeal to men who were "generous and noble minded", and capable of upholding both the prerogatives and dignity of the Crown and "the rights and liberties of the people", as well as men capable of promoting the true interests of the province. Hence, the Tories believed that such a system of appointment secured to the service of the government men who would seek the public good, rather than their own selfish benefit. The appointment of men of such a character could not but:

> nourish that pure and exalted ambition which gives life and energy to public affairs, which rouse the most dignified principles of action, and extinguish that low grovelling policy which only aims at despicable gratifications.

An appointed Legislative Council was viewed as a way of ensuring that only men of "the greatest abilities and integrity" -- Christian men of moral worth and trust -- would be chosen to exercise "the authority and privileges of the Legislative Council". Only British subjects of over 21 years of age were eligible for appointment to the Legislative Council.

As the Upper Canadian Tories were aware, there was a provision in the Constitutional Act that declared it lawful for His Majesty to bestow hereditary titles of honour or rank on any British subject resident in the province. Under the Constitutional Act, members of the provincial aristocracy -- if it were created by the bestowing of titles -- would enjoy a hereditary right to a seat in the Legislative Council. That right would descend from generation to generation through the eldest son, who would be entitled to receive a Writ of Summons to sit in the Legislative Council. Once bestowed, a hereditary right to a seat in the Legislative Council would only be forfeited if the individual were attainted for Treason in a court of law.

Although the nobility in Britain enjoyed a hereditary right to attend the House of Lords, the Upper Canadian Tories were ambivalent concerning whether the members of a potential future aristocracy -- if hereditary titles were to be bestowed in Upper Canada -- ought to enjoy a hereditary right to attend the Legislative Council. It was recognized that the members of the succeeding generation would not necessarily be men of superior qualities and attainments as:

> Whether their sons would inherit those qualifications or not must always be doubtful. (5)

For the Upper Canadian Tories who believed in a meritocracy, it was a matter of serious concern.

A potential Hereditary Aristocracy

The Upper Canadian Tories did not consider a hereditary aristocracy to be a perfect vehicle for public service. From time to time, they cited the potential failings of an upper house comprised of a heredity aristocracy. The Tories defended the existing Legislative Council to which members were chosen for appointment purely on merit – education, ability, achievements, and social standing -- rather than simply ascending to the Council by hereditary right. Nonetheless, the leading Tories were convinced that a hereditary aristocracy had a role to play in Upper Canada, which ultimately must be realized for the good of society. The critical difficulty was the circumstances in which they found themselves.

From the beginning of settlement, and extending into the postwar years, the Tories of Upper Canada held the view that there was a "want of characters sufficiently distinguished" to be selected for the bestowal of hereditary rank and office. It was that situation which prevented their making any unequivocal declaration in favour of hereditary honours and appointments. If a hereditary aristocracy were to perform its proper function, it was essential that the men appointed to the Legislative Council be worthy not only of the honour, but capable of commanding respect and sustaining the independence of character which such an office required.

If men of property and public distinction could not be found in a pioneer society such as Upper Canada, then the creation of a hereditary aristocracy would merely provoke ridicule and frustrate its objective. Therefore, it was not to be encouraged. Indeed, the lack of men of a requisite stature for appointment to public offices was a long-standing problem in the Province of Upper Canada. Earlier, it was a very significant factor in motivating Richard Cartwright -- in his capacity as a member of the Legislative Council, under the administration of Lt. Governor Gore -- to secure the abolition of appointments to the rank of Lord Lieutenant of a County, which was a position that had been created by Lt. Governor Simcoe.

The position of Lord Lieutenant of a County was intended by Simcoe to form the beginnings of a "legal Aristocracy", which was deemed necessary for the proper balance and functioning of the Constitution. The Lord Lieutenants were to be appointed to that rank from among men distinguished for their loyalty and public service in the province, and who possessed the "weight, respect, and public confidence which renders them the natural support of Constitutional Authority". They were to superintend the magistrates of their county, to serve as Justices of the Peace, and to command the militia of the county. Among their proposed militia duties were the organization and training of the county militia, and the making of recommendations -- to the Lt. Governor – of the men who merited a commission as a militia officer when vacancies occurred.

The first Lord Lieutenant that Simcoe appointed was David William Smith, a substantial land owner who possessed, ultimately, some 20,000 acres of land in Upper Canada. Smith was a former British Army officer, a Captain of militia, and a distinguished public administer. He was elected a member of the House of Assembly for Suffolk and Essex in the first legislature of Upper Canada in 1792, and subsequently served as a member of the Executive Council under Simcoe's administration. As such, he fitted the criteria of a man of character, public service and large land holdings that Simcoe had in mind for the formation of a landed aristocracy in the Province of Upper Canada, but few residents of the province did in the pre-War period. There were some large landholders in Upper Canada, but most were land speculators of a questionable character, who favoured the admittance of American settlers into the province to raise land prices.

Unless and until the country could furnish suitable men of character and distinction to enable such honours to be confined only to those who deserved to be so honoured, the Tories did not favour the bestowal of either honorary or hereditary titles. Thus, in 1838 John Beverley Robinson, the Chief Justice, declined an offer of knighthood which was offered by the British government for his services during the Rebellion of 1837. It had never been conferred on Canadian judges previously, and he did not wish "to form an exception", if other distinguished judges of the province were not to be similarly honoured. However, later at mid-century, when Robinson was offered a knighthood on the recommendation of the Governor General, Lord Elgin, it was accepted. Robinson was appointed a Companion of the Bath in 1850, and created a baronet in 1854. At the time, he experienced some misgivings. He feared that "the new system of responsible government" might result in high offices being occupied by men "whom it can hardly be supposed the Sovereign would delight to honor" with a title. (6)

The Upper Canadian Tories were conscious of the fact that the British Constitution had been conferred upon Upper Canada, and the other British North American colonies, "long before they contain[ed] the materials necessary to put it in salutary operation". As such, they expected that the Constitution of Upper Canada would give rise to difficulties and discontent, but were convinced that in time the proper supports would be realized. The British Constitution was an organic constitution which embraced all the interests of a mature society; and it was a constitutional truism that to transfer such a constitution to a colony -- or to any country for that matter:

> without transferring the whole order and conjunction of circumstances in the English government, would prove unsuccessful.

In the meantime, while Upper Canada remained in its rude state, adjustments had to be made in the details of the British Constitution, with some of its elements -- such as a hereditary aristocracy -- deferred. However, the constant aim, which guided the leading Upper Canadian Tories in all areas of endeavour -- politics, religion, education, and even political economy -- was to foster the development and evolution of a mature society which would resemble that of the mother country.

They were dedicated to monarchical institutions, and to the form of society that it typified. Moreover, they were inspired by the hope that:

> in due time, the semblance of monarchy might be more exact. As the countries [sic] increased in opulence, and afforded the materials, distinctions of hereditary rank might be formed, which would add dignity and support to the government, and excite to honourable and patriotic emulation.

In the absence of an hereditary aristocracy, the Tories realized that a proportionately heavier burden fell upon the Established Church and the education system to inculcate "liberal principles" and proper social attitudes. More particularly, they looked to the clergy of the Established Church and the legal profession to set the tone of society through the example of their conduct, bearing, and public service.

Although the Tories had no use for 'pettifogging lawyers', they were convinced from a very early period that the legal profession would emerge as the most powerful profession in Upper Canada -- given the dearth of great landed proprietors and the lack of privileged orders. It was evident that lawyers would come to occupy all public positions of profit and honour in the Province of Upper Canada. Consequently, it was essential that men of the highest talents be found within its ranks. Thus, the law was held out to the young Tories as a profession worthy of ambition, which promised "rank, influence and wealth". When honourably pursued -- by an individual of moral character, knowledge, talent and ability -- a legal career held out the promise of being "more useful to mankind" than any other profession, except for the clerical. (7)

In attempting to account for the anemic development of an aristocracy in Upper Canada, the Tories cited many factors not the least of which was the absence of men of capital. From its very beginning, Upper Canada had been virtually "an asylum of the poor" in that most of its original settlers were refugee Loyalists. Moreover, subsequently, many British immigrants had arrived who were without any substantial capital, or were even in a destitute condition. In a country of little capital, where wealth had to be 'drawn from the soil' – which was a very slow, laborious, and limited process of accumulation – it was difficult to develop a wealthy landed class. Moreover, that difficulty was increased immeasurably by the land policy of the government.

The post-War policy of surveying and granting the land in small lots effectively prevented the purchase and accumulation of large contiguous tracts, and offered no inducement to large capitalists to settle and invest their capital in the improvement of Upper Canadian land, preparatory to opening it for settlement. Furthermore, the existing land granting system acted to discourage the merchants and half-pay officers, from among whom one would expect a landed aristocracy to emerge, from seeking to improve their land. To the contrary, it had the adverse effect of encouraging them -- since their land holdings were scattered through different parts of the Province -- to leave their lands undeveloped in counting on an increase in the population over time to give them a speculative value.

Such a division of the land was neither favourable to the growth of a potential landed aristocracy, nor to the development of Upper Canadian society. It could not but be lamented because it laid the basis "for as wild a Democracy as that of Athens". (8) In sum, instead of a society leavened by an aristocracy of landed estates tended by tenant farmers, and with a substantial class of yeoman farmers of a sound moral and religious character, the province was populated almost exclusively by small farmers of various origins who owned their own land, or would own their land in freehold tenure upon the completion of their settlement duties.

The Upper Canadian Tories were also desirous of establishing a hereditary aristocracy in Upper Canada to strengthen the loyalty of the province. They were convinced that the closer the institutions of Upper Canada approximated those of the mother country, the more "the true nature and spirit" of the monarchy would be perceived and appreciated by Upper Canadians. It would strengthen their feelings and respect for British institutions, and their rejection of American democratic republicanism.

The Tories were concerned about the proper functioning of the Legislative Council whose members were not "either in circumstances or privilege" in a position comparable to that of hereditary peers. Lacking titles and honours, and forming no separate estate with a fixed stake in the land and a hereditary claim to share in the government, the members of the Legislative Council could not serve as an effective curb against the "viciousness" to which popular assemblies were prone when unchecked.

As matters stood during the immediate postwar years, the Legislative Council was found wanting. It was evident that the members:

> can form no standing class in the body politic: each fresh accession to its component parts becomes, as it were, an isolated and incidental thing; there can be no lively sympathy from common interests or privilege; they exhibit no link between the past and the present generations; and they are without the inherent power of ensuring a succession and perpetuating this office.

A hereditary aristocracy was regarded as a vital link in the maintenance of continuity with the past, as a means of strengthening by conduct and example public support for monarchical institutions and the British tie, and as an object of respect which would instill a veneration for "that order of things under which the honours are conferred".

Such an institution was a part of the body politic of the mother country, and an essential element in the institutional system which accounted for "her political and moral greatness" as well as "her prosperity and glory". If Upper Canada were to inherit the full benefit of the British constitution, it was essential that she should enjoy the full complement of British institutions. (9)

Not only was an aristocracy requisite for the maintenance of order in society and the proper functioning of the constitution, but it was in keeping with the order of Providence. All men were not equal in their God-given capabilities and intellectual endowment or, consequently, were they able, unaided, to direct their own efforts to beneficial employment in various areas of life. The nature of man and the needs of society necessitated and gave rise to:

an aristocracy of education, an aristocracy of wealth, an aristocracy of power, an aristocracy of religion, and an oligarchy of government.

Moreover, such a situation was right because "a perfect equality in all things" could only breed "universal anarchy and desolation". The very existence of society depended upon man recognizing the reality and necessity of social inequalities. It was evident that:

man is made for society and mutual dependence, but yet no less for difference of station and the unequal distribution of what we call worldly prosperity.

If man wished to partake of the benefits of society, then it was necessary that all contribute their worth to the whole, from which all in return would receive superior benefits; although, in the nature of things, not in equal proportions. In every activity, which concerned man in his struggle to supply "the wants of common life", whether in producing commodities or establishing government, there were certain principles of organization which could not be ignored.

If individuals were to operate in unison to achieve a required object, it was necessary that they be under the management of a director who possessed the power to command. It was also requisite in manufacturing that the manager be in possession of superior means to effectively finance and direct that effort. If denied access to, and possession of, superior wealth or resources, neither government nor manufacturers could promote the common good.

This necessity was especially evident in industry where men of "superior sagacity" provided employment for other men who, if left to their own devices, would have neither the means nor the knowledge to provide themselves with the necessities and comforts of life in a quantity and quality sufficient to support higher forms of society. All men had to live by productive labour; yet, all were not equally competent to direct its ends.

It was the existence of accumulated wealth which enabled men of ingenuity and enterprise to direct and discipline the industry of others, and provide them with tools, employment, and bread. The nature of man, and the realities of life stemming from that nature, and the concomitant principles of social and economic organization, belied the egalitarian ideals of democratic republicanism. Far from being a cause for lament, inequality was productive of a great deal of good.

The aristocratic form of organization, and the inequalities which sustained it, were also necessary in government itself. Government was essential for the promotion of the wellbeing of all subjects; yet everyone could not devote themselves to governing, even had they the talents to do so. To secure a government of "wisdom and prudence", it was necessary that some men cultivate their mental capabilities far beyond that of their fellow man. Only by receiving support from the labour of others, and enjoying a superior degree of wealth and comfort, could some men attain the leisure (as distinct from idleness) to devote themselves to that mental cultivation requisite in those who form the natural governors of a society. Such an "unproductive aristocracy" of government (in the sense of not producing goods directly by its own labour), was part of the natural order of society and government, and it was such men who enhanced the respectability of society through their weight of character and integrity.

To those who objected to social and economic inequalities, and disapproved of a landed aristocracy, it was pointed out that men who lived from the rents of tenants were no more a "public nuisance" than farmers who rented out their surplus acreage for cultivation, or who hired labourers to work on their farms.

For the Tories, a landed aristocracy was part of "the order of providence", and therefore a necessary element in human society. As the Scriptures attested, society was organic and analogous to the human form of which there were many members, but one body. All the members of the body politic were essential to the well-being of society, and to the keeping of that:

> vast and complicated machinery of human society all moving
> in order, regularity, and harmony; each man knowing and
> humbly keeping his place. (10)

If a landed aristocracy were to evolve in Upper Canada, it was essential that estates be secured by entail and the law of primogeniture. Hence, the Upper Canadian Tories were adamant in their refusal to acquiesce in the continuing efforts of political radicals in the Assembly to modify the primogeniture law under which intestate property in land devolved intact to the eldest male heir. Bills to abolish the law of primogeniture in favour of an equal division of intestate property were introduced in the Assembly during the sessions of 1821 and 1822 by an American immigrant, Barnabas Bidwell and after 1826 in several different sessions by his son, Marshall Spring Bidwell. Several of these bills were passed by the Assembly, but were rejected by the Legislative Council.

In opposing what they regarded as an assault by democratic egalitarianism, the Tories in the Assembly were supported by a leading Old Whig, Dr. William Warren Baldwin – a large land holder -- in marshalling arguments in defence of the law of primogeniture. The Tories argued that any proposed equal subdivision of intestate lands was "a departure from the British constitution", and would prevent Upper Canada growing in its resemblance to the mother country. It was a republican measure, and democratic in its tendency. The law of primogeniture had been abolished in most American states after the American Revolution, and in France by the revolutionaries.

Not only would the abolition of primogeniture be destructive of the harmony of families when men died intestate, but the experiences of Ireland and Lower Canada were cited to prove that a continuous subdivision of property would reduce agriculture to a miserable state. It would prevent younger sons from seeking to rise in importance in other occupations, and eventually -- through generations of sub-divisions -- would "entail a needy population on the Country".

From the time of Magna Carta, a landed aristocracy had been the asserter and protector of the liberties of the people against attempted encroachments by the Crown, and the abrogation of the principle of primogeniture would destroy the possibility of Upper Canada having a landed aristocracy. It would leave the British Constitution, as it applied to Upper Canada, as "a mere shadow" of itself. (11)

By the decade of the 1830s, the Upper Canadian Tories became convinced that the establishment of a hereditary aristocracy was a matter of vital importance -- even an absolute political necessity -- because of the inroads which American democratic republicanism was making into Upper Canada. The province had become the scene of a raging ideological conflict in which the Tories saw themselves as the defenders of British principles against:

> the daily influx of levelling democracy and a fierce spirit of insubordination, which are nourished and encouraged and disciplined by the political leaders of religious sects, who spare no pains to *grind* into their followers those democratical and anti-British principles along with the moral aliment of their religious instruction.

In the great struggle against democratic anarchy, "a Canadian Peerage" -- if duly constituted – was viewed as an essential antidote. Its members would inspire respect, and as a body it would serve to "check that restless spirit of innovation and intrigue" which was plaguing the province.

Moreover, a peerage would not impose any financial burden upon the public. In being landed, the peer would be supported by his own rents. It was estimated that an income of £500 per annum from leased lands would be sufficient to maintain a member of the desired aristocracy; and that in Upper Canada -- as of 1831 -- there were at least two or three gentlemen who were already possessed of such an income. As such, they were judged to be capable of supporting "the necessary dignity of a peerage"; and it was evident that the number of landed gentlemen who would be capable of doing so was increasing year by year.

It was believed that a landed aristocracy, ensconced in the Legislative Council, could contribute much to the political stability of Upper Canada, as well as give a proper tone and feeling to society. A landed aristocracy would in turn be conducive to the maintenance of the Imperial tie. However, by the early 1830s, the Upper Canadian Tories were becoming discouraged by the actions of the liberal-Whig government in Britain which ignored the loyal British subjects of Upper Canada in following a decided policy of conciliating the Reformers of Upper Canada through taking up their so-called 'grievances'. One Tory was moved to exclaim that the ultimate success of the Tory efforts to maintain the Imperial connection was subject to "the proviso, that the Empire were not *reformed* to its dissolution" by the Whigs in the British Parliament. (12)

The House of Assembly

Although the Tories of Upper Canada placed a great deal of emphasis on maintaining the Legislative Council independent of the people, such a stance did not mean that they deprecated the rights of the people or disapproved of their playing a substantial role in the political process. To the contrary, it was essential that the popular branch of the legislature – the House of Assembly, which was elected by the people -- should enjoy undiminished, all "the rights & privileges necessary to maintain its due power and dignity". The people were a vital part of the corporate body and enjoyed a proper, indeed indispensable, share in the constitution which framed the government of the 'nation'.

It was the popular House of Assembly, in conjunction with the Legislative Council, which served to restrain any attempted exercise of arbitrary executive power by the Crown. The elected and the appointed branches of the Legislature, acting together, were the best means that could be devised to control the arbitrary tendencies which were present in all executive authority. However, the purpose of the House of Assembly, in possessing a share in the legislative process, was not to direct and control the executive power.

The Assembly did not have any right to encroach upon the rights and privileges of the other components of the legislative body, but rather had a duty to maintain the balance of the constitution unimpaired. Each branch of the Legislature, in the exercise of its duties and rights and the carrying out of its responsibilities, was equally essential to the welfare of the people. Government was ordained by God, and the members of the House of Assembly and the Legislative Council, as well as the head of state -- His Vicegerent – were subject to the Will of God rather than the will of the people. They were charged by a higher power to act always in accordance with God's moral law in their efforts to promote the common good and well-being of society.

As it stood, the Constitution of the Province of Upper Canada assured to the people the possession of "the real foundation of true liberty, and consequently of solid happiness", which was the right of "being amenable only to laws" made by their own representatives. It was the people of Upper Canada who determined -- through their elected members -- what laws should prevail in the country, and if the laws were "not favourable to virtue", they could only blame themselves. (13)

The Upper Canadian Tories had a very definite conception of how the lower House of the Legislature ought to function, and the specific role of its members in the political process. The elected members were regarded as being responsible to the community as-a-whole, rather than responsible to their constituents. The members of the Assembly were representatives of 'the people', and not delegates sent to Parliament to promote the local interests of their constituents. The words of the renowned English Tory judge, Sir William Blackstone, (*Commentaries on the Laws of England*, 4 vols., 1766-1769), were cited by the Upper Canadian Tories in support of their view: viz. that

> the end of a member's coming to Parliament is *not particular* but *general, not barely to advantage his constituents but the commonwealth.*

For the Tories of Upper Canada, it was the promotion of the common good, and not the "wishes of his constituents", which ought to guide the deliberations and actions of the Assembly member.

The Tories had little patience with members of the Assembly who persisted in bringing forwarded "interested measures" in defence of which, when questioned, they could only:

> allege that they were *instructed* to do so by their *constituents*, & that their *constituents* expect it of them & not that they (the members) have any arguments in favor of their proceedings.

Such rationalizations were abhorred because they were an implicit denial of the very purpose of the House of Assembly and the role of the elected representatives.

The Assembly was viewed by the Tories as being a deliberative body wherein the elected representatives of the people were privileged to meet and participate in debates on the public issues of the day, all of which was supposed to be marked by a sense of propriety and serious, rational argument. Thus, the Tory elite were quite indignant at the boisterous carryings-on by the radical members in the House of Assembly. On one occasion, the organized cheering of the opposition -- upon the passage of the Naturalization bill in May 1828 – caused a great deal of uneasiness among the Tory onlookers. For one member of the House, it was reminiscent of "the Jacobin assemblies of France".

It was noted, with some disgust, that far from being a scene of a calm disinterested deliberation, the House of Assembly "on many occasions resembles a Beer Garden more than anything else"; and that

> Local prejudices, too, are too apt to sway more powerfully than general principles; and the permanent good of a Province is often sacrificed to the petty and temporary advantage of a county or a township.

In the Assembly, "political bartering" was a despicable fact of life with members of one district agreeing to vote benefits for another locality in return for its members voting for the bestowal of government largesse in their area. However, the Tory elite recognized that such pettiness and factionalism, as well as the blatant habit of mixing self-interest rather "deeply with public acts and patriotic professions", were a product of a pioneer life marked by hard struggle. Nonetheless, the bartering of favours in the Assembly was not to be condoned. (14)

Whether Great Britain had been "more generous than wise" in bestowing a representative form of government upon a pioneer colony such as Upper Canada -- where there was initially "almost a total absence of fitting materials for a popular legislature" -- was a moot point. From experience, the Upper Canadian Tories were acutely aware that colonial legislatures impeded good government in that they entailed needless delays, bickering, and expense, and were constantly fomenting discontent in their efforts to encroach upon the rights of the other branches of the Legislature. Almost invariably they contained men with "little claim to respectability" who possessed inflated, even irrational, ideas about their collective authority as members of an Assembly, and who were a constant threat to the decorum of the House.

In being less enlightened than their British counterparts in the House of Commons, the members of colonial assemblies were "more easily swayed by passion or prejudice". It was lamented that both in their very nature and composition, colonial assemblies were prone upon occasion "to engender tumults", and to violate their trust through engendering a spirit of discontent which was disturbing of the peace of society.

Nonetheless, it was realized that good was never unalloyed. Given man's imperfections, such privileges as the Assembly enjoyed -- even if detrimental at times to the peace and welfare of society -- "would be ill exchanged for the stillness of despotism". For it was undeniable that:

> To be governed by Laws, and not by the arbitrary will of any man or number of men, & to have the privilege of *choosing* those who are to have a voice in *making* the laws, are the distinctions of a free people.

For the Upper Canadian Tories, there was little that could be done, but "to make the best of the existing state of things", and by exercising prudence and forbearance, and preaching "brotherly concord" and a due submission to constituted authority, to promote better feeling and perhaps ameliorate the political discord. For not only were selfish – or self-interested -- measures continually pursued in the House of Assembly, but often valuable measures of general import were lost or mutilated in the process; the unfortunate victims of "envy, stupidity & malice".

Nevertheless, things were not as hopeless as they might seem. It was recognized that,

> In all public bodies, there is great difficulty in getting good measures passed in which there is no particular interest concerned, or some passion to gratify.

Even in the best of public bodies, "the attainment of good" required a willingness to compromise, and to accept partial gains. Prudence dictated that it was often necessary to be:

content to give way to the less extended views of colleagues, and to accept of an imperfect measure, rather than lose it altogether.

All men could never be brought into the same way of thinking, since measures of great long-term advantage to the state were often slow to show their benefits. In any case, the occasional defeat of worthwhile measures was not a complete loss. At the very least, when some government measures were defeated, it assured those who differed that they "were in possession of liberty", and not subject to the dictates of the Crown.

Although the British government did not have to grant a representative system of government to the colony of Upper Canada as early as the founding of the province in 1791; nonetheless the Tories maintained that a representative Assembly, once granted, ought not to be revoked by the Imperial government. In regarding the political conflict in Lower Canada, the Upper Canadian Tories were adamant that the essential rights of the Assembly ought not to be infringed regardless of the irresponsible behavior of its Assembly members. In Upper Canada, many of the shortcomings of the Assembly were obviously the result of the immaturity of the provincial body politic, which was amenable to improvement in time. Hence, there was no cause for a complete despair.

The Tory outlook was perhaps best expressed by the Rev. John Strachan who observed:

> We are little people & pleased with little things -- great measures of policy engage little of our attention, but I hope we shall get better.

The real need was for men of independent mind: men who could provide a more enlightened representation, who would strive to overcome narrow views, and who would promote the general good and well-being of society. Men of such character could only be procured in sufficient numbers by means of "a rational plan of education, disseminating moral and religious principles" throughout the province. It was by means of education, more than legal enactments, that 'the good' could be realized because, the great imperfections of national, as well as domestic government, arose from the little virtue and soundness of principle, not only in making laws, but in putting them into execution.

It was a deficiency which could only be rectified by a comprehensive scheme of moral and religious education in a provincial school system under the direction of the National Church. (15)

For the most part the composition of the House of Assembly was such that the Tories were continually fearful that it would abuse its powers. This was not a groundless fear because on several occasions when controlled by a majority of democratic radicals, the Assembly had acted quite arbitrarily. Such was the case in its treatment of two militia officers, Colonels Givens and Coffin, in 1828. In that instance, the two officers were summoned to appear before a Select Committee of the Assembly to furnish some desired information in an enquiry.

In response, the officers informed the Chairman of their inability to obtain leave from their commanding officer to attend the House. The Assembly chose to ignore "the *usual* Courtesy" of forwarding a request to their superior to permit the officers to attend. To the contrary, a Speaker's warrant was issued immediately by the Assembly for their apprehension for contempt of the House. The homes of the two men were broken into; they were forcibly seized and taken to the Bar of the House during a late-night session; and the Assembly – or the radical members still in attendance in the Assembly -- voted to confine them to jail until the end of the session.

Such actions on the part of radical members of the Assembly did not inspire confidence in the judgment or prudence of the popular body. Nonetheless in their public utterances, the Tories maintained that the House of Assembly as an institution -- regardless of the character of its radical members -- had "unquestionably a claim to at least the appearance of respect". They continued to be staunch defenders of its rights, privileges, and immunities, including the power of commitment for contempt which had been so badly misused by the Select Committee of the Assembly. (16)

The Tory view of Representation

In the Tory view, not all men by virtue of their mere existence, were capable of properly exercising the public trust in a legislative capacity. The business of law-making did not necessarily require extensive legislative knowledge in a member, but it was requisite that he be a "liberally-educated man" in possession of "a moderate share of general information". Only through diligent study of the existing laws and the nature of the constitution could the members be competent to legislate new laws and fulfill their proper role in government.

It was evident that members of the House of Assembly, who lacked such a competence and knowledge, would not be guardians of the constitution, but rather its assailants. They would continuously quarrel "about forms and privileges" of which they were ill-informed and, consequently, would be derelict in performing the real duties of government. Such men were unconscious of the fact that as legislators:

> They are [charged] to watch over the welfare of the Province,
> to provide for its wants – to develop its resources, and generally
> to promote its prosperity.

Good government was not easily secured, but rather required a great deal of "thought, wise contrivance, and judicious arrangement". To that end, it was requisite that the elected representatives of the people be men of "leisure and intelligence" who, unlike common labourer, were not "satisfied with shallow sensibilities". Ideally, the men whom the people chose to elect as their representatives ought to be men who had attained a deeper understanding and insight into the realities of life and government through the study of "the history and policy of nations".

The Upper Canadian Tories shared the dismay, which was expressed by Sir William Blackstone (*Commentaries on the Laws of England*), that "the science of legislation, the most difficult of any" could, of all occupations, be regarded as the one requiring no preparation or learning. Indeed, the Upper Canadian Tories were moved to sarcasm in observing that in the United States it was:

a fashionable doctrine, that a man may be a very profound political economist, although his ignorance on all other subjects is quite conspicuous, and his general dullness no less manifest. Nor is *superior* fortune required to confer on him this wonderful intuitive talent in the art of Law making -- in that birth place of genius, political and legislative science, [it] is considered easy and obvious, level to the meanest capacity and most unlettered education.

Regardless of what Americans might lay claim to, the native genius of Upper Canadians was not considered sufficient to qualify everyone to participate in, let alone direct, the business of government. It could only be hoped that Canadians would not seek -- through combining pride with ignorance -- to adopt the American doctrine, but rather would realize that not all men could participate in government. If government were to be carried out "with wisdom and prudence", it was requisite that those of superior intellect, who had cultivated their faculties beyond that of their fellows, should secure election to the Legislature. (17)

The furthering of the true interests of the country demanded that the House of Assembly be composed of men of "property, intelligence and standing in society". Ideally, the members who were elected to the Assembly would be drawn from among the intelligent members of both the commercial and agricultural classes, and complemented by a due proportion of lawyers familiar with the laws of the land and the principles of the constitution.

In such an Assembly, property and knowledge would secure their proper influence, and reason and judgment would be brought to bear on all questions in the pursuit of the common good. In possessing a better understanding of the workings of the constitution, and unmarked by "that jealous suspicion of Government which prevails most with the least informed", an Assembly so composed would seek to promote the welfare of the whole community. Its members, while mindful of the true needs of their own constituents, would be above the influence of "petty and local discontents" such as were excited from time to time by "malicious demagogues" in the House of Assembly.

The ideal member of the Assembly was a man of independent circumstances who desired no office or favour from Government, and in being untrammeled with party ties, would be free and willing to act upon his own convictions. In all spheres of life, the Upper Canadian Tories admired the man of moral character who would stand up for his convictions and judge matters for himself, in being guided by what was right, rather than by "the opinions or censures of others". They expected no less from their legislators.

In the Assembly, the Tory legislators were forthright in proclaiming that in all matters before the House, they would be guided by their own judgment, and their sense of duty would not permit them to sacrifice principle to the wishes of their constituents. If the electorate did not approve of such conduct in their representative, they were advised that they should bestow their suffrage elsewhere.

The proper exercise of the duties of a member of the Legislature required a man who could, and would, "stand on independent ground" in being subject neither to the influence of the Executive nor the whims of the populace; and yet, a man who would be governed in his conduct by an awareness that such independence did not preclude rendering a general support to government, or demand that he be continually opposed to government to prove his independence. In sum, the Tories were opposed to the Reform Party concept that its members of the Assembly were elected delegates of the party and required to vote with the party on public issues. In the House of Assembly, the Tory members voted as independents, and were divided on a number of public issues; whereas the members of the Reform Party voted en masse in support of reform resolutions and bills.

In claiming such an extensive independence for individual judgement and action on behalf of legislators, the Tories assumed that the members of the Assembly – and of the Legislative Council -- would be educated gentlemen, men of "inflexible integrity" who would be possessed of an upright Christian character. As Christian gentlemen, their decisions in the Legislature would be arrived at through bringing to bear -- in a collective capacity -- the fruits of their education, wisdom, personal integrity and good breeding, combined with honesty, judgment, and discernment.

It was considered only right in a Christian nation that the legislators should be "men of Christian principles". In effect, what was desired was the election of God-fearing men who would be guided in their conduct by the Word of God – God's moral law – and an undeviating love of justice, and who would be moved by,

> a deep conviction that they must one day render an account to
> God of the trusts and talents committed to their charge.

To secure the election of such men to the Assembly was a constant concern of the leading Upper Canadian Tories. Although the Tories of York -- as distinct from the Tories of Kingston -- were opposed to the proposed Union of the provinces of Upper and Lower Canada, the Tories were united in favouring a clause in the abortive Union bill of 1822 that provided for an increase in the basic qualification required for election to the House of Assembly. In the Union bill, it was proposed that candidates for election to the Assembly must be worth at least £500 sterling "in Lands and Tenements over and above all rents and encumbrances".

It was felt that such a high qualification would ensure that men devoid of "respectability, interest or influence in the country" would be excluded from standing for election to the House of Assembly of the proposed union of the provinces. As John Macaulay -- a prominent Kingston Tory -- exclaimed, experience had proven it to be,

> an axiom that no man in this country who is worth less than
> £500 is fit to make laws, or to be trusted with a power of
> meddling with the laws fixing the rights of property.

In effect, a high qualification for entry to the House of Assembly would ensure that the members of the Assembly were prominent merchants, professionals (lawyers and doctors), and senior half-pay officers, who presumably would be landed proprietors with major investments in land holdings.

To the same end, the Tories were consistently opposed to the payment of members of the Assembly because they desired to maintain "the motive of honour" and to attract "liberal men of intelligence and candour" to stand for election to the House. The Tories were opposed to the introduction of what they regarded as 'a pecuniary motive' into the political system and, during an 1824 session of the Legislature, rejected a radical motion that the nominal monetary stipend paid to members of the Assembly be replaced by the provision of "liberal wages". To the Tories, the payment of members would encourage "needy demagogues" to seek election to the House. In effect, it was objected that:

> Giving wages to members blasts [the] noble principles of action which ought to direct the representatives of the people, and raises the dregs of the community over the wealthy, the intellect, and [the] wise. (18)

That the representatives of the people should be drawn from the educated social elite among the men of property, was regarded as not only in keeping with the natural order of things, but beneficial to the general welfare.

For the Tories of Upper Canada, the state was a unity within which there could "only be one interest common to all". It was men with a substantial stake in the country who could be counted upon to identify with the general good of the province, and who would be found "interested in promoting its prosperity". They believed that there was a common interest, and unity, which subsumed the various concerns of the different branches of the government, and that the common interest was superior to all individual or local interests.

Such a belief was consistent with the Tory interpretation of the very structure and workings of the Constitution. Thus, it was the King, as head of the nation, who represented the community as-a-whole, and who was responsible ultimately to God for securing the common good of 'the nation'. The unity of the provincial government under the Crown was evident in the fact that it was the King who bestowed the franchise upon the people of Upper Canada in granting the Constitution of 1791, and it was the King, or the King's representative, who called the Legislature into session when its advice or assistance was needed, who determined the duration of the Legislative session thorough the royal prerogatives of prorogation and dissolution. Moreover, the Assembly received its very legislative character from the Crown. Members were sent to the House of Assembly by the people in response to the King, or the King's representative, issuing the writs for an election and, once elected, the prospective members took an oath of allegiance to the King, and not to the people. Moreover, the members could not take their seat in the Assembly, and could not exercise their legislative function, unless and until they had sworn the Oath of Allegiance to the King.

For the Tories, the task of the members of the House of Assembly was not to direct government, but to give voice to "the necessities of the people" which the Crown, once duly advised,

> may consider and weight them against the general good, and grant them if that good will not suffer by it.

It was the Crown which enjoyed an absolute right of veto over Bills that were enacted by the provincial Legislature. The veto was exercised in Upper Canada either by the Lt. Governor acting directly to reject a legislative Bill or, indirectly, by the Lt. Governor reserving a Bill for the Signification of the Royal Pleasure. In the latter case, the Crown possessed a right of disallowance anytime within two years of the passing of a provincial act. (19)

The Franchise

Since the people had an indispensable role to play in the constitution of the state, it was only right that the suffrage should be granted to those who were capable of properly exercising it. The franchise so bestowed was not possessed by the people out of "any natural inalienable right independent of any but themselves", but rather was held "under God and *of the king*, God's Vicegerent over them". Being a granted right, it could be revoked if not properly exercised. It was something which,

> does not belong to any man, just because he is a man, but because of something acquired which he had not by nature, and which is accepted as a proof that he is worthy of holding a higher place in the state than that of simple existence.

Far from being free to do as they pleased with their vote, those who received the privilege of enfranchisement were charged by the King, God's anointed, with both a religious trust and social duty. They were charged to elect only God-fearing men of Christian principles, ability and wisdom, who would seek to promote the common good in their deliberations and votes in parliament. Although man was possessed of free will, and those who were enfranchised were free to vote as they wished, nonetheless voters were duly admonished that in all things "there is a right and a wrong, and it is not a matter of indifference which side we take".

If men were to be elected merely "to forward this or that measure", or were to bestow their votes for purely party and/or selfish interests, then the voter was placing his welfare as well as his very salvation in jeopardy. It was by the negligence of social duties, of which the proper exercise of political rights was one, that man brought suffering upon himself and risked the forfeit of his expectations of 'eternal felicity' in the hereafter.

For the Upper Canadian Tories, it was essential that Christian men be elected to parliament as one of the fundamental purposes of government was to defend and guard God's Church and to encourage the spread of Christian principles among the King's subjects. In the view of the Upper Canadian Tories, the election of men of immoral or infidel principles, was a denial of one's religious duty. It would result in the state being deprived of all positive faith, of its very Christian character, and of all power to act on the side of the Lord Jesus Christ and his Church. (20)

Where the franchise was concerned, there was a real danger in its democratic nature, given that in Upper Canada an almost universal manhood suffrage prevailed. The franchise was based on that of England. Members of the Assembly for counties were returned by men who were in possession of land which was held in freehold, or in other forms of tenure, to the annual value of 40 shillings, and members for the towns were elected by men who owned a dwelling house and lot of at least "a yearly value of £5 Sterling", or who were residents of a town for a year prior to the issue of the Writ of Summons for the election and paid £10 or more in rent per annum. However, in Upper Canada -- where free grants of Crown land were readily obtainable prior to 1826, with the payment of only a small government registration fee -- the 40-shilling freehold property qualification was within the reach of almost every settler.

The existence of such a broad franchise made it difficult to secure the election of better men to the Assembly. The Upper Canadian Tories lamented that in Lower Canada, the existing broadly-based franchise had facilitated the election of 'French demagogues' to the Assembly and the exclusion of the natural leaders of society -- the French seigneurs and their children; whereas, in Upper Canada, the exceptionally-broad suffrage had resulted in the election of men who appealed to popular prejudices. In the Assembly of Upper Canada, the conduct of the radical members was observed to be marked by a lack of "generosity or courtesy" in their dealings with the other branches of the Legislature, and by "a jealous desire" to push every principle and every power to its utmost limits and beyond.

In Lower Canada, the Assembly, which was dominated by its French-Canadian members, was continually engaged in a series of clashes with the Executive. One solution, which several of the leading Upper Canadian Tories advocated, was that the 40-shilling franchise be increased to at least £5, and the property qualification for election to the House of Assembly be doubled. Such an increase in the qualification for voting, and for standing for election, would serve to secure the election of better men in Lower Canada who would act more reasonably. It was regarded as a mistake to bestow such a broadly-based franchise on such "a rude society" because:

> The truth is, it becomes safer to extend privileges of this kind to Society, as it gets more improved, because intelligence, prudence, and good feeling, are calculated to counteract the wildness which naturally prevails in assemblies purely democratic.

Nonetheless, in advocating a restriction of the franchise – where the French Canadians of Lower Canada were concerned – the Upper Canadian Tories readily admitted that there were limits imposed by "the genuine principles of the Constitution". It was requisite that the land be fully represented. It was not the owner or occupier as an individual who was represented in parliament, but "the land", and consequently landowners were entitled to the franchise. Landless men were not. They could not be trusted with control over other men's property.

The belief that it was the land which was being represented in parliament was evident in the opposition of the Upper Canadian Tories to a democratic provision in the Canada Bill of 1840. The Tories were opposed in general to the Canada Bill -- by which the British Government sought to unite the legislatures of Upper and Lower Canada in a new 'United Province of Canada' – but, more particularly, they were also opposed to a provision which it contained for the establishment of district councils whose members were to be elected "by general suffrage". The Tories argued that Upper Canadians had "really, no longing for the extension of democratic principles". Canadians already possessed in practice an almost universal manhood suffrage in electing their representatives to the House of Assembly. In sum, it was the democratic principle itself that the Tories did not want to see enshrined in a parliamentary act.

Nonetheless, although they were vehemently opposed to the principle of universal manhood suffrage, the Tories regarded the right of suffrage as "the most valuable civil right known to our Constitution". They were staunch defenders of the voting rights of those who were legally qualified to vote, and who exercised their right to vote in an orderly manner; although, where Lower Canada was concerned, they favoured a higher property qualification for voting and for standing for election.

During the legislative session of 1821, the Tories had been adamant in defending the rights of location ticket holders to vote in opposing an effort by the Assembly to disenfranchise "a large proportion of the population of the Country". The issue was over whether recent immigrants from Britain who were already British subjects, had a location ticket for their land grant, and were living on their land, were property owners and entitled to vote. The Assembly took the position that British immigrants who had yet to complete their settlement duties and obtain title to their land, were not property owners, and hence ineligible to vote.

The Tories believed that the Assembly -- which contained many American immigrant settlers following the 1820 election – was acting purely from "*party* feelings" in seeking to disenfranchise new immigrants from Britain. Ultimately, the Legislature decided that British immigrants were not entitled to vote until after they had fulfilled their settlement duties and received their land title. In this instance, it was the American settlers of Upper Canada who wanted to restrict the political influence of immigrants. The British immigrant settlers, who were part of an increasingly heavy postwar emigration from Britain, posed an electoral threat to the efforts of the American settlers in Upper Canada to gain control of the Assembly from the Loyalists and their native-born sons. For the most part, the British immigrants were regarded as supporters of the provincial government establishment, monarchical government, and the British tie.

Somewhat later – following the rebellion of 1837 in Upper Canada and the rebellions of 1837-1838 in Lower Canada -- the Tories disapproved of a proposal by the English radical Whig, Lord Durham, that the Governor be given "a discretionary power' to proclaim the suspension of "the Writs of Electoral Districts" where there was a reason to expect disorder or violence. The Tories did not dispute the right of the Crown to suspend the writs; however, they were strongly opposed to the proposal of Lord Durham. His proposed measure would disenfranchise, in one undifferentiated mass, the law-abiding subjects of a district along with the disorderly elements who deserved to be deprived of their vote. As such, the proposal of Lord Durham was opposed by the Upper Canadian Tories. (21)

Political Parties

A whole range of Tory political beliefs -- from a belief in the sovereignty of God, in a common good which was superior to the sum of individual wills, and in the state as a moral entity, as well as their view of the popular branch of the legislature as a place where independent men of character, knowledge and ability would bring reason to bear in deciding what constituted the public good – all combined to sustain the Upper Canadian Tories in their opposition to political parties and extra parliamentary associations. In England, Anglican Toryism was "the creed of the nonpartisan state", and, in Upper Canada, nonpartisan government was the ideal that the Tories strove to sustain in denouncing the organizing tactics and partisan political activities of their Reform Party opponents, both within and outside of the provincial parliament. (22)

It was regarded as unfortunate that men would seek to organize extra-constitutional organizations to exercise an influence upon the electorate and the government, but it was not incomprehensible that men would do so. Although the Tories believed that government should do its best to discourage 'party spirit" and partisan activity; it was realized that:

> There is in all free countries, a party in opposition to the Government. If other causes were wanting, the desire of place alone would produce it, wherever public employments [were] accessible to all by the constitution in force.

In such circumstances, men would invariably band together to promote their own partisan interests and views. Moreover, as a society matured and developed, it was to be expected that factions -- "distinguished by peculiar principles & opinions" – would emerge within the body politic.

Although partisan politics was an understandable phenomenon, nonetheless the Tories deplored the formation of political parties because they were harmful to the peace of society and weakened the unity of the state. Political parties fostered and deepened political animosities, and kept them alive long after the electoral contests which brought them into being were decided. The problem with political parties was that once they were formed to foster a partisan object, there was no way to maintain "the desires of party" within reasonable limits. Experience had shown that:

> the noblest virtues, both public and private, are too apt to perish
> in the contest of parties.

The behavior of the Reform Party members in the House of Assembly caused the Tories no end of discouragement and disgust. They witnessed "head long votes & measures" for "the party", and noted the tendency for new Reform members to "sit in sullen silence", unwilling to listen to any appeals to reason and argument on the issues in question. At the direction of their leaders, the members of the Reform Party were:

> hurried into any and every measure against the Govt by threats
> artfully held out, that if they do otherwise they are not deserving
> of the character [of a Reformer]. (23)

The Radical Threat to the balanced Constitution

In Upper Canada, it was the democratic radicals of the House of Assembly who sought to overthrow the balance of the constitution by encroaching on the prerogatives of the Crown. During the legislative sessions of the 1820s, whenever the radicals managed to a majority in the House of Assembly, a series of resolutions and bills were passed that sought to enlarge the powers of the Assembly. The common aim was to secure control over the revenues of the provincial government and Crown patronage appointments, and, more generally, to promote the partisan interests of the radicals and their various supporting factions.

As of the beginning of the decade of the 1830s, the Assembly was demanding that the clergy reserves land endowment revenues of the Established Church of England be distributed amongst all the religious sects or devoted to education and internal improvements; that the recently-granted Royal Charter for the University of King's College be amended to make the projected university totally non-denominational; that the Legislative Council be made elective; that primogeniture by abolished; that the profitable British Postal Service be taken over by the provincial Legislature; and that "all money's [sic] raised" in the province be placed under the control of the representatives of the people – viz. the Assembly. Moreover, even earlier the democratic radicals of the Reform Party had demanded that the Assembly be given control of the land-granting department of the provincial government; that clerics, judges and sheriffs be barred from sitting in the Legislative Council; and that judges serve during good behavior rather than "during pleasure only".

At various times, the democratic radicals demanded that the Justices of the Peace and the Sheriffs be elected rather than appointed; and that juries be selected by lottery, as in some American states, rather than appointed by the sheriff. In addition, when dominated by the radicals, the Assembly repeatedly refused to vote a permanent civil list. Most of the leading radicals were immigrants from the United States, or recent immigrants from Britain who were admirers of the American democratic republic. They looked to the United States for their political ideas and ideals, and to British radicals for their extra-parliamentary tactics in fomenting public agitations. (24)

In England, the civil list was voted for the life of the monarch, but in Upper Canada the civil list was voted by the Legislature each year. However, in Upper Canada, the civil list had not become a critical political issue between the Crown and the Assembly. Earlier, under the administration of Lt. Governor Simcoe -- by a General Proclamation on the Settling of the Lands of the Crown (7 February 1792) -- one-seventh of the surveyed lands in each township was reserved for the Crown. The revenues received from the leasing of the Crown lands were intended to provide a future revenue – in addition to the Casual and Territorial Revenues of the Crown – to aid in the payment of the cost of the civil government establishment in Upper Canada. Subsequently, with little revenue being raised by the leasing of the Crown lands and little money in the provincial government treasury, the British government had paid the salaries of the Lt. Governor, the officers of the Crown, the Clerks, and the Judiciary from the Military Chest. That arrangement had ceased in 1826, with the formation in England of the Canada Company – a private land development company.

The Canada Company, with a capitalization of £1,000,000 sterling, had agreed to purchase the Crown Reserve lands, and a large tract of wild lands on Lake Huron for £344,375.7s2d, which was to be paid for in annual installments over a period of sixteen years. Through an agreement with the Colonial Office, the Canada Company retained the right to withhold one-third of that sum for the construction of roads and public improvements in the wild lands, with the other two-thirds to be placed at the disposal of the provincial government. With an independent source of revenue, the Lt. Governor no longer had to appeal to the Colonial Office for a British government grant to pay the Civil List, or to submit a request to the Assembly for a vote of monies for the Civil List from the Casual and Territorial Revenues. Hence, although the Reformers gained a majority in the July 1828 provincial election, and were in control of the House of Assembly during the following sessions in 1828, 1829, and the spring of 1830, there was no dispute over the Civil List in Upper Canada.

Following the October 1830 provincial election, the conservatives emerged with a majority in the Assembly, and in next parliamentary session in 1831 voted a permanent civil list for the life of the new sovereign, King William IV. The granting of a permanent civil list placed the provincial administration salaries and the existing annual government grants beyond interference by any future Assembly in which the radical members might possess a majority. The Civil List expenditures were audited by the Inspector-General of Public Accounts, and the report submitted to the Executive Council, and henceforth to the Assembly each year.

The reports of the Lt. Governor on the Civil List comprised a listing of the office holders and the salaries of the Lt. Governor, the law officers, and department heads, and the expenditure on clerical salaries, on the pensions paid, school costs, and the annual grants made to the churches, together with the total expense of the civil list for the previous year. In some sessions, the Lt. Governor might request that the Assembly vote an additional minor funding to meet the 'actual expenses' of the civil administration, when the fixed sums proved insufficient, or he might request that the Assembly approve an addition to the Civil List. In which case, the requested monies were voted by the Assembly to be paid by the Lt. Governor from the Casual and Territorial Revenues which were raised through government fees, import duties, and canal, harbour and road tolls, rents from mills and ferries, as well as from the payments from the Canada Company for the Crown Reserve lands which, after 1831, were subsumed within the Casual and Territorial Revenues. (25) However, where government revenues and expenditures were concerned, a new demand was raised by the political radicals.

As of July 1828, Dr. William Warren Baldwin introduced a new principle of government – the so-called "principle of responsible government" -- which focused on the Executive Council. As initially enunciated by Baldwin, the new principle had two key features. It required that the King's representative, the Lt. Governor, replace his "provincial ministry when they lost the confidence of the people, as expressed by the voice of their representatives in the assembly"; and that the Assembly was to possess the right of impeachment to remove executive councillors upon any evidence of wrongdoing. In effect, the demand was that the Crown appoint its Executive Council members from amongst the leaders of the majority party in the House of Assembly.

William Warren Baldwin interpreted his new principle as constituting simply a reform of the Constitutional Act of 1791 which would supposedly ensure the proper workings of the British Constitution in Upper Canada. In Baldwin's vision, the appointed Executive Council was viewed as a cabinet with the ministers being responsible to the elected representatives of the people in the House of Assembly for the conduct of government, and subject to being dismissed, whenever the Executive Council no longer commanded the support of a majority in the Assembly. The right of impeachment, gave the Assembly a means of removing individual members of the Executive Council for 'wrongdoing', which was not defined. (26)

For Baldwin, the principle of 'responsible government' did not involve a rejection of the sovereignty of the Crown, and would not lead to separation of Upper Canada from Britain. It required only a commitment by the Crown to grant local self-government to the Province of Upper Canada. The Crown would retain control over Imperial trade and defence, but would concede authority over the provincial revenues, provincial government patronage, and local affairs to the provincial government through instructing the Lt. Governor to accept the advice of his Executive Council on local matters. Upper Canada would still be a province of the British Empire under the Crown but, within the Province, the Crown would be bound to appoint members of the Executive Council who enjoyed the support of the elected representatives of the people – the majority party-- in the House of Assembly. Moreover, the Lt. Governor, the Crown representative, would be bound to take the advice of his Executive Council when acting on local matters. (27)

Initially, the demand for 'responsible government' was just one demand amongst various constitutional changes that the political radicals were demanding in an ongoing effort to place the House of Assembly in control of the provincial government revenues and patronage appointments. However, by early 1830s, the various Reform Party factions were united under the banner of 'responsible government', and began to refer to themselves as 'Reformers'.

In contemporary Britain, government was in transition where the meaning of responsible government was concerned. In the traditional system of parliamentary government, each member of cabinet was responsible to the King for the conduct of his department, as well as for any advice tendered. Ministers could be impeached by Parliament for personal misconduct, but the members of the cabinet were not individually or collectively responsible to the House of Commons for the conduct of their departments. Government was carried on in the name of the King, and the defeat of government measures in the House of Commons did not entail the resignation of a ministry. A government could be defeated by the passage of a nonconfidence motion in the House of Commons, but it was a very rare occurrence.

Where the formation of a government was concerned in the British Parliament, it was the King who would invite a prominent member of parliament to form a ministry which, once formed, would be kept in power by a loose alignment -- in the House of Commons -- of the supporters of the individual ministers in the cabinet. There were Tory and Whig political alignments. However, cabinet ministers represented various interests of the realm, had personal power bases, and were not responsible to the 'representatives of the people' in the House of Commons.

Moreover, in Britain, there was a landed aristocracy that controlled the House of Lords, as well as a good many House of Commons seats, and it was prominent members of the landed aristocracy who led and formed the various ministries that governed Britain both before and after the Great Reform Act of 1832. In contrast, Upper Canada lacked a landed aristocracy, and the Tories were convinced that in a single-class society -- of freeholders in possession of the franchise -- the 'principle of responsible government' was a recipe for establishing a pure democracy. For the Tories of Upper Canada, the principle of responsible government, far from being a fulfillment of the British Constitution, was, in its political and social implications, a truly revolutionary principle. (28)

The Tories could not but reject the principle of responsible government on several grounds. If it were to be imposed by the British government, it would destroy the balanced British constitution and the sovereignty of the Crown in making the executive directly responsible to the House of Assembly in provincial matters; and it would bypass the Legislative

Council, thereby rendering the landed interest of that institution a constitutional nullity. Moreover, the 'responsible government' principle was based on a Whig belief in parliamentary sovereignty – the king in parliament acting on the advice of parliament – rather than the tory constitutional view of the king as the sovereign authority in full possession of the executive power, and independent of parliament which was viewed as being a separate legislative and advisory body.

The concept that the members of the Executive Council, who advised the Crown, must be appointed from among the members of the House of Assembly, that the Executive Council had to command the support of the elected representatives in the Assembly to remain in office, smacked of popular sovereignty. It embodied a drastic diminution in the executive power of the Crown, except for Imperial matters, and constituted a denial of the sovereignty of the Crown within Upper Canada. It would place the elected representatives of the people in control of the provincial government, and thereby destroy the balance of the British constitution.

Under a system of 'responsible government', there would be no counterpoise to the tyranny of the majority in Upper Canada where the electorate was based on an almost universal male suffrage. As viewed by the Tories, it would transform the government of Upper Canada into a popular form of government, which raised the threatening spectre of 'mob rule'. More particularly, it was feared that the workings of responsible government would bring about the introduction of party government in which a political party, upon attaining a majority in the Assembly, would be in control of the distribution of government largesse and would be able to make patronage appointments for partisan party purposes. Moreover, for the Tories, the principle of 'responsible government' threatened the destruction of the political connection with the mother country, and the loss of the benefits of the Imperial trade system.

The Tory Outlook on the Constitution

In the Tory view, Upper Canada enjoyed the institutional framework of the British constitution. However, the institutions and social supports of the constitution had to be strengthened, if it were to remain viable over time and capable of promoting the social peace and good order of society. The constitution represented not only the land, but the various interests and social orders of society, and the constitution was well structured in that it fit the natural hierarchical structure of society.

The Upper Canadian Tory elite sought to maintain the British constitution and to reproduce the society, political and religious culture of England, which constituted their cultural heritage. Such a goal was not considered unrealistic because Britain already possessed a mature society which, in the Tory view, was the very embodiment of civilization. English society had evolved with the constitution, under God's permissive providence and in keeping with His scheme of things. For the Upper Canadian Tories, there was no doubt but that the existing British constitution met the needs of man in a civilized state.

The Upper Canadian Tories saw their task as one of maintaining civilization in a wilderness, on the frontiers of settlement, by supporting the constitution and the duly-constituted authorities, by strengthening the institutions of the state, and by building up the social foundations of society, to preclude the frontier population sinking into a less civilized or barbaric state of existence. That effort was part of a broader national policy which aimed at developing the British national character of Upper Canada, and at forming the province gradually – as it evolved and matured as a political society – into the image of a mature English society in all its cultural, social, religious, and political aspects.

The magnitude of the task which faced the Upper Canadian Tories, was well expressed by John Beverley Robinson:

> it should now be felt that we, in this generation, are laying the foundations of a social system, which is to extend its avails upon millions who will soon succeed. The responsibility upon us is great, & upon the measure in which we discharge our obligations, the very happiness of those who are to come afterwards may very much depend. In most human affairs, it is of the greatest consequence to begin well for with communities as with individuals, the force of good habits early inculcated, and steadily persevered in for a time, will easily preserve them in a state to which it would without such a foundation be difficult to raise them by precept or compulsion. (29)

What the Upper Canadian Tories attempted to do, and hoped to achieve in Upper Canada by means of their national policy, was conditioned by their view of the role of the constitution and the institutions of the state in shaping the British national character. It was the Tory view of the British constitution which guided their political actions, and formed part of a broader matrix of beliefs in religion and education that were bound inseparably together. For the Tories, the union of government, religion, and education was essential in any state as they were "the three great pillars of the body politic". Hence, a critical concern of the Upper Canadian Tories was to maintain the existing balance of the constitution in Upper Canada, against encroachments by the House of Assembly. (30)

———————————

Notes

Part Three: The Balanced Constitution

Part Three Divider: Anonymous, *Observations on the British Constitution and on the Proposed Improvement of our Parliamentary Representation* (Edinburgh & London, 1831), 12 & 18f.

Chapter Six - The British Constitution

1. *The Church*, (Rev. A.N. Bethune editorial) extracts from a sermon on "Our National Sins" by the Rev. William Ingraham Kip, Rector of St. Paul's Episcopal Church, Albany, New York, 12 December 1840; *The Church*, 19 September 1840 (Bethune editorial) and 26 April 1844, "Social and Political Catholicism", signed Erieus [Rev. Adam Hood Burwell]; and PAO, Strachan Sermons, Box E, 1 February 1835, St. Matthew 13:33, "Kingdom of Heaven", 3.

2. *Christian Recorder*, March 1820, II, "On the Increase of the Christian Spirit", 60; *The Church*, 24 May 1844, "Social and Political Catholicism" & 12 December 1840, (Bethune editorial on the Kip sermon); Strachan, *A Charge Delivered to the Clergy of the Diocese of Toronto, at the Visitation, April 30, 1856* (Toronto: Henry Rowsell, 1856), 8; and PAO, Strachan Sermons, Box B, 16 December 1837, Hosea 6:5, "Thy Judgments", 2. The quotations are from Strachan, *A Charge*, 1856, 8.

3. PAO, Strachan Sermons, Box E. 1 February 1835, Matthew 13:33, "Kingdom of Heaven", 3; Rev. Adam Hood Burwell, *A Voice of Warning and Instruction concerning the Signs of The Times and the Coming of the Son of Man, To Judge the Nations, And Restore all Things* (Kingston: U.C. Herald Office, 1835), 148; *The Church*, 22 December 1838, "Christian Loyalty"; and *Christian Recorder*, March 1820, Vol. II, "On the Increase of the Christian Spirit", 59-60. The quotation is from *ibid*, 59.

4. *The Church*, 24 May 1844, Erieus, "Social and Political Catholicism". [Man was created, 'in the likeness of God', as a thinking being, with the mental capacity to ultimately comprehend and understand the ways and works of God, and to do so through an assiduous application of man's God-given mental powers over time.]

5. *The Church*, 24 May 1844, Erieus, "Social and Political Catholicism" and 22 May 1841, "Origins of government" by Bishop Horsley. The quotations are from the article of 24 May 1844. The Tory view of the evolution of the British constitution differs from that of the Anglican Whig cleric William Paley (1743-1805), the Archdeacon of Carlisle, whom the Upper Canadian Tories also read. Paley presents an Old Whig view of the evolution of the British Constitution as simply the result of

historical developments, and his concept of the balance of the constitution is strictly utilitarian in being based on power relationships and the differing interests of King, nobility, and commons. There is no role for the Church of England in Paley's view of the constitution or of Christian values influencing its evolution and its efficacy. See William Paley, *A View of the British Constitution* (London: C.G. & F. Rivington, 1831).

[Samuel Horsley (1733-1806), Bishop of Rochester, published works, some posthumously, on theology, Biblical criticism, mathematics, science, and the classics. In the House of Lords, he expounded on the dangers of the revolutionary spirit of the age. See F.C. Mather, *High Church prophet: Bishop Samuel Horsley* (1733-1806) *and the Caroline tradition in the later Georgian Church* (Oxford: Clarendon Press, 1992). William Paley (1743-1805), published works on moral and political philosophy, natural theology, and the evidences of Christianity, as well as his tract on the British Constitution.]

6. *The Church*, 22 December 1838, "Christian Loyalty", 24 May 1844, Erieus, "Social and Political Catholicism", and 19 September 1840, (Bethune editorial).

7. *The Church*, 22 December 1838, "Christian Liberty".

8. *The Church*, 24 May 1844, Erieus, "Social and Political Catholicism", and 22 December 1838, "Christian Loyalty"; *Christian Recorder*, March 1820, Vol. II, "On the Increase of the Christian Spirit", 60; and *Kingston Chronicle*, 28 May 1831, [Rev. A. H. Burwell], "One of the People". The quotations are from "Social and Political Catholicism", 24 May 1844.

9. Burwell, *A Voice of Warning*, 1835, 148-149; and *Kingston Chronicle*, 31 December 1831, [Burwell] "One of the People' (second letter). The quotations are from *A Voice of Warning,* and "One of the People", respectively.

10. PAO, Strachan Sermons, Box A, 9 September 1860, Psalm 72:1, "Give the King thy Judgments", 3-5 & 8; *The Church* (Bethune editorial), 19 September 1840; *Kingston Chronicle*, 31 December 1831, "One of the People" (second letter); and Burwell, *A Voice of Warning*, 1835, 148-149. The quotation and the quoted phrases are from the sermon of 9 September 1860.

11. *The Church*, 25 August 1843, "Responsible Government" signed Digamma, 19 September 1840 (Bethune editorial), and 24 May 1844, Erieus, "Social and Political Catholicism"; *Kingston Chronicle*, 4 February 1832, [Burwell], "One of the People"; Burwell, *A Voice of Warning*, 1835, 148; Strachan, *A Discourse of the Character of King George the Third, Addressed to the Inhabitants of British North America* (Montreal: Nahum Mower,1810, 12 & 15-16; PAO, Strachan Sermons, Box D, 16 December 1837, Hosea 6:5, "Thy Judgments", 12; and *Christian Recorder*, March

1820, Vol. II, "On the Increase of the Christian Spirit", 59-60. The quotations are from Burke, *Reflections on the Revolution in France*, as quoted by "One of the People", 4 February 1832, Digamma, "Responsible Government", and Strachan, *Discourse*, 16, respectively.

12. *The Church*, 26 April 1844, Erieus, "Social and Political Catholicism".

13. *The Church*, 26 April 1844, Erieus, "Social and Political Catholicism". For the Anglican Tory view of human nature, see: the Thirty Nine Articles of the Church of England (1563, finalized 1571), and in particular articles: IX, Of Original or Birth Sin; X, Of Free Will; XI, Of Justification of Man; and XII, Of Good Works.

14. *The Church*, 26 April 1844 & 24 May 1844, "Social and Political Catholicism", Parts I and II. All quotations in this section are from the article of 26 April 1844.

15. *The Church*, 22 May 1841, "Origin of Government"; and *Kingston Chronicle*, 31 December 1831, "One of the People" (second letter).

16. PAO, Strachan Sermons, Box A, Discourse II: "Judge of All", n.d., n.p.; *Kingston Chronicle*, [Burwell] "One of the People", 16 & 30 July 1831 and 31 December 1831 (second letter), and Burke, *Reflections on the Revolution in France* as quoted at length by "One of the People", 4 February 1832, and *The Church*, 25 August 1843, Digamma, "Responsible Government.

17. *The Church*, 25 August 1843, Digamma, "Responsible Government" and 26 April 1844, Erieus, "Social and Political Catholicism"; and *Kingston Chronicle*, 31 December 1831, "One of the People", (second letter), and Burke, *Reflections on the Revolution in France*, as quoted at length by "One of the People", 28 January and 14 February 1832. The quotations are from Burke (as quoted in the 28 January 1832 article); "Social and Political Catholicism"; and "One of the People", 31 December 1831 (second letter); respectively.

18. *Kingston Chronicle*, 14 January 1832, "One of the People".

19. PAO, Strachan Sermons, Box B, [1812], Ecclesiastics 41:3, "Fear not the Sentence of Death", 6; Strachan, *Discourse*, 1810, 55-56; *The Church*, (Bethune editorial), 23 March 1839; and *Kingston Chronicle*, 31 December 1831, "One of the People", and 4 June 1819, (Macaulay editorial). The quotation is from "One of the People", 31 December 1831.

For a contemporary popular account of the Whig view of the evolution of the British Constitution as the growth of freedom and toleration through statute law, see: Jean-Louis de Lolme, *The Constitution of England, or An Account of the English Government; in which it is compared Both with the Republican Form of Government and the Other Monarchies in Europe,* (London, 2nd English edition 1781), 23-50. The de Lolme book was read by the Tories and contributed to the reverence that they had for the British Constitution in protecting 'the rights of Englishmen'.

[Additional historical information has been inserted, into this section of the dissertation chapter, pertaining to the clauses of the Magna Carta, of the Coronation Oath of 1688, and of the Bill of Rights of 1689. See online: the "Magna Carta" text; the Coronation Oath Act 1688 (c.6) as posted by the UK Statute Law Database, National Archives; and the "English Bill of Rights of 1689", posted by the Yale Law School, The Avalon Project, Documents in Law, History and Diplomacy.]

20. *Kingston Chronicle,* (Macaulay editorial), 13 July 1821, and [Rev. A.H. Burwell], "One of the People" (second letter), 31 December 1831. In rejecting divine right absolutism, and his view of the balanced constitution and limited monarchical government, the Rev. Burwell self-identifies as an 'Old Whig' of the school of Edmund Burke. However, the Upper Canadian Tories were not actually Old Whigs, even in their constitutional principles.

For a discussion of the similarities and differences between the Old Tory and Old Whig worldviews, see S.H. Beer, *British Politics in the Collectivist Age* (New York: Vintage Books, 1969), Chapter I, "Old Tory and Old Whig Politics", especially 10-13. For an explanation of the difficulties that the Revolution of 1688 posed initially for Anglican political theorists in their adherence to 'passive obedience', see G.L. Straka, *Anglican Reaction to the Revolution of 1688,* (Madison, Wisconsin: The State Historical Society of Wisconsin, 1962).

[Under the influence of the writings of Edmund Burke on the French Revolution, and with the Tory acceptance of the Glorious Revolution of 1688, it was all too common for some Upper Canadian Tories to associate themselves, mistakenly, with the Old Whigs in a narrow constitutional sense. However, the political principles of the Upper Canadian Tories were not Old Whig. They were Tories in their view of human nature, the Established Church, church-state relations, and in their view of the sovereignty of the king, the Church as an integral part of the Constitution, and the workings of the balanced constitution. The Upper Canadian Tory worldview was that of the older Christian cosmos, and their political philosophy was based on Christian religious beliefs and moral values, as distinct from the interest-group aristocratic politics and parliamentarianism of the Old Whigs of the mid-18th Century.]

21. *The Church,* 25 August 1843, Digamma, "Responsible Government", and editorials (Bethune) of 23 March 1839 & 6 February 1841; and *Kingston Chronicle,* "One of the People" (second letter), 31 December 1831. The quotations are from the "Responsible Government" letter, and the Bethune editorial in *The Church,* 23 March 1839; respectively. Trial by jury, as guaranteed by the Magna Carta was

also viewed as being essential to the preservation of the balanced constitution. As explained by the renowned Tory jurist, Sir William Blackstone, the right to trial by a jury of one's peers precluded the Crown – the executive power – from persecuting opponents through arbitrary acts of imprisonment, property seizure, and/or forced exile. (See Charles M. Haar, ed., *Commentaries on the Laws of England, On Public Wrongs by William Blackstone* (Boston: Beacon Press, 1962), 409-410. This book comprises Vol. IV, of the 1st ed. of 1769.)

22. PAC, Christopher Hagerman, *Speech of C.A. Hagerman, Esq., M.P.P. in the House of Assembly, April 18th 1836, against the adoption of the Report of the Select Committee on the subject of the differences between His Excellency and the Executive Council* (Toronto: J.H. Lawrence, 1836), 14; *Kingston Chronicle*, 10 December 1831, "Cranmer"(submitted by "One of the People"), and 18 February 1820, [Strachan], "Letter no. 4 to Robert Walsh, Esq"; PAO, Robinson Papers, Letters to John B. Robinson, Strachan to Robinson, 16 March 1808, and J.B. Robinson Letter-book 1812-15, Robinson to Robert Loring, 28 June 1814, 120; Burwell, *A Voice of Warning*, 160; Robinson, *Canada and the Canada Bill*, 1840,157; *The Church*, (Bethune editorials), 31 August 1839 & 6 February 1841; and PAO, Macaulay Papers, reel 1, 5 December 1827, Robert Stanton to John Macaulay. The quotations are from the Strachan letter to Robinson, 16 March 1808.

23. *Kingston Chronicle*, "One of the People", 28 May & 6 August 1831; Robinson, *Charge of the Honourable John B. Robinson, Chief Justice of Upper Canada to the Grand Jury of Toronto* (Toronto: Robert Stanton, 1838), 15; J.B. Robinson, *Canada and the Canada Bill*, 1840, 17; and Strachan, *Discourse*, 1810,17-18 & 24. With respect to their concept of a king "above party spirit", the Tories were deprecating the situation which had existed in Britain under George I (reigned: 1714-1727) and George II (reigned: 1727-1760). At that time, the Whig oligarchs -- for the most part under Robert Walpole (prime minister, 1721-1742) -- controlled the king and ran the government, and the monarch appeared to be but a figurehead of the Whig party. (See: Strachan, *Discourse*, 1810, 6). For the Tories, their ideal king was George III (reigned: 1760-1820), who – before his mental deterioration -- actively exercised his executive authority in choosing his prime minister from amongst the members of Parliament who could command support in the House of Commons.

24. *Kingston Chronicle*, 19 November 1819, (Macaulay editorial) and 31 December 1831, [Rev. A.H. Burwell], "One of the People" (second letter); Strachan, *Discourse*. 1810, 20-23 & 43; PAO, Robinson Papers, J.B. Robinson Letter Book, 1812 -15, J.B. Robinson to Robert Loring, 28 June 1814, 120.

25. Strachan, *Discourse*, 1810, 39-40; *Kingston Chronicle*: 14 February 1832, "One of the People" quoting Burke, *Reflections on the Revolution in France*, and 18 February 1820, [Strachan], "Letter No. 4 to Robert Walsh Esq.", and "One of

the People", 10 September 1831 & 31 December 1831(second letter); Strachan, *Sermon of General Thanksgiving*, 3 June 1814, 28; and PAO, Strachan Letter Book, 1827-39, 109. The quotations are from "One of the People", 31 December 1831, and Strachan, Letter Book, 1827-39, 109, respectively. Much of the phraseology used by the Tories is taken from the Burke publication. However, Burke had turned to Richard Hooker for much of his argument against the principles and proceedings of the French revolutionaries.

26. *Kingston Chronicle*, 31 December 1831, [Bethune] "One of the People" (second letter) and 28 January 1832, extracts quoted from Burke, *Reflections on the Revolution in France*; and Strachan, *Discourse*, 1810, 39.

27. *The Church*, (Bethune editorials), 6 January 1838, 13 April 1839 & 6 February 1841; and PAO, Strachan Papers, reel 3, 6 March 1839, "Working of the Union", 1-14.

28. PAO, Strachan Papers, reel 8, "Religious Instruction", n.d., (package 2), 6; and *Kingston Chronicle*, "One of the People", 28 May 1831 & 9 July 1831.

29. *The Church*, (Bethune editorial), 6 January 1838 and 4 April 1840, "Copy of a Despatch from Lord John Russell to the Rt. Hon, C.P, Thomson, dated 14 October 1839"; PAO, Strachan Sermons, Box A, 20 April 1838, Ephesians 4:31-32, "Let all bitterness and wrath ... be put away", 1-2 & 6-7; *Kingston Chronicle*, "One Of the People", 28 May & 18 June 1831; PAO, Strachan Papers, reel 8, "Religious Instruction", n.d., (package 2), 1; and Strachan, *A Charge*, 30 April 1856, 5-6. The quotations are from Strachan, *A Charge*, 6, and "One of the People", 28 May 1831, respectively.

30. Strachan, *A Charge*, 30 April 1856, 6; *Kingston Chronicle*, "One of the People", 28 May & 31 December 1831 (second letter); and PAO, Strachan Papers, reel 8, "Religious Instructions",n.d., (package 2), 1. The first quotation is from Strachan, *A Charge*, 6, and the following two quotations are from "One of the People", 28 May 1831.

31. PAO, Strachan Sermons, Box C, 27 December 1841, John 13:23, "Leaning on Jesus", 2-3. The quotation is from page 2.

32. *The Church*, (Bethune editorials), 6 January 1838 & 12 December 1840; and Strachan, *Discourse*, 1810, 5-17 & 38-39. The Upper Canadian Tory concept of a patriot king appears to have been directly influenced by the ideas of the 18th Century tory politician/statesman, Henry St. John, Viscount Bolingbroke, as set forth in his treatise *The Idea of a Patriot King* (New York: Library of Liberal Arts, 1965, 1st. ed. 1749). However, the Upper Canadian Tory concept of the Patriot King differed in conceiving the king as being a Christian gentleman upholding Christian moral

values in government and in his personal life. Bolingbroke enunciated Tory political principles, but in his political career he was a Machiavellian rather than a true Tory, and in his private life he lacked a Christian moral character.

Chapter Seven - The Constitution of Upper Canada

1 . *Upper Canada Gazette*, "Provincial Parliament of Upper Canada", 8 February 1821, Speech by Attorney General J.B. Robinson, and 15 February 1821, Speeches by Attorney General Robinson and C.A. Hagerman; PAO, Strachan Sermons, Box B, [1812], Ecclesiastics 41:39, "Fear not the sentence of Death"; *Kingston Chronicle*, (Macaulay editorial), 30 March 1821; Strachan, *Discourse*, 1810, 39; Strachan, *A Visit to Upper Canada*, 1819, 137; [Strachan], "Address of the House of Assembly", 5 August 1812, 153 of reprint in Bowler, "Propaganda in Upper Canada"; C.E. Cartwright, ed., *Life and Letters of Richard Cartwright*, 58, Richard Cartwright to Isaac Todd, 1 October 1794; and PAC, Christopher Hagerman, *Speech of C.A. Hagerman, Esq., in the House of Assembly, April 18ᵗʰ, 1836, against the adoption of the Report of the Select Committee on the subject of the differences between His Excellency and the Executive Council* (Toronto: J.H. Lawrence, 1836), 13. On the various courts of Upper Canada, and the judicial personnel, see Frederick H. Armstrong, *A Handbook of Upper Canadian Chronology and Territorial Legislation* (London, Canada: University of Western Ontario, 1967), 105-112.

On the court system, justices of the peace, and sheriffs, see, respectively: William Renwick Riddell, "A Criminal Circuit in Upper Canada a Century Ago", *Journal of the American Institute of Criminal Law and Criminology*, 12, no. 1, 1921, 91-104, Susan Dawson Lewthwaite, "Law and Authority in Upper Canada: The Justices of the Peace in the Newcastle District, 1803-1840" (University of Toronto: Ph.D. Thesis, 2001); and "The Office of Sheriff, Public Goals, and the Clerk of the Crown and Pleas" in *Report of the Commissioners appointed to investigate and report on the state of several Public Departments of the Province* (Toronto, 20 January 1840).

The right of parliament – the Lords Spiritual and Temporal and the Commons - to impeach the King's officers and appointees for "high crimes and misdemeanors" was a medieval right. The most widely-known case in Britain was the failed attempt by the Whig opposition to impeach Warren Hastings in 1788-1795 for his supposed misrule in India. In England, the House of Commons would draw up the articles of impeachment, and the trial would be held before the House of Lords, which would serve as the judge and jury. The accused had a right to defend himself by counsel. The U.S. Constitution of 1787 gave Congress the right to impeach all office holders, including the President and the Vice-President for "treason, bribery, and other High Crimes and misdemeanors". The House of Representatives would impeach, the Senate would try the impeachment, and the office holder would be removed from office, if convicted.]

2. PAO, Robinson Papers, J.B. Robinson Letterbook 1812-15, J.B. Robinson "Memorandum", n.d., n.p.; and PAO, Robinson Papers 1862-1905 (miscellaneous), J.B. Robinson, "Memorandum on the Revenue of Upper Canada", n.d., 15-16.

3. Strachan, *A Visit to Upper Canada*, 1819, 139; PAC, Christopher Hagerman, *Speech of C.A. Hagerman, 18 April 1836*, 3-5, 7-9 & 17. The quotation is from *Speech of C.A. Hagerman*, 8. For the instructions governing the selection and appointment of members of the Executive Council, see PAO, Robinson Papers, 1806-1812, J.B. Robinson draft of the "[Royal] Instructions to Prevost", 22 October 1811, clauses 4,5 & 6, on pages 2-3.

4. Sanderson, ed., *Arthur Papers*, Vol. I, J.B. Robinson to Arthur, 16 April 1838, 77-78; PAO, Robinson Papers 1813-17, Strachan "Reasons against moving the seat of government", 1816, 8; and John Strachan to James Stephen, Assistant Under-Secretary of State, Colonial Office, 18 January 1831, 138- 141 in J.L. H. Henderson, *John Strachan, Documents and Opinions* (Toronto: McClelland & Steward, 1969). The quotation is from the Strachan memorandum.

[See also, The Constitutional Act, 1791 (31 Geo. III, c. 31), clauses XLVI, XLVII & L; and Armstrong, A Handbook, 11-15, for the Executive Council members. The initial act renouncing the right of the king and parliament to levy taxes on the British colonies of British North America and the West Indies, was the Taxation of Colonies Act, 1778 (18 Geo. III, c. 12), which was enacted in a belated effort to placate the American colonists during the American Revolution. In Upper Canada, the Chief Justice was a member of the Executive Council until January 1831. At that time, the liberal-Whig government in Britain declared that the Chief Justices of the colonies could no longer sit in the Executive Council.]

5. PAO, Robinson Papers, Letterbook of J.B. Robinson, J.B. Robinson to Henry John Boulton, 2 January 1816; Robinson, "Future Government of Canada" in *Canada and the Canada Bill*, 1840, 143-145 & 148; *U.C. Gazette* , 15 February 1821, "Provincial Parliament of Upper Canada", Hagerman speech; C.E. Cartwright, ed., *Life and Letters of Richard Cartwright*, R. Cartwright to Chief Justice Alcock, 14 March 1807, 138; and [Strachan], *Address of the House of Assembly*, 5 August 1812, 153 of reprint in Bowler, "Propaganda in Upper Canada". The quotations are from the *Address of the House of Assembly*; and Robinson "Future Government of Canada", 145; respectively.

6. *The Church*, (Bethune editorial), 6 February 1841; John Beverley Robinson, "Plan for a General Legislative Union", 1822, 32; C.E. Cartwright, ed., *Life and Letters*, R. Cartwright to Chief Justice Alcock, 14 March 1807,137; PAO, Robinson Papers, Letterbook of J.B. Robinson, 1814-1862, J.B. Robinson to Lord Glenelg, 6 February 1838, 48, and Journals of J.B. Robinson, J.B. Robinson to Lord Seaton

[Sir John Colborne], 30 March 1854, 37 & 40-41. For Simcoe's Circular creating the "Lieutenants of Counties" and their duties, see, Cruikshank, ed., *The Correspondence of Lieut. Governor John Graves Simcoe*, Vol. I, 245, "Circular Letter to Lieutenants of Counties", 21 December 1794.

7. *Kingston Chronicle* (Macaulay editorial), 7 May 1819; PAO, Strachan Papers, reel # 3, "Working of the Union", 6 March 1839, 2 & 4; De Lolme, *The Constitution of England*, (4th ed., 1784, lst English edition June 1775), xvi; J.B. Robinson, "Plan for a General Legislative Union", 1822, 32; Port Hope, Ontario, Cartwright Family Papers (Private Collection), Richard Cartwright to James Cartwright, 22 January 1807; Strachan, *An Appeal to the Friends of Religion and Literature in Behalf of the University of Upper Canada* (London: R. Gilbert, 1827), 8. The quotations are from De Lolme, *The Constitution of England*, xvi; and Robinson, "Plan for a General Legislative Union", 1822, 32; respectively.

8. Strachan, *Letter to Frankland Lewis*, 1830, 81-82.

9. Robinson, "Plan for a General Legislative Union", 1822, 32; *The Church*, (Rev. A.N. Bethune editorial), 6 February 1841; and *Kingston Chronicle*, 17 December 1831, [Rev. A. H. Burwell], "One of the People". The quotation is from *The Church*, 6 February 1841.

10. *Kingston Chronicle*, 17 December 1831, [Rev. A. H. Burwell], "One of the People". The quotations are from this source.

11. *Kingston Chronicle*, "One of the People", 17 December 1831, and 4 & 11 January 1822, "Provincial Parliament in Upper Canada": speeches of Marshall Spring Bidwell and Major Rogers, and speeches in reply by W.W. Baldwin, and Attorney General J.B. Robinson and Christopher Hagerman; *U.E. Loyalist*, 30 December 1826, "Proceedings in Parliament": speech by the Attorney General. In the postwar period, the political alignments in Upper Canada -- with the exception of the Loyalty Election of June 1836 -- paralleled the British pattern of a whig-radical alliance opposed to the Tories. In Upper Canada, several wealthy, landed whigs – such as William Warren Baldwin -- were aligned with the political radicals in attacking the established prerogatives of the Crown in seeking to place the Assembly in control of government revenues and patronage appointments. However, the political radicals and the liberal-whigs did not share a common social outlook. The whigs of Upper Canada were not democrats or social egalitarians, which was evident when William Warren Baldwin opposed the attempt by the political radicals to abolish the law of primogeniture, and expressed his view that the Crown ought to grant large tracts of land to men of eminence to facilitate the establishment of a landed aristocracy in Upper Canada.

12. *Kingston Chronicle*, 17 December 1831, "One of the People".

13. PAO, Macaulay Papers, reel l, John Macaulay to Jonas Jones, 24 November 1822; *The Church*, 25 August 1843, Digamma, "Responsible Government", and 6 February 1841, (Bethune editorial); [Strachan], "Address of House of Assembly", reprinted in Bowler, "Propaganda in Upper Canada", 153; and Robinson, "Future Government of Canada", *Canada and the Canada Bill*, 146.

14. *Kingston Chronicle*, 4 January 1822, "Provincial Parliament": Hagerman speech; PAO, Macaulay Papers, reel l, 30 December 1821, Christopher Hagerman to John Macaulay, and 3 March 1828, Robert Stanton to John Macaulay; *The Church*, (Bethune editorial), 6 February 1841. In addition to the Blackstone quotation, the other quotations are from Hagerman to Macaulay, 30 December 1821, and *The Church*, 6 February 1841, respectively.

15. PAO, Macaulay Papers, reel l, 24 November 1822, John Macaulay to Jonas Jones, and 23 March 1828, Robert Stanton to John Macaulay; C.E. Cartwright, ed., *Life and Letters of Cartwright*, 118, R. Cartwright, "Memorandum of Transactions in the First Session of the Third Parliament of Upper Canada", 1801; *The Church*, (Bethune editorial), 6 February 1841; PAO, Robinson Papers, Letters to J.B. Robinson, Strachan to J.B. Robinson, 29 February 1816; PAO, Robinson Papers, Charges to the Grand Juries 1829-41, J.B. Robinson, "Charge delivered at Toronto", 25 May 1841; and Strachan, *Sermon on the Death of Cartwright*, 3 September 1815, 33-34. The quotations are from Robinson, "Charge", 25 May 1841, Strachan to Robinson, 29 February 1816, Strachan, *Sermon on Death of Cartwright*, 3 September 1815, 33, Strachan to Robinson, 29 February 1816, and Strachan, *Sermon on Death of Cartwright*, 3 September 1815, 34, respectively.

16. PAO, Macaulay Papers, reel 1, 24 November 1822, John Macaulay to Jonas Jones & 8 January 1823, J. Macaulay to Livius P. Sherwood & 23 March 1828, Robert Stanton to John Macaulay; C.E. Cartwright, ed., *Life and Letters of Cartwright*, 115-118, R. Cartwright, "Memorandum of Transactions", 1801; and Strachan, *Bill for Uniting*, 1824, 6-7.

17. *Kingston Chronicle*, 4 June 1819 & 30 August 1822 (Macaulay editorials) & 24 August 1822, "Heads of Bill for re-uniting Upper and Lower Canada" & 17 December 1831, "One of the People"; PAO, Macaulay Papers, reel 1, 8 November 1822, John Strachan to John Macaulay, and 24 November 1822, John Macaulay to Jonas Jones; and *The Church*, 8 July 1837, "Signs of the Times". The quotations are from the Macaulay editorial of 4 June 1819.

18. *Kingston Chronicle*, 7 July 1820 & 30 August 1822 (Macaulay editorials) & 24 August 1822, "Heads of Bill for reuniting Upper and Lower Canada"; PAO, Strachan

Papers, reel 12, Strachan Letter Book 1844-49, John Strachan to [William] Boulton, 11 December 1844; PAO, Robinson Papers, 1839-42, J.B. Robinson, (draft) letter to *The Church*, 12 April 1842, 2 & 16, and 1823-37, J.B. Robinson, "To the Free and Independent Electors of the Town of York", n.d. [1824]; Strachan, *Sermon on the Death of Cartwright*, 1815, 36-37; PAO, Macaulay Papers, reel 1, 25 February 1821 & 30 December 1821, Christopher Hagerman to John Macaulay, and 24 November 1822, John Macaulay to Jonas Jones, and 8 November 1822, John Strachan to John Macaulay; J.B. Robinson, "Letter to Earl Bathurst" in *Four Pamphlets*, 26 December 1824, 59; *The Church* (Bethune editorial), 3 April 1841; *The Church, Supplement,*12 July 1844, Strachan, "Charge"; PAO, Strachan Sermons, Box C, "Charge', n.d. [1851], Sheet 7, 27; Strachan, *Bill for Uniting*, 1824, 24; and C.E. Cartwright, ed., *Life and Letters of Cartwright*, 120-121, Richard Cartwright, "Memorandum of Transactions", 1801. The quotations are from Strachan, "Charge", 12 July 1844, Macaulay to Jonas Jones, 24 November 1822, and Strachan, *Bill for Uniting*, 1824, 24, respectively.

19. Strachan, *A Visit to Upper Canada*, 1819, 139; *The Church*, 25 August 1843, Digamma, "Responsible Government"; Robinson, "Future Government of Canada", in *Canada and the Canada Bill*, 1840, 157; Kingston Chronicle, 4 January 1822, "Provincial Parliament": Hagerman speech, and 28 May 1831, "One of the People". The quotation is from the latter.

20. *The Church*, 25 August 1843, Digamma, "Responsible Government"; *The Church, Supplement*, 12 July 1844, Strachan, "Charge"; PAO, Strachan Sermons, Box C, Strachan "Charge", Sheet 7, n.d. [1851], 26- 27. The quotation is from Digamma, "Responsible Government", 25 August 1843.

21. [Strachan], "Address of the House of Assembly", 5 August 1812, 153 of reprint in Bowler, *Propaganda*; James [John] Strachan, *A Visit to Upper Canada*, 1819, 138; Robinson, *Letter to Bathurst*, 26 December 1824, 27; Strachan, *Bill for Uniting*, 1824, 12-13; PAO, Macaulay Papers, reel 1, Christopher Hagerman to John Macaulay, 7 March 1821, and reel 4, 7 August 1841, John Macaulay to John Kirby; Robinson, "Future Government of Canada", *Canada and the Canada Bill*, 1840, 151-52; PAO, Robinson Papers, 1839-42, J.B. Robinson, "Remarks on Lord Durham", 23 February 1839, 26; *York Weekly Post*, 15 March 1821, "Provincial Parliament of Upper Canada", speech by Attorney General Robinson. The quotation is from Strachan, *Bill for Uniting*, 13.

22. This paragraph is a composed of the ideas that have been discussed in this chapter, and organized around insights gained from reading S.H. Beer, *British Politics in the Collectivist Age*, (New York: Vintage Books, 1969), chapters 1 & 2. Based on Beer's analysis of Old Toryism, Whig parliamentarianism, and Radicalism, the Upper Canadian Tories were Old Tories in their view of the church-state polity, the moral

role of government, and their view of the king as the sovereign power.

23. PAO, Robinson Papers, Charges to the Grand Juries, 1829-41, J.B. Robinson, "Charge at Toronto", 25 May 1841, 13-14; PAO, Strachan Sermons, Box B, Ecclesiastics 41:3, "Fear not the sentence of Death" [1812], n.p.; Robinson, "Future Government of Canada", *Canada and the Canada Bill*, 1840, 126; and PAO, Macaulay Papers, reel 2, Robert Stanton to John Macaulay, 29 January and 25 February 1835. The first two quotations are from Robinson, "Future Government", 126, and the third quotation is from Stanton to Macaulay, 29 January 1835.

[See also, Sanderson, *Arthur Papers*, II, 52-65, Robinson to the Colonial Secretary, Normanby, 23 February 1839, which is summarized by Craig, *Upper Canada*, 265.]

24. [Historical information on the constitutional demands of the radicals has been inserted from the following sources: Aileen Dunham, *Political Unrest in Upper Canada, 1815-1836* (Toronto: McClelland & Stewart/Carleton Library Series, 1969), 114-118, 121-123 & 150-160; and Craig, *Upper Canada*, 191-194 & 203-209. For a comment on the American influences on the democratic radicals, their character and biases, and their general lack of education (except for their liberal-whig leaders), see Craig, *Upper Canada*, 198-199 & 208-209. Under the Constitutional Act, clerics were banned from the Assembly, but not from the Legislative Council.]

25. Dunham, *Political Unrest*, 35-39; and Craig, *Upper Canada*, 24 & 134-137. For a report by the Lt. Governor to the Assembly with a request for additional funding for the Civil List, see: *Journal of the House of Assembly of Upper Canada, 1st Session, 13th Parliament, Session 1835-7*, F.B. Head, Government House, 14 February 1837 (Toronto: Robert Stanton, King's Publisher, 1837), 461-466.

26. [Craig, *Upper Canada*, 202-203, and Jeffrey L. McNairn, *The Capacity to Judge, Public Opinion and Deliberative Democracy in Upper Canada, 1791-1854* (Toronto: University of Toronto Press, 2000), 43-47. For an overview of the Tory concept of government by an educated elite -- serving in an appointed Executive Council -- versus the Reform concept of government by the representatives of the people in the elected Assembly, which was taken to represent 'public opinion', such as it was formed by the press, see McNairn, 53-62.]

27. [For the Baldwinian concept of responsible government, see: Michael S. Cross, *A Biography of Robert Baldwin, The Morning-Star of Memory* (Don Mills, Ontario: Oxford University Press, 2012), 16-18, 37 & 84; and Gerald Craig, ed., *Discontent in Upper Canada* (Toronto: Copp Clark, 1974), 74-75, Robert Baldwin to Lord Glenelg, Colonial Secretary, 18 July 1836.]

The concept of responsible government, as advocated by William Warren Baldwin, was unique in that – whether Baldwin realized it or not -- it combined three distinct political traditions where the political theory of government was concerned. In its projected workings in Upper Canada, the principle of responsible government was consistent with 18th Century Whig Parliamentarianism in which parliament – or more precisely, the king in parliament – was held to be the sovereign authority, with the king exercising the executive authority in acting on the advice of his ministers who were dependent on the support of the House of Commons. The underlying principle of Whig Parliamentarianism was an understanding that the king would act according to the advice of his Cabinet.

Externally, where the principle of sovereignty was concerned, the concept of responsible government -- as espoused by William Warren Baldwin -- followed the traditional Tory concept of the King as the sovereign power, with the Province of Upper Canada being united to Britain under the sovereignty of the Crown, rather than under the sovereignty of the Imperial parliament.

Thirdly, the division of powers between the provincial parliament and the Imperial parliament, as envisaged by William Warren Baldwin in his concept of 'responsible government', embodied the older medieval concept of a divisible sovereignty under which the Crown could delegate sovereign powers over specified local matters to a subordinate body through the granting of a charter, with the local sovereign authority limited to not passing any laws contrary to the laws of the realm, and owing loyalty and allegiance to the Crown. See Samuel H. Beer, *British Politics in the Collectivist Age* (New York: Random House, 1969), 13-15; and Robert W. Passfield, *Phips' Amphibious Assault on Canada –1690* (By Author, 2011), "Where Sovereignty Lay", 77-81.]

28. [This analysis of the revolutionary nature of the principle of 'responsible government' draws on: Dunham, *Political Unrest*, 154-155; and Craig, *Upper Canada*, 203. See also McNairn, *The Capacity to Judge*, 43-48. More generally, for a summary of conservative arguments against the principle of responsible government during the later Metcalfe crisis of 1843-1844, see McNairn, 251-255.]

[In the United States, the Constitution of 1787 was a constitution of checks and balances. The executive (the President, and his appointed cabinet) was separate from the Legislature which comprised the Senate and the House of Representatives. The President had a veto over bills passed by the Legislature that could only be overcome by a vote of a two-thirds majority of the members of both the Senate and the House of Representatives. Moreover, although the United States was a democratic republic, only the members of the House of Representatives were elected directly by a universal male suffrage, exclusive of black slaves and Indians. The President and Vice-President were elected through an Electoral College which comprises electors from each state, with the number of electors from a state being based on its number of senators and representatives in Congress, and, initially, Senators were selected by the legislatures of the state governments. In effect, even the American republic did not have a purely popular form of representative government such as was being advocated by the Reform Party in Upper Canada with its principle of 'responsible government'.]

29. *Kingston Chronicle*, 31 December 1831, [Rev. Adam Hood Burwell] "One of the People". The quotation is from: PAO, Robinson Papers, Charges to the Grand Juries, 1829-1841, J.B. Robinson, "Charge to the Grand Jury", Toronto, 1 April 1834, 9. The Robinson statement, as quoted, closely parallels an earlier statement of Richard Cartwright on the critical importance of the character of the people in the founding of a viable nation dedicated to promoting the common good of the commonwealth.

30. *Kingston Chronicle*, 28 May & 31 December 1831, [Rev. Adam Hood Burwell], "One of the People". [Since this chapter of the dissertation was written G. Blaine Baker has published several articles on the tory concept of law and the legal professional. See Baker "'So Elegant a web': Providential Order and the Rule of Secular Law in Early Nineteenth Upper Canada", *University of Toronto Law Journal*, 38, 1988, 184-205; and Baker, "The Juvenile Advocate Society, 1821-1826: Self-Proclaimed Schoolroom for Upper Canada's Governing Class", *Historical Papers / Communications historiques*, 20, no. 1, 1985, 74-101.]

Part Four

The National Church

"...it is the duty of every Christian government to support such a religious establishment as may best secure the benefits of [the Christian] revelation to all their subjects. Now, as this divine revelation is intended to promote among all men true morality and purity of life, to become the mother of good works, our cordial in life, and our comfort in death, to bring us daily into the presence of God and our Saviour that we may believe in his holy name, love him with all our hearts, and by making him the object of imitation and the foundation of our faith, ... resemble him on earth, and follow him to heaven; an establishment which produces these excellent effects ought to be cherished by every good government, in its own defence, as the guardian and nourisher of the purest social and domestic virtues."

Rev. John Strachan
A Sermon Preached at York
3 July 1826

"The Honourable and Right Reverend John Strachan, Bishop of Toronto". By
George Theodore Berthon, 1847. Toronto Reference Library.

Chapter Eight

The Concept of a National Church

For the Upper Canadian Anglican Tories, the Church of England was the Established Church of Upper Canada -- the National Church of the province -- and a critical component of their National Policy was to strengthen, extend, and maintain the Church of England in Upper Canada. In that endeavour, the Anglican Tories were motivated not only by their Christian faith and view of the Church of England as a religious institution, but also by their view of the Church of England as a political, social and cultural institution. In that latter respect, their efforts were shaped by their view of the historic role of the Established Church in the proper functioning of the British Constitution and in the formation of the British national character, and their knowledge of the historic prerogatives of an established church, as well as their concept of the Christian duties of the state, and their perception of the religious needs of the pioneer society of Upper Canada.

The Church of England

Where the Church of England was concerned as a religious institution, the Tories believed it to be "the vehicle of true religion" in being a branch of "the one holy Catholic and Apostolic Church". It was, to them, a member of the Church of God, the Universal Church, which comprised the churches of eastern and western Christendom, and was to be found in every country where Christianity prevailed. As a member of the Universal Church, the Church of England adhered to the "Faith, ministry and worship" and all the essentials of the apostolic and primitive Church of Christ, with its ministry constituted in the traditional three orders of bishops, priests and deacons. It was a Church with a lawful ministry, which was governed by ordained bishops who were descended from and directly connected to the Apostles, and ultimately with Christ, and who preached 'the Word' and faithfully administered the sacraments. Above all, it was the Church of the Redeemed, embracing all its baptized adherents, and in being part of the Universal Catholic Church, it was commanded by Christ to make disciples of all nations, without which there could be no salvation.

The catholic and apostolic nature of the Church of England was of the utmost importance to the Anglican Tories as it constituted the basis of their belief that it was a 'true Christian church'. The Anglican clergy continually strove -- through their preaching, teaching, and religious tracts -- to convince Upper Canadians in general that the National Church had not lost or abandoned its pristine Christian character through the passage of time. To that end, the Rev. John Strachan, and the Anglican clerics whom he had educated in Upper Canada, continually set forth their conception of the national Church of England, their interpretation of the impact of the Reformation on that institution, and the worthiness of the Church of England to be the national church of Upper Canada. (1)

In commenting upon the Protestant Reformation of the sixteenth century – as it affected the Church of England -- the Anglican clergy of Upper Canada maintained that the reformers had sought only to purify the Church, rather than to discard her institutions or the gospel which she taught. Consequently, the reformers of the Anglican Church had preserved and restored the gospel of Christ while purging the Church of all corruptions and superstitions accumulated over time. The Anglican reformers of the Church were acutely aware that it was a divine institution, and that it was inviolable in being founded by Christ and his Apostles. Hence, the Anglican reformers were very careful to remove the "superfluous and corrupt" elements that had accrued from man over time, while at the same time they had strived to adhere to the faith, worship and regimen which had prevailed in Apostolic times in all its purity and simplicity. The reformation of the Church of England was a gradual process which was guided not by a desire to innovate, but rather by a dedication to restoration.

It was maintained that, in their piety and wisdom, the Anglican reformers had rejected the "improvident recklessness" which characterized many of the reformed churches and sects, and declined to throw away the good when encumbered by some accidental evil. The reformation of the Anglican Church had restored the purity of the Apostolic Church, and buttressed it through collecting the ancient creeds and liturgies and setting them forth in "the 'scriptural doctrines and offices of devotion" of the Book of Common Prayer. (2)

The clergy of the Church of England, and the Upper Canadian Tories who were adherents of the National Church, were adamant in their insistence that the Church of England did not separate from the Catholic Church of Christ at the Reformation, and that the Church of England was not a newly-founded church based upon doctrines which were devised by the ingenuity of man, such as the churches of Martin Luther, John Calvin, and John Knox. During the Reformation, the Church of England had rejected papal supremacy, but that was part of the restoration and reformation of the English church to apostolic perfection and initial integrity through a reassertion of the original character of the Church of England as an independent branch of the Catholic Church. It was not the Roman Church that had founded the Church of England. It had existed as an independent Christian church until the eleventh century when the 'papal yoke' was imposed upon it. Thereafter, the Anglican Church had struggled -- intermittently, for centuries -- to re-assert its independence, which was finally re-established at the Reformation.

From its earliest days, the Church in England had opposed innovations which were made by the Church of Rome -- such as the introduction of the adoration of images, and the doctrine of transubstantiation -- and had remonstrated continually against the ever-increasing extension of papal power and claims over the Anglican Church. In Tory eyes, the Reformation, as it had unfolded in England, was a conservative undertaking which had aimed at restoring the Church of England to her proper position as an independent branch of the Church Catholic; and it had been accomplished through rejecting papal supremacy and the superstitions and corruptions which had accompanied the supremacy of the Papacy. The Church of England had continued to be the same body that it had been before the Reformation. Neither in the sacraments, nor in the succession of its bishops, did the Anglican Church break with the primitive Church of Christ. (3)

Although the Church of England and the Church of Rome were both regarded as being members of the universal Christian Church, it did not mean that the Church of England was opposed to Protestantism, or that it was not a Protestant church. On the contrary, the Church of England believed in, and preached, "'the great Gospel principles of Protestantism" which were: the redemption of man through Christ's atonement, and the doctrine of 'justification by Faith alone'. The Anglicans were at one with the Protestants in rejecting the Popish doctrine of salvation by merit or good works, and what they regarded as other delusions which only served to obscure the essential truths of Christian salvation. On the other hand, the Church of England repudiated what was regarded as the equally fallacious error of the Antinomian sects who preached salvation by "the efficacy of faith only, without corresponding works".

As viewed by the Tories, the Church of England of the Reformation -- in restoring the gospel of Christ, in rejecting the superstitions and corruptions of the Roman Church, and in maintaining the apostolic succession -- was the 'true religion of Christ'. Moreover, it was the "*via media*", the path of moderation, in occupying the middle ground between the superstitions and corruptions of the Roman Church, and the multiple heresies and fanaticism of the religious sects that had sprang up during the Reformation period. The Anglican Church was regarded as "the bulwark of the Protestant Reformation" through the learning and influence of the theological writings of the Anglican divines on faith, doctrine, worship and spirituality. Not only was the Anglican Church the established national church of England, it was – so the Tories believed -- the Established Church of the Province of Upper Canada.

In the Constitutional Act of 1791, which founded the Province of Upper Canada, the Lt. Governor was authorized to reserve 1/7th of the land in each township survey – the Clergy Reserves – solely for "the Support and Maintenance of a Protestant Clergy". Moreover, as parishes were established within the province, the Lt. Governor -- with the advice of his Executive Council -- was charged with establishing, within each parish, a Parsonage or Rectory "according to the Establishment of the Church of England", and was authorized to endow each parsonage or rectory with part of the lands reserved within each township for that purpose: viz. for the support of 'the Protestant Clergy'.

Once a parsonage or rectory was established, the Lt. Governor was to present a duly-ordained minister of the Church of England "to hold and enjoy" the parsonage or rectory with all the rights and emoluments, terms and conditions, and duties, of an incumbent minister of the Established Church in England. Moreover, the presentation of a minister to a parsonage or rectory was to be "subject and liable to all Rights of Institution, and all other Spiritual and Ecclesiastical Jurisdiction and Authority" of the Bishop of Nova Scotia in accordance with "the Laws and Canons of the Church of England". At the time of the passage of the Constitutional Act, the Bishop of Nova Scotia administered a diocese that extended over Nova Scotia, New Brunswick, St. John's (Prince Edward) Island, Newfoundland, and Bermuda, as well as the newly-created provinces of Upper and Lower Canada.

The Upper Canadian Tories were convinced that the reservation of lands for the support of a 'Protestant Clergy' -- as set forth in the Constitutional Act, and the provisions in the Act for the establishment and support of parsonages and rectories for the Anglican clergy on the same terms and conditions as enjoyed by the Established Church in England -- was proof positive that Church of England was the 'Established Church' of the Province. Moreover, they believed that the provincial government and the parliament of Great Britain were bound by the Christian duty of the state to support the 'Established Church' of Upper Canada, and to safeguard the provisions that had been made in the Constitutional Act for the support and maintenance of the National Church. (4)

The Christian Duty of the State

For the Tories, the Christian faith was necessary to salvation, as well as to the maintenance of social order and public morality in any state. Hence, it was the duty of government "to instruct in her principles, and to rule and obey in her spirit", and the duty of all subjects -- to whom it was preached -- to "receive and believe it". (5)

Every Christian government was held to be under an obligation, a trust, to guard the public morals and to contribute support to render effective the religious instruction of its subjects. A state, as much as any individual, owed its existence to God, and both the state and the individual were equally subject to God's moral law. It was incumbent upon the state to take measures "to secure the benefits of revelation" for all its subjects. And the most effective means of doing so was through a religious establishment comprising ministers of the gospel who were properly educated, trained and appointed for the task. Moreover, the fulfillment of that task required, in turn, government support for an ecclesiastical establishment. A Christian nation which failed to acknowledge its duty to God to secure God's revelation to its people, through providing support for a national church, was viewed as somewhat of an anomaly. (6)

For the Anglican Tories, a national church establishment was in keeping with human nature in serving the religious needs of man. Human nature did not change, and man was by nature a religious being. Throughout recorded history, "all States and people in every age" who had in any way believed in a superior being and an afterlife of some sort, had been distinguished by a religious establishment.

To those who might posit an objection to a church-state connection because of its dating -- where the Christian church was concerned -- from the post-Apostolic era, it was argued that neither Christ nor his disciples had spoken out against church establishments. When a church establishment was introduced in the Roman Empire under Constantine [sic], it did not evoke any objections from among the learned Christians of that day. At the Reformation, none of the leading Reformers had denied the principle of a state-church establishment. Neither "Calvin, nor Beza, nor Cranmer, nor Ridley, nor Knox", ever spoke out against the concept of a church establishment. It was of no little significance that arguments against national church establishments did not become formidable until the French Revolution. At that time, the principle of the separation of church and state was quite novel -- influenced no doubt by the new American republic – and its introduction in France was the product of an "open and avowed Infidelity". (7)

If a state were to perform its true paternalistic function, and be more than "a mere mercenary hireling" governing through fear and force, it was essential that it fulfill its duty with respect to supporting an established church. Religious principles were the source of all moral actions. Hence, a state that neglected to provide for the inculcation of religious principles among its subjects, would not possess a public morality because of its lack of a paternal or Christian character. (8)

The paternal state was an outgrowth of the families which comprised it, and the same sanctions applied to the state as to the family. Just as heads of Christian families were under a sacred obligation to instruct their children in the truths of Christianity, and were not free to abandon them to haphazard instruction or to leave them to their own unaided efforts, so also the state – the other basic social institution – had a paternal function to promote the welfare of its subjects through providing for their religious instruction. (9)

The family formed the very *sine qua non* of society because it was within the domestic circle that all virtues and social relationships commenced. Thus, parents were regarded as being under a very solemn duty to teach their children to fear God, and to provide them with religious instructions as set forth in the Bible to bring their children to Christ. Once Christian values were inculcated within the family, the moral conduct of the children would carry over naturally into the neighbourhood, and hence the nation and mankind.

Upon the young family members going out from the family to take their respective positions in society, it was essential that the Christian values -- which they had imbibed in childhood -- be kept alive and strengthened to "maintain their full influence over the mind" of men. Consequently, the state had a duty to these "children of the community" to continue to provide the religious and moral guidance which had been exercised formerly by their parents. Only in this way could society rest assured that the Christian character which, once stamped upon youthful minds within the family, would not be lost outside of it.

The interests of the parents and the State were one because children who were raised with Christian values and principles would become contented subjects. Men, who were governed in their conduct by the Christian graces – virtue, knowledge, temperance, patience, Godliness, brotherly kindness, and charity -- would "love order", would exercise a due regard for the rights of others, and would be ever anxious "to promote the good of society". Moreover, Christian subjects would inculcate, in turn, the Christian verities in the minds of their own children. (10)

Some form of religion was vitally necessary, in a world so constituted as this one, if government were to exist at all. The very preservation of public liberty and social peace depended upon the presence of a national religion. It was only through a religious establishment that Christian principles could be diffused effectively through every rank and class of society. Men, who were deprived of the means of being good Christians could never be good subjects. Indifference in the performance of the duties enjoined by religion could not help but engender indifference to the performance of the duty owed by the subject to his king.

An established Christian church, such as that of the Church of England, would not only teach men their duty toward God and man and inculcate moral principles of conduct, but would redeem man from his corrupted nature through God's saving grace. Once redeemed, man was enabled to conquer his "selfish passions and appetites" and, in imitation of Christ, to strive for the betterment of all. (11) Were it not for the "sense of virtue" which was preserved and espoused by the Christian Church, "men would soon lose it all, run wild, prey upon one another, and do what else the worst of savages do". (12)

Social order and the best interests of society could only be secured where a sense of pious obligation and moral restraint tempered the spirit of the people. The function of positive law, and the whole system of justice established to administer it, was dependent upon "the sacredness which the public mind attaches to an oath", which in turn was dependent on "some antecedent religious belief". Indeed, to the Tories, the Christian religion was responsible for such social order as man possessed, and for the freedom which grew out of that order. They were convinced:

> that whatever degree of rational and substantial freedom we at this moment enjoy, is to be traced to the influence of pure and undefiled Religion – we are free only in proportion as we are holy. The Church of Christ is therefore the parent of civil and religious liberty. (13)

From a political perspective, loyalty to those in authority had to be based upon more than a calculation of interests or practical benefits, or a shallow adherence resting upon mere habit or education, if it were to be efficacious, at all times and under all circumstances. If government was to be maintained, and the state was to endure, the capricious nature and discordant passions of men had to be counteracted by a stronger bond than mere utility.

The Upper Canadian Tories believed that a true and unselfish loyalty could be realized only within the Christian ethos where each and every man was placed under a sacred obligation to "fear God and honour the king". In a Christian country, allegiance to the legitimately-constituted authority rested not upon mere expediency, but embraced a much higher principle. It rested upon a religious obligation enjoined by God, which all men should, and would, be made aware of through the teachings of the National Church. (14)

To the Tory mind, all the best interests of civil society, the state, and the individual citizen, demanded the dissemination of religious principles and values among the people, and a national Church establishment was the traditional, and most effective, manner of accomplishing that objective. Moreover, the state was duty-bound to render its support to 'true religion' and to ensure that its subjects received the benefits of religion. Since the Church of England was a member of the true Church, and the designated Established Church of Upper Canada, it was requisite that government should provide support for that Church and unite with it in a common cause. In seeking support from the provincial and the British governments for the strengthening and extension of the Church of England in Upper Canada, the Tories were motivated by much more than any supposed self-interest of the Anglican Church. Such actions were a direct outgrowth of the Tory concept of an established Church, and the proper relationship between the Church and State.

The Alliance of Church and State

The Upper Canadian Tories believed that the best interests of civil society, as well as those of religion, were served by an alliance of church and state. While the state had a duty, in fulfilling its God-ordained role, to protect and support an established religion, the religious establishment, in carrying out its Christian function, promoted a spirit beneficial to the maintenance of order in the state and the well-being of its people. Although the state and the church differed in their appointed roles and ends -- the state being charged with the care of civil society, and the church being responsible for the immortal soul of its inhabitants -- both were moral agencies, and their ends were mutually inclusive. The state through positive law, which in a Christian country was based upon God's moral law, enforced an external morality while the Church worked from within to redeem corrupted man and assure him of salvation. (15)

Thus, an alliance of church and State was perfectly natural and proper to facilitate and mutually reinforce the respective efforts of one to the other. In a purely political point of view, such an alliance united the efforts of the two great interests of society which, if unnaturally divorced, would form "two powerful and antagonistic principles". If a contest for supremacy were to develop between the spiritual authority and the temporal power, it would tear a nation asunder in both corrupting religion and fostering insubordination in the state. (16)

The church and the state were not by their very nature mutually antagonistic institutions, or contending forces; although they might be potentially so. The same persons, for the most part, were subsumed within either group, appearing in the character of religionists with respect to the church and as subjects within the state. Hence, their interests in those two capacities were not, and could not be, incompatible. In any struggle between church and state, no one would gain. Encroachments by the state against the church, or by the church upon the state, would in either case prove highly injurious to the welfare of society. (17)

If such a contest were to develop, in the absence of a church-state alliance, the contest would by no means be unequal. A religious body, if comprised of wealth and numbers, could be very influential within a state because of the very means it employed. Through ministers enjoying frequent opportunities of "moulding the opinions of the multitude" from the pulpit and possessing the direction of education – whether independent of the state or not – a religious body had the potential to be a formidable force within a nation for good or evil.

Religion could not enjoy a neutral existence within a state. The very strength and influence that religion possessed over the public mind made it a potentially potent adversary of the state and a force to be feared. Such an independent force, in existing within the realm in the absence of an alliance of church and state, could not but cause those in authority to be apprehensive for their own safety and security. It would compel the state to resort to coercive measures to restrain what could not be controlled by other means. An overt struggle for supremacy would inevitably ensue.

The object of a church-state connection was to avoid such an impasse, and potential turmoil, by uniting the two great interests of society --

the political and the religious -- in a mutually reverential and protective relationship. Through the striking of a balance, or proper adjustment between them, it would enable both elements to be rendered their due, and would immeasurably increase their efficacy in promoting the well-being and good order of society. A proper balance between church and state consisted of avoiding the two potential extremes of Erastianism (the state having an absolute control over the church for state purposes), and theocracy (clerical supremacy over the state).

For the Tories, a church-state alliance was regarded as being highly beneficial to the church. In such an alliance, the church received protection, security of income for her clergy, and the bestowal of rank and power on her 'superior ecclesiastics', which facilitated her spiritual work, and increased in a great measure the influence of the church in the country. However, it was critical that the church-state alliance not interfere with the spiritual character of the church, which must remain completely independent in its religious work in yielding to none in its adherence to its Christian principles. Churchmen and members of the clergy were admonished to have a "bold spirit", and to be ever ready to fight in the cause of truth against any effort on the part of the state to bring about an Erastian system.

On the other hand, in fulfilling his Christian duty to render aid to the Church of Christ under a church-state alliance, the king was promoting the best interests of the state. In possessing the right to a measure of control over the actions of the established National Church, the king ensured that the spiritual power did not increase to the point where it could overshadow and threaten the stability of the throne. History provided numerous examples of the "harm caused to truth" by the supremacy of a Church over the temporal power in the theocratic governments of the Calvinists in Geneva and of the Papacy, at various times, over Roman Catholic nations in Europe.

To achieve a proper balance between the temporal and the spiritual power was no easy task to accomplish, but it was one that had to be attempted in every political system. In that respect, as in many others, Upper Canada was fortunate in having received the full benefits of the Church of England establishment. It was an establishment which, after centuries of conflict between the Bishop of Rome and the English kings, had finally been resolved at the Reformation. The establishment of the Church of England as an independent national church, with the king at its head, had achieved a true equipoise in a church-state alliance that yielded reciprocal benefits, protection, and respect. It was a balance which had only to be maintained to bestow immeasurable good upon Upper Canadian society. (18)

Independency of the Established Church

In Upper Canada, the Tories sought to maintain, strengthen and extend what they regarded as the Established Church of Upper Canada and to facilitate the role of the National Church in the disseminating of religious and moral principles among the inhabitants of the province. They did not see the church-state alliance as involving any compromise of the interests or the integrity of the Church so long as its spiritual independence was maintained. The Anglican clergy set forth their convictions respecting the efficacy of a church establishment in serving the religious needs of the province, and their arguments against those who maintained that the Established Church of England in Britain was a creature of the state.

In that endeavour, the Anglican clerics were at pains to point out that during the Reformation the Church of England had not destroyed, or compromised in any way, the spiritual independence of the Church of Christ. Nor had it compromised its apostolic and catholic character. At the Reformation, England had acknowledged its duty as a Christian nation through bestowing temporal dignities and a "voice in the General Council of the State" on the ministers of the Church of England: viz. the Lords Spiritual – the Archbishop and the bishops of the Church – in the House of Lords. In return, the Church of England had recognized the head of State as her "temporal head" in investing the monarch with a supremacy over the ecclesiastical elements of the church, which was akin to the supremacy exercised by the king in the civil realm. However, the Church had been careful to avoid granting the king, or his temporal legislature, any right to interfere in spiritual matters, either with respect to the doctrines of the Church, her liturgy, or her ministration of the Sacraments. (19)

Although the monarch was declared to be "the supreme head of the Church and clergy of England", that declaration did not encroach in any way upon Christ's headship of the Church as was shown by the insistence of the Church upon the inclusion of the qualifying phrase "as far as is consistent with the law of Christ". The royal supremacy was confined to the ecclesiastical institution, the Church of England, which in virtue of its presence within the royal dominion possessed a national and temporal being in addition to its spiritual character. The monarch presided over "the external apparatus" of the Established Church which he protected and supported, while Christ retained, undiminished, his prerogative as the head of the spiritual Church: the Church of England. (20)

Although the king assumed a measure of control over the Church of England as an ecclesiastical institution, the Church had acted to retain its independence as to its spiritual character and function. The balance, which had been struck at the Reformation between the Church and State, was not dependent upon circumstances for its maintenance, but was rather was governed and defined in law. Statutes passed by Parliament, and articles passed by the Church in convocation, had carefully defined the limits upon the Crown and the extent to which the Church could and would acquiesce in a measure of state control. (21)

The right of 'exterior jurisdiction' which the Church had granted to the king consisted of the traditional prerogatives granted to the civil magistrate by most national churches: the right of convoking national convocations of the clergy, and the right of nomination to bishoprics. Neither one nor the other involved the exercise of any spiritual jurisdiction, and in the latter case the king merely possessed the right to nominate an individual who must be a member of the ordained clergy. Moreover, it was the Church of Christ which bestowed his religious jurisdiction upon a bishop. The ministers of the Church were of her own creation. It was their inviolable right to preach the Word and to administer the sacraments independent of the secular authority. (22)

The Anglican clerics were adamant that the changes which the Church of England underwent at the Reformation had not in any way involved the civil power interfering with her spiritual character. Under Henry

VIII, papal supremacy had been rejected and the monarch declared head of the Church of England by acts of Parliament (the latter embracing the Lords Spiritual and Lords Temporal and the Commons) with "scarcely a change" being made in her religious affairs at all. (23)

It was during the subsequent reign of Edward VI that the Church was restored to apostolic purity, but that was not the work of the civil power. The reforms were carried out by Anglican Church divines. Through the medium of her bishops and clergy assembled in Convocation, and "by the grace of God", the English Church was reformed of its "Popish corruptions". The civil power was merely called upon to give "the sanction of law" to the work of the clergy, and thereby sealed "a mutual alliance" of Church and State against popery. Throughout the Reformation period, the Church of England had successfully maintained its independence in spiritual matters. At no time was the king, or parliament, allowed to define her "constitution, doctrines or usages". (24)

The Church of England had remained what she always had been: "a divine institution", as well as a religious society, whose basis was spiritual, not secular. Much more than a mere civil institution, the Church was "an ordinance of God", which comprised an order of ministers, and their successors, appointed by Him to "keep alive the faith" by instructing mankind through the ages in the ways of salvation. Ministers of the Church derived their authority not from the State, but from Christ in partaking -- through the succession of bishops, in the 'laying on of hands' -- of the commission bestowed by Christ upon his Apostles. Such a body as the Church, although willing to accept State aid and protection to further its God-given task, was not a creature of the State, or necessarily dependent upon the state. Although aligned with the state through the Crown, the Church possessed a distinct purpose and a spiritual being, which was independent of the state. Moreover, the Church retained the same constitution, creed, and discipline as she had possessed in apostolic times long before the advent of the Church-State connection. (25)

As a spiritual body, the Church was under a sacred obligation to defend "the vital doctrines of Catholic truth", and hence its independence, from any or all encroachments by the civil power. Religious truth was not of man, but of God and could not be yielded to any lay body. Although acknowledging the Royal Supremacy as by law established, it was vehemently maintained by the Anglican clerics of Upper Canada that just as "the Crown can make no Statutes without Parliament, neither can it settle doctrines without Convocation". (26)

In sum, the alliance of church and state was mutually beneficial in facilitating the attainment of the interests that they had in common. There were several additional reasons, however, why the Upper Canadian Tories held that religious values needed to be inculcated in the community through an established church which enjoyed government support. These involved their view of the weaknesses and insufficiency of 'voluntaryism' -- the support of a church solely by the voluntary contributions of its members -- and the peculiar benefits which were inherent in the parish system of the Church of England.

Rejection of Voluntaryism

The Tory effort to strengthen and defend the Church of England in Upper Canada was driven not only by their beliefs as to the proper role of an established church in inculcating Christian principles in the people, in saving souls, and in maintaining social order. It was motivated also by a practical consideration and the Anglican view of human nature. The Upper Canadian Tories believed that the Established Church of England in Upper Canada, with the support which was provided for it by the provisions of the Constitutional Act, possessed the only effective means to diffuse Christianity in Upper Canada. It was a province with a population scattered over a wide expanse of territory, which had yet to emerge from its pioneer-settlement phase. They feared also that "mighty as is the influence of truth, when fairly presented to the mind', it was "neither right nor safe" to depend upon the people to procure and provide religious instructions for themselves. (27)

In his corrupted natural state, man suffered from a moral incapacity to readily seek out and embrace the Christian message and way of life, which boded ill for the prospects of religion if left to make its own way unassisted from without. Human nature was such that man's religious needs, unlike his physical necessities, were not compelling. If deprived of food, a craving was induced in man that would increase continually until satisfied; whereas the religious needs of man, in the absence of religious instruction, were not strong enough to induce him to seek to hear the Word. The less man knew of religion, the less he would feel the need of it. If the Christian message were not conveyed to him, he would simply "decline in taste and desire".

If Christianity were to edify man, and assure him of salvation, it had to be taken to the people so that they might be awakened from their "spiritual dormancy", and made to feel a hunger for religion through being exposed to the Christian message. The Church could not wait passively for the people to indicate a desire for religion, but had to take religion to the people through providing places of worship and ministers to preach the gospel and instruct them. The taking of religion to the people was perfectly in keeping with the true missionary principles of Christianity, and was a provision which only an established church, with state support, could adequately secure to the people. (28)

The voluntary principle was not to be relied upon under the best of conditions to provide effectively for the religious wants of a nation, and the peculiar situation of the people in Upper Canada rendered it utterly hopeless for that purpose. With a newly-settled population, which was being augmented continually by new immigrants who were spread thinly over a vast expanse of territory and struggling just to survive and care for their families, little could be spared by the settlers to support a clergyman. Nor was there much incentive for the people to build churches which but few would be able to frequent given the difficulties of travel in many areas of new settlement. (29)

If left to the discretion of individuals as to whether they would support a minister of religion -- even without the peculiar difficulties which Upper Canada posed -- it was feared that many would indulge "their indolence, and their disinclination to exercises of seriousness and reflection". They would neglect the needs of religion entirely, with a concomitant "decay of virtue" and decline of religious knowledge. It was a situation where even the pious and devout who desired to make a provision for religion were incapable of doing so without the aid and support of their fellows who might well refuse to contribute. (30)

In Upper Canada, there were many areas which, long after the early years of settlement, remained deprived of any religion instruction, and lacked "the accommodations so necessary to civilized life". In other areas, "false and-changeful doctrines" were propagated by itinerant preachers of the various dissenting sects who, unchecked by steady instruction in theology, carried men away from "the tenets and practice of sound and scriptural religion", and imbued them with "a contempt of order, propriety, and law". (31)

The Tories deplored what they viewed as the sporadic and frenzied activity of the itinerant sectarian preachers in Upper Canada. The emotional frenzy of religious camp meetings was judged to be insufficient to keep religion alive even in a bastardized form. The "zeal of a sect, or the novelty of change" could suffice for a time in securing support for religion, but "no reliance could be placed upon it as a general and permanent provision". (32) Thus, the preaching and teaching of religion in the Province of Upper Canada could not be left dependent upon voluntary activity and offerings. It needed to be supported by the state, which in Upper Canada meant the the Church of England supported by the Crown through the provisions of the Constitutional Act: viz. the reservation of 1/7th of the land in each township --the Clergy Reserves lands – for the benefit of "the Protestant Clergy"; and the provision for the endowment of parsonages or rectories for the support of Anglican parish priests. (33)

Even in a mature society, such as in England, voluntaryism was open to a further objection in that it failed to provide for the religious needs of the destitute. The Church of England -- because she was not dependent upon the support of her members -- was viewed as pre-eminently "the Church of the poor man". Voluntaryism was fine for the wealthy, the comfortable, and the tradesmen and artisans in a mature society, who could competently support their families and contribute in addition by subscription or by weekly contributions to the maintenance of a Church. However, such a system would not suffice for the poor who had nothing to expend in support of a church. Only in the established Church of England – the National Church -- was a man, regardless of his pecuniary means or lack thereof, assured of receiving the full benefits of religion by his "indefeasible birthright" as an Englishman. (34)

The Tories were quite ready to admit that the Church establishment in England did have its faults. However, they were held to be attributable to the fallibility of the men who comprised the Church, not the Church itself. It was known that, in England, church livings were sought by men who were not properly disposed toward the sacred function, nor motivated to promote the interest of religion and virtue. It was a situation that was deeply deplored because "the salvation of souls [was] not a charge to be lightly undertaken"; however, despite some evident abuses, the Upper Canadian Tories found much to admire in the parish system of the Established Church in England.

Where the independence of the clergy was concerned, the parish system was held to be much superior to the voluntary system. The investiture of the sovereign – the King – with a measure of control over church appointments in return for a public provision for the clergy, was viewed as being much preferable to the clergy being subject to control by the "irresponsible multitude". For the Upper Canadian Tories, the critical concern was always to maintain the integrity of the clergy -- in the administration of their spiritual function – completely independent of coercion and direction from either the government or the people. In contrast, voluntaryism – which was a child of "the spirit of democracy" – was, by its very nature, calculated to enforce the rule of the "rabble rout" over the preaching of the clergy. (35)

In the absence of a permanent provision of state aid -- guaranteed by statute -- for the Established Church, the clergy would be forced to resort to the people of their congregation for financial support. Such a resort raised a fear the regular clergy might be forced to emulate the practices of the sectarian preachers. If so, it was feared that "the minds of the people will be worked upon" by self-seeking ministers to secure financial contributions; that religion would be distorted into "exaggerated doctrines" for increased effect; and that preaching would degenerate into "theatrics" which would be calculated for its effect to please and entertain. In such a situation, it could not be counted upon that clergymen would "at all times speak with that fearless disregard of consequences which the proper discharge of their duties often requires". (36)

The Tories were convinced that voluntaryism could not but lead to preaching taking on the character of a "mode of begging" for financial support. It would destroy the independence of ministers, entail the sacrifices of principle, and render them subservient to the tyranny and insolence of their congregations. Moreover, the learned clerics of the Church of England would be at a disadvantage if the provision of government support was to be replaced by voluntaryism.

Such was the disposition of men that attempts "to edify them in Christian knowledge" would always suffer, and prove less compelling, than doctrines adapted to "the pleasure of the capricious multitude" and presented in such a manner as to "gratify their taste for vehement, impassioned oratory". Under such circumstances, the sober instruction of men in the true tenets of the Christian religion would founder, and the preaching of religion would "fall into the lowest hands" with men of worth and ability shunning the profession. (37)

The Upper Canadian Tories had only to look to the situation of religion in the United States -- which they did -- to see their worst fears about the logical implications of voluntaryism being realized. In America, which lacked a church establishment, ministers were totally dependent upon their congregations for their employment, and could be dismissed at the pleasure of the congregation. Consequently, ministers were often kept in a state of dependency and poverty through being hired -- in many cases after lengthy disputes and contentions among the congregation -- for a mere six months or a yearly term. The result of congregations having the power to dismiss their ministers at pleasure, was that the ministers were forced to "preach as to please, on pain of losing their situations", and the very purpose of preaching was negated. In such a situation, the minister was unable to reprimand the congregation for its faults, or to expound on the harsh truths of Christianity, or to command the respect that was necessary if his instruction were to be heeded. (38)

The Anglican clergy were very conscious of the precarious social status of the clergy in Upper Canada, and they realized that the influence and respectability enjoyed by the clergy was closely connected with the "estimation of religion" in the public mind. Thus, they deplored the anti-clericalism which was fashionable in some European literary circles, and which was spreading to North America. In revolutionary circles, the clergy were accused of seeking worldly goods and preferment. They were denounced as being a "designing and ambitious priesthood", and were charged with indulging in selfishness and hypocrisy in supposedly living at the expense of the poor and oppressed.

What was equally worrying -- following the Napoleonic Wars – was that the circumstances of the clergy appeared to be declining everywhere "towards obscurity and degradation". It was becoming evident that "a Clergyman's learning and virtues" were not sufficient of themselves "to maintain his usefulness and respectability". The conclusion was inevitable: for clergymen to carry out their spiritual function in society, it was necessary that "a comfortable living" be provided through a church establishment. In Upper Canada, it meant that the Church of England had to defend to the utmost its constitutional right to the revenues from the clergy reserves land endowment, which was established for the support of the parish priests of the National Church. (39)

The Parish System

In viewing the frontier settlements of the United States in the post-War of 1812 period, the Upper Canadian Tories concluded that the American Revolution had taught something of value, albeit in a negative fashion. In inaugurating the first political system of any nation to exist without an established religion, the United States – as it had evolved -- proved the utility of a church establishment beyond a doubt. In the United States, a general religious toleration without a church establishment had given rise to a situation where Christianity was "almost totally extinct". In many areas, the Sabbath was generally ignored, and much of the country received no religious instruction at all. In other areas, it was confined to a few towns and had scarcely penetrated the mass of the people in the country. The Americans were "fast approaching to the most general depravity of morals". It was only the rudiments of earlier Christian teaching, which remained "to a considerable extent among the people", that postponed the day of reckoning. However, the symptoms of destruction could already be clearly perceived. It was evident that, within the United States, "anarchy is making rapid strides and the foundations of the social compact are giving way". (40)

If Upper Canada were to avoid going the way of the United States, it was essential that the province take full advantage of the benefits of the Church of England establishment; and that she enjoy the full benefits of the working of the parish system. It was the parish priest, "an integral part of God's visible Church", who fulfilled the essential role in disseminating moral and religious truth, and who through his instruction generated a religious feeling, and gave "support and permanent effect" to Christianity. By the parish system, a priest was placed permanently in each community, and charged to provide religious instruction and education, to arbitrate disputes, and to act as a "moral guardian" for his flock. At all times, he would preach "moderation, temperance, and contentment", and through his influence would encourage industry and benevolence.

The Church establishment, through providing such a man "of piety and education" in each parish, would do much to keep up a sense of religion and "a reverence for what is pure and holy". The parish priest would do so not only through his efforts from the pulpit, but by the influence of his conduct, character, and example, even among those who did not attend religious services. (41)

The influence of example was a consideration not to be taken lightly. The clergyman was counselled to live within his income, and to keep control of his passions at all times, and to provide always a model of proper conduct and upright character. It was believed that the clergyman's precepts would be respected only in so far as "their efficacy is demonstrated by their influence on his own conduct".

In preaching "the pure doctrine of the Bible", and embodying always the epitome of moral worth and moral wisdom, the parish priest could not help but receive deference, affection and respect from the community. As a man of exceptional learning, the parish priest of the Church of England was admonished that he should address himself "to the understanding as well as the hearts of enlightened people" in seeking to dispel ignorance and prejudice, and to instill the spirit of the Gospel through his preaching, ministrations, and example. He was also to foster education by establishing a school for the instruction of the young. In being dedicated to spreading the Christian message, he should never be found shirking in his duty to stand up in defence of 'what is right and good', but should always act "with a spirit of forbearance" in consciously striving "to promote mutual love and good-will" towards all members of society. (42)

Young priests were further admonished that they were under a solemn duty to teach the great truths of religion so that men would not forget that there was a God "shaping their destiny". Man was not sufficient unto himself. The Scriptures contained "certain immutable principles of justice and right" to guide all nations; and if a nation would not serve God, then it would inevitably perish. Religion could not be separated from man's political and social being, and consequently ministers were not to forget that the members of their congregation were also members of society and subjects of the king.

The Anglican priests were instructed to preach all the Christian virtues and to duly admonish the people to act "in the spirit of true loyalty, contentment and obedience". It was the duty of the priest to provide leadership for the people by instruction and example in all areas of life, and to do so through teaching:

> all the qualities, virtues, and principles which become the
> man and the Christian in his individual, domestic, and social
> relations, and which naturally flow from love of God and love
> to our neighbor. (43)

The Church of England was regarded as ideally suited to fulfill the role of a national Church in this respect because she sought not only -- through "the purest form of Christian doctrine" -- to assure her adherents of salvation, but also demanded that they "be good subjects". Her clergy in their education and feeling, both in religion and politics, were at one with "the great principles of the British Constitution". The Anglican clergy would never be found rendering aid or leadership to faction, but rather could be counted upon to condemn any such efforts, from whatever quarter, to destroy the balance in the constitution and society. The Church of England by her very nature and structure was the Church of "orderly government", "balance" and the "middle way", wherein "every member knows and keeps his place". It was claimed, on behalf of the Established Church, that "people so trained must generally grow up good and orderly, and obedient and reasonable subjects" (44)

The ideal parish priest was conceived of as a man of independent mind who would judge matters for himself, and would condemn what he found to be morally wrong in standing by his stated Christian principles and values. He was a man who would distain "base prevarication", and would reject all compromise based on expediency or "timid compliance". An example, which was cited for emulation, was that of the Anglican clerics who, during the American Revolution, had put principle before their own self-interest. They had sacrificed everything that they possessed, including family connections and their livings, in standing by their oath of allegiance to the king, and in choosing to serve and administer to the Loyalists who rallied to the Crown. (45)

The requisite independence of mind and action of the ministers of Christ's Church could only be assured through an established church system. It would preclude clergymen being solely dependent upon their congregations for support, and consequently being too easily swayed -- in situations where feelings and emotions ran high -- to protect their personal interests by giving a lead to faction, as appeared to have been the case with the dissenting ministers during the American Revolution. (46)

Where the independence of the clergy was concerned, the Church of England establishment of Upper Canada was held to possess the best of both worlds. On the one hand, the independence of her clergy was assured through a lawful establishment and the support of the clergy reserves endowment. The lands of the Clergy Reserves – whether leased to produce a revenue, or sold and the monies invested to yield a dividend -- were counted upon to provide a secure income which would render the Church independent of both government and the people. Moreover, the Church of England in Upper Canada also benefited from the zeal of different individuals – in both Upper Canada and England – who were making contributions of land and monies for the building of churches. This was regarded as a very wholesome situation where individual action and zeal served to second the support which was provided by the civil power for the Established Church. It was a system wherein the benefits of a church establishment were combined with voluntaryism, but without suffering the negative effects of a total reliance on voluntary contributions. (47)

An Established Church & God's Moral Law

In the Upper Canadian situation, the Tories did not hold that the Church of England was the only denomination whose ministrations, if supported by the government, would prove efficacious in spreading the Christian gospel; nor did they believe that the Church of England was the only church which would be well received in areas that were destitute of religion. However, in giving effect to an establishment, one denomination had to be selected and provision made for its clergy, and in Upper Canada, the Established Church was the Church of England. A constitutional provision had been made for the support of its clergy through the clergy reserves endowment, as well as for the establishment of parsonages or rectories in keeping with the practice of the Church of England. Therefore, the Tory Churchmen held that the Established Church had an obligation to provide for a parish priest "in each of the two hundred Townships" as soon as possible. (48)

The essential, and indeed the sole exclusive privilege, held by the established Church of England in Upper Canada was the right to enjoy a public provision for the maintenance of its clergy as provided by the Clergy Reserves provision of the Constitutional Act of 1791. In defence of their claim to government support on behalf of the Established Church, the Tories maintained that the rendering of such aid was not an injustice to individuals within the state who might not belong to the national church, nor was it any burden on individuals who were unwilling to contribute to its well-being. The clergy reserves land endowment was granted to the Church of England by the Crown from the wild lands of the Crown, and, in Upper Canada, landowners were exempt in law from being required to paying tithes to the Established Church. (49)

The Upper Canadian Tories believed that man, because he was an "accountable agent", was under a moral obligation -- imposed by God -- "to believe in and support religion". God's moral law was regarded as binding upon all members of a Christian nation – infidels included -- because they were part of a community under God. No one could be allowed to claim exemption from obeying any of God's laws because if but one breach was condoned, and pardoned, what possible justification could there be for enforcing the other injunctions and punishing transgressors? The whole of statute law was founded upon natural justice -- based upon God's moral law -- and it was evident that:

> where moral obligation does not exist, statute law ought never to bind: but where it does exist, a government must have the right to enforce it, or a government cannot be defended on any principle but usurpation and injustice.

If government did not have the right to enforce obedience to God's moral law, then how could government possibly fulfill its function? A right to compel the infidel and others to obey God's moral law was no less valid than the right to enforce the law against theft or murder. Just as the individual could not in his individual capacity choose freely to withhold obedience to positive laws, or the payment of his taxes, so he had no right to object to the designation of an established church.

The provision of support for a national clergy by the state was not of the nature of private contracts and obligations which were entered into voluntarily, were governed solely by the cash nexus, and derived their legal obligation to pay from a voluntary personal commitment. It was a moral obligation which was imposed from without, and originated in a much higher source. To deny the state the right to use statutes to provide for a church establishment in carrying out its moral obligation would be to deprive it of "the moral means of its own preservation". Moreover, such an argument was based upon the fallacious assumption that religious duties could be, or were in any way, separate from civil and political duties. Edmund Burke was quoted to the effect that any attempt to separate religious and civil duties:

> separates morality from duty -- duty to the state -- and it reconciles religion towards God with rebellion against human government, for enforcing a moral law which God has commanded to be religiously observed by all.

It was regarded, to say the least, as incongruous to hold that God could promulgate laws for the governing of mankind and appoint human government to that end, and yet refuse to acknowledge the right of human government to enforce God's moral law.

Government support for the clergy in a nation professing to be Christian, was not only a moral obligation, but a social duty which the welfare of society demanded be performed. It was derived not only from utilitarian considerations, but from the very necessity of the human situation. Man was "made for society and community", rather than being sufficient unto himself; and that being the case, human reason taught that:

the human family should have a religion suited to human wants, and to serve really as a bond of family union.

It was the very good of the community which made it requisite that religion be effectively taught. Religion was the essential foundation of "all morality and virtue, both public and private". Given that reality, it was regarded as absurd to divorce a duty that was owed to society from that which was owed to the civil state and, in consequence, to deny the state the right to enforce the discharge of its moral obligation "by a public and equal system of jurisprudence". Religion was not a private matter, but rather was "common to all". It embraced everyone within its workings, and all members of society were under a universal obligation to acknowledge a national church which was established in law.

The provision of government support for a national church was a duty and obligation that was binding upon every member of the community, completely independent of the individual will or choice. Both the national church and the civil government acted publicly upon the same principle in placing "the good of all" above individual feelings, interests, and wishes in imposing social duties and obligations upon the community which included the obligation to support the Established Church. Such support would normally take the form of a legal enforcement of the right of collecting tithes; however, in Upper Canada, the clergy reserves land endowment was "given as in full equivalent" to the Church of England for surrendering the right to public support through the levying of tithes. (50)

Purpose of the Clergy Reserves

Given such an understanding, the Tories were adamant that the provincial and the Home governments had a duty to safeguard the Clergy Reserves for their original purpose and to aid the Church – through legislation -- in its efforts to render them productive. In keeping with the Tory concept of the role and function of an established church, it was of the utmost importance that the National Church should enjoy a secure source of revenue for the support of its clergy.

From the Tory point of view, an income from a land endowment, such as the Clergy Reserves, was ideally suited to the needs of the church establishment. Once the clergy reserves endowment began to yield substantial revenues, it would enable the National Church to fulfill its purpose in providing access to religious instruction and educational benefits to all who desired it "without money and without price". (51) In fact, the corporate right of the established church to hold property in the form of glebes, or other land holdings, was regarded as an essential element in securing the independency of the national clergy from the state.

Edmund Burke was quoted with approval -- from his *Reflections on the Revolution in France* (1790) – by the Tories in maintaining that the corporate rights of the national Church in holding landed property, gave it a secure source of support because the ownership of such lands was identified with and inseparable from the maintenance of the rights of private property in general. Such property was of the Church, and was beyond either the use or dominion of the state, which could only guard and regulate, but not despoil it. Thus, through enjoying a corporate right to hold property, the Church was rendered independent of being either a pensioner of the state, or dependent upon the "precarious offerings" of its parishioners. (52)

The national policy of the Upper Canadian Tories as it pertained to the strengthening and extension of the Church of England establishment was an outgrowth of a whole matrix of beliefs which revolved around their concept of an established church and its function, under God, in society. Moreover, their concept of the rights and benefits of an established church was evident in the arguments which they marshaled in support of their right to the proceeds of the clergy reserves land endowment, and in seeking to convince others of the justice of their cause. In defending the National Church against the adherents of religious sects who questioned the value and need for an established church in Upper Canada, the Anglican Tories provided a deeper insight into their own beliefs.

Sectarian Arguments against Church establishment

The Upper Canadian Tories were acutely aware of the arguments which religious dissenters raised against the church establishment in both England and Upper Canada, but found them to be very superficial. The arguments of the dissenters focused on the potential defects of a church establishment, and did not obviate the obligation -- enjoined by the Bible -- on all nations to make provision for the teaching of religion.

As viewed by the Tories, the arguments raised against a church establishment by religious dissenters amounted to little more than "an enumeration of practical effects and abuses" in the Established Church in England, and the abuses cited were for the most part unavoidable in being the product of human failings. The Upper Canadian Tories readily acknowledged that there were shortcomings in the Church of England establishment in Britain. Indeed, they were forthright in stating that reforms were needed in the Established Church in England on the grounds of "justice and policy", and not just to:

> humour the times, but because the eternal and unchangeable
> principles of truth and right, and the best interests of religion
> and social order require it.

The Anglican Tory clergy pointed out that the religious dissenters in attacking the defects and abuses in the Church establishment in Britain, whether they realized it or not, were not denying or refuting the principle of church establishment, but were merely denouncing "temporary blemishes". The fallacy in all such arguments was that "they point only to the mode and not to the thing itself."

Otherwise, the arguments against church establishment, as analyzed by the Tories, appeared to resolve themselves into three basic contentions:

first, that it infringed on "the right of private judgment"; secondly, that it invariably became a "political engine to support the state"; and thirdly, that it was inconsistent with either "the true interests of religion" or "the peace of society". The Tories held that:

> These are plausible objections, and abstractly considered, they seem to have some force; but when examined by the test of experience, their strength vanishes away. (53)

With respect to private judgment, any rational being, upon reflection, could not but recognize "the propriety of worshipping God", and that man did not have the right to worship as he pleased and to whom he pleased. In the absence of Revelation, it would have been "proper and expedient" to exercise such a freedom of choice, but the revealed Word of God limited that liberty to the precepts of the true religion as promulgated in the Bible. Such a limitation was of God, not of man, and it could not be considered as being an infringement of individual liberty for the state to facilitate the expounding of that revelation through rendering support to a national church.

In denominating a particular church to be the established church, the state was not dictating to the public in matters of faith, or forcing religion upon any individual in violation of private conscience. It was merely extending a "legal countenance and support" -- in keeping with the duty of every Christian state – to a national Christian church. Under a church establishment in England, individuals retained the basic right, and the only real right, of private judgment which was to absent themselves from the benefits of that national religious institution, and to choose their own form of worship. The existence of a church establishment did not preclude the enjoyment of a freedom of religious belief for others. All other denominations – in lacking only a provision for public support -- were equally as free as the Church of England to administer to their own adherents.

There was nothing to fear concerning the church becoming 'an engine of the state'. State support for the Established Church in England was confined by law to its 'defence and maintenance', and the state did not possess any right to interfere with "the doctrines and ordinances of Christianity". In sum, the argument that a church-state polity would result in an established church serving the secular purposes of the state was unwarranted, and had no application at all to the situation of the Established Church in either England or Upper Canada.

For the Anglican Tories, a church establishment was necessary in Upper Canada if all men were to have the benefits of religion available to them. Whether they chose to partake of them or not was a matter of private judgement. What was indisputable was that there be an established church to make a national contribution to the improvement of public and private morals, which was a matter of a vital concern to the state.

In the abstract, the Tories held to the view that in any state -- as soon as it could be ascertained that the bulk of the people were agreed upon "some points of religious union" -- the government had a duty to form a national church establishment. However, the religious points of union needed to be the "plainest and simplest" possible so that the religious establishment would comprehend a goodly portion of the nation. Nonetheless, it was realized that no religion, no matter how latitudinarian, could encompass everyone. Given the nature of man, for some individuals ever the simplest question, such as "are you a Christian?", would evoke quibbling, while any attempt to define religious principles "would only serve to multiple objections." (54)

Minorities would "clamour, as minorities always do", but for the good of society a national religious establishment ought to be formed. It was not inconsistent with religious liberty and toleration, as individuals retained a freedom of choice to partake of the benefits of a national church, or to reject them in favour of other forms of worship. The Tories maintained that:

> the magistrate should only say, I do not force you to attend the Established Church -- I have established for you the best form of Christianity that I know, but if you are not satisfied and can do better, I shall be glad – I wish you to be religious, and any form of Christianity is better than infidelity.

A state would never find a form of worship to meet all objections. Nonetheless, one denomination needed to be selected for establishment

-- as had been done for Upper Canada -- to accomplish the great ends desired. The great ends were to "promote true morality and purity of life", to sustain piety, to facilitate good works, to bring man to 'fear God and honour the king', and to 'conquer death' through that attaining of salvation. (55)

The question of whether a government -- in a society which enjoyed freedom of religion -- could establish a public religion involved the resolution of two further questions: who should supply religious instruction to the public; and should the state:

> encourage what is allowed on all hands to be useful, or stand an indifferent spectator?

In viewing the political, social, and judicial ramifications of religion, one could not but be conscious of its vital importance if society were going to continue to function in a civilized manner. Not only government, but the whole social organism was dependent upon religion for its proper functioning. It was evident that:

> if an oath be required, either for allegiance, or the due discharge of the duties of any office – if promises are to be believed or performed, then is Religion necessary, for without religion they have no basis.

Thus, the Tories did not countenance the argument of the religious dissenters that a Church establishment in principle was a violation of any freedom or right of private judgment, contrary to the true interests of society, or the source of social discord. The essential importance of religion to man's social welfare required that the state should render active aid to facilitate the propagation of Christianity by supporting a church establishment. (56)

Rejection of the Separation of Church and State

As a paternal institution, the state -- in the Tory view -- had a positive moral role to play in society. There was a practical *raison d'état* for the state to concern itself with public morals, and to designate a state religion. More generally, they believed that:

no form of Government is capable of promoting the good of the community, unless it has such a power over the persons, actions, and properties of the governed as shall turn them to the general benefit, and restrain them from producing evil.

In seeking "to restrain evil and promote the good', a government could either resort to force in order to command obedience to the laws of the country, or could act by encouragement and persuasion to maintain public order. Of the two, public laws and the courts could go only so far in governing the conduct of the members of a state, given that a legitimate Christian government would not employ brute force.

For the preservation of social order what was required was another law, an 'internal law' or conscience, which would always exist and govern conduct in condemning "every species of wrong". This 'law of conscience' was of "infinitely more consequence" than any public law in governing the conduct of man, and it was in the best interest of government to support the institutions – the church, the school and the family -- that formed the conscience of man. Such an action was not a denial of individual freedom; indeed, it was quite the contrary.

If they are able, by encouragement and persuasion, to give it force and energy, prevent its corruption and ensure its proper direction, they are certainly acting favourably to the freedom and happiness of the people; for everything that promotes virtue and religion, promotes happiness and freedom.

The best guarantee and most effective method for shaping the conscience of a citizen, and thereby promoting virtue and religion, was by means of a "liberal religious establishment".

It was a mistaken argument which contended that government involved only a concern with the outward actions of people; and that consequently church establishments were wrong because they represented an assumption of an authority by the state over the minds of its subjects. Such a distinction was meaningless in practice because it would render government useless. It would preclude government from having any role in education, which forms the mind and moulds the character of men, and the Legislature would be denied any right to enact laws because laws – as well as the institutions themselves– give a bias to the public mind.

The involvement of the state in the formation of character through an established church was by no means a denial of freedom of opinion. To the contrary, the Tories were strong defenders of freedom of opinion, as well as religious freedom. However, they believed that the state had an educational role to play in realizing the potential of that freedom through establishing a national church to teach moral values based upon the principles and values revealed by God.

Freedom in the abstract was of little value if the individuals possessing it were incapable of making a rational judgement as to what was in their best ultimate interest. The Tories believed that:

> religious opinions ought indeed to be free, and so ought all our opinions, but a general system of education gives force to this freedom, because it enlightens the mind, and makes it capable of judging with accuracy. And what is a Religious Establishment, but a branch of public education?

Far from representing a curtailment of freedom, a religious establishment had an essential role to play in every state in making freedom a reality. (57)

The Tories totally rejected the dogmatic assertion by "modern infidels" and "political dissenters", that any connection between church and state was unnatural, and that there must be a complete separation of church and state. Such a claim, in the abstract, involved taking the position that either the state was non-Christian or anti-Christian; and that there was no common interest between the state and Christianity. Indeed, if one accepted the contention that a natural hostility existed between the civil and ecclesiastical polity then it would not be any exaggeration to hold that the duties of religion and those of "the ordinary business of life" were distinct and unconnected, which was not the case. Man was accountable for his actions to a higher power.

If church and state were to be entirely separate, an individual serving the state in any capacity, although a Christian in his private life, must be an infidel in office. Such an absurdity was totally unacceptable because there was clearly a definite common accord between religion and the state. It was the duty and business of the state to maintain and promote among its subjects the "principles of good order and general morality" of which religion was the best support or, more correctly, the *sina qua non*. The connection between church and state was perfectly natural and necessary.

Furthermore, from a Christian perspective -- as every Christian was aware -- the workings of Providence were such that:

> irreligion and impiety in a nation will provoke the vengeance of
> Almighty God and produce national visitations from His hand.

For its own wellbeing, the state must recognize and act according to its duty to effectively propagate the principles and values of the Christian religion throughout the populace so that man might live in keeping with God's Will.

In the nature of things, religion and government could not be kept separate and distinct. All men were "amenable to God, and in holding any position of trust were duty-bound to "sanctify their acts as public men by the offices of religions". In the conduct of the affairs of their public office, men who took no note of the principles of religion were incapable of carrying out the true ends of government, and their acts could not but be "displeasing to God and destructive of themselves".

Christ declared that 'my kingdom is not of this world', and admonished Christians to 'render unto Caesar the things that are Caesar's and unto God the things that are God's'. However, Christ did not advocate, or command, a complete separation of church and state. Both the state and the church had legitimate functions to perform, and it was evident that neither should usurp the role of the other. They were to act in harmony to achieve the several ends which they possessed in common.

The fact that there were countries in which church establishments did not always produce perfect peace and order, if it proved anything, evidenced "the wickedness of man or the deficiencies of the form" of church adopted. It did not offer any conclusive argument against the principle of a church establishment or the efficacy of a national church preaching Christian beliefs, principles and values. (58)

Implications for the National Policy

The insistence of the Upper Canadian Tories that the provincial government and the Home Government in Britain should act together as a matter of national policy to strengthen and extend the Church of England in Upper Canada was a natural outgrowth of their view of the role of an established church in a state. It was based on their belief in the shared interest of the church and the state in promoting the common good, social order, and well-being of society. The Tories believed that the Church of England was 'a true church' – a branch of the 'holy Catholic and Apostolic Church' – that the state had a God-ordained duty to support a national church for the dissemination of religion and morality among the people; and that, in the Province of Upper Canada, it was the Church of England that was the established church. And it was provided with state support for its work and maintenance through the clergy reserves land endowment bestowed by the Crown.

Given the pioneer state of settlement in Upper Canada, the Tories were convinced that on practical grounds, as well, that the best means of disseminating religious and moral values, and education to the people, was through the ministrations of a parish priest. In their view, a church-state alliance did not compromise in any way the religious freedom of Upper Canadians, did not violate private conscience, and did not involve any loss of the spiritual independence of the Established Church. Indeed, the clergy reserves land endowment was regarded as a guarantee of the spiritual independence of the church from encroachments by the state, as well as a means of protecting her priests from being entirely dependent on the support of their congregations.

For the Tories, a church-state alliance was in the best interest of both the church and the state. Although the state was charged with the care of civil society, and the church with the salvation of souls, both were moral agencies, and their respective efforts were mutually supportive. In sum, an alliance of church and state was perfectly natural, and promoted the maintenance of the good order, social peace, and the well-being of the people.

In England, the alliance of church and state had disseminated the Christian religion among the nation, had formed the moral character of the English people, had ensured that Christian religious principles would guide the evolution of the British Constitution, and had facilitated the functioning of the parliamentary system of government. The Upper Canadian Tories -- in seeking to strengthen, defend, and extend, the established Church of England in Upper Canada -- believed that the church-state alliance would bestow like benefits upon the people of their Province. The institutional framework existed, and had only to be rendered effective through a cooperation and support among the Established Church of Upper Canada, the provincial government of Upper Canada, and the British Government. Such a united effort would enable the Established Church of the province to secure the happiness, well-being, and salvation of Upper Canadians through its ministrations.

Chapter Nine

The Need for a National Church

In the Tory view, if Upper Canada were to maintain and strengthen its British national character, it was essential that Christian principles be inculcated into the minds of the people, and particularly in the youth of the province, through the presence of institutions capable of providing moral and religious instruction. Both the influence and example of the family and formal schooling were very important to that end, but the role of the Church was pre-eminent and all-inclusive. For the Upper Canadian Tories, the best way to secure the ascendancy of that religious feeling which they held to be essential to the well-being and good order of society was through the means of a national church; and in Upper Canada, which was regarded as being an integral part of the British nation, that church could be none other than the established Church of England. Therefore, as part of their national policy – indeed the very heart of that policy – they advocated that the British government take steps to render effective the establishment of the Church of England not only in Upper Canada, but in all the British North American provinces, to increase the influence of the National Church. The Tory efforts to strengthen and extend the Anglican Church were calculated to serve a political and social purpose, as well as a religious function.

The Political Function

From a political point of view, the Anglican clerics of Upper Canada argued that a national church establishment was the strongest bond of social union because of its ability to inculcate British cultural values in Upper Canadians and to give a British tone and feeling to society. Once fully formed within the province, a British national character would be favourable to the maintenance of monarchical principles and the preservation of harmony between Church and State. The prevalence of good religious and moral principles amongst the people would not only foster and strengthen their attachment to the constitution, but would ensure that Upper Canadians continued to render "a dutiful obedience to civil authority".

In the British North American colonies, a strong national church would contribute immeasurably to the order and stability of society, would support the provincial governments in maintaining social peace, and would greatly strengthen the attachment of the provinces to the British Empire. The British government was advised that a common religious and moral feeling – "a community of religious feeling" -- would unite the colonies more strongly to the mother country than any form of political connection or shared economic interests ever could:

> if these Provinces are worth preserving, the attachment of the inhabitants must be founded on early habits & opinions & these can only be produced and cherished by a proper system of religious and moral instruction.

It was through the minds of the people that permanent attachments of loyalty and feeling were formed. Hence any aid which the British government might provide to effectively establish the Church of England in the colonies – such as monies to support an increase in the number of Anglican clergy -- would prove more efficacious than military expenditures in welding together an Empire "more absolute than any which unhallowed power can hold in subjection". The absence of a uniform system of religious instruction had already cost Great Britain one-half of her Empire in North America, and a neglect to remedy that error could still prove costly in those parts which remained to her, if proper action were not taken. (1)

As viewed by the Upper Canadian Tories, the American Revolution was, if anything, the natural consequence of the folly of successive British governments in failing to provide for the religious instruction of their American colonies. In the absence of an effective established church, dissenting ministers had assumed a direction over the minds of the people, and had undermined their traditional religious beliefs and attitudes toward authority. Moreover, when rebellion broke out, the dissenting clergy had preached and laboured in the revolutionary cause, and made a significant contribution to its ultimate success. The stark contrast between the activities of the dissenting ministers, and the loyalty and service exhibited by the Anglican clergy and their congregations during that rebellion, had proven to the satisfaction of the Tories that an effective religious establishment was essential to the maintenance of the connection with the mother country. Had the national church been established in each of the American colonies as a matter of British policy, and gradually engrossed the direction of education to itself, much bloodshed, expense and suffering would have been avoided. The American colonies would not have separated from the Empire as they did. A lesson had been taught, which the British government was admonished to heed in future policy decisions. (2)

By strengthening the established Church of England in the British North American provinces, the British government would make amends for past failings in its colonial policy, and would halt "the progress of sectarian ascendancy" which threatened to have a deleterious effect upon the political character, social stability and even the military strength of the province. In the immediate postwar period, the Rev. John Strachan complained that religious teachers of the dissenting sects were coming "almost universally, from the Republican states of America, where they gather[ed] their knowledge and formed their sentiments", and their brief sojourns 'on the circuit' in Upper Canada could not be expected to alter their views. He maintained, with respect to the itinerant preachers of the Methodist Episcopal Church, that:

> The Methodist teachers are subject to the orders of the Conference of the United States of America, and it is manifest that the Colonial government neither has nor can have any other control over them, or prevent them from gradually rendering a large proportion of the population, by their influence and instruction, hostile to our institutions, both civil and religious.

Moreover, the activities of some of the sectarian ministers during the War of 1812 did little to calm Tory fears. Most of American sectarian clergy and ministers of the dissenting churches simply returned to the United States at the outbreak of the war, and of those who remained in the province some were at best neutral during the struggle, and several had openly supported the American invaders. One Anabaptist preacher, Elijah Bentley, was arrested, tried, and sentenced to prison for preaching sedition; while an 'American Methodist' preacher, Benajah Mallory, had deserted to the Americans during the war and joined the 'Canadian Volunteers' in pillaging and destroying the properties and livestock of the Loyalist families and the militia officers.

Members of other sects, such as the Quakers, Tunkards and Mennonites, not only had refused to bear arms in defence of the province -- a right which the government had recognized on grounds of conscience -- but had done everything in their power – as pacifists -- to obstruct the local war effort:

> they have been a clog -- leaning to the Enemy -- hiding deserters, obstructing the service by bad example & advice -- holding back their produce or selling it at exorbitant prices – refusing to transport stores -- crying down the Government paper issue.

If Upper Canada were to survive as a country independent of the United States and in possession of a British national character, it was essential that the Church of England, the National Church, attain its proper ascendancy. The American religious sects with their American ties, American leadership, and their democratic religious principles, were an Americanizing influence which posed a potentially dangerous threat to the continued existence of British institutions and the British connection. Their efforts needed to be counteracted by the missionary efforts of a strong national church. (3)

The Religious Duty of the Imperial Government

From a religious point of view Great Britain, as a Christian nation, was considered to be under an "awful obligation" to provide religious instruction for her colonies. The British government was admonished that:

> Religious instruction should be made sufficient and commensurate with the wants of the people in every part of the Empire; nor should it be thought a matter of indifference in colonial policy, or even of secondary consideration. It should take the lead of all others; for to form colonies under Christian principles is one of the noblest and most beneficial purposes which governments can fulfill.

By forming her colonies upon the basis of Christian principles, Britain would be fulfilling the greatest purpose of government, the purpose of Creation, by conferring happiness and the means of salvation upon a goodly number of rational beings. The British Empire comprised one-fourth of the world's population, and if Great Britain would but exert her will and take advantage of her means, she had it in her power to evangelize a large portion of mankind. Britain had the opportunity to "place the moral world upon a new foundation" by providing an effective church establishment in each of her far-flung colonies.

In communicating "the arts, sciences, and letters" and "the arts of civilized life" to her colonies, Britain was acting very commendably, but such benefits were "infinitely inferior" to the dissemination of the truths of Christianity which "determine the destiny of the human race".

> In vain shall Great Britain confer upon Colonies the free government and liberal principles of legislation, for which she is distinguished, if she does not carry with her the revelations of God. Till' she does this, she is unjust to her high station --... Let her therefore no longer leave to individuals or associations the labour of evangelizing her Colonies, or even the whole world – their means are inadequate. (4)

Whether regarded in "a moral point of view", or from "the general interests of Christianity", or "the integrity of the British Empire", it was essential that the British government seek to spread the Gospel in the colonies by actively supporting the National Church. The Empire both in the East, and the West, was and should be regarded:

> as the means, under the high and important destiny imposed on it by the designs of an over-ruling Providence, of carrying those designs into effect, and blessing with light, knowledge and liberty, true, rational, and subordinate, -- those vast regions ... over which He has permitted her to extend her dominions. The view is noble, it is grand, it is magnificent: it is worthy of the wisdom, the goodness, the counsels and the superintendence of Deity.

In the Tory view, the British Empire had both a religious and civilizing role to play in the world. Britain was duty bound not to abandon "the mighty moral and political interests of the human family to the serpents and wolves of democracy and faction". She was counseled to keep her "station and dignity" and to aid her colonies to partake of "her moral greatness and grandeur, and her national prosperity, honor and glory". Religion was of the essence. To what did Great Britain owe her pre-eminence in the arts, commerce, and civilization, and her intelligent and moral population, if not to the values inculcated in her people by the Established Church. (5)

From an Imperial viewpoint, Britain should aid the National Church in her colonies because colonies were a definite asset to the Empire in many ways. Colonies provided a home for Britain's surplus population where her sons could exercise their enterprise and industry profitably in improving and bringing into production the waste lands of the Empire. Moreover, the establishment of new settlements in turn created a demand for British manufactures, and served to develop commercial links between Britain and her remotest colonies.

British emigrants who hazarded the many privations and dangers that had to be overcome to found such settlements for the benefit of the Empire, should not be required to forgo any longer than necessary, the enjoyment of "their most precious rights and privileges" as British subjects. It was a matter of:

> principle that the Colonies of a Country have as good a right to
> receive moral and religious instruction from the Parent State,
> as her laws and Government.

Moreover, of all the colonies, none had a better claim to this "common right of all" than the Province of Upper Canada.

The Loyalists of the American Revolution, in fighting for the Unity of Empire on behalf of Great Britain, had been driven from their home and forced to resort to a wilderness where they were almost totally bereft of the means of securing to their children "the benefits of moral and religious instruction" that they had previously possessed. Not only was the Church of England the national church of the Empire, and hence the established church of Upper Canada, but the receipt of its benefits was regarded as the fulfillment of a pledge which had been made to the Loyalists by the British government when -- so the Tories believed

– the Province of Upper Canada was established as an asylum for the Loyalists and their descendants.

The Loyalists had fought to maintain the Unity of the British Empire and, upon departing from the newly-independent American states, had submitted to a great deal of suffering and deprivation. They had done so to continue to live under the British constitution in its full integrity, complete with its provisions for religious ministrations in accordance with the forms of the Church of England. The pledge of the British government was considered as doubly binding because of the distinguished role which Anglicans were held to have played in opposition to the efforts of the American revolutionaries to foment discontent in the American colonies. It was a belief that, over time, became a positive assertion that the most prominent active supporters of the Crown during the American Revolution were principally Anglicans.

For the Tories, the provisions that were made for the support of the 'Protestant Clergy' in the Constitutional Act of 1791 had solemnly redeemed, in part, the pledge of the British government to the Loyalists, and the founding of the Diocese of Quebec (which comprised Upper and Lower Canada) under Bishop Jacob Mountain in 1793, constituted a further redemption of that pledge. It seemed that the British government had realized that if the colonies were going to become, and remain, firmly attached to the mother country, it must be through the ministrations and influence of a strong, and hence well-supported, established church.

The Challenge faced by the National Church

Despite Upper Canada being entitled to receive the benefits of a national church clergy, little had been done in the interval between 1793 and the War of 1812 to support the ministrations of the Church of England. Just prior to the war, Upper Canada had presented "a very melancholy picture" to the Tories. The province contained "a motley population" which, for the most part, lacked any sense of religion and/or Scriptural knowledge. (6)

The pre-war religious situation in Upper Canada was regarded as lamentable, to say the least, but when properly understood rendered Upper Canadians "objects of compassion rather than censure". The origins of the religious shortcomings among the people of Upper Canada were to be found in the "unhappy situation" of the Loyalists. Having lost their all during the American Revolution, they were forced to retreat to "a pathless wilderness" in which they had had to struggle to regain the benefits of civilization. The British government had done much to provide for the Loyalists in appreciation of their services, and sacrifices, but their spiritual needs were not so easily provided for in such an inhospitable clime. Indeed, the very circumstances and character of the people, as well as the geography of the province, had made it a formidable task to provide for their religious instruction. (7)

In the first place, many of the Loyalist soldiers, through long absences from their families on active service, had "acquired habits unfavourable to calm pursuits of sober industry & regularity of conduct", and had grown neglectful of their religious duties. Once settled in Upper Canada, the lack of proper facilities for dispensing religious instruction and the difficulty of communications over vast expanses of wilderness fostered an indifference to religion. In lacking a parish priest of the Established Church to provide religious and moral instruction, and education, by the turn of the century,

> The rising generation, instead of improving, were in many places more ignorant than their parents, and had still less regard for that religion, to the forms of which, they had never been accustomed.

The difficulty in meeting the religious needs of the Loyalist settlers was further increased by the fact that they were of different religious denominations, and were not moved by that "unity of exertion" which one would expect to find had they been of one denomination. What is more, the American settlers, who had migrated into Upper Canada after the Loyalists, were "accustomed to no regular establishment of religion", and the British immigrants who came out in the early period were marked by little if any religious principles. It was this combination of circumstances that had contributed to the prevailing "coldness and indifference" toward Christianity in the province. Above all, the Loyalists had one great difficulty to overcome, besides which their past habits, the difficulties of communications, and the religious plurality of their settlements, paled: viz. the impact of the wilderness on the mind of the settlers. (8)

It was evident that a few years' residence in the wilderness served to completely transform the attitudes of the settlers. At first, they would feel the need for churches and schools, and would lament that they were unable to immediately attain them, "but, by degrees, such lamentations die away". In lacking churches and living in isolation on farm clearings where they were unrestrained by public opinion, and no longer influenced by the example of those whom they loved, respected and/or feared, the settlers tended to grow careless about religious observances. They became apathetic toward religion, and "indifferent and avaricious" in their attitude toward others.

This process of moral and religious degeneration, and the ill-effects which it was having upon the character of the people, was clearly visible to the Upper Canadian Tories. The Rev. John Strachan described the impact of the wilderness on the settlers as follows:

> [the settlers live] scattered on their farms, cut off from that daily intercourse, which softens and polishes the manners. Confined to family circles, their ideas become selfish and contracted, and they are little disposed to trouble themselves about any other thing than what contributes immediately to their own comfort. Among such a population, social intercourse is very rare, and they seldom meet unless to bargain and traffic. Consequently, the social affections sleep or expire -- their deportment becomes rough and forbidding -- at one time, forward and impudent, at another time awkward and sheepish.

Among the settlers in the wilderness, the best moral and religious habits soon decayed and the better feelings and dispositions – all "sense of decency" and "true piety and virtue" – gave way to an indifference or even a dislike of Christian worship. In the absence of proper religious instruction, habit and custom, and the restraining "force of public opinion", their children lacked any appreciation for the intrinsic value of "spiritual blessings and privileges", and were contemptuous of the Christian rules of life. In such a situation, "the depraved nature of man" and the "hardness and impenitency of the unsanctified human heart", were clearly exposed in the rapidity with which "the passions and appetites" assumed control over men who gave themselves over to a "most irregular and dissolute course of life".

Such a situation was worrisome to the Upper Canadian Tories because:

> With the transition in the exterior circumstances of life, from refinement and elegance to simplicity and rudeness, it is too often thought that there should be a corresponding transition in the moral and religious habits.

In the backwoods, the female sex alone was responsible for whatever sense of humanity and knowledge of religion remained. Within the family, the women sought to "cherish and inculcate some of the principles of social life" in their rude surroundings, but their efforts were adjudged to be insufficient to maintain a moral and religious population. (9)

To the Tories, the Province of Upper Canada, during the early years of settlement, was a society suffering from a moral degeneration, and in such a circumstance, a clergyman had not only to disseminate the Word of God, "but also to preach civilization". Although those who had succumbed to a totally dissolute life were in a distinct minority, still the prevailing transformation in the moral and religious character of the people in the frontier settlements was such as to alarm the Tory elite.

One of the great difficulties which the Tories faced in seeking to improve the moral and religious character of the Province of Upper Canada, was that the tastes of many had become so vitiated that the difficulties in securing religions instruction were often exaggerated, and when overcome, the people "have little or no disposition to support religion or to attend to its institution". Thus, the circumstance which made it imperative for the Established Church to provide moral and religious instruction to the people made that task doubly difficult. Not all the difficulties which the Tories faced were local in origin. In seeking to expand the ministrations of the Church of England on the frontiers of settlement, the Anglican Tories were aware that they were not only engaged in combating the impact of the wilderness upon the mind of the settlers, but also what the Tories regarded as the irreligious and irrational character of the age. (10)

In formulating their national policy during the immediate post-war period, the Upper Canadian Tories were only too well aware that one of the critical problems which they faced in seeking to strengthen and extend the Established Church, was the general apathy toward religion which had prevailed "among the Protestants of all denominations" during the 18th Century, and especially among "the wealthy and fashionable". Moreover, despite the stupendous efforts of the Bible Societies, infidelity still exerted its sway. Indeed, one of the aims of the Bible Society, which was founded by the Tories in Upper Canada in 1819, was to "restore to the gospel that general sense of its great value and importance which seemed to have passed away".

On the one hand, 'the skeptical Philosophers' had "spoken, written against, misrepresented and ridiculed" the Christian religion and, in the more populous areas of Upper Canada, their would-be followers continued, "in the name of liberality", to disparage and disregard religious truth. That men should adhere to such blasphemous opinions was deplorable because they were the product of a false reasoning "which proceeding from laxity of principle to doubt, commonly ends in profligate indifference". However, irreligion was not the only threat to "the true religion'.

By the eve of the War of 1812, in the absence of the ministrations of a regular clergy within a parish system, the province had been "overrun with itinerant Methodist Preachers & Fanatics of all Descriptions" who engaged in a "fanatical revival system" form of preaching that served only to banish the true rational religion from their camp meetings. The Tories were convinced that once the "fires of fanaticism cool down", the emotional preaching of the Methodist circuit riders would leave only a religious indifference in its wake.

Thus, in their efforts "to reclaim" Upper Canadians "to the rational Doctrine and Practices of the Church of England", the Tories were faced not only with the problem of overcoming the debilitating effects and difficulties which were posed by the wilderness environment in the backwoods settlement, but also the need to overcome religious indifference and what they regarded as religious fanaticism. (11)

The general apathy and indifference toward religion of the age also influenced the British government which, since the passing of the Constitutional Act in 1791, had left the Church of England in Upper Canada to find its own way "almost totally unaided by the parent State". The religious health of the colony had been ignored in the pursuit of "pecuniary advantage" with the result that -- by the end of the War of 1812 -- the Anglicans of Upper Canada, as well as the members of other Protestant denominations, were suffering from a lack of religious instruction. To the Tory mind, Great Britain had been "culpably deficient" in meeting "the first care of a Christian nation"; and it was essential that this omission be rectified as soon as possible through providing an effective support for the clergy of the Established Church. (12)

The Established Church of Upper Canada

The Upper Canadian Tories were convinced that the Church of England was the Established Church of Upper Canada. The Constitutional Act of 1791 had bestowed upon the provinces of Upper and Lower Canada a constitution which was a duplicate of the British constitution. As such it conveyed the full benefits and spirit of the British Constitution to Upper Canada, of which the established Church of England was an essential part. The Legislature of Upper Canada in its early years of operation had always acted on the assumption that the Constitutional Act was "an exact transcript" of the British Constitution, and had invariably settled disputes between the various branches of the Legislature through referrals to British constitutional precedents and practices.

It was realized that the Constitutional Act was merely a bare working outline of the British Constitution, and that consequently it had to be interpreted within the spirit and tradition of that constitution as it existed in its full operation in Great Britain. With respect to church establishment, it was of little consequence whether the Church of England was specifically established by colonial law because the National Church was an integral part of the British Constitution. Moreover, it was a fact which was attested to by the terminology, rules and workings of the Church of England which were cited in the Constitutional Act for the establishment of parsonages and rectories.

Moreover, the Tories believed that the government of William Pitt in drafting the Constitutional Act had:

> foresaw that an union of action in the principles of the British Constitution must prevail thro' out the entire British Dominions, otherwise harmony would disappear & confusion ensue. Church & State are so vitally connected in the British Constitution that you cannot injure the one without injuring the other.

For the Upper Canadian Tories, there were no legitimate grounds for doubting that the Church of England was the established Church of Upper Canada, under the direction of the Archbishop of Canterbury, the 'Patriarch of the British Empire'. (13)

The Constitutional Act authorized his Majesty to set aside a land endowment to the value of one-seventh of the Crown lands "for the Support and Maintenance of a Protestant Clergy", and "from time to time" to erect "Parsonages or Rectories" in the townships "according to the Establishment of the Church of England". Moreover, the parsonages or rectories, once created, were for presentation to "an Incumbent or Minister of the Church of England, who shall have been duly ordained according to the Rites of the said Church". To the Tories, the provisions of the Constitutional Act proved conclusively that the Church of England was established in Upper Canada. Moreover, they were strengthened in that belief by their knowledge that the British Government, in its communications with the Lt. Governor of Upper Canada, had always referred to the Church of England as the Established Church of Upper Canada, and their knowledge that the Legislature of Upper Canada, prior to the War of 1812, had concurred in that belief.

The establishment of the Church of England had been recognized by the local government in various ways: the appointment of a clergyman of the Anglican Church to serve as chaplain of the Legislature, its enjoyment of corporation rights, and the marriage acts of 1793 and 1798. Corporation rights had been bestowed upon the Church of England in Upper Canada with the creation of the Diocese of Quebec in 1793. In the same year, the Legislature of Upper Canada had passed an act which provided that as soon as a church was built "according to the use of the Church of England" and a minister appointed to his charge, the householders should elect a representative and the parson nominate another, both of whom would serve as Churchwardens and they, and their successors, would constitute "a corporation to represent the whole inhabitants of the township or parish". Thus empowered, the Church of England as a 'body corporate' could hold property, a right which was denied the other denominations. Consequently, the other churches and sects had to invest their church holdings, and cemetery plots, in the hands of individual members of their congregations.

Furthermore, by the Marriage Act, which was passed in 1793, only the clergy of the Church of England had the right to perform marriages unless the couple to be married lived more than eighteen miles distant from the closest Anglican minister. In which case, the Justice of the Peace was to have the authority to marry them "according to the Form prescribed by the Church of England". This act was further amended by the Marriage Act of 1798 which extended the legal right to solemnize marriages to ministers who were "of the Church of Scotland, or Lutherans, or Calvinists". A minister of the specified denominations who wanted to perform a marriage ceremony was required to apply to the local Justice of the Peace for a license, to offer proof that he was a regularly ordained minister, and to attest that at least one of the parties to be married had been a member of his congregation for a minimum of six months.

Once the Justice of the Peace was satisfied that the requirements of the Marriage Act had been met, the minister was required to take an oath of allegiance to the King before being licensed to perform a marriage according to the rites of his own Church. The Anglican Church ministers faced no such restrictions as they were ministers of the Established Church. In sum, for the Upper Canadian Tories, there was never any question but that the Church of England was the established church of the Province of Upper Canada. The real question was whether, and to what extent, the British government would provide support for the Church in the carrying out of the provisions made in the Constitution Act for implementing its establishment. (14)

From the earliest years of settlement, the Anglican Tories in Upper Canada were anxious to place the Church of England on "a respectable footing" through implementing the provisions of the Constitutional Act for the establishment of parsonages or rectories. They were hampered, however, by problems beyond their control. A major obstacle was the demographic composition of the province. Only "a very small proportion" of the population had been raised in the Church of England in a province where an influx of American immigrants – comprising mainly of "Sectaries or Dissenters" – had come to outnumber the Loyalist settlers over the decade prior to the War. The demographics of the province made the Legislature cautious in asserting the rights of the Established Church in that period – prior to the heavy postwar British immigration into Upper Canada – and, at an early date, made the provincial government conscious of the danger of any attempt to enforce the rights of a church establishment.

The disruption of the War years, and free grants of Crown lands -- which were readily available to immigrants prior to 1826 – made it difficult to lease the clergy reserves lots, and severely hampered the Church of England in securing revenues for recruiting clergymen. It had necessitated also the postponement of the erection of rectories and parsonages. Nonetheless, the Tories were determined to strengthen and extend the ministrations of the Church of England in Upper Canada. (15)

With the exception of efforts made by the Methodists – who were not covered by terms of the 1798 Marriage Act -- to obtain an extension of the right to perform marriages for their ministers, the rights of the Church of England had remained unquestioned in the Legislature before the War of 1812. What the Methodists requested -- and what had been granted to the Church of Scotland, the Lutherans, and the Calvinists -- constituted a diminution of a hitherto exclusive right adhering to the Church of England, but did not involve any denial that the Church of England was the established church of Upper Canada. It was only in the immediate postwar years that the right of the Church of England to enjoy an exclusive benefit from the Clergy Reserves came to be publicly questioned by the political radicals and their sectarian supporters, as well as the extent of the endowment. The establishment of the Church of

England, however, was not questioned initially nor the principle of the union of church and state.

Defending the Clergy Reserves

After the War, a leading member of the Assembly, Col. Robert Nichol, introduced two resolutions -- in March 1817 – which pertained to the Clergy Reserves. The first resolution declared that the Crown and Clergy reserve lots were an "insurmountable obstacle" to the formation of continuous settlement, greatly increased the cost of building and maintaining roads, and were an inducement to Americans to attack the province in the hopes of indemnifying themselves through seizing the reserve allotments. The second resolution declared that the one-seventh proportion of the land being set aside for the clergy endowment was "an appropriation beyond all precedent lavish", and that the clergy reserves lands ought to be sold and a smaller proportion of the proceeds, to be determined by the Legislature, used to endow churches.

In the event, the Legislature was prorogued by Lt. Governor Gore, who strongly objected to several other resolutions which had been introduced into the Assembly that favoured the continuance of American immigration into Upper Canada. The prorogation of the Legislature prevented the resolutions on the Clergy Reserves from being voted on, but the attack on the clergy reserves endowment remained a source of continual worry for the Upper Canadian Tories.

Thereafter, in March 1819, a Presbyterian congregation at Niagara requested that assistance be granted their minister out of the clergy reserves fund on the grounds that in Britain the Church of Scotland was co-established in Upper Canada. Other Presbyterian congregations quickly drew together to take up the argument, and proceeded to organize public meetings throughout the province to gain public support for the claim of the Church of Scotland to a share in the revenues of the Clergy Reserves.

The Tories considered the claim of the Presbyterians to be totally specious, but were already taking steps to defend the interest of the Church in response to the two resolutions which were submitted to the House of Assembly by Col. Nichol. The resolutions were regarded as being "exceedingly pernicious and disgraceful". Although the Legislature could not deprive the Established Church of its reserves endowment, it could excite discontent which, if long continued, would discourage people from leasing the Clergy Reserves. If that happened, it would "very materially impede the progress of the Church".

For the Rev. John Strachan, these developments demanded that the British government send out instructions "informing us what the Established Church is and that the Reserves are for its benefit and for it alone". It was realized, however, that much more than a statement of rights was required if the Church of England were to become effectively established in Upper Canada. It would require a defence of the rights of the Church in the provincial Legislature. (16)

To that end, Strachan began to seek an appointment to the Legislative Council out of a strong desire to strengthen the government and to use his influence in "forwarding the interests of religion and education" in Upper Canada. To his mind, it was "absolutely necessary" that some zealous individual, such as himself, should be appointed in a situation where:

> Great appropriations have been made by [the British] Government for these purposes, but there is nobody of influence interested in rendering them efficient.

The Rev. Strachan considered that his various efforts during the War "to preserve and increase the Spirit of Loyalty" among the people of Upper Canada, and his pre-eminent position as the leading promoter of "true religion and sound education" in the province, merited such an appointment. He had been highly pleased earlier when, in September 1815, he was appointed an "extraordinary member" of the Executive Council in recognition of his services during the War of 1812. Political developments during the year 1817, however, raised a totally new consideration: the need to combat an indifference to the interests of the National Church within the provincial government itself. (17)

Although the prorogation of the Legislature by the Lt. Governor had prevented the clergy reserves resolutions of Col. Nichol from coming to a vote, Strachan expected that the matter would be raised again in the next session of the Legislature. The clergy reserves resolutions, and the failure in the same Legislative session of a bill to provide financial support for the education of young men for Holy Orders of the Established Church, made the Anglican Tories aware of the existence of "a danger to the Church from the prevalence of opinions hostile to her interests in both branches of the Legislature".

It had been anticipated that a bill for the education of clerical candidates – which had provided for an annual appropriation of £500 for ten years for that purpose -- would meet with some opposition in the Assembly. Nonetheless, with the aid of three former pupils of Strachan who possessed seats in the House of Assembly, and his personal influence over several other members, the bill had passed the Assembly only to be rejected in the Legislative Council. No opposition had been expected from the Council. The clerical education bill had been amended to take account of the objections that were raised by the Legislative Council to a similar bill which had passed the Assembly the year before. Hence, it was "in truth their own bill as amended". To the Rev. Strachan, it was:

> certainly considered [to be] the peculiar duty of the Legislative Council to support the Church and, instead of opposing, to be vigilant in cherishing & promoting every measure in her favour.

Strachan was very indignant, to say the least, at such an unexpected turn of events. He was even more so upon learning that the clergy reserves resolutions – submitted to the Assembly by Col. Nichol -- had been "first hatched" by two Legislative Councilors: William Dickson and Thomas Clark. Both men were large landholders who were well known for their opposition to the provincial government with respect to its policy of restricting American emigration into Upper Canada; and they appeared to be bent upon fomenting discontent against the provincial government. (18)

Upon examination of the composition of the Legislative Council, it became clear as to why a measure "having for its object the support of the Church of England Establishment" had met with resistance in that chamber. Of the eight members, four were Presbyterians including Dickson and Clark and their associate Thomas Frazer -- all of who were land speculators with "lands to sell" -- and Neil McLean of Cornwall; one was a Roman Catholic, James (Jacques) Baby, a major landholder who supported the government; and two were Anglicans: Col. William Claus, a Churchman; and the Chief Justice, William Dummer Powell, who was indifferent, if not opposed, to efforts in favour of the National Church.

In being convinced of the necessity of having men who were "judiciously alive" to the best interests of the Church in the Legislative Council, the Rev. Strachan offered to serve the government in that capacity. Previously, he had declined the offer of an appointment to the Legislative Council in contenting himself with his *ex officio* seat in the Executive Council. However, it was the changed political circumstances of 1817 that motivated the Rev. Strachan to actively seek an appointment to the Legislative Council, and to secure his appointment as a regular member of the Executive Council in July 1817.

If appointed to the Legislative Council, Strachan was confident that he could count upon the support of Col. Claus, and could gain the support of Col. Fraser and Col. McLean, as well as the support of the Roman Catholic, Mr. Baby. These men were either close friends, or were "under special obligations" to him personally. In such a case, the bill in support of the education of clerical candidates of the Established Church could be carried through the Legislature and enacted into law with the support of the Lt. Governor, Sir Francis Gore, who was a strong supporter of the interests of the established Church of England.

During the fall of 1817, nothing was accomplished, with the Legislature prorogued and the Lt. Governor absent from the province. The following year, however, the situation took a turn for the better with the arrival in August 1818 of a new Lt. Governor, Major-General Sir Peregrine Maitland, who was a devote Churchman. When the Legislative Council was expanded in July 1820, four of the six new members were Churchmen, inclusive of the Rev. John Strachan and George Herkimer Markland, one of his former pupils. Thus, as of 1820, Strachan appeared to be in a very strong position in the Legislative Council. Moreover, he could count on support from several of his former pupils who were members of the House of Assembly and on a sympathetic Lt. Governor, in his efforts to secure government support for the Church of England to facilitate "the diffusion of moral and religious knowledge" among the people of Upper Canada. (19)

The Postwar Religious Outlook

The beginning of the third decade of the 19th Century seemed to be a propitious time for a concerted effort to evangelize the province. It was noted that "a great change" was taking place in the character of the province. Many of its inhabitants, who formerly had been indifferent towards religion, were seeking religious instruction. Deputations were received from communities requesting that ministers go out to preach to them, churches were being built, and solicitations were received requesting the services of a permanent minister. Life was becoming more comfortable in the older areas of settlement, and the settlers, although unable to give much for the support of a clergyman from their meager earnings, were seeking religious instruction.

The Bible Society of Upper Canada was pleased to find that their efforts to distribute the Scriptures throughout the province were having "a happy effect". Earlier, in the absence of religious instruction and the lack of access to the Bible and religious literature, the wilderness was seen to bring out man's baser instincts, and to vitiate all good feeling and sense of religion. Now that the Scriptures were being made available, the heavily-forested backwoods had a completely opposite effect upon the British immigrant settlers. In being able to read the Scriptures and meditate upon the Word of God, in being free from all distractions, the very experiences of living in the midst of nature served to foster a greater consciousness of man's proper relationship to "the ruler of the Universe". Once in possession of the Scriptures, and living in isolation bereft of any hope of human aid and experiencing continually dangers and threats to their lives in the very nature of their labour, they could not but "feel therefore more strongly impressed than usual with religious truths" and of their "dependence upon God".

Once motivated to turn to "reflection and serious meditation" upon the purpose of life, it was held to be only natural that the settlers would become desirous of receiving religious instruction from a regular clergyman. In such circumstances -- so the Rev. Strachan believed -- all that was required to extend and strengthen the establishment of the

Church of England was to secure a sufficient number of conscientious and zealous clergymen to enable a parish church to be established in all of the settled communities of the province. (20)

The Church of England had only twelve clergymen in the province in 1819, as distinct from five Presbyterian ministers, six Roman Catholic priests, and a very considerable number of itinerant Methodist preachers. Nonetheless, the Rev. Strachan hoped to secure financial support for the Legislature for the education of Anglican clerical candidates and expected more clergymen to emigrate from Britain. Moreover, he was convinced that there was "a favourable disposition" among the people of Upper Canada with respect to the Established Church. As of 1819, the clergy of the National Church were dependent upon the Society for the Propagation of the Gospel in Britain for financial support; however, the Bishop of Quebec was at that time in England seeking to bring the administration of the Clergy Reserves land endowment under the direction of the Church.

If that could be done, it was expected that with proper management the Clergy Reserves would finally yield an income sufficient to place the Church on "a respectable footing", as was originally intended. Once made productive, the reserves endowment would enable a clergyman to be supported in a parish in every settled area of the province. The Rev. Strachan was convinced that:

> We only want Clergymen to have a decided majority in our favour, but ... we must strain every nerve and outpreach, and outpractice our opponents.

Oddly enough, he looked to the United States for inspiration.

For Strachan, the experiences of the Episcopal Church in New York under Bishop John Hobart showed what could be done if a sustained effort were made. In New York, the bulk of the first settlers were Presbyterians and Independents, but their congregations had succumbed "to the affected liberality of the age". They had ceased to instruct their children in the catechisms and basic tenets of their faith and, with the Christian religion falling into disrepute, "their congregations [were] falling into decay". In contrast, the Episcopal Church in being well governed under bishops characterized by "piety, activity and good sense', had tripled its membership in New York alone, and was increasing its adherents in "all the States far beyond other denominations".

On all counts, it seemed to the Rev. John Strachan that both the possibility and the means of constructing their ideal Christian society was within the grasp of the Established Church in Upper Canada. The religious character of the province remained to be formed; and although "heresy, indifference, and infidelity" continued to increase before their very eyes, the Anglican Tory elite never wavered in their belief that:

> If any denomination can succeed in evangelizing this colony, it ought to be the Church of England, and if she does not accomplish this great blessing, the fault will be in her ministry, and not in her Government and principles. (21)

If a truly Christian society were to be constructed in the wilderness of Upper Canada, it would have to be through the exertions of a numerous body of the national clergy in disseminating 'true religion' and extirpating infidelity. Indubitably, an ecclesiastical establishment was "the most effectual channel" for that purpose because it could command sufficient resources to maintain in being a clergy comprised of "intelligent, learned and judicious men". Moreover, in being part of the national clergy, and conscious of belonging to the 'one Holy Catholic and Apostolic Church' as founded by Christ, and "united in one faith", they could not fail to realize their purpose as:

> Their influence will gradually increase with their numbers and they will be able to enforce, with more and more success, the interesting truth, that religion enters essentially into all the interests of individuals, of families, and of states; that it promotes public order and private morals, and is evidently given by the great Author of nature, for the government of the human mind. (22)

A Policy of Religious Comprehension

In their appeals to the provincial and British governments for support to strengthen and extend the Church of England, the Anglican Tories sought to evangelize the Province of Upper Canada and, ultimately, to comprehend the vast majority of the population of Upper Canada within the National Church. In seeking to evangelize the province, the aim was not only the saving of souls, but the placing of the Church of England in a position where it could exert a decisive influence on the formation of 'the British national character' of the province.

With the revival of interest in religion during the decade following the War of 1812, the Upper Canadian Tories were encouraged to make strenuous efforts to extend the Established Church under what they regarded as extremely favourable circumstances. The policy of religious comprehension had three distinct aspects: first, to maintain those who had been raised in the Church of England as adherents; secondly, to win over to the Church those who were indifferent to religion or unattached to another church; and thirdly, to eventually comprehend within the National Church the adherents of the various religious sects of Upper Canada and some of the adherents of the dissenting Protestant churches. The hopes of the Tories in pursuing these objectives were based on how they perceived the religious situation in Upper Canada. (23)

During the immediate postwar period, the Tories of Upper Canada were convinced that as much as one-half of the population of the province was either indifferent to all religion, or had "no decided preference" for any one religious denomination. It was firmly believed that if given a choice, many of these families would generally prefer to receive the ministrations of the National Church, if a parish church were established in each locale. This group was viewed as open to conversion, and if a clergyman were present to exercise a discrete zeal, the greater number could be won to the Church of England. Although many of the irreligious had been, at one time, members of another church or sect, past experience had shown that whenever a clergyman of the Established Church were present, he would secure a large congregation from among them, and even from members of other denominations.

Even those who did not join the Church -- with the sole exception of Roman Catholics -- would have recourse to the Church to have their children baptized, and would "occasionally attend public Worship" in the Church. This was not to say that ministers of the other Protestant churches would not enjoy the same experience in a similar situation, but that the Church of England should exert itself to be the first to be present in the new areas of settlement. Once a minister was established in a community, he would "become the centre of civilization", and his very presence would tend to draw the community together. Although at first, he would dispense "the truths and duties of religion" only to his own adherents, nevertheless in time many who had little or no access to religion would turn to him – if he were "of a mild conciliatory disposition" -- and would adhere to his congregation. (24)

If Upper Canada were to experience the full benefits of an established church -- as England and Scotland did -- it was essential that not only those who were not affiliated to any particular Church be won over to the Church of England, but also that "a fair proportion of the other half" of the population, which already adhered to a Protestant church or sect, be comprehended in time within the Established Church.

From the earliest days of settlement, the Church of England had given religious instruction to the people regardless of their religious affiliation, and had baptized, married, and interred adherents of different religions. Thus, in the Tory view, the Church had developed "peculiar claims on the sympathy and gratitude" of many Upper Canadians. All denominations made use of the Book of Common Prayer – except for the Roman Catholics -- and the children of the various Protestant denominations commonly attended the Sunday schools of the Established Church. This was taken as an encouraging sign, as was the awareness of the Anglican clergy that it was a quite common experience in Upper Canada for new arrivals to convert to the Church of England.

The first Anglican minister in Upper Canada, the Loyalist clergyman the Rev. Dr. John Stuart, had been raised a Presbyterian in Pennsylvania, but converted to the Church of England prior to the American Revolution; while the Rev. John Strachan himself, who had been raised and educated in the Church of Scotland, converted to the Established Church upon his arrival in Upper Canada and, after completing his theology studies, was ordained in 1803. Moreover, two sons of the Loyalist clergyman John Bethune -- the first Presbyterian minister of a congregation in Upper Canada -- had taken orders in the Church of England after attending the Cornwall District Grammar School of the Rev. John Strachan.

Such conversions were not surprising to the Tories, or to Upper Canadians more generally. The real essence of religion for the Anglican clergy was its moral element and the essential Christian values and beliefs; there was no interest in engaging in theological disputations. As defined by the Rev. John Strachan:

> Christianity is a spiritual worship, and its object is to bring men to a nearer conformity to God; for this purpose, it elevates their views above temporal things, and qualifies them for a higher state of existence.

When John Strachan converted to the Church of England, one his former tutors in the Church of Scotland, wrote:

> I have no objection to the Church of Eng., there is no material difference between them, they are but graceless zealots who fight for modes of faith or worship, he can't be wrong whose life is in the right. (25)

Thus, it was taken for granted that a Church of England clergyman, if placed in a parish from the beginning of settlement, would soon attain the adherence of "the greater portion" of the Lutherans, Presbyterians, Congregationalists, and particularly so of the Methodists who were dependent upon itinerant preachers. The [Wesleyan] Methodists had not "distinctly separated" from the Church of England, and it was maintained that both:

> the Lutherans and the Methodists hold the same religious principles [as the Church of England], and as their services are irregular, even while they adhere to their respective forms, they will attend often upon those of the Church. (26)

The Tory effort to comprehend other religious denominations within the Established Church took various forms. Some ministers and their congregations – where the minister was properly educated and regularly ordained in a Protestant church – were approached and encouraged to join the Church of England. As of 1820 a Lutheran minister, the German Loyalist, the Rev. John Weagant had already joined the Church of England, and a large Lutheran congregation near York was reportedly requesting that an Anglican minister be sent. In addition, yet another

Presbyterian minister was in the process of applying for admission to the Anglican ministry.

On the other hand, the Wesleyan Methodists were encouraged to maintain their traditional ties with the Church of England. In *The Christian Recorder* (1819-1821), a publication of the Anglican Church, it was continually stressed that the Rev. John Wesley was "a zealous Churchman" who had opposed all "levellers and Jacobins", and throughout his life had impressed upon his adherents "*not to separate from the Church*". More generally, *The Christian Recorder*, through deliberately adopting a moderate tone, sought to avoid giving any offense to the other religious denominations while seeking to appeal to their religious susceptibilities. As explained by the Rev. John Strachan, the editor of the *Christian Recorder*, his intention was:

> to give no just cause of offence to any while I maintain the purity of our faith, the beauty and excellence of our liturgy and the superiority of our Church Government. (27)

In the postwar period, the Upper Canadian Tories were prepared to enter into a struggle to place the Church of England in a position where it would be enabled to form the religious character, and indeed the 'national character', of the Province of Upper Canada. It was a major undertaking; and yet, it was one in which they were confident of their prospect for success. It was a situation where:

> A wide field is open in Upper Canada for all religious denominations; the majority of the people are still undecided; and of that majority, the greater part will join those Teachers who are the most zealous and attentive to the discharge of their sacred duties.

In the Tory view, the Church of England, as the Established Church, possessed several distinct advantages over other denominations, and not the least of which was the enjoyment of support from the Society for the Propagation of the Gospel in Foreign Parts (S.P.G.) which paid, in large part, the salaries of the Anglican ministers in Upper Canada. Where the funding received from the S.P.G. was sufficient, new congregations could secure a minister at no expense to themselves beyond the erection of a church or "house of prayer".

Moreover, in the estimation of the Rev. John Strachan, the Established Church already possessed a "much more numerous" membership than any other single church in Upper Canada. At various times, it was claimed that as many as one-fifth to one-half of the 200,000 population of Upper Canada were either adherents of, or supporters of the Established Church.

Another advantage which was claimed for the Church of England in its effort to attract "neutrals" and members of the religious sects, was the uniform orthodox discipline of the Church. It was based upon the primitive Christian Church, and its discipline was held to be in keeping with "the habits and the character of the people". For the Anglican Tories, it was a maxim that

> In every supposable state of society, except in a temporary coalition of adverse and discordant prejudices where the object is political power, the Religion which is established by authority, will maintain its just preponderance.

Hence, it was imperative that the clergy reserves land endowment be retained, as intended, for the benefit of the Established Church; and that government aid for the ministers of other denominations be denied or limited in extent. If that were done, under the conditions existing in Upper Canada, there was no doubt in the Tory mind that "the greater portion of the Different denominations will in a few years Conform". (28)

Although the Tory scheme of religious comprehension was based on their political belief in a church-state polity, and their understanding of the role of a national church within the state, it could not be separated from religious self-interest as the leading Tories who supported the religious comprehension scheme were Anglicans. Nonetheless, it also sprang, particularly where the Anglican clergy were concerned, from a deeply felt religious obligation.

A Religious Obligation

The Tories believed that it was their duty as Christians, and "the most sacred of all Christian obligations", to carry the Gospel to all men who were deprived of its blessings; and in Upper Canada, with a large influx of British immigrants in the postwar decades, a rapidly increasing population was being denied access to religious instruction by a lack of parish priests in the new settlements. It was a situation where:

> Both Parents and Children are in very many places shut out from public worship and the sacraments of the Church. Left entirely to secular callings, their minds are by degrees engrossed by temporal, and withdrawn [from] spiritual things. Great then is the obligation that rests upon us to fan the holy flame that has once been lighted up -- and to maintain the saving truth in every heart that has once acknowledged its sanctions.

Christians once redeemed could not be permitted to fall away from the way of God. To the Tory mind, the most effective remedy for religious indifference was the ministrations of "a regular and standing Ministry" of an established church. The Church of England in their eyes had a mission to spread the Christian message, to sustain the faith of its members, and to win back those who had lapsed into indifference. Moreover, as the national church of the British Empire, it had a duty to administer to the spiritual needs of the province.

Whether the people chose to have recourse to her ministrations or not, every effort needed to be made to bring dissenters back into the fold. It was an endeavour that could never be abandoned. The Anglican clergy were admonished to conduct themselves with "Christian love", and with "gentleness and discretion", and to seek always to maintain social harmony while promoting the extension of the Church. Other denominations were to be treated with "the utmost charity", while bending every effort to bring the young and the uncommitted within the Church establishment. Christian charity determined that only persuasion and the "preaching of the Word" should be relied upon to achieve adherents. Indeed, the Tories believed that in any undertaking to win the confidence and commitment of others to one's cause, a resort to coercion was totally unacceptable.

> It is well observed by Mr. [Edmund] Burke that coercion is the ready resource of little minds, but to bring about your purpose by attention to human nature, by indulging innocent prejudices, and consulting honourable feeling, requires much care & is a decisive proof of good talents. (29)

The comprehension of the members of the various religious sects, and the religiously indifferent, into the Established Church was an essential part of the national policy of the Upper Canadian Tories, but a somewhat different attitude prevailed among the Anglican Tories towards the Church of Scotland and the Church of Rome.

The Traditional Churches

The Church of Scotland and the Church of Rome shared common principles and social attitudes with the Church of England which, in the circumstances prevailing in Upper Canada, tended to align them in a conservative common cause. To a common dislike of sectarian religion, on both religious and political grounds, and abhorrence of religious indifference, was added a common fear of the forces of democratic anarchy and infidelity, and of the leveling ideas manifested in the very 'spirit of the age'. All three churches were alarmed -- in living in what they regarded as "a dissolute age" -- at the tendency of men to disparage their superiors, to heap scorn upon religion, and "to speak evil of such things as we do not understand".

All three churches were united by common political beliefs and principles. They abhorred demagogues, who sought to promote discontent among the people, and deprecated innovators and 'men given to change' who refused to accept the natural hierarchical order of society and failed to recognize that a due subordination to God's moral law constituted the very basis of social order. The clergy of all three churches were convinced that Upper Canada lived under "the most mild, wise and equitable government in the world"; and that the political, religious and social benefits that Upper Canadian enjoyed as a British colony should not be sacrificed to address "imaginary grievances" concocted by self-seeking demagogues. It was held that the subversion of legitimate government would only lead to "anarchy and violence", which was far worse than any imperfections in the existing administration of government.

The clergy of the Church of Scotland and the Church of Rome were in accord with the Church of England clergy in maintaining that the state had a role to play in the formation of the moral character of the people; and that the most effective approach was for the church to control education and the state to provide endowments of land and/or salaries for the support of the church and its clergy. Only through the ministrations and teachings of the clergy could "the madness of the people" and "the daring spirit of anarchy" be curtailed.

Although the spokesmen and the clergy of all three churches might disagree, and did, over the extent to which their respective churches should receive government financial aid, and held differing views concerning the clergy reserves endowment, they were united in their common political principles and social beliefs. All three churches believed in a God-ordained moral order, which it was the duty of the church and the state to maintain, as well as in the duty of man to render a strict obedience to the law and a due deference to the authority of the King and his representatives. Moreover, all three churches rejected American democratic republicanism, and had a strong distaste for sectarian religion which they associate with the American revolutionary experience. (30)

Where the three traditional churches were concerned, more than common political principles and social attitudes brought them together. The Church of England and Church of Scotland were both national churches in the United Kingdom – in England and Scotland, respectively -- and the Church of England was established in Upper Canada, so the Tories held; while the Roman Catholic Church had been extended the rights of establishment by the Quebec Act of 1774, at a time when the Province of Quebec encompassed the future provinces of Lower Canada and Upper Canada. Moreover, all three of the "respectable churches" possessed a regularly ordained and learned clergy, and their leading laymen were men of eminence and education. They mixed socially together in York and Kingston where social ties among the laity were often reinforced by similar business and professional interests.

The leading clergymen of the three traditional denominations were noted also for their loyalty to the Crown, and their loyal conduct during wartime. The leading Presbyterian minister in the pre-war period, the late Rev. John Bethune, was a Loyalist who had served as the chaplain of a Highland Scots regiment (the 84th) during the American Revolution. The Rev. John Strachan had distinguished himself during the War of 1812 in strongly supporting the British cause; and the leading Roman Catholic cleric -- a Scots immigrant -- the Rev. Alexander McDonell, had raised a regiment of Highlanders, the Glengarry Light Infantry Fencibles, for service during the War of 1812 and had served as the regimental chaplain throughout the conflict.

Thus, common principles -- religious, moral and political – as well as common loyalties, social attitudes, and fears, mutual respect and fraternization, and a dislike of interlopers such as the American religious sects, drew together the adherents of the three traditional churches. They were aligned politically, despite differences that remained among them over the extent to which the Catholic and Presbyterian clerics should receive government salaries, and differences over a claim that the Presbyterians would make for a half share of the share in the revenues yielded by the Clergy Reserves.

The interests of the Presbyterians and the Roman Catholics were not ignored when – after 1819, under the administration of Lt. Governor Maitland -- the Rev. John Strachan and his protégé, John Beverley Robinson, gained a large say in government appointments and the distribution of Crown patronage. At that time, a system of alliances was constructed between the government bureaucracy in York and the local elites throughout the province, which included members of all three churches. In areas where the Presbyterians formed a major portion of the population, or where the Roman Catholics Highlanders did in the eastern part of the province, their co-religionists in government were consulted over the patronage appointments in their district.

Given such political realities, the Anglican Tories, in their efforts to strengthen and extend the Church of England and comprehend the religious sects, did not have any intention of opposing the granting of some government financial aid to the Presbyterian and Roman Catholic clergy. (31)

Clerical Salaries

During the pre-War period, both the Rev. Bethune of the Church of Scotland and the Rev. McDonell of the Roman Catholic Church were in receipt of a salary of £50 per annum, which had been granted by the British government for their past loyalty and war time service to the Crown. The Rev. John Strachan, for his part, felt that both clerics were men of merit; and that their pension ought to be increased. (At that time, five Anglican clergymen were each receiving a salary of £100 per annum from the Society for the Propagation of the Gospel.) Nevertheless, Strachan maintained that more generally there were limits to, and differences in, the level of support which government ought to bestow upon the clergy of the other two churches.

With respect to the Presbyterians, Strachan held that the government should provide support to any number of congregations in need so long as the minister was "ordained regularly in the Church of Scotland". As of 1819, there were six Presbyterian clergymen in Upper Canada. All of them were regarded as respectable men who were zealous and diligent in disseminating "the truths of Christianity"; although it was lamented that since the death of the Rev. Bethune in September 1815, none of the clergy of the province were regularly ordained in the Church of Scotland or remained in direct communion with the Home church in Scotland. The one proviso, cited by Strachan, was that any government support for the Church of Scotland clergy should not be provided at the expense of the Church of England by diverting income from the Clergy Reserves.

With respect to the Roman Catholic Church, a somewhat different attitude prevailed. Although he had no objection to existing government financial commitments to that church, and had even advised the British government that the existing stipends ought to be augmented, Strachan did not want the government to bestow financial aid to the extent where it would facilitate the Roman Catholic Church to expand in Upper Canada beyond its existing adherents. This attitude was evident earlier, in 1817, when the Rev. McDonell approached the Lt. Governor with a request for financial aid for the Roman Catholic Church in Upper Canada. McDonell had requested -- in support of the establishment of a College for the Education of Catholic Priests -- the grant of salaries of £100 per annum for the support of four school masters and three Catholic priests, as well as for the four priests who were already in the province. It was a request that had struck the Rev. John Strachan as being "truly alarming" and highly objectionable.

The Rev. Strachan pointed out that the Church of Rome was the smallest denomination in the province, and lacked sufficient members to justify such a large establishment; and that the level of support requested, if granted, would place the Church of Rome "above the Established Church of England". Only five of the ten clergy of the Church of England in the province received a government salary, while the Roman Catholic Church was requesting salaries for eleven priests: viz. for four existing priests, as well as for three additional priests and four school masters who would invariably be priests. The object of securing salaries for such a large number of priests, and the monies requested for the establishment of a College for educating Catholic priests, was clearly proselytizing and "the dissemination of Popery" in Upper Canada.

It was also held to be politically inexpedient to grant such a level of financial support to the Roman Catholic Church in Upper Canada. If once granted, it would arouse the Presbyterians and the Lutherans to make similar extensive claims, and with much more reason, as both denominations were more numerous than the adherents of the Church of Rome in Upper Canada. Moreover, the Presbyterians and Lutherans were for the most part Loyalists, while the Roman Catholics of the province – except for the veterans of the Highland Scots Regiment who were settled in Glengarry County – were mostly postwar Scottish immigrants with no claim on government for loyalty and past service.

For the Anglican Tories, it was considered imperative that the provincial government, and the British government, refrain from granting financial aid on an extensive scale to the clergy of any other church in Upper Canada than the established Church of England. Government could, and should, provide financial aid to the respectable churches of Scotland and Rome to administer to their existing adherents, but not to such an extent as to enable them to establish churches in new communities. It would frustrate efforts to bring the bulk of the population within the body of the Established Church, and would foster discord and religious animosity. (32)

View of the Church of Scotland

The Anglican Tories regarded the Church of Scotland as a fellow national church. It was viewed as a church that "professed the same faith", was "sprung from the same great family", and "educated in the same moral and political sentiments". Moreover, it was at one with the

Church of England "as far as the abstract principles of Church & State" were concerned. Nonetheless, for the Anglican Tories, the Church of Scotland had several major shortcomings, and particularly in its form of government. It had departed from the episcopal form of Christian church government, and instituted the Presbyterian system of the Calvinists, which was regarded as responsible for the many divisions which afflicted "the Protestant part of the Christian world". And what was worse, the Church of Scotland had introduced a modified Calvinist system of church government, the congregational system of John Knox.

The internal divisions which had plagued the Church of Scotland were viewed by the Anglican Tories as being directly attributable to its form of church government. Whether governed by the Presbyterian system of John Calvin and Theodore Beza, whereby challenges over the qualification of a minster were referred to an elected presbytery for a decision, or by the congregational system of John Knox, whereby each local congregation had the right to criticize and decide upon the qualification of their minister to preach, the principle was the same. It was the "democratic element" which controlled the church government, and was responsible for the great unrest within the Church of Scotland.

The Anglican Tory view of the form of government of the Church of Scotland was a major reason why the Rev. John Strachan recommended that any Presbyterian congregation which received government aid should have a minister duly-ordained in the Kirk, and why he continually sought to persuade Presbyterian congregations to maintain their direct ties with the Church of Scotland. In the absence of a learned minister and a direct connection with the Kirk, the fear was that -- under the congregational system -- Presbyterianism would fragment in Upper Canada, and would further increase the religious disunity of the province. The Tories were determined to remedy the religious disunity of the province through their policy of religious comprehension, and did not want the government to facilitate a fracturing of the Church of Scotland through providing financial support to autonomous Presbyterian congregations. (33)

View of the Roman Catholic Church

The Anglican Tory wish to deny extensive government financial aid to the Roman Catholic Church in Upper Canada was based on much more than an objection to the claims of the Papacy – through the Pope, the 'vicar of Christ' -- to supreme power and authority over the universal Christian church, or an objection to the Catholic claim of 'papal infallibility'. The Anglican Tories professed to have always maintained "the kindest intercourse" with the Roman Catholics of Upper Canada, and to have kept up "the cordial exchange of the charities of social life". Indeed, such efforts had brought upon the Anglicans the accusation that they "love the Romanists". Nevertheless, the Anglican Tories were acutely aware that "many religious points of the greatest importance" separated them from the Roman Catholic communion, and it was these differences that prevented them from countenancing the extension of the Church of Rome in Upper Canada.

For the Anglican Tories, Roman Catholicism was regarded as a religion that possessed "much truth overgrown with error". It was "*a corrupted Christianity*" that embodied superstitions and "perversions of creed and discipline" which had accrued through centuries of "spiritual darkness and despotism". Over the passage of centuries, the Roman Catholic Church, in refusing to adhere strictly to the authority of the Scriptures, had gradually introduced numerous erroneous doctrines and practices into Christ's Church through accident, time and circumstance, and misfortune. The result was the promulgation of dogmas which were totally unacceptable not only to Anglicans, but Protestants in general.

What was particularly objectionable were the Roman Catholic dogma of 'transubstantiation' (the belief that the bread and wine, when blessed during the Eucharist, were converted into the body and blood of Christ while retaining their appearance as bread and wine), and the papal dogma of infallibility (that the Pope, as the successor of the Apostle Peter and 'the supreme apostolic authority', was incapable of error in expounding upon Church doctrine.) Both transubstantiation, which it was held that the Roman Church continued to espouse "in contradiction to reason, Scripture, antiquity and the evidence of the senses", and the dogma of papal infallibility were regarded as equally fallacious. Moreover, the pretensions of the Papacy to supremacy over all other branches of the Christian church, and the papal claim that Christian unity could only be properly realized under the authority of the Pope, were totally rejected. The papal claim to supremacy was regarded as dangerous to Protestants.

Where the Roman Catholic Church was concerned, the Tories felt that Protestants had to remain upon their guard. Moreover, that was particularly so as long as the Papacy refused to recognize the spiritual jurisdiction of the national churches, and the Roman Church continued to support the persecution of 'heretics' in Catholic countries.

Nonetheless, the Anglican Tories maintained that religious strife should be avoided in Upper Canada as it would invariably injure the religious principles of every denomination. The desire of the Tories was for a social harmony among the Christian churches, and it was held out that if the Papacy would renounce its pretension to a spiritual despotism over the various national churches, then Christian unity might proceed with mutual good will and benevolence. Ultimately, however, it was not just the various unscriptural dogmas of the Roman Catholic Church that were objected to by the Anglican Tories, but the very character of that church which was regarded as marking an important difference between Protestantism and Roman Catholicism. (34)

The Roman Church, in denying its communicants all knowledge of the Scriptures, and refusing "to let the Romish Clergy enlighten their people as much as they are themselves enlightened", degraded man by forcing him to accept a "slavish submission" to the authority of the Doctors of the Church. In denying that the priesthood could err, or were subject to human passions, the Roman Church exercised a thralldom over the minds of men: "a despotism not only over faith but reason, conscience and common sense". In sum, it was believed that where Roman Catholicism attained an ascendancy, "rational freedom" would cease to exist.

In contrast, while Protestantism recognized the role of faith in bringing the individual to an understanding of "what God requires of us", it was realized that priests or ministers, being human, could err. Protestant religious instructors, far from claiming "all dominion over the faith of Christians", sought by adhering to the Scriptures as "the one standard of truth" and preaching the Word, to raise men rather than to degrade them. Protestantism called upon men "to exert their intellect and employ their minds", and through the preaching of the Gospel, sought to uplift "the intellectual as well as the moral character" of its adherents.

Thus, on both religious and intellectual grounds, the Anglican Tories were not in favour of the Roman Catholic religion spreading throughout Upper Canada. There were also political reasons for not wanting the Roman Catholics to ever attain a state of predominance in the province; although that was not a serious concern before the Union in 1841 of Upper and Lower Canada. (35)

The papal claim to possess a spiritual authority over all of Christendom, as the Rev. John Strachan noted, involved a related claim -- which "had never been surrendered" since being reasserted by Robert Bellarmine and the other Jesuit theorists in the 16th Century -- that the Pope had the right to absolve the subjects of a kingdom from their allegiance, if the king should depart from the Roman Catholic Church or refused to acknowledge the spiritual authority of the Pope over the kingdom. Not only did the Papacy assert a right to absolve the people of their duty of obedience under 'a heretical ruler', but it was claimed that the people were justified, indeed obligated, to overthrow such a king whenever they had the power to do so.

Thus, Roman Catholicism was regarded as a potential political danger to any Protestant state within which the adherents of the Roman Church were very numerous. In the Tory view, the Roman Catholic Church in following Bellarmine had departed from its own tradition of the sacred origin of royal sovereignty, and its former denial of any right of active resistance against a legitimate monarch. It had embraced the doctrine of popular sovereignty in holding that all human authority was purely secular in origin, and that rulers were delegates of the people in the secular realm; although subject to the spiritual authority of the Pope where the salvation of man was concerned. Such a political theory with its justification of a right of rebellion by the people, albeit only in response to a ruler being excommunicated by the Pope, ran completely counter to the Anglican Tory belief in passive obedience to legitimate government, as well as the Tory concept of the sovereignty of the Crown. (36)

The attitude of the Upper Canadian Tories, or the Anglican clergy more particularly, towards Roman Catholics was made quite explicit in their reaction to historical developments in England. In viewing the history of England, the Tories approved of the Relief Acts of 1778 and 1791, which repealed the penalties in law the forbade the practice of the Roman Catholic religion and the establishment of Catholic schools, and barred Catholics from the professions. For the Rev. Strachan, the removal of the religious disabilities imposed on Roman Catholics in Britain, was "only right". Christian charity and love, as well as a concern to maintain religious and civil peace and social harmony, and "principles of honour", had required the repeal of the Catholic religious disabilities. The Rev. Strachan upheld the historic granting of a complete religious toleration to the Roman Catholics of Canada and of Britain, but from a historical perspective he held that there had been legitimate constitutional and political grounds for the refusal to extend political rights to the Roman Catholics in Britain.

It was felt that the penal laws imposed on the Roman Catholics of Britain by the Corporation Act (1661) and the Test Acts of 1673 & 1678), and reconfirmed in the Bill of Rights (1689) – "no matter how obnoxious" -- had been rendered necessary in the past to protect the National Church, the Protestant monarchy, and the British constitution, from the threat posed by Roman Catholics at home and from abroad. All Protestants were aware of the 1689 uprising of the Irish Roman Catholics in Ireland, and the uprisings of the Highland Scots Roman Catholics in 1715 and 1745, against the Protestant monarchy. Moreover, there was an acute awareness of the severe persecution suffered by Protestants within the Catholic countries of Europe, and of the invasion threats posed against England by Catholic France -- under Louis XIV and Louis XV – in acting in concert with the Papacy. The Catholic powers and the Papacy had continued to recognize the legitimacy of the deposed James II (1633-1701) as the King of Britain, and, after his death, had recognized his son, James Francis Edward Stuart (1688-1766) as the legitimate King of Britain.

Given the danger posed by a numerous Roman Catholic population to a Protestant state, Strachan held the view that, historically, there was a justification for the retention in Britain of the clauses of the Corporation Act (1661) and the Test Acts (1673 & 1678) – which required the taking of oaths that had the effect of excluding Roman Catholics from public offices, from the military and naval establishments, and from parliament.

On the one hand, extending full political rights to Roman Catholics in Britain was inconsistent with the King's coronation oath to maintain "the gospel and the Protestant reformed religion as established by law" in the threatening situation that England had faced. The critical concern for Strachan, however, was the very political nature of the Papacy, which had necessitated a continuation in force of political restrictions against Roman Catholics in Great Britain. In the view of the Rev. Strachan, it could not have been otherwise for as long as the Roman Catholics continued:

> to acknowledge the spiritual jurisdiction of the Pope, they act directly in opposition to one of the fundamental doctrines of British liberty, which we ratify with an oath, that no foreign prince, person, prelate, state or potentate, hath or ought to have any jurisdiction, power, superiority, pre-eminence or authority ecclesiastical or civil within these realms. As long as the Roman Catholics acknowledge a foreign jurisdiction, their church may become as much a political as a religious institution.

All Roman Catholics had been bound in conscience to follow the dictates of their clergy, who in turn were "bound by oath to obey the Pope". Because of their divided allegiance, no state could count upon the loyalty of Roman Catholics under any and all conditions.

As indicated by the views of the Rev. John Strachan – which were expressed in an 1810 publication -- the wars with revolutionary France and with the France of Napoleon Bonaparte had brought about a change in the Tory attitude toward the Roman Catholics of Britain. The loyalty displayed by the Roman Catholics in support of 'King and Constitution', the declining temporal power of the Papacy, and the disavowal by English Roman Catholics of the Pope's power to depose 'heretical' sovereigns, to interfere in the politics of the nation, and to absolve Romans Catholics of their oaths, was viewed as having rendered their political disabilities superfluous. Indeed, on its part, the Papacy had refused to proclaim Charles Edward Stuart (1720-1788) -- the grandson of James II -- as the legitimate heir to the throne upon the death of his father in 1766 and, as of 1792, the Papacy had recognized the Protestant monarch, King George III, as the legitimate king of Great Britain. (37)

In Upper Canada, the political situation with respect to religion was entirely different than the situation that had prevailed historically in the United Kingdom. The Roman Catholics of Upper Canada enjoyed full political and civil rights as well as religious freedom within the province, as did members of the Protestant religious sects with but two restrictions prior to 1831. Only the traditional churches – of England, Scotland, Rome, and the Lutheran Church – were authorized to perform marriages. That singular restriction on the itinerant preachers of the religious sects had legal implications related to the proper keeping of marriage records and family property rights in law. Secondly, only the Church of England was recognized initially in statute as a corporate body capable of owning property. The other churches and the sects had to have their church lands and buildings registered in the name of a member of their congregation.

In the Canadas (the provinces of Upper Canada and Lower Canada), the Quebec Act (14 Geo. III, c. 83, 1774) had granted Roman Catholics the free exercise of their religion, affirmed the right of their clergy to "hold, receive, and enjoy their Accustomed Dues and Rights", and accorded to Roman Catholics -- upon swearing a simple oath of allegiance and loyalty to the King -- full and equal political rights in accordance with the laws of the province. In Upper Canada, the Tories had no desire to impose political disabilities on the Roman Catholics of the province who were British subjects either by conquest, birth, or naturalization. In Upper Canada, the Roman Catholics were not regarded as posing a political threat.

Although there were significant religious differences between Protestants and Roman Catholics, there was "little animosity" in evidence in the immediate postwar period. The absence of religious strife was attributed by the Tories to the fact that in Upper Canada, Protestantism enjoyed "an undisputed ascendancy" as did the Roman Catholic Church likewise in Lower Canada, which discouraged unequal contests for power and influence within either province. Moreover, the Church of England had "assiduously abstained from controversy" with the Church of Rome. For the Anglican Tories, it was a situation where, although it was the duty of Protestant ministers to bring truth to bear in "exposing the delusions of Romanism", it was held that:

this advocacy of truth can be zealously pursued without the slightest compromise of the gentle charities of life.

In the view of the Tories, the Church of Rome was a Christian Church after all, and Upper Canada in its rude state of society provided a field sufficiently large for the Romanists to labour without fostering antagonisms so long as they confined their efforts to providing religious ministrations to their own adherents.

The Roman Catholic Church was viewed as being a valuable ally in the struggle which was being waged for the defence of civilization. It was noted that a Protestant in looking to Lower Canada, might experience regret:

> to find the majority Catholics, yet when he further considers the very few colonies that have a regular worship, he thinks Lower Canada a vast gainer by the comparison; and is forced to admit that, however, superstitious the Roman Catholic religion may be, and however, great its deviation from pure Christianity, it embraces many sincere disciples of Jesus Christ, and sets its face against everything irreligious or immoral.

In Upper Canada, as the Tories viewed their situation, the main challenge to the Christian character of the province took the form of infidelity and the religious indifference of the age, and the democratic anarchy and republican levelling ideas emanating from the United States. In responding to these threats, the Roman Catholic Church was a force for good, which it was believed should not be alienated.

Although the Tories looked askance at some of the religious and political beliefs of the Roman Catholic Church, they paled when compared with the Protestant religious sects, which combined the worst of Roman Catholic political beliefs – the belief in popular sovereignty, and a right of rebellion by the people – with the lamentable congregational form of church government with its democratic implications. The support of the Roman Catholic Church was welcomed, within prescribed limits, by the Upper Canadian Tories in their efforts to Christianize Upper Canada, to maintain the integrity of the British Constitution, and to strengthen the British national character of the province. For the Tories, the Roman

Catholic Church was, together with the Church of England, a member of the 'one holy Catholic and Apostolic Church' – the Church of Christ -- without which there was no salvation. (38)

The 'American Methodists' Challenge

The one disconcerting note for the Tories -- in the pursuit of their plan to peaceably absorb the religious sects into the Established Church – was sounded by a young probationary preacher of the Methodist Episcopal Church, Egerton Ryerson. In May 1826, Ryerson published a letter in the *Colonial Advocate* in which he attacked the concept of a church establishment, questioned the veracity of apostolic succession, rejected episcopacy as a proper Christian form of church government, and abused the character of the Rev. John Strachan. The son of a prominent Loyalist, Ryerson was an Anglican apostate who had been converted, but recently, to Methodism by itinerant Methodist preachers from the United States.

In his public letter, Ryerson expressed his belief in the doctrines of the Church of England, his admiration for its liturgy, and his support of its Christian principles, but he denounced the union of church and state. He criticized the financial support granted by the government to the Anglican Church in Upper Canada, maintained that a church should be supported voluntarily by its members as was the case with the religious denominations in the United States, and rejected the concept of an established church because it was non-scriptural.

Ryerson argued that Christ and the Apostles had not sought a union of church and state; and that, for the Apostles, "the visible church of Christ" was simply a congregation of believers who gathered to hear the Word preached and to partake of the sacraments. In keeping with the otherworldly character of Methodism, he maintained that true "religious teachers" ought not to get involved in temporal affairs, and the political issues of the day. Their attention needed to be focused on prayer and the preaching of the Word "to call sinners to repentance".

Furthermore, Ryerson denied that an established church was an integral part of the British constitution, or a necessary link in uniting the colony to Britain. He asserted that dissenters were loyal to the British constitution and the mother country. However, their loyalty did not depend on a belief in an established church.

Ryerson rejected the claim – made by the Rev. Dr. Strachan -- that the itinerant Methodist preachers were "uneducated" and mostly from the United States where they "gather their knowledge and form their sentiments". To the contrary, Ryerson argued that the Methodist preachers were largely "born and educated in the British dominions", and were not republicans or "infested with republican principles". Although they were not graduates of a university, the probationary preachers were required to follow a reading list of study established by the Methodist Conference, and were tested on their beliefs and calling by the Elders of the conference. For Methodist "learning and piety' were important, when accompanied by "a consciousness of the divine call", but Ryerson denied that classical learning and knowledge of Latin and Greek were a necessity for ministers of the Gospel.

In a broad ranging attack, Ryerson also questioned the validity of 'apostolic succession' and implied that it had been broken at the time of the English Reformation. In doing so, he raised an old Roman Catholic argument that the consecration of Matthew Parker (1504-1575) as Archbishop of Canterbury in December 1559 was invalid, as the four bishops involved in the 'Laying on of Hands' were bishops who had been dismissed from the Church earlier under the former Roman Catholic monarch, Queen Mary.

Ryerson attacked not only the church-state alliance for being non-scriptural, and the validity of apostolic succession, but also the episcopal form of church government. He argued that the primitive Christian church was governed not by bishops, but by elders or presbyters. Where church government was concerned, Bishop Gilbert Burnet (1643-1715) – a renowned Anglican-whig theologian and historian of the English Reformation – was quoted to the effect that:

> that form of church government is best which is most suitable
> to the customs and circumstances of the people among whom
> it is established.

Thus, episcopacy was condemned by Ryerson for being non-scriptural and held out as a form of church government that was unsuited to the pioneer society of Upper Canada.

In reality, Strachan did not regard episcopacy as being of apostolic origin. In his preaching and published writings, he maintained only that episcopacy was the traditional form of church government; that it had been established by the Church Fathers during the early Christian era; and that it was beneficial for the administration of the church and the maintenance of doctrinal purity amongst the clergy. Moreover, Ryerson's attack on episcopacy as a form of church government was rather ironic. The Genesee (New York) Conference of the Methodist Episcopal Church – to which the Upper Canadian Methodists belonged as of 1826 – was governed by an elected bishop. For Strachan, the Church of England was a divine institution in being a member of "the one holy Catholic and Apostolic Church" – the Church of Christ – but he did not claim that the episcopal form of church government was divinely instituted.

The Methodist Conference had called upon young Ryerson to publicly denounce the aspersions that the Rev. Strachan was casting against the Methodist preachers. However, in doing so, Ryerson showed no restraint. He not only attacked the form and character of the Anglican Church, but slandered the character of the Rev. Dr. Strachan. Ryerson charged that the arguments set forth by Strachan, in support of a church establishment, revealed a "profound ignorance of religion and church history", and displayed "a pitable bigotry" as the church of Christ "as described in the scriptures, [was] very distinct and different" from a church establishment. In his polemic, Ryerson declared; "I scarcely know which to impeach, the Doctor's honesty, or his ignorance".

The virulent attack launched by Ryerson on the church-state alliance, the Anglican form of church government, and the validity of apostolic succession, attracted a great deal of attention in Upper Canada, as did the slanderous nature of his personal attack on the character of the Rev. Dr. Strachan. (39)

On his part, Strachan did not indulge in personal attacks on individual Methodist preachers, and while vocal in commenting on what he regarded as their educational deficiencies, and their supposed American political values, he had refrained from disparaging their religious beliefs. In contrast to Ryerson, Strachan in his publications to that date had emphasized the Christian principles that the Methodists shared with the

Anglicans in seeking to further his scheme of religious comprehension. Given such an aggressive attack on the Church of England by young Egerton Ryerson, it remained to be seen whether the Methodists of Upper Canada would remain true to the otherworldly focus of their revivalist religion, and refrain from involvement in political issues and assaults on the Established Church.

The political radicals in the House of Assembly had managed to secure the electoral support of the American sectarians during the Alien Crisis – which was in the final stages of being settled – through arousing a false apprehension among the public that the Tories wanted to strip resident aliens of their property. In fact, the Tories wanted to confirm the aliens in possession of their property, but sought to preclude the American settlers from voting and standing for public office until they became naturalized British subjects. (40) Now a new menace had appeared.

A leading radical, Dr. John Rolph, was known to have publicly questioned the need for an established church in Upper Canada based on his Lockean-liberal belief in the separation of church and state. Hence, the danger faced by the Tories was that the 'American Methodists' in view of their belief in the voluntary principle, their resentment or envy of the financial support that the Established Church was receiving from the government, and their view of the non-scriptural nature of the church-state alliance (which condemned it in their eyes) – might join the political radicals in campaigning for the disestablishment of the Church of England in Upper Canada.

The Tory Concept of the Church of Christ

For the Anglican Tories, the ultimate responsibility of the Established Church was the salvation of souls, which was in keeping with their understanding of the theology of the Church of England as expounded by the Anglican clerics. It was held that man -- once redeemed through the receipt of God's grace through baptism -- must seek to obey God's Will and assure himself of salvation by "living to Christ" -- in imitation of Christ -- and must realize that in so doing he was engaging in a life-long struggle against sin. Moreover, it was a struggle which could be brought to a successful conclusion only within Christ's Church for:

not only are we under a moral compulsion to receive the Gospel of our Lord, but also to receive it in the way that he has appointed, namely through the Church which he has established."

If man were to know Christ, and to live a life of self-denial, he must seek Christ in prayer, in the study of the Bible, and by partaking of the sacraments. To enable man to attain the promised everlasting life, Christ had blessed man by instituting a Church and a ministry.

The Church was a divine institution which was imbued with the Holy Spirit, and was "not of this world, yet sent into the world to bring it to salvation". The clergy of the Established Church derived their authority from Christ through the Apostles, and were assured of Christ's unfailing guidance in that he had pledge himself to be with them "in their Apostolic capacity" to the end of the world. The appointed task of the clergy was to dispense the sacraments, without which there was no salvation, and to expound upon "the laws of God's moral Government" and the Gospel doctrines in:

> preaching redemption, the doctrine of the atonement, the satisfaction made for sinners by the blood of Christ; the corruption of human nature, the insufficiency of man unassisted by Divine grace; the efficacy of the prayer of faith; and the purifying, directing, sustaining, and sanctifying influence of the Holy Spirit.

The task of the Church and its ministry was to provide the means through which man could attain salvation, by which he was to be encouraged to resort to them, and by which, through church discipline, the true religion could be kept alive.

There was a real danger that corrupted man, because of his "waywardness and self-will", would follow the inclinations of his own heart and become "taken up with a pretense of religion instead of the substance". Hence, it was necessary that he be placed under the direction of "a wholesome and enlightened authority" and guided by "an established ritual and a reasonable service" in his religious worship.

The essentials of religion can no more be maintained without such means than the Political welfare can remain prosperous without law and order and the authority of the magistrate. It is not enough that God has filled the world with inexhaustible blessings, but it is also necessary by human institutions to regulate their mode of fruition and to prevent our perverting them to our own injury and that of Society in general.

It was the Christian Church that maintained, the true faith; and it was within "this visible Church [that] the Church invisible [was] gradually moulded and matured" through the workings of Christ's spirit among the faithful. Membership in the visible Church did not provide an absolute assurance, any more than did external circumstances as to whether an individual would be saved or not. Only "a life of Faith" on the part of the individual could ensure salvation, but the Church did bring Christians together to worship. In this world, those who gave their hearts to Christ were always found in a distinct minority, but the company of their fellows in the visible Church helped sustain faith, while the Church remained "a pledge and proof" that God would not forsake them". (41)

The Church of God was not of any one nation, but rather was universal: the "one holy Catholic and Apostolic Church" established by Christ. It was a Church -- of which the Church of England was but one branch -- that was to be found in all Christian countries. It was destined, in God's good time, to spread Christianity throughout the world. All men were called upon to partake of Christ's atonement, regardless of differences of colour or language, for all men were:

originally the same; possessed of the same corporeal and mental powers, capable of acquiring the same ideas; guided by the same motives; disturbed by the same passions; liable to the same errors; educated in the same universal language and traditions; and gleaning instructions [through] successive generations.

Over time, the descendants of Adam and Eve had multiplied and separated, and had acquired "a different appearance, a different language, and different manners", but God, in his justice, had created "only one species of rational beings"; and all men needed to be saved. (42) Hence, it was the ultimate role of the Established Church of England in Upper Canada -- the National Church -- to evangelize the province and to prepare Upper Canadian through its ministrations for the attainment of salvation and 'everlasting life' on the Day of Judgement.

———————————

Chapter Ten

The Rejection of Sectarianism

To the Upper Canadian Tories, the Established Church was the proper vehicle for inculcating religious principles into the population of the province; and it was requisite, as well as right, that government contribute financially to the support of the clergy of the National Church. The Tories were adamant, however, that the government should refrain from offering financial support to the religious sects. One of the principal aims of the national policy was to comprehend the members of the various religious sects within the National Church, and thus it was essential that nothing be done by the provincial government to foster or strengthen the religious sects in Upper Canada.

For the Tory political elite, the effort to strengthen and extend the ministrations of the Established Church was focused on the strengthening the British national character and loyalty of the province, and on limiting the influence of sectarian preachers whose 'American religious principles and beliefs' were viewed as being a threat to the maintenance of that national character and the traditional social and political order. For the Anglican clerics, however, their rejection of sectarianism was based not only on political and social factors, but their view of the Apostolic Christian Church, religious schism, the traditional role of a church hierarchy, and what was regarded as the non-Christian nature of sectarian religious beliefs. Moreover, the Anglican Tory clerics viewed the sectarian interpretations of the 'right of private judgement' and of 'liberty of conscience' – the two philosophical principles upon which sectarians justified their separation from the National Church – as being based on a fallacious understanding of the Christian religion.

Religious Toleration

Although the Upper Canadian Tories strongly disapproved of dissent, and wished to comprehend all dissenters and sectarians within the Established Church, they did not hold that the maintenance of a church establishment required either the proscription of dissenting churches by law or the persecution of sectarians. To the contrary, they believed in religious freedom and freedom of conscience. For the Tories, a church establishment was not only consistent with a complete religious freedom, it was the very basis of toleration. It was through the teachings of the National Church, in imbuing the province "with the spirit of Christ', that mutual good will and toleration was to be achieved among various religious denominations. A religious establishment was pre-eminently "a branch of public education". Its teachings gave force to freedom of opinion, whether religious or otherwise, and served to "enlighten the mind and make it capable of judging with accuracy".

Only religious values, when effectively inculcated, could break the "sceptre of selfishness" in man, and instill charity and forbearance and the other Christian virtues which give rise to "positive good" and tolerance toward those who differ from us. The laws of man, in being "purely negative in their effect", could not do so. (1)

Religious toleration was also the duty of the state. Although the state was duty-bound to establish a national religion, the Tories believed also that the state should not interfere in any way:

> with the peculiar tenets and modes of worship of those who
> dissent from the national religion, provided there was nothing
> in them hurtful to the general interests of society, or dangerous
> to the lawful institutions of the country.

For the Upper Canadian Tories, the essence of religious toleration and freedom of conscience was the liberty to worship unmolested in any church one might choose to attend, with a concomitant right to educate one's children as one thought best. It was a freedom which did not involve dissenters and sectarians having any right to claim support or financial assistance from government to further their divers opinions and beliefs. The Church of England was willing to extend "a negative toleration" to those outside the pale in the belief that it was 'wrong and inexpedient' to impose "positive pains or penalties" upon sectarians or to proscribe dissenting churches. However, sectarianism was in no way to be afforded "an affirmative countenance" or to receive an encouragement or financial support from government. There was a liberty of conscience in Upper Canada where everyone could choose to adhere to the church or sect that conformed to their beliefs. Moreover, all religious sects were allowed to propound their views, as long as they did not act contrary to law or "give offense or Scandal to Government". (2)

Schism

The fact that the Upper Canadian Tories saw and accepted the need for religious toleration and freedom of conscience did not mean that they approved of schism from the Established Church, or that they were indifferent to religious truth. The established Church of England, in their view, was a member of that 'one holy Catholic and Apostolic Church", in which all were bound to believe. It was a Church which was governed everywhere by bishops who were descended from the Apostles to whom Christ had committed the care of his flock, the dissemination of his teachings, and the bringing of man to salvation; and it was a Church which he had instituted with the promise to be with man always "even to the end of the world". Such a promise was held to have continued in force through the successors of the apostles -- "duly ordained to the same ministry" – with the Church of England enjoying a line of bishops that was descended directly from the apostles "by the imposition of hands". It was a Church in which the "Apostolic doctrine" remained unimpaired, and in which the Church fellowship continued to receive its benefits.

Individuals were at liberty to choose to leave the Apostolic Church so constituted, but in doing so were guilty of committing a sin. God, in being "the God of order", had instituted a church for the benefit of mankind, and separation from it was a sinful act.

A clear difference was recognized between the commission of crimes that required the exercise of coercion on the part of the state, and the commission of sins which, although displeasing in the eyes of God, were to be tolerated -- rather than persecuted -- as the lesser of two evils. Any resort to coercion by the state against those who chose to exercise their freedom of conscience in rejecting the ministrations of the "true religion", was unacceptable and wrongheaded. (3)

Nonetheless, the Anglican Tories could not approve of schism because they believed that:

not only are we under a moral compulsion to receive the Gospel of our Lord, but also to receive it in the way that he has appointed, namely through the Church which he has established by which we understand that visible society on earth which has continued in the Apostolic doctrine and Fellowship since the descent of the Holy Ghost on the day of Pentecost. (4)

All men were under a moral obligation not to desert the true Church of Christ, and the Church itself was bound to preach "so as to vindicate the ways of God to man" because outside of the Church there could be no salvation. Once an individual became, through holy Baptism, a "member of Christ, a child of God and an inheritor of the Kingdom of Heaven", it was incumbent upon the Church to preserve these privileges to him unimpaired. This involved the provision of religious services to all Christians wherever they might be, which entailed a commitment to overcome all impediments and difficulties such as were being encountered in the frontier settlement areas of Upper Canada. The Church was under a Christian obligation to ensure that Christians -- who had once "joined with Christ in Sacramental Union", and been "placed in a state of salvation" with a nature no longer corrupt and sinful -- would not lapse into sin through indifference or by adhering to schismatic sects in the absence of the ministrations of the true Church. (5)

The Tories were convinced that religious dissent originated "solely in fatuous pride" and the "proneness of man" to reject all that partakes of an aura of authority. It was the product of a human desire to be independent of all authority, which if realized in fact would prove destructive of civil society. Every organization, if it were to function, required some form of government to which deference and obedience needed to be rendered by its members, and the Church was no exception. The Church had its own form of government consisting of bishops, priests and deacons (the latter two of whom could not baptize "without the command of the Bishop"), and the very safety and continued existence of the Church was held to be dependent upon "the kind of absolute and preeminent power" which was enjoyed by the bishops under the Apostolic system. Otherwise, without such a dominion being exercised, there could be "as many schisms in the Church as there are Priests". (6)

The power of the bishops, although unquestioned, was by no means either arbitrary or unlimited. It was maintained that such a situation would be completely ahistorical and unsanctioned by the precedents of the primitive Church, as well as inconsistent with its whole being, because:

> the Church is not a heritage to command, but a family to govern, and it was the glory of the successors of the Apostles to do nothing of weight or moment without asking the advice and consent of their Clergy.

The clergy in Convocation or in synods, with the bishops or a bishop at their head, transacted and deliberated upon all Church matters, and it was a system which was "absolutely necessary" if acts of the Church were to carry "due force and authority" in execution. Such a "prudent distribution of power" was held to be "a mark of the true Church". In this respect, it was held to be a matter of some regret that the Church of England in the United Kingdom was deficient in possessing neither a synodical organization, nor an efficient Convocation. (7)

Episcopacy was not "a mere appointment of human wisdom" to be varied or rejected at human whim, but an apostolic institution which was sanctioned by the practice of Christ, who had instituted a hierarchy of church government in appointing two ministerial orders – "the Twelve Apostles and the Seventy disciples" -- subordinate to himself. In appealing to the New Testament to substantiate the validity of episcopacy, the Anglican clerics were aware that with respect to the government of Christ's Church there was "nothing formally or systematically" set forth to guide Christians. However, allusions could be culled which were of "so pointed and decisive" a nature that it was impossible to doubt the existence and development of an organized church polity based on "the principle of three orders": bishops, priests and deacons. The episcopal form of Church government had been universal throughout the Christian Church within half a century of the death of Saint John, and for fifteen centuries no other system but episcopacy was known to the Christian Church. (8)

At the Reformation, many of the leading continental reformers -- among them Philipp Melanchthon, John Calvin, Martin Bucer, and

Theodore Beza -- had acknowledged episcopacy as the proper form of church government, and denounced those who would reject episcopal jurisdiction. They claimed, by way of apology for their own actions, that they adopted a presbyterial system only out of utter necessity. Once they had consolidated and strengthened their presbyterial system of church government, however, they made an about-face. They began to attack the authority of bishops, whom they claimed were "a presumptuous encroachment on the rights and privileges conveyed to Presbyters by the Apostles". In the present day, the Methodists were also guilty of that "infatuation", which was directly contrary to the views of their founder, the Rev. John Wesley (1703-1791), who had refused to countenance such a thing. (9)

In upholding episcopacy against its detractors, the Upper Canadian Tories saw themselves as the defenders, within Christ's Church, of the lawfully-constituted traditional authority against innovators who would impose changes to the detriment of the best interests of the Church, the State, and society. The Tories believed that they were defending the true apostolic Church order in holding to the middle way against "an anomalous alignment of Romish and Protestant Dissent": one seeking to impose a corruption of episcopacy upon the Christian Church, and the other desiring to abolish it altogether.

The Roman Church was a protagonist for a system which -- in bestowing upon one bishop, the Bishop of Rome (the Pope), an overwhelming power and authority over his fellow bishops -- had departed from the discipline of the Catholic Church. It had wrongfully degraded its bishops, (proportionally, as it aggrandized the Pope), to the point where they were unable to perform their proper function within the church. On the other hand, "the advocates of parity of orders" among the Protestant churches and sects -- in holding to a presbyterial form of church government -- were likewise despoiling the lawfully-constituted rulers of Christ's Church of their just authority. Moreover, experience had shown that such a rejection of authority weakened the union of the Christian Church and facilitated schisms.

If a comprehensive Christian Church were to be preserved, and schism avoided, an episcopal system of church government was essential. In its absence, ministerial parity would place within the power of every minister, should he so choose, to form a sect of his own to the detriment of true religion. Both extremes – the aggrandizement of the Bishop of Roman by the Romish Church, and the presbyterial form of church government as instituted by Protestant churches and the sects – were harmful to the interests of the universal Catholic Church, and hence such innovations had to be discountenanced. (10)

Christian Unity

The Anglican clerics among the Upper Canadian Tories were dedicated to realizing the ideal of "a Christian unity" which would embrace all of Christendom. In that respect, the clerics in their hopes and aspirations far exceeded the more limited aims of the Anglican Tory political elite which shared their views, but confined its aspirations to the Province of Upper Canada. Although it was readily admitted by the clerics that their aspiration to achieve a unity of all Christendom was perhaps rather "utopian", nonetheless it was a principle which they insisted could not be abandoned by professing Christians. The hope was expressed that Christian unity could, and would, be achieved through a common agreement upon "the great essentials" of Christianity. Christian unity was held to be achievable in that:

> notwithstanding the diversities of opinion among Christians, the great essentials of our religion are comprised in a small compass: the belief in the existence of a Supreme Being of infinite perfections; in the future state adapted to the moral habits of intelligent beings; that the Scriptures contain the will of the Almighty, revealed to man; that Jesus Christ is the Messiah, through whom alone we can attain salvation; are a sufficient foundation for our religion. (11)

Nonetheless the hope for Christian unity was coupled with an awareness that even in these Christian essentials "small differences of opinion" would invariably arise. Hence, it was concluded that if Christian unity were ever to be achieved, it would have to be based not on a complete uniformity of belief and opinion, but rather simply upon "the Christian spirit".

Two thousand years' experience, if it had proved anything, showed that "mankind will never be of one faith"; and that efforts to achieve a Christian unity based on a doctrinal agreement would only produce "dissention instead of harmony". Unless human nature could be entirely changed, all attempts to realize unity of opinion through reasoning, would "partake of human infirmity" and hence be condemned to failure, or to only a partial success. The best that could be held out for realistically, as capable of achievement, was a Christian unity founded not on:

> the infallibility of the opinion, tenets, doctrines, and decisions of any Church, or set of men, but on that peace and charity, that pure and sublime morality taught in the Gospel.

Such a Christian spirit, in embracing "meekness, forbearance, and brotherly love", would produce whatever unity mankind could possibly attain; and if it did not secure a "unity of mind", which was not to be expected, at least it would augment considerably man's temporal and spiritual good. (12)

In believing, as they did, in the 'one holy Catholic and apostolic Church', the Anglican clerics could not reject the prospect of Christian unity as an ultimate ideal; although admittedly, it appeared to be hopeless of realization. Their desire was to comprehend all Christians within the true Church. A Church which was:

> Catholic in its constitution and government, Catholic in its worship and discipline, as well as Catholic in its doctrinal tenets.

It was hoped that all Christians would be united once again, and live in harmony in adhering to "one faith and one baptism" under "one God and Father of us all". Such a reunion could only be realized if the Romanists would renounce popery, and if the Protestants would seek to "recover the Catholicism" which they had almost totally rejected at the Reformation. Doing so would facilitate the return of the Roman Catholics and Protestant churches and sects to the 'one Holy Catholic and Apostolic Church' to which the Anglican Church continued to belong. It was an ideal which was held out as well worth struggling to achieve, despite any and all discouragements. Moreover, within Upper Canada, it served to encourage the Anglican clerics in their efforts to form an effective church establishment and to extend the ministrations of the Church of England throughout the province. Every individual who was saved by the Anglican Church, in being won over from dissent, would bring Christian unity one step closer to its consummation. (13)

Although the leading Anglican clerics were strong advocates of Christian unity, they did not approve of all movements which purported to lead in that direction. They deprecated all efforts "in the name of liberality" to unite the various denominations by endeavouring to explain away their differences. Where the maintenance of "the essential articles of Christianity" were concerned, and not just "the ceremonial part of religion", such attempts were regarded as nothing but a mockery of true religion. Such movements, on the part of various Protestant sects, were viewed as stemming from an indifference to, or misunderstanding of, true Christianity, and would only result in a fostering of infidelity.

If religion were to continue to be vital, and to command the respect of its adherents, it could not sacrifice all its solid principles to attain a superficial unity. Such an indifference to Christian principles and beliefs was the opposite extreme to that deplorable narrow exclusiveness of principle which had plagued Christianity in the past. Here as elsewhere, a middle way was advocated by the Anglican clerics.

Accepting Christian Differences

The Anglican Tory clerics argued that a Christian, of whatever denomination, should not sacrifice his basic principles and beliefs to facilitate a sham union but rather, in agreeing to disagree, should keep up a Christian intercourse with those from whom he differs in principle. In doing so, he should refrain from disparaging "the peculiar principles' of other Christians as:

> true liberality of sentiment ... consist[s] not in surrendering our
> own sentiments, but in not blaming other people for theirs. (14)

The fact that the Upper Canadian Tories were advocates of toleration for all churches and sects did not mean that they believed "religious truth" to be variable or the discovery of religious certitude either unimportant or unattainable. However, they realized that because of the very nature of religion, and the "infirmity and proneness to error" of mankind, the attainment of any religious certitude, and a common understanding and belief, was fraught with difficulties. Hence, no matter how convinced members of the Established Church were of the truth of their beliefs, they were admonished by the Anglican clerics that modesty and charity should guide all their communications with those who dissented.

To spread the truths of Christianity by compulsion was to act contrary to its very nature because Christianity was intended to depend for its efficacy upon its "moral and persuasive influence" on man's rational nature. The best way to defeat error was not to attack it, but rather to "calmly preach the truth". The task of the parish priest was not to engage in impassioned religious disputes, but rather to minister to his congregation, to provide religious instruction, and to disseminate the Word of God in the community. The Anglican clergy themselves were further admonished, by the Rev. John Strachan, to bear "with charity the occasional heresies, or variances of opinion" among the populace, while speaking out forcefully in defence of what they "believed to be true".

If error could not be corrected by "gentle means" through teaching and preaching the Word, a resort to denunciation would serve only to confirm the advocates of error in their course. Christianity could not be propagated by the sword without defeating its very end, and because "forbearance and mercy" were a large part of the Christian religion, then toleration was "certainly something more than excusable". In sum, toleration – or, more correctly, toleration of error -- was not seen as a virtue, but as a matter of extending Christian charity, forbearance, and mercy to those who were in error. Dissent was not to be condoned, nor supported, because it could not help but undermine "sound principle", and prove destructive of the Christian unity of the nation. (15)

Private Judgment & Liberty of Conscience

For the Anglican clergy, the two basic philosophical principles on which the sectarians justified their withdrawal from the Church of England were unscriptural and fallacious. The sectarians claimed a "right of private judgement" and "liberty of conscience" -- which were held to be superior to all human authority, including the authority of church tradition -- together with a concomitant right for the individual to choose the church and doctrine to which he would adhere. From such a viewpoint, a church became purely "a voluntary society" composed of its adherents. It was a concept that the Anglican Tories found objectionable on several grounds, whether advocated by evangelical Protestants or Lockean liberals.

In the first place, the claims which were being put forth for private judgment were not scriptural. They were irreconcilable with the scriptural injunction – which was "plain, direct and absolute" -- to render obedience to the spiritual rulers set over all Christians. Mankind was clearly commanded to:

> Obey them that have the rule over you, and submit yourselves; for they watch for your souls, as they that must give account. (Hebrews 13:17)

Christ had "solemnly commissioned and ordained" a priesthood to administer to the needs of his flock, and the clergy of the Apostolic Church -- because of the divine institution of their office -- continued to possess an authority which commanded obedience and submission. It was evident that if Christ intended to allow everyone to follow his own judgment in deciding religious matters, he would not have constituted such a ministry to teach men to follow in the way of the Lord.

The Church of Christ was not, and could not be viewed as, a voluntary society which one is perfectly free to join or, once having joined, to reject. It was not in the same category as a debating club, a trading company, or social group, wherein membership involved "no obligation in law or reason". It was written in Scripture:

> He that believeth, and is baptized, shall be saved; but he that believeth not shall be damned. (St. Mark 16:16)

To avoid the commission of a sin, and to avail himself of the benefits of salvation, man must adhere to the Church of Christ.

Secondly, to view the Church as being "no more than a voluntary society", was tantamount to holding that the Church had no existence beyond the believers who adhered to a particular congregation. It constituted a denial of the universal Christian Church, which was established by the blood of Christ.

Thirdly, in a voluntary church, where the private judgment of its members was to be the criterion of religious truth, the pastor was placed in a position of being subject to his congregation. To retain his position, he had to preach to please the congregation, and, in effect, had to look for instruction from the congregation. Such a system was totally incongruous, and out of keeping with "the order of the New Testament" in which the Church was of Christ, and not of man. (16)

Fourthly, there could be no such thing as an absolute right to private judgment, such as was claimed by the sectarians. Such a right was completely inconsistent with the maintenance of any society:

> because as long as every man may be a law to himself, it is impossible to govern a number of such independent private judgments by any general rule.

An absolute right to private judgment could not in the nature of things belong to "associated man" because any society which allowed its members to exercise such a right would immediately dissolve into "its primary elements". It was a truism that:

> man as a member of any constituted society, has no private judgement as long as he remains a member. He is under the collective judgement of the society to which he belongs.

It was a fact that was recognized in the practical workings and governing of all societies, which by universal custom adhered to rules adopted by a majority vote on motions which were put to the members, with the majority -- once ascertained -- being accepted as binding upon all the individuals who comprise the membership. In effect, societies had "a will", when the votes of their members were collected into a majority, but the members did not as individuals. (17)

All sects, despite their protestations to the contrary, were associations that had "their articles of belief, their terms of union, their rules and ceremonies" which regulated their "social worship and conduct", whether written or not. In practice, all religious societies possessed "a received interpretation of the Scriptures", and "a system of doctrines, worship, and discipline", to which the member was bound to adhere upon pain of expulsion. Such rules and laws -- though of man, and not of Christ -- were strictly enforced, with little compassion for those who failed to conform. In effect, the sectarians left "nothing of a public or social nature, to the direction and control of private judgment" where their own congregations were concerned.

Such was the governing force of local custom and usage that members of the various sects could not but conform, even in the absence of formal doctrines and discipline. Although many sects "had no formularies of doctrine and worship" to command an open adherence:

> yet they had forms that governed everything, not only in doctrines and worship, but [that] reached to every punctilio of life, even to set phrases of speech, to a peculiar sound of voice and manner of wearing one's countenance.

No member of a sect could deviate from the accepted rules of conduct without being reproved by his follow members, and if guilty of misconduct the individual would be "dealt with and judged by the whole society". In the personal conduct and bearing, the members of a religious sect were by no means free to act according to their private judgement, but rather were compelled by the force of opinion and the action of the congregation to conform or face expulsion. The same fate awaited any individual who chose to differ in his interpretation of the Scripture from that "received by the society" of which he was a member.

It was evident that the sectarians were appealing to "the pride and self-conceit" of their members, and engaging in a gross deceit in proclaiming a "boundless liberty of conscience" for their own members, while "vilifying the Church of England" for supposedly denying its members their "natural rights to private judgement and liberty of conscience". In actuality, the sectarians were "subject to a collective judgement", and were bound by "their creeds or doctrines, their usages and discipline", whether written or unwritten. It was as much so for the sectarians as it was for the adherents of the Church of England whose ministers and people were held to "a prescribed form of public worship" and a doctrine "set forth in her creeds, articles and liturgy".

The only difference was that the Church of England openly acknowledged that "the private judgment of man" was subject to "the order of the Church". In practice, the Church of England recognized and accepted the only right of private judgment which was consistent with the existence of any society -- and the only right of private judgment which the sects granted their members -- which was the right of the individual to choose to withdraw from the Church. (18)

Even at the Reformation, the Church of England had not had recourse to the private judgment of individuals within her communion to decide religious matters. When the papal control over the English Church was overthrown and the English Church was restored to its former independence of Rome, the reformation was not achieved by the exercise of any rights of private judgment on the part of her communicants. To the contrary, the English Church was re-established by the united action of "the King and Lords temporal and spiritual, and the Commons in Parliament" with the support of the bishops and clergy in convocation. Indeed, the right to the exercise of an "unlimited private judgement" in religion had never been claimed as a principle by the Church of Christ in all its history, or by any Protestant church at the Reformation. It was beyond question that:

> the Bible as explained by every man's private judgement or opinion, is not the doctrine of Protestants.

To the defenders of the Anglican Church, it was obvious that if the Bible were to be interpreted by every man to suit himself, chaos would result. A situation would arise where no doctrine could be held to be heretical or erroneous, and no church could continue to exist in possession of any authority. In religious matters, private judgement had to be "directed and controlled" through a deference being paid to the authority of Scripture and church tradition. Such was the position of all the churches at the Reformation.

Religious Truth

In a Charge to the Anglican Clergy, Bishop Strachan, argued that at the Reformation the Reformers had not rejected church tradition in their dispute with the Romish church. Their dispute with the papacy was "not one of principle, but of fact and degree". The Church of England and the continental reformers -- Martin Luther included – had accepted the legitimacy of all church tradition which could be "traced by direct testimony to the apostolic age", while rejecting only the practices which could not be so verified. In doing so, they repudiate "the dogma of the Romish Church, which places tradition on an equality with Holy Scripture". In effect, they did not deny the authority of tradition, but rejected the Romish claim that:

> men should, upon the mere authority of [church] tradition, receive, as necessary to salvation, doctrines not contained in Scripture. (19)

For the Church of England, the ultimate test of religious truth was to be found in the "Word of God alone", or what could "be clearly proved therefrom". Her adherents were required to believe nothing as being necessary to salvation which could not be "read in Scripture and proved thereby". They enjoyed the freedom to consult the Bible to confirm that the church doctrines were consistent with Revelation; however, the Church of England had never admitted, or advocated, "an unqualified right of private judgment" in religion. Upon finding that the Church doctrine was indeed scriptural:

> it then becomes our duty to receive it with implicit faith, and to preserve it as a sacred deposit intrusted [sic] to our keeping, whole and entire, without adding thereto what to our limited faculties may seem needful, or taking away what we may think superfluous. (20)

This did not mean that the Church of England demanded a blind faith and obedience from her members, but quite the contrary. She required that they "believe with the understanding as well as with the heart". Men were accountable beings who enjoyed both "liberty and responsibility", and they were under a Christian obligation, which the Church acknowledged:

> to examine the foundation of their faith, and to prove all things; that they may hold fast that which is good.

Even children, although they received their faith on authority at baptism, were to be "so taught as to believe with the understanding" by the time they came forward to receive Confirmation. It was asserted that in being:

certain of the truth of her doctrines, the Church fears no honest enquiry. On the contrary, in all her teaching, she aims at enabling her children to give a reason for the hope that is in them, and to be able to contend for the faith which was once delivered to the saints.

Although encouraging "sober and searching enquiry" into the basis of her faith to foster an understanding of the same, the Church did place limitations upon the exercise of the right of private judgment. Her adherents were not abandoned "to the uncertainty of their own reason and judgment", which were fallible in man, nor were they left "to set up their own will and pleasure as the only standard" of interpretation. To the contrary, in their inquiries they were to be guided by the "Scriptures, illustrated and confirmed by the testimony and tradition of the Church". (21)

At the Reformation, where any doubt existed as to the meaning of any aspect of Scripture, the Church of England had accepted the tradition of the Catholic Church in "the ages nearest to Apostolic times" as an interpretive aid. The test applied was to determine how a scriptural passage was interpreted by the Church Fathers, and if it was received by the Church at that time, church members were duty bound "to submit [their] private judgement to the Catholic voice of antiquity".

In that process, the writings of the Church Fathers were very valuable "not as much for the opinions they contain, as for the facts which they attest". Although the Church Fathers were credited with "no powers of inspiration", their testimony was considered as being invaluable as evidence, particularly with respect to church government. Since the Reformation, the fruit of that inquiry was to be found embodied in "the authorized formularies and creeds" of the Church of England and the Book of Common Prayer. Together they contained:

all those doctrines of Scripture which were acknowledged and believed by the Church universal in the primitive age…. (22)

Although the Anglican Church, in interpreting the Scriptures and judging of the truth of Christian doctrine, had drawn upon "the declared voice of the primitive Catholic Church as a help and guide", that source of verification of Christian doctrine was always:

> subordinate to that which she pays to the written Word of God, which she regards, and rightly regards, as the only divine source and standard of religious truth.

The private judgment of man, unaided by the creeds, articles and doctrine of the 'one holy Catholic and Apostolic Church', was not sufficient to arrive at a proper understanding of the religious truth which was contained in the Bible. Where the individual might differ in his interpretation or judgment from that of the Church, it seemed indubitable that he must accept the collective wisdom of the Church, rather than adhering to his own frail judgement. (23)

Necessity of Subordination to the Church

The subordination of one's private judgment to authority and tradition was a necessity not only in religion, but in all areas of life. As an individual, man was not sufficient unto himself. Even those allies of dissent, the Whigs, were aware – in following John Locke -- that in social relations the conduct and opinions of most men were governed by custom and habit rather than "reason, *unaided*". Had not John Locke held that there was a social necessity for "a customary and fixed set of opinions, and habits of thought".

Although the Upper Canadian Tories looked to revealed religion for their ultimate principles of justice, goodness, and virtue, rather than to the authority of reason, they fully concurred with John Locke in the belief in the essential importance of habits, custom, and established opinion in counterbalancing man's "passions and selfishness".

The Tories agreed with liberal-whigs of a Lockean persuasion in that respect, despite there being a great difference in their respective views of human nature and religion, and their differing political theory. The liberal-Whigs held that a lack of proper instruction was responsible for any deficiencies in man's "natural good and noble tendencies"; whereas the Tories held that human nature was corrupted – owing to the Fall – and incapable of improvement except through God's saving grace.

Nonetheless, it was asserted that both Whig and Tory could agree that man was "not a pure emanation of Reason", and that human reason alone was incapable of providing a guide for the living of a moral life. (24)

If society could not function in rejecting "the truths handed down from ages" and in depending solely upon human reason as a guide for conduct, what of religion which by its very nature was "mysterious" and beyond human understanding, and hence the judgement of man.

The Anglican clerics rejected the axiom, which they associated with Socinianism, that: "Where mystery begins religion ends", with its implication that man ought not to believe what he could not "perfectly comprehend in all its modes as well as its essence". To the contrary, they adhered to the axiom that: "Where mystery begins, knowledge ends". Consequently, man had to submit and believe on faith in the authority of divine revelation where religious truth was concerned. Man was unable, through his frail human reason, to completely understand the workings of the ways of God.

Such a reliance of faith was not regarded as being inconsistent with a belief in man as a rational being, because:

> Man is the original contriver of neither the moral nor physical world, nor of the laws on which they are built, and by which they are governed. It is quite as rational therefore for him to reject in nature what he does not understand, and to deny its existence as it is in theology.

For the Anglican Tory clerics, it was as illogical to deny religious truth and the mysteries of religion, which were beyond human understanding and explanation, as it was to deny the existence of physical phenomenon in nature which man could not understand or explain. An example cited was that man could not understand nor explain the properties and composition of light rays, but that did not serve to deny their existence. It was likewise in religion, man could not fully understand all the actions of Providence, such as the existence of suffering and "the apparently unequal distribution of good to individuals and nations"; and yet, that lack of understanding was not sufficient to detract from an abiding faith in "the goodness and righteousness of Providence". It merely went to prove that: "It is not for us to know!" Man must believe on faith, in trusting to God and the means appointed by God for his salvation, rather than to his own private judgement and human reason. (25)

In seeking to strengthen and extend the ministrations of the Established Church of Upper Canada, and to comprehend the sectarians within the National Church, the Anglican clerics acted on the conviction that outside of the Church there could be no salvation. Their actions had a strong religious motivation, in addition to their national policy concerns, in keeping with the belief that:

> God has appointed, under Christ, only one great channel, the Church through which his grace may with full assurance be expected to flow.

That channel was the one Holy Catholic and Apostolic Church of Christ "to which all the promises of the Gospel are addressed". It was a Church which demanded of all her adherents a vital belief "of the whole man, mind, heart, soul and spirit", and a complete belief in all her doctrine as contained in the Book of Common Prayer, her creeds and articles. Private prayer and study of the Word of God, however, were not to be deprecated. Religion did indeed involve a communion "immediate and direct between God and the soul of each believer", but the Christian life was pre-eminently "a corporate life" wherein all were "members of a mystical Society, the Church". The Church could not be discarded in seeking salvation for:

> It is not as an insulated being or individual that a Christian is made a recipient of the blessings of Christ's kingdom, but as a member of that Church for which He died. (26)

An individual could partake of the sacraments -- which were held to be "necessary to salvation" – from a duly-ordained minister only within the Church. This was not to deny that there were other means of achieving a 'state of grace', such as through prayer, scriptural readings, and the hearing of the Word. Each had its place in God's scheme of things, but the sacraments were:

the certain sure witnesses and effectual signs of grace and of God's good will toward us, by which He doth work invisibly in us, and doth not only quicken but also strengthen and confirm our faith in Him.

Of all the sacraments, two were considered by the Church Catholic as being "the principal means of grace": Baptism and Holy Communion. Only through baptism could an individual be regenerated, or reborn, into the Church of Christ and be assure of its privileges; while through communion "a mystical union" was consummated, though eating spiritually of the flesh and blood of Christ, whereby Christ came to dwell in his communicants, and they in him in a state of righteousness, which assured all true believers of the benefits of Christ's atonement.

It was regarded as lamentable that in choosing to follow their own private judgment, rather than submit to the authority of the Church in questions of religious truth, the sectarians of Upper Canada were depriving themselves of access to the sacraments being administered by a duly-ordained ministry. The sectarians were, it was believed, denying Christ and placing their souls in extreme jeopardy. The Will of God had been revealed in Scripture, once and for all. It was the duty of Christians to believe and receive it as given through Christ's Church, rather than for each individual to take it upon himself "to do that which is right in his own eyes". (27)

The Call

In viewing the religious sects of Upper Canada, the Tories were deeply perturbed by the sectarian concept of the workings of 'the call'. It was a belief held by sectarians that "every man" was authorized to preach authoritatively upon religion and to administer the sacraments who honestly believed that he was "animated by a spirit within" to do the work of the Lord. Such a concept was rejected by the Anglican clergy on several grounds. Among them was that it fostered a "low and depreciating sense of ministerial authority"; and that it had a destructive impact upon the unity of the Church. However, the essential objection was "the insufficiency" of a system which depended solely for its veracity and authority upon the testimony of "the human heart".

Such an authority was at best uncertain because what "passes in the heart of man" was not necessarily consistent with the Will of God. In sum, the charge of a minister was too important to be entrusted to men who acted on impulse, at the prompting of their own hearts, especially when it was evident that not every man who felt that he was "called by God to preach the Gospel", was necessarily so chosen. The heart was not to be relied upon. Was it not written in scripture that: "He that trusteth in his own heart is a fool"; and "the heart is deceitful above all things"? Where the authorization of a minister depended upon his feeling 'the call', how could a determination be made "between enthusiasts, fanatics, and pretenders" and God's true ministers.

Such an argument against the sectarian concept of 'the call' did not contradict the belief, on the part of the Anglican clergy, that "the testimony of our own hearts' was necessary to anyone who sought to serve God. Indeed, it was of the essence of a belief in Christ. In objecting to the concept of 'the call', the Anglican clerics were simply asserting that the testimony of the human heart was not sufficient of itself to prove that a ministerial vocation was authorized for an individual by God. An authorization from God to preach the Gospel could be received in only one of two ways: either by a direct intervention of God with an individual to establish his credentials as a minister, or by a transmission of an authority once given – by Christ -- through apostolic succession. The former was objectionable because it implied "a new revelation", or "a miracle", through the supposed working of the spirit of the Lord upon the soul of the individual who was supposedly called to preach the Word.

Such an authorization, which was based solely "upon the vividness of a sudden feeling" and a personal profession of having experienced 'the call' through the direct intervention of God, was not only unscriptural, but totally unchristian. Such a religion was:

> not that of the New Testament; for Scripture, so far from promising a new Revelation, expressed the contrary, that there will be no more. (28)

The character of the Sectarians

More generally, where the sectarians were concerned, the Upper Canadian Tories were alarmed by the character transformation that individuals underwent when they experienced an instantaneous conversion, and became members of a sect. The converted became convinced that they could perceive the workings of God in their soul, which was a proposition that the Tories found incredulous. Nonetheless, the Anglican clergy were willing to make a due allowance for differences of belief. They were aware of the sectarian argument that only those who were "in the light" -- through having experienced an instantaneous conversion -- could receive "the things of the spirit of God", which were denied to "the natural man" who had "no light to discern them".

What the Anglican Tories found totally objectionable was the effect of the conversion experience on the character of the sectarians, and their common assertion that:

> all the converted are kings and priests unto God, whom they
> all know from the least to the greatest, because they are taught
> of God.

In religion, as in politics, the sectarians were marked by a democratic egalitarian levelling spirit which was based on a belief in popular sovereignty and government by the people (the saints). (29)

Such a religious outlook could not but foment Christian disunity and discord. It gave rise to a feeling of self-righteousness, and even a presumptuous attitude which was evident in the conduct and utterances of the sectarians. It was noted of the sectarians that:

> In all their turnings and twistings they plead conscience, new
> light derived from the Gospel or, if these fail, irresistible
> grace.... Everyone is a Patriarch, an Apostle, a Saint filled
> with the Holy Spirit, and all the rest of mankind are corrupt,
> hardened, perverse, the children of Satan.

The self-righteous character of the sectarians was viewed as being detrimental to the best interests of the Church and State in Upper Canada, and disruptive of the harmony of society which the church-state polity was established to promote. It constituted yet another reason why the Upper Canadian Tories looked with disfavour upon the presence of the American evangelical sects, and their itinerant preachers, in Upper Canada. (30)

Instantaneous Conversions

Sectarianism, because of the attitudes that it engendered, was viewed as constituting a potent threat to the religious peace and social harmony of the province. Moreover, the religious belief on which sectarianism was based appeared to be highly questionable: viz. the belief in "instantaneous conversion". The Anglican clergy did not deny that sudden conversions might occur, or that the subjects of a conversion might "know the moment of their arrival". Nonetheless, such conversions, "though not impossible", were not regarded as "the ordinary way of God's dealing with Christians".

Such a phenomenon ran contrary to the Anglican belief in conversion as a progressive and rational process by which a Christian convert, under the influence of the Holy Spirit, would "go unto perfection" gradually. It involved an individual gaining an increase in religious knowledge and attaining a greater "holiness of life". As understood by Anglicans, conversion was not something which would take place instantaneously, in the ordinary course of events, or be attained without faith and a sustained commitment to living a good life on the part of the individual. The sectarian belief in instantaneous conversion was open further to the caution that "impulses may sometimes be mistaken for conversions". (31)

The Anglican clergy believed that "as a *general rule*", conversion to Christianity was "rather a progressive than an instantaneous operation"; and that, in either case, there was no valid test of such conversions other than in the mind of God and, on earth, in the converted person "living to God". In sum, the one visible proof of a true conversion was the living of a godly-life on the part of the person thus regenerated. Indeed, it was on the latter score that instantaneous conversions were considered as being doubly suspect because the very concept, as it was manifest in sectarianism, seemed to transform religion into "a visionary system without solidity and without morals".

For the Anglican Tories, the profession and practice of religion were inseparable, and any doctrine that failed to bring about "a real change of heart and life" could not but be wrong because:

> According to the teaching of the Bible and our holy Church, the conversion of sinners is made to consist of a rational conviction of our sin and a deep sense of danger -- of a heartfelt sorrow at having offended God -- with steadfast purpose of amendment under the influence of the Divine Spirit and the regular employment of all the means of Grace. Such a course will be sure to be followed by resolute perseverance in well doing. (32)

For Christians, instantaneous conversion could not be rejected outright as a fallacious doctrine as long as some doubt remained as to its validity. In viewing its "extraordinary implications", however, the Anglican clerics felt justified in suspending judgment in all cases "till the fruits of righteousness appear".

More generally, although conversion was "a sacred thing between a man's conscience and his God", the Anglican clerics believed that the reality of any Christian conversion could be positively determined. To that end, "the only safe and infallible way of judging of ourselves is by our actions". Just as every tree was known by its fruit, so:

> The nature and degree of inward principles must be determined by their effects. He is the best man who is most remarkable for good works. He loves God most who is most like to him who maintains in all he thinks and does a strick [sic] regard to truth and right, and is most useful and kind to his fellow creatures. (33)

In effect, the Anglican Tories rejected antinomianism (the belief in the sufficiency of faith and God's grace alone as sufficient for salvation, independent of any adherence to moral law and any merit derived from good works), as well as pelagianism (the denial of the original corruption of man's nature and a belief that the human will unaided was capable of social and spiritual good). For Anglicans, man was corrupted by original sin and incapable of persisting in good works until justified in being united with Christ in a state of righteousness, which could only be attained through faith in Christ and his atonement. Good works were the product of justification. Hence, the Anglican Tories held that a man's conduct could be taken as a discernible proof or disproof of his conversion to Christ. True religion was "the root of all true virtue". If an individual were truly converted, and had 'the faith', its effects would be obvious in his life.

Once converted, the principles of religion would transfuse the entire life of the Christian in governing his conduct with the world, in his private being, and in penetrating even "into the recesses of the heart". The ultimate purpose of the Christian religion was the salvation of souls through faith in Christ, but where human conduct was concerned it was the moral element of Christianity that served to guide the converted in living a virtuous and good life in keeping with God's Will. (34)

Camp Meetings

In keeping with their view of a religious conversion as a rational and progressive process in which a Christian convert would continually grow in religious knowledge and holiness of life, with a concomitant lasting effect on his moral conduct, the Tories could not but look upon the camp meetings, or the revivals, of the sectarians without a great deal of disapproval. At such meetings, which could last anywhere from four to eight or even twelve days, numerous individuals would take to "the anxious benches" where they would be "brought out of sin" and "adopted" as Christians, to the accompaniment of "much groaning, weeping, and shouting" while the Holy Spirit descended "miraculously" over hundreds at once.

For the Anglican clerics, camp meetings were regarded as exhibiting "a deplorable fanaticism" and excess, which was such as had to be witnessed to be believed. Of a Methodist camp meeting, it was observed that:

> They will bawl twenty of them at once, tumble on the ground,
> laugh, sing, jump and stamp, and this they call the working of
> the spirit.

The 'American Methodist' camp meetings were regarded as being a travesty of religion. They were viewed as "outrages on truth, religion, order, sobriety and decency". In seeking to gratify "every individual taste and fancy", the meetings provided an "unlimited indulgence to the spirit of anarchy and fanaticism". Moreover, camp meetings gave vent to that demeaning "restless spirit of gossip" for which they were well known.

From the Tory viewpoint, camp meetings were viewed as a counterpart of democratic politics, in that they fomented the same pretensions and impatience of all authority and restraint. They gave rise to pretensions, and a presumptuousness where:

> Everyone, man, woman and child, is a doctor of divinity, and has a gift, and speaks in public or some such, and looks with democratic-pharisaical contempt upon all who do not go with them to the same excess of riot .... (35)

Furthermore, revivals were deplored because they had little permanent effect upon the conduct of those involved. Owing to their very transient nature, they were highly dependent for impact upon "novelty", "excitement" and sudden "outbursts of feeling". It was a fact that was apparently recognized even by their promoters who sought always to hold them in a rapid succession. The enthusiasm which marked such meetings was regarded as a product not of a deep religious conviction, but rather of "blind zeal" and "delusion". It was a situation in which "loud vociferations", "absurd contortions", and "a vehement language", were relied upon to supply the want of any knowledge of true religion. Worst still, it was believed that "enthusiasm" was artificially induced:

> by human contrivance – an artful machinery to excite the animal passions, and disorder the intellect, and banish modesty and decorum, ...

Sectarian preachers were accused by the Tories of adopting the technique of political agitators in aiming their appeals to the "ignorance, pride and presumption" of man. The result was that "some weak persons", in being thoroughly deluded, were seized by "uncommon transports and inward persuasions" which they mistook for the working of the divine spirit within their soul. To the Tories, such emotionalism was "delusive" and "dangerous", as well as being completely contrary in its workings and influence to the character and temper of the true religion. The Anglican clerics believed that in human conduct, or at least in the conduct of true Christians:

Reason must always be the guiding and ruling faculty -- the affections must not lead but follow.

"Warmth" was admittedly an essential component of prayer, but it needed to be accompanied by a well-ordered mind, strengthened by virtue and piety, and free of any offense against God or man. In looking askance at the emotional enthusiasm and verbal outbursts of the sectarians at their religious revivals, the Anglican Tories believed to the contrary that:

> The true spirit of devotion prevails most when there is the most exemplariness of conversation and behaviour; and the greatest degrees of meekness, patience, candour, charity and self-government. (36)

Self-ordained Preachers

Among the factors fostering dissent, with all of its deplorable excesses, none was regarded by the Upper Canadian Tories as being of a greater import than the general "want of principle" of the age and, in particular, the widespread vice of "presumption". It was noted that:

> No man is willing to be thought ignorant even of those things which he has had no opportunity of knowing, and so far does this presumption proceed that men are daily found assuming professions for which they have never made any preparation.

With respect to religion, such an attitude was to be found at the root of all the divisions that prevailed in the Christian world. Such divisions were the product of a "pride and delusion" which begat the belief that man was competent to judge for himself in all matters; and that he was under no obligation "to submit to the word of God and the authority of his Church". Sectarianism was, in effect, but a manifestation in the religious sphere of that social phenomenon of the age. Men who had succumbed to "pride and arrogance" in rejecting their true duty and responsibility, were to be found in all ranks of society, as well as among the "self-ordained Preachers" – who were held to be the "enemies to all regular order and subordination".

Where the sectarian preachers were concerned, the sin of presumption was seen to be present in the concept of 'the call' which embodied the contention that every Christian, when moved by the spirit, was authorized to "preach, pray and administer the Sacraments". In such a system of belief, there was no recognition of any need for a duly-ordained and learned clergy. In denouncing the concept of 'the call', one Anglican clergyman exclaimed:

> The qualifications under it were chiefly a furious zeal, and a loud voice. Ignorance was no impediment, provided that these came in proof of a *call*. (37)

The result of this presumptuous attitude was readily seen in Upper Canada in the prewar and immediate postwar period, when it was noted that the sectarian preachers were for the most part "ignorant enthusiasts". What was even more galling to the Anglican Tories, however, was the fact that 'the sectaries' not only had the presumption to think that such men were proper preachers of the Word of God, but that some sects went so far, "in their delusion", as to deny the need of seminaries to prepare ministers of the Gospel. Sectarians were wont to defend their indifference to formal education, and the resultant low level of education prevalent among their ministers, by pointing out how successful they were in attracting large congregations and numerous adherents. Mere numbers were cited as proof of their possessing "the essential qualifications of able ministers".

From the Tory viewpoint, such arguments were totally unconvincing. Any popularity which was gained, by such means and methods as employed at religious revivals held in camp meetings, was by its very nature ephemeral.

For the Tories, it appeared incongruous that holders of an office in the state needed "a formal and legal delegation of trust" to carry out their public function, without which their acts would be rendered null and void; and yet the spiritual function -- "a higher and holier commission" – could be "discharged by persons not holding their office by an authority recognized in Scripture and sanctioned by the usages of the primitive Church". It was lamented that such a presumptuousness and delusion were characteristic of the age. (38)

On all grounds, the phenomenon of self-ordained clergy was utterly deplored by the Anglican clergy. Such a practice was detrimental to the general character of the clergy, and the best interests of religion. It encouraged and facilitated the overpowering of "modest merit" and "diffident wisdom" by "presumptuous vanity" and "noisy ignorance", and opened the way for the rise of self-seeking men. In lacking the authority and restraint of a duly-ordained ministry under a bishop:

> there was no safeguard for the unity of the Church – no defence against the multiplication of sects and parties from the pride and perversity of men.

Both in practice and theory, sectarianism was viewed as being built upon foundations of sand, and as based upon forms and doctrines merely "of yesterday" in having been introduced at the Reformation and thereafter. Sectarianism was devoid of all tradition and authority, and lacked "any sure system" to maintain unity and coherence. It was open:

> to all the abuses and corruptions, both in discipline and doctrine, that the wavering and unsteady mind of man can produce.

It posed a danger to a well-ordered Christian society which was increased immeasurably by the sectarian tendency "to quote Scripture at random", in paying little or no attention to the context or intention of the passages that were being cited. (39)

Preaching

The dangers that the Tories saw in sectarianism were further augmented by the sectarian elevation of preaching to a predominate position in their scheme of religion, to the detriment of the other 'ordinances of the Gospel'. Of itself, preaching was very liable to abuse. It provided a way for individual preachers to feed and flatter their vanity through the influence that it bestowed upon them. Above all, it was the efficacy of employing preaching as the principal instrument for producing faith and inculcating Christian principles which was questioned.

The Anglican Tory clerics believed that faith was produced by hearing the Word preached and by an avid reading of Scripture. They insisted, however, that if preaching were to be effective, those to whom it was addressed must be prepared to give "an intelligent hearing" to the sermons to profit from them. Such a preparation was best realized through an elementary instruction in the liturgy and catechism of the Church. Moreover, the instruction should come from an authorized ministry that comprised men of piety, superior learning, and knowledge. There was a need for guidance from 'Students of Scripture', who in their conducting of public prayers, the administration of the sacraments, scriptural readings, and explanations of Church doctrine, would provide a necessary supplement to the private Bible reading of their communicants. (40)

The abuses, which were inherent in a system that bestowed an unmerited pre-eminence upon preaching, to the neglect of the other essentials of Christianity, were readily seen in the conduct of the sectaries who had left the Church of England. In the typical fashion of converts, they attacked the Church of England as an 'erroneous and dangerous' institution, while extolling "the exclusive truth" of their new connection and zealously proselytizing others by assuring them of salvation. Yet, experience had shown that some of the same individuals could be found, at a later period, to be just as zealous and exclusive in pursuit of yet another religious system in having rejected their former belief as being erroneous.

Such a pattern of evolution was manifest among several well-known sectarians of whom the classic example was perhaps Dr. Priestley in England, who:

> passed through all the gradations of opinion, from high Calvinism to something only the next remove from pure Deism; and at each separate step, he was clearly right, and all the rest of the world, so far as they differed from him, clearly wrong. – the Schismatic an Independent -- the Independent an Anabaptist, and the Anabaptist an Antenomian [sic], carrying all the force of apparent conviction, and all the zeal of eager proselytism along with him at each step; the present being always essential, and exclusively essential, to salvation; while the last step, which was equally essential while it lasted, is now of no more value than the original point from which the Schismatic first commenced his progress.

If the Christian message was not to be perverted or distorted, and religious indifference bred amidst religious fragmentation, preaching had to be accompanied by Bible reading, instruction by an authorized and learned ministry, and adherence to the Creeds. Each had its due importance in the Christian religion, and none could be dispensed with if a vital faith -- one of the heart embracing a Christian temper and spirit, as well as Christian beliefs -- were to be propagated as delivered by Christ. (41)

The Need for a Learned Clergy

An educated clergy was held to be essential to the Christian religion for many reasons, not the least of which was the very nature of the Bible. A perusal of the New Testament would show that:

> no *system* of divinity is there laid down; that the great truths which concern our everlasting salvation, are not there arranged by rule and method; that the theology of Christianity, in short, is not there taught, or at least unfolded to us, as if it were a science.

On the contrary, the Bible consisted of "Narratives, Prophecies, Psalms and Letters" which contained "general truths" but, in not being obvious, they had to be elicited carefully through the exercise of "a sound judgment". Although "no regular treatises" were to be found in Scripture that did not mean that "all the materials of a regular system" were not contained therein. Everything required "to explain the ways of God to man" was present in the Bible, but it had to be "arranged" to yield the principles and doctrines of Christianity. It required a process that was analogous to that followed in the discipline of physical science.

In that field, all of the elements of physical science were known to be present in nature; yet nature did not appear in any regular order until "the facts" were collected and deductions made which, when classified, yielded "first principles". Similarly, in religion the first principles of Christianity had to be deduced from the Bible. In such a task, only a clergy that was guided by the doctrines and creeds of the Apostolic Church, and aided "by Divine Power, by a superior education, extensive reading, and deep meditation", could be trusted to arrive at "the true doctrine" of Christianity. The need for a learned clergy was proven by the conduct of the sectarians who, in relying on uneducated preachers and lacking any authoritative guide to interpretation, could be heard to cite Scripture in support of "the most wild and opposite opinions". (42)

For the Tories, it was a certainty that Scripture could be interpreted rightly by educated pious men because there could be no divergence between the Will of God, the Word of God which conveyed that Will to man, and enlightened reason. Everyone, including unbelievers admitted that:

> the precepts of the gospel are agreeable to the most enlightened reason -- but surely the voice of enlightened reason is the voice of God.

This did not mean that men of lesser learning or intellectual acumen -- given that all men were not equally endowed intellectually -- could not benefit from reading the Bible. It was believed that "all persons can easily understand the more essential parts" which were necessary for salvation, but there were some passages that were difficult to understand and place in a meaningful context which required information the average person did not "have an opportunity of acquiring". The guidance of educated men of the cloth was essential. It was a truism that all efforts toward understanding necessitated "exertion" as well as "attention and industry"; and it was the clergy of the Apostolic Church who were, above all, eminently prepared and suited for the task. (43)

Until the advent of sectarianism -- accompanied as it was by a disposition "to level all distinctions social, intellectual and spiritual" -- ministers of Christ had always been conspicuously in the forefront of their society in ability and learning: both human and divine. Even the Apostles, contrary to the contention of some who chose to stress their "unlearned state", were very knowledgeable men who well versed in the Old Testament and carefully instructed by Christ himself during daily Intercourse. Thus, it was evident from various considerations that no individual could "assume the sacred office without due preparation". If ignorant men did so, they were not 'called by God', but rather "by indolence or presumption". It was indisputable that ministers of the Gospel had to prepare themselves by "careful study, constant meditation, and fervent prayer", if they were to explain the ways of God to man. (44)

Morality, Religion, and a Learned Clergy

Like all other branches of knowledge, religion had its principles and values which had to be "carefully taught" and properly understood if they were to influence conduct and belief in the moral sphere. Education in the faith was requisite because knowledge of the existence of God was "the foundation of all religion and morals". Faith was "ineffectual if not founded on knowledge of God", without which "there would be nothing".

The conscience of man could not be trusted to distinguish rightly between good and evil if it were not "well informed". In the nature of things, ignorance of the Will of God could not but lead to offensive conduct. To remedy that deficiency of knowledge in man -- by interpreting the Word of God to man, and thereby provide him with a guide to conscience -- was one of the tasks of the ministry of Christ. It was charged with the promotion of "the education, virtue and happiness" of mankind.

In preparing themselves for their vocation, the duly-authorized ministers were required to attain a superior level of mental cultivation which required the attainment of a complete mastery not only of the Biblical revelation, but "of all knowledge human and divine". That was a necessity in view of the comprehensiveness of religion, and a concomitant belief in natural religion in that:

> God should be contemplated in the book of nature, as well as in
> that revelation, and every avenue of knowledge employed that
> may throw light on sacred things.

The ways of God were to be found explicit in God's Works, as well as in Scripture, but to comprehend the moral meaning and the lessons which Nature taught required serious study and a highly developed "moral vision". It was unfortunate that men, for the most part, lacked "a clear moral perception", and were prone to view significant events as mere transient experiences. It was an outlook which discouraged any serious searching for the deeper meaning of the workings of Providence. It was lamentable, in their reactions to life and nature, that:

> the multitude seem satisfied with shallow sensibilities, and thus
> though they may feel much, they learn little.

If the workings of Nature and God's providence were going to promote the moral improvement of man, those who had "wisely learned more" – the clergy -- were under a heavy responsibility to interpret carefully "those voices of the soul" to those less well-informed. For the Anglican Tories, a true understanding and interpretation of both the Bible (God's revealed Word), and of Nature (God's works), was dependent upon a well-educated clergy. (45)

The Church and the Maintenance of Christianity

In interpreting the Bible and conveying the Christian message to mankind, the efforts of educated and pious clerics were not considered to be sufficient, outside of the Church, to overcome the infirmities of human nature. What was feared was "the passion for excitement and novelty" found in man. If left to work its influence unrestrained among even the clergy, human passion would, in time, destroy true religion. If "the faith once delivered to the saints" were to be properly maintained and preached, it had to be through the efforts of a God-ordained clergy serving in, and subordinate to, His Church.

If a clergy existed independent of the guidance and direction of the Church, it could not but breed confusion and chaos in religion because:

> The Church is to the Scriptures what the Judges and Counsellors
> are to the Constitution of the land – its authorized expositors
> .... (46)

From its infancy, the Church had carried out this part of its function through setting forth -- by means of Church Councils -- an authoritative interpretation of Scripture, and by embodying it in her creeds and liturgy. The result was to be found – as compiled by the Church of England at the Reformation – in the Book of Common Prayer. Such formal statements of belief and written forms of prayer were held by the Anglican Tories to be "one of the best safeguards" of orthodoxy. As such, the teachings of the Established Church were immensely superior to the "rash and presumptuous" outpourings of sectarian preachers which were little more than "the feelings, fancies, and infirmities of men". Moreover, the teachings of the Church were equally superior to the thought of learned individuals who relied solely on human reason.

If the true faith were to be maintained uncorrupted by "a Socinian or a Pelagian bias", written forms were essential. This fact was attested to by the evolution of Calvinism in Geneva. In the absence of written forms of prayer and creeds, over time Socinianism had subverted the principles of Calvin, which was a process that had been repeated in Ireland and England and among American Presbyterians and Congregationalists where a rationalist approach was being taken to religious belief.

In contrast, the Church of England possessed a "permanence" and "stability" in having a liturgy that was "unaffected by the weakness, the corruption, the false opinions, or evil motives of men". Its members still adhered to one faith in a Church which was unmarked by "discordance in doctrine, precept or discipline". In her written forms, episcopal hierarchy, and her learned and lawful ministry, the Apostolic Church possessed, together with the Bible, all the elements of permanence which were necessary for maintaining orthodoxy and properly expounding the Word of God. It was a permanence and security which 'the sectaries', who were "connected by no bond of union, no common principles of order, and no subordination", could not hope to possess. (47)

The non-Christian nature of Sectarianism

Although the Anglican clergy viewed the means and methods that the sectarians employed in disseminating their evangelical religion – camp meeting, revivals, a strong emphasis on preaching, and the employment of self-ordained preachers – as constituting a threat to the maintenance of orthodox Christianity, the critical objection to sectarianism was its non-Christian nature.

Sectarians called themselves Christians; yet, they denied the tenets of scriptural religion, rejected "everything that is peculiar to the Gospel", quoted Scripture at random in being oblivious to the context and, in their conduct, acted "directly at variance with the general tenor of the sacred scriptures". Their religious notions were such that the Church became in their hands "a lawless democracy" wherein everyone could do what was "right in *his own eyes*" and worship "according to the dictates of his own conscience", rather than according to "the Will of his Maker".

In the view of the Anglican Tories, sectarian beliefs fostered a system wherein every man was free to form his own religion "to suit himself", and sectarianism begat a religion that was not of God, but of man. It was apparent among sectarians that:

> The idea of such a thing as authority in the premises of a divine revelation to man, and the like constitution of a particular society called the church ... is held in sovereign contempt; ....

In almost totally lacking any adherence to the truths of Revelation, the sectaries placed their faith instead in "miraculous interpositions of Providence", which was a corruption of the true religion. (48) The sectaries not only rejected the Christian church tradition, but Christianity itself, which was made clear in their concept of personal salvation. It was a belief, as expressed by themselves, that:

> "Piety and religion ... consist in private good and personal exertions; and everyone understands that as a free agent, he ALONE IS TO WORK OUT HIS OWN SALVATION";

and that,

> "Christ has taught us that *the only way to salvation lies in good deeds and in faithful and personal prayers, and that every man's happiness depends upon himself*".

Such sectarian statements of belief were directly contrary to "the leading tenets of Christianity". The sectarians denied the need for Christ's atonement in the redemption of man, rejected any reliance on the authority of the learned clergy of Christ's Church to interpret Scriptures in keeping with Church tradition and established Christian doctrines, and denied that salvation was dependent on the ministration of the sacraments by a duly-ordained clergy within the apostolic Catholic Church. (49) In addition, the sectarians were condemned for destroying the unity of the Christian Church, as were the non-conforming churches.

In the view of the Anglican clergy, both Holy Scripture and history condemned those who would break the unity of Christianity in separating from the 'one Holy Catholic and Apostolic Church'. In the Bible, the dividers of the Church were declared to be "enemies of the Church", and the history of dissent was marked by continual divisions with the non-conforming churches constantly giving rise to separatist religious sects. Such was ultimately the fate that awaited the dissenting churches in deserting the truth of Christ as embodied in His Church. They were a product of man, not of God, and consequently in being human creations and "called after men" – whether of Luther, Calvin, Knox, or Wesley -- they could not but "gradually disappear".

It was indubitable that:

> The Church is only one body of which our Lord is the head, as there is one Spirit, one Faith, one Lord, and one God and Father of all. (50)

One of the most lamentable aspects of dissent and sectarianism was that the "sin of separation" from Christ's Church constituted -- in its very nature -- an act of "deliberate insubordination". It was an act that was symptomatic of:

> nay often the cause and first beginning of an unhumbled, willful, self-dependent, contentious [and] jealous spirit – a spirit which is too frequently accompanied or followed by coldness, pride, and infidelity.

Such a spirit, which was born of "presumption", "pride" and "reliance on self", was inconsistent with Christianity in that it encouraged men to oppose their own "self-will" and "private judgment" to "the revealed will of God and to those who have the Rule over us". It was a spirit which was fostered and played upon by sectarian preachers to inculcate among their followers a deep hostility toward the clergy of the Established Church, and a preference for their own "effusions of ignorance" in preference to the teachings of "men of rational piety and competent learning".

True faith demanded a "uniform obedience to the Will of God" and the forsaking of all "schemes of Religious change, the pursuit of novelties, and dreams of innovation in the Church of Christ". The means of propagating and propounding the faith had been appointed by Christ and his Apostles. Once His Church was established, it became the duty of all Christians to maintain it in "its full efficiency" and, likewise, where Revelation was concerned:

> God having declared his Will it becomes our duty not to question, but to obey.

For the Anglican Tories, the Church of England was a branch of the 'one Holy Catholic and Apostolic Church' to which subordination was due on the part of all true Christians in the province. (51)

In separating from the Church of Christ and attacking the God-ordained ministry of the Established Church, the sectarians were not only acting contrary to the best interests of religion and God's Will, but were destroying the peace and order of a society under a Christian government. Leaving aside the interests of religion and morality, even from a strictly utilitarian standpoint the influence of a standing ministry was regarded as constituting a strong support for the "public comfort and security of society", as well as for private happiness. Any movement which sought to undermine a standing ministry was viewed by the Anglican Tories as a potential threat to public order; and that was particularly the case with sectarianism.

The sectarian preachers by their very interests were the opponents of "all regular order and subordination". It was held that:

> They breed licentiousness of opinion, they make the common people disputers, and not religious -- unsteady in their faith, or rather of no faith. (52)

Freed from the religious duties which restrain and guide conduct, and under the influence of a "blind intemperate zeal", sectarianism threatened "no small disorder" to any nation. For the Anglican Tories of Upper Canada, it was a cause of some foreboding. In the nature of things, as "truth" would have it:

> Religious democrats, to order foes,
>
> Must soon, she roars, the civil power oppose ....

Sectarianism was a threat to the order and well-being of a Christian society because of the very values and attitudes that it preached. In its otherworldly and inward-looking consciousness, sectarianism precluded the development of a national spirit, or a social conscience, among its followers. It was observed of 'the sectaries' that:

> They have no national feelings, no regard for the public welfare and prosperity of the nation; if they proceed prosperously, what is the rest of the world to them. In their private relations also, they loose [sic] all that sympathy and affection which bind society together; everything centres in the Tabernacle, and in its good fortune only they rejoice; they have arrived at a stoical apathy by a very different principle from that of Zeno.

Thus, the religious zealots of the religious sects of Upper Canada, like the wise man of the Stoics, could be seen to have arrived at a detachment from public concerns which could not but prove detrimental to the best interests of the state. The National Church could not fulfill its function to form the national character of the province, and to promote national unity through the influence of Christianity, if sectarianism, with its non-Christian character and lack of either a Christian social conscience or a national spirit, were to become widespread in the absence of an effective Church establishment. (53)

In the opinion of the Upper Canadian Tories, the best interests of the state and the Church dictated that the religious sects ought not to receive any encouragement from the provincial government. They were to be tolerated, but sectarianism could not be approved or condoned. One of the prime objectives of the national policy was to form and strengthen the British national character of Upper Canada; and it was a policy objective that could only be achieved if the bulk of the population were to be comprehended within the Established Church wherein alone a national character could be properly formed.

The policy of religious comprehension was in keeping with the traditional concept of the role of an established national Church to which the Upper Canadian Tories adhered, as well as a product of a Tory desire to limit the growth of the sects whose religious principles were regarded as being synonymous with American democratic republicanism. More particularly, for the Anglican clergy their strong support for a policy of religious comprehension was also a product of their deeply-held religious beliefs, their view of the non-Christian nature of the dissenting sects, and their fear of the insubordinate and self-centred attitude which sectarianism fostered, as well as its seemingly-inherent hostility towards a church establishment. Ultimately, however, the Anglican clergy strove to encompass the sectarians within 'the one Holy Catholic and Apostolic Church' to ensure their salvation, because in rejecting the Church of Christ they had placed their souls in jeopardy. (54)

———————

Chapter Eleven

Human Nature and Christian Redemption

The Tory effort to strengthen and extend the National Church, and to increase its effectiveness in disseminating the Christian religion in Upper Canada, had both a political and a religious dimension. On the one hand, it was a product of their concern to maintain order and harmony in the state, and to promote the happiness and liberty of Upper Canadians by inculcating in the public mind the moral and religious values which they held to be essential to that end. On the other hand – particularly for the Anglican clerics among the Tory elite -- there was a more profound religious basis for extending the ministrations and teachings of the established Church of England. For the clerics, it was a critical part of their effort to evangelize the province. It was a commitment born of their religious view of human nature, their concept of man's purpose here on earth, and their belief in God's Providence and His scheme of redemption. In sum, it was the Christian religious beliefs and worldview of the Upper Canadian Tories that governed what they sought to achieve. It was to enable Upper Canadians to enjoy peace, order, and social harmony, in living a life of virtue, self-denial, and good works, with the ultimate aim of attaining salvation and everlasting life. It was the Anglican clerics who were in the forefront in articulating the Tory religious beliefs and worldview.

The Corruption of Man

For the Upper Canadian Tories, the Biblical account of Creation and man's fall from grace was central to their concept of the purpose of life, and formed the basis of their assessment of man's needs in all areas of human endeavour, his strengths and weaknesses, his potentialities, and the requirements of his situation. In brief, they believed that in the beginning God had created "an order of rational Beings", in his own image, to render "a peculiar service" to Himself; and that His creature, man, was by his nature preconditioned to be perfectly happy in serving God and living in paradise with Him. In his prelapsarian state, man had religion, and all his faculties, both spiritual and physical, were perfectly attuned to his soul and not subject to any inclination, affliction or appetite contrary to God's Will. Sin was totally absent, and man lived "in perfect Unison" with God: "His mind was God's mind and his will, God's Will".

Nonetheless, man was created with a free will, had chosen to disobey God, and his rebellion had "deformed the Creation". Sin had entered into the life of man, and "every faculty of the Soul and body became depraved, and the image of God [was] almost entirely defaced". The goodness of man was lost, his knowledge of divine things was corrupted, and his moral sense was weakened. Guilt replaced innocence, terror succeeded love, and man fell into "Ruin, misery and Death". In his fallen state, man still possessed his former faculties and powers, but they were now corrupted, greatly weakened, and misdirected.

In sum, man was rendered "spiritually ignorant", and because of his corrupted nature was no longer capable of pleasing God. In his heart, man was "at enmity with God" and his fellow man. His apostasy had left him "subject to evil affections and passions" -- such as envy, contention, pride and covetousness – which bred hatred and ill-will. In his fallen state, bereft of religion and left to the mercy of his appetites, there was no crime or corruption which human nature was incapable of committing.

The reasons for man's first disobedience and rebellion, "against the God of all perfection and of goodness", was "a mystery … far beyond the reach of [human] understanding fully to explain". However, there was no doubt as to the presence of sin in the world, of man's depravity, and his consequent need for redemption and reconciliation with God. Fortunately, redemption was not beyond man's reach. The Scripture revealed that:

> we are placed on earth as Probationers for heaven; and that for this great end and for the working out of our salvation we are supplied with various means of Grace and knowledge, and have been made the subjects of a special spiritual discipline.

Christian Redemption

The Christian religion was given to man by God, in his 'infinite wisdom, goodness, and mercy', to reveal to man "his lofty destination", to enable him to regain "that state of perfection and happiness, for which [he was] designed" by the Creator, and to restore to him "the Image of God".

Scripture taught man how he was to conduct himself in this life if he were to realize "the great end of our being -- a holy life", and how to attain salvation. Man was commanded to love God, not the world, and to obey His commandments, if he were to attain everlasting life.

In seeking redemption, man was totally dependent upon the dispensations which were provided by the Christian religion. Because of his contrary nature, man was incapable "unaided" of rendering the obedience which was required of him, or consequently of making any progress toward "a purer state". It was Christianity alone that addressed the fallen nature of man, and set forth the purpose of life for man's benefit. It was Christianity that set forth "the perfect law of righteousness by which man could judge his conduct", and that provided the means by which the character, as well as the state of mankind, could be changed.

In sum, the object of God's communication with man through the Gospels was to bring man to "a perfect conformity to the divine character", and to which end the central doctrine of the Christian religion was that of "man's absolute dependence upon the atonement of Christ for salvation and upon the holy spirit for sanctification". Only Christianity embraced the doctrines which were essential to "the temporal and eternal happiness of man". Christianity could reconcile "God's perfect holiness and man's sinfulness" by bringing about a reformation in the life of man, and a "renewal of heart conducive to the perfecting of his nature". Through the Christian religion, man was provided with "a moral governor, a moral redeemer, and a moral sanctifier" -- the Father, the Son, and the Holy Spirit – to enable him to obey God's Will, as well as know it, to the end that man might attain a state of righteousness once again. (1)

In the Christian scheme of redemption, God, in his mercy, sent his son -- in the nature of man --to deliver 'the fallen race of man' from the misery which was incurred in punishment for breaking God's law, and to restore man to his proper nature. Christ through his suffering and death had redeemed man, and placed him in "a state of justification". Christ had done so by taking upon himself all of man's sins, and then ascended into heaven from which the Holy Spirit was sent to sanctify all men that they might enjoy "the benefits of that redemption which [Christ] had purchased with his blood". Through his sacrifice, Christ removed "the stain of original sin", and thereby redeemed man, if he accepted the atonement, but Christ was also the embodiment of 'the perfect nature' which man was called upon to pursue.

Christ was 'the Word made flesh', and he had revealed all that was essential to man to know in this life. On the one hand, Christ revealed that God was a God of love, tenderness and mercy, the friend and benefactor of man, and made evident "the whole will of God relative to man and the whole method of salvation". On the other hand, in being both God and man in one person, Christ provided a perfect example -- covering all areas of life -- of how man should act and live, and "an infallible guide" to happiness both here and hereafter:

> The life of the blessed Jesus was the most exact pattern of every virtue. In him we behold an example of the most ardent love and dependence upon God, of the most tender affection to mankind; we see the most perfect filial reverence for his heavenly Father, the most unreserved submission to His Will, the most entire satisfaction with his dispensations, the most perfect example of prompt and cheerful obedience to his commands; and in his intercourse with the world what kindness and condescension, what eagerness to relieve distress, how indulgent, how generous was he to all mankind, both friends and foes! To him every duty was sacred; with what alacrity did he comfort the afflicted, console the troubled soul, inform the ignorant, and encourage the weak and timid.

Scriptures revealed that Christ was "the mediator between God and man", the Saviour who "satisfied the divine justice" and delivered the human race from sin. Christ was at one with God, the all in all, the object of worship and of faith "through whose name and mediation all prayers [were] to be offered up" to God. By his atonement, Christ restored man "to the capacity of mercy and favour" and provided the means of his salvation. Through his sacrifice, Christ:

> hath ratified the new convenant, by which salvation is made attainable, and is really tendered to all upon reasonable and equitable conditions. By this convenant, God is willing to

dispense mercy and pardon to any man sincerely believing and seriously repenting, and He further promiseth inestimable blessings to such as shall continue in an obedience suitable to man's natural infirmity and proportionable to the assistance afforded. ... all men are invited, exhorted, and intreated [sic] to entry into it, and to partake of its advantages. (2)

The Gospels called upon man to obey God's law if he wished to have everlasting life, and promised that God, if sincerely entreated, would bestow the gift of His grace and spirit upon man through Christ to enable fallen man to effect "a thorough change of life" and to do his duty in submission to God's Will.

God in His goodness, love and mercy, was ever ready to forgive and promote the eternal happiness of His creatures, but "no man [could] be saved unless his return [was] attended with a willing obedience". The Gospel scheme of redemption required human co-operation, for man was possessed of a free will, and could refuse to partake of the covenant and remain in sin. In sum, "everything happened through the power of God", but man had been given "a certain sphere of action" for which he was accountable. In his corrupted state, he was still able to discern and appreciate what the Christian faith offered, and was capable of recognizing "the good". Thus, the first step required of man in seeking salvation was a sincere repentance in the sense of becoming aware of the evil of sin, and being truly grief stricken and humbled by the knowledge of his transgressions against God and his own "ignorance, weakness and corruption".

In such a state of sincere repentance, man was capable of understanding the Christian message, for:

> The principal qualification for hearing the word of God consists in an honest and a good heart --... free from all evil dispositions and corrupt passions which blind the eyes, distort the understanding and obstruct the admission of divine truth -- a heart perfectly free from prejudice, from pride, from vanity, from self-sufficiency and conceit – a heart sincerely disposed and earnestly desirous to find out the truth and firmly resolved to embrace it when found.

It was necessary that redemption commence with a change of heart because man, in his fallen state, was at enmity with God, and the will of fallen man was opposed to God's Will, but salvation could be achieved only through faith. Since faith came to the heart by hearing the Word of God preached and through studying the Bible, and a good heart "enlightened the understanding" and alone was receptive to God, a change of heart and faith in Christ were "inseparably connected with true repentance".

Faith

A "faith of the heart" was a necessary step in man's redemption because man knew little about 'the power of God' and much that was essential to man's salvation was beyond human comprehension. The natural wisdom and mental energies of man were quite limited, and "Scriptures address[ed] some truths solely to our Faith not to our reason". Man was commanded to obey, to surrender both the heart and the understanding to God's authority, on faith alone. It was not for man to question what was beyond his comprehension. There was much that man had to accept for which he had "no means or ground of argument" – such truths as the presence of Christ in the Sacrament of Holy Communion, and the resurrection of the dead. There was much that was mysterious and miraculous in Christianity which had to be accepted on faith and on authority, but which nonetheless, though ill-understood, was essential to man's present and future happiness. (3)

By 'faith alone' was man justified, for only if he received Christ as his Saviour and believed in the atonement could man be saved. To believe, or have faith, meant to know that there was an 'invisible world', and that the things of this world are not sufficient for man's happiness. It was through faith alone that man came to yield a willing obedience to the Divine Will; to realize one's total dependence upon God and accountability for one's actions here on earth; and to look beyond the present and seek for good in God alone.

Faith was "more than a formal doctrine". It was a matter of heart, a temper, a spirit, and a state of mind, which governed a man's conduct not for a moment, but over the whole course of his life. It motivated him to follow the example of Christ in continually seeking to do good in subordination to God's Will. Faith and obedience were essentially "one and the same", and "constitute the way of Salvation".

God's Grace

If man were truly repentant and had faith, then he could partake of 'the new convenant', and appropriate to himself the benefit of Christ's atonement. Through baptism, he could enter into the convenant of grace and become a member of the Church of Christ -- "the kingdom of heaven upon earth" -- which included all who were lawfully baptized. Outside of the Church, there was no salvation, for:

> except a man be born again of water and of the Spirit -- of the Spirit operating as water by cleansing and sanctifying the Soul -- he cannot see the Kingdom of God.

Through holy baptism, the faithful received "the free gift of God's grace", which was the antidote to their depravity. It washed away man's sins, and caused him to be reborn into righteousness. Thereby, man was regenerated. With the assistance of God's grace, in his new state of redemption man was enabled to do God's Will and to work out his own salvation "under proper care and discipline". Once in a state of righteousness, man would know what was required of him. And he would enjoy the possession of a spiritual power which was sufficient to enable him to control his passions and appetites, and to rise above "such corruption of nature as might still remain". He would be able to do his duty, and ensure himself of salvation. (4)

Having "joined with Christ in sacramental union", and having received the gift of God's grace -- the workings of which were "far beyond the comprehension of human understanding" – man's ultimate salvation was still conditional. It would dependent upon his obeying God's commandments, and maintaining his faith in Christ. In sum, with God's grace, man was enabled to "work out his own salvation", and in a state of righteousness had the power to do God's Will, but ultimately salvation depended upon whether the individual had the will to respond to the promptings of his conscience in rendering obedience to God. Through Christ, and Christ alone, man could do what was required of him, but too often men failed in their Christian duty solely through a lack of will.

Faith and Reason

The maintenance of true faith consisted of man keeping his will subordinate to his reason, and thus living in conformity to God's Will. In a state of righteousness, man could understand what was required of him, but that did not mean that he could understand all the mysteries of the Christian dispensation. To the contrary, there were things that had to be believed and acted upon through trust. Yet human reason could still serve as a guide to understanding what had been revealed. Although certain doctrines might transcend reason, in God's creation there could be no opposition between faith and reason. "Faith [was] only reason sanctified", for:

> the precepts of the Gospel are agreeable to the most enlightened reason, but surely the voice of enlightened reason is the voice of God.

Christian Liberty

For the true Christian, life was "a state of trial", a struggle, in which he must strive to maintain himself in his new state of righteousness and, with the aid of the divine spirit, must seek to conquer sin and "all wicked inclinations". While he remained in this world, the Christian was engaged in a struggle between human nature and grace, as well as between the flesh and the spirit, from which there was no escape. He was required to discipline himself and to exercise temperance, forbearance and self-denial, in resisting the temptations of the moment, while persisting in rendering obedience to God's law. In doing so, the Christian would gradually approach closer to the divine perfection, and thereby assure himself of salvation. The aim and object of the sincere Christian must always be to recover his true nature -- the image of God -- and to achieve a state of Christian liberty wherein in being free from "the guilt & power of sin", he could willingly obey God's commandments because his desires would be "all in conformity to the divine will".

The State of Righteousness

In his state of righteousness, the Christian enjoyed "the means of grace" and knowledge of God's law which enabled him to discharge his duties, but it was not to be expected that man could ever render a perfect obedience. The most that was expected of him was that he would pray to God for assistance, and strive to do his best. Nevertheless, man was a rational being, who possessed a freedom of choice, and was accountable for his conduct. However, he was not alone. The Christian religion provided not only the power to enable man to do his duty, but also a means of encouraging him to do so.

Through Baptism, the Church raised man to a state of righteousness and secured to him the benefits of Christ's atonement, but it was also duty bound to help the Christian preserve what he had been given, and to increase it. Through the sacrament of Holy Communion, the true believer, in becoming a full member of that body in communion with Christ, renewed the convenant and received a further accretion of grace for his benefit. Moreover, the Church, in preaching the Christian message, continually sought to hold the duly baptized to 'the right ways', not by compulsion, but by exercising "a moral and persuasive influence" in keeping with man's nature and God's intent.

Christianity was intended to appeal to man's "moral and intellectual nature" and to carry conviction by reason and argument, and "warnings and admonitions". Hence, the Church was charged to strive to enlighten the understanding, 'to move the will' and to awaken the conscience, so that the redeemed might continue to strive to work out their salvation in "going unto perfection". In the Christian scheme of redemption, it was evident that for Christians:

> to do God's will and to take care of our Souls is ... our common
> and indispensable work -- the one thing needful for us all. (5)

A Life of Virtue

In seeking to work out his salvation in 'going unto perfection', it was not enough that the Christian merely believe in Christ's atonement. Through faith in Christ man was justified, but faith had to be joined to "a life of virtue" to ensure salvation. Those who persisted in evil doing, regardless of how fervent their faith, could not expect forgiveness. Christianity was much more than a set of dogmas or beliefs. It required "a living to Christ", in the spirit of Christ, with the redeemed seeking always to progress in holiness, grace, and knowledge in this life.

To live a life of virtue, in forsaking all evil-doing, man had to render an absolute obedience to the Will of God by keeping his commandments inviolate; and that was possible, given man's nature, only for those who had the faith. "Purity of life" was inseparable from true faith because faith was the "animating principle which produces this conformity of the will and affections to the Will and law of God".

Good Works

Faith did not ensure that the Christian would be virtuous and engaged in good works, given the nature of temptation, and man's possession of a free will. Nonetheless, a life of virtue was inseparable from true faith for only the redeemed through God's grace had the power to persist in doing good works. In turn, a life of virtue was one marked by a progressive increase in "good works of practical holiness". The true Christian persisted in doing good works not for reasons of personal satisfaction or any pleasing consequences to be derived from it, but rather out of a sense of duty. God commanded man to do good and His Will must be obeyed, regardless of whatever its 'temporal effects' or the probability of success might be.

An increase in the progress of holiness through good works, accompanied by prayer, would invariably result in "the growth of grace in the heart". The pursuit of 'the good' required the assistance of God's grace, and the more good works that man pursued the greater would be the spirit of God in him. The growth of grace in man was regarded as analogous to that of a seed growing in a garden. The Christian did not know how grace would grow in his heart any more than the gardener knew how the seed grew in his garden, but it was equally necessary that they be cultivated. In both cases, although "human means may and ought to be employed, ... it [was] God alone that [gave] the increase".

Nonetheless, good works alone could not save man. They were the result of faith and a pure heart, rather than a prerequisite of justification. In the Christian scheme of redemption:

> the conversion of sinners ... consists of a rational conviction
> of our sin and a deep sense of danger -- of a heartfelt sorrow

at having offended God, with steadfast purpose of amendment under the influence of the Divine Spirit and the regular employment of all the means of Grace -- such a course [was] sure to be followed by resolute perseverance in well doing. (6)

To 'proceed unto perfection' involved not only the doing of good works, or acts of virtue, by the Christian, but also demanded that he strive to attain a progressive increase in religious knowledge. He must become more and more knowledgeable about "the whole scheme of the Gospel", but not so much in an intellectual sense as in a comprehension of the moral and divine nature of religion. The aim of Christianity, according to the Anglican clergy, was to bring about a restoration of the image of God in man, and to restore man "to the divine nature" through "the infinite enlargement of our nobler faculties", our moral and intellectual powers and capacities, and the freeing of man from "all low and sinful propensities".

An increase in religious knowledge would promote in turn -- and was inseparable from -- a progressive increase in "holiness of life" as the Christian, with the faith of his heart, "becomes better acquainted with the meaning and excellence of the Holiness of God". As he grows in love, the redeemed is better able:

> to form more adequate conceptions for the Divine Love, and thus his Faith becomes the Shining light which shineth more and more unto the perfect day. (7)

Imitation of Christ

In progressing toward perfection, the Christian had to be guided by his religion for man was incapable of improving his moral and intellectual powers in the absence of the direction of the Gospel. In seeking to advance in holiness, grace, and knowledge, it was to Christ that man must look. Christ provided both the means of improvement and the example to be emulated. On the one hand, the Christian must realize:

> that in whatever we do Christ should be in our thoughts for since it is through him alone that we have the power to do any good thing so unless we do it for his sake, it is not good. From Christ our obedience comes and towards him it must look – he

tells us without me ye can do nothing, and no work can be good without grace and love.

On the other hand, in seeking "to be perfect as God is perfect", the Christian must strive to imitate Christ who revealed the perfect character and behavior for man. Christ, as man, showed that man could live a holy and Godly life, could keep his passions and appetites under control, could faithfully discharge his duties, and could act benevolently towards his fellows "without counting the cost". Above all, Christ had shown "that human nature under the guidance and support of the Spirit of God is capable of a high degree of moral perfection". Thus, young Christians -- in both Church and school in Upper Canada -- were admonished, in 'going unto perfection', to:

> Never think that you have reached the pinnacle of wisdom, of virtue, or of piety. Set not limits to the good you perform, nor consider any degree of moral or intellectual improvement beyond your reach.

Young Christians should:

> add to their Faith, virtue; and to virtue, Knowledge, and to Knowledge, temperance, and to temperance, patience, and to patience, Godliness; and to Godliness, brotherly Kindness, and to Brotherly Kindness, Charity.

In doing so, they would experience an eternal "progressive felicity". (8)

God's Superintending Providence

In the great work of salvation, man was aided and guided by the doctrines and precepts of revealed religion, but he was also encouraged to discipline himself through knowledge of God's superintending Providence. Scriptures revealed that God's providence and moral government extended over all creation wherein he "directs all things by the rules of consummate wisdom and goodness". Benevolence and justice were its ruling principles, and God's Providence promoted, "the best interests of all living creatures" and their happiness in so far as they were capable of being so. God was continually shaping man's destiny and exercising his protection and guidance over both man and nature.

Everything that happened was of God, and in accordance with His Will.

> He cares for every one of us, everything which happens to us comes from Him, from whom nothing but good can come. He orders all, directs all, comprehends the present and the future, nothing can resist His Will or frustrate His designs, and He brings all things to the Glorious issue which He intended.

Man had to have faith in God's moral government, and in Christ into whose "care and providence" the whole system of creation was placed. God was the creator of order, and the whole order of nature was arranged to provide support for man's moral and spiritual being.

It was the spirit of God which had brought order and form out of what had been a shapeless void, and it was God's active Providence which kept the world from dissolving "into its primitive Chaos". If man were to prosper, and avoid death and destruction, he must accept the God-ordained order on trust, and contemplate God in forsaking all "schemes of happiness" which were not in keeping with what "God has formed for us". To aid man in that endeavour, and to keep his thoughts upon "the operations of God" in the face of "worldly seductions and delusions", Christian worship had been provided as well as the Scriptures. Moreover, man could trace -- in part -- the system of God's providence in nature and human events, and could learn the lessons that they taught.

An Evolving Grand Design

To know religious truth did not require a resort "to any profound inquiries or reasoning, or to any form of abstruse and mystical doctrine". It demanded only the 'opening of the heart' to faith and the eyes to God's work. The natural world provided strong evidence of the workings of the divine spirit in its constant and orderly motion, and its governing laws which bore "the impress of a steady and undeviating design". The all-prevailing harmony and regularity of motion, and the remarkable "adaption of means to the end", as seen everywhere, were such as to rule out mere chance as an explanation, and "proved beyond contradiction, the superintendence of the Deity". Everything, bespoke progress, a design being carried forward, whether seen in the order of the universe, the instinct governing the actions of 'lower animals', or the conscience of man: "the voice of truth in the hearts of all rational beings turning them into harmony with the intimations of God's law[s] which were externally made for them".

It was evident that the spirit of God enlivened and directed everything to His purpose in keeping with His grand design. All was in accordance with His Will for:

> if in the subordinate parts of creation, change and even seeming disorder, are introduced, this only shows us that there is no blind necessity at work, but that we are ever in the hands of a Being who can say to every appearance of chance and mutability, "Hitherto shalt thou come and no farther. (9)

The seeming disorders in "the subordinate parts of creation" were not a denial of God's absolute sovereignty over all that occurred, but rather were indicative of the fact that God's Providence permitted man the freedom to work out his own salvation on earth in keeping with the requirements of his nature. A situation existed where:

> the System of the world depends in a way unknown to us on God's Providence and on human agency. Every event, every cause of action has two faces or aspects -- in the one it is divine and perfect, and in the other it is marked with Sin and Imperfection because it belongs to man.

All of nature, both animate and inanimate acknowledged God, and acted in accordance with His Will "with unerring precision". Neither the stars, nor the seasons, sought to change their position or rotation, and even 'the brute creatures' were true to the instincts implanted in them. It was man "who alone knew God" and resisted God because of man's sinful nature which was inherited from the Fall. It was man who introduced disorder into the world where peace and harmony ought to reign. Man alone was insubordinate:

> He turns from God to that which is right in his own eyes -- he makes a law for himself -- he becomes selfish & therefore sinful.

Nonetheless, man possessed a conscience, and God in his mercy had provided the means whereby man could change his nature, if he would but have faith and accept Christ as his Saviour. In keeping with man's nature and the purpose of life, God set forth what constituted "the good", and gave man the power to pursue it. Moreover, the knowledge of God's Providence was intended to persuade man that his happiness depended on his faithfully serving God. This was as it had to be, for:

> Man cannot be happy 'til he becomes good, and goodness, according to the moral and intellectual constitution of the human mind, is not a thing to be produced in it by a direct act of power, but only by the influence of persuasion and by motives of reason. (10)

In the pursuit of happiness, man therefore was at liberty to enter into, or to reject, the convenant of God's grace, but was admonished that the workings of Providence were such that he would suffer ill consequences if he decided wrongly. Man had to be aware that:

> God who knows all things regulates his conduct towards the human race according to their actions and character. The good He must approve of and reward -- the bad He must discountenance and punish for He is holy and just and good and His holiness and justice and goodness require that He should render to every man according to his works.

For the Anglican clerics, the hand of God could be readily seen in directing the growth and movement of the universe. Given their belief in an active Providence, they maintained that if Christians, in their state of righteousness, did not seek to recover His true or original nature in 'going unto perfection' and in cultivating "all those graces & virtues which produce harmony & peace", that God's judgements would bring suffering and "temporal calamities" upon them, as was the case with unredeemed man.

This did not imply any defect of God's mercy, but rather was the result of man's "own wickedness, idolatry and disobedience" -- the inevitable consequence of any and all violations of God's moral law. Indeed, it was maintained that most of the miseries of this life could be avoided, and happiness attained, if it were not for man's corrupted nature, for:

> The Physical evils are few, partial & transitory: they pass away like a fleecy cloud ... & are forgotten. It is the passions of men which are continually overflowing, & dealing around them destruction & death. From their baleful influence, there is no escape since those who are able to regulate their own affections, are plunged into calamity by the rashness of others.

The Moral Governance of God over the Nation

The aim of Christianity and the workings of God's providence was not only to save souls, but to produce a Christian nation – "a holy nation, a peculiar people" -- for nations as well as individuals had, in effect, a moral personality and a religious character. Nations were subject to chastisement at God's hands -- either directly or indirectly -- for their moral degradation and irreligion. The history of the Jewish people, as well as that of other nations, exposed the pattern of God's judgment.

Whenever the Jews rejected God, became idolatrous, hypocritical and licentious, and trampled "on the rules of justice and social order", they immediately suffered for their sins. When vice flourished, disorder, destruction and conflict soon followed. Irreligion inevitably gave rise to factions which weakened the character of the people and sapped their "national energy". In such a state, they were easily defeated by their enemies, and were thereby punished for their transgressions.

The hand of God was not always clearly visible in passing events, but man could be sure His spirit was ever present and active, for:

> In His dealings with the children of Israel, God from the very first declared that every departure from the law and admission of Idolatry would be followed by temporal calamities.

Jewish history illuminated "the moral Governance of God" which superintended the course of every nation, and enabled man "to read passing events" and understand their cause and the purpose that they were accomplishing.

Viewed from "a religious point of view", temporal calamities served to instruct man in the workings of Providence, and thereby acted "to sustain Faith". The miseries that nations endured during times of economic depression were instrumental in recalling men to God, and in highlighting the essential role which Providence played "in the government of nations", for:

> When gliding pleasantly along the stream of prosperity, we forget our dependence upon God -- we feel no want, we experience no pain & we are little inclined to serious reflection, or moral improvement. What then is left to bring us back to the knowledge of ourselves. Scripture is indeed open, but our minds are too much dissipated to peruse them & we are not yet so much acquainted with our own imperfections as to believe that we stand in need of assistance. (11)

Long continued, prosperity invariably produced indifference to religion which brought deplorable political and social consequences. In prosperous times, Governors would come to place their trust in their own plans and wisdom in guiding the development of the nation and its resources; and the people, all too readily, would succumb to "a licentiousness, both of mind and of body". Inevitably, God would act to recall man and suddenly, despite "the guidance of fixed and scientific principles" of political economy, all production and enterprise would halt as man received a chastisement for his sins.

In such a manner, through the workings of Providence, man would suffer from adversity through which even "the most unthinking" were brought "to a serious consideration of the supreme and moral Ruler who governs the universe". Temporal rulers, in their new-found wisdom, were brought to realize that there was a government higher than their own; and that, in the rush for "improvements and changes", they must heed God's law if any permanent advance were to be achieved in the human condition.

Mercantile adventurers learned, from bitter experience, the difference between 'spirited enterprise' and 'rash speculation', and the people were reminded of the value of a religious-moral life:

that there is a severe and religious poverty, and simplicity, which
is preferable, amidst all its hardships, to the gross indulgence
of licentious habits, or even to an unchecked improvement in
intellect and knowledge, if these are unaccompanied with a
similar improvement in piety and moral government.

Indeed, national disasters invariably brought out whatever virtue
remained in man, and produced a deeper piety and gave rise to good
works and feelings of charity which outlasted the events which gave rise
to them.

God's moral law and governance covered all aspects of life; and, in
retrospect, it was clear that seemingly unexpected calamities were
"exactly according to the regular laws of providential arrangement".
Visitations of God's judgment were provoked by the irreligion,
presumptuousness, and the errors of selfish men who acted in ignorance
"of Divine wisdom, of Divine power, [and] of Divine law". (12)

Man, because of his misdeeds, did "merit and demand the chastisement
of Providence"; yet, the suffering that he experienced, when properly
understood, was beneficial and served a higher purpose. Even the
political upheavals of the French Revolution -- although destructive of
social order and domestic peace and productive of a great deal of misery
and irreligion -- had yielded great benefits. In retrospect, it was evident
that the disorders had provided lessons for both ruler and subject. France
and all the nations of Europe, as a result of the French Revolution and
the revolutionary wars, had undergone "a severe process of purification"
which attested to the continuing governance of God's Providence.

> Many of the most oppressive relations of society have been
> softened and removed. Forms of Government have been
> ameliorated -- the opinions and habits of nations have become
> more just -- prejudices weakened and a corrector knowledge
> diffused among the people & above all a deeper impression of
> the excellence of the Gospel and the inestimable benefits which
> it is certain to confer upon all who embrace it.

Moreover, the development of better communications between nations
had brought about "a more rapid diffusion of knowledge and information",

which would bring an amelioration of suffering or additional misery to nations depending on whether they heeded the lesson that had been taught and henceforth guided their conduct according to Christian principles. Ultimately, there was one certainty, that "all will at length be overruled for good by the moral Government of God".

Moral Good & Evil

The workings of Providence were such that "all things were directed for the advantage of the good", and even the presence of evil in the world and the afflictions which men suffered, were "necessary in this stage of [man's] being, to the very existence of moral good". God could have removed all suffering and evil from life,

> but where would have been the moral influence of such a dispensation on the thoughtless and wayward spirit of man? Would he not instantly have lived still more to himself, and his own thoughts, and his own ways, and still less to those of God, than he does at present, with so many fears and anxieties hanging over him, and so many chastisements at hand to recall him?

The existence of pain and disappointment was necessary to the enjoyment of success and pleasure. Evil was not an end in itself, but was employed by God to further his "benevolent designs" for:

> We must never forget that we live under a convenant of grace -- a convenant which offers pardon and forgiveness to the frailty of man, but that to produce these effects God assumes the character of a righteous ruler and equitable judge, and as men behold in the order of nature dispensations producing great sufferings as a means of public good, so is it ordained that every deviation from His moral laws is inseparably followed by the endurance of suffering in one form or another. (13)

The true Christian was aware of the need to obey God's law, and could trace the directing power of God in the actions of man. Viewing the career of despots, such as Napoleon Bonaparte, from a religious point of view, the true Christian could see God's providence at work as the conqueror, spurred on by pride and an insatiable ambition to ever greater conquests, eventually brought about his own defeat. God works in mysterious ways; and indeed,

> His mighty power is never more wonderfully displayed than in directing the passions of men, however wild or irregular, to the accomplishments of His judgments while they appear in the meantime entirely free, & to be only following the bent of their own inclinations.

Nonetheless, it was erroneous to presume that man could understand all the workings of God's Providence or witness "a complete display of His moral government in the present life". Man could see "the impartial goodness of God" in nature; that vice was "commonly ... the Instrument of its own punishment"; and that Providence was "continually producing happiness, and not misery". Scriptures assured man that:

> all things, even the most untoward, *work together for good to them that love God*; that is, to those who conform themselves to His Will, and are fervent in their imitation of His perfections.

That being said, it was the good as well as the wicked who shared in the suffering and pain of this world, and often the good suffered "the greater share for their means [were] not so great to escape as the wicked who stop at nothing". Such an outcome was out of keeping with all human conceptions of moral justice, and incomprehensible to all but the followers of Christ to whom all had been made known.

The Day of Judgement

Christ had not only redeemed man, but revealed that there was "a future state of retribution", a day of final judgment, when the dead, "both the righteous and the wicked", would be resurrected to be judged "according to their deserts". On that day, the wicked would be condemned to eternal misery, and the good, who had accepted Christ and "walked in his way", would receive everlasting life – "eternal felicity". The judgement day, as revealed by Christ, was:

> the fundamental law of God's moral Government by which the distribution of rewards and punishments are finally adjusted on the principles of justice and mercy.

Man was not intended to be completely happy in this life of trial, for true happiness was to be found only "beyond the grave". For man, the hope of resurrection to eternal life was of "the highest moral import" and, as explained by the Rt. Rev. John Strachan:

> The belief of this principle is indispensably necessary for our consolation and obedience. It is the animating principle of a holy life for it assures us that our good works are not only remembered but rewarded also. (14)

The Day of Judgment was the culmination of the Christian's life, when "those who [had] done their duty as men and Christians" in 'going unto perfection' would be freed from "gross desires and inclinations" and no longer be subject to their passions and appetites. On that day,

> our spirits ... shall then be made perfect, [and] will pass on still from one degree of perfection to another through the immensity of ages – and as they advance in improvement our Happiness will be continually increasing to all Eternity.

To enable man to attain everlasting life "in perfect Unison" with the mind of God, was the ultimate end which all the works of God and his governing Providence were intended to promote. The Christian revelation was provided by God to encourage fallen man to prepare himself for a future state of eternal happiness and perfection, to provide direction on how to do so, and to admonish him of the suffering and miseries, and ultimate damnation, which would be the lot of all who refused to obey God's Will. (15)

A Striving for Perfection

The Upper Canadian Tories believed, as expressed by the Anglican clergy, that "man was intended for rational happiness and progressive improvement"; and that God gave man the power -- once redeemed -- to work out his salvation in 'going unto perfection'. The power required was not of man, nor the direction. The power was under the control of the Holy Spirit, but since man possessed a free will -- "a co-operating will" -- he was able to choose whether to seek "what is good". Thus, he was accountable for his actions, and would receive his just deserts in this life, and ultimately on the Day of Judgment.

Man could not be perfect as God was perfect, but as a Christian he must strive to attain that perfection which consisted of "the more or less perfect agreement of [his] will with God's directing spirit". To achieve that unison required an effort of self-denial on the part of all professed Christians, for:

> The effect of power or grace bestows upon them no intrinsic merit. It is the faith and readiness with which they suffer themselves to be led which God accepts and counts as righteousness through a mediator.

And that mediator was Jesus Christ. (16)

In keeping with their religious beliefs pertaining to the corruption of human nature, the purpose of life, the nature of God's Providence, and His scheme of redemption for man, the Upper Canadian Tories were bound to extend the ministrations of the National Church – the established Church of England – throughout the Province of Upper Canada. Such an effort was essential to enable Upper Canadians to live a moral life in imitation of Christ and, ultimately, to attain salvation and achieve an everlasting life. Moreover, given the Tory belief in the crucial role of a National Church, in forming the moral and religious character of the nation, and the role of education in the formation of the mind and character of youth, it was requisite that a 'national' system of education be established in the Province of Upper Canada under the direction of the National Church.

———————

Notes

Part Four: The National Church

Part Four: Divider: Quotation: John Strachan, *A Sermon Preached at York, Upper Canada, Third of July 1825, on the Death of the Late Lord Bishop of Quebec* (Kingston, Macfarlane, 1826), as quoted in J.L.H. Henderson, *John Strachan, Documents and Opinions* (Toronto: McClelland & Stewart Ltd., 1969), 90.

Chapter Eight - The Concept of a National Church

1. *Christian Recorder*, February 1821, vol. II, Strachan, "The Episcopal Church in the United States and the Rt. Rev. Bishop Hobart's Charge", 415; PAO, Strachan Sermons, Box D, St. Luke 114: 23, "Compel to come in", 12 December 1847, 6-7, and Acts 2: 47, "The Church", 24 July 1842, 2. The Upper Canadian Anglican Tory stress on 'apostolic succession' though similar to that of the Tractarians of the Oxford Movement was not derived from that source. Strachan, and his students through him, were first exposed to the apostolic character of the Church of England much earlier in the writings of Dr. Hobart, the Episcopal Bishop of New York, whose works included six books (published 1804-1811) on the Episcopal Church. (See John Strachan, *A Letter to the Rev. Thomas Chalmers, D.D. Professor of Divinity at the University of Edinburgh, on the Life and Character of the Right Reverend Dr. Hobart, Bishop of New-York, North America* (New York: Swords, Stanford & Co., 1832), and A. N. Bethune, *Memoir of John Strachan*, 1870, 139, quoting from Strachan's work on Hobart.)

Initially, Strachan was attracted to the Oxford Movement, but with reservations as revealed in his correspondence. In a letter to the Rev. John Henry Newman, Strachan wrote: "I have found so much in accordance with my own heart and with my own principles in the tracts of the times"; and "in the tracts of the times I was delighted to discover the results at which I had slowly and laboriously arrived carried still further". (PAO, Strachan Papers, reel 3, Strachan to the Rev. J.H. Newman, 15 August 1839). Nonetheless, Archdeacon Strachan was not an adherent of the Oxford Movement. He pointed out elsewhere that "almost all that is valuable in the Oxford Tracts was time immemorial the doctrine of the Scotch Episcopalians or Non-Jurants". (John Strachan to James Strachan, 8 August 1844.) Moreover, Strachan considered himself to be "a true churchman, and neither high church nor evangelical". The quotations are from John Strachan to his brother, James Strachan, 8 August 1844, and from Strachan to William Tucker, 1853, as quoted in J.L.H. Henderson, ed., *John Strachan Documents and Opinions* (Toronto: McClelland and Stewart, 1970), 282, respectively.

It is puzzling that Strachan denied that he was 'high-church' which by definition encompassed Anglicans who emphasized 'ritual, priestly authority, the sacraments, and the historical continuity with Catholic Christianity' to which one might add a belief in the church-state alliance. With the possible exception of an emphasis on 'ritual', the Rev. Strachan subscribed to all the classic definitions of 'high-church' Anglicanism. However, he may have associated 'high church' with Anglicans who viewed the priesthood as a sacerdotal caste and dwelled on theological minutiae; whereas the emphasis of Strachan was on the moral tenets of the Christian religion and the saving of souls.

In fact, there was a major difference between Newman and Strachan in the conclusion drawn from the 'laying on of hands' in the consecration of the Anglican clergy. For Newman, apostolic succession led to a view of the Church clergy as a sacerdotal caste, with God's grace and salvation coming to man through the clergy preaching and administering the sacraments, which derived their validity from a personal apostolic succession of the clergy. (For a brief summary of Thomas Arnold's analysis of Oxford Movement and Newman's concept of apostolic succession, see Basil Willey, *Nineteenth Century Studies, Coleridge to Matthew Arnold* (New York: Columbia University Press, 1950, 1st ed. 1949), 60-63.)

Strachan differed in interpreting apostolic succession in a doctrinal sense. It was viewed as constituting a proof positive that the Church of England was the 'true religion', a branch of the Catholic Church, and therefore assured of God's guidance and aid in its mission, which was to inculcate Christian religious values into man as a social being as well as the saving souls. Religion for Strachan always carried a very heavy moral import, and he continually stressed the efficacy of religion as an ethical standard of conduct. In his view of Christianity and the Bible, there is much in common between Strachan and the religious writings of Samuel Taylor Coleridge (1772-1834). See: Willey, *Nineteenth Century Studies*, 39-58, Coleridge on 'Religion and Morality', 'The Interpretation of Scripture', and 'The Constitution of Church and State'.

2. *Christian Recorder*, February 1821, vol. II, Strachan "Bishop Hobart's Charge", 412; *The Church, Supplement*, 12 July 1844, Strachan, "A Charge"; Strachan, *A Charge Delivered to the Clergy of the Diocese of Toronto, at the Visitation, April 30, 1856* (Toronto: Henry Rowsell, 1856), 10; and PAO, Strachan Sermons, Box B, St. Matthew 20:23, "Sit on my right hand", 15 December 1856.

3. Strachan, "A Charge", *The Church, Supplement*, 12 July 1844; PAO, Strachan Sermons, Box C, Strachan "Charge" (rough draft), sheet 2, n.d. [1857]; and *The Church*, 17 May 1844, "The Roman Catholic Church not the Mother Church of

England; or, The Church of England, the Church originally planted in England" by Rev. T. B. Fuller, Rector of Thorold, Canada West. For the historical details of the Acts at the Reformation which brought about the rejection of papal supremacy, and how they were interpreted by Anglicans, see "On Private Judgment, no. III" signed S.D., *The Church*, 5 July 1844.

[The Roman Catholic Church believed in transubstantiation: that in the Eucharist (Holy Communion) the bread and wine transubstantiate into the physical and spiritual body and blood of Christ. Anglicans believed that the faithful in partaking of the bread and wine of the Eucharist, in remembrance of Christ's atonement for the sins of man, were receiving the spiritual body and blood of Christ.]

4. PAO, Strachan Sermons, Box B, St. Matthew 20:23, "Sit on my right hand", 15 December 1850; [Strachan], "Bishop Hobart's Charge", *Christian Recorder*, Vol. II, 412, February 1821; and A.N. Bethune, *Lectures, Expository and Practical, on the Liturgy of the Church of England* (Toronto; Henry Rowsell, 1862), 65.

[The Antinomians, who believed in 'justification by faith alone', did not see the need for any positive law, or external institutions to enforce obedience to the law. They believed that those who had 'the faith' would know right conduct and would be self-motivated to live a moral life and to obey God's law. Anglicans also believed in 'justification by faith alone', but held that good works flowed from faith and were the mark of the good Christian living a Christ-like life in 'progressing unto perfection'. Hence, good works could not be divorced from righteousness – the establishing of a relationship with God through Christ.]

5. *Kingston Chronicle*, 6 August 1831, [Rev. A. H. Burwell], "One of the People".

6. Strachan, *Church of the Redeemed, a Sermon preached the 5th October 1836* (Toronto: R. Stanton, 1836), 49; Strachan, *A Letter to the Rev. Thomas Chalmers*, 1832, 46; Strachan, "Address of the Archdeacon of York", *The Church*, 1 June 1839; Strachan, *Sermon on the death of the Lord bishop*, 1826, 15 & 17; Strachan, *A Letter to the Right Honorable Thomas Frankland Lewis, m.p.* (York: R. Stanton, 1830), 100; and PAO, Strachan Papers, reel 8, Strachan, "Religious Instruction", n.d., package 2, 3.

7. Rev. A.H. Bethune, *Thoughts upon the Lawfulness and Expediency of Church Establishments and Suggestions for the Appropriation of the Clergy Reserves in Upper Canada, as far as regards the Church of England: a Letter to C.A. Hagerman, Esq., M.P., Solicitor General of Upper Canada* (Cobourg:

R.D. Chatterton, Printer, 1836), 7-11; PAO, Strachan Papers, reel 8, Strachan, "Religious Instruction", n.d., package 2, 3; and Strachan, *Life and Character of Hobart*, 1832, 46.

[Constantine the Great (306-337 A.D.) introduced toleration for the Christian religion within the Roman Empire in 313 A.D., and subsequently became an adherent of Christianity. It was the Emperor Theodosius I, by the Edict of Thessalonica (380 A.D.), who established Christianity as the state religion of the Roman Empire.]

8. *Kingston Chronicle*, 6 August 1831, [Rev. A. H. Burwell], "One of the People"; and Strachan, *The Church of the Redeemed, A Sermon preached 5th Oct. 1836 to Clergy of the Established Church* (Toronto: R. Stanton, 1836).

9. Rev. A.N. Bethune, *Thoughts upon Church Establishments*, 1836, 6; and Strachan, *The Church of the Redeemed, A Sermon*, 1836, 51-52.

10. *Kingston Gazette*, 18 February 1812, Strachan, "Reckoner – No. 50"; and PAO, Strachan Sermons, Box B, vol. II, Corinthians 3:17, "Spirit of the Lord", 6 July 1821, 9-12.

11. *Kingston Chronicle*, 28 May 1831 and 23 July 1831, [Rev. A.H. Burwell], "One of the People"; Strachan, *Sermon on the death of the Lord Bishop*, 1826,16-17; Strachan, *A Letter to Frankland Lewis*,1830,12; *The Church*, 17 February 1838, (Bethune editorial).

12. Bethune, *Thoughts upon Church Establishments*, 1836, 12, quoting the Rev. William Wollaston, *The Religion of Nature Delineated* (1st. ed. 1722, 2nd ed., 1724). [Wollaston was a Church of England priest, school teacher, and scholar, whose book had a major influence on the promotion of Natural Religion in the 18th Century, and established the philosophical basis for British Deism. The Upper Canadian Tories were not deists, but their clergy were well-read in theological and philosophical works.]

13. Strachan, *The Church of the Redeemed*, 49-50; *Kingston Chronicle*, 30 April 1831, "Address of the Legislative Council"; Bethune, *Thoughts upon Church Establishments*, 1836, 6; and *The Church*, 17 February 1838, (Bethune editorial). The quotation is from *The Church of the Redeemed*, 49-50. [Those who doubt that there is a direct connection between the presence of Christian religious beliefs and the presence of a strong public morality, religious toleration, and civil rights in a state, need only to look at the numerous present-day failures to establish civil and religious liberty in non-Christian states. With but a few rare exceptions, only in countries where historically men were educated in the

Christian faith in reading the Bible, has civil and religious liberty and religious tolerance truly evolved and taken hold among the populace; although today that attainment is shrouded in an imposed Lockean-liberal rhetoric which ignores the historic Christian character of most of the free societies of the modern world.]

14. *The Church*, 23 June 1838 and 24 May 1844, (Bethune editorials); PAO, Strachan Papers, reel 8, "Religious Instruction", n.d., package 2, 6.

15. Bethune, *Thoughts upon Church Establishments*,1836, 12-13; and Port Hope, Ontario, Cartwright Family Papers (private collection), Strachan to James Cartwright,14 December 1803 and 12 March 1804.

16. Bethune, *Thoughts upon Church Establishments*, 1836, 13.

17. *The Church*, 7 June 1844, "The Monarch's Headship in the Relations of Church and State, Part II" derived from the Rev. A. Boyd, M.A., Curate of the Cathedral of Derry, *Episcopacy and Presbytery* (London: R.B. Seeley and W. Burnside, 1st ed., 1841). [The Boyd book was written in defence of the Church of England and its belief in Apostolic Succession. It was a response to attacks launched in print against the Church of England by several Presbyterian ministers in Northern Ireland. The Boyd publication underwent numerous editions during the 1840s.]

18. *The Church*, 7 June 1844, "The Monarch's Headship in the Relations of Church and State, Part II"; PAO, Strachan Papers, reel 8, "Religious Instruction", n.d., package 2, 6; and Strachan, *Charge Delivered to the Clergy of the Diocese of Toronto at the Primary Visitation, 9 September 1841* (Toronto: H & W Rowsell, 1841), 17.

19. PAO, Strachan Sermons, Box E, Psalm 68:19, "Blessed is the Lord", 25 September 1865, 3.

[The spiritual independence of the Church of England was also protected by the Coronation Oath of 1688 by which the king swore to uphold the rights and privileges of the Established Church, and to maintain the laws of God and the true principles of the Gospel. Moreover, the power of the estates of the realm in Parliament – inclusive of the Lords Spiritual – was judged to be sufficient to preclude the king encroaching upon the spiritual independence of the national Church.]

20. *The Church*, 22 May 1844, "Relations of the Church and State, The Monarch's Headship, Part I", derived from Boyd, *Episcopacy and Presbytery*.

21. *The Church*, 22 May 1844 and 7June 1844, "The Monarch's Headship". Part I & II. William MacVean, ("The Erastianism of John Strachan", *Canadian Journal of Theology*, vol. xiii, 1967, 189-204) discounts the contention that Strachan had Erastian intentions, and comments very generally upon the importance for Strachan of the rule of law in governing the relationship between Church and State. The title of this article is completely misleading and inappropriate, given its argument.

22. *The Church*, 7 June 1844, "The Monarch's Headship, Part II". The Royal Instructions to successive Governors of the Canadas show that the British government fully intended to exercise its right to nominate the Bishop of Quebec, and any future bishops should a new diocese be created. It was also so understood in Upper Canada. See, for example, PAO, Robinson Papers 1806-1812, J. B. Robinson copy of the 'Royal Instructions to Prevost', 22 October 1811, 30.

23. *The Church*, 5 July 1844, "On Private Judgment, no. III", signed S.D.

24. *The Church*, 19July 1844 and 2 August 1844, "On Private Judgment', no. IV and V", signed S.D.

25. *The Church*, 26 April 1844 (Bethune editorial); and *The Church*, 22 May 1844 and 7 June 1844, "The Monarch's Headship", Part I and II.

26. PAO, Strachan Sermons, Box C, "Charge" (rough draft), Sheet 3, n.d., 9-10. Bishop Strachan, as he expressed himself in this Charge, was indignant and alarmed over the Gorham case in England where the Judicial Committee of the Privy Council, with a majority of lay members, was allowed to rule on Church doctrine -- in this case the doctrine of Baptismal Regeneration. The Committee ruled in March 1850 that an Evangelical clergyman of the Church of England – the Rev. George Gorham – was free to adhere to any view he liked on infant baptism. Gorham did not believe in the Anglican doctrine that infants, thorough the receipt of God's grace in baptism, entered into the Church of Christ and were regenerated.

Strachan refused to acknowledge that a lay tribunal had any authority to decide upon church doctrine. He maintained that just as "the Crown can make no statute without Parliament, neither can it settle doctrines without Convocation". In England, fourteen prominent Anglican priests, including Archdeacon Henry Edward Manning, left the Church of England for the Roman Catholic Church over this instance of the interference of a temporal court in a matter of Anglican Church doctrine.

27. *Christian Recorder*, October 1820, vol. II, "On Religious Establishments", 284; and Strachan, *Letter to Frankland Lewis*, 1830, 103.

28. Strachan, *Letter to Frankland Lewis*, 1830, 107-109; and Bethune, *Thoughts upon Church Establishments*, 1836, 18-19. This argument, as set forth by Strachan and Bethune, was based largely on a treatise published by the Rev. Thomas Chalmers, Professor of Moral Philosophy at St. Andrew's University, Scotland, on the "Use and Abuse of Literary and Ecclesiastical Establishments" (1827). Strachan, who was a graduate of King's College, University of Aberdeen, corresponded with the Rev. Chalmers for many years. [Chalmers was the leader of the 'evangelical party' within the established Church of Scotland. He believed as well in the spiritual independence of the national church from encroachments by the state. At a later date, when the courts upheld an established right of large landholders to select the minister for their respective parishes, Chalmers, who championed a 'non-intrusion principle', led over 400 ministers out of the Kirk – in the great Disruption of May 1843 – to form the Free Church of Scotland. However, Chalmers continued to believe in the principle of a church establishment and its national benefits.]

29. Strachan, *Sermon on the death of the Lord Bishop*, 1826, 18; Strachan, *Letter to Frankland Lewis*, 1830, 109; *The Church*, 11 August 1838, 21 November 1840 & 8 May 1814 (Bethune editorials); and *The Church*, 21 November 1840, "Speech of Mr. Justice Hagerman Before the Upper Canada Clergy Society".

30. Bethune, *Thoughts upon Church Establishments*, 1836, 15; and *Christian Recorder*, October 1820, vol. II, "On Religious Establishments", 281. This argument was drawn largely from the Rev. William Paley, *The Principles of Moral and Political Philosophy*, (London, 1st ed.,1785), Book VI, Chapter 10, "Of Religious Establishments and of Toleration", and applied to the Upper Canadian situation by Bethune and Strachan.

31. Strachan, *Sermon on the death of the Lord Bishop*, 1826, 18; and *The Church*, 11 August 1828 (Bethune editorial).

32. Rev. A.N. Bethune, *Thoughts upon Church Establishments*, 1836, 15. As noted, the Upper Canadian Anglican clergy derived several of their arguments in favour of Church establishment from the works of the Rev. William Paley, an Anglican whig cleric in England. However, they could not, and did not, agree with his basing the necessity and value of religion upon its general utility. Otherwise, they agreed wholeheartedly with Paley that religion played an essential role in the moral sphere; and they were conscious of the utilitarian aspect of religion in society and the state. The Upper Canadian Anglican clergy, however, always remained acutely aware that the primary role of the Christian religion was the salvation of souls through the atonement of Christ and the bestowal of God's grace.

33. *The Church*, 21 November 1840, "Speech of Mr. Justice Hagerman before the Upper Canada Clergy Society."

34. *The Church*, 21 November 1840, (Bethune editorial). In characterizing the Church of England as the 'poor man's church", Bethune quoted with approval the views of Archibald Alison, whom he referred to as "the Christian historian of the French Revolution". However, in Upper Canada, the Church of England did not always live up to its ideal concept of itself as the 'Church of the poor man'. Bethune in an editorial (*The Church*, 27 March 1841) denounced the "vicious system" of pew-selling and pew-letting, which closed "many of our churches" to the poor. He sought to return to the ideal of "the Poor man's Church" by providing a free service in his church at least once every Sunday. [Archibald Alison, a Scots historian, was the author of a monumental conservative history of the French Revolution: viz. *History of Europe from the commencement of the French Revolution in 1789 to the restoration of the Bourbons in 1815* (10 volumes, 1833-1843).]

35. *The Church*, 21 November 1840 (Bethune editorial); and PAO, Robinson Papers, John Beverley Robinson Diaries, 6 January [1817], 19-21.

36. Bethune, *Thoughts upon Church Establishments*, 1836, 16; and *The Church*, 26 August 1837, "The Voluntary System". The Tory argument in this paragraph draws on the work of Isaac Taylor, a prolific English writer, philosopher, and member of the Church of England, who defended the principle of a Church establishment and condemned religious dissenters for joining with "the irreligious" in attacking the Church: viz. Anonymous [Isaac Taylor], *Spiritual Despotism, by the Author of Natural History of Enthusiasm* (New York: Leavitt, Lord & Co, 1835), see especially "Voluntary Principle", 45-47.

37. Bethune, *Thoughts upon Church Establishments*, 1836, 16; and Strachan, *Life and Character of Bishop Hobart*, 1832, 45.

38. *Christian Recorder*, October 1820, vol. II, "On Religious Establishments", 284; [Strachan], *Hypocrisy Detected: in a letter to the late firm of Haldane, Ewing and Co. with a Preface containing the narrative of Mr. James Reid, a missionary sent by these gentlemen to Upper Canada* (Aberdeen: J. Booth Jr., 1812), 113; *Kingston Gazette*, 21 April 1812, Strachan, "Reckoner No. 58"; and Strachan, *Life and Character of Bishop Hobart*, 1832, 45.

39. Strachan, *Letter to Frankland Lewis*, 1830, 103-101. In this work, Strachan quotes liberally from the writings of Dr. Chalmers. Attacks on the clergy were the common stock in trade of the French philosophes, or "modern Pagans", during the 18th Century, and of their English radical followers in the 19th

Century. See Peter Gay, *The Enlightenment: an Interpretation, The Rise of Modern Paganism* (New York: Vintage Books, 1966). [One of the factors in the perceived decline of respect for learned clerics was the spread of the 'spirit of capitalism' in Upper Canada and, in particular, the Lockean-liberal view that "money answers all things". Even Adam Smith, in setting forth his theory championing economic self-interest (*The Wealth of Nations*, 1776), recognized that the new liberal order would result in a decline in moral virtue and a denigration of education in favour of the practical man of action and of accumulated wealth.]

40. *Kingston Gazette*, 21 April 1812, [Strachan], "Reckoner - No. 58"; [Strachan], *Hypocrisy Detected*, 1812, 112; *Christian Recorder*, October 1820, vol. II, "On Religious Establishments", 281 & 283; Strachan, *Sermon on the death of the Lord Bishop*,1826, 17; and PAO, Strachan Papers, reel 8, "Religious Instruction", n.d. package 2.

41. *Christian Recorder*, October 1820, vol. II, "On Religious Establishments", 284; Strachan, *Church Fellowship: A Sermon preached September 5, 1832 at the Visitation of Lord Bishop of Quebec* (York: R. Stanton, 1832), 22; *Christian Recorder*, October 1820, vol. II, "On the Duties and Advantages of a Parish Priest" (From the *Monthly Magazine* of January 1811), 285-286; Bethune, *Memoir of the Right Reverend John Strachan*, 143; *Kingston Gazette*, 21 April 1812, [Strachan], "Reckoner – No. 58".

42. Strachan, *A Sermon on the Death of Rev. John Stuart, Preached at Kingston, 25th August 1811* (Kingston: Charles Kendal, 1811), 30; and *Christian Recorder*, October 1820, vol. II, "On the Duties and Advantages of a Parish Priest", 286; Strachan, *Letter to Frankland Lewis*, 1830, 110-111; and Strachan, *Life and Character of Bishop Hobart*, 1832, 34.

43. *The Church*, 12 December 1840 (Bethune Editorial); Strachan, *A Charge Delivered to the Clergy of Toronto*, 9 September 1841, 21; *The Church, Supplement*, 12 July 1844, Strachan "'Charge"; Bethune, *Memoir of the Right Reverend John Strachan*, quoting a speech by Strachan of 9 September 1841. The quotation is from Strachan, *A Charge*, 9 September 1841, 21.

44. Strachan, *A Charge delivered to the Clergy of Toronto*, 30 April 1856, 6; and *Kingston Chronicle*, 28 May 1831 & 18 June 1831, [Rev. A. H. Burwell], "One of the People".

45. Rev. John Strachan, D.D., *Sermon on the death of the Rev. John Stuart*, (Kingston: Charles Kendall, 1811), 24. Strachan held up Stuart, a Loyalist Anglican clergyman, as an example of the principles, exemplar character, and

conduct of a parish priest. Richard Cartwright was another example held up for his Loyalist pedigree and Christian character and conduct. Cartwright was studying for the Anglican ministry at the outbreak of the American Revolution, and sacrificed everything for his allegiance to the king. His studies were interrupted, and consequently he was not ordained into the Anglican priesthood. See Strachan, *A Sermon on the Death of the Honourable Richard Cartwright, Preached at Kingston, 3rd September 1815* (Montreal: W. Gray, 1816), 24-25.

46. Strachan, *Letter to Frankland Lewis*, 1830, 13-14; and PAO, Robinson Papers, 1823-37, J.B. Robinson to R. Wilmot Horton, 24 December 1828, 30-32. The Rev. John Strachan, and his former students, were thoroughly familiar with the contemporary histories of the American Revolution, and were acutely aware of the role played by dissenting ministers and sectarians in supporting the American rebellion. The Upper Canadian Tories did not have access to the manuscript of Peter Oliver, "The Origin & Progress of the American Rebellion to the Year 1775 in a Letter to a Friend", London, 11 March 1781. However, they held a similar view of the role of the dissenting ministers in actively supporting the American Revolutionaries.

For Peter Olivers's view of American Revolution, see: Adair, Douglas and John Schultz, eds., *Peter Oliver's Origin and Progress of the American Rebellion: a Tory View* (San Marino, California: Huntington Library, 1963), 41-42, wherein Oliver comments that the "dissenting clergy were strongly tinctured with Republicanism"; and that "the Clergy being dependent on the People for their daily bread, by having frequent intercourse with the People, imbibed their Principles". This argument was further buttressed by a footnote taken by Oliver from an even earlier article, dated 4 January 1772, which made the observation that "the Boston clergy have temporized against their own judgments, in compliance with the prejudices of their people".

47. Strachan, *The Church of the Redeemed, A Sermon*, 1836, 50.

48. Strachan, *Letter to Frankland Lewis*, 1830, 109-110.

49. *Christian Recorder*, October 1820, vol. II, "On Religious Establishments", 284; *The Church*, 26 August 1837, "The Voluntary System"; [Strachan], *Hypocrisy Detected*, 1812, 112; PAO, Strachan Papers, reel #8, "Religious Instruction", n.d., package 2; Strachan, *Letter to Frankland Lewis*, 1830,101.

50. *Kingston Chronicle*, [Rev. A. H. Burwell], "One of the People", 31 December 1831; and Spragge, ed., *Strachan Letter Book, 1812-1834*, Strachan to the Lord Bishop of Quebec, 18 March 1816, 104. Both quotations are from "One of the People".

51. Strachan, *Letter to Frankland Lewis*, 1830, 101.

52. *Kingston Chronicle*, 28 January 1832, [Rev. A.H. Burwell], "One of the people". This article includes a number of lengthy quotations from Edmund Burke, *Reflections on the Revolution in France* (1790).

53. PAO, Strachan Papers, reel 8, "Religious Instruction", n.d., package 2, 3-4; *Kingston Chronicle*, 31 December and 10 September 1831, [Rev. A.H. Burwell], "One of the People"; [Strachan], *Hypocrisy Detected*, 1812, 109; *Kingston Gazette*, 21 April 1812, "Reckoner - No. 58"; and *Christian Recorder*, October 1820, vol. II, "On Religious Establishments", 281. The quotations are from "One of the People", 10 September 1831; and *Hypocrisy Detected*, 109, respectively.

54. *Kingston Gazette*, 21 April 1812, "Reckoner - No. 58"; [Strachan], *Hypocrisy Detected*, 1812, 109-112; *Christian Recorder*, October 1820, vol. II, "On Religious Establishments", 281-284; Strachan, *Life and Character of Bishop Hobart*, 1832, 47. See also [John] Strachan, *A Visit to Upper Canada*, 1820, 126; and Strachan, *Letter to Frankland Lewis*, 1830, 100.

55. [Strachan], *Hypocrisy Detected*, 1812, 111-112; *Christian Recorder*, vol. II, October 1820, "On Religious Establishments", 284; PAO, Strachan Papers, reel 8, "Religious Instruction", n.d., package 2; and *Kingston Gazette*, 21 April 1812, [Strachan], "The Reckoner – No. 58". The same argument is presented almost verbatim in each of these sources. The quotation is from *Hypocrisy Detected*, 112.

56. *Kingston Gazette*, 21 April 1812, [Strachan], "Reckoner - No. 58"; [Strachan], *Hypocrisy Detected*, 1812, 109-110; and *Christian Recorder*, vol. II, October 1820, "On Religious Establishments", 281-82. The quotations are from *Hypocrisy Detected*, 109.

57. *Christian Recorder*, October 1820, vol. II, "On Religious Establishments", 282-283; *Kingston Gazette*, 21 April 1812, [Strachan], "The Reckoner No. 58"; [Strachan], *Hypocrisy Detected*, 1812, 110-111. The quotations are from "The Reckoner – No. 58, "On Religious Establishments", 282, and *Hypocrisy Detected*, 111, respectively.

58. PAO, Strachan Papers, reel 8, "Religious Instruction", n.d. package 2; and Bethune, *Thoughts upon Church Establishments*, 1836, 24-25 & 8-9; *Kingston Gazette*, 21 April 1812, [Strachan], "The Reckoner – No. 58". The quotation is from Bethune, *Thoughts upon Church Establishments*, 25.

Chapter Nine - The Need for a National Church

1. Metropolitan Toronto Central Library (MTCL), Strachan Papers, Strachan to Wilmot Horton, Undersecretary of State for the Colonies, 15 May 1827; Spragge, ed., *Strachan Letter Book*, 81, Strachan to Col. Harvey, May 1815, and xiv-xv, [Strachan], Report to the Colonial Office, 5 June 1824; Strachan, *An Appeal to the Friends of Religion and Literature in Behalf of the University of Upper Canada* (London: R. Gilbert, 1827), 20; Strachan, *Sermon on the death of the Lord Bishop of Quebec*, 3 July 1825; 25-29; J.G. Hodgins, ed., *Documentary History of Education*, vol. I, 220, Strachan, "Table of the Religious State of Upper Canada as it respects the Established Church", 1827; PAO, Hodgins Papers, "Report of the Select Committee To Which was referred the Petition of Bulkley Waters and Others, entitled The Petition of Christians of all Denominations in Upper Canada" (Chairman: M.S. Bidwell), March 1828, 110, reply of John Beverley Robinson to the report; Strachan, *Observations on a Bill for Uniting the Legislative Councils and Assemblies of the Provinces of Lower and Upper Canada in One Legislature* (London: W. Clowes, 1824), 29; and *The Church* (Bethune editorial), 3 March 1838. The quotations are from the reply of J.B. Robinson to Bidwell's report, March 1828, 110, and from Strachan's letter to Col. Harvey, May 1815, respectively.

The essence of Anglican Toryism as a political philosophy -- as espoused by the Rev. Strachan and his young Tories -- was the belief that there was an essential connection between the Christian religion and morality, social order, and the proper functioning of the British Constitution. At an earlier date, the English Tory, Lt. Governor John Graves Simcoe, shared that belief in the interdependence of church and state, and sought to strengthen the Church of England in Upper Canada. See Simcoe to Henry Dundas, Secretary of State, 6 November 1792, and Simcoe to the Archbishop of Canterbury, 30 December 1790, as quoted in Alan Wilson, *The Clergy Reserves of Upper Canada: A Canadian Mortmain* (Toronto: University of Toronto Press, 1968), 16-17.

Dr. John Rolph, in resisting the efforts of the Tories to strengthen the Established Church of England in Upper Canada, bespoke an attitude typical of 19th Century Lockean-liberals, and religious dissenters, who were proponents of a separation of church and state. He declared: "I do not think that attachment to the British Government can, or ought to, depend upon religious forms or creeds". (Bidwell Committee Report, March 1828, 11.)

2. Strachan, *Observations on the Provision for the Maintenance of a Protestant Clergy in the Provinces of Upper and Lower Canada* (London: R. Gilbert, 1827), 1-2; Strachan, *Observations on A Bill for Uniting*, 1824, 29; Spragge, ed. *SLB*, xiv, [Strachan], Report to the Colonial Office, 5 June 182; and Gladstone

Papers, vol. 272, fol. 59-62, Strachan to W.E. Gladstone, 22 January 1840, reprinted in E.R. Fairweather, "John Strachan on Church and State: Two letters to William Ewart Gladstone", *Canadian Journal of Theology*,1966, 284.

3. Robinson, "Letter to Earl Bathurst", 26 December 1824, 54; Hodgins, *DHE*, vol. I, 213, Strachan, Memorandum to Maitland, March 1826; MTCL, Strachan, *Canada Church Establishment, Letter to R.J. Wilmot Horton*, 16 May 1827, 1; Spragge, *SLB*, 92, Strachan, "Remarks to be sent to Sir George Murray", [spring 1815]; and Cruikshank, "J.B. Robinson", 202. The quotations are from Strachan, *Canada Church Establishment*, 1827, 1, and Strachan, "Remarks to be sent to Sir George Murray", 92, respectively.

The Upper Canadian Tories were not alone in regarding the American religious sects as an Americanizing influence hostile to the British government, and the established Church of England. With respect to the 'American Methodists', even some of their own adherents in Canada shared the same feelings about the views of their American ministers. In May 1812, a Montreal Methodist Society declared their dislike of American Methodist ministers in complaining that the latter were "in general bitter enemies to our good old King & Government .... Therefore, we are often stigmatized as a set of Jacobins, when in fact only our spiritual guides are so; but they being our head, we the body are supposed to be defiled and corrupted in the Sorbonian Bog of Democracy, which we abhor". (Quoted by G.S. French, *Parsons & Politics: The Role of the Wesleyan Methodists in Upper Canada and the Maritimes from 1780 to 1855* (Toronto: Ryerson Press, 1962), 70 & 71-73. See also *Parsons & Politics*, 84, note 116, P. Glassford to J. Taylor, 23 November 1820, who is quoted as commenting that: "The political sentiments of the American Preachers frequently slip out, Shewing their inveterate hatred of the British Government".

By the 48 Geo III. c.1, (1808), Tunkers, Quakers and Mennonites were exempted from military service upon providing proof of their religious connection, and paying a fine of twenty shillings. See J.S. Moir, ed., *Church and State in Canada 1627-1867: Basic Documents* (Toronto: McClelland and Stewart, 1967), 152-153.

4. Hodgins, ed., *DHE*, vol.1, 220, Strachan, "Table of the Religious State of Upper Canada as it respects the Established Church", 1827; and Strachan, *Sermon on the death of the Bishop of Quebec*, July 1825, 27-29. The quotations are from Strachan, "Table" 220, and the Strachan sermon, 29, respectively.

5. *Kingston Chronicle*, 10 September 1831, [Rev. A. H. Burwell], "One of the People"; and Strachan, *Sermon on the death of the Bishop of Quebec*, 3 July 1825, 16-17. The quotation is from "One of the People", 10 September 1831.

6. Strachan, *Sermon on the death of the Bishop of Quebec*, 3 July 1825, 1 & 12; Hodgins, ed., *DHE*, vol. I, 220, Strachan, "Table of the Religious State of Upper Canada"; Spragge, ed., *SLB,* 24-25, Strachan to Lord Teignmouth, 1 November 1812, and xiv, Strachan, "Report to the Colonial Office", 5 June 1824; *Christian Recorder*, vol. I, March 1819, 3-5, [Strachan], "History and Present State of religion in Upper Canada"; James Strachan [John Strachan], *A visit to the Province of Upper Canada in 1819* (Aberdeen: J. Chalmers, 1820) 35; PAO, Strachan Papers, Strachan to Dr. Brown, 27 October 1803; Sanderson, ed., *The Arthur Papers*, vol. I, 103-104, Strachan to Sir George Arthur, 2 May 1838; Strachan, "Religious State of Upper Canada", Appendix No. I, 37-41, in Strachan, *Provisions for the Maintenance of a Protestant Clergy*, 1827; *The Church*, 11 November 1837, Strachan, "Address to the Clergy of the Archeaconry of York", 13 September 1837. The quotations are from Strachan, *Sermon*, 12, and Strachan to Dr. Brown, 27 October 1803, respectively.

7. Spragge, ed., SLB, 2, Strachan to Lord Teignmouth, 1 November 1812; and *Christian Recorder*, vol. I, 3-5, March 1819, [Strachan], "History and Present State of Religion in Upper Canada".

8. *Christian Recorder*, I, 3-5, March 1819, [Strachan], "History and Present State of Religion"; and PAO, Strachan Papers, Strachan to Dr. Brown, 27 October 1803. The quotations are from Strachan to Brown, 27 October 1803, and "History and Present State of Religion", 5, respectively.

9. *Christian Recorder*, I, 3-5, March 1819, [Strachan], "History and Present State of Religion"; Strachan, *Sermon on the death of the Bishop of Quebec*, 1825, 18-19; *The Church*, (Bethune editorial), 8 May 1841; Hodgins, ed., *DHE*, I, 220, Strachan, "Table of the Religious State of Upper Canada", 1827. The quotations are from Strachan, *Sermon*, 19, and *The Church*, 8 May 1841, respectively.

10. Strachan, *Sermon on the death of the Bishop of Quebec*, 1825, 18; *The Church* (Bethune editorial), 8 May 1841; and *Christian Recorder*, I, 4, Strachan, "History and Present state of Religion". The Upper Canadian Tories did not regard the 18th Century as the 'Age of Reason', but rather held that moral philosophy had degenerated therein from the level it had attained under earlier thinkers – the Ancients and the Scholastics.

11. PAO, Cartwright Letterbook, IV, 345, "Memoir respecting the present State of the Episcopal Church in U.C. & the Means of its Amelioration submitted to his Honour Major General Brock", 26 February 1812; *Kingston Chronicle*, 23 July 1819, [Rev. A.H. Burwell], "One of the People"; Strachan, *Sermon on the death of the Bishop of Quebec*, 3 July 1825, 20; *Christian Recorder*, vol. II, 359, December 1820, "Bible Society of Upper Canada".

12. Strachan, *Sermon on the death of the death of the Bishop of Quebec*, 1825, 25-26; Hodgins, ed., DHE, I, 220, Strachan, "Table of the Religious State of Upper Canada", 1827; and Spragge, ed., *SLB*, 121, Strachan, "Questions put by the Bishop 9 July 1816 & their Answers".

13. *The Church*, (Bethune editorial), 3 March and 11 July 1840; PAO, J.B. Robinson Letterbook 1812-15, John Beverley Robinson, "Memorandum", n.d.; James [John] Strachan, *A Visit to Upper Canada*, 1820, 137; *U.C. Gazette*, "Provisional Parliament of U.C." quoting Christopher Hagerman speech of 15 February 1821, and a speech of Attorney-General Robinson, 8 & 15 February 1821; *Kingston Chronicle* (Macaulay editorial) 30 March 1821; *York Weekly Post*, "Provincial Parliament" (Hagerman speech) 22 February 1821; PAO, Strachan Papers, reel 6, John Macaulay to J.B. Robinson, 22 February 1850; Gladstone Papers, vol. 272, fol. 59-62, Strachan to W.E. Gladstone, 22 January 1840, reprinted in E.R. Fairweather, "John Strachan on Church and State: Two letters to William Ewart Gladstone", *Canadian Journal of Theology*, 1966, 284. The quotation is from Strachan to Gladstone, 22 January 1840.

14. "The Constitutional Act, 1791" reprinted in part in Moir, ed., *Church and State in Canada*, 108-110; *Christian Recorder*, vol. I, March 1819, "History and Present State of Religion in Upper Canada"; Strachan to W.F. Gladstone, 22 January 1840, in Fairweather, *CJT*, 284; Spragge, ed., *SLB*, 142, Strachan to the Lord Bishop of Quebec, 10 November1817; *The Church*, (Bethune editorial), 3 March 1338; PAO, Robinson Papers, 1806-1812, "Royal Instructions to Prevost", 22 October 1811, 26; A.H. Young, "The Church of England in Upper Canada 1791-1841", *Queen's Quarterly*, 1930, 163; Moir, ed., *Church and State*, editorial comment, 154, and 142-143, "An Act to confirm and make valid certain marriages heretofore contracted in the Country now comprised within the Province of Upper Canada, and to provide for the future Solemnization of Marriage within the same" (33 Geo IIII, c.5,1793), and 146-147, "An Act to extend the provisions of 33 Geo III,c.5" (38 Geo III, c. 4, 1798); and E.A. Cruikshank, ed., *The Simcoe Papers*, I, 236, Richard Cartwright to Simcoe, 12 October 1792.

Much has been written by Canadian historians pertaining to the question of whether or not the Church of England was established in Upper Canada. J.S. Moir (*Church and State in Canada*, 108,150 & 154) is of the opinion that the Church of England was established or at least enjoyed "a limited establishment"; and A. H. Young (*Queen's Quarterly*, 1930, 147-152), took the position that the Church of England was never legally established in Upper Canada, but that it was "endowed". According to Young, the British government had intended from the time of the Conquest of Canada to establish the Church of England but had not done so; yet the various colonial governors invariably referred to the Church of England as the Established Church. See also, Alan Wilson (*The Clergy Reserves*, 9-10 & 15) in quoting a speech of William Pitt, 12 May 1791.

The only common agreement among the various historians is that regardless of the intention of the British government to establish the Church of England in Upper Canada, little was done on behalf of the Church, either before or after the founding of Upper Canada in 1791. See Wilson, *The Clergy Reserves*, 10-12; Young, "The Church of England in Upper Canada", 149 & 154; and A. H. Young, "Lord Dorchester and the Church of England", *Canadian Historical Association Review*, 1926, 60-65.

15. PAO, Cartwright Letterbook, IV, 344, Richard Cartwright, "Memoir respecting the present State of the Episcopal Church in U.C. & the means of its Amelioration submitted to his Honour Major General Brock", 26 February 1812; Port Hope , Cartwright Papers (Private Collection), Strachan to James Cartwright, 25 January 1807; Cruikshank, ed., *Simcoe Papers*, I, 235-236, Richard Cartwright to Simcoe, 12 October 1792, and IV, 134, Simcoe to the Duke of Portland, 8 November 1795; and Moir, *Church and State*, 204-206, "Report of Archdeacon John Strachan on the establishment of the Upper Canadian Rectories", 12 October 1837.

16. Spragge, *SLB*, 138, Strachan to Lt. Governor Gore, 22 May 1817, & 104, 130, 142, Strachan to the Lord Bishop of Quebec, 16 March 1816, 17 May 1817 and 10 November 1817, & 148, Strachan to Rev. Sir, October 1817, & 194, Strachan to the Rev. George Mountain, 27 July 1819; *Kingston Chronicle*,12 February 1819, "For the Kingston Chronicle"; MTCL, Strachan Papers, Strachan to Bishop of Quebec, 12 May 1817; Wilson, *Clergy Reserves*, 58-59, & 61; Moir, *Church and State*,161; and McVean, "Erastianism of Strachan", 200.

17. George W. Spragge, "Dr. Strachan's Motives for Becoming a Legislative Councillor", *Canadian Historical Review*, xix, 1936, 397-398; Spragge, *SLB*, 81, Strachan to Col. Harvey, May 1815, & 108, Strachan to Lt. Col. Clifford, 25 April 1816, & 129, Strachan to Lord Bishop Mountain, 12 May 1817. The quotation is from Strachan to Col. Harvey, May 1815.

18. Spragge, *SLB*, 136, Strachan to Francis Gore, 22 May 1817, & 129, Strachan to the Lord Bishop, 12 May 1817; MTCL, Strachan Papers, Strachan to the Lord Bishop, 12 and 17 May 1817. The quotations are from Strachan to the Lord Bishop, 12 May 1817.

19. Spragge, *SLB*, 129-131, Strachan to the Lord Bishop, 12 May 1817 & 146, Strachan to Lt. Governor F. Gore, 15 November 1817, & 134, Strachan

to Hon. and Rev. A. Hamilton, 4 August 1817, & 156, Strachan to Hon. and Rev. Chas. Stewart, 16 February 1818; MTCL, Strachan Papers, Strachan to the Lord Bishop of Quebec, 6 July 1819, 13 December 1820 & 19 February 1821; and Spragge, "Strachan's Motives", CHR, 398. The Rev. John Strachan was appointed a regular member of the Executive Council on 25 July 1817, and was appointed to the Legislative Council on 10 July 1820 along with three Churchmen: Joseph Wells, Duncan Cameron and George Herkimer Markland. A Presbyterian Angus McIntosh of Sandwich, was also appointed in 1820, but never attended a session.

Thereafter, both the Executive Council and the Legislative Council continued to receive accretions to their number from among young professional men who were either former students of the Cornwall District Grammar School of the Rev. John Strachan, or were close friends or associates of Strachan and/or John Beverley Robinson. The transformations of the Executive and Legislative councils, and the commanding presence of the Rev. John Strachan, gave him a decisive influence over the conduct of both bodies until he resigned from the Executive Council in November 1835 and ceased to serve in the Legislative Council in February 1841. See F. H. Armstrong, *Handbook of Upper Canadian Chronology and Territorial Legislation* (London, Canada: Lawson Memorial Library, University of Western Ontario, 1967), 13-14, "Chronological List of Members of the Executive Council", & 13-14, "Chronological List of Members of the Legislative Council". For a list of the Cornwall Grammar School pupils, compiled in 1833, see A. N. Bethune, *Memoire of John Strachan*, 147-148.

20. *Christian Recorder*, I, 12, March 1819, "History and Present State of Religion in Upper Canada"; [John Strachan], *A Visit to Upper Canada*, 1820, 124-125; Spragge, *SLB*, 134, Strachan to Rev. A. Hamilton, 11 August 1817; and *Christian Recorder*, II, 358, December 1820, "Bible Society of Upper Canada" (Committee Report).

21. *Christian Recorder*, I, 10-12, March 1819, "History and Present State of Religion in Upper Canada"; Spragge, *SLB*, 200, Strachan, "Memorandum on the Religion of the Province", 18 January 1820, & 156, Strachan to Hon. and Rev. Chas. Stewart, 16 February 1818; [John Strachan], *A Visit to Upper Canada*, 1820, 123-124; *Christian Recorder*, II, 412-413, February 1821, "Episcopal Church in the United States"; and *The Church*, 25 November 1837, Strachan, "Address". The quotations are from Strachan to Rev. Chas. Stewart, 16 February 1816, and Strachan, "Address", 25 November 1837, respectively. [What the Rev. Strachan failed to foresee was that the pre-war American settlers -- who were gaining the right to vote after a residence of seven years in Canada -- would return a large number of representative to the House of Assembly in the 1820 election. The American members of the Assembly were primarily

members of evangelical sects who were proponents of the separation of church and state, and were opposed to the provincial government providing financial support for the clergy of the Church of England and/or for the education of Anglican clergy.]

22. *Christian Recorder*, II, 413, February 1821, "Episcopal Church in the United States"; and PAC, Strachan Papers, Extract on "Church Fellowship", 5 September 1832. [The reference for this quotation is missing from the extant draft of this chapter of the dissertation. The quotation is from one or other of the cited works of John Strachan.]

23. *Christian Recorder*, vol. II, 441, February 1821, "York Committee of the S.P.C.K." [Society for Promoting Christian Knowledge]. The policy of religious comprehension which Strachan implemented in the years following the War of 1812 did not originate with him. It represented a traditional Anglican attitude, and was a reflection of historical reality. Throughout the 18th Century, dissenting sects followed a recurring pattern of springing up, and then gradually declining and returning within the fold of the established Church of England. (See Robert Kelley, *The Transatlantic Persuasion: The Liberal-Democratic Mind in the Age of Gladstone* (New York: Alfred A. Knopf, 1969), 22, for the English Tory view of dissenters.)

With respect to the policy of religious comprehension on behalf of the Church of England in Upper Canada, the absence of ministers of other persuasions in the very early years strengthened this bias of mind among the Anglican Tories. For example, as early as 1784 the Rev. Dr. Stuart, the first Anglican minister in Upper Canada, gave his opinion that if the Church of England could place clergymen in the new settlements before other ministers were available, "many of the Catholics & Dissenters might be led to conform to the Established Church". See: Richard A. Preston, ed., *Kingston before the War of 1812* (Toronto: Champlain Society, 1959), xciii.

24. Spragge, *SLB*, 73, Strachan, "A Report of the State of Religion in Upper Canada", 1 March 1815, and 118, [Strachan], "Questions put by the Bishop, 9 July 1816 & their Answers"; PAO, Hodgins Papers, "Report of the Select Committee" [Bidwell Report], 14, March 1828, testimony of John Beverley Robinson; Strachan, *Letter to Frankland Lewis*, 1830, 105-106; [John Strachan], *A Visit to Upper Canada*, 1820, 125-126; Spragge, SLB,199, [Strachan], 'Memorandum on the Religion of the Province for the Lt. Governor', 18 January 1820.

25. Strachan, *Letter to Frankland Lewis*, 1830, 106; Spragge, *SLB*, 200, Strachan 'Memorandum on Religion', 18 January 1820 & xiv, R. Macleod to

Strachan, 7 October 1809; *Christian Recorder*, I, 5, March 1819, "History and Present State of Religion"; A.N. Bethune, *Memoire of the Right Reverend John Strachan, First Bishop of Toronto* (Toronto: Henry Rowsell, 1870), 2-3,9 & 16; and Strachan, *Poor Man's preservative against popery, on the character and genius of the Roman Catholic religion and sacraments* (Toronto: G.P. Bull, 1834), 34. The quotations are from *Poor Man's preservative*, 34, and Macleod to Strachan, 7 October 1809, respectively.

Anglican Toryism in Upper Canada, as evidenced in the writings of the Rev. John Strachan and the clerics whom he trained, maintained a very heavy emphasis upon morality, human reason, and the general Christian values and beliefs, as opposed to any dogmatic concern with theology *per se*. This was not to say, however, that they were indifferent to theology, far from it. Their religious beliefs and values were in keeping with "the rationalist Anglican tradition" which evolved from the work of the Anglican Divine, Richard Hooker (1554-1600) in his *Of the Lawes of Ecclesiatical Politie* (Eight volumes, 1593-1601), in which the traditional doctrines and beliefs of the Christian church were sustained. Among their contemporaries, the religious views of the Upper Canadian Tories had much in common with the mature religious writings of Samuel Taylor Coleridge (1772-1834) in England, and Thomas Arnold (1795-1842) of Rugby. (See, Basil Willey, *Nineteenth-Century Studies*, 39 -58 & 60-77.)

26. Strachan, *Letter to Frankland Lewis*,1830,106; Spragge, *SLB*, 200, Strachan, 'Memorandum on the Religion of the Province', 18 January 1820, and 75, [Strachan], 'Report on State of Religion', 1 March 1815, and 118, "Questions put by the Bishop, 9 July 1816, & their answers". The quotation is from Strachan, *Letter to Frankland Lewis*, 106.

The Anglican Tories were not alone in thinking that they shared "the same religious principles" with the Methodists in their emphasis on the moral essence of Christianity. The Rev. Egerton Ryerson held the same view. (See C.B. Sissons, ed., *Egerton Ryerson: His Life and Letters*, vol. I (Oxford: Oxford University Press, 1947), 23-29, and vol. II, 324; and the *Kingston Chronicle*, 7 January 1832). Methodism, which originated in the Church of England, was marked by a strong Christian moralism and viewed itself as adhering to "the common, fundamental principles of Christianity". The evangelical movement that became known as Methodism, was founded by the Rev. John Wesley (1703-1791), an Anglican priest. (For Wesley's definition of 'a Methodist', see G.S. French, *Parsons & Politics*, 14.) However, what Strachan ignored in his argument of the similarity of the religious beliefs of the Methodists with the Anglicans was the 'American Methodist' religious experience which differed from the English Wesleyan Methodists. The 'American Methodist' preachers were opposed to a church establishment, and were focused on preaching, instantaneous conversions, the emotional religious experience of 'camp meetings', the 'inner light', and a personal spiritual communication directly with God.

It was the English Wesleyan Methodists who had not "distinctly separated" from the Church of England; whereas the American Methodist Episcopal Church had separated from the British Wesleyan Conference in 1784 to establish a totally independent American church with a distinct Calvinist theology. In turn, the Methodists of Upper Canada separated from the American Genesee Conference in 1828 to form an independent Methodist Episcopal Church for Canada. By the 1840s, if not earlier, the Anglican clergy were much more astute in their analysis of evangelical sectarianism, and no longer viewed the 'American Methodists' and the other sects, who believed in instantaneous conversion, as sharing common Christian beliefs.

27. Spragge, *SLB*, 43-44, Strachan to Your Honor, 6 September 1813 & 199-200, 'Memorandum on Religion', 18 January 1820; PAO, Macaulay papers, reel 1, Strachan to John Macaulay, 20 August 1820 & 10 April 1820. The quote is from Strachan to Macaulay, 20 August 1820. The Anglican Tories continuously appealed to the English Wesleyan Methodists of Upper Canada to maintain their connection with the Established Church of the province. See, for example, the *Christian Recorder*, vol. II, December 1820, "Southey's Life of Wesley"; *The Church*, (Bethune editorial), 15 December 1843; and Strachan, *Church Fellowship, A Sermon preached Wednesday, September 5, 1832, at the Visitation of the Honorable and Right Rev. Charles James, Lord Bishop of Quebec* (York: R. Stanton, 1832, 24).

The Upper Canadian Anglican Tories felt a close kinship with the English Wesleyan Methodists and their adherents, but abhorred the itinerant "American Methodist" or "Yankee Methodist" preachers of the Methodist Episcopal Church who extended their preaching circuits into Upper Canada. In 1820, the Tories were chagrined to learn that the English Wesleyans had agreed to leave the Province of Upper Canada to the ministrations of the American Methodists. The Tories regarded the earlier Methodist dispute as a contest for power, and could see no religious object which could be promoted by the American Methodists refusing to relinquish the province to the Wesleyans. In the immediate postwar period, the Upper Canadian Tories had strong political reasons for objecting to the presence of American preachers in Upper Canada, regardless of the particular sect to which they belonged. (*Kingston Chronicle*, Macaulay editorial, 10 November 1820.) Only later would the Anglican clerics develop a critique of sectarianism on religious grounds.

28. *Christian Recorder*, I, March 1819, 12, "History and Present State of Religion", and II, February 1821, 42, "Religion in India"; Strachan, *Observations*

on a Bill for Uniting, 180; Strachan, *Letter to Frankland Lewis*, 1830, 106; Spragge, *SLB*, 144, Strachan to the Lord Bishop of Quebec, 10 November 1817, & 199-201, Strachan, 'Memorandum on Religion', 18 January 1820. The quotations are from the 'History and Present State of Religion', 12, and "Religion in India", 42, respectively. The second quotation, which pertains to an established Church maintaining its predominance, was intended to apply to the situation in India, but the reasoning also applied to Upper Canada. In the Canadian context, it proved to be a very prophetic statement.

The number of adherents of the Established Church in Upper Canada was not easily attainable in the absence of a census in the early period. In his early pronouncements, the Rev. John Strachan tended to include all of those who were not specifically members of other churches or the sects -- viz, those who had not actively rejected the national church by the action of joining the congregation of another religious community -- as being members (actual, or lapsed, or potential) of the Church of England. That practice, of course, placed Strachan at the centre of a storm of protest, which was provoked in 1827 by the publication of his Ecclesiastical Chart estimates of the number of adherents which the various denominations enjoyed in Upper Canada. The Methodists similarly counted anyone who attended a revival camp meeting in any community as one of their adherents.

29. PAO, Strachan Papers, Extract from *Church Fellowship*, 5 September 1832; *Christian Recorder*, I, March 1819, 12, "History and Present State of Religion", and II, February 1821, 441, "York Committee of S.P.C.K."; *The Church*, 12 July 1844, Strachan, "A Charge"; Strachan, *Letter to Frankland Lewis*, 1830, 106-107; and Spragge, *SLB*, 8, Strachan, "Life of Col. Bishoppe", December 1813. The quotations are from the Church Fellowship extract, 5 September 1832, and Strachan, "Life of Col. Bishoppe", December 1813, respectively.

30. S.F. Wise, "The Origins of Anti-Americanism in Canada" in D.W.L. Earl, ed., *The Family Compact: Aristocracy or Oligarchy?, Issues in Canadian History* (Toronto: Copp Clark, 1967), 143-145; S.F. Wise, "Upper Canada and the Conservative Tradition", *Profiles of a Province*, (Toronto: Ontario Historical Society, 1967), 25; Moir, *Church and State*, 162-163, "Memorial to Earl Bathurst from Members in Canada of the Church of Scotland, 12 November 1820"; Rev. John Burns, *True Patriotism, A Sermon preached in the Presbyterian Church, Stamford U.C., June 3, 1814, the day appointed for Provincial Thanksgiving* (Montreal: Habun Mower, 1814), 3-15; PAO, Macaulay Papers, reel 2, Rev. A.H. Burwell to John Macaulay, 1 September 1831; and PAO, Strachan Sermons, Box D, 16 December 1837, Hosea 6:5, "Thy Judgments", 7.

This paragraph draws heavily upon the insights of Professor Wise, but has been expanded upon in consulting the sermons of two Presbyterians ministers -- the

Rev. Burns and the Rev. Spark -- and the Anglican Tory sources cited. For a more detailed exposition of the moral and political values of the Church of Scotland, see the Rev. Alexander Spark, D.D., *The Connexion between the Civil and Religious State of Society, A Sermon, preached at the opening of the new Scotch Church, called St. Andrew's Church, on Friday, the 30th day of November 1810* (Quebec: John Neilson, 1811); and Spark, *A Sermon, preached in the Scotch Church in the City of Quebec, 21 April 1814, being the day appointed for a General Thanksgiving* (Quebec: John Neilson, 1814). [See Robert Lochiel Fraser, "Burns, John" and James H. Lambert, "Spark, Alexander", *Dictionary of Canadian Biography*, vols. VI & V, respectively.]

31. S.F. Wise, "The Origins of Anti-Americanism in Canada", 143-144; Wise, "Upper Canada and the Conservative Tradition", 25-28; Wise, "Tory Factionalism: Kingston Elections and Upper Canadian Politics, 1820-36", *Ontario History*, LVII, 1965, 205-225; R.A. Bowler, "Propaganda in Upper Canada" (MA thesis, 1964), 43-44; William MacVean, "Erastianism of Strachan", *CJT*, 1967, 202; Cruikshank, ed., *Correspondence of Simcoe*, I, Richard Cartwright to Simcoe, 12 October 1792, 235; and Spragge, *SLB*, 75, [Strachan], "Report on State of Religion", 1 March 1815. In discussing the conservative political tradition in Upper Canada, Professor Wise does not mention the Lutherans, which was perhaps because they were not very numerous, or consequently politically significant in Upper Canada. The Anglican Tories, however, regarded the Lutherans as sharing similar political, social, and religious principles, which was why Strachan believed they could be easily comprehended within the Church of England. The Wesleyan Methodists, as distinct from the 'American Methodists', were another religious community which would have supported what Professor Wise views as a conservative alliance.

32. Spragge, *SLB*, 7, Strachan, "Report on State of Religion", 1 March 1815; *Christian Recorder*, 1 March 1819, "History and Present State of Religion", 14-15; Young, "Church of England in Upper Canada", *Queen's Quarterly*, 156- 157; Spragge, ed., *SLB*, 200, Strachan, "Memorandum on Religion", 18 January 1820, & 144, Strachan to the Lord Bishop, 10 November 1817 & 13 December 1820; and PAC, Strachan Papers, 'Extract from a Sermon on Church Fellowship', 5 September 1832. Apparently, there was no expectation that the Church of Rome would secure converts in Upper Canada from among the Protestant churches and sects, or even from among the indifferent to religion. Consequently, the Rev. John Strachan was deeply shocked by the conversion of a prominent Anglican, John Elmsley, to Roman Catholicism. In response to that conversion, Strachan wrote: *The Poor Man's Preservative against Popery, Part I, Containing an Introduction on the Character and Genius of the Roman*

Catholic Religion, and the Substance of a Letter to the Congregation of St. Jame's Church, U.C., occasioned by the Hon. J. Elmsley's Publication of the Bishop of Strasbourg's Observations on the 6th Chapter of St. John's Gospel (Toronto: G.P. Bull, 1834).

[John Elmsley jr. (1801-1863) was the son of a former Chief Justice of Upper Canada. Upon the death of his father in 1805, the widow and her young children returned to England where John was educated in law. In 1825, Elmsley jr. returned to Upper Canada to manage the large landholdings acquired earlier by his father. As an educated gentleman and man of social prominence, he soon became a member of the Tory elite, and was appointed to the Executive Council in 1830 and the Legislative Council in 1831. In September 1831, he married a Roman Catholic and -- two years later -- converted to the Roman Catholic Church. See Henri Pilon, "Elmsley, John", *Dictionary of Canadian Biography*, vol. ix.]

33. PAO, Strachan Sermons, Box D, Hosea 6:5, "Thy Judgments", 16 December 1837, 7; *U.E. Loyalist*, 1 December 1827, "A Hater of Hypocrites"; PAO, Macaulay Papers, reel 2, Rev. A.H. Burwell to John Macaulay, 1 September 1831; PAC, Strachan Papers, "Extract on Church Fellowship', 5 September 1832; *The Church*, 24 May 1844, "Presbyterianism (From the Times)"; Spragge, SLB, 75, "Report on State of Religion", 1 March 1815; and *Christian Recorder*, 1, March 1819, "History and Present State of Religion", 14.

The Church of Scotland, which the Anglican Tories saw as having much in common with the Church of England -- with the exception of its congregational form of church government -- was not the Calvinistic church founded during the Reformation by the Rev. John Knox (1514-1572). During the 18th Century, with the restoration of lay patronage, the nobles and gentry were enabled to appoint moderate ministers to parishes, and by mid-century moderates had taken over the Scottish Kirk from the strict evangelical Calvinists. The moderates of the Church of Scotland placed a heavy stress upon rational religion, moral philosophy, and Christian ethics, rather than on theology, religious dogmas and enthusiasm. Hence during the early 19th Century, the Church of Scotland under the moderates had much in common with the Church of England.

Ultimately, the ongoing differences between the moderates and the evangelical Calvinists in the General Assembly of the Church of Scotland would lead to "the Disruption of 1843", when the evangelical ministers left the Kirk to establish the separate Free Church of Scotland. There was also another moderate church in Scotland, the Episcopal Church of Scotland. The father of John Strachan was a member, and John Strachan, as a youth, attended some services in the Episcopal Church of Scotland.

The Anglican Tories were well aware of the political philosophy of John Knox, and in particular his justification of rebellion. See: *The Church*, 5 July 1844, "The Principles of a Demagogue". Calvinism was notorious for its justification of a right of rebellion on the part of "inferior magistrates", if not by private persons. The English Civil War (1642-1651) and the Commonwealth experiences were ever present in the minds of the Upper Canadian Tories.

34. Strachan, *Church Fellowship*, 5 September 1832, 23; *The Church*, (Bethune editorial), 28 July 1843, and 12 July 1844; Strachan, "A Charge"; Strachan, *The Poor Man's Preservative against Popery*, 1834, i, viii-ix,13-14; Strachan, *A Charge Delivered to the Clergy of the Diocese of Toronto, at the Visitation, April 30, 1856* (Toronto: Henry Rowsell, 1856), 31; PAC, Rev. Adam Hood Burwell, *A Voice of Warning* (Kingston: U.C. Herald Office, 1835), 156-159; *The Church*, 6 September 1844, "The Papal Supremacy (From Dr. Hey's Lectures in Divinity)".

[The cited work was: Dr. John Hey, *Lectures in Divinity, delivered in the University of Cambridge from 1780 to 1795*, 1st. ed., 1796 (Cambridge J. Smith University Printer, 2nd ed., 1822)]. The Anglican Tories never attempted to hide their view of the Church of Rome from their Roman Catholic associates at any time, but they did not belabour the point. Only in response to a particular event, the conversion of John Elmsley in 1834, did Strachan dwell at any length upon Roman 'corruptions and superstitions': viz. *The Poor Man's Preservative against Popery*.

35. Strachan, *The Poor Man's Preservative against Popery*, i-ix & 53; and *Kingston Chronicle*, 23 July 1831, [A.H. Burwell], "One of the People"

36. *Kingston Chronicle*, 23 July 1831, "One of the People"; and *The Church*, 5 July 1844, "The Principles of the Demagogue (From Dryden's Postscript to Pere Mainbourg's History of the [Catholic] League)". See also, Rev. A.H. Burwell, *A Voice of Warning*, 1835, 151-152; and *The Church* (Bethune editorial), 12 July 1844. In 1831, the Rev. A.H. Burwell became concerned that 'the Jesuits' in the United States were spreading Roman Catholicism at an alarming rate. At that time, Burwell made clear his objections to Roman Catholic political theory, and its implications for a Protestant country. Likewise, *The Church* became concerned with the Catholic threat to Upper Canada in the 1840s. That later alarm was in response to the Union of the Canadas in 1841, the growing strength of Ultramontanism among the French Canadians of Canada East (Lower Canada), and the great influx of Irish Catholic immigrants during the Irish famine years of the mid-1840s.

For a summary of the political theory of the Italian Jesuit priest, Robert Bellarmine (1543-1621) -- concerning the right of the Pope to depose a heretical ruler and absolve his subjects of obedience – see Sabine, *A History of Political Theory*, 386- 391. On Bellarmine and the Jesuit theorists of the Catholic League in France, see J.W. Allen, *A History of Political Thought in the 16th Century* (London: Methuen, 1923), 343-353.

37. Strachan, *Discourse*, 1810, 24-26. The quotation is from page 26. The belief of the Upper Canadian Tories that, historically, there was a justification for the imposing of political disabilities on Roman Catholics in Great Britain in the late 17th Century was not as intolerant as it might appear. Even Whigs, such as John Locke in his *Letter Concerning Toleration* (1689), while advocating complete toleration for all religious sects and churches on the grounds of a separation of Church and State, made an exception of the 'Fifth Monarchy men' and the Roman Catholics. The grounds for refusing to extend full civil rights to Roman Catholics was the threat that they posed to civil government because of their foreign allegiance to the Pope, and the refusal of the Papacy to recognize the legitimacy of the Protestant monarchy of Britain.

More generally, Protestants were oppose to granting access to public offices and political power to Roman Catholics because of memories of the persecutions and burnings at the stake of the Protestant martyrs during the reign of the Roman Catholic monarch, "Bloody Mary" -- Queen Mary I (reigned 1553- 1558) -- as well as the conduct of the English Roman Catholics in supporting the royal absolutism practiced by the Catholic monarch, King James II, prior to his forced 'abdication' during the Glorious Revolution of 1688. Moreover, English Protestants were alarmed at the continuingly severe persecution of Protestants on the continent by the European Catholic powers with the encouragement of the Papacy. In England, Roman Catholic religious disabilities were removed during the late 18th century but, as of the early 19th Century, the opposition in Britain to a full political emancipation for Roman Catholics focused on the Irish problem. See Ursula Henriques, *Religious Toleration in England, 1787-1833* (Toronto: University of Toronto Press, 1961).

The statement by Strachan that the English Roman Catholics had disavowed the Pope's claim of possessing a right to depose 'heretic' sovereigns, to interfere in national politics, and to absolve Roman Catholics of their oaths of allegiance, in all probability was in reference to statements made much earlier in England by a Catholic Committee which submitted a "Protestation" (1788) to Prime Minister, William Pitt (the Younger) that affirmed their rejection of the various political powers claimed by the Papacy. (See: Henriques, *Religious Toleration*, 168).

[The Corporation Act of 1661 and the Test Acts of 1673 & 1678, in combination, required all civil and military office holders, members of a city government, a corporation, and of parliament, to swear the Oath of Allegiance, the Oath of Supremacy which recognized the King as the Supreme Head of the Church of England and an Oath of Passive Obedience, and to take communion in the Established Church of England, and to renounce transubstantiation. These Acts – referred to collectively as the Test Acts – effectively excluded Roman Catholics from public office, as well as religious dissenters. However, parliament passed an annual indemnity act, which enabled dissenters to hold public office until 1828 when the passage of the Sacramental Test Act (9 Geo. IV, c. 17) repealed the requirement of the Test and Corporation acts that office holders had to take communion in the Church of England. Roman Catholics in Britain continued to be excluded from public office by the other requirements of the 'Test Acts' until the passage of the Catholic Emancipation Act of 1829.]

38. Strachan, *Poor Man's Preservative against Popery*, 1834, 3; *The Church*, (Bethune editorial), 31 October 1840, and 5 July 1844, "The principles of the Demagogue"; Robinson, *Letter to Earl Bathurst*, 26 December 1824; [John] Strachan, *A Visit to Upper Canada*, 1819, 22-23. The quotations are from *The Church*, 31 October 1840, and Strachan, *A Visit to Upper Canada*, 22-23, respectively. The granting of religious toleration and civil rights to Roman Catholics within the Province of Quebec – by the Quebec Act of 1774 -- was intended to win the support of the French Roman Catholics for the Crown. When the Province of Quebec was divided into two provinces by the Constitutional Act of 1791, the Roman Catholic Highlanders in Glengarry County and the French Canadian Roman Catholics in the western part of the new Province of Upper Canada benefitted from that earlier legislation. [Online: Solon Law Archive, The Quebec Act, 1774 (14 Geo. III, c. 83, clauses IV, V, VI, VII & VIII.]

In the postwar period, the Anglican Tory view of the Roman Catholic Church in Upper Canada as being an ally in defending Christianity and the traditional social order against the forces of infidelity and anarchy was not unique. In Britain, following the onset of the French Revolution, Burkean conservatives saw Roman Catholicism as a counterpoise to the revolutionary threat emanating from France. However, in Britain -- in contrast to Upper Canada -- anti-Catholic prejudices were too deeply seated to permit that sentiment to predominate over the traditional antipathy felt by English Protestants towards the Papacy. Moreover, the Irish Roman Catholics possessed a deep-seated animosity towards the Crown, and the Church of England in Ireland.

[In Britain, it was the Duke of Wellington, as Prime Minister (Jan. 1828-Nov. 1830) and leader of the Tory party, who eventually took the lead in Parliament to secure the passage of the Catholic Emancipation Act of 1829 which removed all political disabilities in law from Roman Catholics in Britain. Wellington was acutely concerned about the political danger posed by enfranchising Catholic voters in Ireland where the Roman Catholic clergy were under the direction of a foreign power: the Papacy. Nonetheless, he secured the passage of the Catholic Emancipation Act in an effort to quell civil unrest in Ireland. See Karen A. Noyce, "The duke of Wellington and the Catholic question", in Norman Gash, ed., *Wellington: Studies in the Military and Political Career of the First Duke of Wellington* (Manchester: Manchester University Press, 1990), 139- 157.]

39. [This section has been inserted in the original dissertation text to broaden the historical context with the respect to the emergence of an open opposition to the church-state alliance in Upper Canada. See: "A Review of a Sermon, Preached by the Honourable and Reverend John Strachan, D.D. at York, Upper Canada, third of July 1825, on the Death of the late Lord Bishop of Quebec, by a METHODIST PREACHER", *The Colonial Advocate*, 11 May 1826. On the contrasting worldviews of Strachan and Ryerson, see William Westfall, *Two Worlds: The Protestant Culture of Nineteenth Century Ontario* (Kingston-Montreal: McGill-Queen's University Press, 1989), 20-49, and especially 24-27 for a broader analysis of Ryerson's attack on the Rev. Dr. Strachan. For some additional comment on the strident nature of Ryerson's style of argument, and his proclivity for seeking to totally demolish the position and character of anyone with whom he disagreed, see: R.D. Gidney, "Ryerson, Egerton", DCB, XI.

The two different religious worldviews in evidence were: the Anglican (Tory), with its emphasis on reason, tradition, and the principle of order and subordination; and the 'American Methodist', which was focused on religious feeling and emotion, revivalism, and the 'inner light' which reflected a direct and personal encounter of the individual with God. Methodist revivalism fostered both a tendency towards withdrawal into otherworldliness, as well as an affinity with political radicalism through a shared rejection of the existing hierarchical social order and the concept of an established church. (Westfall, *Two Worlds*, 38-45). Under the leadership of the Rev. Egerton Ryerson, the Upper Canadian American Methodists aligned themselves with the democratic radicals in attacking the church-state polity of Upper Canada.]

40. On the Alien Question, see Craig, *Upper Canada the Formative Years*, 114-123 & 188-189; and Patrick Bode, *Sir John Beverley Robinson, Bone and Sinew of the Compact* (Toronto: The Osgoode Society, 1984), 96-97 & 125-130.

41. Provincial Archives of Ontario (PAO), Strachan Sermons: Box A, 16 February 1866, Hebrews 12:1, "All Saints a Cloud of Witnesses", 1-53; and

Box D, 25 December 1838, Ephesians 1:10, "All things in Christ", 3, 7-8 & 12 December 1847, St. Luke 14:23, "Compel them to come in", 6-7 & 30 November 1853, Revelation 21:22, "The Lord Almighty and the Lamb", 13; and Box E, 7 June 1832, Psalm 127:1, "Except the Lord build the house, they labour in vain", 6-7; Strachan, *Sermon on the death of the Lord Bishop*, 1826, 31; and *The Church* (Bethune editorial), 1 December 1838. The quotations are from the sermons: "Compel them to come in", 12 December 1847, 6; *Sermon on the death of the Lord Bishop*, 1826, 31; and "The Lord God Almighty and the Lamb", 30 November 1853, 13; respectively.

42. PAO, Strachan Sermons: Box B, 10 January 1830, Isaiah 55:10-11, "Certainty of God's word", 6-9 & 12 December 1847, St. Luke 14:23, "Compel them to come in", 6-7; and *Kingston Gazette*, 22 January 1811, [John Strachan], "Reckoner - No.4". The quotation is from the Reckoner article.

Chapter Ten - The Rejection of Sectarianism

1. Strachan, *Letter to Frankland Lewis*, 1830, 100, quoting the English Whig, Charles James Fox (paraphrased here), on the connection between religious establishments and toleration; *Christian Recorder*, II, 283, "On Religious Establishments", October 1820; Strachan, *Charge to the Clergy of Toronto*, 1841, 121; Bethune, *Memoir of John Strachan*, 188, quoting with approval the charge to the clergy of Toronto of 9 September 1841; and Rev. A. H. Burwell, *Voice of Warning*, 1835, 10.

2. Strachan, *Life and Character of Bishop Hobart*, 1832, 46; Burwell, *Voice of Warning*, 1835,10; Strachan, *The Church of the Redeemed, A Sermon*, 1836,55; *The Church* (Bethune editorial), 12 July 1844; Strachan, *Letter to Frankland Lewis*, 1830, 101; PAO, Robinson Papers, 1806-1812, J.B. Robinson draft of the '[Royal] Instructions to Prevost', 22 October 1811. The quotation is from Strachan, *Life and Character of Bishop Hobart*, 1832, 46.

3. PAO, Strachan Sermons, Box D. St. Luke 14:23, "Compel to Come in", 12 December 1847, 6-7 &11, and Box E, St. Matthew 6:10, "Thy Kingdom Come", 24 June 1844, 10. The Rev. John Strachan, and his pupils through him, were first exposed to the apostolic character of the Church of England at an earlier date in the writings of the Rt. Rev. Dr. John Henry Hobart, Episcopal Bishop of New York (State), whose writings included six books (published 1804-1811) on the Episcopal Church. (See: Strachan, *A Letter to the Rev. Thomas Chalmers, D.D., Professor of Divinity at the University of Edinburgh, on the Life and Character of the Right Reverend Dr. Hobart, Bishop of New York, North America* (New York: Swords, Stanford & Co., 1832, and the Rev. A.N. Bethune, *Memoir of John Strachan* (1870), 139.)

As Strachan made clear somewhat later, he considered himself to be "a true churchman, and neither high church nor evangelical ...." (PAO, Strachan Letter Book 1853-4, 321, Strachan to William Tucker, 1853, as quoted in Henderson, ed., *John Strachan*, 282.) In sum, Strachan was a Churchman in the 'via media' tradition of the Anglican theologian, Richard Hooker. During the late 19th Century, there were three major movements within the Church of England: Anglo-Catholicism (High Church ritualism); Evangelicalism (Low Church); and Broad Church, the latter of which was associated with Thomas Arnold of Rugby and emphasized tolerance, liberality, and Christian unity within the Church. In Upper Canada, the Anglicanism of the Church of England clergy -- under the influence and teachings of Archdeacon Strachan -- contained elements of all three movements. (On Thomas Arnold and Newman, see Basil Willey, *Nineteenth Century Studies, Coleridge to Matthew Arnold* (New York: Columbia University Press, 1950, 51-101.)

In defending the church-state polity, apostolic succession, and the authority of the Church, Strachan partook of High Church Anglicanism; in his emphasis on justification by faith alone, his emphasis on preaching, Biblical revelation, the salvation of souls, and on evangelizing the province, he partook of the leading elements of Evangelical Anglicanism; and in his call for religious comprehension based on the spirit of Christianity, on reason, liberality and tolerance, and his strong emphasis on the moral element of the Christian religion, he partook of Broad-Church Anglicanism. Indeed, Strachan always stressed the efficacy of the Christian religion as an ethical standard for the conduct of man, and tended to judge whether an individual was truly a Christian or not by observing whether the conduct of the individual was consistent with that of a Christian.

4. PAO, Strachan Sermons, Box D, St. Luke 14:23, "Compel to Come in", 12 December 1847, 6.

5. PAO, Strachan Sermons, Box D. Acts 2:47, "The Church", 24 July 1842, 5, and Box A, Daniel 6:10, "A Sermon for the benefit of the Young", February 1865; and *Christian Recorder*, I, 141, "Corruptions of Human Nature", June 1819.

6. *Kingston Chronicle*, [Rev. A. H. Burwell] "One of the People", 31 December 1831; and The Church (Bethune editorial), 16 February 1844; and PAO, Strachan Sermons, Box E. St. Matthew 6:10, "Thy Kingdom come", June 1844, 9.

7. Strachan, *Church Fellowship*, (5 September) 1832, 18.

8. *The Church* (Bethune editorials), 15 May 1841, 20 October 1843, 29 December 1843, 5 January 1844 & 12 January 1844; and Strachan, *Life and Character of Bishop Hobart*, 1832, 14.

9. *The Church* (Bethune editorial), 29 December 1843.

10. *The Church* (Bethune editorial), 10 November 1843; PAO, Strachan Sermons, Box E, St. Matthew 6:10, "Thy Kingdom Come", 24 June 1844, 12; PAO, Macaulay Papers, reel 2, Rev. A. H. Burwell to John Macaulay, 3 September 1831.

11. *The Church* (Bethune editorial),15 May 1841; and *Christian Recorder*, I, 455, "On the Increase of the Christian Spirit", February 1820. The quotation is from the latter.

12. *Christian Recorder*, I, 455-456, "On the Increase of the Christian Spirit", February 1820.

13. *The Church* (Bethune editorial), 15 May 1841; and *Christian Recorder*, I, 456, "On the Increase of the Christian Spirit", February 1820. The Rev. A. N. Bethune, an Anglican clergyman, was the son of a Loyalist, a former student of the Rev. John Strachan at the Cornwall District Grammar School, and had studied for the priesthood under the direction of Strachan. Bethune acknowledged that in writing on Christian Unity, "we have been much aided in our inquiries and strengthened in our opinions by arguments and facts adduced by the authors of the 'Tracts for the Times' [1833-1841] and other kindred writers". However, Bethune added that these writings "were the work of individual Christians", had "no authoritative force", and were to be condemned "when they err".

The Upper Canadian Tories -- as Anglicans -- shared religious beliefs with the Tractarians of the High Church "Oxford Movement", but were not connected with that movement within the Anglican Church in England. [The word "Catholic" was used in the passage quoted in the sense of its true meaning: viz. "universal". The reference was to the 'one holy universal and apostolic church' of Christ, not to the Roman Catholic Church which the Tories viewed as but another branch -- somewhat corrupted -- of the universal church of Christ.]

14. PAO, Strachan Sermons, Box E, St. Matthew 20:16, "Many will be called, few chosen", 23 December 1804, 11-13. The quotation is from 11-12. Here Strachan appears to be referring to the various 'Restoration Movements' which were launched by some Protestant churches and sects, during the 19th century, in seeking to promote Christian unity.

15. *Christian Recorder*, II, 411, "Episcopal Church in the United States and the Rt. Rev. Hobart's Charge", February 1821; PAO, Strachan Sermons, Box C, St. Luke 8:15, "Keep the Word", 10 February 1828,1; *The Church*, "Authoritative Ministerial Teaching", 2 August 1844; Strachan, *Life and Character of Bishop*

Hobart, 1832, 15 & 35-37; [Strachan], *Hypocrisy Detected*, 1812, 74; *Christian Recorder*, II, 287, "On the Duties and Advantages of a Parish Priest", October 1820; and *Kingston Chronicle*, "One of the People", 6 August 1831 & 31 December 1831.

16. *The Church*, 31 May 1844 & 2 August 1844, "On Private Judgement", signed S.D., Parts I & III.

17. *The Church*, 21 June 1844, "On Private Judgement", Part II, signed S.D.; and *The Church*, 20 September 1844, "A Supplement to the Articles on Private Judgement", signed S.D. The quotations are from the articles of 20 September and 21 June, respectively.

18. The Church, 21 June & 2 August 1844, "On Private Judgement", Parts II & III; and The Church, 20 September 1844, "A Supplement to the Articles on Private Judgement". The quotations are from the article of 21 June 1844.

19. *The Church*, 5 July 1844, "On Private Judgement", Part III; and *The Church, Supplement*, 12 July 1844, Strachan, "A Charge to the Clergy of Toronto". The quotation is from the "Charge".

20. Strachan, *A Charge delivered to the Clergy of Toronto*, 9 September 1841, 17; PAC, Coventry Family Papers, vol. 13, "Reminiscences of John Strachan", n.d., 91; and *The Church, Supplement*, 12 July 1844, Strachan, "Charge to the Clergy of Toronto". The quotation is from the latter source.

21. *The Church, Supplement*, 12 July 1844, Strachan, "Charge to the Clergy of Toronto".

22. *The Church* (Bethune editorial), 20 June 1840; *The Church*, 23 February 1844, "The Apostolical Fathers", signed B; and Strachan, *A Charge delivered to the Clergy of Toronto on the 9th September 1841*, 16-17. The quotation is from the *Charge* of 1841.

23. *The Church, Supplement*, 12 July 1844, Strachan, "A Charge to the Clergy of Toronto".

24. *Kingston Chronicle*, 30 July 1831, "Assemblage at York", signed QPO. The view of human nature, which is expressed in this article, is that of the Whigs who were Lockean-liberals. However, the argument as to the importance of custom and habit in the preservation of social order was in accord with the view of the Tories. The Whigs were not the only admirers of John Locke. The Rev. John Strachan referred to Locke in passing as "the profound Locke". Strachan was in accord with many of Locke's views on education; but, definitely not in

accord with Locke's view of human nature and revealed religion, Locke's view of the ultimate purpose of education, or of Locke's man-centred worldview and emphasis on individualism and materialism.

25. *Kingston Chronicle*, 7 January 183[2], "Philosophical", signed 'One of the People'; PAO, Strachan Sermons, Box A, 10 January [1836], Isaiah 55: 10-11, "Certainty of God's Word", n.p. The quotations are from the "Philosophical" article by 'One of the People' [Rev. Adam Hood Burwell].

26. *The Church, Supplement*, 12 July 1844, Strachan, "A Charge to the Clergy of Toronto"; and PAO, Strachan Sermons, Box C, n.d., 181, "Charge" (draft), Sheet #2. Both quotations are from the *Charge* of 12 July 1844.

27. *The Church*, 12 July 1844, Strachan, "A Charge to the Clergy of Toronto".

28. *The Church*, 2 August 1844, "Authoritative ministerial Teaching"; and [Strachan], *Hypocrisy Detected*, 1812, 99. The quotations are from the article and the pamphlet, respectively.

29. *The Church*, 31 May 1844, "On Private Judgment", Part I.

30. [Strachan], *Hypocrisy Detected*, 1812, 86.

31. *The Church* (Bethune editorial), 31 March 1838; PAO, Strachan Sermons, Box A, 22 February 1860, 1st Thessalonians 5:6, "Let us not sleep", 9, and Box A, 26 September [1847?], Hebrews 6:1, "Advancement in Religious Knowledge", 24-29. The quotation is from the latter source, 26.

32. *The Church* (Bethune editorial), 31 March 1838; PAO, Strachan Sermons, Box B, 26 June 1806, 2nd Timothy 3:16, "Lecture 1", 5 & 7-8, and Box A, 26 September [1847?], Hebrews 6:1, "Advancement in Religious Knowledge", 29. The quotation is taken from the latter source.

33. PAO, Strachan Sermons, Box A, 22 February 1860, 1st Thessalonians 5:6, "Let us not sleep", 8; *Kingston Gazette*, 19 May 1812, [Strachan], "Reckoner - No. 62". The quotation is from the Reckoner article.

34. Rev. A. N. Bethune, *Lectures on the Liturgy*, 1862, 65; Strachan, *Sermon on the death of Cartwright*, 1815, 52-53; MTCL, Strachan Papers, J.L. Brown, Aberdeen, to John Strachan, 6 April 1820; Port Hope, Cartwright Family Papers (Private Collection), Strachan to James Cartwright, 11 June 1804; and PAO, Strachan Sermons, Box D, St. Matthew 19:17, "Importance of Commandments", 26. While teaching at the village of Kettle in Scotland, John Strachan came under the influence of the local minister, Dr. James Brown for a brief period prior to the departure of Brown in 1796 to take up an appointment

as the Chair of Natural Philosophy at the University of Glasgow; they continued to correspond thereafter. Brown held that the teaching of morality was "the grand object of our religion, to which all its doctrines and institutions ultimately converge". For Brown, as conveyed in his letter to Strachan, Christianity was a moral system within which "worth makes and marks the man" in his progress towards "the great end of our being -- a holy life".

35. *Kingston Chronicle*, 28 May 1831, [Burwell], "One of the People"; and Spragge, *Strachan Letter Book 1812-1834*, vii, Strachan to James Brown, 13 July 1806; and PAO, Strachan Sermons, Box A, 22 February 1860, 1st Thessalonians 5;6, "Let us not sleep", 7. The quotations are from the letter of 13 July 1806, and the article of 28 May 1831, respectively.

36. PAO, Strachan Sermons, Box A, 22 February 1860, 1st Thessalonians, 5:6, "Let us not sleep", 5-6; *Kingston Gazette*, 19 May 1812, [Strachan], "Reckoner - No. 62"; and *Kingston Chronicle*, 28 May 1831, "One of the People". The first quotation is from "One of the People", and the two following quotes are from the "Reckoner- No. 62", respectively.

37. *Kingston Gazette*, 3 March 1812, [Strachan], "Reckoner – No. 52"; [Strachan], *Hypocrisy Detected*, 1812, 83; PAO, Strachan Sermons, Box D, 12 December 1847, St. Luke 14:23, "Compel to Come in", 10; *Kingston Chronicle*, 28 May 1831, "One of the People". The quotations are from the Reckoner- No. 52 and the "One of the People" articles, respectively.

38. PAO, *Richard Cartwright Letter Book, 1809-1812*, (microfilm), IV, Richard Cartwright to John Strachan, 18 March 1809, 298; [Strachan], *Hypocrisy Detected*, 1812, 51-52 & 58; *Kingston Chronicle*, 7 January 1832, "Rev. Mr. Ryerson's Answer to Sir John Colborne's Reply to the Petition of the Episcopal Methodists (15 December 1831)"; and *The Church* (Bethune editorial), 3 October 1840.

39. [Strachan], *Hypocrisy Detected*, 1812, 83-84; *The Church*, 23 February 1844, "The Apostolical Fathers"; and *The Church* (Bethune editorial), 3 October 1844. The quotations are from the editorial of 3 October and the article of 23 February 1844, respectively.

40. *Christian Recorder*, II, 410- 411, "Bishop Hobart's Charge", February 1821; and PAO, Strachan Sermons, Box A, 10 August 1856, Romans 10:17, "Faith Cometh by Hearing", 13-27.

41. *Christian Recorder*, II, 411, "Bishop Hobart's Charge", February 1821; PAO, Strachan Sermons, Box E, 5 July 1840, 1st Corinthians 3:3, "Evils of Divisions",7, and Box A, 21 October 1832, Acts 4:13, "The Boldness of Peter

and John", 30. The quotation is from the "Charge" article.

42. *The Church*, (Bethune editorial), 12 January 1844; PAC, Coventry Family Papers, vol. 13, "Strachan Reminiscences", n.d., 92-93; *The Church*, 11 November 1837, Strachan, "Address to the Clergy of the Archdeaconry of York (13 September 1837)". The quotation is from *The Church*, 12 January 1844. For an Anglican view of 'the authorized English version of the Bible' see *The Church* (Bethune editorial), 3 May 1844.

43. *Kingston Gazette*, 16 July 1811, "Reckoner - No. 28"; PAO, Strachan Sermons, Box B, St. Luke 15:7, "Repentance", n.d, n.p., and Box A, Acts 4:13, "The Boldness of Peter and John", 21 October 1832, 48-49; and *The Church* (Bethune editorial), 20 February 1841. The quotation is from the "Reckoner - No. 28".

44. PAO, Strachan Sermons, Box A, 21 October 1832, Acts 4:13, "The Boldness of Peter and John", 1-10, 19-21, 29-32 & 41- 43.

45. PAO, Strachan Sermons: Box E, 26 November 1852, Hebrews 6:1, "Let us go unto Perfection", 1; Box E, 7 June 1832, Psalm 127:1, "Except the Lord build, labour is lost", 6-7; Box B, 26 June 1806, 2nd Timothy 3:16, "Lecture 1",10; and Box A, 21October 1832, Acts 4:13, "The Boldness of Peter and John", 32 & 43. See also [Strachan], *Hypocrisy Detected*, 1812, 84; and *The Church*, 8 July 1837, "Signs of the Times". The quotations are from the sermon of 21 October 1832, 32, and the "Signs of the Times" article, respectively.

46. Bethune, *Lectures on the Liturgy*, 1862, 5; and *The Church* (Bethune editorial), 20 February 1841. The quotation is from the Bethune editorial.

47. *The Church* (Bethune editorial), 20 February 1841; PAO, Strachan Sermons, Box B, 2nd Timothy 3:16, 26 June 1806, "Lecture 1", 1- 4, and Box E, 17 October 1847, Joshua 24:15, "Choose whom ye will serve", 10; PAC, Coventry Family Papers, vol. 13, "Reminiscences of John Strachan", n.d., 93-96; *The Church* (Bethune editorial), 29 March 1844; Strachan, *Sermon on the death of the Lord Bishop*, 1826, 13-14. For an excellent analysis of the evolution of Calvinism at the hands of American evangelicals see: Alan Heimert, *Religion and the American Mind, From the Great Awakening to the Revolution*, (Cambridge, Mass.: Harvard University Press, 1966).

[The Anglican Tory claim that the Church of England was free from "discordance in doctrine, precept or discipline" could no longer be put forth in such strong terms by the end of the period under study. By the mid-19th Century, a strong evangelical Protestant wing would emerge within the Church of England clergy in Canada West (Upper Canada). It was led by Irish immigrant Anglican priests, who were formerly part of the Anglo-Irish Protestant Church Ascendancy in Ireland. Nonetheless, the evangelical movement within the Church of England in Canada did not occasion a schism, or a disruption, such as was experienced by the Church of Scotland in 1843. (See: James J. Talman, "Cronyn, Benjamin", *DCB*, vol. X.)]

48. PAO, Strachan Sermons, Box E, 23 May 1835, 1st Corinthians 12:11, "One and the self-same spirit", 1; [Strachan], *Hypocrisy Detected*, 1812, xxxiv & 83; and *Kingston Chronicle,* "One of the People", 14 May & 18 June 1831. The quotation is from the 18 June 1831 article.

49. *The Church,* 15 December 1843. In this issue, the editor comments on and quotes from an article in the *Christian Guardian* newspaper of the Methodist Episcopal Church. The two quotations are from the original *Christian Guardian* article, with italics and capitalization added by the editor of *The Church*, the Rev. A. N. Bethune. The Anglican Tory clerics of Upper Canada were not the first to comment on the non-Christian nature of dissent. The Anglican divine, Richard Hooker (1554-1600) -- in the Preface to his multi-volume study, *Of the Lawes of Ecclesiastical Politie* – provided an analysis of Puritanism which parallels the Upper Canadian Tory analysis of the religious doctrine of the sectarians. Strachan possessed a complete edition of Hooker's works, which is now held by the Trinity College Library, University of Toronto. The Anglican clerics of Upper Canada were steeped also in the published works of the Anglican divines of the 18th Century.

For a superb analysis of the non-Christian "gnostic mentality" of Calvinism, from which many sectarians derived their doctrine, see Eric Voegelin, *The New Science of Politics*, (Chicago: University of Chicago Press, 1952), and, particularly, Chapter IV, "Gnosticism – The Nature of Modernity"; and Chapter V, "Gnostic Revolution – The Puritan Case", which contains his comments on Hooker's analysis of the same, 135-152.

[Historically, Gnosticism was a belief in self-divinization that appeared in the 2nd Century A.D. As a belief system, it was based on the "Gnostic Gospels", which were long lost and rediscovered only recently. The several Gnostic sects believed that the entire material world, including man, was corrupt, but some individuals had within them a 'divine spark' of God from the spiritual world of perfection, goodness and light. For man to achieve salvation, the 'divine spark', which was trapped in a corrupt body, needed to be awakened by a 'Light Messenger' to re-establish its connection with God, the source of Divine Light. It was a mystical experience of acquiring Gnosis, which was interpreted as knowledge of God – spiritual truth -- in a personal transcendent communion with God. Spiritual truth was not achieved through study and intellectual pursuits, but rather was received by the individual directly from God through a personal and immediate religious experience. Once freed from darkness, the soul of those who were saved would be re-united with the Supreme God at death, on the Day of Judgement.

The 'saved' saw themselves as living on a 'mystical higher plane of existence' in possessing a higher and deeper knowledge of God. They were viewed as being otherworldly in living for the spiritual world, and "being in the world, but not of the world". Morality was regarded as an inner integrity, which was born of the possession of 'the light'. Gnostics had no use for ethics, or for external rules of conduct which were regarded as purely of this corrupt world. Rules and conventions formulated by man were irrelevant to salvation, as were good works.

Some Gnostic sects, the so-called Christian Gnostics, saw Jesus Christ as the Life Messenger – a revealer or liberator -- who took on a human form to lead humanity to the light of God. He did so through conveying to man the living Word of God, which was captured in the Gospels of the Bible; yet Christ was not regarded as the Saviour of man. For the Gnostics, Christ was a pure spirit, and only appeared human to man. Hence, the physical suffering of Christ for the sins of man, and the Atonement had no meaning. Salvation was achieved not through the sacrifice of Christ and faith in Christ, but through a personal religious experience in gaining divine knowledge directly from God. (Source: Internet articles, "Gnosticism")]

50. PAO, Strachan Sermons, Box D, St. Luke 14:23, 12 December 1847, "Compel to Come in", 7-8, and Box E, 17 October 1847, Joshua 24:15, "Choose whom ye will serve", 10. The quotations are from the sermon of 12 December 1847, 8. [Prior to the early1840s, the Anglican clergy had refrained from directly attacking the religious beliefs of the sectarians. However, with the church-state alliance – which embodied Anglican beliefs – being under a constant attack by the Reformers and their sectarian supporters during the 1830s-early 1840s, the Anglican clergy began to retaliate in setting forth what they regarded as 'the unchristian nature of dissent'.]

51. PAO, Strachan sermons, Box E, 5 July 1840, 1st Corinthians 3:3, "Evil of Divisions",10-13, and Box D, 12 December 1847, St. Luke 14:23, "Compel to Come in", 7; and [Strachan], *Hypocrisy Detected*, 1812, 86. The quotations are from the sermon of 5 July 1840, 11 & 13, respectively.

52. [Strachan], *Hypocrisy Detected*, 1812, 59 & 71. The quotation is from page 71. Strachan, in commenting on sectarianism in this pamphlet, refers

specifically to the Haldanite sect in Scotland and the American Methodists. [The Haldanites had their origin in 1797 when the Haldane brothers, Robert and James, formed a society devoted to the propagation of the Gospel. The society soon separated from the Church of Scotland, and spread across Scotland where their tabernacles and meeting houses were open to all Christians who professed simply a belief in Christ. Their religion was based strictly on the evidence of Scripture and fellowship in Christ. All creeds and confessions, and clerical titles and vestments, were rejected. The Haldanites elected their church elders, and preached the Gospel, Christian charity, and forbearance. By 1840, if not earlier, the Haldanites were beginning to be absorbed by the Scottish Baptists with whom they shared many similar religious doctrines and beliefs. See *Evans's Sketch of the various Denominations of the Christian World, and of Atheism, Deism, Mahometanism, &c*, 18th edition (London: Longman & Co., 1841), 267-291, "The Haldanites".]

53. [Strachan], *Hypocrisy Detected*, 1812, xxxiv & 59-62; and *Kingston Chronicle*, "One of the People", 28 May 1831. The quotations are taken from *Hypocrisy Detected*, 62 and xxxiv, respectively. The source of the poetic couplet on 'religious democrats' has not been identified – perhaps Alexander Pope?

54. [William Westfall (*Two Worlds, The Protestant Culture of Nineteenth Century Ontario*, 1989), has pointed out that there were two different Protestant worldviews in conflict in early 19th Century Upper Canada that fostered a deep division on cultural issues: the evangelical Protestant worldview of the religious sects, and the traditional Christian worldview held by the Anglican Tories. By mid-century, the evangelicals – in becoming more respectable socially – began to adopt the traditional Christian worldview. For example, the 'American Methodists' came to reject the emotional religion of the camp meeting, and self-professed preachers with their emphasis on emotive preaching. The Methodists began to demand an educated and regularly-ordained clergy, to emphasize the role of the sacraments in salvation, and to build churches that rivalled the Anglican churches. Moreover, the evangelicals became less unworldly and inward looking. The Rev. Egerton Ryerson even recommended to Methodists a sermon by Bishop Strachan on the Christian duties of man.

Ironically, Bishop Strachan did live to witness the evangelicals being re-absorbed into the traditional Christian church, but it was not by joining the Church of England. It was through the evangelical sects in Upper Canada transforming themselves into traditional Christian churches, and adopting the traditional Christian worldview which was based on the Protestant Bible that was produced by the scholarly divines of the Church of England.]

Chapter Eleven - Human Nature and Christian Redemption

1. Provincial Archives of Ontario (PAO), Strachan Sermons: Box A,10 August 1856, Romans 10:17, "Faith Cometh by hearing", 27-32 ; and Box B, 8 July 1806, Lecture 3, "Belief in God", 1-2 & 2 October 1825, Jeremiah 6:16, "'Stand in the good way", 81 & 10 January 1830, Isaiah 55:10-11, "Certainty of God's Word", 3,7, 9-13 & 26 August 1816 , Lecture 10, "Forgiveness of Sins", n.p.; and Box D, 19 November 1847, Matthew 19:17, "Importance of the Commandments", 3-5, 12, 26 & 25 September 1852, Galatians 6:9, "Let us not be weary of well-doing", 2-3, 6 & 30 November 1853, Revelation 21:22, "God Almighty and the Lamb", 4-6, 11; and Box E, 13 October 1824, II Corinthians 13:5 "Examine Yourself", 8; and Port Hope, Cartwright Family Papers (private collection), Richard Cartwright to James Cartwright, 13 September 1803.

See also published sources: *Christian Recorder*, I, 136-137, June 1819, "Dissertations on the Christian Doctrines No. 4: The Corruption of Human Nature" & I, 283, October 1819, Strachan, "On Missions" & 294-295, "Chalmer's Sermons", & 297-298, "Divinity of Christ"; *The Church*, 6 February 1841, "Preventing Grace"; *Kingston Chronicle*, 6 August 1831, [Rev. A.H. Burwell], "One of the People"; and Strachan, *A Charge Delivered to the Clergy*, 1856, 5-6. The quotation is from the sermon, "Let us not be weary of well-doing", 25 September 1852, 2-3.

2. PAO, Strachan Sermons: Box A, (folder II), "Discourse VI", 344 & 25 December 1847, St. John 1:29, "The Lamb of God", 29 & 8 July 1806, Lecture 3, "Belief in God", 7 & 15 December 1850, Matthew 20:23, "Sit on my right hand", 2-3 & 8 April 1855, I John 3:16, "Love of God", 3-5; and Box C, 15 January 1809, Romans 6:5, "Resurrection", 6-9; and Box D, 19 November 1847, Matthew 19:17, "Importance of the Commandments", 5 & 30 November 1853, Revelation 21:22, "God Almighty and the Lamb", 5-6 & 25 December 1859, "All things in Christ", 3-6 & 26 December 1865, St. John 18:37, "Bear witness unto the truth", 30-33; and Box E, 4 January 1824, Colossians 3:11, "Christ is all in all", 4 & 22 October 1848, Romans 12:5, "One body in Christ", 5.

See also published sources: *Christian Recorder*, I, 131, June 1819, "Corruptions of Human Nature" & 173, July 1819, "Dissertations on Christian Doctrines No. 5" & 216-217, August 1819, "The Appointment of a Mediator No. 64" & 297-301, October 1819, "Divinity of Christ" & 468, February 1820, "Letters of Henry Kirk White to his Brother Neville"; and *Christian Recorder*, II, 126, June 1820, "Analysis of Four Sermons on Universal Redemption" &173, July 1820, "'A Discourse on the Religion of the Indians in North America, delivered, before the New York Historical Society, December 20, 1819 by Samuel Farmer Jarvis, D.D.". The quotations are from "Divinity of Christ", October 1819, 300, and "Analysis of Four Sermons on Universal Redemption", June 1820, 126, respectively.

3. PAO, Strachan Sermons: Box A, 10 August 1856, Romans 10:17, "Faith cometh by hearing", 27-33 & 25 December 1847, St. John 1:29, "The Lamb of God", 5-6; and Box B, 2 October 1825, Jeremiah 6:16, "Stand in the good way", 8; and Box C, 10 February 1828, St. Luke 8:15, "Keep the Word", 2 & 7 April 1839, St. Mark 12:26-27, "God of the dead & of the living", 3 & [1851], "Charge", Sheet 7, 26; and Box D, 28 March 1830, Isaiah 1:16, "Wash ye make ye clean", 1-7, 22-23, 33-34 & 26 December 1865, St. John 18:37, "Bear witness unto the truth", 25; and Box E, II Corinthians 13:5, "Examine Yourself", 7. See also a published sources: *Christian Recorder*, I, 219, August 1819, "Appointment of a Mediator" and 294-296, October 1819, "Chalmer's Sermons". The quotation is from the sermon on St. Luke 8:15, "Keep the Word", 10 February 1828, 2.

4. PAO, Strachan Sermons: Box A, February 1865, Daniel 6:10, "A Sermon for the benefit of the Young", 24-26 & 26 September 1867, Hebrews 6:1, "Advancement in Religious Knowledge Necessary", 2-5; and Box B, 28 March 1830, Isaiah 1:16, "Wash ye make ye clean", 4-14, 27-28 & 24 July 1842, Acts 2:47, "The Church", 2-5 & 17 February 1847, St. Luke 9:23, "Self-Denial", 22-24 & 19 November 1847, Matthew 19:17, "Importance of the Commandments", 3-4, 8, 12-13, 21-31, 34-35, 43; and Box E, 19 May 1839, Romans 8:14, "Led by the Spirit of God, they are the sons of God", 1 & 5 July 1840, I Corinthians 3:3, "Evil of Divisions", 7.

See also published sources: Strachan, *A Charge Delivered to the Clergy*, 1856, 5-6; *Christian Recorder*, I, 301, October 1819, "Divinity of Christ" & 468-469, February 1820, "Letters of Henry Kirk White". The quotation is taken from the sermon, Romans 8:14, "Led by the Spirit of God, they are the sons of God", 19 May 1839.

5. *Christian Recorder*, I, 468-469, February 1820, "Letters of Henry Kirk White"; PAO, Strachan Sermons: Box A, February 1865, Daniel 6:10, "'A Sermon for the benefit of the Young", 24-30, & 45-50 & 3 August 1806, I Corinthians 10:31, "Whatsoever ye do, do all to the glory of God", 1 & 26 September 1867, Hebrews 6:1, "Advancement in Religious Knowledge necessary", 1, 7-9; and Box B,, 2 October 1825, Jeremiah 6:16, "Stand in the good way", 9-11; and Box C, 6 January 1822, Colossians 1:10. "Wait worthy of the Lord", 8 & 10 February 1828, St. Luke 8:15, "Keep the Word", 1; and, Box D, 28 March 1830, Isaiah 1:16 "Wash ye, make ye clean", 14-18, 39-43 & 14 April 1839, Deuteronomy 7:22, "Little by little", 1 , 4 & 17 February 1847, St, Luke 9:23, "Self- Denial", 17-24 & 25 September 1852, Galatians 6:9, "Let us not be weary of well doing", 2-3, 6; and, Box E, 19 May 1839, Romans 8:14, "Led by the Spirit of God, they are the sons of God", 1; and Box B, 6 July 1821, II Corinthians 3:17, "Where the Spirit of the Lord is there is liberty",1; and PAO, Strachan Papers, MS 13, n.d., Strachan to Bethune, "Monthly Tracts on the Resurrection No. 1", 3-4. The quotations are from the sermons on "Do all to the glory of God", 3 August 1806, 1, and "Let us not be weary of well doing", 25 September 1852, respectively.

6. PAO, Strachan Sermons: Box A, 25 December 1847, St, John 1:29, "The Lamb of God", 18-20 & 26 September 1867, Hebrews 6:10, "Advancement in Religious Knowledge necessary", 1-2, 24-30, 55-56; and Box B, 26 August 1816, Lecture 10, "The Forgiveness of Sins", n.p.; and Box C, 6 January 1822, Colossians 1:10, "Walk worthy of the Lord", 7-8; Strachan, *The Life and Character of the Right Reverend Dr. Hobart*, 1832, 8; and *Christian Recorder*, I, 287-288, October 1819, "On Missions". The quotation is from the sermon "Advancement in Religious Knowledge necessary", 26 September 1867, 29-30. Man could not attain perfection in this life, but in once in a righteous state, he could 'progress unto perfection' in living a moral life in imitation of Christ.

7. PA0, Strachan Sermons: Box A, 10 August 1856, Romans 10:17, "Faith cometh by hearing", 39-40 & 26 September 1867, Hebrews 6:1, "Advancement in Religious Knowledge necessary", 24, 34-35, 38; and Box B, 30 March 1806, II Corinthians 4:3, "If Gospel hid", 8; and Box D, 30 November 1853, Revelation 21:22, "The Lord God Almighty and the Lamb", 6; and Box E, 2 May 1830, Hebrews 3:7, "Harden not your hearts", 8; and Strachan, *A Charge Delivered to the Clergy*, 1856, 25-26. The quotation is from the sermon "Faith cometh by hearing", 10 August 1856, 39-40,

8. PAO, Strachan Sermons: Box A, (folder I), Discourse I, John 1:17, "Constant agency of the Deity", 276 & 25 December 1847, St. John 1:29, "The Lamb of God", 17-20; and Box B, [1812], Ecclesiastics 41:3, "Fear not the sentence of death", 6 & n.d., St. Luke 15:7, "Repentance", n.p. & 6 July 1821, II Corinthians 3:17, "Where the Spirit of the Lord is there is liberty", 6 & 5 March 1851, I Corinthians 19:25, "Everyman that striveth for mastery", 2; and Box C, 21 February 1847, St. Luke 19:16, "Pound gained Ten", 4; and Box D, 2 May 1830, Hebrews 3:4. "Harden not your Hearts but hear", 1-2 & 17 February 1847, St. Luke 9:23, "'Self Denial", 40 & n.d., Matthew 21:9, "Cometh in the name of the Lord", 3 & 30 November 1853, Revelation 21:22, "The Lord God Almighty and the Lamb", 6; and Box B, 4 November 1855, Psalm 29:11, "Lord will give strength", 2-3; Strachan, *A Charge Delivered to the Clergy*, 1856, 24-26; and Strachan, *The Christian Religion Recommended in a Letter to his Pupils* (Montreal: Nahum Mower, 1807), 11-12. The quotations are taken from the sermon on "Self-Denial", 17 February 1847, 40-41, the published letter on *The Christian Religion*, 1807, 12, and the sermon "Lord Will give strength", 4 November 1855, 3, respectively.

9. PAO, Strachan Sermons: Box A, (folder I), Discourse I (printed), St. John l:17, "On the Constant Agency of the Deity", 271-281 & (folder II), Discourse VI (printed), St. John 3:16, "Love of God manifest in Christ", 344-345 & (folder I), Discourse II (printed), Genesis 18:25, "Judge of All" , 293- 294 & 10 January 1830, Isaiah 55:10 -11, "Certainty of God's Word", 2-4; and Box B, 26 August 1816, Lecture 10. "Forgiveness of Sins", n.p. & 2 October 1825, Jeremiah, 6:16, "Stand in the way of God", 10 & 20 March 1852, II Kings 4:26, "And she answered, it is well",

3 & 8 April 1855, I John 3:16, "Love of God", 2; and Box D, 30 November 1853, Revelation 21:22, "God Almighty and the Lamb", 13 & 26 December 1865, St. John 18:37, "Bear Witness to the Truth", 16, 20-23; and Box E, 19 May 1839, Romans 8:14, "Led by the Spirit of God, they are the sons of God", 1; *Christian Recorder*, I, 292-293, October 1819, Strachan, "Chalmer's Sermons"; and MTCL, Strachan, *Sermon of General Thanksgiving*, 1814, 6. The quotations are from the sermon "Bear witness to the Truth", 26 December 1865, 23 and Discourse I, "Constant Agency of the Deity", 274, respectively.

The printed discourses, which are undated, appear to have been removed from a book and inserted into the two folders. The content of the discourses is very similar to Strachan's article in the *Christian Recorder* on "Chalmers Sermons", which suggests that the discourses in the two folders were taken from a publication by Chalmers. The Scottish divine, Dr. Thomas Chalmers (1780-1847), was a minister of the Church of Scotland – the 'moderate' 18th Century Church -- and a professor of science and mathematics at the University of St. Andrew's, who underwent a conversion in 1810 when he embraced evangelicalism. Sometime after settling in Upper Canada, John Strachan began to correspond with the renowned Dr. Chalmers. It was Chalmers who subsequently led "the great disruption of 1843" that resulted in the founding of the breakaway Free Church of Scotland.

10. PAO, Strachan Sermons: Box A, (folder I), Discourse I, St. John 1:17, "Constant Agency of the Deity", 277 & Discourse II, Genesis 18:25, "Judge of All", 290-292 & (folder II), Discourse VI, St. John 3:16, "'Love of God manifest in Christ", 341-342; and Box B, 8 April 1855, I John 3:16, "Love of God", 2, 7; and Box E, 6 January 1848, Isaiah 60:3 "Brightness of the Rising", n.p. The quotations are from the sermons "Brightness of the Rising", 6 January 1848, n.p., "Love of God", 8 April 1855, 7, and Discourse VI, 341, respectively.

11. PAO, Strachan Sermons: Box A, (folder I), Discourse II, Genesis 18:25, "Judge of All", 294 & 10 January 1836, Isaiah 55:10-11, "Certainty of God's will", 7 & 8 April 1855, St. John 3:16, "Love of God", 2; and Box B, 6 July 1821, "Where the Spirit of the Lord is there is liberty", 3; and Box C, 16 March 1806, Hebrews 12:11, "Chastening yieldeth righteousness" 2-3; and Box D, 16 December 1837, Hosea 6:5, "Thy Judgements", 1-5; and Box E, 16 August 1836, Psalms 30:54, "Joy Cometh in the Morning", 2. The quotations are from the sermons 'Spirit of the Lord', 6 July 1821, 3, "Chastening yieldeth righteousness", 16 March 1806, 2, "Thy Judgements", 2, and "Chastening yieldeth righteousness", 3, respectively.

12. PAO, Strachan Sermons: Box A, (folder II), Discourse VI, St. John 3:16, "Love of God manifest in Christ", 379-390; and Box C, 16 March 1806, Hebrews 12:11, "Chastening yieldeth righteousness", 1, 3. The quotation is from Discourse VI, 380-381.

13. PAO, Strachan Sermons: Box A, (folder II), Discourse VI, St. John 3:16, "Love of God manifest in Christ", 343, 384; and Box D, 16 December 1837, Hosea 6:5, "Thy Judgments", 3-4; and Box E, 16 August 1836, Psalms 30:54, "Joy Cometh in the Morning", 1-2. The quotations are from the "Thy Judgements', 16 December 1837, 4, Discourse VI, 343, and "Joy Cometh in the Morning", 16 August 1836, 2, respectively.

14. PAO, Strachan Sermons: Box A, (folder I), Discourse I, St. John 1:17, "Constant Agency of the Deity", 278- 279 & Discourse II, Genesis 18:25,"Judge of All", 289-290, 295 & (folder II), Discourse VI, St. John 3:16, "Love of God manifest in Christ", 342 & 26 September 1867, Hebrews 6:1, "'Advancement in Religious Knowledge necessary", 9-11; and Box B, 30 March 1806, II Corinthians 4:3, "If the gospel hid", 2, 5-7, 11 & 26 August 1816, Lecture 10, "Forgiveness of Sins", n.p. & 15 December 1850, Matthew 20:23, "Sit on my right hand"; and Box C, 16 March 1806, Hebrews 12:11, "Chastening yieldeth righteousness", 2-3; and Box D, 25 December 1865, St. John 18:37, "Bear witness to the Truth", 30-39; Strachan, *Sermon for General Thanksgiving*, 1814, 3-6; and Spragge, ed., *SLB*, 65, Strachan to Richard Cartwright, 25 June 1814. The quotations are from "Chastening yieldeth righteousness', 16 March 1806, 3, Strachan, *Sermon for General Thanksgiving*, 1814, 6, "Sit on my right hand", 15 December 1850, 1, and "Advancement in Religious Knowledge necessary", 26 September 1867, 10-11, respectively.

15, PA0, Strachan Sermons: Box A, (folder II), Discourse I, "Constant Agency of the Deity", 275; and Box B, 26 August 1816, Lecture10, "Forgiveness of Sins", n.p. & 19 May 1839, Romans 8:14, "Led by the spirit of God, they are the sons of God", 1; Strachan, *The Christian Religion Recommended*, 1807, 32. The quotation is from "Forgiveness of Sins", 26 August 1816.

16. PAO, Strachan Sermons: Box B, 8 April 1855, I John 3:16, "Love of God", 1-2. The quotation is from page 2. Strachan rejected millenarianism in discounting the prospect of any divine intervention bringing about a change either in the Church, or in "the moral nature of man", to usher in an earthly millennium. He believed that the struggle against sin would continue for mortal man until the end of the world.

Part Five

Education & the National Character

"The peace and happiness of the community, the preservation of our institutions and of all that is valuable in society, depend upon the character of the people, and essentially upon their intelligence, there is no object of greater importance in Legislation, or possessing a more imperative claim upon the public revenue, than the establishment of Public Schools, which must ever be the basis upon which the peace, good order, and prosperity of society are to rest."

Archdeacon John Strachan
President, General Board of Education
February 1829

"The Home District Grammar School (1816-1829)". *Robertson's Landmarks of Toronto*, 1894. Toronto Reference Library.

Chapter Twelve

A National System of Education

In their efforts to preserve and strengthen the British national character of Upper Canada, and thereby resist the inroads into the province of infidelity and American democratic levelling principles, the Tories did not overlook the importance of education. A vital part of their National Policy, and indeed a crucial element in their plans for extending the National Church, was the establishment of a national system of education under the direction of the Church of England clergy. At the close of the War of 1812, the Tories were very conscious of the fact that they were engaged in combatting the spread of ideas which threatened to destroy "the moral fabric of society". It was 'a battle for the mind of man', which could be won only through the establishment of a proper system of moral and religious instruction in a provincial system of education.

A critical National Concern

As part of their national policy, the leading Upper Canadian Tories, among whom the Rev. John Strachan was the most pre-eminent, called upon the provincial government to establish a general system of education for the entire province. What they envisaged was the provision of three levels of schooling: a common (elementary) school system; an extension of the existing eight District (secondary) Schools; and the founding of a university to which the entire youth of Upper Canada, of all religious denominations, would have access. It was believed that the 'true prosperity' of the province, as well as the very survival of civilization, depended upon the inculcation of proper habits and opinion in youth; and that if the traditional Christian order of society were to be maintained and the social order preserved, a general system of education was desperately needed in the immediate postwar period. In the projected system of education, the National Church was to play a major role. (1)

The education of youth was a matter of national concern, and of great importance from a political point of view, because of the Tory belief that:

> it is only by a well instructed population, that we can expect to
> preserve our excellent Constitution, and our connection with

the British empire, or give that respectability to the country, which arises from an intelligent Magistracy, and from public situations filled with men of ability and information.

In such unsettled times, such as the Tories were experiencing following the period of revolutionary upheavals in the former American colonies, and in France and much of western Europe, it was believed that if "true and rational freedom" were to survive, the youth of Upper Canada must be provided with a proper education. They had to be made aware of the perfections of the British constitution – "the best practical form of government" -- as well as be inspired with patriotic feelings. Once conscious of the merits of their own institutions, they would then be able to hold their own in argument, or in arms, against both "the friends of despotism... and of democratical tyranny".

Within that context, District Grammar Schools, and especially a university, were viewed as vehicles for bringing together "the promising youth" of the province and "the sons of the most salient families". The intention was that the young men of Upper Canada would become united in friendship and interest, and "acquire similar, views and modes of thinking".

In being united in "respectability and thought", and increasing continuously in numbers, such a group of young men -- upon taking up positions among the learned professions, on the bench, and in the Legislature -- would prove capable of influencing the conduct of government, as well as the development of the national character of the province. Public offices would be filled with men of "greater intelligence and more confirmed principles of loyalty" than had hitherto been the case. Moreover, such men would be capable of quietly checking any leaning towards the United States on the part of "any portion" of the population, and would be able to "overmatch any tendency to disaffection that might appear".

Once such a general system of education was established, it would be only a matter of time until the influence and example of the graduates of the school system would impart a strong 'British feeling', or tone to the manners and opinions of the inhabitants of this province: when their just partiality for our mother-country, their love for our gracious sovereign, and their veneration for our laws and institutions, together with the sound moral and religious principles which they have imbibed, shall spread and take deep root in the country, till the warmest patriotism, and the purest piety, adorn the banks of the impetuous St. Lawrence.

The establishment of a general system of education -- culminating in a university -- was thus regarded as a very important 'national' concern. Both the loyalty of the population, and the very "peace, good order, and prosperity" of the province, depended upon "the character of the people", which was to be formed in large part through education. (2)

An American Cultural Threat

Education could not be neglected if a province having a British national character were to survive in North America. To the Tory mind, it was obvious that if British feelings were not inculcated in the minds of the young, they would eventually acquire American values and principles. Thus, a university was regarded as being of a critical value in preventing such an occurrence because:

it would establish by degrees a line of discrimination between the Canadians and the United States founded upon different manners and modes of thinking which could not easily be done away.

In sum, the projected provincial school system was counted upon to instill a British national character in the youth of the province, and the university was to form the character and values of the future leaders of public opinion in the province to preclude them succumbing to American democratic republicanism.

Upper Canada, because of its geographical position, was particularly vulnerable to the influence of American ideas and, within five years of the War of 1812, it was obvious that American publications and polemics were having a strong impact upon the public mind of Upper Canada. The province was becoming more and more Americanized with each passing year, and very little was being done by the provincial government to inoculate Upper Canadians against that contagion. For the Tories, such a deplorable development was partly due to the lack of a university in Upper Canada. In the absence of a Canadian institution of higher learning capable of providing "a liberal education", the youth of Upper Canada had to resort to Britain or the United States for the completion of their education. Moreover, as few could afford the expense of going to England or Scotland to attend university, many were finding their way into American schools.

Both "reason and policy" dictated against permitting such a situation to continue. Where the youth of Upper Canada were concerned, an American education was objectionable on moral and religious grounds, as well as political interest. In the United States, in contrast to every other country, morals and religion did not form the basis of the education system. In that country, "the domestic, the social, and religious virtues" were not taught, or given the pre-eminence they deserved, in the education system. Consequently, American schools were totally lacking in discipline and order. Moreover, it was noted that:

> politics pervades the whole system of education: the school books from the very first elements are stuffed with praises for their own institutions and breathe hatred to everything English.

It was maintained that American schools strove to impress upon youthful minds "a hatred" of King George III by "calumniating his memory", and declaring him to be "a sanguinary oppressor" and "a tyrant". To the Tories, it appeared that young men who went to the United States from Upper Canada for their schooling would "learn nothing but anarchy in Politics and infidelity in religion". Invariably, upon their return they were found to have disappointed the better hopes of their family and friends.

Thus, for the Tories, there was a real danger in the youth of Upper Canada being educated in the United States.

> To such a country our youth may go strongly attached to their native land and to all its establishments, but, by hearing them continually deprecated, and those of America praised, these

attachments will, in many, be gradually weakened, and some may become fascinated by a liberty which has degenerated into licentiousness, and imbibe, perhaps, unconsciously, sentiments unfriendly to things of which Englishmen are proud.

Even if they should escape incurring prejudices hostile to British institutions, the youth of Upper Canada who were educated in the United States would not possess the same deep feeling and attachment to the various establishments of Upper Canada and the mother country, as they would if "carefully nurtured" in a British system of education. Therefore, given the impracticability of students going to England to complete their education, it was essential that the Province of Upper Canada establish a complete system of education of its own. (3)

A need to combat 'Modern Skeptics'

For the Tories, a general system of education – under the direction of the Established Church -- was required also to combat the efforts of infidels, or "modern skeptics", who were bent upon undermining religion "in the minds of the young". In looking at the recent history of Europe, it was observed that such men were involved constantly in striving to discredit religion by denying the existence of God, the Judgment Day, and all "moral distinction". Skeptics were engaged in vehement attacks upon Christianity, and were seeking to destroy the influence of the clergy by depicting them as "a set of dangerous men, directed by deceit or blinded by superstition, to whom no principles belonged but intolerance, bigotry, and narrowness of mind". In disparaging Christianity and declaiming upon the self-sufficiency of man, the infidels were not above claiming for themselves all "candour, freedom of discussion, truth and universal benevolence". Yet, their actions belied their words, for they were men who:

> with moderation on their lips, persecute with unrelenting cruelty, [men who were] bigoted amidst their liberality and furious amidst their toleration, and [who,] while anxious to pull down Christianity, [knew] of nothing to substitute in its room.

This was not to say that the defenders of Christianity were innocent of all wrongdoing and wickedness in all ages. The Upper Canadian Tories readily admitted, and deplored, that this was not the case. What they feared, however, was that if the 'blasphemy' and 'doubts' which were being expressed by the infidels, and their "bold assertions and specious invectives", were left unchallenged, and that religious principles were not inculcated through education, those who, in the beginning, despised such arguments, would eventually come to believe them.

In Europe, such appeals to the vanity of man had succeeded in "rendering irreligion fashionable" and in 'deluding thousands'. However, the explanation for that phenomenon, as well as the antidote, was perfectly clear to the Upper Canadian Tories:

> With shallow men the fashion is everything, whether in their mode of dress or of thinking. On this principle, we account for those furious enthusiasts of the present day for undefined liberty and unrestrained licentiousness: a few centuries ago they would have been the murderers of the Albigenses [sic], and the promoters of the crusades. It was reserved for them to exhibit in this enlightened age the astonishing Phenomenon of men preaching humanity, liberality, and toleration, while they are persecuting with violence not for believing too much, but because some men still presume to believe in demonstration, and for fear of retaining any portion of Christianity, these enthusiasts have not only rejected its doctrines, but the moderation, the charity, [and] the piety it enjoins.

Given the nature of man, and the impact of infidelity on Europe, there was an obvious need to:

> fortify the minds of the rising generation against the inflammatory and profane writings of profligate men who hating God and the best interests of man spread abroad their profane and pestilent ... torrents.

In the immediate postwar period, the Tories were of the view that the "floodgates of infidelity" were no longer open in Europe with the defeat of Napoleon and the restoration of the traditional monarchies. Moreover, Upper Canada was judged to be in no immediate danger from the blasphemous declamations of infidels. Nonetheless, the Tories held that:

> the days of seduction having passed away, the best method of guarding against their return is to give our children a religious education. (4)

A Need for Direct Government Action

For the Upper Canadian Tories, all of the best interests of society -- social, political, moral and religious -- were dependent upon and promoted by a proper system of education. Given such a belief, they could not but lament the lack of a proper system of education in Upper Canada, and seek to remedy that deficiency.

Since the extension of the benefits of education to the youth of the province was beyond the slender resources of the Established Church, the situation could be remedied only by the people themselves coming forward to pay for the education of their children, or by government action in supplying financial support. The exigencies of the situation, however, were such that only the provincial government was in a position to establish a general system of education in Upper Canada.

Past experience had shown that the people could not be relied upon to secure education for themselves, any more than they could secure their own instruction in religion. The impact of the wilderness upon the minds of Upper Canadians was the same with respect to education as it was where religion was concerned. When the first settlers came to Upper Canada, they were desirous of securing an education for their children. However, their inability to pay teachers -- owing to their impoverished circumstances -- and the great distances which separated them from their neighbours, prevented their doing so.

In time, the settlers ceased to feel the need of schools and, as their circumstances improved, they made no effort to establish them. The result was, by the turn of the century, that "the rising generation instead of improving, were in many places more ignorant than their parents". The situation had been rectified somewhat in 1807 when the provincial Legislature established eight district schools – one in each District of the province. However, the settlers continued to show a distressing tendency to value the labour of their children above any knowledge and formal education that they might acquire by being permitted to attend a District School.

Nonetheless, despite public apathy, the Tories saw a definite need for increasing the number of district schools. They sought to complete the system of education by establishing a proper provincial common (elementary) school system, and a provincial university. Moreover, they called for direct government action in support of a 'national' school system. (5)

The Development of a Respectable Society

At the close of the War, the Upper Canadian Tories were also acutely concerned about maintaining and increasing the 'respectability' of the province. They witnessed "the great difficulty" which the provincial government had experienced, and was experiencing, in securing educated men of 'independent character' to fill its various appointments. Both the Legislative Council and the Executive Council required new members, more magistrates were needed, and the character of the House of Assembly left much to be desired; yet there was a dearth of "proper persons" who could provide "efficient leadership", if appointed or elected.

In the case of the Assembly, it was hoped that the Crown lawyers might secure election and provide some direction for that body. Otherwise, in the view of the Tories, the future character of that House remained questionable. It was noted that:

> There are few merchants sufficiently disinterested & the country is too young to have produced many Characters retired & at their ease.

A general system of education was regarded as the only means of rectifying that deficiency through producing a respectable body of men upon whom the province could draw for public service, in various capacities. In effect, the projected system of education was counted on to produce a governing class – a political class of educated and respectable men who would be dedicated to public service.

More generally, it was held that a general system of education – culminating in a provincial university – would not only contribute to the respectability of the province, it would attract a better class of emigrant from Britain, and would provide "a liberal education" for the sons of the merchants and for the youthful heirs of the large landholders of Upper Canada – the future proprietors of landed estates – whether they intended to enter the professions or not.

The Needs of the Professions

The three professions -- medicine, the law, and the church -- required the establishment of a university to ensure that high standards of conduct and learning were maintained or attained as the case might be. Hitherto, medicine had not been an attractive profession, but with the increasing wealth of the settlements, it promised to become so; yet there was nowhere in Upper Canada that medical knowledge could be acquired. Medical doctors had to have access to formal instruction. In the absence of a university in Upper Canada, they had to go to Britain -- if they had the financial resources -- or to resort to the United States. The latter resort was totally unacceptable. The Tories lamented the fact that "three-quarters" of the medical practitioners in the province had attended American schools, and it was "presumed that many of them are inclined towards that country".

The law was attracting numerous readers, but many lawyers were ill-prepared for their profession. A university was required to upgrade their education and set stricter standards for admittance to the bar. In addition, the National Church was suffering from a severe shortage of clergymen, and it was felt that only a university could provide the numbers needed. The direction of the education of clerical candidates by individual ministers had proved "most unsatisfactory" in that only a limited number of students that could be accommodated. Moreover, the Tories believed that the province, as a whole, would benefit from the presence of a university in Upper Canada as it was to the members of the legal profession – as well as the clerical profession -- to whom they looked to set the tone and character of the province. (6)

To the Tory mind, it was essential that the legal profession should be "the repository of the highest talent" and, to that end, law students needed to attend a central university where they might receive a good professional education as well as a sound moral and religious training. Lawyers were pre-eminently the governing class of the future:

> Lawyers must from the very nature of our political institutions -- from there being no great land proprietors -- no privileged orders -- become the most powerful profession, and must, in time, possess more influence and authority than any other. They are emphatically our men of business, and will gradually engross all the colonial offices of profit and honor.

In view of such an expectation, the Upper Canadian Tories were particularly anxious to instill the right values in the minds of the young men of the law because that profession was open to peculiar dangers. It was a matter of critical concern that lawyers be made strongly aware of the fact that they were "accountable beings" for it was "a maxim of universal experience, that men are wicked in proportion to the strength of their temptation". Because of the nature of their business in dealing with other men's property, lawyers were more strongly tempted than other professions. As any nation increased in wealth, the principles of natural law invariably became covered over with "a multitude of laws of expediency" which enabled "petty fogging lawyers" to become rich by "delaying justice and defending wrong".

Of all the professions, the law required above all "a mind strongly impressed with a deep and clear sense of justice to keep steadfast its integrity", which only a proper education could produce. A good lawyer ought to possess a strong sense of justice and, while being precise in his interpretation of the law, should be guided by its general sense and by benevolent feelings. If the laws were so interpreted, there was:

> a great good which a lawyer of superior talents and inflexible integrity, might effect in preventing wrongs, and terminating contentions, directing the doubtful, and instructing the ignorant. (7)

Thus, a concern to secure the education of the future law profession was a very important impetus to Tory plans for establishing a university in Upper Canada. An even more compelling motive, however, was the need to secure a formal education for the young men who were desirous of entering the priesthood of the Established Church.

The Needs of the Established Church

The Anglican Tories believed that if the Church of England were to eventually comprehend the bulk of the population of the province within its fold -- an essential component of the National Policy -- it must have clergymen who were natives of the province and educated therein. However, the education of a native clergy posed a particular problem owing to the high standards of education to which Anglican clerics were expected to attain. Clergymen of the Established Church were expected to be men of above average learning in advance of "the public mind" in their general knowledge of all fields of knowledge. It could not be otherwise, as the clergy of the National Church were duty bound "to be able to address themselves to the understanding as well as the hearts of an enlightened people". A university education was required of the Anglican clergy in Britain, and Upper Canada could demand no less.

In sum, a university was needed to provide clerical candidates with both "a liberal and a theological education". There was also a concern that, in the rude circumstances of Upper Canada, the Anglican clergy might fall into imitating the sectarian preachers. They were regarded as being generally "ignorant enthusiasts" who either neglected, or were indifferent to, a formal education in theology or any other discipline. The belief of the sectarians that "every Christian man" if he received "the call", and were thus moved by the spirit, "may preach, pray and administer the sacraments", alarmed the Anglican Tories. It made them even more conscious of the need to provide a university education for their own clergy:

> We can't descend to the level of the denominations around us.
> We require a much better educated and higher qualifications in
> our clergy.

A university in Upper Canada was viewed by the Rev. John Strachan as being "essentially a Missionary College" as the needs of the Established

Church were greater than that of the other professions. A university would provide the numerous clergy which would be required to inculcate Christian principles in the population of the province, both from the pulpit and in the schoolroom. Thus, a university would contribute to the extension of the ministrations of the Established Church in the province, as well as contribute heavily to the formation of the mind and character of the British subjects of the Province of Upper Canada.

From a more strictly religious point of view, it was argued that a university would serve as "a rallying point of the Protestant faith", and would give leadership to the Protestant denominations of Upper Canada in a situation where its immediate neighbor in Lower Canada was overwhelmingly Roman Catholic. Moreover, the teaching and example set by the highly-educated Anglican clergy would give a British tone to society, and the projected university would facilitate the extension of the ministrations of the National Church as well as serve a political purpose.

In the immediate postwar period, the Tories were deeply concerned that the sectarian preachers in Upper Canada, who were for the most part of American origin, were impregnated with American principles and sentiments. If the youth of Upper Canada were to be kept loyal to British institutions and principles, and not become Americanized, it was believed that the government of Upper Canada, and especially that of Great Britain, must act to establish a university for:

> It is evident that, if the Imperial Government does not step forward with efficient help, the mass of the population will be nurtured and instructed in hostility to all our institutions both civil and religious. (8)

In the Tory mind, the establishing of a 'national system' of education, culminating in a university, was inextricably linked with their plans for the extension of the Established Church. Both efforts were mutually sustaining and reinforcing. A church establishment was regarded as being "one branch of public education" because of the values it disseminated. Hence, the clergy were expected to play a major role "in fostering education by establishing schools". In that endeavour, the efforts of the clergy were being hampered by a lack of funds and their paucity of numbers in the Province of Upper Canada.

The Duty of the State

The public benefits to be derived by the founding of a university were well articulated by the Upper Canadian Tories. However, their appeal to government – both at the provincial and Imperial level -- for the establishment and funding of a national system of education, was based on a deeper matrix of beliefs. It was a product of their concept of the 'duty' of both Church and State, and their belief as to the proper relationship that ought to exist between the Church, the State, and education. In sum, the Tory call – after the War of 1812 -- for the government to establish a national system of education stemmed from much more than their awareness of existing deficiencies in the education of youth, the Americanization threat, and the political dangers to which the province was particularly vulnerable.

The Tories believed that the State had a Christian duty to promote the education of its people. The conduct of the schools, and much of the actual teaching, was held to be the preserve of the Established Church, but it was the State which was held to be responsible for supporting a general system of education. That belief in turn was a natural outgrowth of the religious beliefs of the Upper Canadian Tories, their view of the duty of government and the basis of social order, and their understanding of God's scheme of things. (9)

One of the fundamental beliefs of the Tories was that government, in conjunction with the Established Church, must found and control a system of education because the inculcation of religious values in youth was essential to the present well-being and future happiness of its subjects. In the very nature of things -- the "moral and physical disposition of things" as instituted by God -- it was necessary that man obey his Maker. If a nation were to receive the blessings of Divine Providence and escape retribution at His hands, both ruler and subject had to act in subordination to God's will as revealed in the Bible. God had so constituted the world, and the nature of man was such, that human government could not prosper and function properly without religion.

For the Tories, the Christian religion was "the only true source of morality and public order". Only instruction in Christian principles – inclusive of both "the duties of morality and the doctrines of revelation" -- could produce in a people "a temper and spirit" sufficient to ensure a subordination to God's will, and secure that obedience 'to the powers that be' which was necessary to the continuance of "social peace and national unity". Religious principles were the basis of moral actions, as well as of allegiance to the sovereign. A civil state had to rest upon a religious foundation; otherwise, it could have neither "a moral and religious social system" nor a paternal government.

If government were not to rule solely by brute force, in being oblivious to all moral considerations, then it must possess the right to form the religious and moral character of its subjects. In accordance with God's scheme of things and for the benefit of man, it was:

> the duty of every government composed of Christians, to pay the first attention to the interests of religion, and lay the foundation of public prosperity in public virtue, and of public virtue in private individual instruction in the religion which our Creator has given us.

In effect, it was a duty of the state, which was held to be analogous to that a father, "to pour the spirit of contentment & tranquility over the infant minds" by providing the children of the province with moral and religious instruction. For the Tories, the family was but a microcosm of the state and the origin "of all virtue and happiness". Once children leave the family to "take their place in Society", they became "children of the community" and responsibility in turn devolved upon the state to see that religious principles continued "to maintain their full influence over the mind" of the young through the ministrations of a national church and the teachings of a national system of education. (10)

The Requisites of Human Happiness

Since "God governed the world, and ruled over all things, human and divine", the teaching of the Christian religion could not be separated from education and politics. The very purpose of government was to promote the "good of the community" over which it ruled, and the amount of happiness and prosperity which man experienced was in turn dependent upon whether his actions were in accordance with God's Will. By means of his natural powers of observation and reasoning, man could learn much of what was required of him, but his human observations and reasoning powers were limited in seeking to attain knowledge of what constituted true happiness here on earth.

From their conception of God, their view of "the constitution of things", and their view of human capabilities and "the numberless sources of enjoyment everywhere presented", men could know that they were intended to be "ultimately happy". Since God was good, it was evident that He intended man to be happy; and that all His works were designed to promote that end.

Such an understanding was not to deny that the world was full of misery, dishonesty, tyranny and injustice, or that even virtuous men suffered numerous afflictions. The present life, in the reasoning of the Tories, was not formed on a plan of happiness or of misery but, it was undeniable that -- barring accidents, which might thwart the natural effects of the existing order of things -- virtue promoted happiness, and vice bred nothing but misery. The afflictions which men suffered were largely self-imposed, but were of a real value in that they revealed how God wanted men to live, and brought the individual to a greater awareness of himself, his situation, and his dependence upon others.

In the existing scheme of things, man learned the need for temperance, self-denial, and the value of moral restraint, discovered his own weaknesses, and became conscious of how little material things -- power, riches, or popular applause -- could contribute to his real happiness in the face of accident and death. Experience taught that idleness invariably leads to evil and corrupts the heart, while labour, though a burden, was necessary to the attainment of a good and comfortable life. Chastened by his experiences, man, in exercising his rational faculties, could see that for his own good he must seek to promote "the useful and good" in all his worldly pursuits.

Nonetheless, the experiences of life and man's rational capacity were not sufficient to enlighten either the subject, or his government, as to man's true happiness. Human reason was insufficient to guide man to attain true happiness, or government to promote it. To achieve that end, Revelation was given as a guide to both, and, "when rightly understood", was perfectly suited to man's needs. It contributed solely to his happiness:

for if we consider the various dispensations of revealed religion, we shall find, that however different the form, the end was always and ultimately the same -- that they were adapted to the social progress of man, and constitute so many parts of one great and comprehensive scheme for the improvement and happiness of the human race, which commenced with the fall of Adam, and will be completed when all they that are in their graves shall hear the voice of the Son of God and shall come forth -- they that have done good unto the resurrection of life, and they that have done evil unto the resurrection of damnation. (11)

The Christian religion, as revealed in Scriptures, provided for the whole constitution of man, body and soul, in setting forth clearly not only the rules of conduct for this life, which could be learnt – if imperfectly -- from the nature of things, but also revealed his ultimate destination and the purpose of life.

Religion served as a powerful sanction for proper behaviour as it made clear that not only was the degree of happiness which man could attain in this world dependent upon his own actions, but most importantly the very salvation of his soul and his attainment of eternal felicity could be placed in jeopardy by his actions. The Christian religion was not contemptuous of worldly things, but rather provided "spiritual objects of contemplation" -- a plan of salvation -- which moderated man's desire for temporal things, refined his passions, and "elevated the soul".

The Christian religion was essential to man's happiness for the latter, although dependent in part upon worldly comforts, depended in large measure upon man's ability to govern his passions and appetites and not succumb to "an intemperate pursuit" of pleasure, wealth, and honours, which were pursuits that would only result in torment and discontent. Contentment was a virtue which was central to the happiness of man; and yet without religion it was unattainable in living an active life -- as opposed to a contentment which was derived from an indifference to things of this world. For the Tories, asceticism and otherworldliness in religion were not in keeping with one's Christian duties toward oneself and one's fellow man.

In this world, as it was constituted by God, true contentment was dependent upon the hope of a future life. Amidst the struggles and disappointments of this life, contentment, and hence happiness, were to be found only in the promise held forth by the Christian religion of the life to come. Such a promise:

> raises our desires to a more refined and exalted species of happiness which is independent of time or of fortune -- which consists not in the abundance of riches -- but in the tranquility of mind, which arises from the due government of our appetites and passions; ... [and] that anticipation of immortal bliss founded in a good conscience and a full observance of faith in the merits of our Lord Jesus Christ.

Scripture informed man that his true happiness was to be found in love of God and subordination to the divine Will, and called man to the performance of his duties. Man was provided with precepts for his guidance, which were "admirably adapted to the nature and constitution of man", and standards of right and wrong which were in accord with his own reason.

Everything was subject to God's governance, and man would be happy or miserable in so far as he sought to conform to the perfections of his Maker. In deviating from the prescribed rules of conduct, man "debased his nature" and neglected his proper station which was assigned to him by God. In God's scheme of things:

> true happiness [for men] depends upon the perfecting of their nature and ...the nearer they rise to a conformity to the will of God the more delight they shall enjoy.

In this life, there was "nothing light, nothing indifferent". Everyone, of whatever station he occupied in the order of things, had his duties to perform and must be content with his lot, and all were to look to God as "the standard of excellence". With a "well-regulated temper", a good conscience, and "a confident assurance of divine favour", man could experience tranquility in this life in his "progress toward perfection". However, his ultimate happiness was to be found only in the re-union of the mind of man with "the infinite Being who made it".

Man was originally made in the image of God, and consequently was wise and holy before 'the Fall'. If he were to be true to his nature and be happy, he had to seek to attain that perfection again:

> the consequence of ... Wisdom and Holiness was the greatest happiness, for such is the constitution of things, that happiness is inseparable from Wisdom and Holiness -- God is infinitely wise, and Holy, and he is therefore infinitely happy.

Such were the requisites of human happiness. In God's scheme of things, if government were to realize its proper paternal function and promote the happiness of its subjects, it must have the right – and, in the Tory mind, it did have the right of the father -- to provide for the religious and moral instruction of "its children" as well as for their physical well-being; and it was duty-bound to do so. Hence, they called upon the provincial government to establish a 'national system' of education under the direction of the Established Church.

The Requisite Unity of Church, State, and Education

To secure the happiness and security of its citizens, it was necessary that government should provide "*a Religious and Pious Education*" with training in good morals, but also that government should provide security from internal upheavals and external attacks, as well as seek to foster loyalty among the people and to promote national prosperity. To the Tories, however, it was evident that these attributes of good government could not be realized:

> where there is no state religion, and where the government, [in seeking to make] religion the basis of moral instruction and the source of loyalty, does not provide for and superintend the entire education of the people. (12)

In this world, government was "the only legitimate schoolmaster", and religion embodied all the moral and political truths, and was "the means of reconciliation between man and God". These truths needed to be inculcated "into the human heart and mind" through education. The teaching of the moral and political truths of religion would serve "to purify the affections to a fit condition for the exercise of man's citizenship under the divine paternal government".

In sum, the Tories believed that a truly Christian state there must be a "union and joint co-operation" of the institutions of government and religion in the establishment of a system of education in which Christian moral and political principles "should exclusively predominate". For given the nature of man and society in God's creation, such a system and the truths that it embodied were "the spring and principles of [the] political and moral life and prosperity" of the nation. In effect, government, religion, and education were "co-equal and co-essential", and had to act in conjunction in any "well-regulated state", with Christian principles providing "a public standard" of morality.

"The truths essential to the well-being of a state" had to be duly recognized, and acted upon, for the good of its citizens. That was as it should be, for:

> Christianity is Truth .... She is the foundation of government
> and the object of Education, and the end of government is to
> instruct in her principles, and to rule and obey in her spirit. (13)

Not only was the fulfillment of the purpose of the State dependent upon the union of government, religion, and education, but the very safety, strength and well-being of the nation was dependent upon their working in harmony -- and with "the most beneficent efficiency" -- within a Christian polity. In a highly-idealized conception – somewhat exaggerated for effect -- one Anglican Tory – the Rev. Adam Hood Burwell – declaimed that were the States united with a National Church and a national education system, it would produce:

> a system which shall embrace every true interest of every
> individual of a state; which shall absorb in itself every source
> of influence, patronage and power both moral and physical, and
> monopolize all the affections, and all the integrity, and all the
> loyalty, and all the allegiance, and all the strength of a nation;
> under which there would be perfect rational liberty and security
> to the subject, and perfect subordination and obedience to
> the ruler.

When the institutions of government, religion and education – "the three great pillars of the body politic" – were united, they were capable of "forming the national manners, and character, and heart, and soul, by the Christian faith". In being united, they were capable of securing the attachment of Upper Canadians to the government, and of preserving the due balance of society. However, when separated they were of a far lesser value, and even acted at cross purposes.

Upper Canada possessed an Established Church which, it was maintained, had only to be strengthened and extended to fulfill its proper function, but the government had to act to establish a system of education for:

> if education is left to private adventure or the will of the people, there is no moral and political contagion but may be imported from abroad or manufactured at home, and instilled into the minds of youth.

It was necessary in all things that there be a fixed standard and principles, and hence it was only right that the youth of the province should be educated "in the national faith" by means of the National Church clergy teaching within a national system of education. With government support, and in being based on Christian principles, a national system of education would be able "to form the citizen for his country by the influence of the religion of the country".

Government, religion and education could not be separated one from the other, or left to the dictates of individual conscience, without destroying "the true notion of loyalty". The Americans had divorced government from religion, and religion from education; and in that country "the Majesty of the people [was] omnipotent, ... self the object of Loyalty, and inclination the rule of allegiance".

The American system of separating government from religion, and religion from education, was the inverse of the proper order of things. The "will and opinion of the people" could not be the "all in all" in matters of government, religion and education on practical grounds as well as principle, for:

> in fact, there is not in any country one man in fifty who does not think as he is directed by some other than himself: for if the government does not form his mind for him some demagogue

or party will, and direct it for him too. The Almighty people cannot think nor act but as they are directed. (14)

If the State were to command the affections, loyalty and allegiance of its subjects, and ensure its own endurance, certain principles had to be recognized and inculcated in the people. First, that the State possessed the right to define the nature of allegiance and its extent, as well as the right to teach the subject his duty. These rights were of the essence of "the family compact". Just as the father did not consult his children about their duties, but exercised his superior wisdom and strength to provide for their "moral and physical necessities", so to the State had to do the same if it were to exercise a paternal government. It was a situation where:

> the subject is by the necessity of his condition both ignorant to devise and weak to execute the means of safety to his person and property, and therefore the state does it for him.

In turn, these basic rights entailed a further obligation on the part of the state: that of forming the minds of its subjects to their allegiance by means of educating them "on certain selected, definite, and fixed principles". Since allegiance was ultimately dependent upon the strength of religious feeling – "its power over the conscience" -- the state was bound to provide for both a national religious establishment and a religiously-based education system. (15)

In the nature of things -- according to the Upper Canadian Tories -- both the preservation of the state, and the performance of its true purpose, necessitated a state-controlled education system, wherein Christian principles were disseminated under the direction of the clergy of the Established Church. However, it was an arrangement that was considered as being as beneficial for the citizen as it was necessary to the state.

In a properly constituted Christian polity, a reciprocal relationship was held to exist between the state and the subject where education was concerned. On the one hand, the education system in being based on religious principles, would guarantee a loyal, contented, and obedient population living "in perfect subordination"; and, on the other hand, it would serve to produce educated men of Christian principles who could act to restrain the ruler and secure 'the rights of the subject' in his person and property. Most importantly, such a system was believed to be essential to the maintenance and vitality of "true liberty", and the continued happiness of the people of Upper Canada.

The Defence of Rational Freedom

To the Tories, who saw themselves as living in an age in which the traditional Christian polity was under assault by detractors who were espousing revolutionary doctrines, it was of the essence that religious principles should be effectively disseminated throughout the province. The Tories were convinced that unless a national system of education -- closely connected with the Established Church -- were established to educate the youth of the province in Christian principles, then 'democratic anarchy' and 'infidelity' would prevail. All sense of order, and hence all freedom and happiness, would be destroyed.

Much of the success of 'innovators' in securing public support for their attacks on the Church and State was regarded as attributable to the fact that they were addressing "uninstructed minds". Hence, there was an urgent need "to fortify the minds of the rising generation against the inflammatory and profane writings of profligate men". Christian principles had to be taught to deepen man's rather limited understanding as to what constituted his true happiness. For the Tories, human nature was such that:

> we are too much disposed to look for the Sources of felicity beyond ourselves -- to place it in changes and alterations, in acting by absolute self will, in being free from all restraints -- and constrained by no law -- limited by no authority & with the full power of doing whatever we please. But were all this granted instead of happiness we should reap misery. (16)

A system of public education was thus needed not only to instruct the people in "the duties of morality and the doctrines of revelation", but also to clearly set forth "the just government of God" in His Creation. Moreover, the people had to be made aware of the lesson that history taught with respect to the methods employed by demagogues, and the misery and suffering which they inflicted upon mankind in their headlong rush to destroy all that was good and honourable in human society and government.

It was assumed by the Tories that such teachings in a national system of education would render the youth of the province immune to what was referred to as "the craft and deceptions of grievance mongers and the sowers of sedition." The people, in being products of such an education system, would realize that men who indulged "a querulous disposition" were the true enemies of freedom. They were undermining the social order and harmony of society in continuously denigrating established institutions, in showing a lack of respect for "received opinions and the experience of the wise", in refusing to extend to magistrates and men of rank and station their due deference, and in failing to recognize the necessity of such distinctions for the proper functioning of society. Under close scrutiny by enlightened minds, the selfish motives of demagogues would be exposed, and their deceptions unmasked. Thus, education would promote social unity by bringing together both subject and ruler in a mutual desire to further the general good, and to heal "the spirit of suspicious jealousy" which all too often separated them.

In the Tory view, agitators and demagogues were invariably intolerant of any opinion but their own, were contemptuous of the laws, and were set on undermining public order by attempting to convince the people of their "absolute independence in public and private conduct". Where these destabilizing efforts were successful, the results were often fatal to liberty as the people invariably became "forward, self-sufficient, presumptuous and licentious".

> In such cases, every little disappointment -- every imaginary grievance -- every wanton desire of change produces a ferment & Threatens the public peace -- Everyone carves out his own method of redress and persecutes his designs by the dictates of his own corrupt will.

Only Christian principles, properly inculcated in the public mind, could counteract such a tendency and render citizens capable of defeating the fallacious arguments of demagogues and infidels. Education would make them aware that:

The licentious reprover -- the slanderous scoffer -- is not solicitous for the cause of liberty but for his own interests. [In] pretending to be its promoter, he makes it subservient to his passions. But [true] liberty ... consists in the restraining of our appetites and passions -- seeking happiness not so much in outward as in inward perfection – in willing nothing but what God wills and in doing nothing but what is in conformity to the divine will. (17)

To the Tory mind, religion had to be the basis of government and education for liberty was an outgrowth of order, and could only be enjoyed in a truly Christian state where both ruler and subject acted in subordination to God's law and prospered accordingly. In the nature of things, the promotion of virtue and religion in the province would strengthen liberty and increase happiness, for freedom and happiness were inseparable. It was held that true liberty, or:

rational freedom, consists in the greatest attainable degree of public and private prosperity, in connection with the means of producing the greatest attainable degree of public and private virtue.

If men were to live peacefully together, and to enjoy freedom as well as the happiness, security and the comforts which society could yield, then all citizens -- rulers, magistrates and subjects -- must be bound by the rule of law, but laws could only go so far in maintaining order in a state. For the preservation of tranquility, it was necessary that citizens should exercise a due self-restraint and reject all unprincipled actions, and to that end, they must be imbued with "a love of order".

A love of order was held to be "essential to the very being of any State" for it "induced [men] to conform to the laws and to promote the welfare of the community". Consequently, it was "the foundation of mutual faith, confidence and security". Good laws alone were not sufficient to sustain 'true liberty' or make men good:

for the laws are negative in their effect, -- it is religion alone that instills positive good, and breaks the sceptre of selfishness.

> It is only the practical influence and operation of faith and piety
> that can soften the heart, and introduce those sacred charities and
> protecting virtues which are ever blessing and ever blessed. (18)

Indeed, freedom and happiness were dependent upon good laws, but the
execution of these laws and even the making of them was dependent
upon the vital presence of "virtue and soundness of principle" in both
legislator and subject, which only a general system of moral and religious
education could ensure. The real security for liberty was to be found in
the very character of the people -- their love of order -- and that in turn
was dependent upon, and inseparable from, religion:

> To give steadiness & effect to this love of order we must
> call in the aid of religion, which is the only firm and lasting
> foundation upon which the tranquility and security of a people
> can be strengthened & established. What are the true supports
> of Authority but the love of religion. The experience of all
> nations teaches us, that neither the unassisted dictates of reason
> nor the active principle of public spirit nor the punishment of
> the civil magistrate are effectual checks upon men's appetites
> and passions if we leave out a belief of a God & a Providence,
> or cease to cultivate those affections of the heart which that
> belief tends naturally to produce. The fear of God must be
> always considered as the surest foundation of freedom -- it
> forms & fixes every virtue of the heart, gives life and motion to
> every good principle of the mind, directs the hopes and fears of
> men to their proper objects & supplies the unavoidable defects
> of human laws.

It was the fear of God -- in acting upon the conscience of man -- that
supplied "an internal law" which, in being ever present, was much
more effective in governing the conduct of the citizen than the public
law. For the Tories, it was the principles which were sanctioned by the
Christian religion that were the basis of order in any state, and the very
happiness and freedom of its members was dependent upon the strength
of those principles. Thus, it was believed that in the best interests of the
state and society at large, religious instruction had to form the basis of

any education system established in Upper Canada so that the youth of the province might have instilled in their hearts "the fear of the Lord". (19) To that end, it was requisite that the projected national system of education be placed under the direction of the established Church of England, the National Church of the Province of Upper Canada.

———————————

Chapter Thirteen

Education, Religion and Morality

To the Upper Canadian Tories, the stability of the state and the happiness of the people were dependent upon the predominance of moral principles in the public mind; and that belief in turn necessitated that the State act to establish a school system to disseminate moral values. Education was expected to serve a critical moral purpose in forming the character of youth, but, on a deeper level, the Tory educational plans were the product of a much more strictly religious motivation. In keeping with their view of the purpose of man's life here on earth, God's scheme of things, and the dependence of morality on religion, the Tories believed that any system of education which was to be established in Upper Canada must be religiously based, and under the direction of the Established Church. It was a belief that was clearly enunciated by the Anglican clerics in their sermon exhortations to their congregations and in their religious and educational publications.

A Religiously-based system of Education

To the Tory mind, whether instruction took place in the Church, the family, or the school, it must be in keeping with the teachings of the Christ's Church. They believed that:

> the great and true object of Education is to bring religion to bear upon all the faculties of the Soul since it consists in the process of training that Soul for heaven.

Man was an accountable being, and parents and teachers in educating their children were "directing immortal spirits". Hence, children needed to be brought up "in fear and nurture of the Lord". For the Tories, it was critically important that the minds of youth be carefully inculcated with "correct and fixed principles of action" -- based upon the beliefs and values of the Christian religion. Moreover, it was requisite that Christian principles take "deep root in the heart" for:

> Unless this be done while we are young, how shall we give account in the day of Judgment or how shall we sanctify our hearts …. how shall we know God and his Son, Jesus Christ,

whom to know is eternal life, and keep ourselves unspotted from the world.

It was the principles which were imbibed in youth that would determine not only the conduct of the man in this world, but also his "acquittal or condemnation" on the Day of Judgement. Thus, it was requisite that every public system of education be founded upon moral and religious instruction. Given God's scheme of things, it was evident that students must be:

taught that it is essential to their happiness here and hereafter that they should first seek the kingdom of God and his righteousness -- a command given by the Son of God himself; and [that] no system of Education can be right which does not enforce this as the foundation and beginning of all knowledge. (1)

Education had to be based on religion for "without knowing God, all knowledge is vain". It was requisite that instruction render man a moral being, and "make him the true worshipper of God and the self-denying friend of his species". Not all students were capable of making great advancement in the sciences, but all could be sincere Christians and good members of society if provided with a proper moral and religious education.

Children under sixteen were not capable of studying religion as a science, but could be instructed in the practical rules of Christianity and made aware that they were responsible beings. To that end, they must be taught "correct principles of religion and virtue"; and:

that there is a God above, our Friend, our Benefactor, the Creator of all things; and that it is only by imitating His moral perfections, as brought home to our hearts and affections by our blessed Redeemer, that we can render ourselves worthy of the rank we hold in the scale of beings, and enjoy solid pleasure in this life, and in that which is to come.

Education was needed to prepare children "for the stations in society which they are designed to fill" by their God-given intelligence, aptitudes, and abilities. They needed to be taught the useful subjects of the arts and science, but the primary and most essential task of education was to inculcate good principles and to make children "lovers of Religion".

In the Tory system of values, practical knowledge was of a great utility to man, but was purely secondary to the teaching of Christian virtue. Religion could not be confined to the Church or the home, and the school curriculum limited to such practical subjects as arithmetic, geography, and algebra, for:

> Education requires much more: it is to give your pupils a moral training favorable to the good order of society, to the performance of their duties to God and man, and to become useful to them here and hereafter.

In sum, a formal system of education was required to provide the youth of the province with a good grounding in morals and practical subjects to prepare the student for whatever business of profession he might take up in life. However, for the Tories – as articulated by the Anglican clerics among the Tory elite – the education of youth involved a much higher purpose, for:

> the ultimate object of all education and knowledge is to raise man to the feeling of his own moral worth, to a sense of responsibility to his Creator and to his conscience for every act, to the dignity of a reflecting, self-guiding, virtuous, [and] religious member of society. (2)

Disagreement with Modern Educational Theorists

In adhering to their belief that the primary function of education was to inculcate moral and religious principles in youth at an early age, the Tories were well aware that they were going against "the opinions" of several of the leading educational theorists of their epoch who advised that moral and religious principles should not be taught to the young. The "modern educational theorists" argued that the minds of children must be kept free from "early prejudices"; and that they should come by their principles through "clear conviction" rather than having them impressed by authority. The 'modern theorists' maintained that only when the reasoning powers were well developed in adolescence would youth become capable of judging morals and religious matters for themselves, and only then would such principles carry conviction through understanding. Otherwise, they would not carry enough conviction to influence future conduct.

For the Tories, the problem with such a theory of education was that adults were not "always disposed to submit to reason" in determining their conduct, any more than children. In youth, the mind and body were "small and weak", and both needed to be nurtured. Children had to be taught to walk and speak, and the mind needed be supplied with "correct notions [to] give strength and precision to its expanding powers". Moreover, in advocating that moral and religious principles not be taught to children, the 'modern educational theorists' failed to take account of the fact that in the nature of things:

> prepossession or prejudice must be the first foundation of all our principles. No person can reason without admitting things of which he has never examined the truth; he must be satisfied with the report of those who have; for a whole life would not be sufficient to investigate one tenth part of the principles generally received. Indeed, what we are enabled afterwards to believe from rational conviction, must, at first, be received as true without proof.

Children must be taught what to believe 'on authority'. In seeking to educate youth, it was only right that the youthful mind be imbued with "such principles as will not require to be extirpated, but confirmed, when [the pupil] becomes enlightened". (3)

In the Tory view, it was dangerous to postpone instruction in morals and religion until the reasoning power of youth grew capable of making proper value judgments, and of giving a rational assent to them. If the mind of youths were not inculcated with good principles, then bad principles and habits would fill the void as man in his fallen state was prone to evil. Moreover, such was the nature of man that a bad character, once formed, would inhibit the imbibing of new ideas, and it would prove difficult to eradicate bad principles -- no matter how false, absurd or ridiculous they might be – even by resorting to "the most vigorous reason".

Children who were raised "in forgetfulness of God" could not but be "wicked and miserable" in being left as "slaves of their passions and appetites". Vice did not have to be taught, but virtue "required instruction and a wise education" if the natural innocence of childhood were to be strengthened and kept alive. The cultivation of proper habits early in life was thus of the utmost importance; and, once formed, good habits invariably exercised "a powerful influence" on conduct thereafter.

Men in this life were what they were -- "good or evil, useful or not" -- for the most part due to the education they received. In effect, a moral education or the lack thereof was the great source of virtue or wickedness, respectively; and education – when properly based on moral and religious principles – was the great vehicle for the improvement of man's condition. Although it was believed that learning made men better, it was recognized that there were limits to what man could attain. The Rev. John Strachan, for one, expressed his belief that:

> it may be proved that the greater part of vice is owing to the want of knowledge, I had almost said the whole -- But as our knowledge never will be perfect, wickedness will always in some measure prevail.

In the nature of things, it was evident to the Tories that religion could not be separated from education if the best interests of the youth of the province, and society at large, were to be fostered. (4)

Rejection of secular systems of Education

In keeping with their belief that religion could not be separated from education, the Upper Canadian Tories deplored the tendency -- which they saw developing in the United States and in Europe -- to separate religion from education. In formulating plans for the establishment of a general education system for Upper Canada, the Rev. John Strachan was well aware of recent educational reforms. He welcomed "mechanical improvements" such as the Bell-Lancaster monitorial system, which facilitated the education of larger numbers of students through the older students monitoring the younger students and helping them with their lessons. In England, both Dr. Andrew Bell and Joseph Lancaster were active in promoting the establishment of elementary schools based on the monitorial principle, but they differed in that Bell's monitorial school system was religiously-based; whereas Lancaster excluded religion from the curriculum of his monitorial schools.

In Tory eyes, it was "a false liberalism" to exclude religion from education or to favour a secular system of education, such as prevailed in Prussia. Only a religiously-based system of education could bring about "what above all things, must be desired -- a reformation of the national morals". To learn "to read, write, cipher, and sing" was useful for the common business of life, but true prosperity and "the national welfare" would not be promoted by any educational system which was indifferent to religion.

Under the direction of the National Church, education was "invaluable and indispensable" to man's wellbeing. However, separated from moral and religious principles, knowledge was mischievous and even dangerous for:

> any other than a religious education, leads to pride, selfishness, and conceit; and, instead of reforming the heart, promotes our ability of doing evil.

In Europe, the fruits of secular systems of education were readily seen by the Tories -- as of the early 19th Century -- in:

> the perversion of public principle, the daily weakening of the bonds of union between the humble ranks of society and their natural guardians and protectors, growing insubordination, disregard to the laws, increase of crime, the denunciation of good men, mockery of religion, impatience of just control and salutary restraint, contempt of sound learning and experience, and the interruption of honest industry. (5)

Most importantly, religion could not be separated from the educational process because for the Tories 'knowledge' was by definition "a seeking after God", through the study of the Will and nature of God both in "His spiritual manifestations" and" His external works". Much remained to be known with respect to the nature of things, and it was only right, as well as necessary, that man should seek to extend his intellectual horizons so long as he realized the essential role which religion had to play in guiding his inquiries, for:

> The progress of human knowledge can never be arrested, nor, when rightly understood, is it opposed to Divine law. They are not rivals or enemies, but in the closest agreement, for they both came from God. The written Word and the unwritten page of nature equally manifest His power and glory, and both are essential to social improvement. The Gospel of Salvation and of human knowledge join hand in hand in promoting the moral and mental amelioration of our fallen race.

In the view of the Tories, it had to be recognized that although human and divine knowledge were mutually complementary, neither could be properly understood or fully known by the human intellect unaided.

They observed that a secular education far from furthering inquiry into spiritual truth actually served to hinder it, for all too often men so educated came to distain religion, and were filled with "a spirit of doubt" which rendered them "morally incapable" of understanding the Word of God. Indeed, it was evident that:

> The natural man trusting to his extensive knowledge of Science and the works of nature and demanding certain proof and evidence for everything that he does not fully understand, receives not the things of the Spirit for to him they are foolishness, his mind is darkened in regard to Spiritual things because he had no desire to find them true.

Religious truth could be known, or was made known, only to those who accepted Christ as their Saviour and who consequently, with their minds "rectified and illuminated" through the entry of the Holy Spirit, saw all things. In effect, faith was a necessary prerequisite for gaining spiritual knowledge; man must believe that he might know.

Man in "his pride of intellect" could not understand the Scriptures or arrive at sacred truth through mere speculation. Only through faith and holiness of life could he progress in acquiring divine knowledge. Men of superior intellect, if deprived of a religious education, were incapable of knowing what even "the simple and comparatively ignorant mind" -- once enlightened by faith -- could understand.

The Pursuit of Knowledge

Although the Tories believed that religion was the basis of 'true learning', they by no means felt that a simple faith was sufficient to meet all of man's needs. Man was duty-bound to develop his God-given capabilities, and especially his reasoning powers. It was the one faculty and ability which set him apart from the so-called 'brute beasts of creation', and which enable man to grow in knowledge.

Ignorance was regarded as a deplorable evil for the uneducated man was incapable of comprehending the workings of Providence or of understanding "the book of nature". Hence, the uneducated man remained "an insulated being in the midst of society" – a man who would "die having never lived", because ignorant of the unity of all things. In contrast, the religious man who sought to develop his mind through study acted, in doing so, to promote his own well-being. In sum, 'true learning' could not but be accompanied by a growth of wisdom and virtue which, in the nature of things, were essential to man's happiness.

Nevertheless, man could not know everything. He must recognize that there were mysteries, known only to God, which were beyond human comprehension. There was much that was essential to man's life which was by its very nature incapable of the proofs demanded by the "natural man"; however, such matters should not be excluded from education on that account. Divine knowledge needed to be sought in Scriptures to supplement what man could know from the study of nature.

In the pursuit of knowledge man must guard against being "led away by vain and idle thoughts", for:

> To inquire into things proper for us to know is a laudable and noble pursuit, but to institute a set of inquiries for the express purpose of overturning the evidence of God, or because we

doubt of His truth, can never be sufficiently reprobated …. Such inquiries are vain, for it is impossible for us ever to acquire any knowledge of future events.

Everything in God's creation had its law and principle and was subject to "a happy law of harmony and concord", and man was no exception. Scriptures revealed the Will of God, and set forth all that man was required to know and the duties he must fulfill, if he were to attain happiness in this life and the hereafter. Where spiritual truth was concerned, it was sufficient that man must believe and obey. To do otherwise, or to question, was both pretentious and unavailing. It amounted to "a wish to see with the eyes of God, to be perfect as He is perfect", and such was not the nature of man.

Science and Religion

Even in seeking scientific knowledge -- knowledge of "those portions of knowledge deemed secular" -- religion was required to place the discoveries of science within a proper context. Because of the unity that existed between His Will and His works, all study of exterior nature served to "expand our conceptions of the power, wisdom, benevolence, and superintending providence of God". Indeed, it was the most critically-important purpose of education and study. In sum, a proper understanding of God's works, as seen in nature, required an exposure to the teachings of divine revelation wherein "the plans and operation of God [were] more clearly unfolded". In the nature of things, "true knowledge" had to be pursued in conjunction with a religious education; and, in that pursuit, the Christian religion was "the root and trunk of the tree of Education". (6)

To the Anglican Tory mind, any system of education which studied man simply "as a physical being confined to this world" neglected the better part of man's nature. In the first place, man as a "reflecting being" would never by content if his horizons were limited to his physical surroundings and, secondly, as a moral and religious being, man was capable of developing his moral character and of responding to sentiments and feelings which were extraneous to physical science. Therefore, education must seek to enlighten and purify "the heart and spirit" and to enable as well as inform the mind. If moral philosophy, or moral science, was to be part of the curriculum, religion could not be ignored. On all counts, a religious education was requisite for man to properly understand his own being, as well as the world around him.

It was maintained that "history proved", in the lives of Lord Bacon and Sir Isaac Newton, that religion did not "cramp the intellect or discourage the attainment of science", but actually aided in its advancement. For the Tories, religion could not be divorced from education, or science taught in a secular school environment, without negative consequence. The Rev. John Strachan expressed his belief that:

> Nothing can be more beautiful than science and religion combined; they are, indeed, intimately entwined. God is to be worshipped in the works of nature, as well as in the works of grace: united they raise man to the highest standard of excellence which it is possible for him to attain in this lower world; but, if they are to be separated, leave us religion to purify our hearts, and not science, which, without its companion, only enlarges our power of doing evil.

Moral experiments, such as the mechanics' institutes which provided education for all classes of society, particularly artificers in their off-hours, were regarded as being highly commendable undertakings; yet they suffered from a deficient program. In confining their interest to the "demonstrative or experimental sciences" to the exclusion of religion, they added much useful knowledge to the mind of their attendees, but did nothing to elevate the character and soul in "taste, delicacy, pure virtue or religion". The ill-effects of that neglect were readily seen in that many mechanics' institutes quickly "degenerated into political clubs and hot-beds of infidelity". If it were going to truly benefit man, education must be based on moral and religious instruction.

Those who sought to exclude religion from education were viewed as acting on false principles. Indeed, they were regarded as being most illiberal in seeking to exclude the teaching of religion from the schools. Even if one left all religious arguments aside, Christian theology and morality had had a profound impact upon "the literature, civilization and destinies of [western] nations" for some eighteen hundred years. Hence, it should be studied at least as "a branch of history" if western man were to understand his civilization. (7)

In sum, the Tories disagreed entirely with those who -- in recognizing only the physical part of man's being -- sought to confine education exclusively to "the experimental sciences". They differed strongly also from those who, while recognizing the need for education to have a moral basis, nonetheless called for the exclusion of the teaching of "the dogmas of religion" from education in favour of the teaching of "pure morality only". To the Tories, such a position was objectionable on several grounds.

Morality and Human Nature

All such efforts to teach morality in the absence of religion did not take into account that man was an accountable being, and that all past attempts to teach morality independent of religion had resulted merely in the spread of infidelity. Almost invariably, children so taught had grown up "equally destitute of morals and religion". In his fallen state, man was incapable of devising, sanctioning, or living up to any proper code of morality in the absence of revealed religion. It was requisite that any system of moral education established for the benefit of man had to be based on the Christian religion, because of his very nature.

Although the Tories believed that man in his fallen state was "prone to evil and wickedness" and incapable of redeeming himself, or of living a good life unaided, they by no means held that man was ignorant of all moral or religious ideas, or utterly depraved and totally alienated from God. At one point, the Rev. John Strachan sought to provide a rational explanation for the view of human nature held by the Upper Canadian Tories. He quoted, with approval, a passage from a sermon by Dr. Thomas Chalmers, the renowned preacher of the Church of Scotland, to the effect that:

> The general approbation of virtue and detestation of vice, which have universally prevailed, prove that the moral sense was not annihilated, and that man did not become by the fall,

an unmixed, incorrigible mass of pollution and depravity, absolutely incapable of amendment, or of knowing, or discharging, by its natural powers, any part of the duty of a dependent rational being.

In his own sermons, the Rev. Strachan maintained that fallen man was still a moral and religious being; and that, though "the heart, the passions, the will, and the understandings" were corrupted by the Fall, all knowledge of right and wrong was not destroyed in the heart. Man, as distinct from 'the brute beasts of creation', was a rational animal capable of reflecting upon human actions and could appreciated virtue and could "relish emotions Spiritual and heavenly".

The rational faculty of man included "a moral sense" or conscience which monitored his conduct. Conscience was a law "engraven on the hearts" of all men great and small, and was independent of revelation or outward circumstances; yet it was in accordance with God's moral law. It condemned all evil doing, approved of good conduct, and rendered men miserable or happy according to their actions. Moreover, man was also a religious being because:

The foundation of religion exists in various degrees in every human soul however it may be directed, purified or debased. As reason and certain affections are common to all men, so the better part of our nature may be justly considered [to be] of a religious character.

In effect, man by his very nature was possessed of a "rational religion" to guide his conduct. On the one hand, man possessed a conscience, an innate sense of right and wrong, and by his reason, in the absence of revelation, he could "in some measure Know God" and be aware of the existence of a future state, of Providence, and the need of prayer and public worship. The truth of this assertion was attested to by the existence of such beliefs and "some kind of Religion or Worship in all nations", including those where no revelation was known to exist. Moreover, the working of the conscience was dependent for its effectiveness upon "a fear of future retribution", or a day of judgement, which in turn presupposed some knowledge of God.

In the absence of revelation, man was capable to some degree of knowing of God through studying "the book of nature" -- God's Works. He could begin to understand what was expected of him in this life by attention to the example set by the conduct of children. Man's natural religious character was seen at its best in youthful minds which, sheltered from temptation and error, "see things as they really are in all their truth and freshness". The religious nature of youth was evident in their humble and trusting nature which consisted of:

> Love for relations and friends -- reverence for elders -- honour for authorities -- respect for existing institutions -- humility and loyalty -- a sense of shame at what is unseemly -- a desire to rise in the scale of Being -- a disposition to take things on trust and believe what we do not see -- gratitude for kindness -- readiness to forgive.

Nevertheless, although man's fallen nature was not totally depraved, and his reason was aware of God's moral law and capable of knowing religion to some extent, this "natural religion" was adjudged to be insufficient to enable man to live up to what was required of him. (8)

To the Tory mind, man was not sufficient unto himself, and his "reason, *unaided*" was not capable of preserving him from evil. Reason was, and should always be, "the guiding and ruling faculty" in control over man's affections, but the numerous follies to which mankind succumbed proved that "its dominion over the passions [was] at best precarious". In general, men preferred virtue to vice but, all too often, that inclination had little influence upon their actions.

Motivated by "ambition, pride & interested views", men were seen to put aside "the powers of reason and assume the nature of beasts" in following their passions and appetites in being oblivious to all standards of morality and justice. In such situations, they readily succumbed to vice and became habituated to indulging their passions and taking a pleasure in "uproar and licentiousness" from which human reason could not restrain or reclaim them. To the contrary, the maintenance of virtue required patience and vigilance and the cultivation of settled habits, which few individuals would persist in acquiring on their own.

Moreover, there were definite limits to the competence of human reason for "man [was] not a pure emanation of Reason". There were many things in God's creation that were "beyond the power of [human] reason fully to comprehend or understand". This was particularly true of the Christian religion which by its very nature was mysterious, and involved beliefs that man had to accept on faith in being beyond his comprehension, but no less necessary to his well-being. Man could judge of the evidences of God's creation, but the "nature of religion" was beyond his understanding. Moreover, if man sought to overstep the limits of human reason, then he risked turning "this admirable faculty" into "a principle of destruction, not of edification" where human happiness was concerned.

Ancient & Modern Moralists

In the absence of revelation, the ancient philosophers, such as Plato, Aristotle and Cicero, had sought to construct a system of morals and religion for the betterment of mankind, but with little success. Restricted within "the narrow scope of human vision", the systems which they constructed were invariably speculative, complex and abstruse, and their concepts of virtue were "ambiguous and frequently false". Rather than providing binding principles of action, they all too frequently proved to be matters of dispute, "fostering pride and contention and failing to purify and improve the heart".

Although the ancient philosophers rose above "the superstitions of the people", and developed some idea – although rather confused – of the immortality of the soul, and Plato, in particular, realized that it was by the interposition of God that order was maintained in all things, the ancient philosophers were "incapable of forming a rational worship". Moreover, even if they had been able to arrive at a true system of morality, it would still have been insufficient as a rule of life.

All such moral systems which had been devised by man were deficient because they lacked universality and certainty, as well as any sanction to enforce virtuous action. The philosophers of the Greek schools, in their pride, disdained to enlighten the common people, and there were many areas of life, such as the condition of the lower orders, to which their concern did not penetrate. Too often the virtue of the ancients was for public consumption. It was a heroic virtue, dependent upon popular applause, and incapable of providing "consolation and inward repose". It did not "afford true and solid comfort, much less any happiness" to those suffering from the afflictions of this world.

Deprived of, or separated from knowledge of God's superintending providence, and judging everything according to "present fitness or propriety" or personal benefit, the difficulties and misfortunes of life brought only suffering upon man. In being "pleased with secondary causes", man not only failed to learn the lessons which were being taught in adversity, but most importantly, was under no compulsion to act in a virtuous manner for:

> all rules of life, except the Christian, want a proper sanction or
> obligation to enforce them and are therefore imperfect.

Socrates had "despaired of making men better, unless a teacher should descend from heaven"; he was conscious of his inability to motivate men to live up to his own example of virtue.

Modern philosophers, "to whom the world is everything", claimed that human reason was sufficient to ascertain moral and religious truth but in reality "their sublime notions of found morals, and divinity are from those very scriptures they revile". In seeking to separate morality from religion, they faced the same problem as the ancients.

To secure virtuous conduct, modern philosophers sought to ground their moral system on utilitarian considerations which they derived from their peculiar view of human nature. Utilitarianism was a moral philosophy and code of ethics which – as summarized by the Rev. John Strachan -- was based on the belief:

> that it is impossible for man to act without the appearance
> of some good to be procured by the action, for a love of life
> and a desire of self-preservation are implanted in our nature;
> consequently, we avoid misery and torments.

The belief of the utilitarian philosophers that virtuous conduct could be based simply on a weighing by the individual of whether an action promoted some good or happiness, and produced pleasure rather than pain, was viewed by Strachan as totally incredulous. The Disciples of Christ had "courted poverty, ignominy and death" in the service of God, thereby proving to the contrary that "self-preservation and the love of life" were not inviolable or absolute principles of human nature. Often virtuous conduct involved accepting sacrifices and suffering not in keeping with "any immediate pleasure it produced".

It was allowed that present utility could lead to virtuous conduct, but it was held to be defective as a criterion of judgment as it provided "no certain obligation to virtue" for the generality of mankind. Unquestionably, moral systems of human construction wedded to this life were incapable of rendering a people virtuous, and consequently were an unsatisfactory basis upon which to found a moral education, for:

> Human reason & Philosophy unassisted by religion are too weak to stem the tide of the passions or to bring solid comfort and nourishment to the heart. (9)

Christianity and the Teaching of Morality

The Christian religion had to be the basis of any educational system which purported to teach morality because Christianity was not only unique and distinct from all moral systems of human construction in having a sanction sufficient to govern man's conduct, but it supplied all their deficiencies. In contrast to the uncertainty and confusion of human systems, God had revealed His Will directly to man in plain and simple terms in the Gospel, and had instructed man as to how he should conduct his life if he wished to attain happiness in the present life and in the hereafter.

Scripture provided "a perfect law of righteousness" for guidance which was "admirably adapted to the nature and constitution of man" because perfectly "in accord with [the] presumptions of right and wrong which Reason affords". God had revealed principles of virtuous conduct -- veracity, purity, charity and piety -- which man could only grasp obscurely by means of his own natural reason.

Christianity was "the foundation of true morals" for man was incapable of accurately judging or devising in whole the proper principles of morality strictly on the basis of his experience. In effect, as the Rev. John Strachan expressed it, the connection between reason and revelation, or natural religion and revealed religion, was such that:

> Reason is the compass by which we steer our course, and revelation the polar star [by] which we correct its variations.

Christianity was "the perfection of natural religion" and "the perfection of reason". In sum, Christianity explained what was unclear to human reason where moral doctrines and concepts were concerned, as well as what was incomprehensible to philosophers "of earth-bound vision" where purely religious doctrines were concerned. Moral principles adhered in the nature of things, and were part of the eternal truth of God's creation. Consequently, since man was made in the image of God, any system of morality which was "just and true to the wants of [man's] nature" had to be founded upon the Christian religion. (10)

By means of his moral sense, man could distinguish right from wrong, but only instruction in the Christian faith could keep the conscience uncorrupted and enable it to have a decisive influence over the actual conduct of man. In the nature of things, if education were to produce moral, virtuous and religious beings, then it must be based upon revealed religion. Man possessed "many natural and honourable powers" as a moral and religious being, but they were not sufficient for him to realize his purpose in life,- which education ought to further, or to please God. For unaided by revelation:

> we know not enough for our happiness, and we cannot yield Him that perfect service which His Holiness requires.

Christianity not only provided just and true precepts for man's guidance, but was "the root of all true virtue" for religion transformed the whole being of man and governed his minutest actions. Other moral systems accepted man as he was, focused on this life, and "took cognizance of external acts only". On the contrary, Christianity 'entered into the heart', and demanded "internal purity and benevolent dispositions". The Christian religion comprised religious doctrines, in addition to moral precepts, by means of which the nature of man could be transformed and given the power to do what was good. Moreover, it provided "a sanction or obligation" to encourage or compel the Christian to virtuous action.

The "man of the world" might act virtuously from various motives, but such a morality was inferior to that of the true Christian, for Christianity demanded much more.

> The Christian lives in such a manner as to qualify himself for the acceptance, as well as the enjoyment of future happiness. -- The first has only to cultivate justice, prudence, temperance & benevolences; to these the Christian must add constant piety, humility, resignation and charity.

In referring all things to God, the Christian acted not from present concern or comfort, but rather out of Christian duty. Even in adversity, the Christian adhered to virtuous conduct in receiving "consolation and inward repose" from his religion in being secure in the knowledge that on the Day of Judgment all would be redressed. In sum, morality could not be divorced from religion if moral principles, once taught or inculcated, were to continue to be effective for life in governing human conduct. (11)

In formulating their plans for the establishment of a provincial system of education, the Upper Canadian Tory elite -- under the leadership of the Rev. John Strachan – was heavily motivated by their Christian beliefs. As Christians, the Tories believed that man was an accountable being; and that education, above all else, must prepare the student to fulfill his purpose in life and, ultimately, to prepare him to face the Day of Judgement. Hence, there was a need to teach religious principles to youth, which demanded a religious content in education as did the teaching of morality.

For the Tories, it was a certainty that if moral values were going to effectively govern the conduct of man, morality could not be separated from the Christian religion. The needs of man's nature and the purpose of his being determined that moral values must be taught to youth in the education system, and to be efficacious, morality had to be based on religion. Hence, religion had to form the basis of any system of education which was to be established in Upper Canada; and that necessity was reflected in the education system that the Upper Canadian Tories strove to establish as part of their National Policy.

Chapter Fourteen

Education and the Condition of the People

In establishing a general system of education for the Province of Upper Canada, the Upper Canadian Tories – and the Rev. John Strachan in particular – were acting in accordance with their religious beliefs and Christian outlook on life, but they were motivated as well by their concern for the condition of the people. In addition to its religious and moral function, a religiously-based system of education was viewed as a vehicle for attaining the betterment of all ranks of society through the formation of the public character of the province. A 'national' system of education, open to all ranks of society, would increase the respectability of the province, and would strengthen and maintain the existing social order, as well as promote social peace and harmony. The Tory religious beliefs, and their understanding of the purpose of education and the benefits to be gained by 'proper learning', determined not only the system of education that they were striving to establish -- one under the control of the state and the direction of the Established Church – but also what was to be taught, who should be the beneficiaries of that education, when and where religious and moral values should be taught, and by whom and to what purpose.

A Christian Education

To the Tory mind, education was a life-long process which commenced in childhood with the efforts of parents, and then teachers, to inculcate into "the infant mind" principles and values which would serve to guide and order the conduct of the pupil throughout this life, and in preparation for the life to come. To achieve that end, it was requisite that all classes of society be provided with the benefits of education; and that "the Gospel, and the Gospel only, [be] the basis of education". Only Christian principles, as taught by the National Church and conveyed to the child by ardent teachers, could serve to develop "a Proper character", to ensure the peace and harmony of society, and to "guide [man] through time and prepare [him] for eternity".

As Christians, the Tories believed that:

> the principles of religion [were] ...the best calculated for the improvement of human nature and [for] promoting the welfare and true happiness of society.

Religion could not be separated from education any more than the soul from the body. For to fulfill its social and religious purpose, education had to act upon "the whole inner man". Indeed, the heart of man was the central focus of the social concern of the Tories, as well as of their religious scheme of redemption. It was in the heart, so they believed, that were to be found:

> the sources of that pride and of those prejudices which unsettle
> the moral restraints and disorganize the machinery of society.

It was religion – the Christian religion alone -- which could "destroy the power of evil in the heart", improve man's corrupted reason, and raise man's desires above worldly concerns, pleasures and appetites. If the "holy purpose of education – to produce on earth the society of heaven" – was to be realized, religious principles had to be inculcated in every youth of the province through a universal system of education open to all.

That being so, the Tories did not believe that the teaching of the doctrines and precepts of religion to pupils in a school system was sufficient alone for the forming of a proper moral character in youth. To the contrary, religious instruction had to be accompanied by the inculcation of "religious habits". Teachers could give instruction in the truths of religion, but religious habits could "only be formed at home". Christian principles had to be brought to exercise a controlling influence over conduct of the young; and, in that endeavour, the doctrines of religion were "only the materials" upon which a thoroughgoing "moral and spiritual training" ought to be based.

In the Tory view, education could not be confined to "the mere intellectual" in disregard of its practical social implications, for:

> in the business of education …we must take care to touch the
> heart, to enlist the feelings – to engage the affections, to mould
> and purify the habits, to guide the conscience -- to discipline
> the body, to govern the will.

Parents were admonished that they should commence the inculcation of religious principles in their children "as soon as children know when they do wrong". It was to be done with "great tenderness and delicacy" in taking account of the "freedom and indulgence" required on account of their age. An accurate knowledge of the truths of religion was not required in children so much as a good grounding in its principles to render the child capable of understanding the practical implications of religious principles in human relations.

To the Tory mind, children, despite their limited capacities, were capable of understanding what was required, for:

> surely... a child may be taught obedience to his parents, to be kind and affectionate to his companions, to be mild, charitable and humane; to behave with the strictest propriety in his intercourse with the world; to be faithful and honorable, to conquer perverse and wicked habits, to subdue degrading habits, and to restrain the turbulence of passion.

This did not mean that education ought to be confined to the moral precepts of religion to the exclusion of Christian doctrines, or that the latter were "too difficult or abstract" to be comprehended by children. On the contrary, children needed to be made aware of Christ's atonement and brought to Christ. To that end, the truths of religion had to be taught in full, step by step, and all questions answered as they might arise. Where Christian principles were concerned "by teaching some and concealing others, we build upon a foundation that can never stand".

The inculcation of Christian principles and religious habits was of the essence for as the character of youth were formed "so would go the man"; and, in the nature of things and in keeping with "the better part of his nature", man could be happy and at peace only if he returned to God and lived in obedience to His Will. In sum, it was held to be in the best interests of society that parents and the schools seek to form "the national manners, and character, and heart, and soul" of Upper Canadian youth through the inculcation of Christian principles and religious habits. (1)

A Universal System of Education

The formation of a 'national character' was a critical function of any system of education. However, the Tory insistence that the provincial government was obligated to work with the Established Church to establish a universal system of education -- open to all classes and ranks of society "high and low, rich and poor, old and young" -- stemmed from a complex of motives and concerns: religious, moral, and social.

In the first place, the Tories believed that it was a duty of every Christian government to bring to bear "the ennobling and sanctifying operation" of a proper system of education upon all its subjects to ensure that they would be instructed in "the way, and the truth, and the life". To that end, it was essential that everyone, including the poor, be educated so that they might be able to read the Bible and come to know, believe, and understand its leading doctrines and precepts. The example to be followed here, as always, was that of Christ who had sought continually "to reform the people" through his teachings, and who had concentrated his effort on the ignorant and the poor. For the Tories, the poor could not be denied access to education for, even on the grounds of charity, they had as much of a claim to public support as the sick and destitute had for comfort and aid.

The religious motivation for establishing a universal system of education in Upper Canada was reinforced in the Tory mind by a critical concern for the moral character of the province. They believed that ignorance invariably fostered vice, and all the other evils which afflicted man; while education sustained civilization by inculcating "firm sentiments of moral and religious wisdom" which served "to enlarge the understanding and elevate the sentiments". Through education, "the national mind" could be raised above "the mere selfish pursuits of gain" or the indulgence of the appetites, and endowed with "higher and holier aspirations". It was believed that education was particularly necessary in regard to morality for the uneducated were blind to "the nature of moral obligation" and unable to comprehend either "the sublime doctrines" of the Christian religion or "the awful sanctions" which were the best guarantee of moral conduct. In sum, it was believed that:

Before the gift of Christianity can be attended with beneficial consequences, it must be preceded by some degree of knowledge and general improvement in those who receive it. -- The mind must be accustomed to reflect and meditate, before it can contemplate with profit the grand mysteries of our Holy Faith.

Not all men were capable of comprehending 'the evidences' of Christianity, but all, if properly educated, could know what was required of them and govern their conduct accordingly. Thus, for the Tories, the diffusion of education among all ranks of society was requisite on both religious and moral grounds which -- given their belief that religion could not be separated for morality-- meant that Upper Canada had to have a religiously-based system of education. Religious and moral concerns, however, were only a part – although an essential part – of their motivation in striving to establish a universal system of education in Upper Canada. A system of education, open to all, was requisite as well to serve a social purpose in maintaining public order and social harmony.

Educating the Poor

In witnessing the postwar popular unrest in England, the Upper Canadian Tories were particularly concerned to secure the education of the lower orders of society. On the one hand, they felt duty-bound as Christians to foster and support policies which would contribute to "the amelioration of the temporal as well as the spiritual condition of the destitute and distressed", and education was held to be a primary means by which that could be accomplished. The Tories were anxious that the poor be taught "every useful and improving branch of knowledge", as well as "the great practical and saving truths" of Christianity. On the other hand, the desire to educate the poor was motivated as well by an anxiety and concern for the maintenance of the social order.

Religion was regarded as "a constraining principle" which would provide an antidote to 'the poison' that was being spread by infidels and demagogues whose effusions were aimed particularly at the lower orders of society. In the absence of "a sound and religious instruction", the public mind was susceptible to the delusions which were being preached by infidels and demagogues who were bent on fomenting social unrest and political disorder. The history of the French Revolution was regarded as being the most tragic example of what would occur in the absence of an educated people with a strong public character.

The Socializing effect of Education

To the Tory mind, a proper education – religiously based – was needed to render the lower orders "content with their situation". It would bring them:

> to a high pitch of conscientious duty, sobriety of mind and practice, and unmurmuring endurance, and which alone [could] raise them too above the low temptations of sensuality, or give to the intellectual improvement of their minds its genuine influence upon their hearts and spirits, or bear them through the furnace of affliction with a patriotic and Christian patience.

As Christians, with their eyes fixed firmly on immortality, they would realize the insignificance of worldly things and would not "feel uneasy, discontented & angry at passing circumstances and events". Under the influence of Christian principles, they would possess "a patient tranquil [and] resigned spirit", and be governed by feelings of peace, kindness, justice, charity and good will towards their fellow man. They would know that all, regardless of rank, were "equally responsible before God & all members of the same family & destined to be tried before the same impartial tribunal". Moreover, such an education would encourage them to put "a lasting good" before present gratification, and to seek to avoid that 'general improvidence' and 'thoughtless indulgence' to which the lower orders were prone.

Through learning to provide in better times for adversity, the suffering of the poor would be eased during hard times -- which always fell heaviest upon them -- and they would be less inclined to turn to crime and disorder. Nonetheless, it was realized that the education of the lower orders was not without its dangers. It was held that:

> their religious knowledge should be made to keep pace with their advancement in other things, for without the meek and charitable influence of Christianity upon their hearts, their superior information will only render them more obstinate and untractable [sic]. (2)

To the Tory mind, a religiously-based education was the best support of social order not only because of the type of character it formed, but also as to the duties which it prescribed and the religious sanction that it provided to enforce adherence. In the Christian scheme of things, as interpreted by the Anglican Tories, religion embraced man's domestic and social life, and was "an active principle" which set forth the duties that man owed both to God and to his fellow man.

Teaching the Duties of Life

If man were to 'progress in holiness', then self-examination, private prayer, and a pious acceptance of God's Providence were required, but religion also demanded the performance of the duties of this life. The Christian religion taught that man was the creator of neither his being, nor his various faculties; and that the purpose of life was not "to gratify sense and to serve appetites and passions". To the contrary, the Christian religion taught that man was created by God for His own purposes which required man to "discharge … various duties as [a] rational and social [being] in preparing for eternity". In sum, God -- a far wiser and more powerful being –had placed men in the different stations of life which they occupied, so that each might perform his prescribed duties "to God, Society and himself".

To that end, Scripture commanded that they love God with all their hearts and "labour diligently in their several callings" and to do their duty in going unto perfection. If man were to ensure himself of salvation, he must faithfully discharge his temporal as well as his spiritual duties, for:

> no worldly business can excuse a man from the neglect of God
> and of his own soul -- nor can any pretense of Faith be made
> to serve as an apology for sloth or idleness in any honest
> worldly calling.

In the nature of things, these duties -- the social, domestic and strictly spiritual -- were inseparable for they were:

> interwoven with each other and in proportion as they are
> disjointed, the duty is the worse performed and the privilege
> the less enjoyed.

Indeed, the duties which pertained to man's secular concerns were "subordinate to things essentially spiritual"; and yet they were an integral part of man's spiritual life.

> Even while we render to Caesar the things that are Caesar's and unto God the things that are God's, we must still keep in mind that Caesar's portion is to be given for God's sake and as evidence that we love God.

It was God's Will -- as revealed in the Gospels -- that the Christian in His service should strive to "unite piety with daily duty", and "spiritual and social excellence", in bringing into "union and harmony the religious and the social character of man". It was a philosophy which would be reflected in the teachings of the schools under the superintendence of the Anglican clergy. (3)

The Acquisition of Knowledge and Understanding

In keeping with God's scheme of things, everyone -- regardless of his particular position in the social hierarchy -- had God-given talents and abilities of one sort or another to cultivate, and a character which must be improved and maintained, for:

> the life which God has given us ... is a great and important trust for the right management of which we are all responsible, and it comprehends many other trusts each requiring to be religiously discharged in whatever rank of life we are placed and which we dare not neglect without incurring blame and ultimate ruin -- We have duties to perform, a race to run -- a sphere of activity to fill, obligations to meet -- all of which imply a responsible condition and a religious and moral character.

If man were to attain "eternal felicity" on the Day of Judgment and escape damnation, it was essential that he develop his talents to the best of his abilities and make a positive contribution to the good of society. Abstention from committing evil acts and a strict obedience to human laws was not sufficient, in the absence of well-doing, to ensure salvation.

To that end, man must be "diligent in [his] station" and seek to improve his mind and perfect his nature through imitating the graces of Christ.

Not only man's reasoning powers and bodily health, but even the diverse "natural tempers, dispositions, propensities and inclinations" of mankind could and ought to be improved. However, everything depended upon the development of man's moral and intellectual powers which could only be attained by dint of human effort. The acquisition of knowledge and understanding required 'attention and industry'.

Learning was essential to salvation, for 'true learning' could not but foster wisdom and holiness, and hence happiness both in the present life and the hereafter. Through the acquisition of religious knowledge and faith, Christian virtue was implanted in the heart. Christian virtue entailed not only a humble, trusting and truthful nature, but also a sense of compassion for those less fortunate and a desire to do good in aiding the distressed and promoting "the order and felicity of Society".

In the truly virtuous man, "self was annihilated". All actions proceeded from a sense of duty, and the mind of the virtuous man – when it was not employed in seeking to further the good of mankind – was occupied in "the contemplation of the infinite perfections of God" for the purpose of imitating them. For the virtuous man, the intimate connection between the present and the future life was clear, as was the realization that "all things depend upon God".

The development of his rational capacities was a duty which man owed to himself and to God, as well as his fellow man. With a virtuous heart, man could do what was expected of him, and the development of his understanding both fostered and strengthened Christian virtue which:

> appears in its greatest perfection in the man whose mind is extensively cultivated, whose understanding is accurate and his knowledge profound, whose dispositions and habits are its warm supporters, and all subservient to the promotion of his true happiness.

Learning to Strive to perform the Duties of One's Station

All men were not equal in their capacity to learn, but all children could be taught, and could comprehend, what was necessary to attain salvation, and could be made aware that man was an accountable being. In his "wisdom and goodness", God had endowed each individual with sufficient powers to fulfill his particular trust and, on the Day of Judgment, each individual would be rewarded or condemned accordingly. Both in school and from the pulpit, children and parishioners were admonished by the Anglican clergy that:

> Glorious and immediate is the reward of him who faithfully discharges the duties of his Station, however lowly that station may be, from a principle of obedience to God and a steadfast regard to His Will -- In the careful performance of the work given him to do, he feels that he is discharging the duty of a Christian. God who surveys all, comprehends all and how the General order -- the highest Perfection and happiness -- shall be maintained and advanced, hath placed men in this station -- Therefore however humble my occupation, however difficult or laborious -- however trifling or uncertain their success here, I stand working where God wills that I should work. I am therefore occupied in His service and this connection gives dignity to my labours and makes them a source of honour and felicity.

The proper performance of one's occupation, in whatever rank, was set forth as a duty which ought to be discharged willingly and faithfully as "a service done to God". It should not be the occasion of "disquietude or misery".

> By thus acting, we prove our reverence for the institutions and regulations which God hath established; we acknowledge His wisdom, His kindness -- submit ourselves entirely to His Will, allow ourselves to be guided and governed by Him in all things, act and work as it were upon the same plan by which God acts and are, in the language of Scripture, workers together with him.

Those who were dissatisfied in their station, or neglected their duties to God, society and themselves, and failed to strive for the perfection that they were called upon to pursue, were forewarned that they would not attain comfort and contentment in this life. And, on the Day of Judgement, they would be condemned to 'eternal death'. (4)

Aspiring to Excellence in One's Position

All men were not equal in talents, but all were duty-bound to develop their talents to the fullest for the benefit of society as well as themselves, and to cultivate a Christian moral character. Each man was required to strive to be the best of whatever he was, to make the best of his lot in life and through perseverance, patience and self-denial, to apply himself to the utmost of his abilities in the profession or occupation in which God had placed him.

Young men of a superior talent and ability were expected to "aspire to excellence", to "cherish a laudable ambition", and through "application, ability, diligence and integrity" to attain distinction in their profession. All youth were admonished to focus their ambition on becoming the best of whatever God willed one to be, which was signified by the talents and abilities that He allotted to each.

In God's scheme of things, no one was precluded from "rising into a superior class". On the contrary, one's position in society was relative to the individual's peculiar God-given talents and the use to which they were put. Efforts to advance "one's condition" – or social position – as long as it resulted from "activity of the mind and love of excellence" were natural, and "if properly directed" were quite laudable. However, students were cautioned that there were limits to striving which had to be recognized. To seek to raise oneself to a higher position was commendable, but no one should in the process "despise the obscurity of his station" or "that portion of bliss" which it afforded. Nor should anyone form unreasonable expectations as to his own capabilities and just deserts. The individual must remain aware that everyone had his allotted role to play in society, and -- given that Tory belief -- students were admonished that:

a man's true consequence [was] not to be measured by his own conceit, or his place in society determined by his own presumption. For when he steps out of the sphere in which he ought to move, and invades another unprepared and uncalled by lawful means, he is quite out of his element, and has lost his real consequence among men.

Learning to Be Content with One's Station

The Upper Canadian Tories were firm believers in an aristocracy of talent and ability, and a society wherein those of a superior God-given talents and abilities could ascend to a higher station in the social hierarchy through education and personal achievement. What concerned the Tories in the immediate postwar years, however, was the 'levelling spirit' and presumptuousness which was evident among the lower orders which took the form of individuals seeking to enter into professions and occupations for which they were ill-prepared, ill-educated, and ill-suited. Hence, the sermons of the Anglican clergy, and of the Rev. John Strachan, in particular, preached a message that emphasized being content with one's station in the 'natural' social hierarchy. It was a message that was conveyed as well to students studying in the grammar schools where most of the teachers were Anglican clerics.

Those who were envious of their superiors and bent on "plans of aggrandizement" were cautioned that man was prone to overestimate the happiness which a change of condition would bring, and to underestimate the sacrifices which it would entail. Not only would such an effort multiply his cares and worries but, once embarked upon, his desires would inevitably expand and "the whole soul [become] absorbed with rising in the world". Peace of mind and ease would give way to impatience and "anxious expectation". He would lose the ability to derive satisfaction from any situation which was not an immediate step to something better. In such a "fever of ... mind", the overly-ambitious man would become indifferent to virtue and incapable of resuming or enjoying the pleasures that were yielded by his original state.

The envious and discontented were cautioned that true felicity could be found only in a religious life; and that, in the feverish pursuit of "riches and elevated rank", they would reach a point of no return where:

> Chagrin -- melancholy -- envy -- hatred and other wretched
> passions ... rack your soul and these growing by indulgence
> render you completely miserable. The Sympathy of your
> Friends only inflames your pride and confirms your restlessness.
> Nature possesses no charms for you -- To your distorted eye all
> is gloomy and disordered. (5)

If man were to be truly happy, he must learn "to contract his desires" and
be brought to realize the unreasonableness of feeling discontented with
his particular station in life. Everyone as a member of society received
its benefits, and everyone in his station -- as "subjects of God's kingdom"
-- ought to readily and willingly contribute to that society in accordance
with their God-given talents and abilities. Rather than being envious
of the advantages that were enjoyed by his superiors, the discontented
individual was advised to take account of the comforts that he actually
enjoyed over those below him in the social hierarchy.

From the pulpit, and in the classroom, the Anglican clerics further
cautioned that what constituted happiness varied from individual to
individual, with age, and "with the different Ranks of Society"; and
that consequently:

> supposing you [were] raised to the condition of one whose
> happiness you envy. Is it certain that [your] enjoyment will
> be equal to his? Perhaps neither your power of body nor of
> mind fit you for his situation – and the difficulties which you
> must encounter may poison your joy. Your different shares of
> sensibility will produce very unequal degrees of happiness.

Where the social order was concerned, the Anglican clergy admonished
both youth and their parents that they must be "content with things as
they were" for:

> The gifts of fortune are not so partially distributed as we may
> at first imagine – We presume that the Author of our nature
> has given us that temper, understanding and taste which will
> qualify us for that place in the System [that] we were ordained
> to fill.

The poor and the restless were assured that the allurements and glories of this world were insignificant when compared to life eternal, and the perfection to which the soul of man was called to aspire through "the only begotten Son to God". In this life, perfect happiness could not be attained by man. In sum, what the Anglican clerics taught was that the path to true happiness was to be found in faithfully striving to cultivate one's own talents, in striving to carry out the duties of one's station in obedience to God's commandments, and in preparing oneself for the life to come through living a moral life in keeping with God's Will.

In sum, the Upper Canadian Tories believed that those who were discontented with their allotted station in life, and sought happiness in attempting to usurp a superior position, were "pursuing a delusive phantom". In doing so, they would but "inflame their malevolent passions", and bring soul destroying "cares and anxieties' upon themselves. They would incur God's displeasure for refusing to obey His Will and failing to accept "that subordination which [was] the order of nature". (6)

A Natural Subordination & Interdependence

For the Tories, it was evident that in God's scheme of things there was subordination among men, as well as in the natural world. Those who accepted their station in life and labored to fulfill their respective duties were admonished not to regard themselves as unfairly treated. On the contrary, a due subordination was necessary, as well as highly beneficial, both for the individual and society.

What the Anglican clerics taught was that in nature some of God's creations, whether animal, vegetable or 'inert matter', were superior to others in terms of their properties or faculties – viz. their strength, beauty or intelligence—and yet, everything, and every animal, had its use and "all subsist by their dependence upon one another". The governing principles were obviously subordination, plenitude and interdependence. In nature, everything was not on a level, or of the same character, and nothing was inutile, redundant, or incomplete, and all objects or beings were "mutually connected" one with another. Subordination and interdependence were in keeping with the order of God's creation, and there was little doubt that such principles were intended also to apply to human society where a like subordination and interdependence was manifest.

Where "the gifts of God" were concerned, there was no equality of division for:

> men [were] placed from their birth by the hand of Providence
> in different situations of rank, power, and wealth; ....

Moreover, that "natural inequality" extended even to their character and abilities as there was an "infinite diversity in the tempers, dispositions, and talents of men". The differences in intelligence, aptitudes, interests, and feelings were a clear indication that "one is formed to rule, another to obey". Such was the intention of the Creator, and it was a situation that had to be accepted, for:

> it was of little importance to determine, even if possible, whether
> this difference of character [came] from the original constitution
> of individuals ... or from the particular circumstances in which
> they happened to be placed. Perhaps in original temperament,
> all mankind [were] nearly on a level and the extreme diversities
> in character depend chiefly on causes foreign to the individual.

Whether attributable largely to nature or circumstance, it was indisputable that there were differences of character among mankind. It was 'the Fall' that had originally corrupted man's moral nature to a greater or lesser extent, "but undoubtedly in very different degrees". Hence, all men could not be brought to the same level of knowledge, attainments, or exalted station, even if subject to the same instruction and discipline.

Some men were intended to occupy superior positions in society and others to labour in inferior positions; and, although seemingly inexplicable, it could not be doubted that it was in keeping with God's Will. Therefore, it was both right and just. And it was a worldview that the Tories –through their teachings -- were intent on inculcating into the youth of the province. (7)

A Society of Mutual Dependence & Benefit

The Tories believed, and taught, that subordination was not only in keeping with the diverse talents and abilities of man, but was required to satisfy his nature and his wants. Man was a social being who could not live a solitary or independent life without being "rendered wretched". The securing of the common necessities of life, not to mention the maintenance of civilization, required that men combine their different talents and resources and place themselves under the direction of some among them who were more capable of directing their efforts and keeping them acting in unison for the benefit of all. In such a manner, "the general comfort & happiness" of all were advanced; and all, despite their differences of rank or station, were mutually dependent -- one on another – to meet their mutual needs and wants.

Within the social organism, everyone was free "to follow his own business unmolested"; and yet everyone was dependent on his fellows in a situation where:

> the happiness of one is subservient to that of his Neighbour -- Private Interest is inseparably connected with the interest of the community, and the union and happiness of the whole acquire a degree of strength and a security which the unnatural disjointed systems of solitude and selfishness could never attain.

Within society, everyone had his allotted role to fill for the benefit of both himself and society as a whole; and no occupation, however inferior, was to be despised for each had its duties and rights, and all were necessary to the proper functioning of society:

> The Magistrate requires the aid of his people – the Master of his servant – They are all dependent upon one another, as they subsist by an exchange of good offices. And all are independent as far as one is entitled to the countenance and protection of another. The lowest order enjoys its peculiar comforts and privileges and contributes equally with the higher to the support and dignity of Society.

Man's future happiness, as well as the good of society and his own well-being, demanded that he faithfully fulfill the duties of his station and strive "to cultivate the social virtues". This was in keeping with God's scheme of things, and should not be the cause of anger and discord. Compared to the prospect of immortality, the things of this life were "of little importance"; and students had to come to understand that it was:

> much more rational and becoming to bow to His Will, to submit
> with patience and resignation to all His dispensations.

To the Tory mind, a religiously-based system of education -- through the Christian values it would inculcate in youth and the duties it prescribed and sanctioned -- was a mainstay of the social order. Thus, the desire of the Tories to establish a religiously-based education system in Upper Canada stemmed from a social concern – the need to teach Christian values to support the existing social order– as well as from religious and moral concerns; all three motivations of which were inextricably interwoven where the formation of character was concerned. (8)

The Formation of Character

For the Tories, the formation of a common 'national' character among the settlers of Upper Canada – a 'British national character' -- was of the essence of the National Policy in its political, religious, educational and social aspects. It underlay their efforts to extend the ministrations of the Established Church in Upper Canada, to maintain the balanced British constitution, to defend the Church-State polity of Upper Canada, and to establish a universal system of education – open to all -- under the direction of the Established Church. The Church, the State, and education had an essential role to play in the development and sustaining of the 'national' character, as did the family and the individual himself.

Given their religious outlook on the purpose of life and their worldview, the Upper Canadian Tories held that it was the duty of parents to see that the "intellectual and moral powers" of their children were cultivated; and that their children were instructed in the "arts and accomplishments" which would prepare them to properly "perform the duties they owe themselves". The primary focus of education within the family, as within the school, was 'the formation of character'; and it was the mother of the family who was viewed as the primary influence in imparting moral and religious values to her children in the home. In addition, at the elementary school level, one of the primary purposes of a formal system of education was to support the home in 'the formation of the character' of the youth of the province.

Whether approached from a strictly religious, moral or social point of view, the living of a Christian life, the attainment of one's proper place in society, and the fulfillment of the duties of one's station, was dependent upon "firmness of character". Men were born with different talents, and consequently formed different "objects of ambition". However, the attainment of whatever position in life a youth was best suited to fulfill as an adult, depended not only upon his God-given talents, but also upon diligence and "steadfastness and perseverance in pursuit" of the object of his ambition. Above all, it required a strong character and application. Students were admonished that natural talents alone, if "unaccompanied with firmness and energy of mind", would not bring success in any endeavour.

Men were responsible beings who would be called to give account on the Day of Judgement for the use and improvement that they had made in their God-given talents and in fulfilling the duties of this life. Given such beliefs, the Upper Canadian Tories consciously strove to develop the character of their children and to promote the education of youth. Where education -- both informal and formal -- was concerned the formation of character was of the essence; and in that endeavour the family, the Church and the school, had a crucial role to play. (9)

The Tories held that a man's character could be improved only through the development of his moral and intellectual powers; that only the saving grace of the Christian religion could enable man to improve his character in any lasting sense; and that any improvement had to come about under the direction of Christian principles. For the 'going unto perfection' consisted of attaining and cultivating Christian virtues. That belief, in turn, was reflected in the values which the Tories sought to inculcate in their children, and in the way in which they went about it.

The Education of Youth

Families were expected to provide an informal instruction in religion to their young children --before they received a more formal instruction in the Church and school -- to ensure that religious values were inculcated in youth and the proper admonitions duly delivered. Children were also to be taught how to approach life and what was expected of them.

In the Tory view, children needed to be made aware, by their parents and mentors, of how 'precious' their time on earth was, and of the need to study and apply themselves while young. Their future consequence in this world, as well as in the next, depended upon their own exertions. God might call them at any time to give an account of themselves, and they must not "forget the future in the present".

Children were exhorted continually to seek to rise by their own merit, and to excel at whatever occupation or profession which might be chosen for them, according to the assessment of their talents and abilities made by their parents and others – their teachers – who were better able than themselves to judge of their capabilities. Everyone, it was explained, could not be the best of their particular profession or occupation; yet that was what one must strive to be, for:

> If you lose the race after every effort to gain the victory, you
> lose with honour, but to be distanced is always disgraceful.

At the same time, children were to be cautioned that in pursuing their studies in school and/or in preparing for a profession, that learning was not everything; they must also be 'good', and seek always to cultivate the social virtues. They must be brought to realize that 'man did not live for himself alone'. They were admonished to strive "to shew a good heart to advantage" by setting a good example of proper conduct for others, and were cautioned that they must avoid being "idle, ignorant and rude" while making the best of the educational and professional opportunities at hand.

Such admonitions were well summarized in a letter which young John Beverley Robinson received from his mentor, the Rev. Dr. John Stuart

-- an Anglican Loyalist minister -- upon Robinson commencing his studies under the Rev. John Strachan's at the Cornwall District Grammar School:

> I need not attempt to enumerate the Advantages in your Power, while in this desirable Situation. Neither, I hope, need I caution you to turn them to your future Profit, by Industry, Assiduity & a strict Regard to moral Conduct. I trust that your own good sense will suggest to you that you are now laying the Foundation of the Character which you will sustain through Life whether you will be an useful and respectable Character in Society, or the contrary. (10)

Emulating Men of Eminence

As teachers, the Anglican clerics constantly set before their pupils the lives of eminent men of virtue from the Bible and from history, especially Jesus Christ and the virtuous heroes of Antiquity; and the Rev. John Strachan made a point of publishing biographical sketches and sermons upon the death of eminent men of Upper Canada. It was believed that such examples of holy and virtuous lives served as "proper objects of imitation" for youth; that youth would be inspired by them with 'a love of virtue'; and that such examples would foster in youth a desire to attain a preeminence in their field of endeavour – a distinguished reputation -- which would last beyond their particular lifetime.

The Upper Canadians who were held up for emulation were men of eminence in their community. They were men who were seen to have advanced "with probity and honour" in their careers, and to have achieved distinction by dint of their industry, application and study, or who had unselfishly served in some public position. In effect, they were men of stature who were described as having distinguished themselves by their benevolence, their inflexible justice, public virtue, wisdom, knowledge, and private worth, and who were possessed of an independent, firm and honourable character, a pious heart, and a sincere patriotic dedication to promoting "the best interest of their Province".

Nonetheless, the holding up of the lives of good men for emulation, parental blandishments in the home, and exhortations from the pulpit on Sunday, were not adjudged sufficient to properly form the character of youth, or to prepare them for life in the community at large. It required, as well, the imposition of a learning process and a disciplined study that could be found, for the most part, only within a school system that was organized on "a rational plan of education". Such was the school system that the Anglican Tory elite strove to establish in the Province of Upper Canada, with a standardized curriculum and system of discipline calculated to form the character of the youth of the province and to prepare them to live a good and productive life in keeping with God's scheme of things. (11)

The Grammar School Curriculum

What the Tories hoped to achieve in establishing a general system of education was clearly evident in the curriculum which the Rev. John Strachan -- in his position as President of the General Board of Education (1822-1833) -- established for the District Grammar Schools. The grammar school curriculum, and his defence of the same, reflected the deeper religious, political, and social values of the Upper Canadian Anglican Tory elite.

The grammar school curriculum was designed by Strachan to avoid the narrowness of either a purely classical or a strictly commercial education, while yielding the benefits of both. The District Grammar Schools provided a five-year course of study, with each school comprising 60 to 65 students in total. Among the breadth of subjects taught were English Grammar, Spelling, Reading, Writing and Elocution, Latin Reading and Grammar, Greek grammar and composition, and French, Mathematics --Algebra, Euclid (Geometry), Trigonometry -- and the study of selected classical authors; as well as such useful subjects as Arithmetic, Geography, Civil and Natural History, Bookkeeping, Surveying, Navigation, the Construction of Maps, Elements of Astrology, and Commerce. Included in the curriculum were courses on the Old and New Testaments, and a study of the truths of the Christian religion as set forth in a work by Hugo Grotius: *De Veritate Religionis Christianae* (1st. ed. 1627).

With respect to religion, students who were members of the Church of England were taught the Church catechism, and non-Anglican students -- if their parents gave their permission -- were to be given instruction in religion and explanations of the Scriptures, within a context where religion was to be presented as "a practical rule of life" rather than "as a science". All students were to be made aware of "the practical use" of what they had to learn, and how it would benefit them "in the business of common life". Arithmetic, for example, was to be applied to solving problems at hand; Geography to involve the study of the locality; and Astronomy to be applied to navigational problems.

Such a broad course of study was justified on the grounds that the District Grammar Schools had not only to prepare students for whatever profession they should follow in life, but also had to prepare and qualify those students who wished to continue their education at a university. Thus, the education provided for the students had to be "most respectable", and on a par with the public schools of England so that those who desired, or could afford, to complete their education at an English university would not suffer any disadvantage. (12)

The Tory stress on the immediate social and practical utility of a formal education served yet another purpose. The Tories were convinced of the value of a traditional education in the Classics, but to attract public support for the district grammar school system, the 'useful' subjects were emphasized. Hence, the public was informed that the scope of the curriculum was designed to include subjects that were usefulness in business and everyday life, that were a necessary prerequisite to further study of "the higher branches of abstract science", and that were requisite "to discipline the mind". Indeed, the latter was the primary argument set forth in defence of maintaining Classical studies in the curriculum of the District Grammar Schools. In maintaining the necessity of having classical studies as part of the District Schools curriculum, the Tories faced what they described as "violent attacks" on the part of "ignorant, fanatics, and anarchists" who -- it was asserted -- wished to follow the French despot, Napoleon Bonaparte, in proscribing the teaching of the Classics in schools.

To the contrary, the Rev. Strachan maintained that the study of the language and literature of the Ancients was not a waste of time. Not only were the professions of law and medicine, and the clerical calling, dependent upon a knowledge of Latin, but such an education was "a mark of distinction which evinced intelligence, liberality, delicacy and nobleness of sentiment" and set a man apart as a 'gentleman'. Such studies were held to develop "habits of industry and perseverance", and an accurate and penetrating mind "of enlarged views" which, although capable of generalizing, yet would be "accustomed to trace matters to first principles". Moreover, Classical literature portrayed the lives of men who exhibited "genuine patriotism" and a respect for "the dignity of human nature". Thus, it was held that Classical studies could not but inspire like feelings in all who sought "to penetrate into the origin and progress of human knowledge".

The Classics provided excellent examples of public virtues: constancy, contempt for wealth and power, patriotism, magnanimity, justice and bravery, which were invaluable in forming the character of youth. It was maintained that:

> By means of [the study of the Classics] ... the grandest powers of the human Soul are awakened, the noblest sentiments are excited, the most august forms of virtue, beauty, and order are made to fasten on the mind, it becomes enraptured with virtue and inspired with the desire of imitation.

Such a broad course of study -- which embraced the Classics and religious studies (the Old and New Testaments), as well as the more strictly practical subjects and the realm of science -- was counted upon to build character, and to ensure that every student would find some area of study which would be "adapted to his taste and capacity". To serve its purposes, the curriculum had to be very broad and demanding, but it was felt that there was no reason why "boys of moderate ability" – if they applied themselves diligently under the direction of "a vigilant teacher" -- could not complete the entire grammar school program. For the Tories, the character of the teacher was of the utmost importance, as was the conduct and government of the schools which was adjudged to be equally as important as the curriculum in forming the character of the students and the governing principles of their mind. (13)

The Teaching Profession

To the Tory mind, teaching was a most respectable and responsible profession; and it was essential that strict standards be applied to those who sought to enter its ranks. The Tories insisted that only men of superior learning and upright character, who were British subjects and preferably Anglicans, were acceptable as teachers for the youth of Upper Canada. That insistence stemmed from the importance which they attached to the function of the teacher in developing the faculties and character of youth, and in instilling values and beliefs which were perceived as being beneficial for the state as well as for the good of the student.

In addition to teaching the courses of study, the teacher was expected to inculcate religious principles, and to instill a sound sense of judgment in his students by teaching them how to separate "the specious from what is proper". The teacher was charged as well with impressing upon his students the need to practice the social virtues, and of making the student aware of his duty to serve the state. To the Tory mind, the teacher was duty-bound to provide support for the stability of government by inspiring students with a love of country and loyalty toward their Sovereign, and to teach his students about the perfection of the British constitution that they might be able to defend it against the arguments of despots and democrats. The teacher was also charged with ensuring that a concern for promoting the public good was foremost in the minds of his students.

To that end, the teacher was encouraged to emulate:

> the ancients [who] trained up their youth to be useful to the State and taught them to despise every advantage inconsistent with its welfare.

The character of the students was to be formed so that whatever position they might attain in life, they would act always with "dignity and disinterestedness" in both their public and private lives. Teachers were expected to apply themselves to produce learned young men who would be "good members of society", as well as, in the case of the more-gifted young men, subjects who would be capable of serving with honour and distinction in the State, the Church, or the Judiciary, to the benefit of their country. In all respects, teachers were regarded as having a crucial role to play in realizing the hopes which the Tories held out for the education of the youth of Upper Canada.

Discipline and Good Habits

In addition to a belief in the necessity of procuring competent teachers of a good character for the schools, it was also believed that the success of any education system was largely dependent upon the establishment of a proper system of discipline in the schools. Indeed, it was held that discipline was what a formal system of education could provide which was lacking when education was confined to instruction by a private tutor, or by the parents, within the home. (14)

In contrast to the views of some educational theorists of their own day, the Upper Canadian Tories were not of the opinion that "children should be governed by reasoning them into compliance or that instruction should always be given under the form of pleasure". Although the Tories agreed that children were quite susceptible to arguments regarding proper conduct, nevertheless they held to the view that in practice it was requisite that children be taught 'on authority' within a school system where correction could be "judiciously applied".

For the Tories, one of the major purposes of education was to instill good habits in youth which would aid them to control their passions, but they held that it could be done only if "a regular and uniform discipline" were maintained in the schools. To the Tory mind, the purpose of a formal education was to prepare the student for life, and the classroom was a microcosm which had to be organized in keeping with their ideal of how a well-ordered society should function. In effect, the school was regarded as a socializing agency and, in its conduct and government, the school needed to promote discipline, which contributed to the formation of a proper character in youth. (15)

The Governance of the School

In the Tory scheme of education -- as set forth by the Rev. John Strachan -- the conduct and government of the school were under the direction of the teacher, but students were expected to participate fully in their education. The learning environment was to be structured to instill knowledge in the most efficient manner, and to develop a sense of responsibility in youth, as well as increase their capabilities, by encouraging them to take an active part in their own education. While striving to excel in their own studies, students were to be involved in teaching through the practice of appointing the more-advanced students to act as monitors to aid in the instruction of the less-advanced students.

Students were also to be actively involved in the learning process by means of the 'question and answer' method of teaching. Rather than learning by rote, the practice in the Grammar Schools – under the superintendence of the Rev. John Strachan -- was to require students not only to answer questions put to them by the teacher, but to formulate questions themselves and test the comprehension of their peers by questioning them on the lesson. It was a method of teaching that was regarded as invaluable for several reasons. It served to awaken the interest of the students in the subject matter, and quickened their comprehension; it enabled the teacher to judge how well a lesson had been understood and to ascertain which students required additional explanations; and, it permitted the students to be ranked at the head or foot of each school class or particular subject of study, depending upon their daily performance. This latter consideration was of the utmost importance for it was in keeping with the Tory belief that education should proceed on the principle of the emulation of the better students by the less-accomplished students.

The system of ranking students was not regarded as unfair or prejudicial to the less-accomplished students as numerous opportunities existed for a student to excel. The diversity of subject matter was such that if a student were ranked low in one class, he might well head another more suited to his interests or talents. An "honourable emulation" was considered to be both noble and useful in society at large, as well as in the school. It was the purpose of the system of government, which the

Tories wanted to see established in the school system, to assess merit, to enforce the discipline which was required to form the character of the student, and to encourage students to excel in imitation of the better students. (16)

The system of government that was advocated for District Grammar Schools was similar to what the Rev. John Strachan had established in his Cornwall District Grammar School during the pre-war period. It provided a wide measure of student participation and responsibility. The teacher was aided in governing the school by 'censors' who were appointed from among the older students in rotation. The 'censors' were responsible for taking care of the school property, setting out the books and pencils, reporting on attendance, and serving as monitors for the less-advanced students when required.

Most importantly, the 'censors' were charged with keeping a daily register of the lessons taught, and the names and rankings of those who excelled or did poorly in every class, as well as the names of students who misbehaved. These entries were in turn summarized in a weekly register, which was supplemented by a monthly register, a "Book of Merit", in which the teacher recorded the names of the top two students in each class and of those who distinguished themselves by good conduct. The purpose of the elaborate recording system was to ensure that justice was done in the meting out of rewards and punishments.

By associating students in the discipline of the school, and in the keeping of detailed records of conduct, it was felt that "infallible evidence" was provided concerning the just deserts of the students, and all "suspicion of partiality", favouritism, or arbitrariness, was avoided through the students being judged by their peers. If the system were to fulfill its purpose, it was of the utmost importance that the students were able to see that justice was done in the meting out of rewards and punishments.

Where the assessment of merit was concerned, the aura of impartiality and fairness was maintained through a two-step process. Initially, each entry in the daily register was read out the following day in class where the students were free to point out any inaccuracies that required correction, and, at the close of the school year, the student body as a whole chose a committee of their peers to inspect the registers to ascertain those who should be awarded the school prizes. If any student felt aggrieved, he was permitted to request that another committee be chosen to examine the registers. In that manner, the students who excelled over the entire school year were recognized and rewarded; and there was no doubt left in anyone's mind, but that justice had been done.

With respect to the meting out of punishment, there was a like scrupulous concern that justice prevail. When a student was accused of an offense by another student, "a regular trial" was instituted, and the matter was carefully investigated by the student body which, if need be, was free to select -- from among their peers -- a jury to decide the case. Punishment was never applied until the student had been heard in his own defence, and his guilt had been established beyond any doubt. Once that had been determined, punishment could be enforced. However, it was noted that often the pain of undergoing the trial itself was deemed sufficient to redeem the offender. If not, he was assigned lines to memorize, and/or was confined to his quarters. The object of the system was not to inflict physical punishment.

At the Cornwall District Grammar School, corporal punishment was discountenanced, and was resorted to only in cases of immoral conduct. Indeed, the Rev. John Strachan had found that the placing of the student body under the control of "a just discipline" -- which governed "the conduct of every scholar at all times and in all places" -- resulted in the instilling of good habits of conduct, which enabled corporal punishments to be all but discarded. That was particularly the case with students who boarded at the school and lived under the direct supervision of the teacher. Based on his teaching experience, Strachan asserted that:

> corporal punishments may with good management be entirely dispensed with; but this can scarcely be effected when the scholars are much at home, and neglected or indulged by their Parents. It is, nevertheless, certain that by making a boy's rank depend on his behavior and acquirements and keeping up a constant exertions and watchfulness, it may be nearly accomplished.

Moreover, it was asserted that corporal punishment would rarely be needed in schools that were placed under good teachers who were "both loved and feared" by their students. (17)

The need for a formal system of Education

The system of education, which the Tory elite strove to implement in Upper Canada was based on a well-thought out program of instruction for the grammar schools. It included a prescribed curriculum, as well as a method of teaching and of conducting a school, which were calculated to supply the deficiencies of informal instruction in the home and the Church. To the Tory mind, the advantages which such a system of formal education provided over other means of instruction were basically three-fold.

In the first place, the school system was intended to accustom students to being under a strict and just discipline which served to form good manners and habits in an environment which approximated that of society at large. Within the school, the conduct of the students could be placed under the governance of "many salutary restraints and regulations" and the "vigilant review of a great number of [their] equals". Such a discipline was regarded as being of the utmost importance for it was believed that only those who were brought up in "a habitual subjection to precept and just authority" were capable of controlling their passions and regulating their temper to the benefit of both society and themselves.

Secondly, the students who pursued a formal education in such a school environment would develop "habits of diligence and application", which were the true basis of future advancement in a profession or of success in a business; and thirdly, a formal education taught students "to think accurately".

Thirdly, men who did not have their minds formed by "a systematic education" were often confused in their thinking, and were prone to accept "rash opinions" or arguments which were deduced from erroneous principles, without "sifting them to the bottom". This latter failing was of an especial importance because only men who had been taught to think for themselves and to have the courage of their convictions, were fit to properly fill any public office. And, one of the primary purposes of a 'national' education system was to produce a governing class for the Province of Upper Canada. (18)

The forming of an Aristocracy of merit and ability

The Tories held that all children needed to receive an education, but that did not mean that they should all receive the same amount of education. On the one hand, it was accepted that every individual had different God-given learning abilities and talents, and was suited to a particular occupation and position in society for which education should prepare them. Moreover, there was also a distinction made between the children of the poor and those "of the higher and more opulent classes of society". In general, it was expected that the former would devote only "a short time" to the pursuit of an education in the Common School system. Consequently, it was held that the education for the poor, at the elementary school level:

> ought to be directed to the acquisition of that information which will render them content with their situation and, at the same time, prepare them for a purer state of existence. To read and write their own language [in the vernacular], and to cast accounts, in addition to religious instruction, comprehend all that can be readily advantageous to the mass of society.

The children of the superior classes of society were expected to receive "a more liberal course of instruction" by advancing further through the education system – to a District Grammar School, with the best students progressing on to university. It was expected that the governing and professional class of the next generation would come from among these students who received a higher education, and from among whom "an aristocracy of literature" would emerge. However, the differences in education were not regarded as unfair because advancement through the educational system was to be determined solely on the grounds of "natural ability" and "superior wisdom". (19) Scholarships were to be provided by the state to aid outstanding students in the elementary school to advance to the District Grammar Schools in situations where families were unable to support the cost of a higher education for a gifted child. (20)

Through the establishment of provincial government scholarships for gifted students from poorer families:

> the door to a liberal education would be opened to all the inhabitants, and the children of the farmer and mechanic might be found deservedly filling the highest offices of the Colony to which they had arisen by their superior talents, fostered by the benevolent institutions of the Province. (21)

All men were not born with the same talents or abilities, and that "natural inequality" in talents and abilities, and capacity for learning, which was reflect in the various ranks of society was -- to the Tory mind – "highly beneficial" to society in general. (22) So long as merit and ability, as assessed in large part through the educational process, were the determinants of one's position in society, a governing aristocracy was perfectly natural. It was in keeping with the principle of "the division of labour" whereby each man was to devote his talents and abilities -- in whatever position to which he was best suited -- for the benefit of all. Indeed, it was held that:

> Rank & office when allowed a free circulation as in the British Empire presents the most desirable state of Society which can be conceived -- it is a safeguard of freedom, the source of the highest enjoyment Physical and intellectual, and a subject of honest pride & exaltation. (23)

A proper system of education would teach the youth who were destined to form the next governing and professional class how to govern others and to respect the lessons which history taught them. They would learn to fill whatever office or professional position that they might come to occupy with dignity, to be kind and considerate of others, and to give "a ready obedience to the just commands of superiors". (24)

They would be made aware of the need to strive to win the affection and admiration of those whom they might command by seeing to their needs and treating them in a conciliatory manner, while seeking to excel in the performance of the duties of their rank. (25) Above all, they would be made to realize the importance of maintaining their character unblemished in the knowledge that it was the immoral conduct and neglect of duty on the part of the governing class in France which was largely responsible for the political upheavals of the French Revolution and the spread of "democratical principles".

In such a system of education, youth would be taught:

> that in order to be respected by others, they must never fail to respect themselves; that high principle, unspotted integrity, and an unremitting regard to public decorum, a reverence for religion, and attention to the feelings of inferiors, ought never to be separated from rank and station.

A formal system of education was counted on to promote the moral and intellectual improvement of all of the youth of the province, to give them a basic education, and to teach them useful subjects in preparing them for life. Where the more advanced and gifted students were concerned, it was intended to produce young men who would be imbued with "the social graces", and who would form an 'aristocracy of talent and ability' fit to govern the province and to give a tone of respectability to its public life. (27)

In sum, the education system -- that the Rev. John Strachan strove to establish -- was counted on to produce a governing aristocracy which would be composed of 'gentlemen' who would know what it was:

> To be bred in a place of estimation; to see nothing low or sordid from one's infancy; to be taught to respect one's self; to be habituated to the censorial inspection of the public eye; to look early to public opinion; to stand upon such elevated ground as to be enabled to take a large view of the widespread and infinitely diversified combinations of men and affairs in a large society; to have the leisure to read, to reflect, to converse; to be enable to draw and court the attention of the wise and learned, wherever they are to be found; to be habituated, as in armies, to command and to obey; to be taught to despise danger in the pursuit of honour and duty; ... ...to be led to a guarded and regulated conduct, from a sense that you are considered as an instructor of your fellow-citizens in their highest concerns, and that you act as a reconciler between God

and man; to be employed as an administrator of law and justice, and to be thereby among the first Benefactors to mankind; to be a possessor of high science or liberal art; to be amongst rich traders, who, from their success, are presumed to have sharp and vigorous understandings, and to possess the virtues of diligence, order, constancy, and regularity, and to have cultivated an habitual regard to commutative justice.

Such men comprised a natural aristocracy, the very backbone of the nation. They were the natural governing class, the leaders of society, and the upholders of the social order. (28)

Thus, the motives which impelled the Upper Canadian Tories to establish a general system of education in Upper Canada – in keeping with the education component of their National Policy -- were quite mixed. They comprised a concern for the social and political stability of the province and the well-being of its people, as well as a desire to produce respectable and well-educated members of the professions, and a political elite of merit and ability which would be capable of governing and promoting the public good of the province through the proper exercise of authority. To achieve such aims required the establishment of a formal system of education which was to form the character of the youth of the province in keeping with Christian principles. The education system was to impart practical knowledge and a knowledge of God's works, and to prepare the youth of the province for the living of a good and productive Christian life.

Ultimately, the way in which the Upper Canadian Tories sought to respond to such a mixture of social, political and moral concerns was determined by their religious outlook, beliefs and values, inclusive of their view of human nature. It was their religion which provided the basic rationale for the Tory drive to establish a 'national' school system in Upper Canada, and for the curriculum and discipline that they wished to see established therein. (29) In the words of Archdeacon John Strachan:

The great object of the whole system was to make the Scholars good as well as wise; to lead them to the habitual exercise of that practical virtue which is founded upon the Divine principles of Christianity. To this all other attainments ought to be subordinate and the Teacher should never forget that his instruction should not be merely for time, but also for Eternity. (30)

Thus, it was believed by the Tories that if a Christian character could be inculcated into the province, through a 'national system' of education, then the Province of Upper Canada, as well as Upper Canadians individually, would receive God's blessings, would experience prosperity in this life, and, eventually, would attain "eternal felicity" in the life to come. To the Tory mind, this was the essential purpose of education to which all other concerns were derivative, and subordinate. The system of education that they strove to establish in Upper Canada mirrored that fact. (31)

Notes

Part Five: Education and the National Character

Part Five Divider: The quotation is from PAO, Journal of the House of Assembly, Appendix 16, [John Strachan], "Report of the President of the General Board of Education", 5 February 1829.

Chapter Twelve - A National System of Education

1. Spragge, ed., *Strachan Letter Book*, 29, Strachan to Marquis Wellesley, 1 November 1812, & 81, Strachan to Col. Harvey, [1815] , & 75-76, "Report on Education", 26 February 1815, & 90 & 92, "Remarks to be sent to Sir George Murray", [1815]; Strachan, *Discourse*, 1810, Note II, 47; *Christian Recorder*, I, 266, September 1819, "To the Editor" & II, 190-194, July 1820, "Respectful Demeanour towards constituted Authority, a Christian Duty" & II, 296-299, October 1820, "Hartford's 'Life and Principles of Thomas Paine'; PAO, *Journals of the House of Assembly*, 1829, Appendix 16, [Strachan], "Report of the President of the General Board of Education", 5 February 1829; PAO, Strachan Papers, "Extract of a Despatch from the Right Hon'ble Earl Bathurst K.G., and an accompanying Memorandum from Lieutenant Governor Maitland to Earl Bathurst, delivered by J. B. Robinson, February 1823; James [John] Strachan, *A Visit to Upper Canada*, 1820, 127 & 131; Hodgins, ed., *Documentary History of Education*, I, 213, Strachan, "Memorandum to Lt. Governor Maitland", March 1826; and *The Church*, 6 May 1837, "Church Prospectus" & Editorial (Bethune), 3 November 1828.

The arguments presented by the Tories in favour of establishing 'a national system of education' in Upper Canada, remained remarkably constant over the two decades following their initial enunciation by the Rev. John Strachan in the immediate postwar period, 1815-1820. His education policy was expounded upon in different levels of detail in the various primary sources cited, which cover a wide time span. For the actual contribution of Strachan to education in Upper Canada, see J.D. Purdy, "John Strachan's Educational Policies, 1815-1841", *Ontario History*, LXIV, 1972, 45-64; G.W. Spragge, "John Strachan's Contribution to Education, 1800-23", *Canadian Historical Review*, XXII, 1941, 147-158; George W. Spragge, "The Cornwall Grammar School of John Strachan, 1803-1812", *Ontario History*, XXXIV, 1942, 63-84; and Alison Smith, "John Strachan and early Upper Canada, 1799-1814", *Ontario History*, LII, 1960, 159-173.

2. Spragge, ed., *SLB*, 29, Strachan to Marquis Wellesley,1 November 1812, & 75-76, "Report on Education", 26 February 1815; *Christian Recorder*, I, 52, April 1819, "History and Present State of Education in Upper Canada"; [John Strachan], *A Visit to Upper Canada*, 1820, 101; PAO, Robinson Papers, J.B. Robinson Letter Book, 54, "Letter to Earl Bathurst", 26 December 1824; R.C. Good, ed., Strachan Letter Book, 1827-39, (unpublished M.A. thesis, University of Toronto Rare Book Room), xix, Strachan letter, 8 August 1811; *Kingston Gazette*, 3 September 1811, "An Address delivered by the Rev. Mr. Strachan at the last annual examination of His School, August 8, 1811"; Hodgins, ed., *DHE*, I, 212 - 213, Strachan, "Memorandum to Maitland", March 1826; Strachan, *An appeal to the Friends of Religion and Literature in Behalf of the University of Upper Canada* (London: R. Gilbert, 1827), 5-10; PAO, *Journals of the House of Assembly*, 1829, Appendix 16, [Strachan], "Report of the President of the General Board of Education", 5 February 1829. The quotations are from the 'Present State of Education', April 1819, 52, and from Strachan 'Address of 8 August 1811', respectively.

3. [John Strachan], *A Visit to Upper Canada*, 1820, 131; Spragge, ed., *SLB*, 29, Strachan to Marquis Wellesley, 1 November 1812 & 68, "Education in Lower Canada", 14 February 1815 & 75, 'Report on Education', 26 February 1815, & 78-79, Rev. Strachan and Rev. Addison, "Memorial on Education", 1815; PAO, Robinson Papers, Letters to J.B. Robinson, Strachan to Robinson, 10 June 1822; PAO,, Macaulay Papers, reel 1, John Bethune to John Macaulay, 21 December 1810; Hodgins, ed., *DHE*, I, 212, Strachan, 'Memorandum to Maitland', March 1826; *Kingston Chronicle*, 14 July 1820, [Strachan], 'Letter to Robert Walsh'; *Christian Recorder*, I, 52, April 1819, "History and present State of Education in Upper Canada"; Strachan, *An appeal on Behalf of the University*, 1827, 4-5; and J.B. Robinson, *Canada Bill*, 1840, 25. The first quotation is from Strachan to Wellesley, 1 November 1812, and the two following quotations are from Strachan, *An Appeal*, 1827, 5.

4. Strachan, *The Christian Religion Recommended in a Letter to his Pupils* (Montreal: Nahum Mower, 1807, 5-10; *Christian Recorder*, I, 444, February 1820, "History and Present State of Education in Lower Canada"; PAO, Strachan Sermons, Box A, 25 March 1821, Jeremiah 13:23 "Can the Ethiopian Change his Skin", 13-14. The first two quotations are from *The Christian Religion Recommended*, 1807, 9 & 5-6; the third quotation is from "Can the Ethiopian Change his Skin" 25 March 1821, 13; and the fourth quotation is from "History and Present State of Education in Lower Canada", February 1820, 444.

5. [John Strachan], *A Visit to Upper Canada*, 1820, 127; *Christian Recorder*, I, 5, March 1819, "History of Religion in Upper Canada"; Strachan, *Sermon*

on the Death of the Lord Bishop, 1826, 18; Strachan, *An appeal in Behalf of the University*, 1827, 22; Strachan, *Letter to Frankland Lewis*, 1830, 108-109; PAO, *Journals of the House of Assembly*, 1829, Appendix 16, Strachan, "Report of the President of the General Board of Education", 5 February 1829; and Spragge, ed., *SLB*, 76, 'Report on Education', 26 February 1815 & 143, Strachan to the Lord Bishop, 10 November 1817.

6. Spragge, ed., *SLB*, 91, 'Remarks to Sir George Murray', [1815] ; *Christian Recorder*, I, 52, April 1819, "History and Present State of Education in Upper Canada" & 177-179, July 1819, "The Confessor, No. 5"; and Hodgins, ed., *DHE*, I, 213, Strachan, "Memorandum to Maitland', March 1826, & 53-54. The quotation is from 'Remarks to Sir George Murray'.

7. Strachan, *An appeal in Behalf of the University*, 1827, 8; Hodgins, ed., *DHE*, I, 213, Strachan, 'Memorandum to Maitland', March 1826; Cartwright Family Papers, Port Hope, Strachan to James Cartwright, 12 March 1804; MTCL, Strachan, *A Sermon on the Death of the Honourable Richard Cartwright, Preached at Kingston, 3 September 1815* (Montreal: W. Gray, 1816), 23-24. The quotations are from Strachan, "Memorandum to Maitland', March 1826, and Strachan, *Sermon on the Death of Cartwright*, 24, respectively.

8. *Christian Recorder*, I, April 1819, "History and Present State of Education in Upper Canada"; Strachan, *An appeal in Behalf of the University*, 1827, 14-18; Hodgins, ed., *DHE*, I, 213, Strachan, 'Memorandum to Maitland', March 1826; *Kingston Gazette*, 3 March 1812, [Strachan] "Reckoner -No. 52"; Strachan, *Hypocrisy Detected*, 1812, 51-52, 58 & 83; PAO, Richard Cartwright Letter Book 1809-1812, IV (microfilm), 298, Richard Cartwright to John Strachan, 18 March 1809; Strachan, *Bishop Hobart*, 1832, 34; and PAO, Strachan Papers, Strachan Letter Book 1844-49, Strachan to J, Biddle, n.d,; and Strachan, 'Memorandum to Maitland', March 1826, respectively.

As of the 1840s, the Anglican Tories began to feel a sense of unease about the large numbers of Irish Catholic immigrants arriving in the ports of Canada East (Lower Canada). Thus, a university, which would be open to all denominations of Christians and under the direction of the national Church of England, came to be viewed as also having a vital role to play in sustaining Protestantism in Upper Canada.

9. Strachan, *Letter to Frankland Lewis*, 1830, 111; *Christian Recorder*, I, 44, April 1819, "History and Present State of Education in Upper Canada"; Hodgins, ed., *DHE*, 213, Strachan, 'Memorandum to Maitland', March 1826; *Kingston Gazette*, 21 April 1812, [Strachan], "Reckoner - No. 58"; and Spragge, ed., *SLB*, 90, Strachan, 'Remarks to Sir George Murray', [1815].

10. Strachan, *Church of the Redeemed, A Sermon preached 5th October 1836* (Toronto: R. Stanton, 1836), 39; PAO, Strachan Sermons, Box A, 21 October 1832, Acts 4:13, "The Boldness of Peter and John", 43 & Box B, 6 July 1831, II Corinthians 3:17, "Where the Spirit of the Lord is there is Liberty", 9-12; *Kingston Gazette*, 18 February 1812, [Strachan], "Reckoner – No. 50"; Strachan, *Sermon on the Death of the Lord Bishop*, 1826, 16; *The Church* (Bethune editorial), 17 February 1838; and *Kingston Chronicle*, 28 May 1831, [Rev. A. H. Burwell], "One of the People". The quotation is from the latter source.

11. Strachan, *A Charge Delivered to the Clergy of the Diocese of Toronto, at the Visitation, April 30, 1856* (Toronto: Henry "Rowsell, 1856), 8; *Kingston Gazette*, 21 April 1812, [Strachan], "Reckoner - No. 58" & 16 July 1811, "Reckoner – No. 28"; PAO, Strachan Sermons, Box B, 30 March 1806, II Corinthians 4:3, "If gospel hid", 7, & Scottish Speeches, "Whether the misery or happiness of man be greater", [late 1790s], 31-33, & Box E. Hebrews 13:5, 24 September 1824, "Be Content with such things as ye have", 1; *Christian Recorder*, II, 409-410, February 1821, "Episcopal Church in the United States and the Rt. Rev. Hobart's Charge"; and Strachan, *Sermon on the Death of Cartwright*, 1816, 9-16. The quotation is from 'Episcopal Church in the United States', 409-410.

12. PAO, Strachan Sermons: Box B, n.d., St. Luke 15:7, "Repentance", Box D, 19 November 1847, Matthew 19:17, "Importance of the Commandments", 1-2, Box E, 24 September 1824, Hebrews 13:5, "Be Content with such things as ye have' 13, & Box E, 22 February 1829, Matthew [16:27?], "Your good Works glorify the Father", 1; *Kingston Gazette*, 16 July 1811, [Strachan], "Reckoner - No 28"; *Christian Recorder*, I, 301, October 1819, "Divinity of Christ"; and *Kingston Chronicle*, (Macaulay editorial), 10 December 1819 & [Rev. A. H. Burwell], "One of the People", 6 August 1831. The four quotations are from: "Be Content with such things as ye have", 24 September 1824, 3, "Repentance", n.d., "Importance of the Commandments" November 1847, 2, and "One of the People", 6 August 1831, respectively.

13. *Kingston Chronicle*, [Rev. A.H. Burwell], "One of the People", 6 August & 31 December 1831. The quotation is from the 6 August 1831 article.

14. *Kingston Chronicle*, [Burwell], "One of the People", 6 August 1831 & 28 May 1831; *The Church*, (Bethune editorial), 6 January 1838; and PAO, Strachan Papers, reel 8, package 2, n.d., Strachan, "Religious Instructions", 1. All three quotations are from "One of the People", 6 August 1831.

15. *Kingston Chronicle*, [Burwell], "One of the People", 6 August 1831. The quotation is from the same source.

16. *Kingston Chronicle*, [Burwell], "One of the People", 6 August 1831; Strachan, *Sermon for a General Thanksgiving*, 1814, 25-29; Strachan, *The Christian Religion*, 1807, 5-10; *Christian Recorder*, I, 444, February 1820, "History of the Present State of Education in Lower Canada"; PAO, Strachan Sermons, Box A, 25 March 1821, Jeremiah 13:23, "Can the Ethiopian Change his Skin", 13, & Box B, 6 July 1821, II Corinthians 3:17, "Where the Spirit of the Lord is there is liberty", 1. The quotation is from 'the Spirit of the Lord', 6 July 1821, 1.

17. *Kingston Chronicle*, 6 August 1831, [Burwell], "One of the People"; Strachan, *Sermon for a General Thanksgiving*, 1814, 27-29; PAO, Strachan Sermons, Box B, 6 July 1821, II Corinthians 3:17, "Where the Spirit of the Lord is there is liberty", 6-8; and *Christian Recorder*, I, 303, October 1819, Strachan, "A Sermon". The quotations are from 'the Spirit of the Lord', 6 July 1821, 8 & 6-7, respectively.

18. *The Church*, 6 May 1837, "Church Prospectus"; PAO, Strachan Sermons, Box B, 6 July 182, II Corinthians 3:17, "Where the Spirit of the Lord is there is liberty", 6-9; Bethune, *Memoir of John Strachan*, 1870, 188, reprint of a Strachan, 'Speech' of 9 September 1841; *Kingston Chronicle*, 28 May, 23 July, & 6 August 1831, [Burwell], "One of the People". The quotations are from "One of the People", 23 July 1831, and the Strachan 'Speech' of 9 September 1841, respectively.

19. PAO, Strachan Sermons, Box B, 6 July 1821, II Corinthians 3:17, "Where the Spirit of the Lord is there is liberty", 9; *Christian Recorder*, II, 283, October 1820, "On Religious Establishments"; and Strachan, *Sermon on the Death of Cartwright*, 1816, 34. The quotation is from 'the Spirit of the Lord', 9.

Chapter Thirteen - Education, Religion and Morality

1. PAO, Strachan Sermons: Box A, February 1865, Daniel 6:10, "'A Sermon for the benefit of the Young", 8; 32, 33, 44 & 26 September 1867, Hebrews 6:1. "Advancement in Religious Knowledge necessary", 13, 15, 18, 21-22; and Box B, 6 July 1821, II Corinthians 3:17, "Where the Spirit of the Lord is there is liberty", 9-10; Strachan, *Address to the Synod*, 1860, 47- 48; and *Christian Recorder*, I, 445, February 1820, "History of the Present State of Education in Lower Canada". The quotations are from "A Sermon for the benefit of the Young", February 1865, 8, "Advancement in Religious Knowledge necessary", 26 September 1867, 21; and *Address to the Synod*, 1860, 47-48.

2. PAO, Strachan Sermons: Box A, 25 March 1821, Jeremiah 13:23, "Can the Ethiopian Change his skin", 13-14 & 25 December 1847, St. John 1:29, "The

Lamb of God", 21; Strachan, *A Charge Delivered to the Clergy*, 1856, 16; The Church, 22 March 1844, "Educational System in Prussia" (From "The Notes of a Traveller on the Social and Political State of Prussia &c." by Samuel Laing, Esq.); PAO, *Journals of the House of Assembly*, 1829, appendix 16, "Report of the President of the General Board of Education", 5 February 1829; *Kingston Gazette*, 3 September 1811, "An Address delivered by the Rev. Mr. Strachan, at the last annual Examination of His School, August 8,1811"; Bethune, *Memoir of John Strachan*, 1870, 28; MTCL, Strachan, *The Life and Character of the Right Reverend Dr. Hobart*, 1832, 32; *Christian Recorder*, I, February 1820, "History and the Present State of Education in Lower Canada". See also G.W. Spragge, "The Cornwall Grammar School under John Strachan, 1803-1812", *Ontario History*, 1942, 70. The quotations are from Bethune, *Memoir of John Strachan*, 1870, 28, quoting Strachan, *A Charge Delivered to the Clergy*, 1856, 16, and "Educational System in Prussia", 22 March 1844, respectively.

In referring to religion 'as a science' to be taught, the Tories were thinking in terms of natural philosophy which focused on the investigation, observation, and understanding of 'the works of God' in Nature, and which was taught within a Christian belief system rather than as a secular modern science.

3. *Kingston Gazette*, 3 September 1811, Strachan, *An Address at the last annual Examination*; and *Christian Recorder*, I, February 1820, "History of the Present State of Education in Lower Canada", 445. The quotation is from Strachan, *An Address*.

In deprecating 'modern educational theorists' who argued against inculcating moral and religious principles in the young before their rational powers were fully developed, Strachan was probably referring principally to Jean Jacques Rousseau (1712-1778). See R.L, Archer, ed., *Jean Jacques Rousseau, his educational theories selected from Emile, Julie and Other Writings* (New York: Barron's Educational Series, 1964). The educational theories of Rousseau rest upon two basic premises: 1) that "the greatest of all blessings is not authority but liberty where the man who is really free only desires what he can perform, and he can then perform all that he desires" (*ibid*, 90); and 2) that "the first promptings of nature are always right; there is no original corruption in the human heart" (*ibid*, 97). From these premises, Rousseau argues that education should be based not on teaching 'from authority', but on a well-regulated liberty.

Children should not use their intellect till it has acquired all its faculties.... The first education therefore should be purely negative. It consists, not in teaching virtue or truth, but in guarding the heart from vice and the mind from error. (*ibid*, 99)

In sum, Rousseau was opposed to teaching moral values to the young. In contrast, the Tories insisted on the critical importance of inculcating moral values, and hence religious values, in youth at an early age. The Tories differed also from Rousseau in believing in original sin, and in being aware of its implications for education.

4. *Kingston Gazette*, 3 September 1811, Strachan, *An Address at the last annual Examination*; Strachan, *A Letter to the Rev. A.N. Bethune, Rector of Cobourg on the Management of Grammar Schools* (York: R. Stanton, 1829), 45; Port Hope, Cartwright Family Papers (private collection), Strachan to James Cartwright, 13 September 1803; Strachan, *Life and Character of the Right Reverend Dr. Hobart*, 1832, 29; *Christian Recorder*, I, 266, September 1819, (Strachan editorial) & 444, February 1820, "History of the Present State of Education in Lower Canada"; PAO, Strachan Sermons: Box A, 25 March 1821, Jeremiah 13:23, "Can the Ethiopian change his skin", 13 & Box B, Scottish Speeches, 9 March 1799, "Discourse on ... duties", 8-11 & n.d., "Which of the two, the miser or Spend thrift, the most hurtful to Society", 13. The quotation is from Strachan to James Cartwright, 13 September 1803.

The educational views of John Strachan, on the critical importance of education in forming the character and understanding of youth, closely parallel those of John Locke (1632-1704) whom Strachan cited with approval. On Locke's educational theories, see: John Locke, "Some Thoughts Concerning Education" (1693) in J.L. Axtell, ed., *The Educational Writings of John Locke, A Critical Edition with Introduction and Notes* (Cambridge: Cambridge University Press, 1965). On the critical importance of 'early habits', see 129, 138 & 146.

Although the Tories agreed with John Locke on the critical importance of education in forming the character of youth for civil society, on teaching methods, and on the development of the student's reasoning powers; yet they differed in several essentials where the nature of man and the ultimate purpose of education were concerned. The epistemology of John Locke denied the Christian belief in 'original sin' and held that the character of youth could be formed simply by establishing a proper learning environment. To the contrary, the Tories believed that requisite first step in character formation was for a child to be baptized into the Christian Church and receive God's grace; otherwise, in lacking God's grace, fallen man was not susceptible to improvement in any lasting sense. Moreover, moral values had to be based on religious beliefs to effectively govern human conduct..

5. Strachan, *Life and Character of the Right Reverend Dr. Hobart*, 1832, 27-29; *The Church*, (Bethune editorials), 5 May 1838 & 22 March 1844; *Christian Recorder*, I, 44, April 1819, "History and Present State of Education in Upper

Canada" & 445, February 1820, "History of the Present State of Education in Lower Canada". The quotations are from "History and Present State of Education in Upper Canada", April 1819, 44, and Strachan, *Life and Character of Hobart*, 1832, 28, respectively.

The Bell-Lancaster monitorial system was developed independently by an Anglican minister, Dr. Andrew Bell (1753-1832), while serving as a military chaplain in Madras, India, and Joseph Lancaster (1778-1838), a Quaker schoolmaster in London, England. The monitorial system involved employing older, more advanced pupils to monitor and tutor groups of younger, less advanced pupils. During the first decade of the 19th Century, both men strove to establish schools on the monitorial system for the education of the poor. They differed in that Bell's schools were established in conjunction with the Church of England, and Lancaster's were non-denominational schools. Moreover, Lancaster used corporal punishment to enforce disciple; whereas Bell employed rewards – medals and badges -- for good behavior and achievement.

In Britain, a National Society was founded in 1811 to establish an elementary school system in England and Wales to provide education for the poor on the Bell system in keeping with the teachings of the Church of England. Most of the schools were erected adjacent to a parish church, and by the early 1830s upwards of 12,000 schools were established within the British Empire – largely in England and Wales -- on the Bell system. Earlier, in 1808, a Society was founded to promote the establishment of schools on the Lancasterian monitorial system. The Lancasterian society was dependent on the raising of funds by public subscriptions for the education of the children of the poor, and after an initial period of success in founding schools, it had a less lasting impact than the Church of England system in providing education for the poor. See: Rev. Andrew Bell, *Instructions for Conducting Schools through the Agency of the Scholars Themselves; comprising the Analysis of an Experiment in Education made at the Madras [Orphanage] Asylum, Madras, 1789-1796* (London: multiple publishers, 1816, 5th ed. enlarged); and Joseph Lancaster, *Improvements in Education, Abridged, containing a complete epitome of the System of Education Invented and Practiced by the Author, Joseph Lancaster* (London: by the Author, 1808, 1st ed. 1803).

6. Strachan, *Life and Character of Hobart*, 1832, 29 & 32- 33; Strachan, *A Charge Delivered to the Clergy*, 1856, 22; PAO, Strachan Sermons: Box A, 29 August 1819, St. Luke 16:31, "If they hear not Moses and the Prophets, neither will they be persuaded tho' one rose from the Dead", 20-23, & 10 January 1836, Isaiah 55:10-11, "Certainty of God's Word", 2, & 26 September 1867, Hebrews 6:1, "Advancement in Religious Knowledge necessary", 38-44; and Box B, Scottish Speeches, 1795-99, 59, "Arms or literature"; *The Church*, 18

January 1840, John Toronto, "Reply" & 13 March 1841, (Bethune editorial); *Christian Recorder*, I, 446, February 1820, "History of the Present State of Education in Lower Canada", & II, 286, October 1820, "On the Duties and Advantages of a Parish Priest" (from Monthly Magazine, January 1811), Point X. The quotations are from Strachan, *A Charge*, 1856, 22, "Advancement in Religious Knowledge necessary", 26 September 1867, 43-44, and "If they hear not Moses", 29 August 1819, 20-21, respectively.

7. Strachan, *Life and Character of Hobart*, 1832, 29-32; MTCL, Strachan, *The Christian Religion Recommended in a Letter to his Pupils* (Montreal: Nahur Mower, 1807), 14; and *The Church*, 18 January 1840, John Toronto, "Reply". The quotation is from the *Life and Character of Hobart*, 1832, 31.

8. PAC, Coventry Family Papers, vol.13, 91, "Reminiscences of John Strachan", n.d.; PAO, Strachan Sermons: Box A, 25 December 1847, St. John 1:29, "Behold the Lamb of God", 30-34; and Box B, Scottish speeches, 1795-99, n.d., "Whether a nation be more indebted to arms or literature",58, & 9 March 1799, "Discourse on Duties", 8, & 6 July 1821, II Corinthians 3:17, "Where the Spirit of the Lord is there is liberty", 2; and Box E, 13 October 1824, II Corinthians 13:5, "Examine Yourself", 7-8, & 2 May 1830, Hebrews 3:7, "Harden not your heart", 2, & 17 October 1847, Joshua 24: part of 15, "Choose you this day whom ye will serve", 3, & 7 February 1841, "Love not the World", 3.

See also *Christian Recorder*, vol. I, 295-296, October 1819, "Chalmers' Sermons", 295-96, & 260-261, September 1819, "Dissertations on the Christian Doctrines No. 7: Divinity of Christ", and vol. II, 244-245, September 1820, "Annual Report on the Madras School"; and Strachan, *Hypocrisy Detected*, 1812, 110. The first quotation is from "Chalmers' Sermons", October 1819, 295-296, and the second and third quotations are from the sermon, "Behold the Lamb of God", 25 December 1847, 32.

In his discussions on human nature in 1819, and in his sermons following that date, the Rev. John Strachan adhered consistently to the Anglican view of human nature as 'corrupted' after the Fall, as distinct from the Calvinist view of the 'total depravity of human nature'. However, in the earlier period there is one letter extant in which Strachan, to the contrary, affirmed his belief in the "utter depravity of man by nature" (Bethune, *Memoir of John Strachan*, 58, Strachan to Dr. Chalmers, n.d.). This indicates a transition in Strachan's thought – presumably under the influence of his Anglican divinity studies -- away from the Calvinist view of human nature which he had imbibed in Scotland during his youth. On the other hand, in his comments on 'the moral sense of man', Strachan clearly drew on the early sermons of the Rev. Thomas Chalmers of the Church of Scotland and his knowledge of the works of the Scottish Moralists.

[As of 1819, Thomas Chalmers was renowned in Scotland for his preaching at the Tron Church and subsequently the Church of St. John in Glasgow. Thereafter, in 1823, Chalmers received an appointment at St. Andrew's University where he further distinguished himself as a moral philosopher and as a theologian. Years later, in 1843, Chalmers would lead the exodus of evangelical Presbyterians – ministers and parishioners -- from the Church of Scotland into the Free Church of Scotland which he was instrumental in establishing.]

9. *Kingston Gazette*, 24 December 1811, [Strachan] "Reckoner No. 42"; PAO, Strachan Sermons: Box A. 3 August 1806, I Corinthians 10:31. "Do all to the Glory of God", 9-16; Box B, Scottish Speeches 1795-99, n.d., "Whether a nation be more indebted to arms or literature", 58, & 9 March 1799, "Discourse on duties", 8, & n.d., St. Luke 15:7, "Repentance", n.p., & 30 March 1806, II Corinthians 4:3, "If gospel hid", 4; and Box E, 17 October 1847, Joshua 24: part of 15, "Choose you this day whom ye will serve", 3; [Strachan], *Hypocrisy Detected*,1812, 84 & 110: Strachan, *The Christian Religion Recommended*,1807, 18-27; and *The Church*, (Bethune editorial), 23 May 1840. The quotations are from "Do all to the Glory of God", 3 August 1806, 14; Strachan, *The Christian Religion Recommended*, 1807, 27; and "Do all to the Glory of God", 16, respectively.

[Utilitarianism is a political philosophy and system of ethics that was developed in England by a prominent philosopher, social reformer, and so-called "Philosophical Radical" -- Jeremy Bentham (1748-1832). Utilitarianism was refined subsequently by another English philosopher, political economist, and theorist of individual liberty, John Stuart Mill (1798-1832). See: Jeremy Bentham, *An Introduction to the Principles of Morals and Legislation* (1788); and J.S. Mill, *Utilitarianism* (1863). Strachan's critique was directed at the Bentham work; J.S. Mill had yet to publish his work at that date.]

10. PAO, Strachan Sermons: Box A, n.d. (folder I), Discourse I, St. John 1:17, "Constant Agency of the Deity", 277, & n.d., Romans 13:11 & 12, "High time to Awake out of Sleep", 14, & 3 August 18060 I Corinthians 10:31, "Do all to the Glory of God", 1, & 20 December 1807, St. Matthew 8:9, "For I am a man under authority", 9, & 4 March 1832, I Timothy 3:16, "Without Controversy", 23- 24; and Box B, 30 March 1806, II Corinthians 4:3, "If Gospel hid", 7-8, & 26 June 1806, II Timothy 3:16, "All scripture is given for instruction in righteousness", 1-2, 8-9, & 8 July 1806, Lecture 3, "Belief in God", 1; and Box D, 4 March 1832, I Timothy 3:16, "Mystery of Godliness", 6; and Box E, 4 January 1824, Colossians 3:11, "Christ in all in all", 3, & 22 February 1839, St. Matthew 5:16, "Your good works", 1; PAC, Coventry Family Papers, vol. 13, n.d., "Reminiscences of John Strachan", 91-92; *Kingston Gazette*, 16 July

1811, [Strachan], "Reckoner - No. 28"; and Strachan, *The Christian Religion Recommended*, 1807, 29. The quotation is from Strachan, "Reminiscences", 92.

11. PAO, Strachan Sermons: Box A, 3 August 1806, I Corinthians 10:31, "Do all to the Glory of God", 2; and Box B, 30 March 1806, II Corinthians 4:3, "If Gospel hid", 8; and Box E, 13 October 1824, II Corinthians 13:5, "Examine Yourself", 7, & 23 September 1855, St. John 3:12, "Ye believe not"; Strachan, *The Christian Religion Recommended*, 1807, 30; and *Kingston Gazette*, 1 January 1811, [Strachan], "Reckoner - No. 1". The quotations are from the sermons, "Examine Yourself", 13 October 1824, 7 and "If Gospel hid", 30 March 1806, 8, respectively.

Chapter Fourteen - Education and the Condition of the People

1. *Kingston Gazette*, 3 September 1811, "An Address delivered by the Rev. Mr. Strachan, at the last annual examination of His School, 8 August 1811"; PAO, Journals of the House of Assembly, 5 February 1829, Strachan, "Report of the President of the General Board of Education", Appendix 16; *Christian Recorder*, I, 43, April 1819, & II, 43-44, February 1820, Strachan "History and Present State of Education in Upper Canada", & II, 243-244, September 1820, "Annual Report of the Madras School in New Brunswick, for the year 1820", & II, 301, October 1820, "The Resurrection of Christ"; *The Church*, 6 May 1837, "Church Prospectus", & 5 May 1838 and 8 March 1844 (Bethune editorials), & 18 January 1840, John Toronto, "Reply to the Teachers of the Sunday School"; PAO, Strachan Sermons: Box A, February 1865, Daniel 6:10, "A Sermon for the benefit of the Young", 5-7, 24-26, 30, & Box B, 25 December 1847, St. John 1:29, "The Lamb of God", 35, & 6 July 1821, II Corinthians 3:17, "where the spirit of the Lord is there is liberty", 10-11, & Box D, 28 March 1830, Isaiah 1:16, "Wash ye, make you clean", 23-24. The quotations are from "The Resurrection of Christ", October 1820, *The Church* (Bethune editorial), 5 May 1838, "A Sermon for the benefit of the young", 7, and [Strachan], "An Address", 8 August 1811, respectively.

2. PAO, Journals of the House of Assembly, Appendix 16, 5 February 1829, Strachan "Report of the President of the General Board of Education"; *Christian Recorder*, I, 43, April 1819, Strachan, "History and Present State of Education in Upper Canada", & II, 446, February 1820, "History of the Present State of Education in Lower Canada", signed N.N.; & II, 286, October 1820, "The Duties and advantages of a Parish Priest", & II, 417, February 1821, "Religion in India"; *The Church*, (Bethune editorials), 5 May 1838 & 8 March 1844, & 6 May 1837, "Church Prospectus"; PAO, Strachan Sermons: Box A., n.d.,

(folder II), Discourse VI (printed), St. John 3:16, "Love of God Manifested in Christ", 383-387; Box B, 8 July 1806, Lecture 3, "Belief in God", 6-7; Box D, 30 November 1853, Revelation 21:22, "God Almighty and the Lamb", 7; and Box E, 24 September 1824, Hebrews 13:5, "Content with things as they are", 16; and Strachan, *Christian Religion*, 1807, 5-10. The quotations are from "Religion in India", February 1821, 417, Discourse VI, 385, and "Education in Lower Canada", February 1820, 446, respectively.

J. D. Purdy in "John Strachan and education in Canada 1800-1851" (University of Toronto: Ph.D. Thesis, 1962), 11, argues that Strachan's desire to educate all classes of society, rather than limiting education to "the children of the socially prominent families as it was in England", was "largely derived" from the Scottish school system. In Scotland, everyone attended parish schools where advancement depended on merit and ability, rather than wealth and position. No doubt, Strachan was influenced by his familiarity with the Scottish national education system, but his striving to establish a national system of education open to all was based on religious, moral and social concerns that were related to the development of the national character in the youth of the province.

[In England, John Locke favoured the education of 'the genteel class', with the children of the poor to be placed in "working schools" where they would receive only the rudiments of education while being put to work to earn their keep. In contrast, the Church of England supported the 'National Society for the Education of the Poor in the Principles of the Christian Church', which was formed in 1811 to establish schools in England and Wales on the monitorial system – the Madras or Bell system – that was developed by the Rev. Dr. Andrew Bell, an Anglican clergyman. Thousands of monitorial schools were founded in the parishes of England and Wales over the next two decades by parish priests for the education of the poor. The Rev. John Strachan was thoroughly familiar with the Bell system, both in its aim to establish a school system to educate the poor and its monitorial method of teaching which paralleled his own concern.]

3. PAO, Strachan Sermons: Box A. 3 August 1806, I Corinthians 10:31, "Do all to the Glory of God", 1-2; Box D, 25 September 1852, Galatians 6:9, "Let us not become weary of well doing", 7-17; Box E, 11 February 1835, Matthew 13:33, "Kingdom of Heaven – leaven", 3, and 2 May 1830, Hebrews 3:7, "Harden not your Hearts", 1, 4-5. The quotations are from the sermon, "Let us not become weary of well doing", 25 September 1852, 13-14 & 15, respectively.

4. PAO, Strachan Sermons: Box A. 25 December 1847, St. John 1:29, "The Lamb of God", 38-39; 3 August 1806, I Corinthians 10:31, "'Do all to the Glory of God", 6; Box B, Scottish Speeches,1795-99, "Prosperity or Adversity", 75, & "Whether a nation be more indebted to Arms or literature", 59, & St.

Luke 15:7, "Repentance", n.p., & 9 March 1799, "Discourse on Duties", 6-8, 11-12; Box C, 10 February 1828, St. Luke 8:15, "Keep the Word", 12, & 19 November 1847, Matthew 19:17, "Importance of the Commandments", 1; Box E, 29 June 1806, St. Matthew 25:25, "Thy Talents", 12-14. & 29 January 1826, Psalm 19:11, "In keeping them there is great reward", 11-12, & 2 May 1830, Hebrews 3:7, "Harden not your hearts", 1, & 1 February 1835, St. Matthew 13:33, "Kingdom of heaven -- leaven", 2, & n.d., St. Mark 12:42, "And there came a certain poor widow", 6-7; and *Christian Recorder*, I, 446, February 1820, "History of the Present State of Education in Lower Canada". The first two quotations are from the sermons, "And there came a certain poor widow", n.d., and "Glory to God" 3 August 1806, 6, and the following two quotations are from the sermon "In keeping them there is great reward", 29 January 1826, 11-12 & 12, respectively.

5. PAO, Strachan Sermons: Box B, 13 April 1834, Acts 20:34. "My Necessities", 3-4, & 10 November 1849, St. Luke 20:38, "God of the Living", 7; and Box C, 25 December 1805, St. Matthew 28:5, "Ye Seek Jesus", 10-12 & 10 February 1828, St. Luke 8:15, "Keep the Word", 11-12; and Box E, 24 September 1824, Hebrews 13:5, "Content with things as ye have", 7-10; PAO, Robinson Papers 1862-1905, 23 June 1862, J.B. Robinson, "Address to the Law Society", 13-15; and *Kingston Chronicle*, 10 December 1831, [Rev. A.H. Burwell], "One of the People". The quotations are from "One of the People", 10 December 1831, and the sermon, "Content with things as they are", 24 September 1824, 7, respectively.

6. PAO, Strachan Sermons: Box A, n.d. (folder II), Discourse VI, (printed.), St. John 3:16, "Love of God manifested in Christ", 348-49; Box B, 13 April 1834, Acts 20:34, "My Necessities", 2-3; Box C, 25 December 1805, St. Matthew 28:5, "Ye Seek Jesus", 12; Box E, 24 September 1824, Hebrews 13:5, "Content with things as ye have", 6-11, & 29 January 1826, Psalm 19:11, "In keeping them there is great reward", 15. The quotations are from the sermon, "Content with things as ye have", 24 September 1824, 10 & 6, respectively.

7. PAO, Strachan Sermons, Box A, n.d., (folder I), Discourse II (printed), Genesis 18:25, "Judge of All", 285-286; Box B, n.d., St. Luke 15:7, "Repentance", n.p.; Box C, 10 February 1828, St. Luke 8:15, "Keep the Word", 10-11; and Box E, 24 September 1824, Hebrews 13:5, "Content with things as ye have", 4-5. The quotations are from the sermons, "Keep the Word", 10 February 1828, 11, and "Content with things as ye have", 24 September 1824, 5, respectively.

8. PAO, Strachan Sermons, Box A, n.d. (folder I), Discourse II (printed), Genesis 18:25, "Judge of All", 286, & Box B, 24 September 1824, Hebrews 13:5, "Content with things as ye have", 6, 12-16; PAO, Strachan Papers, reel

3, 6 March 1839, "Making of the Union", 6; and *Kingston Chronicle*, 17 December 1831, [Burwell], "One of the People". The quotations are from the sermon, "Content with things as ye have", 24 September 1824, 6, 7 & 13-14, respectively.

9. PAO, Strachan Sermons, Box B, Scottish speeches, 1795-99, "Ought a Father to take home his seduced daughter or to disown her", 37, & 1 January 1865, I Chronicles 29:15, "Days on earth are like a shadow", 28-29, and Box C, 21 February 1847, St. Luke 19:16, "Pound gained ten", 2-3.

10. For examples of the type of advice, admonitions, and instruction which were continually impressed upon the minds of the young Anglican Tories by their parents and mentors, see: PAO, Macaulay Papers, reel 1, Ann Macaulay to her son, John Macaulay, October 1807, 26 January 1808, 19 April 1808, 2 June 1808, and 5 July 1808, and John Strachan to John Macaulay, 2 April 1808; PAO, J.B. Robinson Papers, Letters to J.B. Robinson and Emma Walker 1803 -1822, Rev. Dr. Stuart to J.B. Robinson, 23 April 1805, 30 June 1808, and 17 August 1809, and John Strachan to J,B. Robinson, 16 November 1807 and 25 July 1809. The quotations are from Strachan to J.B. Robinson, 25 July 1809, and the Rev. Dr. Stuart to J.B. Robinson, April 23, 1805, respectively.

The cited letters reflect in detail Anglican Tory values and the Tory outlook on life, and show that there was a definite correlation between the education values and principles publicly espoused by the Anglican Tory elite and the admonitions that mothers gave their children in the home of the Anglican Tories. To that end, compare the letters above with several of the sermons and writings of the Rev. John Strachan: viz. PAO, Strachan Sermons, Box B, 13 April 1834, Acts 20:34, "My Necessities', 2 & I Chronicles 29:15, "Days on Earth are like a shadow", 1 January 1865, 25-30, & Box E, 22 October 1848, Romans 12:5, "One body in Christ", 5; and *Kingston Gazette*, [Strachan], "Reckoner No. 5", 29 January 1811 and "Reckoner No. 33", 20 August 1811.

11. Metropolitan Toronto Central Library (MTCL), Strachan, *A Sermon on the Death of Rev. John Stuart, preached at Kingston, 25 August 1811* (Kingston: Charles Kendal, 1811); PAO, Strachan Sermons, Box B, 1812, Ecclesiastics 41:3, "Fear not the sentence of Death", n.p.; Box E. 22 October 1848, Romans 12:5, "One body in Christ", 5; MTCL, Strachan, *Sermon on the death of Cartwright*, 20; Spragge, ed., *Strachan Letter Book*, 5-6, "Life of Col. Bishoppe", December 1813, & 103, "Inscription on Mr. Cartwright's Grave"; and Bishop A.N. Bethune, *Memoir of John Strachan*, 1870, 27, "Address of the Rev. John Strachan to his pupils at the annual Examination at Cornwall, August 1807".

12. MTCL, Strachan, *A Letter to the Rev. A.N. Bethune, Rector of Cobourg, on the management of Grammar Schools*, 6 October 1829 (York: Robert Stanton, 1829), 3-6, 21, 34 & 41-42; *Christian Recorder*, I, 44, April 1819, [Strachan], "History and Present State of Education in Upper Canada"; and *Kingston Gazette*, 3 September 1811, Strachan, "Annual Address to his pupils".

For the course of study pursued in the common schools see J. George Hodgins, ed., *Documentary History of Education in Upper Canada*, (*DHE*) I, 182, "Course of Study pursued in the Common Schools" (1820-21). For the university curriculum proposed by the Rev. Strachan, see Spragge, ed., *Strachan Letter Book* (SLB), 69, 14 February 1815, Strachan, "A Scheme for two Schools and a College". Another publication, Strachan, *A Letter to the Rev. A.N Bethune, Rector of Cobourg, on the Management of Grammar Schools*, 1829, 5-7, provides a year by year breakdown of the subjects and authors studied in the grammar schools. A description of a typical school day in Strachan's school can be found in George W. Spragge, "The Cornwall Grammar School under John Strachan, 1803-1812", *Papers & Records of the Ontario Historical Society*, XXXIV, 1942, 67-71.

13. *Kingston Gazette*, 3 September 1811, "An Address delivered by the Rev. Mr. Strachan, at the last annual Examination of His School, 8 August 1811"; PAO, Strachan Sermons, Box B, Scottish Speeches 1795-99, "Whether Communicating or receiving knowledge be the more pleasant", 1799, 27-28, & "Whether ought a man to value his life or reputation", n.d., 86; and MTCL, Strachan, *A Letter to the Rev. A.N. Bethune, Rector of Cobourg, on the Management of Grammar Schools*, 1829, 8 & 28-29. The quotation is from 'Communicating knowledge', 27-28.

[For an overview of education in France under Napoleon, see: Internet, Napoleon-Series.org/education, J. David Markham, "The Revolution, Napoleon, and Education". Earlier, John Locke (*Some Thoughts Concerning Education*, 1693) rejected the teaching of the classical curriculum in schools, and the teaching of Latin and Greek, in favour of a strictly practical education in the vernacular language. In Upper Canada, it was the democratic radicals who were vehemently opposed to the teaching of the Classics, and Latin and Greek, in the District Grammar Schools, presumably because an education in the Classics was one of the attributes of 'a gentleman'.]

14. Spragge, ed., *SLB*, 77, "Report on Education", 26 February 1815; PAO, Strachan Sermons, Box B, Scottish Speeches 1795-99, "Whether Communicating or receiving knowledge be the more pleasant", 1799, 27-29; and *Kingston Gazette*, 3 September 1811, "An Address delivered by the Rev.

Mr. Strachan, at the last annual Examination of His School, 8 August 1811". The quotation is from the "Report on Education", 26 February 1815.

15. *Kingston Gazette*, 3 September 1811, "An Address delivered by the Rev. Mr. Strachan, at the last annual Examination of His School".

16. Strachan, *A Letter to the Rev. A.N. Bethune, Rector of Cobourg, on the Management of Grammar Schools*, 1829, 10 & 36; Hodgins, ed., *DHE*, 43 quoting Bishop Fuller's sermon (1867), and Strachan's comments in the *Christian Recorder*, I, 182, 1819; *Kingston Gazette*, 3 September 1811, Strachan, "An Address delivered by the Rev. Mr. Strachan, at the last Examination of His School". Strachan employed monitors – "censors" -- at his school in keeping with the Bell-Lancaster system, but he expressed the opinion that their use was severely limited. He held that monitors could be used on occasion to teach the rudiments of the simpler subjects to the younger, or less-advanced, pupils, but that otherwise the system was "too mechanical" and unsuitable for teaching subjects which demanded explanations that only a teacher could give. See PAO, Strachan Papers, 21 October 1809, Strachan to Dr. Brown.

17. MTCL, Strachan, *A Letter to the Rev. A.N. Bethune, Rector of Cobourg, on the Management of Grammar Schools*, 1829, 10-14; and PAO, RG18, "Second Report", 14 December 1832, testimony of John Strachan, 10-11; and *Kingston Gazette*, 3 September 1811, Strachan, "An Address delivered by the Rev. Mr. Strachan at the last Examination of His School". The quotation is from Strachan, *Management of Grammar Schools*, 1829, 12.

18. Bethune, *Memoir of John Strachan*, 1870, 26-28, quoting Strachan, "Address of Strachan to his pupils at the annual examination in August 1807"; Strachan, "Introduction" to a book on Arithmetic published by Strachan in 1809 as quoted in Henry Scadding, *Toronto of Old: Collections and Recollections* (Toronto: Adam, Stevenson & Co., 1873), 106-07; James [John] Strachan, *A Visit to Upper Canada*, 1819, 127; *Christian Recorder*, I, 44, April 1819, Strachan, "History and Present State of Education in Upper Canada"; PAO, Macaulay Papers, reel 1, Strachan to John Macaulay, 13 November 1822; and *The Church*, (Bethune editorial), 8 March 1844.

19. *Christian Recorder*, I, 446, February 1820, N.N., "History of the Present State of Education in Lower Canada".

20. PAO, Strachan Papers, February 1823, "Memorandum", [Maitland to Bathurst], 2; and James [John] Strachan, *A Visit to Upper Canada*, 1819, 130; and Spragge, ed., *SLB*, "Report on Education", 26 February 1815, 77.

21. MTCL, Strachan, *An Appeal to the Friends of Religion and Literature in Behalf of the University of Upper Canada* (London: R. Gilbert, 1827), 7. See also James [John] Strachan, *A Visit to Upper Canada*, 1819, 130-131.

22. PAO, Strachan Sermons, Box B. n.d., "Repentance", n.p.

23. PAO, Strachan Papers, reel 3, 6 March 1839, Strachan, "Making of the Union", 6.

24. Bethune, *Memoir of John Strachan*, 1870, 28, quoting Strachan, "Annual Address, August 1807".

25. PAO, Robinson Papers, Letters to J.B. Robinson, Strachan to John Beverley Robinson, 16 September 1812.

26. MTCL, Strachan, *Sermon for General Thanksgiving*, 3 June 1814, 26.

27. *Kingston Gazette*, 12 March 1811, [Strachan], "Reckoner No.11"; and PAO, Macaulay Papers, William Macaulay to Ann Macaulay, 18 May 1815.

28. Edmund Burke, *Letter from the New to the Old Whigs* (1791), as quoted in *The Church*, 22 May 1841.

29. *The Church*, (Bethune editorial), 8 March 1844, & 18 January 1840, John Toronto [Strachan], "Reply to the Teachers of the Sunday School"; and PAO, Strachan Sermons, Box B. 6 July 1831, II Corinthians 3:17, "Where the Spirit of the Lord is there is Liberty".

30. Strachan, *A Letter to the Rev. A.N. Bethune, Rector of Cobourg, on the Management of Grammar Schools*, 1829, 44; and *The Church*, (Bethune editorial), 8 March 1844. See also, Rev. A.N. Bethune, *Memoir of the Right Reverend John Strachan, First Bishop of Toronto* (Toronto: Henry Rowsell, 1870), 42-43, in quoting Strachan, "Appeal to the Clergy and Laity of the Diocese of Toronto", January 1850. The Strachan quotation is from Bethune, *Memoir*, 42.

31. [While copy-editing the education chapters of the abortive Ph.D. dissertation for this publication, the author thought seriously about preparing a new chapter for insertion on "The Establishment of a National System of Education". It would focus on the Upper Canadian Anglican Tories achievements in education with respect to the Common Schools, the District Schools, various legislative acts pertaining to education, and the General Board of Education, as well as in the establishment of the University of King's College (established 1843/ secularized 1849), and its successor Trinity College (1851). The intention was

to further illustrate the dictum that 'ideas influence actions'. However, much has been published already on the establishment of the system of education in Upper Canada and the role of the Rev. John Strachan in that process; although no existing treatment has adopted a Tory perspective on the subject, or seriously critiqued the motives of the liberal secularist and sectarian opponents of the Anglican Tory national system of education.]

[For a more recent overview of Strachan's arguments in defence of a national system of education, see Curtis Fahey, *The Anglican Experience in Upper Canada, 1791-1854* (Ottawa, Canada: Carleton University Press, 1991), 64-75. For the nature of the attacks by the sectarians and the Reformers on the national education system and, more particularly, on the King's College Charter and the endowment of King's College, see: Fehey, 74-82.]

Conclusion

Upper Canadian Anglican Toryism

A Clash of Ideologies

Richard Hooker: Theology and Political Philosophy

John Locke: Political Philosophy and Religion

The Upper Canadian Tory Worldview

Old Tory vs Old Whig

The Glorious Revolution of 1688

Ideas Influence Actions

Upper Canadian Anglican Toryism

———————————

Conclusion

Upper Canadian Anglican Toryism

This present study has reconstructed the ideas of the Upper Canadian Anglican Tories -- their values, principles and beliefs – as they pertained to their worldview, and more particularly to the constitution of Upper Canada, religion, and education. In doing so, the study has made explicit the underlying political thought – the political philosophy -- of the Upper Canadian Anglican Tories. It completes the original intention of the author to resolve an historiographical controversy of the early 1970s as to whether the Upper Canadian Tories were true Tories in adhering to the 'pristine toryism' of Richard Hooker, the Anglican theologian of the English Reformation, or whether their beliefs, values and principles were those of the Old Whig parliamentarians of the 18th Century. At the same time, this study has addressed a secondary intention which was to gain a deeper understanding of, and explanation for, the positions taken by the Upper Canadian Tories on the public issues of their day through the reconstruction of their political principles, values, beliefs, and worldview.

A personal goal was to produce a lasting scholarly work in intellectual history that would transcend time and serve to lay the basis for the writing of a Tory history of Upper Canada – a history focused on the men who were consciously striving to establish a separate 'nation' on the North American continent. It was to be a traditional conservative polity, based on timeless Christian moral values, the union of church and state, loyalty to the Crown and the British Empire, and the preservation of a (idealized) 'British national character', that would remain separate and distinct from the American democratic republic to the South which embodied Lockean-liberal values.

This conclusion follows the original concept for the study. It sets forth the political philosophy of Richard Hooker, and the political thought and behavior of the Old Whigs of the 18th Century, which are analyzed in comparison with the ideas, values and beliefs of the Upper Canadian Anglican Tories to determine whether the Upper Canadian Tories were true Tories or Old Whigs. In addition, Lockean-liberal ideas, values and beliefs are analyzed and compared to those of Upper Canadian Anglican Tories to determine to what extent if any, the thought of the Anglican Tories – their constitutional, religious and educational ideas, and their worldview -- was influenced by the Enlightenment values set forth in the works of John Locke.

A Clash of Ideologies

What this study has revealed is that the Province of Upper Canada -- in the two-decades following the War of 1812 -- was the scene of a veritable ideological battle, which the Tories referred to as "a battle of ideas". It brought into conflict three different worldviews: the God-centred Christian worldview of the Anglican Tories; a secular man-centred worldview of the Lockean-liberal Reformers; and an emotional 'inner light' millenarian worldview of the Protestant evangelical sectarians who aligned themselves politically with the Reformers in attacking the Tory establishment. A fourth ideology in the 'battle of ideas', egalitarian democratic republicanism, emerged in the early 1830s. It was based on American Jeffersonian agrarianism and Jacksonian Democracy and represented an extension -- to their logical conclusion -- of the Lockean beliefs in the compact theory of society and government, individual natural rights, popular sovereignty, and the separation of church and state.

In Upper Canada, the Tory establishment was under a persistent attack by democratic radicals, evangelical Protestant sectarians, liberal-whigs, and eventually egalitarian democratic republicans, who were aligned under the umbrella of the Reform Party in championing the principle of 'responsible government'. It was a constitutional principle that was based on the concept of popular sovereignty. It required that the members of the Executive Council must have the support of a majority of the House of Assembly to hold office, and that the Lt. Governor must take the advice of his Executive Council on local matters. On their part, the Tories were convinced that the implementation of the principle of responsible government would destroy the balance of the British Constitution by transferring political power, and provincial government revenues and patronage, into the hands of the majority party in the House of Assembly and would foster the development of partisan party politics. However, the constitutional conflict in Upper Canada was not just a power struggle, it was born of differences in ideology between the Tory establishment and its diverse attackers.

In Canadian history, there has been a general lack of understanding of the conflicting ideologies that fostered a veritable 'battle of ideas' in

Upper Canada following the War of 1812, and that was responsible for the disaffection and political struggles waged in the Province. That lack of understanding can be attributed -- where the Tories of Upper Canada are concerned -- to a belief among Canadian historians that the old Toryism of the 16th and 17th centuries had faded away following the Glorious Revolution of 1688, and that Toryism was no longer a viable political philosophy as of the early 19th Century. The prevailing view, as articulated by Terry Cook ("John Beverley Robinson and the Conservative Blueprint for the Upper Canadian Community", *Ontario History*, 1972), was that the conservative values espoused by the Upper Canadian Tories were not derived from "the pristine Toryism of Elizabeth and Hooker", but, rather, were derived from the 18th Century 'whig notions' of order, authority, hierarchy, obedience and deference. In sum, it was maintained that the so-called 'tories' of Upper Canada were actually 'Old Whigs', as distinct from the liberal-Whigs of the American Revolution who had set forth their political values and beliefs in the Declaration of Independence of 1776.

The characterization of the Tories of Upper Canada as Old Whigs was based on the cultural and social values that the Upper Canadian Tories shared with the Old Whigs, and their common adherence to the 18th Century British 'balanced constitution'. However, a determination as to whether the Anglican Tories of Upper Canada were true Tories or Old Whigs, or even Lockean-liberals with 'a tory touch', requires a comparative analysis of the whole matrix of values and beliefs held by the Upper Canadian Tories with the pristine Tory political philosophy of Richard Hooker, the political thought of the Old Whig parliamentarians of the early 18th Century, and the Lockean-liberal political philosophy of John Locke. (1)

Theology and Political Philosophy: Richard Hooker

Given that the political philosophy of the Upper Canadian Anglican Tories was anchored in the Christian religion, it raises the question as to what extent the Upper Canadian Tories -- particularly the Anglican clergy – adhered, in their theology and political philosophy, to the orthodox traditional religion of the Church of England as formulated by the Anglican theologian, Richard Hooker (1554-1600) during the English

Reformation. That question can be resolved through an examination and analysis of the beliefs, values and the worldview of Richard Hooker as set forth in his momentous work, *Of the Lawes of Ecclesiastical Politie* (vols. 1-4, 1593, vols. 5-8, posthumously).

During the English Reformation, Richard Hooker undertook to prepare a defence of the Elizabethan Anglican Church against the threat posed by the Puritans – Calvinist Biblical literalists—who based their religion strictly on Holy Scripture, preached resignation to the Will of God as set forth in Revelation, and demanded that the Church of England abandon its 'Catholic rites' and episcopacy in favour of the Presbyterian system of church government: Pastors, Doctors, Elders, and Deacons. The Puritans were fiercely anti-Roman Catholic and viewed 'fallen man' as being totally corrupt and damned to perdition, unless he were a member of 'the godly' who were predestined for salvation by the free grant of God's grace.

In defending the doctrine and discipline of the Church of England, Hooker set forth a religion of hope, that was based on faith, reason, revelation, law and tradition. In defending the national church, he provided a novel justification for a national state-church polity under the temporal headship of the monarch; and an argument that the Church of England was part of the universal (Catholic) church of Christ through apostolic succession. In his great work of theology and philosophy, Hooker drew on church tradition, medieval cosmology, and the work of Thomas Aquinas (*Summa Theologica*, 1265-1274) which had synthesized Aristotelian philosophy with Christian doctrines in taking account of the Aristotelian conception of law, of man as a rational being, and of the capacity of human reason to attain knowledge of God through the study of nature. In his great work, Hooker systematically erected a coherent system of ethics and law that embraced the Christian religion and the whole of man's life.

Hooker rejected the Puritan belief in Scripture as the sole source of religious truth and guide to man's conduct, as well as the Calvinist belief in the utter depravity of human nature. For Hooker, God's moral law (God's Will) was immanent in Nature, as well as revealed in Scripture, but had to be interpreted through man's reasoning power. In keeping with the cosmology of the medieval scholastics, and the Elizabethan worldview of his day, Hooker saw man as living in an hierarchically-ordered universe, a cosmos, governed by laws emanating from God's reason, and binding upon even God Himself. The whole universe was thus rationally ordered and kept in harmony by the operation of laws – eternal, divine and natural -- which operated in their respective spheres. Since God was conceived of as 'right reason', there was a complete harmony in the workings of the eternal, divine and natural laws of the universe.

It was a universe that, in keeping with the medieval concept of the Great Chain of Being, was marked by order and degree which linked the lowest inanimate and animate forms upwards to God, with man -- in view of his possession of a reasoning power and a soul -- occupying the apex of the animal world. It was an organic order characterized by plenitude and subordination, wherein the perfection of every creature consisted in its acceptance of its assigned role or station in life in acting in subordination to God's Will.

However, man differed from the other animals of creation in that he did not fulfill his role purely by instinct, but rather possessed a free will and was able to act contrary to God's Will.

For Hooker, man was above all a rational being, and the function of his reason was to discover the laws – the voice of God – which adhered in Nature (the Natural Law) so that man might come to know God in all the ways in which he revealed himself. Man's perfection, and his happiness and well-being, consisted in his bringing both his desires and his conduct into keeping with God's Will (His moral law) as conveyed in Scripture and inherent in Nature.

The entire cosmos was conceived of as being governed by law: an Eternal Law (that set forth the eternal purpose by which God does all things and that governed the workings of the universe); a Divine Law (the Will of God as revealed in Scripture), a Natural Law (which governed Nature, both animate and inanimate), and a moral law (which was subsumed within the Divine Law and Natural Law), as well as a Positive Law (or human law, which governed man's outward acts and provided penalties to enforce the precepts of natural and divine law). The purpose of the moral law, conveyed in the Divine Law of Revelation and the Natural Law, was to direct man toward the attainment of goodness and virtue, and to restrain him from misconduct. The Divine Law and the Natural Law conveyed the Will of God, where God was conceived of as goodness and wisdom, and right reason. In effect, man lived in a universe governed by laws established once and for all in keeping with an eternal rationality. The only partial exception was the Positive Law which was to be based on right reason and to serve the same end in directing man's conduct. In so far as positive laws enforced the observance of God's moral law contained in the Divine Law and the Natural Law, they were permanent, but where they related to conventions and regulations pertaining to government, the church as an institution, or society, positive laws were changeable in being dependent on changing circumstances.

For Hooker, human reason had a major role to play in religion not only in interpreting Scripture and understanding the Natural Law, but also in guiding the establishment of God's Church – in taking account of church tradition -- where explicit details could not to be found in Scripture. Through his reasoning power, man could know that there was a God, and that He was truthful, before accepting His revealed Will on faith. In effect, Hooker set forth what would become – by the 18th Century – one of the basic premises of natural religion: that there were religious truths and moral values which could be discerned in Nature by man's reason in the absence of Revelation. Through his reasoning power – according to Hooker -- man could come to know the existence and attributes of God, the duties of man as revealed in Nature, the difference between good and evil, and even the immortality of the soul (as Plato had divined). Hence, the Christian religion was based on reason, as well as Scripture, in the sense that God's law – God's Will – was immanent in Nature as well as revealed in Scripture and could become known through human reason; although there were 'mysteries' of religion that were beyond the comprehension of human reason.

The God-given eternal laws established for man – the divine, natural, and moral laws -- prescribed man's duties, set forth 'the good' that man was to pursue, and were intended to govern man's conduct. God's laws were the embodiment of pure reason and were intended to bring about the happiness of man in living in subordination to God's Will. However, the truths that could be known, or ascertained, through human reason were not sufficient for man to attain salvation.

In keeping with the Christian doctrine of original sin, Hooker held that man's reasoning power and will was so corrupted by 'the Fall' as to render him incapable of fully knowing and submitting to God's moral law whether revealed in Scripture or discerned in Nature. In his unredeemed state, whatever man sought to do would invariably tend towards evil, and his senses would mislead him as to what was 'the good' and virtuous. Hence, man needed the bestowal of God's grace to quicken his reason and strengthen his will.

Only with the aid of God's grace could man properly understand the good found in both Nature and Scripture, and be able to discipline his will so as he would be able to act continually in subordination to God's Will. Moreover, the attainment of salvation was dependent on man gaining knowledge of the mysteries of the Christian religion, which were beyond the reach of human reason because they were not found in Nature. Man could not attain salvation through human reason alone. Salvation could be attained only through knowledge of Christ's atonement, and through having faith in Christ as the son of God and the savior of mankind, and through the receipt of God's grace, and that essential knowledge could be found only in Scripture. Moreover, to be saved, man had to assent by faith, and not by reason. In sum, there was a crucial distinction between reason and revelation. In following the Thomistic theory of knowledge of the Dominican priest, and scholastic philosopher, Thomas Aquinas (1225-1274), Hooker set forth two distinct orders of knowledge: that known by reason; and that known by faith. Both reason and faith played a central role in the Anglican religion, but reason was applicable only to the natural order. In addition to reason and faith, for Hooker the teachings and ministrations of the Church also played an essential role in the attainment of salvation.

It was through the Church preaching the Word, administering the sacraments, and leading the prayers, that the means were provided by which men could receive the knowledge and grace required to be able to save himself and to continue to live a good and virtuous life. In sum, in the Christian scheme of redemption, as set forth by Hooker, both reason and revelation had a role to play, as well as the Church. The role of the Church in preaching was crucial in bringing man to have faith -- as unredeemed man was slow to understand and believe -- and the ministration of the sacraments was essential to man's salvation, particularly the sacrament of baptism (by which, through God's grace, the believer was sanctified and regenerated), and Holy Communion (by which the faithful were united with Christ in righteousness through partaking, spiritually, of the body and blood of Christ). Although man was tainted with original sin, he was still a rational being and capable of seeking redemption and ultimate salvation. However, he was not self-sufficient. Man could not attain redemption without a faith in Christ as the son of God and in Christ's atonement. It was the bestowal of God's grace through the sacrament of baptism, which enabled man to 'go unto perfection' towards salvation. Man could not be perfect in this life, but, once redeemed, he could approach perfection through restraining his selfish passions and living a moral life in subordination to God's Will.

Within Hooker's theological-philosophical defence of the Anglican religion was a whole corpus of political thought which was thoroughly medieval, and which formed a natural component of his moral and religious thought. The political philosophy melded social, cosmic, and political principles, as well as moral and religious values, and reflected the Tory concept of authority as it existed in Elizabethan times. In the more strictly political aspects of his work, Hooker set forth a theory of the origin and purpose of government, a concept of sovereignty, a view of the English Constitution in Church and State, and a view of the historical evolution of the institutions of the church and state.

For Hooker, government originated in the needs of human nature, and its origin was almost coeval with the formation of society in that the continued existence of the one implied the need for the other. Government was a natural outgrowth of man's natural sociability and reasoning powers which moved him to associate with others. It was a product of man's consciousness of a need for law to restrain himself and his fellows from inflicting injuries on one another. The purpose of government was to promote the common good and to keep each component of the social hierarchy functioning in harmony, and that was to be done by means of the making of laws. Society could not function without law, which in turn required a government to promulgate and enforce it. Law was the very soul of the body politic in binding society together and animating it towards the attainment of the common good. In effect, the very happiness of the people depended on the making of good laws which, in the nature of things, were laws that were consistent with God's moral law and right reason.

For Hooker, governments were originally constituted when a community gave its consent to the formation of a governing body under a governor who would exercise his authority for the common good. In effect, all legitimate government rested upon an initial consent of the people, which was the basis of authority and the right of the government to command obedience. However, once a government was legitimately established, and sanctioned by God, there was no right of resistance. If the ruler ordered an action contrary to God's moral law, the people could exercise a right of passive disobedience, but otherwise Hooker commanded a passive obedience to all legitimately-constituted governments of whatever type. He believed that monarchy was the best form of government, but did not hold that any one type of government was sanctioned by God. The form of government differed from state to state and depended on the historical evolution of the nation and the character of a people. The monarchical form of government was not divinely prescribed, and in Hooker's political theory there was no justification for divine right absolutism.

Richard Hooker died before the accession of the Stuart monarchs to power in Britain and their claim to the exercise of a divine right absolutism unrestrained by law or custom. However, Hooker was aware of the influential writings of the renowned French jurist, Jean Bodin (*Six Livres de la république*, 1576), in which it was argued that there must be an absolute sovereign power in any well-ordered state to maintain national unity and public order. In a monarchy, the absolute sovereign power resided in the king, and -- for Bodin -- that power was inalienable and unchallengeable. The king's will, his sovereign command, was the sole source of law and the monarch was not subject to any human legal restraint, or legal prescription, in the promulgation of laws or their enforcement.

For Bodin, the king embodied both the legislative and executive functions of the state, and the magistrates held a delegated power from him. The French 'parlement' served only an advisory role when the three estates – the Clergy, the Nobility, and the Commoners – were summoned by the king. However, according to Bodin, all Frenchmen were citizens of the state, and a citizen was defined simply as a subject of the sovereign. Although the sovereign enjoyed an absolute power, he was expected to make laws in keeping with God's law -- the Natural Law -- which embodied the eternal standard of right, but there was no right of resistance should the sovereign promulgate oppressive laws.

In contrast, Hooker held that sovereignty resided with God. Once the authority of the king was established by the consent of the people – tacit or otherwise – he was sanctioned by God to hold the power to enforce the law over every individual and interest in the realm; yet, the king did not enjoy an arbitrary power. His power was restrained by the purpose of government (to promote the common good), by the laws of the commonwealth to which he was subject, and by the constitution of government in England whereby the King in Parliament made the positive laws -- which gained their legitimacy based on the consent of the representative of the people -- and the king, in his separate executive capacity, enforced the laws of the realm. Moreover, the proper functioning of the Constitution, with respect to the royal supremacy over the Church, necessitated that the king be a Christian.

A novel feature of the political philosophy of Richard Hooker was the concept of a Christian commonwealth on a national scale. In the Christian church-state, all Englishmen were regarded as being members of both the Church and the State, and the first duty of the State was to promote religion. Religion and politics could not be separated, and the state and the national church were rightfully closely allied. The national Church of England was held to be a member of the universal (Catholic) Church of which Christ was the spiritual head, and wherein the national branch of the Catholic Church in England – the Church of England -- was under the temporal headship of the monarch. The royal supremacy over the national church was justified as being scriptural in keeping with the 'godly prince' of the Old Testament who possessed the right and the duty to govern in both the ecclesiastical and the civil sphere subject only to the dictates of Scripture. The 'godly prince' was the supreme governor over all persons and things in his dominion, which was essential to prevent anarchy and disorder in church and state by precluding a divided allegiance. However, the royal supremacy was not viewed as compromising the spiritual independence of the Church.

A distinction was made between the Church as a supernatural body governed by God's revealed Will and headed by Christ, and the external institution of the Church which embraced the Church government and the congregations physically gathered together to worship. It was the Church as a human society, and as a form of ecclesiastical government, that was under the control of the civil magistrate, but not spiritual matters. Hooker specifically rejected the political use of religion by the state -- in an Erastian sense -- as advocated by Niccolo Machiavelli in his *Discourses on Livy* (1531). For Hooker, the promotion of the Christian religion by the state was essential to the happiness of the people of England. As such, it was the ministrations of the Church – in preaching the Word and administering the sacraments – that was essential for the redemption of the people, which would enable them to live a happy life in subordination to God's Will and, ultimately, enable them to attain salvation.

Hooker readily admitted that the episcopacy and the liturgy of the Church of England (as embodied in the Book of Common Prayer and the Creeds of the Church) were not scriptural. He took the stance that such matters were left to man's discretion, but, argued that the episcopacy and liturgy of the Church of England were justified on the grounds of church tradition. He denounced efforts to introduce innovations in the Church simply for the sake of change or present preference. (2)

The Upper Canadian Anglican Tories were orthodox Anglicans in adhering to the theology, cosmology and political philosophy expounded by Richard Hooker, to his view of the union of church and state, and to his argument that the royal supremacy comprised strictly a temporal rule that did not compromise the spiritual independence of the Church. They also rejected the concept of the king possessing an absolute sovereign power. For the Tories of Upper Canada, the king as a Christian was restrained by a fear of God: the Day of Judgement, and God's Providence which -- in the nature of things -- punished those who violated God's moral law. In addition to God's moral law, the king was constrained by his God-given duty to promote the common good of the nation, by the English Common Law, and by the workings of the balanced British Constitution, as well as by 'the rights of Englishmen' as embodied in statutes of the Constitution. More generally, the Upper Canadian Tories were firm believers in Hooker's concept of the rule of law – divine law, natural law and moral law -- and they shared his emphasis on reason, revelation and church tradition as the essence of the Christian religion. There were several differences in outlook, but these were surprisingly minor given the great lapse of time between the late 16th and the early 19th centuries. (3)

Scientific and Enlightenment Influences on the Tories of Upper Canada

The Upper Canadian Tories embraced the scientific advances of the 17th Century which were characterized by the scientific method of Francis Bacon (1561-1626), new scientific discoveries in astrology, mathematics, physics, biology and chemistry, and, more explicitly, the new Copernican heliocentric model of the universe, and the law of universal gravitation and the law of motion of Isaac Newton (1693-1727). However, all such scientific advances were assimilated within the Christian framework of belief of the Anglican Tories. The scientific discoveries represented but a further welcome knowledge of the wonders of God's creation, and an increase in knowledge of the mind of God as revealed in His works.

Likewise, the Upper Canadian Tories embraced the 18th Century idea of progress -- of human improvement -- and held that progress was being made in the arts and sciences, and in improvements in the living conditions and moral character of the peoples of western Europe, following the upheavals of the French revolutionary wars. Nonetheless, the Tories continued to adhere to their view of man as tainted by original sin and in need of redemption. The 18th Century Enlightenment concept of God as a clockmaker, who created and set in motion a mechanical-mathematical universe, did not pose an intellectual problem for the Tories. They continued to believe in a universe governed by the laws of God and the concept of God's active Providence working -- in the world that He had created -- to discipline man in the moral sphere.

Similarly, the concept of evolution – as it existed in their day, prior to the publication of the evolutionary theory of Charles Darwin at the mid-nineteenth century -- did not pose an intellectual problem for the Tories, or negate their belief in the Biblical account of creation, the Great Chain of Being, God's active moral Providence, or in a universe governed by the laws of God. The contemporary concept of evolution, which focused on the adaptation of a species to its environment – "adaptation in kind" -- and selective breeding, had no impact on the Upper Canadian Tory worldview. The Darwinian theory of the random evolution, by natural selection, of all species from a common original ancestor did not have a serious impact on the public mind until the late 19th-early 20th centuries. Only after decades of controversy did *The Origin of the Species* (1859) -- and, more particularly, *The Descent of Man* (1871) in which Darwin applied his evolutionary theory to human evolution -- give rise to a new worldview. Ultimately, Darwinism undermined the faith of many Christians and, more particularly, the faith of members of the evangelical denominations who believed in Biblical literalism. However, the devastating impact of Darwinism on the Christian worldview post-dated the lives of the Upper Canadian Anglican Tories.

In sum, the Upper Canadian Tories held a cumulative view of scientific advances. Indeed, the latest scientific discoveries were taught by the Rev. John Strachan at his Cornwall District Grammar School (1803-1811) and at his Home District Grammar School (1812-1822). The Tories of Upper Canada were unaware that a new science paradigm was emerging that would prove highly destructive of faith in the traditional Christian theology, cosmology and teleology. (4)

Religion and Political Philosophy: John Locke

In seeking to determine whether the Upper Canadian Tories were true Tories – or Old Tories – in the tradition of the 'pristine toryism' of Richard Hooker, there remains a question as to what extent, if any, the Anglican Tories of Upper Canada were influenced by the works of John Locke and 18th Century Enlightenment values. The Tories of Upper Canada did not follow Francis Bacon in separating reason from revelation, but they did admire some elements of the works of John Locke (1632-1704) whose writings had a major influence in the formulation of the 18th

Century Enlightenment concepts of human nature, natural law, natural religion (natural theology), and 'enlightened self-interest' individualism. The extent to which the Upper Canadian Tories were influenced by, or rejected, the religious and political ideas and the 'liberal worldview' of John Locke can be ascertained through an analysis of several of Locke's major works.

Following the Glorious Revolution of 1688, John Locke published several works that had a transforming impact on political thought during the 18th Century Enlightenment, and on the development of Whig-liberalism. Among his most influential publications on politics and religion were: *Two Treatises on Government* (1688); *A Letter Concerning Toleration* (1689); and *The Reasonableness of Christianity* (1695). In his writings, Locke acknowledged his indebtedness to the 'judicious Hooker'. Locke adopted the basic premises of Anglican Toryism: the Christian belief in God the Creator of the universe and of all things animate and inanimate in a universe of order governed by the laws of God, and in man as a rational being, as well as the belief in the laws of Nature that could be known by human reason and that were a reflection of Divine Law as revealed in Scripture. However, Locke brought about a revolution in political theory through introducing several new concepts and beliefs.

Where Locke differed fundamentally from Richard Hooker was in their contrasting views of human nature, on the purpose of government, the role of revealed religion, and what constituted 'the Good'. Locke discarded the God-centred, 'ancient political philosophy' of Anglican Toryism with its identification of 'the Good' with conforming to God's moral law in obedience to the Will of God. He replaced the God-centred political philosophy of orthodox Anglicanism with a man-centred 'modern political philosophy' – bourgeois liberalism – that focused on individual rights and personal freedom, property rights, laissez-faire government, the separation of church and state, religious toleration, and the pursuit of individual self-interest and personal happiness as the purpose of life.

Where human nature was concerned, Locke discarded the Christian belief that man was corrupted by 'the Fall' and in need of redemption to be able to live a life of goodness and virtue. To the contrary, Locke asserted that man was perfectly capable of living a good and virtuous life in accordance with the Natural Law without any recourse to divine revelation and the ministrations of the Church; that human reason alone was sufficient to know God's moral law as revealed in Nature; and that the Natural Law conveyed all that man needed to know to live a good and virtuous life and assure himself of eternal salvation.

In yet another novel departure, Locke asserted that man was endowed by his Maker with certain inalienable and indefeasible natural rights to 'life, liberty and property'. The older belief of Richard Hooker in man as a rational social being with duties, responsibilities and rights -- that adhered to his specific position in a functional, God-ordained, natural social hierarchy -- was jettisoned in favour of the existence of universal natural rights that pertained to man as an individual.

For Locke, the state of nature was a place of peace, mutual assistance and good will, wherein the individual was free to follow his enlightened self-interest and to enjoy the fruits of his own labour. It was a state of nature wherein property was created by the labour that the individual invested in a piece of land to enclose it and make it productive. In sum, man was completely free and self-sufficient in the state of nature. He enjoyed self-evident natural rights, and the Natural Law that governed the world was readily known through human reason. However, there was a lack of security for the individual.

According to Locke, government was founded by the people to provide a better protection for the preservation of their individual natural rights. He introduced the concept of a social contract whereby free individuals had supposedly consented to enter into society and to establish a government to make and enforce laws for the protection of their person and property. In effect, the legitimacy of government and its right to rule rested on the consent of the governed, and the power of government was limited. The role of government was to establish and enforce positive laws – based on the Natural Law – for the protection of private property, the preservation of the God-given natural rights of the individuals comprising the nation, and the enforcement of the sanctity of contracts. No longer did government have a duty to promote the common good and well-being of the nation. Government ceased to possess any overriding ethical, moral or religious purpose in a society composed of individuals following their own enlightened self-interest in pursuing their personal happiness and well-being.

Given the premise that government was based on the consent of the governed, Locke held that if a government violated the trust of the people through engaging in 'a long train of abuses' of individual natural rights, then its right to govern would be forfeit. Power would revert to the people. It was 'the people' who possessed the supreme power and who, when faced by a tyrannical government, had the right to install a new government. Hence, the power and prerogatives of the government were strictly limited by the indefeasible and inalienable natural rights of the governed, and 'the people' possessed 'a lawful right' of rebellion to resist tyranny.

For Locke, human reason and the Natural Law provided all that man required for guidance in government and life, and the Church was simply a voluntary organization which individuals joined -- of their own free will -- for public worship. Hence, Locke advocated the separation of church and state, as well as religious toleration on the grounds that human reason could not discern supernatural truths. To which he added that even if the 'true religion' could be known, any attempt to impose a religious uniformity on society would lead to social disorder and violence. Moreover, since the Natural Law was but a reflection of Divine Law, and could be known through human reason alone, there was no need for perceptive individuals to rely on Scripture for moral guidance.

Given that man was no longer viewed as being corrupted by original sin, there was no longer any need, on the part of discerning individuals, for a faith in Christ as the son of God and in Christ's atonement, or for the ministrations of the Christian Church in administering the sacraments (principally Baptism and Holy Communion) to convey God's saving grace to redeem man from his fallen state and to unite him in righteousness with Christ. According to Locke, natural man was sufficient unto himself, and perfectly capable of living a good life in a society based on individual rights – inclusive of the right of private property – wherein the public interest was identified solely with the freedom of the individual to pursue his own happiness and well-being.

Where his concept of natural law was concerned, Locke believed that man could achieve happiness through adhering to the moral law provided by a beneficent God for the benefit of mankind, and would so out of his own 'enlightened self-interest'. However, in yet another work, *An Essay Concerning Human Understanding* (1690), he espoused a different moral system and sanction for moral conduct. In a novel theory of morality, Locke postulated that 'things are good or evil, only in reference to pleasure or pain'; and that all of the sensations that man can experience – physical and emotional -- were reducible to 'a desire to enjoy pleasure and avoid pain'.

Man could learn what caused pleasure and what caused pain from his senses and reflection. Moreover, he could regulate his moral conduct -- in seeking to attain the good and the avoidance of evil -- according to the sensations that he experienced. In keeping with his epistemology – his theory of knowledge – that all ideas were derived from the senses and reflection, Locke produced an empirical system of morality and moral conduct based on sensations, rather than obedience to God's Will and the fear of a future Day of Judgement. Such an empirical system of morality and standard of moral conduct was far removed from the traditional rationalist natural law concept of morality that was adhered to by Richard Hooker, and by Locke in his earlier *Two Treatises on Government* (1688).

In a study of the Christian religion (*The Reasonableness of Christianity*, 1695), Locke took a rationalist approach to an examination of the New Testament to discern the foundations of the Christian faith. He concluded that Christianity was essentially a moral system – based on God's revealed Will – which provided guidance for the living of a good and virtuous life of good works for the purpose of attaining eternal salvation. In effect, the Christian religion was intended to provide man with moral guidance "in the way of salvation", as interpreted by the rationalist John Locke.

From his analysis of the Gospels of the New Testament, Locke concluded that Christianity was founded upon several basic beliefs: a belief in Jesus Christ as the Messiah (the son of God); a belief in the necessity of repentance by the individual; and a belief in the necessity of partaking of the sacrament of baptism to receive God's grace and live a moral life of good works sufficient to attain salvation. These were the foundations of the Christian faith that God had made, and 'declared to be so'. However, what Locke valued in the Christian religion was the expounding of God's moral law in a clear and readily understandable fashion for the guidance of the labouring masses -- such as "the day-labourers, tradesmen, the spinsters and dairy-maids" and "the hand used for spade and plough" -- who lacked the time and the inclination to discern God's moral law in Nature, and who needed "to hear plain commands" to secure their obedience. Locke valued also the Christian concept of the Day of Judgement for its impact in encouraging the masses to live a moral life. In effect, Locke treated Christianity as simply a support for rational religion. The latter was based on a knowledge of the Natural Law, which the more discerning members of society could comprehend "by the light of reason", but the laboring masses needed a more readily understandable moral law which was enforced by the fear of God and the Day of Judgement.

Where Christianity was concerned, Locke argued that Christians needed only to agree on the fundamentals of their faith to live according to God's Will and attain salvation. Otherwise, Christians possessed a freedom of conscience to hold their own beliefs, and a freedom of religion to worship as they pleased. Men might differ over aspects of religion and their interpretations of Biblical passages, but that was inconsequential where salvation was concerned. As such, Locke disparaged the priesthood for their impositions – elaborate creeds and rites -- on the Christian religion, and noted that neither priests nor a priesthood were mentioned in the Gospels. For Locke, the Christian religion was primarily a moral system which was based on rules of conduct that God revealed, and prescribed, to guide man in enabling him to live a good life and attain eternal salvation. As such, Christianity constituted a reasonable system of beliefs for the masses. (5)

The works of John Locke had a profound effect on the development of a belief in self-evident natural rights and natural religion (natural theology) among the intellectual elite of the 18th Century Enlightenment. And his works were instrumental in fostering deism. However, that was not the case with the Upper Canadian Anglican Tories of the early 19th Century.

The Tories did not concur with the religion beliefs of the 18th Century deists who rejected Revelation, the supernatural elements of the Christian religion, and organized religion itself. The deists believed simply in natural religion (natural theology): that man was naturally good; that a beneficent God had created a world for the happiness of man; and that man in simply following his reason and discerning God's Moral Law in Nature, could live a good and virtuous life which was sufficient to attain salvation. The deists – who included Anglican Whigs, Latitudinarian Anglican divines and, inexplicably, even some English political Tories – separated reason and revelation, and saw no need for revelation (revealed religion) to set forth what was needful for man to know to live a good and virtuous life. They saw no need for man to be redeemed – justified through faith in Christ. For the deists, the established Church of England was valued principally for its social value in inculcating moral values into the masses, and for its role in sustaining the social order through the propagation of a belief in a future rewards and punishment for man on the Day of Judgement. (6)

The Upper Canadian Tory Worldview

In contrast to the views of John Locke and the Enlightenment deists, the Upper Canadian Tories continued to adhere to the unity of reason and Revelation. They maintained, in common with Richard Hooker, that there were mysteries of religion that were beyond human comprehension, and that 'fallen man' had need of a faith in Christ as the son of God, in Christ's atonement, and in God's transforming grace, as well as access to the ministrations of the apostolic Christian Church to be redeemed. It was the Church that interpreted the revealed Word of God – the parables of the Gospels -- for the guidance of man, that administered the sacraments, and that provided guidance and support to aid the redeemed to adhere to a life of goodness and virtue in seeking to attain salvation through 'progressing unto perfection'.

Moreover, the Anglican Tories of Upper Canada maintained the traditional Anglican belief -- as enunciated by Richard Hooker -- that the happiness of man consisted of living in subordination to God's Will – His moral law -- as revealed in Scripture and inherent in Nature (Natural Law). They did not concur in the transformation of the Natural Law, by

John Locke, from a restraining concept -- embodying a subordination to God's Will -- to a liberating concept with the individual enjoying inalienable natural rights and a freedom of conduct that were superior to the sovereign power and laws of the nation. For the Upper Canadian Anglican Tories, the Natural Law conveyed rules of moral conduct that man needed to follow to ensure his own happiness and well-being, and the civil rights of Upper Canadians rested not on an arbitrary declaration of some abstract natural rights principles, but on the historic 'rights of Englishmen' that were embedded in the principles and statutes of the British Constitution and the Common Law.

The Tories of Upper Canada did not share the rejection of the concept of original sin by John Locke, or his view that man was endowed by a benevolent God with certain inalienable and indefeasible natural rights – to life, liberty, and property – which could be known through human reason; or that both society and government were formed by a contract for the sole purpose of preserving the natural rights of the individuals comprising the nation; or that 'the people' had a right to resistance against a legitimate government, if judged to be tyrannous.

For the Tories of Upper Canada, in their view of British politics, it was 'the interests' of the realm -- as represented in the House of Lords and the House of Commons -- who were responsible to act to maintain the balance of the constitution and the rule of law against any usurpations attempted by the Crown, just as it was the responsibility of the Crown to unite with the Commons against any usurpations attempted by the Nobles, and for the Crown to unite with the Nobles against any popular uprising. Once a legitimate government was formed by the consent of the people, whether tacit or otherwise, there was no right of resistance. There was only an obligation of passive obedience on the part of the people. What the Tories of Upper Canada feared above all was rule by 'the mob' – a mobocracy. Hence, their abhorrence of democracy, and their ardent support for the principles of the balanced British Constitution -- as embodied in the Constitutional Act of 1791 in Upper Canada -- and their resistance to encroachments against the powers and prerogatives of the Crown by the House of Assembly.

The framework of beliefs adhered to by the Upper Canadian Anglican Tories was that of the Christian worldview and the theology of the

Church of England as espoused by Richard Hooker with its necessary balance of reason and Revelation, its respect for tradition, and its belief in fallen man's need for redemption and subordination to God's Will -- God's moral law -- to attain happiness in this life and everlasting life. As such, the Tories of Upper Canada rejected the novel beliefs of the Enlightenment in the sufficiency of natural religion and human reason for enabling and guiding man to live a good and virtuous life. Among the natural religion beliefs that the Tories rejected were: that man was naturally good; that human reason could discern from Nature -- from God's moral law immanent in Nature -- all that was necessary to live a good and virtuous life; that the living of a moral life was sufficient in itself to attain salvation; and that the Christian Church was of value principally for its role in teaching morals to the unenlightened masses and for providing a support for the maintenance of the social order.

More generally, the Upper Canadian Tories rejected the Enlightenment tenet that 'man was the measure of all things', and the novel 'natural religion' and 'individual natural rights' precepts of John Locke. Otherwise, because of their belief in the union of reason and revelation, the Anglican Tories of Upper Canada could readily incorporate -- into their Christian belief system -- the new scientific knowledge emerging from the 17th Century scientific revolution, and the work of the desists in producing new evidences for the existence of God in Nature and arguments from design for the existence of God, the Creator. For the Tories, there was no conflict between reason and revelation – each of which had its proper sphere – or between the Christian religion and science, or between Christianity and the idea of human progress.

The Political Thought of the Upper Canadian Tories

Where the origin of government was concerned, the Upper Canadian Tories were at one with Hooker in viewing man as a natural social being, but they differed in that the Tories saw government as originating in the paternal rule of the father within the family, rather than evolving from society more generally. However, they were in accord that government was a natural outgrowth of man's social nature, and was established for the promulgation and enforcement of positive laws – in keeping with God's moral law -- to govern the behavior of man, as well as to better promote the common good and harmony within the social hierarchy. In addition, for the Upper Canadian Tories, government had evolved in keeping with God's permissive Providence, and one of its duties was to promote and defend the established National Church.

Where sovereignty was concerned, the Tories of Upper Canada conceived the sovereign executive power as being separate from the legislative role of parliament, with parliament acting only in an advisory capacity to the government of the realm. (In Upper Canada, the Tories viewed the Lt. Governor – the king's representative – as exercising a delegated authority from the sovereign Crown in Britain, with an appointed Executive Council acting in an advisory capacity, and the Legislative Council and the House of Assembly exercising strictly a legislative function.) In contrast, Hooker held to the medieval view of the king in parliament, with the laws enacted by parliament deriving their authority from the consent of the people through their delegates in parliament, and the king acting as the executive in enforcing the laws passed by parliament.

The Upper Canadian Tories were influenced by the 18th Century political theorists who held that there had to be a single sovereign power in each state, but the Tories rejected the political theory of Jean Bodin that the sovereign must wield an absolute power to ensure the peace, order and stability of society, and that the sovereign must possess both the executive and legislative functions of government. The Upper Canadian Tories continued to adhere to the concept of a limited constitutional monarchy in their view of the legal restraints on the power of the monarch, and the political restraints through the functioning of the 18th Century balanced, or mixed, British Constitution.

Both Hooker and the Tories believed that God was the ultimate sovereign, but they differed in their view of his sanctioning of the monarch's authority. For the Tories, the King was God's vicegerent in exercising a delegated sovereign power; whereas for Hooker, God sanctioned the rule of a king who governed with the consent – tacit, rather than direct -- of the people. Both Hooker and the Upper Canadian Tories held that monarchy was the best form of government; although Hooker believed that God was indifferent to the form of government so long as a government acted in keeping with God's moral law. It was the people of a state who would decide what form of government was best suited to themselves. In contrast, the Upper Canadian Tories viewed the British Constitution as having evolved in keeping with the Christian principles of the English people, and God's permissive providence, which gave the limited constitutional monarchy of Britain, and the balanced British Constitution, somewhat of a religious aura.

Where the concept of a monarchy limited by law – a limited constitutional monarchy – was concerned, the Upper Canadian Tories focused on the specific limits on the monarch in the principles and statutes of the British Constitution, in the Common Law, and the interest of the House of Lords and House of Commons in resisting any attempt by the king to usurp the balance of the Constitution. Moreover, there was a religious restraint imposed on the king by his duty – in his position as God's vicegerent -- to uphold God's moral law.

Where the character of the king of the Christian commonwealth was concerned, the Upper Canadian Tory concept of the Patriot King owed more to the 18th Century, Tory statesman, Henry St. John Bolingbroke (*The Idea of a Patriot King*, 1749) than to Hooker's concept of the Old Testament 'godly prince'.

For Hooker, there was no right of rebellion against a legitimately-established government. Subjects had a duty to yield a 'passive obedience' to a government sanctioned by God. The Upper Canadian Tories did not share that view. They held that neither the monarch nor the people had a right to usurp the balanced British Constitution, and that usurpations were not to be acquiesced in. Hence, the Tories were staunch admirers of the Glorious Revolution of 1688 in England which was effected by the Nobles of the House of Lords, with public support, in upholding the constitution, the rule of law, and 'the rights of Englishmen' against the usurpations of King James II. Likewise, they were opposed to the effort of William Lyon McKenzie to overthrow the balanced constitution, and they argued that Upper Canadians had suffered no grievance sufficient to justify a rebellion. In effect, the Upper Canadian Tories clearly believed, in keeping with Locke, that there were 'unlawful' acts on the part of a government -- such as England had experienced under King James II – that justified a rebellion; although they differed from Locke as to where the right of resistance rested. For the Tories, there was no popular right of resistance external to parliament.

Both Hooker and the Tories shared a belief in the natural union of church and state, and accepted the royal supremacy over the national church. There was a consistent view that the king was merely the head of the temporal and ecclesiastical component of the church, and that the Church retained its spiritual independence with church doctrine and spiritual matters being decided by the bishops in Convocation.

The Upper Canadian Tories adhered to Hooker's concept of the Christian Commonwealth as applied to the nation state, his defence of episcopacy on the grounds of Church tradition, and his concept of apostolic succession with respect to the Church of England being a member of the universal (Catholic) Church. The Upper Canadian Tory scheme of religious comprehension was based on the concept of the Christian Commonwealth which the Anglican Tory clerics hoped to realize in Upper Canada through establishing churches and parishes with 'a spiritually independent' cleric ensconced in each parish. The clerics were to preach the Word, administer the sacraments, and provide a voice of moral authority in their community, while striving to form the Christian character of the province. What the Tories conceived of as 'the British national character' of the province was to be strengthen through the teachings of the Church as dispensed from the pulpit, through the preaching of 'the Word' to gain converts to the National Church, and through Anglican clerics teaching in the schools of the province.

What is beyond dispute is that the basic religious beliefs, values and principles of the Upper Canadian Tories, and their underlying political philosophy, were derived from "the pristine Toryism of Elizabeth and Hooker", with but a few significant variations that comprised primarily the incorporation of the concept of the 18th Century balanced British Constitution, new advances in scientific knowledge, a somewhat different view of the limits on the power of the king, and a limit on the duty of 'passive obedience' in situations where a monarch betrayed his trust and engaged in oppressing his people. Moreover, although the Upper Canadian Tories believed in religious toleration, they held that religious toleration had acceptable limits – historically -- based on past needs to resist overt threats to the maintenance of public order, to the preservation of the state, and to religious freedom itself by religious zealous, or any church or sect that sought to impose its own particular theological beliefs on the state. In effect, the ethical principles of God's moral law took precedence over any religious beliefs that violated, what the Tories regarded as, the universal standard of morality.

Religious Toleration and Lockean liberalism

Both Hooker and the Tories were opposed to coercion in religion, as was John Locke. For Locke, religious toleration was a product of his indifference, if not antipathy, to organized religion and his dismissal of denominational differences over theological doctrines as unimportant where salvation was concerned. For Hooker, as for the Upper Canadian Tories, a forced conversion to the Established Church was a denial of the essence of Christianity and, more particularly, a denial of the need for an individual to have a sincere faith in Christ to attain redemption and union with Christ in his Church. The Upper Canadian Tories believed in, and supported, religious toleration (the refraining from coercing, or imposing legal constraints, against the members of a minority faith), freedom of conscience (the right to hold one's own religious beliefs) and freedom of religion (the right to worship publicly as one pleased).

In Upper Canada, there was freedom of conscience, freedom of religion, and a complete religious toleration. There were no religious restrictions on Upper Canadians beyond the Marriage Act, which had excluded sectarian preachers from performing marriages until the Act was modified in 1831. However, the motivation for maintaining the marriage act to that date was social, not religious, and involved a professional certification concern. The highly-trained and well-educated clergy of the traditional churches did not want their social status and professional standing undermined by the state recognizing a legal right of ill-educated and self-proclaimed sectarian preachers to perform the marriage ceremony. In an increasingly secular age, the ordained clergy of the traditional churches were highly aware that they were suffering from a declining social status and moral standing within their communities, and – as of the 1820s – by a growing lack of respect for professional accreditations and higher education in a frontier community.

In Upper Canada, voting was governed simply by a property franchise, with no other restrictions or encumbrances. Evangelical sectarians, members of the dissenting churches, and Roman Catholic immigrants, once they took the Oath of Allegiance to the King and received their land patent, were eligible to vote, to stand for election to the provincial parliament, and to receive appointments to public office. There was nothing in the Oath of Allegiance to which evangelical sectarians, dissenters, and Roman Catholics could not subscribe -- based on their religious beliefs -- and hence nothing that precluded their full participation in the government and politics of the Province of Upper Canada. Although the Anglican Tory clerics strove to establish a Church of England parish system in Upper Canada, they readily renounced any right to the collection of parish tithes. The Rev. John Strachan played a prominent role in securing the passage of the Tithe Act of 1823 in the hope – a disappointed hope as it turned out -- that the renunciation of the traditional right of the established Church of England to collect parish tithes would pacify the evangelical sectarians and put an end to their attacks on the clergy reserves land endowment of the National Church.

In viewing the history of England, the Upper Canadian Tories were aware of the revolutionary threat that the Puritans had continued to pose against the monarchy and the Church of England following the English Civil War (1642-1651), and the threat that the Roman Catholics of Britain had posed to the Protestant establishment in England during the brief reign of James II (1685-1688). After the Glorious Revolution, there had remained a strong fear that the English Roman Catholics would seek to overthrow the Protestant establishment with military support from the European Catholic powers – in particular, from King Louis XIV of France. Hence, the Upper Canadian Tories saw a historical necessity for the imposition, and maintenance in force, of the Corporation Act (1661) and the Test Act (1673) that precluded Dissenters and Roman Catholics from attaining public positions, seats in government, and commissions in the Army and the Royal Navy. Such political restraints on Dissenters and Roman Catholics were regarded as having been necessary for the peace, order and security of the English nation during threatening times.

Nevertheless, circumstances had changed by the 19th Century. In viewing the contemporary religious situation in England, the Upper

Canadian Tories were convinced that the Roman Catholic components of the population no longer posed a serious political or military threat to the nation. Moreover, the Tories of Upper Canada had no quarrel with the Toleration Act of 1689 that had removed political restraints on Dissenters in England. More generally, they considered that penal laws of that nature were no longer necessary in contemporary Britain. Hence, the leading Tories of Upper Canada advocated that Roman Catholics be granted a complete toleration in the mother country, and welcomed the passage of the Sacramental Test Act of 1828 – that removed the requirement that government officials take communion in the Church of England -- and the passage of the Catholic Emancipation Act of 1829, by the Tory government of the Duke of Wellington.

The Upper Canadian Tories did not agree with the intransigent stance taken by the leader of the ultra-Tories in England – Lord Eldon -- who in 1829 caused a split in the Tory party by refusing to support the government of the Duke of Wellington over the issue of Catholic Emancipation. (Oddly enough, in supporting Catholic Emancipation in Great Britain, the Upper Canadian Tories did not express – in so far as has been determined – any concern about its impact on the Protestant Ascendancy in Ireland.) For the Upper Canadian Tories, the Roman Catholic Church establishment in Lower Canada was viewed as an ally in defending Christianity and the traditional social order against democratic anarchy, irreligion, and secularism.

In Upper Canada, the Roman Catholic Church was an established church in law, and Catholics enjoyed a complete freedom of religion and freedom of conscience. More generally, Upper Canadians were free to attend, and to worship, in any church or with any sectarian congregation that they wished. There was no imposition of tithes for the benefit of the established Church, and no political restrictions on dissenters or Roman Catholics to keep them from voting or holding public office. However, what the Tories expected in return from the Protestant church dissenters, the evangelical Protestant sectarians, and the Roman Catholics, was toleration for the National Church, its prerogatives, and its peaceful enjoyment of the endowments that were bestowed by the Crown. However, the Church of England did not receive a 'live and let live' tolerance from the other religious denominations.

The National Church came under persistent attacks – from the leading clerics and laymen of the other religious denominations, from the infidels of the radical press, and from the Reformers in the House of Assembly who were, for the most part, adherents of the dissenting churches or of the evangelical religion sects. Among the evangelical sects, it was the 'American Methodists' who were the most relentless in their attacks, and not only on the prerogatives and endowments of the National Church. They were religious zealots who in their attacks went so far as to deny the establishment of the Church of England in Upper Canada, to denounce episcopacy as being a non-scriptural form of church governance, and to join with the democratic radicals in seeking to destroy the church-state alliance through political activism.

Where Lockean-liberalism was concerned, the Upper Canadian Tories shared the liberal values of religious toleration, freedom of conscience, and freedom of religion. However, the Tories were not in accord with Locke's advocacy of the separation of the church and state, his view of natural religion as sufficient for an educated man's spiritual needs, his man-centred concept of the universe, or his view of the Church as primarily a moral force in society for the support of the social order and a place where the religious simply gathered to pray. In the political sphere, the Upper Canadian Tories rejected Locke's views on the origin of government in a social contract, his claim that government was established solely for the preservation of 'life, liberty, and property' of the individuals comprising a nation, his concept of God-given inalienable natural rights pertaining to the individual, and his concept of popular sovereignty with 'the people' possessing a supposedly 'lawful right' to rebel against a tyrannical government. In sum, the Upper Canadian Tories were not Lockean-liberals in their political philosophy.

Old Tory versus Old Whig

Although the basic religious beliefs, values, and principles of the Upper Canadian Tories, their political philosophy, and their worldview, were clearly derived from "the pristine Toryism of Elizabeth and Hooker", a question remains as to what were the distinctions between the Old Tories and the Old Whigs in England, and to what extent did the Tories of Upper Canada share, or adopt, aspects of the Old Whig political thought.

In his classic study, *British Politics in the Collectivist Age* (1965), Samuel H. Beer maintains that political culture "is a major factor in explaining the political behavior of individuals, groups, and parties". Thus, Beer focuses on what he sees as the distinct political cultures that existed during different historical periods in Britain. He identifies five different types of political behavior that characterized the different stages of British political development. He conceives "the modernization of British politics" as marked by the evolution from the Old Tory politics of the 17th Century, to the Old Whig parliamentarian politics of the 18th Century, to the Liberal and Radical politics of the 19th Century, through to the Collectivist politics of the 20th Century which, in the latter case, was characterized by two new forms of political organization and representation: Socialist Democracy and Tory Democracy.

The work of Samuel Beer provides a ready framework for determining to what extent the Upper Canadian Tories adopted Old Whig values, principles and beliefs, as distinct from Old Tory concepts and ideas, and for placing the politics of Upper Canada within the broader field of the history of political thought in Britain. However, in contrast to the British political experience, Upper Canada did not evolve through distinct historical stages of political behavior. Within post-War of 1812 Upper Canada, Old Tory, Old Whig and Liberal and Radical political ideas were present at the same time, and brought about a clash of ideologies.

What emerges from the following analysis of the political thought and values of the Old Tories and the Old Whigs, is a confirmation of the conclusion that the Tories of Upper Canada were true Tories, rather than Old Whigs, as well as a realization of the timelessness of Anglican Toryism as evidenced in the continuity of ideas – values, beliefs and principles – as found in the political philosophy of Richard Hooker during the Elizabethan Age, in the political philosophy of the Old Tories in 17th Century England, and in the political philosophy of the Upper Canadian Anglican Tories of the early 19th Century.

In England, the Old Tories and Old Whigs shared a common belief in man as a social being, in government as having evolved from the family, and in a natural social hierarchy. Both the Old Tories and the Old Whigs believed in the legitimacy of a landed aristocracy playing the leading role in society and government, and in the duty of those in authority to promote the common good of the nation and to maintain a state of harmony between the various orders and interests of society. There was a common belief as well in the concept of society as a functional hierarchy -- based on mutual duties and responsibilities -- that was essential to the maintenance of social order and stability, and the proper functioning of society and the government itself. However, the basic premises on which the social order rested were viewed differently by the Old Tories and the Old Whigs.

For the Old Tories, there was a God-created cosmic order of authority, subordination and degree, in both nature and human society which was conveyed in the concept of the Great Chain of Being. The social order was part of a divine plan wherein men had duties and responsibilities imposed by the position that they occupied in society as it had evolved under God's permissive Providence, and each social component had a God-given functional purpose in His grand scheme of things. Men were born with different God-given talents and abilities which were intended to suit them to fulfill a particular position and function in the social hierarchy. Society was viewed as being both corporate and hierarchic, in which there were fixed interests comprising the nobles, and the commonality and the corporate communities – legally-created boroughs, institutions, incorporated towns, and guilds – in an organic state. However, the social hierarchy was fixed in a hereditary sense in that the aristocracy and the gentry were regarded as being the natural-born leaders of society, and were expected to provide leadership and guidance for their local community and support for its various interests in parliament.

The Old Tories were believers in an active Providence guiding the evolution of society in keeping with God's purpose; whereas the Old Whigs, as exemplified by Edmund Burke (1729-1797), held a more sociological view of the natural social hierarchy based on the historical evolution of the nation. Although Burke occasionally employed the Great Chain of Being imagery to convey the natural hierarchical order of society, he did not base his argument on Christian cosmology or on God-given talents and abilities. In his justification for a natural hierarchical society – as summarized by Samuel Beer -- there are appeals to history, experience, historic function, prescription, and a practical concern about maintaining stability and order in society. For Burke, society was an organism that grew over time – 'a partnership down through the ages' – and that had evolved in keeping with human needs. Burke believed in a natural aristocracy, but it was a product of circumstances, education and breeding. His natural aristocracy was composed of men who were educated in virtuous conduct, who had the time to read and reflect, and who were habituated to honour and duty, and capable of taking 'a larger view' of affairs. In effect, the 'natural leaders' of society for Burke were the great peers of the realm, the landed gentry, the leading merchants and manufacturers, and the yeomanry – the 'fixed interests' of the country – whose interests were represented by the great aristocratic Whig families in parliament.

Burke was a supporter of the hereditary monarchy, but denied that monarchy was established by divine right, and that monarchy was better than any other form of government. The best form of government was that which was best suited to the character of the people. However, on pragmatic grounds, Burke held that a monarchy based on hereditary right was the best guarantor of the preservation of the civil liberties as it precluded potential conflicts over the succession. Burke believed in a God-given natural law, but did not base his political writings on Scripture and Christian doctrines.

The Tories of Upper Canada believed in the natural social hierarchy, but did not distinguish between the Old Tory and Old Whig premises in justifying their concept of a natural social hierarchy. They espoused both the divine plan argument of the Old Tories, as well as the sociological argument of Edmund Burke. However, the Upper Canadian Tories believed that the social ranks of society were not fixed hereditarily, in God's scheme of things. To the contrary, the Upper Canadian Anglican Tories believed that youth of superior God-given talents and abilities were to be found throughout society.

Upper Canada lacked a landed aristocracy and gentry to provide leadership for society, hence a natural governing elite had to be created to occupy positions of authority. To that end, the Upper Canadian Tory sought to establish a national system of education in which youths of superior talents and abilities – regardless of their social origins – could be identified, tutored and provided with financial support from the state, to further their education. It was through education that the natural hierarchical social order was to be sustained through ensuring that those who were born with superior God-given talents and abilities would attain their proper position in society.

The Upper Canadian Tories believed in a natural hierarchical society, but their social order was based on the concept of a meritocracy in which careers were open to men of talent, education, and moral worth, who were loyal to the Crown and the established order. They were men who were 'bred' to positions of authority, but it was through a national system of education -- administered by the established Church of England -- which was open to all ranks of society, and in which the inculcation of a Christian moral character was of a vital importance. For the Tories of Upper Canada, one's social position was not pre-ordained. Man had free will, and only those who had faith in Christ, who were redeemed, and who lived a moral life in applying their God-given talents and abilities in promoting the common good, would attain, and maintain, their proper position in the natural social hierarchy.

Both the Old Tories and the Old Whigs were supporters of the hereditary monarchy, but where they differed dramatically was in their interpretation of the balanced British Constitution, the location of the sovereign power, their view of the established Church of England, and their concept of parliamentary representation.

For the Old Tories of the 17th Century, the balanced British Constitution consisted of a legislature composed on King, Lords, and Commons, which guaranteed that the rights and liberties of Englishmen would be defended from encroachment, or from being overthrown, by the ability of any two components of the legislature to unite in opposition to any attempted encroachment by the third component. God was the sovereign power, and the king, in his separate executive role, was God's vicegerent who was to govern in keeping with God's moral law, and in seeking to promote virtuous conduct and the common good. The King was viewed as embodying the unity and common interest of the nation. Parliament was viewed as simply an advisory body, with the King choosing his ministers from amongst the leading members of the House of Lords. In contrast, the Old Whigs of the 18th Century differed in where they located the sovereign power, and their view of the sovereignty.

In the late 16th Century, a novel concept of sovereignty emerged based on the argument that a well-ordered state needed to be government by an absolutist sovereign power. The absolutist concept of sovereignty was a product of political theorists who were troubled by the problem of maintaining peace, order, and political stability in nations wracked by religious conflict, and religious wars, during the Protestant Reformation. One early, and highly influential publication, was that of a French jurist, Jean Bodin (*Six Livres de la république*, 1576), who presented a pragmatic argument that there must be an absolute sovereign power in each state to maintain national unity and public order in the face of religious divisions. A similar argument was introduced into England by the Stuart monarchs, based on an earlier tract by King James VI of Scotland (*The Trew Law of Free Monarchies*, 1598).

King James VI -- subsequently King James I of the kingdoms of England, Scotland and Ireland -- propounded a novel absolutist political theory which the Stuart monarchs, and particularly his grandson, King James II, sought to implement. It combined the traditional concept of the divine right of kings (that all authority is derived from and sanctioned by God) with the traditional Anglican religious belief in the duty of passive obedience (that is owed to a legitimate monarch), to forge a new theory of divine right absolutism. It was a theory that as God's lieutenant "the king makes the law, and not the law the king", and that all subjects owed an absolute passive obedience to a lawful king. The king was responsible only to God for his conduct, and the people had no right to sit in judgement.

Both the Old Tories and the Old Whigs rejected the theory of divine right absolutism. Moreover, there was little support in England for a divine right absolutism form of royal government, even among the moderate Roman Catholic supporters of the Stuart monarchy. The Old Tories believed in the traditional concept of the divine right of kings, and in the principle of passive obedience to a legitimate government, but had no concept of a king unrestrained by the Common Law and the 'Rights of

Englishmen' as embedded in statutes of the Constitution. They viewed the king as holding a delegated sovereignty – from God -- with the King in his sovereign capacity holding the right to initiate legislation in parliament, to govern the country with the aid of his appointed ministers, to enforce the law, to control coinage, and to oversee the 'high matters of state': trade and commerce, the collection of taxes, foreign affairs, the making of war and peace, and the promotion of the well-being of the nation. However, the Old Tories had no concept of the king's sovereign power being above the law and absolute within the realm.

The Old Whigs did not recognize the king as holding the sovereign power in the nation, and rejected the principle of passive obedience on the part of the subject. For the 18th Century Whigs, the 'Supreme Legislative power of the Nation" was embodied in the three estates – King, Lords, and Commons -- in parliament. Under the balanced constitution, all three branches were regarded as being co-equal in consenting to legislation; and that equipoise of power – or separation of powers -- was viewed as essential to the preservation of the 'rights of Englishmen', and for the passage of legislation for the common good and well-being of the nation.

After the political settlement of the Glorious Revolution of 1688, the Whigs held that the king did not possess or exercise a sovereign power independent of Parliament, and no longer was the king viewed as representing the unity of the nation and as the promoter of the common good. Parliament came to be regarded as a deliberative body, wherein the interests of the nation were represented by the members who formed a body competent to determine – through rational debate -- the common good and the national interest. Moreover, for the Whigs, Parliament was held to be the sovereign body of the nation in holding the right, by the consent of the people, to govern the country. During the Whig Ascendancy (1715-1760), Whig ministers – members of the great families of the landed aristocracy -- ran the British government. They governed in the name of 'the King in parliament', and George I and his successor George II were reduced to being mere figureheads.

Under the new concept of government --18th Century Whig parliamentarianism -- the balanced British Constitution consisted of the king, lords and commons in Parliament, and the sovereign power was regarded as residing in 'the king in Parliament': parliamentary sovereignty. The sovereign power was exercised by the 'King's Government' – the Prime Minister and his cabinet – governing in the name of the king in carrying out the wishes of Parliament. Ministers were still considered responsible to the king, but it was recognized that a ministry had to be able to command a majority in Parliament, and especially in the House of Commons, to retain power. Under the new system of Whig parliamentarianism, which grew out of the Glorious Revolution settlement of 1688-1689, it was Parliament that exercised control over government spending, taxation, trade and commerce, and the other 'high matters of state'.

During the Whig Ascendancy, the concept of the role of parliament in government, and the role of the king underwent a total transformation under the influence of Locke's political theory. His arguments pertaining to government founded on the consent of the people, the natural rights of life, liberty and property, on the right of resistance against a tyrannical government, and for religious toleration, came to have a significant influence on the evolution of whig-liberalism in England, and in Great Britain more generally. However, his theory of individual rights did not have much of an impact initially. For the Old Whigs, 'the people' were represented by the aristocratic families, and their supporters in the House of Commons who were dependent for their election on a Noble patron. The members of Parliament were regarded – according to Burke – as providing 'a virtual representation' of the various interests of the country. The role of government was viewed in terms of balancing the different interests of 'the fixed interests' of the realm – the Crown, the landed Aristocracy, the Church and the commonality – and in terms of protecting the 'life, liberty and property' of Englishmen.

In contrast to Whig parliamentarianism, the Upper Canadian Tories held a different view of the British constitution and the respective roles of the king and parliament. The Tories of Upper Canada continued to adhere to the earlier Old Tory view of the King as God's vicegerent in wielding a delegated sovereign power that was distinct from the legislative function of the monarch. They believed in the balanced British constitution, but it was the Old Tory legislative balance of King, Lords and Commons, in parliament. Sovereignty resided outside of Parliament in the office of the king, and it was the king who represented the unity of the nation and exercised the sovereign power in his executive capacity. However, the Upper Canadian Tory concept of sovereignty did not convey an absolute power.

The King was to exercise his delegated sovereign power – delegated from God -- in keeping with God's moral law; he was subject to the rule of law (the Common Law); and his powers were limited by the principles and statutes of the British Constitution which embodied 'the rights of Englishmen'. Indeed, one of the primary functions of the king – according to the Upper Canadian Tories -- was to uphold the 'rights of Englishmen'. The Tories of Upper Canada were admirers of King George III (reigned: 1760-1820) who acted in a sovereign capacity, appointed his own ministers, and was a devote Christian of a strong moral character. Before his descent into 'madness', George III was viewed as fitting the Tory ideal of a patriot king.

The Old Tories and Old Whigs of England differed also in their interpretation of the evolution of the British Constitution. For the Old Tories, the British Constitution had evolved in keeping with the Christian religious principles of the English people and God's permissive Providence, and its proper functioning depended upon the Christian character of the people. Moreover, the Church of England was regarded as being an integral part of the British Constitution, which was evident in the presence of the Lords Spiritual in the House of Lords, and the role of the Archbishop of Canterbury in the coronation ceremony. In contrast, the Old Whigs viewed the evolution of the British Constitution from a sociological, rather than a religious perspective.

The Old Whigs viewed the British Constitution as evolving from circumstances and events, and from the conflict between the king and the aristocracy for power. Some Whig political theorists even attributed the evolution of the British Constitution to the native 'genius' of the Anglo-Saxon race, and to the recovery of the ancient liberties of the Anglo-Saxon people which had been subverted by the Norman Conquest. The Old Whigs, as indicated by Edmund Burke, retained the belief that the proper working of the constitution relied on the character of the people, and that the best form of government was the one which was best suited to the character of the people in any nation. For Britain, that was a hereditary monarchy and the balanced or mixed constitution as interpreted by the Whig parliamentarians. However, the Old Whigs did not consider that the monarchical form of government was, necessarily, the best form of government for a colony.

The Old Whigs admired the Church of England -- as Burke attested -- for its 'sublime principles', but valued the Church establishment principally on utilitarian grounds. The Church of England was regarded as the bulwark of public order in terms of the impact of its teachings – its religious and moral principles --in maintaining a due order and subordination among the masses. In a Christian Commonwealth such as England, the church and state were -- for Burke – were integral parts of the same body, and the maintenance of religion was the principal concern of the magistrate for its support of the social order and the promotion of the common good.

The Tories of Upper Canada shared the Old Whig belief that there was a direct relationship between the teaching of the Church of England and the maintenance of the social order. However, the Anglican Tories of Upper Canada valued the Established Church for far more than its general social utility and moral force on society and government. They were strong supporters of the alliance of church and state, and never ceased to believe in revealed religion and the essential religious function of the Church of England in the salvation of souls.

Where the role of the members of parliament were concerned, there was a definite difference between the Old Tory view and that of the Old Whigs. Under the Old Tory regime, the members of parliament were regarded as being elected delegates – 'attorneys' -- who were expected to be advocates for the various 'interests' of their community. The interest of the landed aristocracy found expression in the House of Lords, the interest of the Established Church of England through the Lords Spiritual in the House of Lords, and the diverse corporate, institutional, and community interests of the nation found expression within the aggregate of the elected members of the House of Commons. The members were not in parliament to govern the nation, but rather to assent to taxes requested by the King, to seek to secure the enactment of legislation for the benefit of their local corporate interests, and/or to request a redress from the King for a specific grievance. It was the king who represented the national interest, who governed the nation, and who promoted the common good through his royal government. It was the King alone, with the advice of his appointed courtiers or ministers, who was responsible for dealing with the 'great matters of state'. The Speech from the Throne, at the commencement of each session of Parliament, set out the program and policies of the Crown for which a vote of monies would be requested from Parliament.

In contrast, during the Whig Ascendancy of the 18th Century, the members of Parliament were no longer viewed as delegates who were bound to represent and advance the local interests of their constituents. As articulated by Edmund Burke, members of Parliament came to be viewed as representatives of the nation, who were expected to set aside their local interests and to act in the national interest in promoting the common good. In the new 18th Century concept of parliamentary government -- which was championed by the Old Whigs -- the ideal member of parliament was a man of independent means, free of outside influences, who – while keeping in mind the interests of his constituents – was expected to support policies that would promote the general interest and common good of the nation, as defined by parliament. More generally, members of parliament were expected to be skilled legislators who would engage in rationale debate, and who would exercise their mature judgement and wisdom -- in keeping with an 'enlightened conscience' and 'the eternal rules of justice and reason' – in deliberating on 'the great matters of state'. To that end, candidates for election to the House of Commons were to be men of moral character, wisdom, and of 'a high quality of mind'

In Upper Canada, the Tories were adherents of the Old Whig concept of representation as enunciated by Edmund Burke and other prominent Whigs, with one major additional attribution. For the Tories of Upper Canada, it was essential that the members of the House of Assembly be men of a Christian moral character, as well as possessed of the qualities cited by Edmund Burke. However, by the late 18th Century, the Old Whig concept of representation had gained a wide acceptance among British politicians, both Whig and Tory. In fact, the Tories of Upper Canada cited the English jurist and Tory politician, Sir William Blackstone, (*Commentaries on the Laws of England*, 1766-1769), in maintaining that members of the House of Assembly were representatives of the community as-a-whole, and not simply delegates of their constituents or of a political party. In sum, the Upper Canadian Tories viewed the Legislature Council and the House of Assembly as deliberative bodies where public issues were to be decided through rational debate. In that respect, the Tories of Upper Canada shared the Old Whig view of parliamentary representation, but it was a view that the Tories of contemporary England had adopted as well.

More specifically, for the Tories of Upper Canada, the ideal members of the Legislature were 'liberally-educated men' of property, intelligence and standing in the community -- from the agricultural and commercial classes, and the legal profession – who would be capable of bringing wisdom, prudence and good judgement to bear during debates and in the enacting of legislation. For the Upper Canadian Tories, however, good government required not only the enacting and enforcing of good laws, it required action to promote the welfare and prosperity of the province through trade and commerce, 'national' economic development policies, the construction of transport facilities, and the exploitation of provincial natural resources. Above all, the Tories of Upper Canada were men of faith – Churchmen -- whose conduct and actions were guided by their religious beliefs -- inclusive of a belief in the Christian concept of original sin, in the Protestant doctrine of 'salvation by faith alone', in Christ's atonement, God's saving grace, the redemption of man, God's moral law, Providence, and the Day of Judgement, salvation and an afterlife.

Emergence of the liberal-Whigs

During the course of the 18th Century -- under the growing influence of the political philosophy of John Locke -- the Old Whigs were transformed into liberal-Whigs from whom the Upper Canadian Tories differed dramatically in most respects. The liberal-Whigs came to view society as comprised of individuals, rather than the Old Tory and Old Whig concept of corporations, orders, and 'interests', and viewed government as constituted primarily to defend the life, liberty and property of the individual. In the early 19th Century -- the post-Napoleonic Wars period – the liberal-Whigs favoured a uniform property franchise for voting in assuming that men of property would possess the requisite intelligence, education, and character to participate in government, and they held to a new concept of society within a secular worldview.

Society came to be viewed by the liberal-Whigs as comprised of classes – an upper, middle and lower class – with the middle class conceived of as possessing the best qualities of the nation in its belief in 'the maintenance of order and the security of property, and its declared hostility to corruption and oppression'. The liberal-Whigs in parliament were fervent in their commitment to parliamentary reform. They favoured an extension of the franchise to include the middle class, a reform of the riding boroughs to attain an equality of population, and the creation of new ridings to encompass the centres of commerce, trade, and manufacturing that lacked representation in parliament. In addition, the liberal-Whigs were committed to laissez-faire government, free trade, the development of manufacturing, religious toleration (inclusive of Catholic emancipation), and the elimination of the politics of what they deemed 'special interests'. Moreover, they held a novel view of political parties.

The liberal-Whigs regarded their Whig political party as a legitimate grouping of rational individuals who shared common principles, and who freely combined to facilitate the passage of legislation to promote the common good of the nation, which they identified with the liberal-Whig program of reform. In contrast, the Old Tories had deplored political parties. They were regarded as factions bent on promoting partisan interests that were detrimental to the common good of the nation. (7)

The Tories versus liberal-Whigs and Old Whigs

The Upper Canadian Tories thought in terms of a property franchise, and the personal qualities that land ownership conveyed, but they rejected the liberal-Whig concept of a society composed of rational individuals. The Tory concept of an ideal society was one in which a landed aristocracy played an essential role in both society and government, and they lamented the absence of a landed aristocracy in Upper Canada. The Tories of Upper Canada did not view politics in terms of individualism, and rarely talked in terms of classes, but rather viewed the political system in terms of social orders within a natural, God-ordained, social hierarchy. Moreover, they rejected the liberal-Whig concept of political parties. For the Tories political parties were associated with factions and partisan politics. The Upper Canadian Tories did hold some social ideas, values, and beliefs in common with the Old Whigs of the 18th Century, but there were vast differences in their political thought and their religious values as well.

With respect to the historic Old Whig politics, the Upper Canadian Tories did share the social concepts of order and deference, a belief in a natural hierarchical society, a belief in primogeniture and in hereditary rights, and in duties and rights related to one's position in society, but these social values and beliefs, and the concepts that underlay them, were common earlier among the Old Tories in their day. In addition, the Upper Canadian Tories shared the Old Whig belief in the 18th Century balanced, or mixed, British Constitution, but differed over the location of the sovereign power. Where parliamentary representation was concerned, the Tories of Upper Canada adhered to the Old Whig view of the members of parliament being representatives of the nation and bound to promote the common good of the nation. Thus, the Upper Canadian Tories rejected the earlier 17th Century Old Tory view of the members of parliament as delegates bound to promote the 'interests' of their local constituency. However, by the 18th Century the English Tories had rejected the delegate concept of representation as well.

Where the Tories of Upper Canada differed dramatically from the Old Whigs was in their view of the role of religion in society, in the state, and in the evolution of the British Constitution. That difference between the Tories and the liberal-Whigs was encapsulated in the dichotomy of the union of church and state versus the separation of church and state. The Upper Canadian Tories did share the liberal-Whig view of the ideal member of parliament as being a property holder of intelligence, education, and character, but the Tories added a qualification that the ideal member ought to be a man of Christian moral values.

On the other hand, the Tories of Upper Canada rejected the 19th Century British liberal-Whig view of political parties, the new liberal concept of society as a body of individuals divided into three classes, and liberal-

Whig individualism. The Upper Canadian Tories rejected also the concept of parliamentary sovereignty – the king in parliament -- that the liberal-Whigs inherited from the Old Whigs. Moreover, the Tories differed from the liberal-Whig view that the purpose of government was simply to protect the life, liberty and property of the individual, and differed as well from the liberal belief that man – guided only by human reason and his enlightened self-interest -- could attain a lasting happiness in this life. Not only did the Upper Canadian Tories differ from the liberal-Whigs in their political, constitutional, and religious values and beliefs, but they differed at a deeper philosophical level in their cosmology and teleology, their view of reason and natural law, and of human nature. More generally, it was a difference based on the Christian faith of the Tories of Upper Canada in contrast to the natural religion secularism of the British liberal-Whigs.

In the Province of Upper Canada, it was the Reformers who adhered to the concept that the members of the House of Assembly were delegates of their constituents. Initially, the Reform members regarded themselves as delegates who were bound to pursue the local and sectional interests of their respective ridings, but once the Reform Party began to organize for elections, and to set forth an election platform, the Reform members of the House of Assembly were held to be delegates of the Reform Party. They were bound to vote for the party platform and for party resolutions and motions.

The Glorious Revolution of 1688

Toryism did not cease to be a viable political philosophy following the Glorious Revolution of 1688. Well over a hundred years later, the Upper Canadian Tories continued to adhere to the traditional Anglican Tory political philosophy as espoused by Richard Hooker and, for the Tories, the revolution did not mark a new departure, or a revolution in politics or in political and social values. For the Tories of Upper Canada, the revolution settlement of 1688-1689 marked the culmination of the evolution of the British Constitution to its full "consistency and perfection" in so far as anything of man could approach perfection. For the Tories, the constitution had evolved in series of struggles to maintain an equipoise between the tyranny of one (royal absolutism) and the tyranny of the many (mob rule), in keeping with a guiding standard: the eternal principles of justice and morality as revealed by God.

The 'final perfection' of the Constitution embodied a series of attainments: Magna Carta (1215); the right to petition the Crown (1406); the Petition of Right (1628); the Habeas Corpus Act (1679); the right of parliament to impeach the king's ministers for misconduct (1681), and finally – following the 'Revolution' of 1688 – the Coronation Oath of 1689 and the Bill of Rights of 1689. For the Upper Canadian Tories, the British Constitution – which was restored during the Revolution of 1688 --established a limited constitutional monarchy that embraced the vital principles of society and government in a balanced form of government. It was a royal government that preserved the 'true liberty' of the subject, and that vindicated 'the natural rights of man' which, for the Tories, were defined as: 'the right to paternal government based on God's moral law, and subordination to God's Will rather than the arbitrary will of an earthly sovereign' or the general will of the mob.

In sum, the Upper Canadian Tories were adherents of the 18th Century balanced British constitution of 1688-1689 – as they interpreted it -- and the rule of law. For the Tories, the King, Lords, and Commons each had their respective duties and responsibilities under the constitution and within the compass of the law, and where government was concerned the three branches of the legislature were expected to enact laws in keeping with God's moral law, and everyone, including the king, had to obey the laws of the realm. Moreover, there was a common duty to maintain the balance of the constitution, to protect and promote the National Church – the established Church of England – and to maintain inviolate 'the rights of Englishmen' which were reconfirmed and solidified in the revolution settlement of 1688-1689.

Historically, the revolution was instigated by the leading Lords Temporal and Spiritual of the House of Lords in resistance to the royal absolutism of King James II -- a zealous convert to Roman Catholicism -- and in opposition to his policy of Catholicizing England which was undermining the Church of England and the supremacy of the Protestant religion. As the legitimate heir in the royal succession, King James had initially enjoyed the support of the Tories in parliament, but had been opposed by the Old Whigs who -- during the reign of Charles II – had brought forward a series of bills in Parliament that aimed at excluding James from the royal succession: the Exclusion Crisis, 1679-1681. The Whigs objected to a Roman Catholic ascending the throne of England. However, before ascending the throne, James had gained a widespread popularity among the English people in declaring before the Privy Council that:

> I have been reported to be a man of arbitrary power, but I shall make it my endeavor to preserve this government both in church and state as it is now by law established. I know the principles of the Church of England are for monarchy, and the members of it have showed themselves good and loyal subjects, therefore I shall always take care to defend and support it. I know too that the laws of England are sufficient to make a king as great a monarch as I can wish, and as I shall never depart from the just rights and prerogatives of the crown, so I shall never invade any man's property.

The Declaration was printed and read by the Town Criers in the towns and villages of England, and had had a very positive effect in rallying support for the succession of James to the Throne. However, subsequently, the actions of King James belied his public professions as he strove to establish a system of divine right absolutism in England while seeking to Catholicize the country.

Once in power, James dissolved Parliament and established an inner Royal Council composed of Roman Catholics that carried out all government business in the name of the King, while ignoring the Privy Council. He raised taxes without consulting parliament, surrounded himself with Roman Catholic Francophiles, including a Jesuit priest who became his principal advisor, established close ties with the Royal Court of Louis XIV of France, and appointed Roman Catholic diplomats to represent England abroad. The King's Printer was ordered to publish translations of French Catholic political and religious works, including the works of a French bishop and theologian, Jacques-Bénigne Bossuet -- a tutor of Louis XIV -- who was a staunch defender of divine right absolutism and a leading apologist for the Roman Catholic religion.

These acts had a negative effect on English public opinion as did the extreme cruelty exercised, at an early date, by the newly-appointed Lord Chief Justice, George Jeffreys, in the 'Bloody Assizes' that followed the defeat of a rebellion by the Protestant Duke of Monmouth at the Battle of Sedgemoor (July 1685). Monmouth was executed, 74 or more of his Protestant 'army' were hanged, drawn and quartered, and upwards of 800 others were transported to the West Indies as indentured servants. Moreover, political unrest had increased when James proceeded to build up a professional standing army of 40,000 men, which was partially quartered in private homes in the garrison towns of England.

With Roman Catholics constituting only one-fiftieth of the population of England, James sought to win support from the Dissenters -- and their acquiescence in the pro-Catholic policies of his royal government -- by the issuing of a Declaration of Indulgence (1687). The Declaration suspended the Test Acts oaths which precluded Roman Catholics and Dissenters from public office. It was an act of toleration for political purposes, the implications of which alarmed the Tory supporters of King James as well as the Whigs. Both political interests were united in insisting that the King had no right to suspend an Act of Parliament. The Dissenters were initially pleased when James appointed Dissenters, as well as Roman Catholics, to public positions and as officers in the army and navy, but were taken aback when James immediately established a Commission of Ecclesiastical Causes (1687) that prosecuted Protestant preachers who denounced Roman Catholicism from their pulpits. In effect, government and military appointments were opened to Dissenters, but at the cost of the imposition of a censorship on the freedom of speech of their preachers.

The Anglican clerics, the Tories, and the Whigs were alarmed further when the Ecclesiastical Commission disregarded the charter rights of Magdalen College, Oxford, in ordering that Roman Catholic priests be made fellows of the Anglican College. When the fellows refused, they were removed and replaced with Catholic fellows, which turned the college into a Roman Catholic seminary. For the Dissenters, it raised a fear that if the Roman Catholic government of James II could violate the charter rights of the established Church of England with impunity, they would have no defence in law to restrain the king from any future attack against the Dissenting churches and chapels. Two further events proved decisive.

In April 1688, when James ordered that the Declaration of Indulgence be read from the pulpits of the Church of England, the Archbishop of Canterbury and six bishops forwarded a signed petition to the king in which they proclaimed their loyalty to the King, but stated that under the constitution the king did not have the authority to dispense with a statute of parliament. Consequently, the Indulgence was illegal, and the Bishops could not 'in honour and conscience' read the Indulgence "in the House of God during a divine service". Subsequently, when the Bishops' petition was widely published by private printers, the seven prelates were arrested, charged with seditious libel, and jailed in the Tower of London to await trial.

All over England, there was an outpouring of popular support for the imprisoned bishops from among the nobility, the populace, and Protestant clerics, inclusive even of the Dissenters who were benefiting from the Declaration of Indulgence. The imprisoning of the Anglican bishops was regarded as an attack on Protestantism by a Roman Catholic monarch. When the seven bishops were brought to trial on June 8, 1688, they were found 'not guilty' of sedition, and were freed, but that did not serve to dissipate a strong public antipathy that had been aroused towards the 'Popish government' of James II.

 The second decisive event was the receipt of news of the birth, on June 10,1688, of a son and heir of James II, which presented the reality of a permanent Roman Catholic dynasty in England. In response to a growing public unrest, leading Protestant nobles – inclusive of both Tories and Whigs -- sent an invitation to Prince William of Orange (the Stadholder -- chief minister of state-- of the Republic of the United Netherlands), to invade England, and promised William military support upon his landing. The Prince of Orange was married to the eldest daughter of James II, the Princess Mary, who had been raised a Protestant at the insistence of King Charles II after his younger brother -- the future King James II -- converted to Roman Catholicism. Moreover, the Prince of Orange was a leader in the resistance of the Protestant powers to an expansionist France under Louis XIV who was bent on spreading Roman Catholicism, by warfare and forced conversions, over the entire European continent.

When Prince William landed in England on 5 November 1688 with a Protestant army of 15,000-20,000 men, the Archbishop of Canterbury and three Bishops of the Church of England were summoned to a conference during which King James personally demanded that the Church issue a declaration condemning the invasion and denouncing rebellion. The Bishops expressed their loyalty to the King but, after reminding James of the injuries that he had inflicted on the Church of England, they refused to issue a declaration dealing with 'temporal matters, political and military'. It was a severe blow to James at a time – during the 17th Century -- when Old Tory values prevailed among the people of England, and Anglicans heeded the voice of the Bishops of the National Church.

With the Church of England standing by, Protestant Lords joined the Prince of Orange within days of his landing, and in the North, West and South of England, Protestant Lords raised their forces in defence of the Protestant religion and against the arbitrary rule of King James II. Moreover, the commanding officers of the English Army and the Royal Navy soon declared their support for the Protestant religion. King James was left in a hopeless situation with a Royal Army that was greatly weakened by massive desertions, and that was of a doubtful loyalty, except for several regiments of Irish Roman Catholics. Rather than risk losing a decisive battle, James fled to France, and the Prince of Orange moved on London where he received an enthusiastic welcome from large crowds.

To provide a revolution settlement, Prince William – in acting upon the advice of his supporters among the English Protestant Nobility – summoned a Convention Parliament to sanction what had taken place. The Convention Parliament (December 1688-January 1689) declared that King James had abdicated by fleeing the capital and throwing the Great Seal of office into the Thames River, and offered the throne to the Princess Mary and her husband, the Prince of Orange. A Bill of

Rights ("An Act Declaring the Rights and Liberties of the Subject and Settling the Succession to the Crown", February 1689) was enacted that confirmed the legal limits on monarchical power, the rights of parliament, and the civil rights of the subject; that declared James II had abandoned the throne; and that recognized King William III and Queen Mary II as joint monarchs of the three kingdoms of England, Scotland and Ireland. In addition, the Bill of Rights excluded Roman Catholics, and anyone who married 'a Papist', from the royal succession to the throne. With the succession settled, the Convention Parliament was progued by the new monarchs, and King William formed a royal government administration composed of the leading Protestant Nobles of the country, inclusive of both Tories and Whigs, which sought – initially -- to govern in a non-partisan manner.

For the Archbishop of Canterbury and Bishops of the Church of England, who had supported the Prince of Orange out of a need to defend the National Church, the revolution posed a crisis of conscience in that the Anglican clerics were believers in the divine right of kings and passive obedience to a legitimate monarch, and the legitimacy of James II as King of England was not in question. However, the crisis of conscience was alleviated by the belief that James had abandoned the throne in fleeing to France, and the fact that the Princess Mary was the legitimate heir to the throne in the Protestant royal succession. The infant son of James, in being a Roman Catholic, was excluded from the royal succession to the throne by an Act of Parliament: the new Bill of Rights. Moreover, the achievement of a change in regime almost without bloodshed, and the widespread acceptance by the populace of the new joint monarchs – King William and Queen Mary -- reinforced the belief that God sanctioned the new regime which rested on the consent of 'the people'.

It was a rationalization that was in keeping with the political philosophy of Richard Hooker. In his magnum opus on ecclesiastical polity, he had maintained that the best form of government was the one best suited to the character of the people, and that once a government was legitimately established with the consent of the people, it was sanctioned by God. In effect, the government of King William and Queen Mary was accepted by the people; whereas the previous royal government, which acted on the novel principle of divine right absolutism, was not.

The revolution restored a royal government based on the principle of a limited constitutional monarchy. It was the accepted traditional form of government of the English people prior to the Stuarts ascending the throne and attempting to usurp the constitution in acting on their novel political theory of divine right absolutism.

On their part, the Whigs set forth a strictly political justification for the rebellion as enunciated by an Anglican-whig cleric – and future Bishop of Salisbury -- Gilbert Burnet (*Enquiry into the Measures of submission*, 1688). Burnet maintained that King James by subverting the laws upon which his authority was founded, had destroyed his own power and the legitimacy of his right to govern, and that 'the people' had a right to act to preserve their English liberties and property – as defined in positive law – against a king who sought to subvert them.

Parliament did not play a role in the revolution of 1688 as it was not in session for the past three years, and the leading Dissenters in England – but not their co-religionists -- had remained aloof during the invasion by the Prince of Orange. The Revolution of 1688 was an Anglican achievement by the leading Nobles of the realm – both Tory and Whig – and the Prelates of the Church of England, acting in defence of the Protestant religion, the rule of law, the Church of England establishment, and 'the rights of Englishmen', in opposition to the royal absolutism and the threatening pro-Catholic policies of James II in both domestic politics and foreign relations.

It was a revolution that drew the support of almost the entire English nation as King James -- during his four-year reign -- had managed to alienate the Church of England clerics, Tory Churchmen and moderate Tories, the Old Whigs, the radical Whigs (later liberal-Whigs) among whom John Locke was a leading figure, and the Nonconformist or Dissenting churches and sects. The Rebellion of 1688 was even acquiesced in by moderate English Roman Catholics who were opposed to the arbitrary government of James II and his close association with the expansionist and absolutist government of Louis XIV of France. Even the Papacy, under Pope Innocent XI, was opposed to the intolerant Gallican Catholicism that Louis XIV was imposing on France, and his conquered territories, through the forced conversion of Protestants. (8)

In sum, the Revolution of 1688 was national uprising that was conservative in its nature. It constituted a change in government that aimed to preserve the traditional political and religious culture of England against the threatening divine right absolutism and the Gallican form of Roman Catholicism that King James and his Jesuit advisors sought to impose on England. It was not a political revolution based on Lockean-liberal principles. The political theory of John Locke, which justified a rebellion of the people against a royal tyrant – as presented in his *Two Treatises on Government* – postdated the revolution by a year and was inspired by the revolution.

It was the renowned whig historian, Thomas Babington Macaulay in his monumental multi-volume study, *The History of England from the Accession of James the Second* (1848) who imposed a liberal-Whig interpretation on the Glorious Revolution of 1688 in drawing on the political theory of John Locke. In the Whig interpretation, the revolution was hailed as a victory for the English people who supposedly rose against 'tyranny in the state and the persecution of the Church'; the Convention Parliament was held to have 'deposed' King James and bestowed the throne on William and Mary; and the revolution was characterized as marking the triumph of parliamentary supremacy in the long struggle between 'the people' and the kings of England.

Macaulay justified the revolution on the grounds of what he referred to as 'the Whig theory": that government was established to serve the people, and that the people had a right to depose a king – James II -- who "grossly, systematically, and pertinaciously" violated the law. Macaulay maintained that the only claim on which the rule and authority of the king rested was the consent of the people, which was the sole basis for the legitimacy of the subsequent rule of King William and Queen Mary. For Macaulay, the revolution settlement represented the triumph of liberal-Whig principles, but that was not the case historically. The Upper Canadian Tories held a more historically-accurate view of the basically conservative nature of the Glorious Revolution of 1688 from a strictly constitutional and church-state polity viewpoint. For the Tories of Upper Canada, the revolution was undertaken to restore the rule of law, a limited constitutional monarchy, and 'the rights of Englishmen'. It constituted a rejection of the novel divine right absolutism of King James II, and a defence of the National Church and the Protestant religion against the efforts of the King and his Jesuit advisors to Catholicizing England. The revolution was not based on any theory of popular sovereignty, or whig parliamentary principles, despite what Macaulay asserted later in his monumental liberal-Whig history. (9)

More recently, an American historian, Steve Pincus (*1688: The First Modern Revolution*, 2009), in taking a broader view of the international and political economy repercussions of the Revolution of 1688, and its impact on the society, government and economy of the English state, has argued that the English revolution was a transforming event on a national level. Both James II, and the victors of 1688 were 'modernizers' who followed a similar path in undertaking to create a royal government with a centralized bureaucracy, a professional standing army and an efficient navy, who favoured an interventionist state that would foster economic development and trade for the benefit of the nation, and who had imperial ambitions in seeking to capture and expand overseas trade.

The main difference was that King James sought to establish an absolutist state government to pursue his modernization projects, and looked to the France of Louis XIV as an ally in contending with the commercial trade threat posed to England by the Dutch Republic. James did not fear a European continent dominated by France, or the aggressive Catholicizing policy of Louis XIV. Rather, James was bent on Catholicizing England, and his vision was focused on the creation of an overseas English empire. In contrast, the Protestant supporters of William of Orange (the Williamites) wanted to preserve the limited monarchical government of England, and favoured close relations with the Dutch Republic. They were alarmed at the expansionist policies of Louis XIV and his Gallican Catholic state, which threatened the independence of the Protestant states of Europe and even the very survival of the Protestantism in Europe.

Both the Whigs and Tories of England were committed modernizers of the state apparatus and the military, and favoured a mercantilist policy, but differed in foreign affairs. The Whigs wanted to go to war immediately with France to resist the expansionist policies of Louis XIV, which England did in joining a coalition of European powers –

both Protestant and Catholic – in the War of the Grand Alliance (1689-1697) that pitted England, the Dutch Republic, Austria, the German territories of the Holy Roman Empire, Spain, and the Duchy of Savoy, against France. In contrast, the English Tories favoured a 'blue water policy' focused on the defence of Britain and her overseas colonies, while remaining aloof from any direct involvement of troops, ships, and monies, in the fighting of wars on the European continent.

The Whigs and Tories differed further as the Whigs sought an expanded overseas trade based on the development of manufacturing in England; whereas the Tories favoured the development of an overseas trade based on landed wealth. According to the Pincus interpretation, the political economy, economic life, and character of the English state was totally transformed by the modernizing policies of James II and, subsequently, by the Williamite Tories and Whigs, with England emerging as the first modern state, and sharing with the Dutch Republic the distinction of being the first two nations to engage in a global economy. (10)

Be that as it may, the Upper Canadian Tory interpretation of the Glorious Revolution of 1688 as a conservative event continues to be valid in a narrower political view of the revolution in terms of the preservation of the balanced British Constitution, the confirmation of the 'rights of Englishmen', and the successful defence of the traditional church-state polity of the English state. Subsequently, the liberal-Whigs would come to favour free trade, laissez-faire government, and an inclusive religious toleration; whereas the English Tories would continue to adhere to mercantilist policies – the Navigation Laws, Colonial Trade Preferences, and the protection of English agriculture. The English Tories accepted the Toleration Act of 1689 that granted religious freedom to Nonconformists (primarily Baptists and Congregationalists), but continued to defend the Test Acts that precluded Roman Catholics and Nonconformists from public office and military appointments.

In contrast, the Tories of Upper Canada were proponents of a complete religious freedom for all residents of Upper Canada, and for the unfettered political rights of British subjects -- under the law -- to vote and hold public office, which included any foreign immigrants who became property holders and took the Oath of Allegiance to become naturalized

British subjects. In the economic sphere, the Tories of Upper Canada were strong supporters of the retention of the Navigation Laws and the Colonial Trade Preferences system, and believed in an interventionist state: viz. the duty of government to promote national economic development policies for the well-being of the nation. Although at one point – immediately following the War of 1812 -- the Rev. John Strachan did advocate a policy of free trade, and cited the authority of Adam Smith (*The Wealth of Nations*, 1776) on the economic benefits of free trade.

The Christian Patriot King Concept

In holding that the sovereign power resided in the King, the Upper Canadian Tories were upholding a decidedly Tory view of the British Constitution. Nonetheless, their idealized concept of a Christian Patriot King was uniquely Upper Canadian Tory; although the idea of a patriot king was clearly derived from a political treatise of the 18th Century, English Tory, politician/stateman, Henry St. John, Viscount Bolingbroke (*The Idea of a Patriot King*, 1749).

Both Bolingbroke and the Upper Canadian Tories shared a common belief with respect to the power and function of the king, and the requisite patriotism and moral character of a good king. They shared a belief that the sovereign power exercised by the king belonged to his office, and not to him personally, and that the king ruled within a limited constitutional monarchy. Both the king and the people were subject to the common law of England and the principles and statutes of the constitution. Moreover, there was a common conviction that the balanced legislature of the British Constitution – King, Lords, and Commons – was an effective guarantor of the liberties and rights of the people, as well as an effective restraint on any attempt by the King, Lords, or Commons to encroach upon, or overthrow, the balance of the constitution. In his monarchical role (executive role), the patriot king was viewed as representing the unity and general interest of the nation. He would govern in the interests of the common good -- above political parties and factions -- while maintaining the rule of law, and promoting the happiness and well-being of his people.

Both the Upper Canadian Tories and Lord Bolingbroke rejected the concept of monarchical absolutism, while retaining a belief in the divine right of kings. For the Tories, the King was God's vicegerent on earth who was duty bound to govern in accordance with God's moral law, which was known by both revelation and reason. For Bolingbroke, the linkage was not so direct. A king who governed in keeping with the God-given Natural Law and who promoted the happiness of his people, was sanctioned by God in fulfilling the purpose of his institution. Both believed that a hereditary monarchy was the best form of government; that there was no right of rebellion against a legitimate government; and that there was a natural harmony of interest between the king and the people in seeking to promote the common good.

For the Upper Canadian Tories, the power of the king was circumscribed and limited, and the 'rights of Englishmen' protected, by statute law in the British Constitution: the Magna Carta (1215), the Petition of Right (1628), the Habeas Corpus Act (1679), and -- following the Glorious Revolution of 1688 -- the Coronation Oath (1689) and the Bill of Rights (1689).

For Bolingbroke, the idealized patriot king was a man of sense and virtue, of a strong moral character, who knew his duty, was incorruptible, good natured, generous, and well educated. However, Bolingbroke, a theist, made no mention of the Christian religion, or the National Church, in the kingdom of the patriot king, and his concept of the common good consisted simply of the promotion of 'private security and public tranquility', national wealth, power and fame, a national spirit, and 'the greatest good' of the nation. The patriot king would achieve these objectives, in a pragmatic manner, by upholding the constitution and the laws of the state, promoting free trade, commence and agriculture, defending the national interest, avoiding high taxes and public debt, and by strengthening the 'maritime defence' of the realm.

To the contrary, for the Upper Canadian Tories, the patriot king must be a Christian as only a morality based on religious belief could effectively govern human conduct and ensure the provision of good government, and only a regenerated man could adhere consistently to God's moral law in the performance of his public duties. (Moreover, the King was the temporal head of the Church of England.) In his personal life, the patriot king was expected to set an example for his people, and to win their loyalty through living a life of the purest morals and virtuous conduct, and in being a gentleman of peace and moderation. For the Tories of Upper Canada, the duties of the Christian patriot king included not only the promotion of the happiness and welfare of his subjects, the common good and the national interest, and the upholding of the constitution, but also the encouragement of the 'true religion' and virtue among his subjects, and the fostering of the arts and sciences which revealed the works and the mind of God.

The moral character of the patriot king was central to both Bolingbroke and the Upper Canadian Tories, but for Bolingbroke, the formation of character was simply a matter of education, and the inculcation of moral values in the royal youth. Moreover, Bolingbroke did not acknowledge the Tory view that the Church of England was an integral part of the British Constitution, nor did he recognize -- what the Upper Canadian Tories regarded as -- the critical role played by the national clergy in inculcating Christian values in the different orders of society. According to the Tories of Upper Canada, it was Christian values that had guided the historical evolution of the British Constitution, and it was the dissemination of Christian values among the people—by the Anglican clergy – that had played, and was playing, an essential role in the functioning of the balanced constitution and the maintenance of the social order.

For the Tories, fallen man needed to be redeemed through faith in the atonement of Christ, through receiving the Grace of God through the sacrament of baptism, and through the ministration of the sacraments and preaching of the Word by the national clergy, if he were to live a moral life. And it was the clergy that had formed, and continued to form, the national character of Englishmen in teaching obedience to legitimate authority, the governance of the passions and the will, and Christian charity and brotherly love, public virtue, moderation, peace and forbearance. (11)

The National System of Education

For the Tories of Upper Canada, education was one of the three great pillars – education, religion and the constitution – that comprised the foundation of any state. Education formed the national character of the state, strengthened national unity, and promoted the well-being of the people and the respectability of the country. Where education was concerned, the Anglican Tory clerics of Upper Canada were heavily influenced by the educational ideas and teaching methods advocated by John Locke (*Some Thoughts concerning Education*, 1693), whom the Rev. John Strachan referred to as 'the profound Locke'. However, Locke held a decidedly different view of the purpose of education. His treatise was written to provide instruction for the English gentry on the form of education and instruction best suited for a 'young gentleman'. For Locke, it was the responsibility of the family to educate their children, and he believed that parents had a duty to ensure that their children were well-educated for their own future benefit and happiness, and for "the welfare and prosperity of the nation". The purpose of education was to produce a rational, thinking being, with a love of knowledge and self-improvement, who would question the authority of custom and accepted beliefs.

Where the learning process was concerned, Locke rejected rote learning, the conventional memorization of long passages of Latin prose, and teaching by the threat of physical punishment and the ready use of the Rod. He encouraged teachers to teach to the level of comprehension and understanding of their pupils, but rejected any suggestion that teachers should reason with their young pupils to enhance understanding. Since the reasoning power of young children was undeveloped, Locke admonished teachers and tutors to teach from authority in imparting ideas and precepts. He recommended that teachers and tutors be encouraged to make learning interesting and appealing to pupils at their particular level of comprehension and understanding, to take advantage of the natural inquisitiveness and desire for knowledge of the pupils, and to provide encouragement by rewards, praise, and commendations. Moreover, Locke advocated that an element of play should be introduced into the school day, as well as physical activities to produce young men of a sound mind and body. Nonetheless, Locke maintained that pupils still needed restraint and disciple, which was to be enforced by a 'fear' of the Rod; although the Rod was to be applied very sparingly, and only for serious character offenses. Great severity in disciplining a child was deplored, and denounced, as detrimental to his character development.

The Upper Canadian Tories were in accord with the teaching method advocated by John Locke, as indicated by the teaching methods practiced, and advocated, by the Rev. John Strachan during his teaching career. In addition, the Tories shared with Locke a belief in the vital role of education in character development.

For Locke, teachers had a crucial role to play in the formation of the moral character of youths, and in installing good living habits to guide the actions of pupils throughout their adult life. However, given their lack of a well-developed reasoning power, young children were not able to discern God's moral law in Nature and, consequently, had to be taught the moral values embodied in the Bible. At a young age, children were to be taught "a true notion of God" as the Creator of the universe, "of all things", and of "all our Good", were to be taught to pray, and to hold God in reverence and love. However, Locke recommended against any effort being made to teach the 'incomprehensible' mysteries of religion, and the supernatural elements. It was further recommended that pupils commit to memory the Lord's Prayer, the Creeds (presumably the Nicene Creed and the Apostle's Creed) and the Ten Commandments. Once a pupil learned to read, teachers were to focus on the passages of the Bible which contained moral lessons and principles that the pupil needed to absorb. Pupils were to be discouraged from simply reading the Bible. It was beyond their comprehension and uninstructed readings would yield little of a lasting value.

The ideal product of education for Locke, was a useful and able man of a good moral character, schooled in good habits, with a well-developed reasoning power that would enable him to exercise a self-restraint in controlling his appetites, while acting in accordance with his enlightened self-interest and the prescriptions of God's moral law emanate in Nature. Education had a role to play not only in the formation of a moral character, but also in the formation of the mind and the reasoning power of the individual. In the epistemology of Locke (*An Enquiry concerning Human Understanding*, 1689), all knowledge was gained from experience – sensations and reflections – in a process in which ideas were the material from which knowledge was gained, and which led to the development of the understanding and the forming of wider associations. Hence, it was essential that pupils be exposed to ideas and experiences at a young age.

What Locke desired for the gentry was a 'practical education' focused on useful subjects and the inculcation of moral values. He had little use for the traditional system of education focused on the study of the Classics, 'abstract notions of Logic and Metaphysics', the learning of ancient languages (Greek and Latin), and theology. The purpose of education, as Locke envisaged it, was to produce 'gentlemen' (the sons of the aristocracy and the gentry) capable of managing their estates, as well as well-educated and useful men (the sons of the merchants and manufacturers) who would be able to enter the professions and the world of commerce and industry. He advocated that children be taught in the vernacular language, but recommended that the sons of the aristocracy and the landed gentry be taught French and Latin as well, which were requisite for their 'calling' as a 'gentleman'.

Although Locke rejected the traditional classical curriculum, he admired the ethical writings of the Ancients. He recommended that, as the reasoning power of the pupils developed, they should read (in translation) Tully's *Offices* in which the Roman orator and statesman, Marcus Tullius Cicero (106-43 BCE) set forth moral precepts for all public offices and social situations. He also advocated that the great men of Antiquity – those who were noted for their moral courage and virtue -- should be held up as examples to be emulated, and that their works be read in translation rather than as exercises in the learning of the Latin and Greek languages.

Where the 'modern' concept of natural law was concerned, Locke recommended that the young 'gentlemen' be encouraged to read – in translation -- Samuel von Pufendorf (*de Jure naturali & Gentium*, 1744) on the 'natural Rights of Man', the founding of society, and 'the duties of man and citizen'; and Hugo Grotius (*De jure belli et pacis*, 1625) on the principles of natural law common to all states in war and peace.

For Locke, the most important concern was to educate the future leaders of society, and that was to be done, for the most part, by private tutors. Otherwise, Locke was prepared to leave education in the hands of the local parish schools of the Church of England where pupils could be taught to read and write, to do sums, and to be industrious, while being inculcated with moral (and religious) values sufficient to recognize the difference between right and wrong. (12)

The Upper Canadian Tories found much to admire in the teaching methodology of John Locke, his emphasis on the importance of education in the formation of the moral character of youth, and his emphasis on the importance of teaching 'useful subjects'. They also shared his beliefs in the importance of forming good habits in youth, and in the inculcation of moral values at a young age, and a belief in his dictum that in nine cases out of ten, what a man became in life was determined by his education. Moreover, the Tories followed Locke in holding up 'examples' of men of moral courage and virtue from Ancient history for pupils to admire and emulate. In addition, the Rev. Strachan provided 'examples' of men of moral courage and virtue from the contemporary era: viz. two Upper Canadian Loyalists --Richard Cartwright and the Rev. John Stuart of Kingston, as well as King George III who was characterized as being a 'Patriot King'. Moreover, in the Upper Canadian education system, pupils were encouraged to excel through emulating the character and achievements of the more outstanding students.

Under the administration of the Rev. John Strachan, as President of the General Board of Education (1822-1833), pupils were admonished that life was short, that they needed to apply themselves to their studies and avoid idleness, and that they must develop their God-given talents and abilities in preparation for living a good, productive, and God-fearing life. Moreover, pupils were exhorted to strive to excel in whatever occupation or profession that "might be chosen for them" based on their God-given talents and abilities, their apparent interests and aptitudes, and their application and achievements while in school. Above all, they were counselled that they must 'rise on their own merit', and must always cultivate the social virtues and live their life in keeping with God's moral law.

Where the Upper Canadian Tories differed greatly from Locke was in their beliefs that education served a broader national and religious purpose beyond inculcating moral values and useful knowledge in an individual; that a full classical curriculum in combination with the teaching of 'useful subjects' would constitute a proper education for a 'gentleman'; and that moral instruction, if it were to be effective in governing the conduct of the pupil throughout his lifetime, must be based on Christian religious beliefs. More precisely, the Tories did not share Locke's view of human nature as highly malleable in a proper learning environment, or his dismissal of the Christian concept of original sin. The Tories differed also as to whom should have the opportunity to receive an education befitting a 'gentleman'.

In contrast to Locke, the Upper Canadian Tories did not believe in confining higher education to the established social elite through instruction in private schools or by tutors. To the contrary, the Tories strove to establish a state-supported 'national system' of education under the direction of the National Church. The Tories viewed a national system of education as having an essential role in the strengthening of the British national character of the province, in promoting national unity through uniting the people of the province by shared national feelings and values, and in ensuring political stability. Education was counted on to foster patriotism, loyalty to the Crown, and a commitment to the unity of the British Empire. Moreover, a well-educated population was viewed as being essential to ensure that public offices and the professions of the province would be filled with men of knowledge, ability and sound moral values. Given the lack of a landed aristocracy in Upper Canada, the school system was counted on to produce a governing elite. In effect, for the Tories, the education system was viewed as a means of 'breeding' an aristocracy of merit to serve 'the nation' in government, public offices, the judiciary and the professions: medicine, law, and the Church.

The education system was open to all ranks of society. It had to be to fulfil its national purpose, but also in keeping with the Tory beliefs that the natural social hierarchy was based on God-given talents and abilities, and that superior God-given talents and abilities were found among all ranks of society. Hence, it was essential that the poor be admitted to the Common (elementary) Schools, and that government bursaries be provided, by the Legislature, to enable the 'clever poor' – the intellectually gifted – to proceed to the District Grammar School level, and hopefully beyond to the projected university. The idea was to ensure that the 'clever poor' would be enabled to attain their proper 'station' in society – the position that they were intended to fill based on their God-given intelligence, talents and abilities, with the proviso that they must be of a good moral character and assiduous in applying themselves in school and, subsequently in their professional calling.

Pupils of lesser intellectual capacity from poor families, and most of the sons of farmers, were expected to attend only the local Common School to receive an elementary education aimed at teaching them reading, writing and arithmetic, at forming their moral character, and at strengthening their patriotism through the development of a British national character, before they joined the workforce. The sons of the social elite were expected to proceed to the District Grammar School where further progress would depend on their individual talents, abilities and application. Students were admonished that young men of superior God-given talents and abilities had a duty to "aspire to excellence", to "cherish a laudable ambition", and to excel in their 'stations' through 'application, ability, diligence and integrity'.

For the Upper Canadian Tories, the national system of education had to be under the direction of the established National Church. In that belief, they were influenced by the traditional role of the Church in the provision of education, their negative view of independent schools, and, most critically, by their view of human nature, morality, and the ultimate purpose of education. In sum, it was their Christian religious beliefs that account for their rejection of a secular education system.

For the Tories, government was "the only legitimate school master" with a duty to maintain a necessary union of church, state and education, and to promote national unity. Education had to be centrally controlled by the State and under the direction of the National Church because a proliferation of independent schools would produce 'a myriad of different values and beliefs', and, without a religious basis, education would foster 'democratic anarchy and infidelity'. The Tories believed further that a secular education – in separating religion from education -- would produce 'pride, selfishness and conceit' in the individual, and it would weaken the harmony of interests between the different orders of society through undermining the sense of noblesse oblige. In the absence of the teaching of Christian values -- charity, forbearance, love of others, and self-denial – youth would indulge their selfish passions and disregard their social duties. In contrast, a religiously-based education would promote public order, social harmony, the common good, and the living of 'a good life'.

The Tories were not in accord with the belief of Locke that the teaching of moral precepts from the Bible was sufficient to inculcate moral values into the character of young pupils. Locke maintained that man was born with a mind that was a blank slate – a tabula rasa – upon which ideas were imprinted from the senses, and that the character of man could be moulded by teachers instructing pupils in moral precepts at a young age. To the contrary, the Tories believed that the senses of man were corrupted by 'the Fall', and that man was incapable of living a godly and moral life in his fallen state.

To be rendered capable of living a consistently good life, man needed to be redeemed through hearing 'the Word', believing in Christ's atonement, receiving the Grace of God through baptism, and attaining a state of righteousness in union with Christ through Holy Communion. Without being redeemed into righteousness, man was not susceptible to moral improvements in any lasting sense. Hence, young pupils needed to hear the Christian message, and their moral lessons had to be based on Christian beliefs. Moreover, moral precepts in the abstract carried no compulsion; whereas, in the Christian religion, good behavior was sanctioned by a fear of God and the Day of Judgement.

As Christians, the Tories believed that man was both a physical and a spiritual being, and was accountable for his conduct here on Earth. Hence, pupils had to be taught what was essential to man's happiness and future salvation: viz. living in subordination to God's Will (God's moral law) as revealed in Scripture and discerned in Nature. For the Anglican clerics especially, education was intended to foster the development of knowledge of God in both His spiritual manifestations (the study of the Bible) and His extensive works of Nature (Natural Philosophy). To that end, it was essential that youth be competent to read and understand God's Will as revealed in the Bible, and that the reasoning power of youth be developed sufficiently, together with their growth in religious knowledge, to understand the meaning of what was being read.

Man had a duty to develop his God-given abilities to the fullest, to extend his reasoning power, and to grow in knowledge. An uneducated man would not be able to understand the workings of Providence, or to discern God's Moral Law immanent in Nature, or be able to place the discoveries of science within a proper Christian context. Education also had a political purpose. It was intended to inculcate feelings of loyalty to the Crown and the Province, as well as a strong British feeling --encapsulated in the 'British national character' -- a veneration for the laws and institutions of a constitutional monarchy. In addition, the education system was intended to foster an aversion to the 'profane works of demagogues' and to the political and cultural values of the secular American democratic republic.

Teachers – many of whom were Anglican clerics in the provincial education system – had a religious duty to 'bring students to Christ'. Without the inculcation of a strong moral character based on Christian religious beliefs, all education of youth was held to be in vain. It would merely increase man's capacity to do evil. Hence, it was essential that the direction of education be under the National Church to ensure that the future leaders of society would be men of a strong moral character and values, sanctioned by religious beliefs. Education needed to act upon the 'Inner Man', which only religion could do, to purify the heart. The teaching of religion was needed in schools 'to destroy the power of evil in the heart, to improve man's corrupted reason, and to raise man's desires above worldly concerns'.

For the Upper Canadians Tories, only the inculcation of Christian moral values and religious beliefs in pupils would produce adults who were possessed of a 'love of virtue and order' and who would be 'good members of society'. The finest product of the education system was held to be the educated 'gentleman' who was committed to serving God and his fellow subjects in promoting the public good, and who would act with honour and distinction in the State, the professions – law, medicine and the Church – and in the Judiciary.

In the Grammar schools of Upper Canada -- under the administration of the Rev. John Strachan -- students were exposed to a full classical curriculum, together with 'useful subjects' and courses in religious knowledge, during their five-year course of study. According to the Rev. Strachan, 'all areas of human knowledge' were taught within a Christian framework of interpretation with an emphasis on explaining the practical application of the subject matter, its value in building character, and/or its utility in discipling the mind.

The stated justification for such a broad curriculum, comprising the traditional classical subjects, a wide variety of 'useful subjects', and religious courses (Old and New Testaments), was that it would prepare students to fulfill a variety of roles in life. The intention of such a broad course of study was that students would be able to focus on the subjects suited to their own particular talents, abilities and interests; and that the students who excelled, and received a 'gentleman's education', would be competent to enter the projected King's College in Upper Canada or any British university. Subsequently, they would serve as the leaders of their community in the professions, the Church and government, and the judiciary as well as in education.

The Upper Canadian Tory concept of a 'national' system of education, supported by the state and under the direction of the National Church, would have been totally foreign to John Locke. It was contrary to his belief in laissez-faire government, his belief that the role of government was simply to protect the life, liberty and property of the individuals comprising the nation, and his advocacy of the separation of Church and State. It was the Tory belief in education as having a critical role to play in the inculcation of a British national character, in sustaining public order, and in inculcating moral values, that underlay their National Policy effort to establish a universal system of education in the Province of Upper Canada: viz. an elementary Common School system, a District Grammar School system, and the projected King's College university. It was an education system that was based on the religious, social and moral beliefs of the Anglican Tories, but was influenced as well by the familiarity of the Rev. John Strachan with the national system of education in Scotland, and the Scottish tradition of the universities and parishes providing bursaries to aid the clever 'lad O'pairts', from poor families, to attain a higher education. (13)

The Rev. John Strachan was born and raised in Scotland, and had received the benefit of the Scottish national system of education. He belonged to a poor working-class family and, as a youth, it was the winning of a bursary for scholarly achievement that had enabled him to attend King's College, University of Aberdeen, where he managed to support himself by teaching school during the summer months. Strachan graduated from King's College (MA,1797), and taught in local village schools before emigrating to Upper Canada in December 1799 to take up a position as tutor to the children of two prominent Upper Canadian merchants, Richard Cartwright and Robert Hamilton of Kingston. Once in Upper Canada, Strachan converted to the Church of England, and commenced his theological studies under the Rev. John Stuart, a Loyalist Anglican cleric, who had been educated at the College of Philadelphia (BA, MA), prior to the American Revolution. Strachan was ordained in 1803, and assigned to the nearby Cornwall parish. There he established the Cornwall District Grammar School to which the political elite, among the Loyalist and British immigrant families, sent their sons to be educated, and boarded in the local community. (14)

Strachan was a very earlier promoter of the idea of a 'national system' of education for Upper Canada, and was in the forefront in calling on the Legislature to vote monies for bursaries to aid the pupils from poorer families. Most of the Loyalists who settled in Upper Canada had been dispossessed of their property and worldly possessions during the American Revolution in fleeing the American rebels. Thus, the Loyalist settlers and their descendants were responsive to the establishment of a 'national' system of education and the Tory effort to secure grants from the Legislature to enable gifted pupils from poorer families to attain a higher education. On the other hand, the democratic radicals, evangelical sectarians, and the dissenting churches, were opposed to the establishment of a national system of education under the superintendence of the established Church of England.

Ideas influence Actions

An underlying theme of the present study was that "ideas influence actions", and that to truly understand what the Upper Canadian Tories and the leaders of the various opposition groups were seeking to accomplish, an historian must penetrate 'the mind' of the leading historical actors of each group to comprehend their peculiar worldview, and the matrix of political, cultural, moral, and religious values and beliefs that underlay their thought processes. In effect, this study was based on the belief that what the leading protagonists in any historical action sought to achieve, and their approach to doing so, was ultimately guided and governed by how their situation and circumstance were perceived and conceptualized within the distinct mental framework of their own cultural group or community.

In this treatment of the ideological struggle – the 'battle of ideas' – underway in the Province of Upper Canada in the two decades following the War of 1812, it is obvious that there was a definite connection between the differing ideas -- values, beliefs and principles, and worldview –of the various political interests in Upper Canada and their respective stances on the political issues of the day. In effect, this study shows clearly that 'ideas influence actions'. It confirms also a perceptive declaration by the late historian and metaphysical philosopher, R. G. Collingwood (*The Idea of History*, 1963) -- that a historian ought to seek 'to think himself into the historical event' because 'to comprehend the thought expressed in an event is to already understand the historical event'. (15)

To understand the stand that the Upper Canadian Tories took on the public issues of their day, one needs to look no further than the values, beliefs, principles, and worldview of the Anglican Tory mind of Upper Canada. A focus on the ideas and the national policy of the Upper Canadian Tories yields a much deeper understanding of the history of Upper Canada than currently exists. It explains the motives and aims of the men who were governing the province in terms of what they (the Anglican Tories) were striving to achieve, and why they stood in defence of primogeniture, the church-state alliance, the balanced British Constitution (in resisting encroachments by the House of Assembly and the principle of 'responsible government'), the clergy reserves endowment, and prescriptive rights of the established Church of England, as well as their efforts to establish a 'national system' of education under the superintendence of the Established Church, their defence of an hierarchical society and a governing meritocracy of 'gentlemen' (in opposition to democratic levelers), their stance on the Alien Question, and their focus on loyalty, their insistence on the constitutional importance of the king as the sole executive power, and their staunch defence of the British Imperial connection.

Likewise, if one wants to understand why a rebellion occurred in Upper Canada in a society of private property owners, who paid no direct taxes or the tithe, had the vote, and were among the freest people in the world in living under a limited constitutional monarchy and the rule of law, one needs only to understand the political culture of the rebels. The rebels were mainly American immigrants who were imbued with democratic republican political values and beliefs – including a belief in American 'manifest destiny' -- and many of whom were evangelical sectarians who believed in an egalitarian democracy and longed for the overthrow of the traditional political, religious and social order and its replacement by 'the rule of the saints' – themselves.

As early as 1799, Richard Cartwright had warned that the influx of American settlers into Upper Canada constituted a potentially dangerous source of disaffection as men do not change their political principles upon crossing a border. Similarly, the Tories were uneasy about the influence of the 'American Methodist' preachers who were extending their circuits into Upper Canada, both before and after the War of 1812. Leaving aside the objectionable emotional religion of the 'inner light' evangelical sectarians, the Tories were alarmed by the political views reportedly expressed by the itinerant preachers in disparaging King George III as a tyrant and praising the American revolutionary experience. It was the potent mix of American democratic republican values and sectarian religious beliefs among the American settlers of Upper Canada that sustained the democratic radicals during the 1820s, and accounts for the support that William Lyon Mackenzie received in his abortive coup d'état attempt of December 1837.

Upper Canadian Anglican Toryism

From this study, it is evident that the Anglican Tories of Upper Canada were indeed true Tories in their political philosophy and theology, and that their national policy ideals were based on their Christian faith, their traditional concern with the perennial problem of the maintenance of public order in any state, and their worldview. In their social, religious and political ideas, they retained the essence of the traditional Anglican Toryism of the age of Queen Elizabeth I as articulated and expounded by the Anglican divine, Richard Hooker. It was a unified system of political thought that transcended time, and embodied a concept of human nature (fallen Man/original sin), a theory of the origin of society and government, and a belief in the traditional Christian cosmology and teleology, and in absolute God-given moral values. What distinguished a true Tory from Old Whigs, and liberal-Whigs – as well as from the democratic radicals and the egalitarian democratic republicans of Upper Canada – was the centrality of the Christian religion to the Tory political philosophy.

Anglican Tories, whether in Elizabethan England or Upper Canada, believed in the union of Church and State, in a natural social hierarchy, and in an epistemology—a theory of knowledge -- that recognized both human and spiritual knowledge, that recognized the limits of human reason where spiritual matters were concerned and that held religious knowledge could be gained through Reason, Revelation and the teachings of the Church. In sum, Upper Canadian Anglican Toryism was a decidedly Christian political philosophy based on timeless theological beliefs, moral values, and political principles as enunciated by Richard Hooker in his 16th Century magnum opus, *Of the Lawes of Ecclesiastical Politie*.

The Upper Canadian Tories shared with the Old Tories a belief that human happiness required living in obedience to God's Will (God's moral law) in keeping with God's superintending Providence, and a belief that, once redeemed, the purpose of life for man was to 'go unto perfection' through living a godly and moral life in imitation of Christ in controlling selfish passions and abjuring the seeking after personal gratification and material wealth for its own sake. The Anglican Tories of Upper Canada were Churchmen, who believed in the concept of a national church, the union of church and state, in a national system of education based on religion, and the need for the institutions of the state to form the national character of the people on a sound moral and religious basis. Above all, they believed that life on earth was but a trial period for man in 'going unto salvation', with salvation and everlasting life for those who possessed a faith in Christ and lived their lives in imitation of Christ.

The Tories believed also in civil duties as well as civil rights, public virtue, the concept of the common good, the historic 'rights of Englishmen', and in the balanced British Constitution under the sovereignty of the Crown and the rule of law. They believed in representative government with the House of Assembly being elected on a property franchise, and the Legislative Council being appointed from among educated gentlemen of a strong moral character and prominence in their local communities. The provincial Parliament was viewed as an institution for rational debate on public issues, and as an advisory body to the Lt. Governor, who exercised a delegated sovereign power from the King. Although the Tories recognized the principle of the sovereignty of the Crown (the King); they held that the King's representative in Upper Canada ought to follow the advice of his appointed Executive Council on purely local matters. Moreover, the Lt. Governor was bound to obey the law in carrying out his constitutional function and his Instructions from the Crown.

One of the major concerns occupying a conservative ruling elite in any state is the maintenance of a stable political order, and that was the case in Upper Canada. The Upper Canadian Tories believed that the maintenance of public order was dependent on the people acting in keeping with a common system of moral values; and that it was the Christian religion that provided 'an eternal moral order and eternal verities' to govern the conduct of man. However, morality was insufficient of itself to form a national character unless it were based on religious beliefs. Hence, in the founding of a state, the 'three great pillars of the body politic' – the constitution, religion, and education – had to be united to form a uniform national character among the people which, in the Loyalist Asylum of Upper Canada, was appropriately the formation of a 'British national character'. In addition, for the Anglican clerics, man was held to be accountable to a Higher Power for his moral conduct, and the Christian faith 'provided the principles and rules of conduct by which all men ought to act'.

The ideal type of government for the Upper Canadian Tories was a meritocracy with public offices, at all levels, being in the hands of well-educated Christian 'gentlemen' of a strong moral character. What the Tories envisaged was an aristocracy of merit, selected and 'bred' through a national education system, that would be dedicated to public service and the promotion of the common good, and that would evince public virtue and patriotism. Anglican Toryism was a true philosophical conservatism, rather than a 'situational conservatism' bent on simply defending an established order against fundamental change.

The Tories of Upper Canada were not immune to the 18th Century Enlightenment emphasis on Natural Law, but they viewed Natural law within the older medieval worldview. For the Tories, Natural Law was but a reflection of Divine Law within a rational universe governed by laws emanating from God, who embodied 'right-reason'. They shared with the Lockean-liberals and the Deists a belief that God's moral law could be discerned in Nature. However, for the Tories, the living of a good life of moral rectitude was insufficient to attain salvation. Since human nature was corrupted by 'the Fall', man needed to be redeemed through faith in Christ and the saving grace of God, but since the mysteries of the Christian religion were beyond the comprehension of human reason, man needed both reason and revelation to attain salvation.

As Protestants, the Tories believed in 'justification by faith alone', and that faith could be evoked by hearing 'the Word' and coming to believe in Christ as the Saviour and in Christ's atonement. Redemption depended on the faithful receiving God's saving grace through baptism, and achieving a union with Christ in righteousness through partaking of Holy Communion. Once redeemed, the righteous were enabled to live a godly and moral life in imitation of Christ in anticipation of a future salvation upon the resurrection of the dead on the Day of Judgement. In sum, the Tories were true believers in Biblical Revelation as containing the Word of God for the guidance of man 'in the way of salvation'.

The Tories of Upper Canada denounced the anarchy and infidelity of the French Revolution, and what they regarded as its underlying cause of its excesses: viz. the rejection by the revolutionaries of the Christian religion and God's moral law, and the embrace of a secular doctrine of individual natural rights and a belief in an unrestrained popular sovereignty. As enunciated by Thomas Paine (*The Rights of Man*, 1791), the French revolutionaries adhered to several revolutionary doctrines: that man as man was possessed of inalienable natural rights – to liberty, property, security and resistance to oppression – that all men were born equal, that the people were sovereign, and that the law was simply 'an expression of the will of the people'. It was a novel concept of popular sovereignty and of law that was based on a belief expressed by Jean-Jacques Rousseau (*The Social Contract*, 1762) that sovereignty resided in the people of the nation collectively, and that 'the general will' of the people would produce good laws to govern society.

Although the Upper Canadian Tories were not as eloquent as the Old Whig, Edmund Burke (*Reflections on the Revolution in France*, 1790) in his denunciations of the political beliefs of the French revolutionaries, they shared his fear that any government based on 'the general will' of the people -- in the absence of a God-given system of morality, the rule of law, and any concept of self-restraint -- would lead to anarchy, infidelity and a tyranny of the majority. For the Tories of Upper Canada, the progress of the French revolution, in its anti-clericalism and social upheaval, anarchy and bloodshed, and the Reign of Terror and the emergence the Napoleonic dictatorship with its ideology of 'total war', provided an abject lesson for any government on the dangers of democracy and infidelity.

Constitutionally, the Upper Canadian Tories believed in a limited constitutional monarchy, and the balanced legislature of the British Constitution with sovereignty residing in the king, and were strong supporters of the traditional 'rights of Englishmen' and of religious toleration. Moreover, they totally rejected the concept of divine right absolutism. The Tories of Upper Canada accepted the Revolution of 1688, which they interpreted as an effort by the Lords Temporal and the Lords Spiritual to conserve and protect the balanced British Constitution, the historic 'rights of Englishmen', and the Protestant Religion, against the divine right absolutist form of government and the Catholicizing polices of James II that were aimed at converting England to Roman Catholicism.

The Tories conceived of the Province of Upper Canada as being a Loyalist Asylum, and were committed to building a conservative society in Upper Canada based on traditional Christian values and beliefs, and loyalty to the Crown and the British Empire. To preserve, and strengthen, the British national character of Upper Canada, they sought to establish a national system of education, to extend the ministrations of the established Church of England, and to defend the balanced 'British Constitution' against the efforts of the democratic radicals and liberal-whigs to overthrow the balance of the constitution in favour of the popular branch, the House of Assembly.

Behind the Tory nation-building policies, and effort to restrict the flow of American settlers into Upper Canada, was a desire to establish a separate 'nation' in North America. It was to have a staunch 'British national character', which was envisaged as capable of resisting American cultural values and the lure of egalitarian democratic republicanism, and a sufficient strength, with the support of British military forces, to resist any expansionist threat posed by the United States. What is evident is that Upper Canada had a soul – in the Aristotelean sense of an inner organic principle that animates and gives life to a being [or a nation] -- and its soul was Anglican Toryism. It was a political philosophy that guided the young Tories in their nation-building ideals, and in the formation of their national policies to strengthen and defend the Province of Upper Canada.

Notes

This Conclusion is based primarily on the readings and research conducted by the author while in the History Graduate School of McMaster University. Prior to departing from McMaster University, the author had a rough concept in mind for the writing of a conclusion, and was proceeding with the necessary research, but had yet to put pen to paper. The sources cited are largely the works that the author studied while in graduate school, but in being primary sources and classic monographs pertaining to political ideas, they are timeless. The several more recent works that have been consulted, can be identified by their date of publication.

1. Terry Cook, "John Beverley Robinson and the Conservative Blueprint for the Upper Canadian Community", *Ontario History*, LXIV, 1972, 79-94. Since this conclusion was originally conceived, William Westfall has published a study -- *Two Worlds. The Protestant Culture of Nineteenth Century Ontario* (Kingston & Montreal: McGill-Queen's University Press, 1989) – in which he identifies two different 'cultural patterns' within an ascendant Protestant religious culture in Ontario during the period from 1820 to 1870: viz. the 'religion of order', as exemplified by the Church of England; and the 'religion of experience' of the evangelical sects, as exemplified by the ['American'] Methodists and their leading spokesperson, the Rev. Egerton Ryerson. Westfall does not comment on the various political cultures of Upper Canada.

2. Richard Hooker, *Of the Laws of Ecclesiastical Polity*, C. Morris ed. (New York: Everyman's Library, 1968), Books I, II & V. Among the commentaries consulted were: Norman Sykes, "Richard Hooker" (in F.J.C. Hearnshaw, ed., *The Social and Political Ideas of Some Great Thinkers of the Sixteenth and Seventeenth Centuries,* London: 1967); Christopher Morris, *Political Thought in England, Tyndale to Hooker* (London: 1965); Alexandro P. D'Entréves, *The Medieval Contribution to Political Thought: Thomas Aquinas; Marsilius of Padua, Richard Hooker* (New York: The Humanities Press, 1959); and George H. Sabine, *A History of Political Theory* (London: 1968). For the political philosophy of Jean Bodin, and his concept of absolute sovereignty, see Sabine, *A History of Political Theory*, "Jean Bodin", 399-414. As Sabine points out, there were several inconsistencies in Bodin's novel theory of royal absolutism. According to Bodin, the absolutist king had no right to alter the law of succession, the French 'parlement' held the right to assent to taxation, the property of the state was inalienable, and the property of [noble] families was sacrosanct. Otherwise, the will of the sovereign was the law of the land.

3. This argument is not intended to imply that the Anglican Tories were simply

disciples, or blind followers, of Richard Hooker. To the contrary, the Rev. John Strachan – the fountainhead of Upper Canadian Toryism – was not only well-read in the works of Richard Hooker, but also read widely in the published works of the Elizabethan divines, the Cambridge Platonists of the 17th Century, and the Latitudinarians of the 18th Century, as well as the Tractarians of the 19th Century. His readings also included political theorists such as John Locke, the writings of Christian laymen such as William Ewart Gladstone, the works of radicals such as Thomas Paine, Richard Price, and Joseph Priestly, as well as works of the 18th Century Scottish Moralists. Strachan was familiar with the major works of the philosophes of the Enlightenment, including the radical works of Jean-Jacques Rousseau, and subscribed to the leading English and Scottish quarterlies of his day. He was also heavily influenced in his religious thought by the works of the Rt. Rev. John Henry Hobart (1775-1830), the Bishop of the Episcopal Church of New York State.

4. For the cultural and intellectual impact of the 17th Century science revolution on Europe, see Roland N. Stromberg, *An Intellectual History of Modern Europe* (New York: Appleton-Century Crofts, 1966), 3-5 & Chapter Two: "The Scientific and Intellectual Revolution of the Seventeenth Century". On the scientific advances and origins of the scientific revolution, see: Herbert Butterfield, *The Origins of Modern Science, 1300-1800* (Toronto: Clarke, Irwin & Co. Ltd, 1957). See also Thomas Kuhn, The *Structure of Scientific Revolutions* (Chicago: University of Chicago Press, 1970). In his original publication of 1962, Kuhn set forth a then-novel concept that a period of revolutionary scientific advances can result in a paradigm shift to a new framework of thought and understanding. On the complexity of Darwin's evolution theory, responses to his theory, and its impact on society and science in the late 19th Century, see Peter J. Bowler, *Charles Darwin: The Man and His Influence* (Cambridge University Press, 1996), 109-201.

5. This summary of the political philosophy of John Locke is drawn primarily from George H. Sabine (*A History of Political Theory*,1963) 517-540. The summary of the empirical moral theory of Locke is based on chapter 22, "Of Modes of Pleasure and Pain" in *An Essay on Understanding* (1690), and the summary of Locke's view of Christianity is based on a close reading of an online copy of *The Reasonableness of Christianity, as delivered in the Scriptures* (London: Awnsham and John Churchill, 1695.)

6. On deism, see: Leslie Stephen, *History of English Thought in the Eighteenth Century*, vol. I (London: Smith, Elder & Co, 1876), and especially 91-222. The Anglican Tories of Upper Canada rejected deism, and Latitudinarianism, but found much of worth in the arguments of the Anglican-whig cleric, William Paley, in his defence of natural theology (natural religion), and his argument

from design – the watchmaker analogy – for the existence of God: viz. *A View of the Evidences of Christianity* (1794), and *Natural Theology: or, Evidences of the Existence and Attributes of the Diety, Collected from the Appearances of Nature* (1802). Although the Tories welcomed the arguments of William Paley for the evidences of God in Nature and his Natural Law writings, they rejected his utilitarian view that the chief value of the Christian religion was in its moral values and social utility. For the Tories of Upper Canada, the ultimate purpose of the Christian religion was the salvation of souls.

7. On the Old Tory and Old Whig political cultures, see: Samuel H. Beer, *British Politics in the Collectivist Age* (New York: Random House/Vintage Books,1969), xi-xiv & 3-33 and 34-39, "Liberal Individualism". See also, Charles Parkin, *The Moral Basis of Burke's Political Thought: An Essay* (New York: Russell & Russell, 1956). On the political theorists mentioned, who espoused the necessity of an absolute sovereign power within a state, see Sabine, *A History of Political Theory*: 399-414, "Jean Bodin", and 391-397, "The Divine Right of Kings/James I". The English Tories abhorred the totally unlimited, amoral, and arbitrary -- 'might makes right' -- concept of absolute sovereignty espoused by Thomas Hobbes (*Leviathan, or The Matter, Forme and Power of a Common Wealth, Ecclesiastical and Civil*, 1651). On the political philosophy of Hobbes, his absolutism, materialism and individualism, see Sabine, 455-475. In the 17th Century, the English Tory Party rejected both royal absolutism and parliamentary sovereignty, while adhering to the sovereignty of the king, the rule of law, and a belief that the Established Church was an integral part of the Constitution, see: Keith Feiling, *A History of the Tory Party, 1640-1714* (Oxford: Clarendon Press, 1965, 1st. ed. 1924). On English government during the earlier reign (1558-1603) of Queen Elizabeth I, when statute law was a recognized limit on the sovereignty of the Crown, see: G.R. Elton, *England Under the Tudors* (London & New York: Methuen, 1974, 1st. ed. 1955), 395-429.

8. Gerald M. Straka, *Anglican Reaction to the Revolution of 1688* (Madison, Wisconsin: State Historical Society of Wisconsin, 1962), viii & 1-96. Some additional historical information on the policies of James II have been added to this section from Steve Pincus, *1688, The First Modern Revolution* (New Haven: Yale University Press, 2009), including the quotation which is from page 96. See also online text: "The English Bill of Rights, 1689", The Avalon Project, Yale Law School. Straka argues that the social contract had no role in the justification of the 1688 rebellion by those involved in it; that it was a conservative undertaking upon which the Whigs subsequently imposed their political theory; and that the position of the Church of England in supporting the new regime amounted to a rejection of the divine right of hereditary

succession for the adoption of the divine right of providential election. Straka maintains that the Jacobites -- who continued to support the claim of James II to the Crown -- were principally Roman Catholics, supplemented by a small number of Anglican clerics and laymen, who continued to hold to a belief in the divine right of hereditary succession.

9. Straka, *Anglican Reaction*, VIII & 118-121; and Lady Hanna Macaulay Trevelyan, ed., *The Works of Lord Macaulay, Complete in Eight Volumes, Vol. II, The History of England* (London: Longmans, Green & Co., 1866), 146-183 & 256-433, and especially 392-397 & 407 on 'the Whig theory' and interpretation of the Revolution of 1688 as set forth by Macaulay.

10. Steve Pincus, *1688, The First Modern Revolution*, and especially 3-10 & 474-486. In an exhaustive analysis of various political and religious tracts, polemics, and private papers, Pincus concurs that the revolution of 1688 was conservative in nature as an immediate political event -- given the absence of revolutionary political and social ideas. However, he concludes that it was a truly revolutionary event in its repercussions for the foreign and imperial policies of England, and its impact on the political economy and the economic life of the English people, and that, in keeping with modern revolutions, it was a popular revolution that was highly divisive and violent in its aftermath in Ireland and Scotland.

11. Henry St. John Bolingbroke, *The Idea of a Patriot King* (New York; Library of Liberal Arts, 1965, 1st. ed. 1749). In religion, Bolingbroke was a Theist who rejected revealed religion, as well as Natural Religion in denying that moral values could be discerned in nature through human reason. He admired Bacon and Locke, and favoured an empirical theology of sorts in which the existence of God was derived from the argument from design. He maintained that moral values could be deduced by observation and reflection on the behavior of one's own neighbours. The Anglican Tories of Upper Canada owed nothing to Bolingbroke beyond his concept of the 'patriot king'. On the ill-digested and somewhat contradictory religious ideas of Bolingbroke, see: Leslie, *History of English Thought*, I, 177-184.

12. John Locke, *Some Thoughts concerning Education* (London: A & F Churchill, 1693). On the 'useful' subjects that Locke recommended by taught, see 212-233. There is an inconsistency in Locke's comments concerning what is to be taught concerning God and religion. He maintains that young children ought not to be exposed to the 'mysteries of religion' or 'the other Spirits' (Jesus Christ and the Holy Ghost) that were beyond their capacity to understand; yet, he recommends that the pupils memorize the Creeds (the Nicene Creed, and the Apostles' Creed), which set forth the mysterious, or supernatural, aspects of the Christian religion.

13. On the curriculum recommended for the District Grammar schools of the province in each year of a five-year program, see: John Strachan, *A Letter to the Rev. A. N. Bethune, Rector of Cobourg, on the Management of Grammar Schools* (York: R. Stanton, 1829).

14. John Strachan, "Autobiography", 1800, extract in J.H.L. Henderson, ed., *John Strachan, Documents an Opinions* (Toronto: McClelland & Stewart, 1969), 1-8, 11 & viii. On the Scottish national system of education, and the bursary system for aiding gifted pupils from poor families, see: James Scotland, *The History of Scottish Education, From the beginning to 1872*, Vol I (London: University of London, 1969), 37, 44-45, 60 & 85; and H.M. Knox, *Two Hundred and Fifty Years of Scottish Education, 1696-1946* (Edinburgh: Oliver & Boyd, 1953), 3,7 & 9.

15. R.G. Collingwood, *The Idea of History* (Oxford: Oxford Paperbacks, 1963), 213-214. See also, Robert W. Passfield, *Military Paternalism, Labour and the Rideau Canal Project* (Bloomington, IN: AuthorHouse, 2013), Appendix: "Cultural Values", 226-230.

Appendices

Appendix A – The Loyalist 'tories' and Anglican Toryism

Appendix B – Conservatism in the Modern Era

———————————

Appendix A

In preparing an Introduction for the projected Ph.D. dissertation, during the winter of 1973-1974, the author saw a need to incorporate comment on the nature of 'the conservatism' of the Loyalists of the American Revolution with whom the Upper Canadian Tories closely identified. Several recently-published articles in Canadian history journals had argued that the Loyalists of the American Revolution shared a common Lockean-liberal ideology with the American revolutionaries, despite their political differences. That assertion raised a serious question as to why the Anglican Tories of Upper Canada identified so closely with the Loyalist tradition, if indeed the Loyalists were Lockean-liberals (liberal-whigs). Was it simply a case of empathy on the part of the Upper Canadian Tories for the Loyalists who had suffered a tragic loss at the hands of the American revolutionaries, or were there 'true Tories' among the Loyalists who fled from the new American Republic? To resolve that question, the author proceeded to analyze the nature of the conservatism of the Loyalists of the American Revolution. That analysis is reproduced herein as originally written.

The Loyalist 'tories' and Anglican Toryism.

In Canadian historiography, there is a wide disagreement as to the nature of the 'conservatism' of the Loyalists of the American Revolution who settled in Upper Canada, and their subsequent contribution to the conservative tradition in Canada.

S.F. Wise ("Upper Canada and the Conservative Tradition", 1967) has argued that the Canadian conservative tradition is a product of the intermingling of "two streams of conservatism" in Upper Canada during the two generations which preceded the union of the provinces of Upper and Lower Canada in 1841. The Loyalist embodied one stream of conservatism, which Professor Wise views as "an emotional compound of loyalty to the King and Empire, antagonism to the United States, and an acute, if partisan sense of recent history". The other intermingling stream, he sees as being "the Toryism of late eighteenth century England", which provided "a more sophisticate viewpoint" and was brought to Upper Canada by its first governor, Lt. Governor John Graves Simcoe, and his government officials.

In sum, for Professor Wise both streams of conservatism in Upper Canada were infused with a counter-revolutionary outlook. In its origins, Canadian conservatism was viewed as being a product of the intermingling of the 'emotional conservatism' of the Loyalists who opposed the American Revolution, and of British Toryism which was reinvigorated by Edmund Burke in his denunciations of the French Revolution. Professor Wise has also attributed the longevity of the emotional conservatism of the Loyalists to a "psychological need" to accept their history, and to justify their actions to themselves in retrospect. (1)

In his interpretation of the conservatism of the Loyalists, Professor Wise ignores the observation made by the Canadian philosopher, George Grant, (*Lament for a Nation*, 1965) that there was a deeper "moral significance" in the Loyalist experience; and that the Anglican Loyalists, in opposing the American revolutionaries, "appealed to the older philosophy of Richard Hooker". (2) Moreover, William Nelson (*The American Tory*, 1961), in his examination of Loyalist motives, has concluded that among the Loyalists that he studied, there were two groups -- the "Anglican High Tories" and the "Whig theoreticians of the Revolution" -- that did differ "in fundamental principles". The basic difference rested in their political philosophy: the "organic conservatism" of the Anglican Tories, as distinct from the "Lockean individualism" of the revolutionaries.

Nelson argues that it was recent immigrants from Britain, particularly the Anglican clergy, who took the lead in opposing the Revolution; and that the Anglican minorities in the northern colonies were for the most part true Tories. Moreover, it was the Anglican clerics and Anglican minorities from the northern colonies who comprised a significant component of the Loyalist migration to Upper Canada following the American Revolution. According to Nelson, it was their religion which motivated and provided the ultimate justification for their actions. Hence, based on his analysis, Anglican Toryism was present in Loyalism from the beginning among the orthodox Anglican Loyalists. It was inseparable from their adherence to the Loyalist cause. (3)

To date, little has been resolved concerning the nature of the 'conservatism' of the Loyalists who migrated to Upper Canada. A recent article by David V. J. Bell, "The Loyalist Tradition in Canada", 1970) denies that Toryism was present in the American colonies in the 18th Century. Bell asserts that the arguments which were employed by the whigs and tories prior to the American revolution, show that despite "important differences in outlook", the two groups shared "virtually identical" Lockean-liberal assumptions and values, and were not separated by ideology. (4) Terry Cook, ("Conservative Blueprint", 1972), has expressed an agreement with the assertion of David Bell. According to Cook:

> Since nearly all public men in the eighteenth century shared ... Whig assumptions [on sovereignty, order, hierarchy, and the balanced constitution], it is possible to agree that the gentlemen destined to become Tories and Whigs during the American Revolution were all really Whigs, that their values were indeed virtually identical. (5)

However, the assertion of Bell and Cook that the American tories were liberal-whigs who shared the same Lockean-liberal assumptions and values as the revolutionaries, but were loyal to the Crown and Empire in opposing the democratic republican ideas of the revolutionaries, is highly questionable. Such an argument does not allow for the presence of 'true Tories' among the Loyalists who opposed the American revolutionaries. It merely confirms that Toryism was a rather weak voice which was easily lost in a revolutionary debate that took place within what was almost a monolithic Lockean-liberal political culture in the American colonies during the period of the revolution. (6)

Nonetheless, despite the assurance of Nelson that there were true Tories -- Anglican Tories -- among the Loyalists, what precludes any comprehensive association of Anglican Toryism with the conservatism of the Loyalists who settled in what became the Province of Upper Canada, was the fact that Anglican families comprised only one component element of the Loyalist migration. Moreover, not all Anglicans in the Thirteen Colonies were *ipso facto* tories, and supporters of the Crown and Empire, in the event they had the courage to stand up for their convictions.

The establishment of the Church of England in a colony, and even its predominance, did not necessarily ensure the prevalence of an Anglican Tory system of values and beliefs. For example, in colonial Virginia prior to the American Revolution, the Church of England was established and included almost the total population of the colony within its membership;

yet the wilderness environment and the circumstances of the colony prevented the effective dissemination, or retention, of Anglican values and principles among its adherents. (7)

In Virginia, Anglicans remained for the most part ignorant of theology, and the organization of the Church was 'congregational' in practice, with all that that implied. (8) Gradually, under the congregationalist system of church government, the Established Church of Virginia was transformed until, by the 18th Century, it was primarily a social institution which served as "the bulwark of decency", moderation, and upholder of religious toleration which characterized that colony. (9) Neither the theology of the Church of England, nor the moral and political philosophy embodied in its teachings, nor the Anglican episcopal form of church organization were familiar to the adherents of the Established Church of Virginia. By the time of the American Revolution, Virginians had fallen into "secular habits". (10)

In Virginia, members of the Established Church were oblivious to the deeper meaning, principles and values of Anglicanism, as well as unconscious of its characteristic reverence for authority, and belief in the balance of liberty and authority and self-denial. What the Church of England in Virginia did teach was a reverence for the traditional 'rights of Englishmen' which inspired the American Revolution; and it was the Anglicans of Virginia who supplied the leadership – together with the Congregationalists of New England – for the American revolutionaries. (11)

The situation was different with respect to recent Anglican immigrants from Britain who were settled in the American colonies. Indeed, that was particularly the case for the immigrant Church of England clergy who took the lead in seeking to organize resistance to the activities and propaganda of the revolutionaries. Two of the leading Loyalist spokesmen were Anglican clerics: the Rev. Charles Inglis (1734-1816), Rector of Trinity Church, New York, and the Rev. Jonathan Boucher (1759-1804), pastor of St. Barnabas Church, Upper Marlboro, Maryland. (12) Both clerics based their opposition to the revolution on principles and philosophical arguments which were derived from the traditional Anglican cosmology and political philosophy. In sum, it was among the recent Anglican immigrants, and the Anglican minorities who were settled in the northern colonies, that the older Tory values and principles of the Church of England were retained, and had not been supplanted by Lockean-liberalism. (13)

In Upper Canada, the Anglicans among the Loyalists exiles were from these two particular groups of American colonials. For the most part, they comprised either recent English Anglican immigrants to the American colonies, or former members of Anglican settlements in the northern American colonies. The actual number of the Anglican Loyalists who settled in Upper Canada, and who had opposed the American Revolution out of a conscious rejection of the Lockean-liberal values of the revolutionaries, is unknow and not relevant to the present argument. What is historically significant is that there were true Tories among the Loyalist families who settled in what became the Province of Upper Canada.

Such a statement is not intended to deny that there were many so-called 'tories' during the American Revolution who adhered to Lockean-liberal values in opposing the American revolutionaries. Nor does it deny that there were Loyalists whose opposition to the revolutionaries was based simply on an emotional response of loyalty to the traditional institutions of government with which they were familiar, as well as Loyalists who simply had the misfortune of having backed the losing side in the conflict.

Nonetheless, there were Anglican Churchmen and clerics among the Loyalists who were keenly aware of the deeper "moral significance" of the Loyalist experience and the Loyalist rejection of the American Revolution (1776-1783). In their values, principles and beliefs, these Anglican Loyalists were 'true Tories' who – in the words of George Grant -- "appealed to the older philosophy of Richard Hooker" and rejected the Lockean-liberal principles, values, and beliefs that were being espoused by the leading American revolutionaries. (14)

In Upper Canada, it was the political philosophy of the Loyalist Anglican Tories – which was derived from the theology of the Church of England, and was expressed in the older principles, values, and beliefs of that National Church -- that had a strong and lasting influence in the formation of the Upper Canadian conservative tradition, and the conservative interpretation of the American Revolution. It was the Anglican Tory philosophical element in the Loyalist experience with which the Upper Canadian Tory elite identified, and associated themselves. Moreover, both the emotional conservatism of the larger body of the Loyalists and the Toryism of the Anglican Loyalist leadership were reinvigorated during the period of the conservative reaction to the excesses of the French Revolution (1789-1799).

In sum, there were three streams of conservatism that intermingled to form a nascent Canadian conservatism. These comprised the two major steams of conservatism that entered Upper Canada with the Loyalists: an emotional or 'situational conservatism', which was focused simply on a defence of the existing colonial social and political order, the Crown, and the Imperial connection; and a philosophical conservatism – Anglican Toryism -- which was embodied in the Anglican Loyalist settlers and their refugee clerics. These two streams of conservatism were found in the Loyalist experience, and were further reinforced and invigorated by the Anglican Toryism of late 18th Century England which was brought to Upper Canada by British government officials and 'High Church Anglican' immigrants from England following the founding of the Province of Upper Canada in 1791. For a time, the three conservative elements combined to establish a viable conservative political culture in the Province of Upper Canada, under the leadership of the Anglican Tory elite of the province.

Notes

1. S. F. Wise, "Upper Canada and the Conservative Tradition" in Edith Firth, ed., *Profiles of a Province, Studies in the History of Ontario* (Toronto: The Ontario Historical Society, 1967), 20-33, and especially 20. See also S.F. Wise, "Colonial Attitudes from the Era of the War of 1812 to the Rebellions of 1837", in S.F. Wise and Robert Craig Brown, *Canada Views the United States* (Toronto: Macmillan of Canada, 1967), 21-22. J.J. Talman ("The United Empire Loyalists", *Profiles of a Province*, 3- 8) points out that most of the 5,960 Loyalists who settled in what became the Province of Upper Canada, were farmers and minor property holders from upstate New York; whereas, in contrast, among the 35,000 Loyalists who settled in Nova Scotia and New Brunswick there were a significant number of professionals, gentlemen, and former public office holders. Other than a loyalty to the Crown, Talman says little about the beliefs of the Loyalists or their legacy.

2. George Grant, *Lament for a Nation, The Defeat of Canadian Nationalism* (Toronto: McClelland & Stewart, 1965), 63.

3. William Nelson, *The American Tory* (Boston: Beacon Press, 1961), 17, 72-80, 85-115 & 186-188. Numerous articles have been published on the question of the motives of the Loyalists. The Nelson book and an article by H.A. Morton ("The American Revolution: A view from the North", *Journal of Canadian Studies*, VII, 1972, 43-54) provide the best insights into the meaning of the Loyalist experience and tradition.

4. David V. J. Bell, "The Loyalist Tradition in Canada", *Journal of Canadian Studies*, V, 1970, 22-33.

5. Terry Cook, "John Beverley Robinson and the Conservative Blueprint for the Upper Canadian Community", *Ontario History*, LXIV, June 1972, 79.

6. The comments of Gad Horowitz on the American political culture are pertinent here. See Gad Horowitz, "Conservatism, Liberalism and Socialism: An Interpretation", *Canadian Journal of Economics and Political Science*, 32, 2, 1966, 10-13.

7.Daniel J. Boorstin, *The Americans: The Colonial Experience* (New York: Random House, 1958), 24-25 & 132; and Clarence L. Ver Steeg, *The Formative Years, 1607-1763* (New York: Hill & Wong, 1964), 74-74, 88 & 90. Among the factors cited for contributing to the breakdown of traditional Anglican religious values and beliefs in Virginia were: the great distances between churches, the dearth of Anglican ministers, and the lack of a colonial bishop to enforce conformity of belief and ritual.

8. Boorstin, *The Americans*, 125-127, 134 & 137; and Ver Steeg, *The Formative Years*, 89. The absence of a central clerical authority to enforce discipline and maintain orthodoxy in Virginia resulted in the local vestries usurping the episcopal power. The power of the vestries, composed of leading laymen of the parish, was further strengthened by the local practice of refusing 'to present' a clergyman for induction into his parish. As a result, the clergyman was denied tenure, and could be dismissed by the vestry at will. It was, in effect, a congregationalist system by which "the supervision of the clergy and the definition of religious practices fell into the hands of the leading lay members of the parish". (Boorstin, 127).

9. Boorstin, *The Americans*, 133. Boorstin regards the transformation of the established Anglican Church of Virginia -- which saw it retain its traditional catholicity and its moderate and tolerant spirit, while shedding "its atmosphere of hierarchy and of excessive reliance on ritual" -- as a 'purification' of the Church. To the Anglican Tories of Upper Canada, however, such a development would have been viewed as a religious degradation. It was an awareness, by the Upper Canadian

Tories, of the transformation that the Anglicanism had undergone in the American colonies, and the reasons for the same, that motivated them to strive to make the Church of England 'effective' in Upper Canada, and the clergy 'independent' of the financial support of both the government and their own congregations.

10. Van Steeg, *The Formative Years*, 90.

11. Boorstin, *The Americans*, 131.

12. The Rev. Jonathan Boucher returned to England at the outbreak of the hostilities which brought on the American Revolution. Subsequently, he published: *A view of the Causes and Consequences of the American Revolution in Thirteen Discourses, Preached in North American between the Years 1763 and 1775; with an Historical Preface* (London: G.G. & J. Robinson, 1797). The Rev. Charles Inglis remained in New York as the Rector of Trinity Church during the American Revolution, while the city was in the hands of British troops. He returned to England after the Revolution, and was subsequently invested as the first Bishop of Nova Scotia, with a diocese that comprised the Maritime Provinces, Newfoundland, and the old Province of Quebec, as well as Bermuda. In 1793, a separate See of Quebec was created under Bishop Jacob Mountain which comprised Upper and Lower Canada. The Rev. Inglis published two significant works during the American Revolution: a political treatise, [Charles Inglis], *The True Interest of America Impartially Stated in Certain Strictures on a Pamphlet intitled Common Sense, by an America*. Second Edition. (Philadelphia: James Humphreys, 1776); and an historical appeal for loyalty to the King and Constitution: [Charles Inglis]. *Letters of Papinian in which the Conduct, present State and Prospects of the American Congress are examined* (New York/ London: J. Wilkie, 1779).

13. Nelson, *The American Tory*, 17, 72-90 & 186-188. Boorstin (*The Americans*, 124-125) has argued that one of the reasons why the Congregationalists of New England and the Anglicans of Virginia "became more practical and less interested in dogma" was due to the absence of theological opponents challenging them to defend and articulate their beliefs. Where the situation in Virginia was concerned, one could argue that the lack of a robust preaching and teaching of the principles, values, and beliefs of the Church of England, and the failure to inculcate Anglican beliefs and values into the youth of the parishes, left the adherents of the established Church of England open to succumbing to the Lockean-liberal principles and beliefs of that era, which they did as of the mid-18th Century.

14. William Nelson, in his analysis of the political debate of the revolutionary era, refers to the 'true tories', among the American tories, as "organic conservatives" or "Anglican High Tories".

Appendix B

This piece was originally composed as a section of the dissertation Introduction. It was intended as a comment on the relevance of the study on the Upper Canadian Tory Mind to an argument raised by a Canadian political philosopher, George Grant, concerning the lack of viability of an organic conservative political ideology in our modern technological age.

Conservatism in the Modern Era

To suggest that the present study -- on the Upper Canadian Tory Mind -- may have a relevance for the present-day, is not to say that history teaches lessons that can guide future conduct, or that past certitudes provide a guide to the resolution of current problems. This study is not intended to apply Tory political thought to present controversies, such as the question of the viability of a conservative political ideology in the modern technological age, and the related question of Canada's fate. (1)

Nonetheless, the subject matter of this study cannot be divorced totally from present concerns. That is so because of the nature of Toryism as a timeless philosophy of human nature and society, and the fact that the Upper Canadian Tories addressed themselves to similar questions in their own day when faced with political opponents who were espousing Lockean-liberal principles, values and beliefs. Hence, the present study might well help conservative thinkers to come to grips with the seeming dilemma which our modern technological society poses for the viability of a true conservative philosophy of society and government in our era. It will do so through setting forth the beliefs, values and principles of a conservative political philosophy, Anglican Toryism, which embodies timeless and immutable principles which were held to be in keeping with God's scheme of things and the needs of man's nature.

George Grant (*Lament for a Nation, The Defeat of Canadian Nationalism*, 1965) has asserted that conservatism is not a viable political ideology in our modern era in which capitalism, liberalism, faith in progress, and the demands of technology have all combined to deny the validity of the basic premise of conservatism. Grant maintains that it is the predominance of such a complex of man-centred values that renders impossible any hope of preserving traditional institutions and standards over time, and consequently conservatism has been deprived of any meaningful role to play in our modern society. Capitalism is "a way of life', with profit-making as its ultimate aim and value to the detriment of all other values and traditions which might conflict with, or inhibit, the realization of that purpose; and liberalism, with its emphasis on individual freedom and its faith in material progress, has proved a perfect vehicle for the spread of the spirit of capitalism.

In North America, an all-pervasive liberal-capitalism denies the validity of any assertion that man must recognize values other than his own wants and personal interests, or that there should be limits to change. Liberalism regards freedom as the essence of man. Thus, men are free "to do what they want", and "to make the world as they choose" unrestrained by "any conception of good that imposes limits on human freedom". Moreover, the liberal doctrine of progress holds that emancipation is to be achieved through the conquest of nature by technological means. It is this complete commitment of modern man to technology and the meeting of the demands of technology which, according to Professor George Grant, not only denies the basic premise of conservatism but renders a conservative philosophy obsolete for all practical purposes. (2)

The essence of the argument being presented by Grant is that:

> A [conservative] political philosophy that is centred on virtue must be a shadowy voice in a technological civilization. When men are committed to technology, they are also committed to continual change in institutions and customs. Freedom must be the first political principle – the freedom to change any order that stands in the way of technological advance. Such a society cannot take seriously the conception of an eternal order by which human actions are measured and defined. ... Without the concept of such an order, conservatism becomes nothing but the defence of property rights and chauvinism, attractively packaged as appeal to the past.

In our modern age – according to Grant -- conservatism cannot be a viable alternate political ideology in a technological civilization in which a liberal capitalism predominates, and in which its assumptions permeate all the media and deprive the public of the knowledge of any alternative value system. Moreover, it is modern man who is receiving, and wishes to continue to receive, the maximum benefits of the technological age. Technology has brought stupendous benefits to modern man, who is oblivious to, or uninterested in, seeking any deeper meaning in life. (3)

This assertion has a deeper significance which is made plain in another publication by George Grant (*Technology and Empire, Perspectives on North America,* 1969). Therein, he comments that:

> Western technical achievement has shaped a different civilization from any previous.... This achievement is not something simply external to us, ... It moulds us in what we are, ... in our actions and thoughts and imaginings. Its pursuit has become our dominant activity and that dominance fashions both the public and private realms.

As interpreted by George Grant, "practical conservatives" of the nineteenth century, in the face of the growing ascendancy of liberalism, had two options open to them in political life. The "more honest" used what influence they possessed to fight "rearguard actions" in defence of what was and ought to be in defending the traditional order and timeless values; and the "more ambitious" accepted the age of progress and made use of appeals to "a moribund past" to mask class, imperial, or national interests. It was a portent of what was to come for "conservatism must languish as technology increases". If conservatives wish to receive popular support, they must commit themselves to "a dynamic technology"; yet, if they do so, they cease to be true conservatives for such a commitment precludes the maintenance of anything over time. In sum:

> They are not conservatives in the sense of being the custodians of something that is not subject to change. They are conservatives generally, in the sense of advocating a sufficient amount of order so the demands of technology will not carry the society into chaos.

In sum, as argued by George Grant, true conservatism is no longer a viable political philosophy in our modern age. Hence, for Grant, the fate of Canada – a country founded upon true conservative values – is clear. It is evident in the defeat of Canadian nationalism, which is inexorably linked with the impossibility of conservatism in the modern age. Canada will inevitably lose its national cultural identity, and be absorbed into the omnipresent liberal-capitalist American culture. (4)

Given that assertion of Professor Grant, this study of the Upper Canadian Tory Mind will have historical value in setting forth the long-lost political ideology of the true conservatives of Upper Canada – the Anglican Tories -- and what they held to be the timeless values and beliefs pertaining to the meaning of life. It will lead to a better understanding of what Canada once was and – as argued by George Grant -- what Canada can no longer be: a true conservative society in the modern technological era, which is dominated by an all-pervasive liberal-capitalism, technological imperatives, and a belief in continual progress and unlimited individual freedom.

Addendum by Author: June 2017

If the late George Grant were writing today – in our present age of 'modern liberalism' -- one surmises that he would see a role for conservativism in the maintenance of our timeless Judeo-Christian moral values against the 'moral relativism' that characterizes modern liberalism. One suspects that he would denounce also the modern liberal beliefs in 'globalization', 'multi-culturalism', 'pan-nationalism', and 'open immigration', as being destructive of Canada's sovereignty as a nation, its heritage, and its cultural identity, and would be critical of 'identity politics' as a modern form of tribalism that is destructive of any concept of a 'common good' that transcends individual and group interests.

Notes:

1. The debate over the viability of an organic conservative political ideology in our modern technological age was sparked in Canada by the publication of *Lament for a Nation, The Defeat of Canadian Nationalism* (Toronto: McClelland & Stewart, 1965) by George Grant.

2. Grant, *Lament for a Nation*, 42, 56-58, 66 & 72.

3. Grant, *Lament for a Nation*, 42, 74, 76 & 94. The quotation is from 72-73.

4. George Grant, *Technology and Empire, Perspectives on North America* (Toronto: House of Anansi Press, 1969), 73-74 & 66-68. The quotations are from pages 15 and 67, respectively.

Index
Upper Canadian Anglican Tory Mind

Index to Conclusion
Upper Canadian Tories as 'true Tories'

CPSIA information can be obtained
at www.ICGtesting.com
Printed in the USA
LVHW040957090119
603052LV00004B/13/P